Routledge Revivals

British Colonial Theories 1570-1850

British Colonial Theories 1570-1850

Klaus E. Knorr

With A Foreword
by
H. A. INNIS

First published in 1944 by University of Toronto Press

This edition first published in 2018 by Routledge
2 Park Square, Milton Park, Abingdon, Oxon, OX14 4RN
and by Routledge
52 Vanderbilt Avenue, New York, NY 10017, USA

Routledge is an imprint of the Taylor & Francis Group, an informa business

© 1944 by Taylor and Francis

All rights reserved. No part of this book may be reprinted or reproduced or utilised in any form or by any electronic, mechanical, or other means, now known or hereafter invented, including photocopying and recording, or in any information storage or retrieval system, without permission in writing from the publishers.

Publisher's Note
The publisher has gone to great lengths to ensure the quality of this reprint but points out that some imperfections in the original copies may be apparent.

Disclaimer
The publisher has made every effort to trace copyright holders and welcomes correspondence from those they have been unable to contact.
A Library of Congress record exists under ISBN:

ISBN 13: 978-1-138-39255-7 (hbk)
ISBN 13: 978-1-138-39260-1 (pbk)
ISBN 13: 978-0-429-40212-8 (ebk)

BRITISH COLONIAL THEORIES

British Colonial Theories
1570-1850

By
KLAUS E. KNORR

WITH A FOREWORD
by
H. A. INNIS

UNIVERSITY OF TORONTO PRESS

COPYRIGHT, CANADA, 1944
UNIVERSITY OF TORONTO PRESS
REPRINTED 1963, 1964, 1968
PRINTED IN THE UNITED STATES OF AMERICA

TO

MARIANNE T. KNORR

TABLE OF CONTENTS

	PAGE
FOREWORD by H. A. INNIS	xi
PREFACE	xvii

CHAPTER

PART I

I.	INTRODUCTION	3
II.	COLONIAL THEORIES: 1570-1660	26
	The Spreading of the Gospel	28
	The Northwest Passage	32
	American Gold and Silver	34
	Strategic Considerations	37
	Get There First	38
	Nursery of Seamen	38
	The Transatlantic Fisheries	40
	Outlet for Surplus Population	41
	The Transportation of Criminals and Undesirables	48
	Colonies as Sources of Raw Materials	50
	Colonies as Markets	56
	The Augmentation of Revenues	59
	The Opposition to Colonization	59
III.	COLONIAL THEORIES: 1660-1776	63
	Strategic and Naval Considerations	63
	Theories on Population and the Colonies	68
	Colonies as Sources of Raw Materials	81
	Colonies as Markets	95
	Anti-Colonial Arguments, Misgivings, and Deprecations	105
	Josiah Tucker and the Colonies	117
IV.	THE OLD COLONIAL SYSTEM: BASIC OBJECTIVES, CONCEPTIONS, POLICIES	126

PART II

V.	INTRODUCTION	155
VI.	ADAM SMITH AND THE DISSENTERS	175
	1. Adam Smith and the Empire	175
	2. The Dissenters and the American War of Independence	195

CHAPTER	PAGE

VII. COLONIAL THEORIES: 1776-1815.................... 201

    I. 1776-1782... 201

    II. 1783: The American Intercourse Bill............... 213

    III. 1784-1815
        Population and Emigration........................ 219
        Colonies as Markets.............................. 228
        Colonies as Sources of Raw Materials.............. 230
        Colonies as Outlets for Surplus Capital........... 233
        The Financial Burden of Empire................... 234
        The English "Physiocrats"........................ 236
        Aversion to Empire, Imperial Expansion, and Imperial Wars... 241
        The Empire as the Basis of Seapower............... 244
        The Mission of Empire............................ 246
        Summary.. 248

VIII. BENTHAM, JAMES MILL, AND RICARDO.......... 251
    The Colony Trade.................................... 251
    The Colonial Empire as a Source of Power............ 256
    Penal Settlements................................... 258
    Colonies as a Source of Wars........................ 259
    The Finances of Empire.............................. 260
    The Interest of the Few Versus That of the Many..... 262
    Population, Emigration, and Colonies................ 264
    The Question of Separation.......................... 266
    Utilitarianism as a Temper of Thought............... 267

IX. EMIGRATION AND COLONIZATION: 1815-1850...... 269
    "The Shovelling out of Paupers"..................... 269
    Systematic Colonization............................. 294
    Surplus Capital and Surplus Labour.................. 296
    The Problem of Over-Production...................... 299
    Foreign Trade or Colonization....................... 300
    The Main Principles of the Wakefield System of Colonization 309
    The Multiplication of Little Englands and Colonization by Order of Providence................................. 310

X. THE FALL OF THE OLD COLONIAL SYSTEM...... 316
    Huskisson's Changes in the Colonial System.......... 316
    The Problem of the Sugar Duties..................... 317
    The Problem of the Timber Duties.................... 325
    Trade and Empire.................................... 332
    The End of the Navigation System.................... 342
    The Significance of Economic Theory................. 347

CHAPTER		PAGE
XI.	SOME ADDITIONAL ITEMS IN THE BALANCE-SHEET OF IMPERIALISM	350
	Expense	350
	The Spoils of Empire	356
	The Political Backwash of Imperial Rule	358
	Power and Prestige	360
	The Pride and Glory of Empire	364
	The Spread of Peace, Order, and Civilization	366
	The Question of Separation and Anti-Expansionism	371
XII.	THE WHITE MAN'S BURDEN	376
	The Campaign against Slave Trade and Slavery	376
	The Missionary Movement	379
	The Aborigines' Problem	382
XIII.	THE PROBLEM OF CONVICT TRANSPORTATION	389
XIV.	A NOTE ON THE LAKE POETS AND THOMAS CARLYLE	396
	The Lake Poets	397
	Thomas Carlyle	400
XV.	THE MIDDLE CLASS AND THE EMPIRE	406
INDEX OF NAMES, BOOKS, AND PERIODICALS		417
INDEX OF SUBJECTS		424

FOREWORD

IN a survey of British colonial theories from 1570 to 1850, published at this time, the author has placed the English-speaking world under heavy obligations. It covers the period of the old Empire and of the readjustments of the second Empire which followed the failure of the old after the revolt of the American colonies, ending with the emergence of free trade, and is significant to the history of the American colonies and of the British Commonwealth of Nations, as outlined by Professor McIlwain. The discussion fills a notable gap in the important work of Marshall, Beer, Professor Viner, and Professor Heckscher in recent years in the field of mercantilism and is complementary to the detailed studies of Professor Gerald Graham and Professor A. R. M. Lower. For the first time we can envisage the problems of mercantilism in a maritime empire. Our debt is increased by the wealth of quotations which Dr. Knorr has included which indicate the extent of the literature and enable the student to continue immediately with further study of the problems. Combing of the literature widens our understanding of the significance of Adam Smith and of the peculiar implications of the expansion of Great Britain to the study of political economy. Literature of the period reflects the character of the long struggle in which principles of the subject were hammered out in relation to the immediate demands of the Western World.

The survey ends with the decline of devices adapted to the draining of supplies of gold from other European countries and the beginning of concentration on the production of gold which became conspicuous after the discoveries in California and in the Pacific after 1848. The problem of production[1] of precious metals tends to displace the problem of trade. It marks the end of the problems of industrial and short-term credit following improvements in communication and transportation. The American Revolution followed the conflict between an aggressive short-term commercial credit region in the American colonies and the powerful political long-term credit regions engaged in producing staples for the mother country. Long-term credit was the essence of vested interests maintaining a monopoly under favourable British legislation as in

[1] See H. A. Innis, "Liquidity Preference as a Factor in Industrial Development" (*Transactions of the Royal Society of Canada*, 1943, section II, pp. 1-31).

the case of the sugar planters of the West Indies in opposition to the Atlantic colonies, of the fishing interests of the West Country in opposition to Newfoundland, of the fur trade of the Hudson's Bay Company against the St. Lawrence, and of the timber trade under colonial as against Baltic interests. The significance of theoretical interest in the broad problem of the wealth of nations shown in the writings of the period was in the undermining of the shelter of vested interests of staple industries requiring long-term commercial credit. The Reform Acts opened the way to the destruction of rotten boroughs as hiding places. The failure of the old Empire and the pressure of short-term credit in the manufacturing areas of Great Britain opened the way for free trade and the third Empire. The demands of new staples adapted to the industrial needs of Great Britain under free trade compelled the development of responsible government in the staple-producing regions to create devices for borrowing extensive capital for the construction of canals and railways. Responsible government and the decline of colonial preferences compelled a reorganization of imperial cost accounting and the setting up of new systems of allocation. The spread of economic theory lagged in the colonies with the result that protection took the place of colonial preferences. New vested interests such as the investors in Great Britain and the new industrialists in the colonies supported the growth of local autonomy.

The emergence of responsible government and the third Empire marked a stage in the constitutional evolution of Great Britain and the Western World beginning with feudalism and the emphasis on land, supported by the position of Great Britain as a frontier and an exporter of wool as a staple to Europe, and continuing through the adjustment of feudalism and land to the demands of the sea and trade. Feudalism and primogeniture contributed to expansion of maritime trade. The Crown with its monopolies was inadequate to the demands of maritime trade, and parliament with statutes of regulation encroached on its powers. In turn Crown and parliament proved inadequate to the demands of active commercial units in the American colonies and adjusted their position in the second and third Empires only after the colonies had rebelled. But the adaptability of the British Constitution was in sharp contrast with the rigidity of the French. The strength of feudalism in France and the power of the Crown reinforced by the Church favoured the conquest of land. French institutions were adapted to continental expansion. Centralized control fostered the occupation of North America by military rather than naval development. The spirit of feudalism and the army was evident in measures of defence shown in the construction of forts on the line of principles developed by Vauban. But continental expansion, reliance on feudalism and land, the importance of the army and forts made enormous demands on expenditures and in turn on the fiscal mechanism. Whereas naval expansion was a part of maritime trade, and the Navigation Acts favoured ships and maritime trade, military expansion on land implied severe burdens on trade and finance. Continental expansion under the French assured monopoly control over the St. Lawrence and the Mississippi, extensive contacts in trade with an aboriginal civilization, consequent sharp fluctuations in the supply of furs as a staple product and in the demand for furs as a luxury product, and sharp changes in income with strains on the economy of France and her colonies. Maritime expansion under the English assumed competition along an extended coast line and a large number of relatively short rivers, between populations with standards of living comparable to the mother country, and with a monetary system gradually extended on the basis of specie obtained under mercantile policies and gradually increasing the efficiency and regulation of the laws of supply and demand. A maritime economy tended to be characterized by stability and a continental economy by violent fluctuations. The characteristics of a continental economy in France were extended to the continent of North America, and the characteristics of a maritime economy in England were extended along the Atlantic seaboard. For both economies the problem of new areas proved too difficult, but the flexible character of the British Empire provided the base for the commercial civilization of the Western World. Competition between regions along the Atlantic seaboard was effective in adjusting relations between them, whereas competition between drainage basins on the continent was monopolistic in character and subject to intense difficulties whether they were controlled by the same European power, as in the case of the St. Lawrence and the Mississippi, or by separate European powers, as in the case of the St. Lawrence and Hudson Bay.

In the second Empire the adjustment of Crown and parliament in relation to the demands of Nova Scotia proved more rapid along the Atlantic seaboard than in the St. Lawrence. Nova Scotia was dependent on the expansion of maritime trade, and the St. Lawrence on the military control of a conquered people and the exploitation of land under the Crown. Traditions of parliament and the assemblies in the old Empire continued in Nova Scotia in the new

Empire, but delay in the establishment of assemblies in the St. Lawrence region and the emphasis on land and the feudal system strengthened the traditions of the Crown. The long struggle between the executive and the assembly in the St. Lawrence was in sharp contrast with the development of government in Nova Scotia. Newfoundland as a result of the vested interests of shipping in the West Country in England occupied a marginal position in the first Empire and in the second. New England regarded Newfoundland in the old Empire as an extension of Great Britain under the Navigation Acts where goods could be warehoused to avoid the costs of direct contacts with England. The policy of the West Country in denying a separate entity to Newfoundland was exploited by New England. In the second Empire the support of Nova Scotia to settlement in Newfoundland, especially during the Napoleonic Wars, and the weakening of the position of the West Country brought the long-delayed institution of the courts, recognition of ownership of land, and the long struggle for representative institutions and responsible government.

Dr. Knorr has described the background of the development of flexibility in the British Empire. His study throws fresh light on the fundamental problem of western civilization—that of the impact of ideas or rather of the conditions under which ideas emerge and take root. Decline of censorship of the press prepared the ground for the rich crop of ideas which proceed from the press. The censorship of France restricted an interest in problems of colonial theory. Ideas sprang from the wealth of vested interests concerned in colonial development, and extensive publication favoured the weeding out of the impractical. Political economy grew from the soil of commercial activity. The emergence of the broad study of policy came with the background of trade and industry. A study of the wealth of nations followed a study of the wealth of separate interests. The significance of the broader approach to policy was evident in its wholesale revision which followed publication of *The Wealth of Nations* and the revolt of the colonies. The reading of Malthus and the census of 1801 led Selkirk to undertake his colonial experiments in the St. Lawrence region and in the Red River. The population problem introduced by Malthus had its impact on emigration and the spread of imperialism. Ricardo's theory of rent undermined the position of the landed aristocracy and paved the way to free trade.

The flexibility characteristic of Anglo-Saxon traditions described by Dr. Knorr has its implications for Western civilization and particularly for Canada. Without an international organization with flexibility as its essence Canada would lose her freedom in the friction between blocs of power in the United States and in the British Empire. Consolidations of power compel further consolidations of power, and intensification of nationalism compels further intensification. The significance of the colour problem to Western civilization is evident in the demand for consolidations of power in the United States and in the British Empire. Continued insistence on flexibility is the basis of effective development in the British Commonwealth of Nations including Eire, and of advance to an efficient world organization based on co-operation rather than on power. Ominous trends have been evident in the growth of nationalism, the tyranny of opinion, which has become more powerful since the turn of the century, and the rise of bureaucracy, particularly in the war period, and with it the obsession with detail and the administrative complexity and rigidity which characterized the mercantilism of the first Empire.

The British Commonwealth of Nations and particularly the autonomy of Canada were a result of the strength of the democratic tradition of the United States. A powerful country without a strong foreign policy permitted survival. A drift from democratic traditions in the United States and the development of nationalistic or imperialistic trends implies interference in Canadian affairs, and a drift from democratic traditions in Canada in nationalism or imperialism invites interference. A small nation with survival dependent on international organization is exposed to grave dangers as a result of the temptation to play a large part in world affairs, to assume the role of interpreter between larger powers, and to accentuate national pride in manifest destiny. "Collaboration" with large powers almost certainly involves playing a game without the picture cards or of being used as a pawn. On three notable occasions the results of Canadian interference have been roughly as follows—the Alaska boundary dispute with Canada against the United States and Great Britain and consequent antagonism to both, the Anglo-Japanese Alliance[2] in which Canada co-operated with the United States, and the Ottawa Conference in 1932 in which Canada co-operated with Great Britain in formulating a policy to meet the offensive tariff measures of the United States

[2]See J. B. Brebner, "Canada, the Anglo-Japanese Alliance and the Washington Conference" (*Political Science Quarterly*, March, 1935, pp. 45-58). Professor Brebner tends to neglect the influence of Ambassador Harvey. See W. F. Johnson, *George Harvey* (Boston, 1929), chap. XXXII.

and incurred the antagonism of Great Britain by her aggressiveness in pressing for a point of meeting in Canada and in taking advantage of a weak government. The dangers are increased by the complexity of domestic difficulties in race and religion. Census returns point to the impending struggle and the necessity of concern with external rather than domestic problems. It may be urged that we should resist pressure to become professional chestnut savers, that we should dig in our own garden, that solution of our domestic difficulties would compel the respect of large powers and in turn compel the closer relations between Great Britain and the United States essential to world peace,[3] but a small bilingual nation has no such alternative. Switzerland appears to have been compelled to turn inward rather than outward and to have passed through periods of difficulty and the mercenary stage,[4] but she has an entirely different geographical background. All this, however, belongs to a later period than that described by Dr. Knorr, though we can reach no successful solution without following the road which he has described in the conflicting arguments of the period of the first and second Empire.

H. A. INNIS

The University of Toronto,
March, 1944.

[3]"For God's sake, do not drag me into another war! I am worn down, and worn out, with crusading and defending Europe, and protecting mankind; I *must* think a little of myself. I am sorry for the Spaniards—I am sorry for the Greeks—I deplore the fate of the Jews; the people of the Sandwich Islands are groaning under the most detestable tyranny; Bagdad is oppressed—I do not like the present state of the Delta—Thibet is not comfortable. Am I to fight for all these people? The world is bursting with sin and sorrow. Am I to be the champion of the Decalogue, and to be eternally raising fleets and armies to make all men good and happy? We have just done saving Europe, and I am afraid the consequences will be that we shall cut each other's throats. No war, dear Lady Grey! —no eloquence; but apathy, selfishness, common sense, arithmetic! I beseech you, secure Lord Grey's sword and pistols, as the housekeeper did Don Quixote's armor" (Feb. 19, 1823, Sydney Smith to the Countess Grey, Lady Holland, *A Memoir of Reverend Sydney Smith*, New York, 1855, II, p. 288).

"Each time Mr. Wells and my other architectural friends anticipate a great out-burst of post-war activity and world-planning my heart contracts. To me the chance for future society lies through apathy, uninventiveness and inertia" (cited in Lionel Trilling, *E. M. Foster*, Norfolk, 1943, p. 173).

[4]Marshall Ney to a Swiss general, "We fight for honour! You for money!" The Swiss General to Marshall Ney, "Yes, Marshall!, we both fight for what we have not got" (*The Autobiography of William Jerdan*, London, 1853, III, p. 65).

PREFACE

THE purpose of this study is to present and examine significant British colonial theories on the advantages and disadvantages resulting to the mother country from the establishment and maintenance of oversea colonies. For what reasons was the building and the preservation of Empire thought profitable or unprofitable to the British nation?

From the very beginning of English colonization up to the present, this question occupied the minds of British writers and politicians. No single argument or any inter-related set of arguments, no theory in other words, remained unchallenged over any length of time. Sometimes the continuous debate among politically influential and intellectually articulate groups on the pros and cons of empire slackened and arguments became stereotyped; sometimes the discussion was exceedingly lively, the change of ideas rapid, and mortality of arguments high.

The development of colonial theories influenced motives that produced action and significantly fashioned the formulation of policies. Action by responsible statesmen in framing expansionist and imperial policies must receive the sanction of the politically influential. This process necessitates discussion which is facilitated by the formulation of theories.

Not that policy-making is exclusively influenced by the objective merits or demerits of theoretical alternatives. Traditions, prejudices, self-interest, and inertia enter significantly into the picture. Irrational pride of empire, for example, may determine a large portion of the ruling groups to disregard well-established arguments put forth by anti-imperialist circles. It is a widely accepted assumption that the theories and opinions of ruling groups are determined by their own selfish interests as to power, prestige, and income. However, the realization of such selfish interests is in turn governed by opinions and theories on the nature of particular advantages and on the methods by which such advantages can be secured. In this sense, theories produce action and, therefore, are relevant data.

Various reasons may be advanced for the purpose of furthering any particular policy. These different reasons may carry different weight both with those who proffer them and with those to whom they are addressed. It is necessary, therefore, to distinguish between the relative weight of imperialist and anti-imperialist arguments. This is most difficult when the representatives of a particular interest-group stress specific arguments because they appear popular but are irrelevant to the objective this group has chiefly in mind. Yet wherever there are rival groups of influential persons and a sufficient amount of freedom of speech, as obtained in Great Britain throughout the period considered in this study, such subterfuge will not escape exposure.

Colonial arguments and theories change because ruling groups revise their set of ultimate ends or discover fallacies in prevalent conceptions regarding the methods of arriving at such ends. Most important of all, change is the result of a modified distribution of political power and social prestige.

As suggested in the foregoing paragraphs, colonial theories are not produced in a vacuum. They are acted upon by theories on related subject-matters. Theories of population and international trade in particular and theoretical considerations of power and welfare in general influence and are influenced by colonial theories. All these theories are, in turn, the product of the political, social, and cultural setting of an age in a particular country. Factors such as technological progress and religious movements are found to have had a definite bearing on the development of colonial theories and major social and political changes are seen reflected in changes of imperial thinking.

Covering a period of nearly three centuries, the present study cannot be expected to furnish a detailed examination of the exact cultural and social genesis of specific colonial arguments. Such an exhaustive undertaking could have been conducted only for a very limited period of time. In the case of Great Britain, moreover, major lines of social and cultural causation as well as of the relationships of different ideas have fortunately been established by reliable historians. In the following it must suffice to make reference to their conclusions.

Writings and speeches of the day form an immense storehouse for the student of British colonial theories. Indeed, he is faced not with paucity but with a vast abundance of source material. It was necessary, therefore, to adopt the method of critically selecting representative statements. In respect of every single argument care has been taken to examine a sufficiently large number of statements in order to avoid unwarranted generalizations. The most typical of these arguments are quoted verbatim. It has been thought useful to include numerous statements issued by mediocre writers and politicians whose utterances are usually more typical than those of their more brilliant contemporaries.

This study is interested not in persons but in ideas. Authorship is deemed of importance merely in so far as it indicates, in broad manner, the political and social genesis of arguments offered. Attention is focused on major arguments and theories. Their discussion is arranged topically as well as chronologically. Because contemporary events in British history—wars, peace treaties, industrial progress, social change, etc.—exerted an important influence on colonial theories, the chronological has not been subordinated to the topical. Hence, this study is divided into relatively extensive chronological periods within which arguments and theories are discussed on the basis of topical classifications.

Colonial arguments and theories referring to the particular cases of Ireland and India have been excluded from the present study. No doubt, the English planted their first colony in Ireland and until the Union with England in 1800, Ireland was in fact an English colony. But there are important differences between Ireland and other British colonies. The same holds true of India. English writers usually considered these two dependencies as cases *sui generis* and their arguments and theories were, therefore, not immediately applicable to these two colonies.

This study was written originally as a doctoral dissertation under the supervision of Professor Jacob Viner of the University of Chicago. To him, scholar and teacher *par excellence*, I am greatly indebted for arousing my interest in the subject and providing much helpful criticism. Professor Harold A. Innis and Professor V. W. Bladen, both of the University of Toronto, gave me generous advice. Professor Bladen also furnished valuable editorial assistance. Grateful acknowledgments are due also to Professor Quincy Wright of the University of Chicago and Professor J. B. Condliffe of the University of California. They all read the manuscript and made helpful suggestions. For devoted editorial assistance I owe much to my wife. Finally, I wish to express my sincerest gratitude to the Canadian Social Science Research Council for granting a subsidy without which publication would have been impossible at this time.

KLAUS E. KNORR

Stanford University, California,
April, 1943.

PART I

CHAPTER I

INTRODUCTION

THAT set of policies which shaped the relations between Great Britain and her colonial empire, from its birth until the American War of Independence, is usually referred to as the "Old Colonial System." As this system is structurally part of the so-called "Mercantile System," the theories underlying it are mercantilist theories. The fact that mercantilist thought antedated the establishment of English trans-oceanic colonies suggests the usefulness of outlining its fundamental principles. Such an approach to the subject matter under consideration would indicate the particular frame of mind in which the first English writers on the desirability of possessing oversea colonies were inclined to view the actual possibility of colonizing.

To the reader of recent literature it seems customary to start a discussion of the "mercantile system" or of "mercantilism" by pointing out the inutility of these terms. It may be acknowledged that the mercantilists failed to leave to their successors a system of thought intellectually as consistent as that of Thomism, of Physiocracy, or of the classical school of economics.[1] Writing at different stages between, roughly, the sixteenth and the nineteenth centuries, representing different social classes and interest-groups, having received different kinds of training, and often marshalling all their arguments with a view to advocating some particular policy, the mercantilists produced a bundle of doctrinal elements which, far from dovetailing, are incapable of exhaustive systematic demonstration. It is quite true that mercantilism does not mean "exactly the same thing at different times, or in different places at the same time."[2] It is likewise true that with regard to most major doctrines of mercantilism, there are not only some mercantilist writers who attacked and disproved them (without thereby ceasing to be mer-

---

[1] This is the opinion of A. V. Judges, "The Idea of a Mercantile State," *Transactions of the Royal Historical Society*, 4th series, XXI (1939), 41 f.

[2] Conyers Read, "Mercantilism: the Old English Pattern of a Controlled Economy," *The Constitution Reconsidered*, ed. C. Read (New York, 1938), p. 63.

cantilists), there are also cases in which the very demonstration of such doctrines is, to our minds, self-contradictory.³

Yet in spite of these admissions and qualifications, the "mercantile system" was more than just an uncoördinated maze of opportunist expedients of statecraft.⁴ It can hardly be denied that there are some basic principles which bestow upon the writings of the various mercantilists more than a topical unity. From a formal point of view, it seems most fruitful to regard the "mercantile system" as a "variegated fabric of economic ideas,"⁵ the major threads of which can be separated for purposes of analysis. Or, to employ a more abstract phrase, the reviewer is confronted with a "shifting combination"⁶ of diverse doctrinal tendencies which even themselves are frequently in a "state of flux."⁷ Regarded from the point of view of substance, some of these "major threads" or "doctrinal tendencies" will be outlined below.

The mercantilists, of course, were mainly concerned with a programme of conduct on the part of state, corporation, and individual. Planned conduct supposedly being determined by ends and means, they provided their contemporaries with theories as to both. In order to understand their conception of the ends involved, it seems useful to study briefly the international and national environment of the "mercantile state" with the view of discovering the particular tasks with which historical realities (to the shaping of which the practitioners of the "mercantile system" only partially contributed) confronted them.⁸

Regarding the external environment which the state and its rulers had to face, the early development of mercantilist thought was accompanied by the gradual disintegration and final collapse

---

³Jacob Viner, *Studies in the Theory of International Trade* (New York, 1937), chaps. I-II.

⁴As is the opinion of Judges, "Idea of the Mercantile State," p. 50.

⁵E. A. J. Johnson, *Predecessors of Adam Smith* (New York, 1937), p. 4.

⁶P. J. Thomas, *Mercantilism and the East India Trade* (London, 1926), p. 3.

⁷E. S. Furniss, *The Position of the Laborer in a System of Nationalism* (Boston, 1920), p. 8.

⁸To appreciate the significance of such a study, however, it should be emphasized that both the theorisers and the practitioners of the "system" may have, at least partly, misinterpreted these historical realities, that they may have overstressed one task as against another, and that they may have resorted to incompetent, inadequate, or misconceived means in attempting to tackle these tasks. They also may have had in mind private ends of their own. With regard to all these aspects of the problem there was nothing inevitable about the conclusions at which the mercantilists arrived. This fact has been frequently overlooked by economic historians.

of the medieval system of European unity and the simultaneous emergence of a number of monarchical nation-states which stood to each other in a relation of absolute independence and legal equality.[9] The consummation of this change has been repeatedly described and traced in its diverse political, economic, social, and cultural aspects. Hence, it is only necessary here to point out some of its more important implications. During the Middle Ages the state was a rather loosely knit unit permitting a great deal of intrastate diversity in some spheres as well as interstate uniformity in others. The rulers of the ascendant nation-states were exceedingly conscious of their own separate personality and deliberately cultivated this separateness.[10] All universalist and internationalist ties being loosened or jettisoned in the course of this process,[11] there remained for the regulation of interstate relations no principle but that of force in one form or other. The state-system which thus emerged was often characterized by an aggressive desire among the rulers to effect a maximum extension of territory under their sovereignty or of resources under their absolute control. The salient feature of this international system, therefore, was the existence of antagonistic drives coupled with the almost total lack of any common and, hence, unifying, interest. Thus there was no common desire for the maintenance of peace except during short periods of exhaustion following prolonged warfare. Even then such a desire for peace was in most cases little more than a wish for a period of rest or for a truce. It will be shown below that the then current conception of international trade likewise excluded any notion of a common good of which all states partook.

It was this absence of the recognition of a community of interests among the nation-states which retarded the evolution of a universally binding legal framework replacing that of medieval Europe which had been discarded. Community of interest against the aggressor existed only temporarily among a certain number of states which combined against the most powerful and voracious of their kind. But the principle of the balance of power, based though it was on a temporary community of interest, was never

[9]Cf. Charles Dupuis, *Le Principe de l'équilibre et le concert européen* (Paris, 1909), chap. I; R. B. Mowat, *The European State System* (London, 1923).
[10]Cf. M. J. Bonn, *The Crumbling of Empire* (London, 1938), pp. 15 ff.
[11]Cf. Jacopo Mazzei, "Potenza mezzo di ricchezza e ricchezza mezzo di potenza nel pensiero di mercantilisti," *Rivista Internazionale di Scienze Sociali*, XLI (1933), 4; René Gonnard, *Histoire des doctrines économiques* (Paris, 1930), p. 69.

capable of producing a steady equilibrium. In the last analysis, it was but a "calcul de forces."[12] Power being inherently an ever-inconstant factor, the power relationships between the various states were bound to be in flux.[13] The pursuit of an equilibristic policy, therefore, implied a perpetual *balancing* of power. There was always some pretender intent on tipping the balance in his favour. The inherent instability of the system of alliances upon which balance-of-power diplomacy rested was augmented by the fact that in the overwhelming majority of cases sheer military victory settled nothing permanently. Given underlying conditions conducive to the generation of conflicts, conflicts are bound to emerge.

The consequences of this situation are evident: the occurrence of war as the ultimate method of testing relative power relationships and as the ultimate regulator in international affairs, had to be constantly reckoned with, and preparedness in its military, economic, and diplomatic aspects appeared as a constant objective in shaping politics. It likewise necessitated ever-alert watchfulness and jealousy toward actual and potential rivals. The need of sustained vigilance and preparedness and the psychological condition of omnipresent jealousy, therefore, seem to be the most remarkable features of this state-system.

To quote some contemporary opinions, Thomas Hobbes was fully aware that absolute national sovereignty and the absence of universal power-enforced laws[14] were conditions responsible for the frequent occurrence of wars. He observed that "in all times, Kings, and Persons of Soveraigne authority, because of their Independency, are in continuall jealousies, and in the state and posture of Gladiators; having their weapons pointing, and their eyes fixed on one another."[15] He also testified to the instability of peace and the resulting necessity of constant preparedness: "For Warre, consisteth not in Battell onely, or in the act of fighting, but in a tract of time, wherein the Will to contend by Battell is sufficiently known . . . the nature of War, consisteth not in actuall fighting; but in the known disposition thereto, during all the time there is no assurance to the contrary. All other time is PEACE."[16]

Similarly, Francis Bacon revealed the essence of balance-of-power diplomacy by stating that, as regards the king's neighbours,

---

[12]Dupuis, *Le Principe de l'équilibre*, p. 14.   [13]*Ibid.*, pp. 93 ff.
[14]Cf. Thomas Hobbes, *Leviathan* (1651) (Everyman ed.; London, 1940), p. 66.
[15]*Ibid.*, p. 65.   [16]*Ibid.*, p. 64.

INTRODUCTION 7

"there can no general rule be given (the occasions are so variable), save one, which ever holdeth; which is, that princes do keep due sentinel, that none of their neighbours do overgrow so (by increase of territory, by embracing of trade, by approaches, or the like) as they become more able to annoy them than they were."[17] On the necessity of preparedness he remarks that "the best way to continue a secure peace, is to be prepared for a war. Security is an ill guard for a Kingdom."[18] And the author of *A Discourse of the Common Weal of This Realm of England* wrote: "Wise men saie that in peace men must looke and provide for warre..."[19]

The above quotations show how keen observers, penetrating beneath the surface of events, viewed the basic patterns of contemporary international politics. Even England's geographical insularity could not produce a confident feeling of security at a time when she did not enjoy unchallenged naval superiority over the narrow seas. Her growing participation in oversea colonization, furthermore, led to increased involvement in power politics. Colonial empires were founded in opposition to each other.[20] Their increase and defence reacted directly on power alignments and power politics in Europe, and *vice versa*. A system of the colonial balance of power emerged which not only became part of the European balance of power, but also multiplied the causes of conflicts and rendered them more acrimonious than before.[21]

The majority of modern writers on mercantilism suggest, usually without adducing sufficient evidence, that "state-making," that is, the primary objective of unifying and consolidating the

[17]Francis Bacon, "Of Empire," *Essays* (Everyman ed.; London, 1936), p. 58.

[18]Francis Bacon, *A Letter of Advice to the Duke of Buckingham* (1616), in James Spedding (ed.), *The Letters and the Life of Francis Bacon* (London, 1872), VI, 20.

[19]E. Lammond (ed.), *A Discourse of the Common Weal of This Realm of England* [1581] (Cambridge, 1893), p. 84.

[20]Bonn, *Crumbling of Empire*, p. 25.

[21]In exceptional cases this intimate connection between European and colonial power politics was suspended. At the beginnings of English colonization, informal war in America was deemed compatible with formal peace in Europe. Thus Drake (referring to the line of demarcation established by the Treaty of Tordesillas in 1494) coined the phrase of "no peace beyond the line" (cf. Adolf Rein, *Die europäische Ausbreitung über die Erde* [Potsdam, 1931], p. 184). The Anglo-French agreements of 1686 and 1687 stipulating that acts of violence in America were not to be considered as a *casus belli* in Europe, may be mentioned as an example of a reverse relationship (cf. Max Savelle, *The Diplomatic History of the Canadian Boundary, 1749-1763* [New Haven, 1940], Preface, p. x). However, agreements of the latter type were usually, sooner or later, disregarded.

national state and/or that of strengthening the state's power with regard to its role in the international arena, constituted the predominant motives of the mercantilists and the influential among their contemporaries.[22]

As to the first assumption, the case of England differed somewhat from that of continental European states. In England, the development of a strong and thoroughly unified and centralized state preceded the appearance of an extensive mercantilist literature.[23] As far as the second assumption is concerned, the foregoing considerations seem to suggest that considerations of power, with a view to national self-preservation, must have been uppermost in the minds of the ruling class. However, sweeping generalizations should be avoided. Professor Viner pointed out that in England an aggressive national spirit had emerged before the development of mercantilist theorizing as a predominant current of thought.[24] This fact in itself does not, of course, invalidate Professor Heckscher's thesis of the predominance of power considerations in mercantilist reasoning. If one thinks of the impact of power politics, gradually growing in weightiness, upon the minds of policy-makers and theorizers, it seems safe to assume that their reactions were evoked over a long period of time before they assumed a more articulate form. Furthermore, while nationalistic aggressiveness is conceivable without leading to mercantilist theories of conduct, surely there is nothing essentially incompatible about these two phenomena.

But was power really *the* ultimate end[25] which theorists and practitioners of mercantilism had in mind? Comparing mercantilism with post-mercantilist thought, as represented by Adam Smith, Professor Heckscher declared that "the most vital aspect of the problem is whether power is considered as an end in itself, or only as a means for gaining something else, such as the well-being of the nation in this world...."[26] Applying this standard of judgment he arrived at the conclusion that, in spite of the lack of clear-cut demarcation, "there can be no doubt that an essential

---

[22]Cf. Gustav Schmoller, *The Mercantile System* (New York, 1896), p. 50; E. Heckscher, *Mercantilism* (London, 1935), I, 21; E. Lipson, *The Economic History of England* (London, 1931), III, 1; Thomas, *Mercantilism and the East India Trade*, p. 3; Johnson, *Predecessors of Adam Smith*, pp. 3 ff.; Furniss, *Position of the Laborer in a System of Nationalism*, pp. 5 f.

[23]Viner, *Studies*, p. 111. [24]*Ibid.*

[25]The end of internal unification of the state is disregarded in the following discussion.

[26]*Mercantilism*, II, 16.

distinction is discernible here. . . . Adam Smith's argument was undoubtedly that the endeavours toward opulence must make such sacrifices as security demanded. For him, power was certainly only a means to an end. . . . Mercantilists usually believed the reverse, and mercantilism as a system of power was thus primarily a system for forcing economic policy into the service of power as an end in itself."[27] Thus, Professor Heckscher inferred that post-mercantilist reasoning favoured the promotion of both wealth and power, but considered the latter end to be distinctly subordinate to the former. To the mercantilists, on the other hand, attainment of power had been the primary objective. They had esteemed wealth only in so far as it was productive of power.

Professor Viner opposed this interpretation. He pointed out that the evidence so far adduced by students of mercantilism does not justify the conclusion "that there was substantial difference in these respects between the seventeenth and the nineteenth centuries. For both periods power and wealth were both ultimate ends, i.e., valued for their own sakes. In neither period were they ordinarily regarded as conflicting ends, and on the contrary it was the general view in both periods that the attainment of the one was a means to the attainment of the other; power bred wealth, and wealth power."[28]

In answer to this criticism, Professor Heckscher somewhat recanted his former doctrine.

The ends of statesmen in the economic field between, say, the beginning of the sixteenth and the middle of the eighteenth centuries were of course diversified; but I think it may be said that at least two tendencies played a very great part, i.e., that towards the unification of the territory of the State economically, and the use of the resources of their countries in the interests of the political power of the State. . . . But important as this was in itself, it does not constitute the most characteristic contrast to what came later . . . the most important difference did not lie in the choice of ends, but in opinions as to the best way of achieving those ends; i.e., in the choice of means. . . . I agree with my critics on that point to the extent of admitting that both "power" and "opulence" . . . have been, and must be, of importance to economic policy of every description. But I do not think that there can be any doubt that these two aims changed places in the transition from mercantilism to laissez-faire.[29]

That every ruling group strives at all times for the attainment of diverse ends is an assumption that need not be proved. The

[27]*Ibid.*, p. 17.
[28]Jacob Viner, "Mercantilism," *Economic History Review*, VI (1935-6), 100.
[29]E. F. Heckscher, "Mercantilism," *Economic History Review*, VII (1936), 45-8.

exclusive pursuit of one object solely is unthinkable. But regarding this diversity of ends, the attitude of the majority among the ruling class very likely is patterned after some vague[30] scale of preferences.[31] Ordinarily there is also an extremely complicated relationship between means and ends, i.e., the same phenomena, power and wealth, may be regarded at the same time as ends in themselves and as means to the attainment of either. Furthermore, if different periods are compared, even the attainment of the same end may be pursued by different means.

Professor Viner certainly is right in observing that to mercantilism as well as to post-mercantilism, both power and wealth were ultimate ends. There were, however, two remarkable differences. It was the consensus of opinion in both periods that wealth bred power. The majority of mercantilists, as will be seen, also assumed that power bred wealth. During the post-mercantilist period, however, there was an increasing tendency to assume that power was largely attained at the expense of wealth. It was Adam Smith who popularized the idea that opulence and power were incompatible ends and that considerations of power, though necessary in the interest of national self-preservation, conflicted with considerations of plenty. The Manchester School, later on, sharply stressed the fundamental antagonism between these two ends.[32]

The other difference lies in a different conception of "wealth." It is not quite clear what the mercantilists understood wealth to be, but they certainly did not subscribe to the definition of it advanced by economic liberalism. It would be wrong to assume that the mercantilists had no concern for the welfare of the broad masses of the people, but progressively greater satisfaction of their material wants was not a guiding idea to them. Mercantilists did not think in terms of a consumer-oriented economy. Wealth to their minds, in the first place, was identical with the wealth of the ruling class, and wealth of the national community was wealth which, through their political control of the state, could be mobilized for the needs of ruling groups. The masses of the people, as will be

---

[30]Such a scale of preferences will be clearly differentiated only by the lucid and abstract thinker.

[31]If a ruling class is composed of different groups, especially as regards major interests, then the majority opinion of each single group may differ as far as this scale of preferences is concerned. For example, opinions of English landholders and English merchants may have differed in this respect.

[32]The attitude of the Manchester School toward the ends of power and wealth will be further discussed in the second part of this study.

seen, were rather regarded as components of national wealth in the latter sense.

Finally, it must be kept in mind that, strictly speaking, power in itself is seldom wanted as an ultimate end. No doubt, its very accumulation may be a process enjoyable to those who command power. Apart from this, power may be wanted for the sake of the prestige and influence it confers upon the ruling class, for the preservation of national independence in a world ruled by power diplomacy and war, for the purpose of aggrandizement, or for the promotion of wealth (sectional or national) if it is assumed that power breeds wealth and profits.

It has been suggested above that the accumulation of power with the view to preserving national independence in a world characterized by power diplomacy and frequent warfare, necessarily must have been a major consideration of the English ruling class. With the advent of anti-mercantilist thought, however, Britain was relatively much more powerful than she had been during the mercantilist period.

Changes in the external environment of the nation and a declining belief in the theory that power breeds national wealth and sectional profits, therefore, partly account for the fact that considerations of power in contrast to considerations of plenty were weightier in the mercantilist than in the post-mercantilist period.

The assumption that power is productive of wealth is manifest in contemporary consideration of the relationship between maritime power and trade. Bacon observed that "the wealth of both Indies seems in good part but an accessory to the command of the seas."[33] Sir John Borough likewise emphasized mastery of the sea as a prerequisite to the acquisition of wealth through the medium of foreign trade.[34] Daniel Defoe wrote: "'Tis for this, that these Nations keep up such a Military Force; such Fleets and such Armies to protect their Trade, to keep all the Back-doors open. . . . Trading Nations are obliged to defend their Commerce. . . . If the Doors of our Commerce are shut, we must open them. . . ."[35] Henry Elking, after describing England's superior power, concluded that "there is no doubt but our Merchants, whose Ships are pro-

---

[33]Francis Bacon, "Of the Greatness of Kingdoms and Estates," *Essays*, p. 96.

[34]Sir John Borough, *The Soveraignty of the British Seas* (London, 1651), p. 115.

[35][Daniel Defoe], *The Evident Approach of a War* (2nd ed.; London, 1727), pp. 13, 30.

tected, their Interest assisted in foreign Courts, will reap the Benefit of a Naval Power for Years to come...."[36] And speaking before the House of Lords, Lord Haversham asserted the mutually beneficial relationship between maritime power and trade: "Your Fleet and your Trade have so near a relation, and such mutual influence upon each other, they cannot well be separated; your trade is the mother and nurse of your seamen; your seamen are the life of your fleet, and your fleet is the security and protection of your trade, and both together are the wealth, strength, security and glory of Britain."[37]

Charles Davenant formulated the principle of trade following the flag: "To be in a lasting condition to cope with the Dutch in trade, we must, as well in time of peace as war, have a fleet in readiness strong enough, upon all occasions, vigorously to assert our dominion of the Sea: trade has ever been observed to follow power, and to be influenced by it.... No profession of men sooner feel the effects of national increase, or decrease in reputation, than merchants."[38] These quotations bear testimony to the mercantilist belief that the power and prestige of a strong state will further its foreign trade.

If the exigencies of England's position in a world ruled by the principles and forces of power diplomacy and the conviction that the external power of the state serves the function of promoting foreign trade, determined the theorizers and practitioners of mercantilism to render their state as powerful as possible, then it seems pertinent to enquire into mercantilist reasoning on the means by which this power could best be gained and preserved.

In formulating policies designed to further the external power of the state, mercantilist writers followed two different lines of approach.[39] First, they advocated the organization of economic activity towards increasing particular components of power. Secondly, they favoured the accumulation of a general reservoir of economic resources, or national wealth in general, from which power could be drawn when required.[40] Among the various ingredients of power most frequently stressed by mercantilist

---

[36] [Henry Elking], *The Interest of England Considered* (London, 1720), p. 38.
[37] William Cobbett, *The Parliamentary History of England*, (London, n.d.), vol. VI, c. 598. Henceforth these records will be referred to as *Parl. Hist.*
[38] Charles Whitworth (ed.), *The Political and Commercial Works of Charles D'Avenant* (London, 1771), V, 457.
[39] The distinction made between these two approaches was, of course, vague and is only discernible if mercantilist literature is regarded as a whole.
[40] Cf. Heckscher, *Mercantilism*, II, 31.

writers are "treasure" or "money" or "bullion," specific raw materials and products like naval stores (i.e., products which had to be imported into Great Britain), and specific implements like ships. To this list must be added population which, as a basis of power, was viewed from a quantitative and from a qualitative aspect. The former aspect, as will be shown later, was never an important factor in English mercantilist calculations. During the last decades of the sixteenth century and the first half of the seventeenth century, England was generally considered to be over-populated, and even later mercantilist writers were usually not interested in mere numbers. They desired the largest possible number of *employed* people, thus introducing a qualitative consideration. In addition, skilled artisans and well-trained seamen were deemed indispensable to the building up and the preservation of power.

Apart from the item of "treasure," the need felt for all these ingredients of power is self-explanatory. On the function of "treasure" the bulk of the mercantilists did not only hold remarkably confused and fallacious opinions, but the very term was employed with a great deal of ambiguity and often used interchangeably with "wealth" and "riches." While one extreme school of mercantilist writers absolutely identified "treasure" with "wealth,"[41] their more analytical contemporaries ascribed to the precious metals certain functions vital to the working of the national economy. Among these functions are those of serving as a state treasure, as stores of wealth, as capital, and as a circulating medium.[42] Although with respect to every single one of these functions of "treasure," a relationship can be construed, connecting it with the potential power of the state, the two most important aspects for the purpose of this study are those of the precious metals serving as a state treasure and as a desirable form of accumulated wealth.

Suviranta holds that when the English mercantilists pleaded for the hoarding of bullion, they did so for the purpose of providing for the safety of the nation in cases of emergency.[43] This was probably true at an earlier period up to the beginning of the sixteenth century.[44] However, the need for hoarded bullion as a

[41]Cf. Viner, *Studies*, pp. 21 f.

[42]*Ibid.*, p. 22. See also Professor Viner's discussion of the mercantilist theories on these functions (*ibid.*, pp. 22 ff.).

[43]Br. Suviranta, *The Theory of the Balance of Trade in England* (Helsingfors, 1923), p. 115.

[44]M. Beer, *Early English Economics* (London, 1938), p. 63.

state treasure for emergency cases is, in the later period, very rarely mentioned in the pertinent literature.[45] Still references to "treasure," "bullion," or "money" as the true "sinews of war" are exceedingly frequent. The following citations will serve as samples:

... and then yf his grace should want, in time of warre, specially sufficient treasure to paie for armore, weapons, tacklinges of shippes, goounes, and other artillarie, necessarie for the warre, that could by no meanes have his subiectes wheare with to bie the same, what should his grace be in, and his Realme? Surely very ill. And thearfore these coines and treasures be not with out cause called of wise men bellorum, that is to saie, The senowes of warre....[46]

Since Moneys haue obtained the title of the sinews of war, and the life of Commerce: I hope that the accumulating thereof may properly be called the Praeheminent study of Princes....[47]

There be three main parts of military puissance, Men, Money, and Confederates.[48]

... for they [treasure] and the army are like a ship at sea, which must be well-provided with anchors and cables and victuals; money is to them all this, nay, everything.[49]

For although Treasure is said to be the sinews of the War, yet this is so because it doth provide, unite & move the power of men, victuals, and munition where and when the cause doth require....[50]

Money is necessary for the purchasing of many Provisions for War by Land or Sea, as Arms, Victuals, Ammunition, materials for Shipping, and many others, which being gotten, yet neither Souldiers nor Seamen will now adventure themselves at the mouths of Cannon and Musket without pay, whereof the further Consequence is that the Prince and Nation which hath the greatest Treasure, will finally have the Victory, and probably with little or no fighting. For being enabled by their Treasure to keep themselves in a posture of War, they will oblige their Enemies to the like Expence, till their Armies and also their Councils will dissipate. This shews the difference between the ancient and the present Course of War.... But

---

[45]Viner, *Studies*, p. 23.

[46]*A Discourse of the Common Weal of This Realm of England* [1581], pp. 86 f.

[47]Gerard Malynes, *The Center of the Circle of Commerce* (London, 1623), Preface.

[48]Francis Bacon, *Considerations Touching a War with Spain* (1624) in J. Spedding (ed.), *Letters and Life of Francis Bacon*, VII, 498 f. On other occasions Bacon plays down the value of treasure as the sinews of war (cf. "Of the True Greatness of Kingdoms and Estates," *Essays*, pp. 90 f.), but his intention in doing so was only to stress the even greater importance of subjects of sufficiently martial disposition (*ibid.*, p. 91).

[49]Thomas Violet, *Mysteries and Secrets of Trade and Mint-Affairs* (London, 1653), p. 35.

[50]Thomas Mun, *England's Treasure by Forraign Trade* (1664), in J. R. MacCulloch (ed.), *A Select Collection of Early English Tracts on Commerce* (London, 1856), p. 190.

since the Wealth of the Indies came to be discovered and dispersed more and more, Wars are managed by much Treasure and little Fighting, and therefore with little hazard to the richer Nation. . . . Also Money will command the Service and Lives of any poorer and rougher Nation, It will purchase the Assistance of Forreign Princes, It will indear their Ministers, open their Cabinets, engage true and close Correspondencies, and poison their Councils: It will pass unseen through Rampiers, Fortifications, and Guards, into Cities and Forts, and will surprize them without the tedious hazards of Seiges; It will purchase Governors and Generals, and like Lightning will consume the Heart of a poorer Nation, whilst its Countenance and Outside shall remain fresh.[51]

Hereby the Nation will be abundantly Enriched, and Money being the very Life of War, and Sinews of all Publick Action, we shall be enabled to bring the World into a Dependent Awe. . . . For, Since the introduction of the New Artillery of Powder Guns, &c. and the Discovery of the Wealth of the Indies, &c. War is become rather an Expence of Money than Men, and Success attends those that can most and longest spend Money: Whence it is that Princes' Armies in Europe are become more proportionable to Purses than to the Number of their People; . . .[52]

Thus Money raises Armies. . . .[53]

Money, it is true, has of late been more than ever, been among us regarded as the main Engine of war. . . .[54]

Similar statements appeared with regard to the ascendancy of Spanish military power and Spanish mines in America.

And in very deede it is moste apparaunte that riches are the fittest instrumentes of conquests, and that the Emperour turned them to that use.[55]

. . . it is his [the Spanish King's] Indian gold that endangereth and disturbeth all the nations of Europe; it purchaseth intelligence, creepeth into counsels, and setteth bound loyalty at liberty in the greatest monarchies of Europe.[56]

. . . now let us a little consider the enemy wee are to encounter, the king of Spaine. They are not his great territories which make him so powerful, and so troublesome to all Christendomes. . . . No, sir, they are his mines in the West Indies, which minister fuell to feed his vast ambitious desires of universall monarchy; it is the money he hath from thence, which makes

---

[51][William Petyt], *Britannia Languens* (1680), in MacCulloch, *Collection of Early English Tracts on Commerce*, pp. 11 f.

[52]James Whiston, *A Discourse of the Decay of Trade* (London, 1693), pp. 2 ff.

[53]Daniel Defoe, *A Plan for the English Commerce* (1728) (ed. Oxford, 1927), p. 40.

[54]John Brown, *An Estimate of the Manners and Principles of the Times* (5th ed.; London, 1757), p. 92.

[55]Richard Hakluyt, *Discourse on Western Planting* (1584), in C. Deane (ed.), *Documentary History of the State of Maine* (Cambridge, 1877), II, 52.

[56]Sir Walter Raleigh, *A Voyage for the Discovery of Guiana* (1596), in *Works* (ed. London, 1751), II, 149.

him able to levy, and pay souldiers in all places; and to keep an army continually a foot, ready to invade and endanger his neighbours.[57]

An analysis of even these few quotations will clarify some interesting points. The authors of the *Discourse of the Common Weal of This Realm of England* and of *Britannia Languens*, as well as Raleigh and Whiston, were fully aware of the epochal changes which the art of warfare had undergone during the sixteenth century. The prominent features of this transformation were the regular employment of the mercenary infantryman and artillerist and the increasing employment of artillery in the field as a manoeuvrable arm.[58] The conduct of war had become a much more expensive undertaking than before. Thus the aforementioned writers enumerated the various uses to which money could be put: it was necessary for the purchase of arms, ammunition, and naval stores, for the hiring of soldiers and sailors, for the conduct of espionage services, for the bribing of officials in hostile countries, for the buying of allies, for subsidies to confederate powers, etc. Hence the frequent references to money as the "sinews of war."

What the mercantilists meant by terms like "money" and "treasure" in this connection is very difficult to construe. Writers like the author of the *Discourse of the Common Weal of This Realm of England* and Violet may have had in mind large quantities of the precious metals in the state treasure. On the other hand, authors like the writer of *Britannia Languens*, Malynes, Bacon, Mun, Whiston, and Defoe either referred to "money" as "plenty of gold and silver within the country,"[59] or general wealth. Whichever opinion was held in the individual case is immaterial for the purpose of this study. Important, however, is the conclusion that an abundance of precious metals was highly valued in order to bolster the power of the state.

Some of the mercantilists surely identified financial power with a large national stock of bullion and indulged in what French writers like to call "l'illusion chrysohédonique."[60] Others, in a more or less confused way, may have thought of general wealth in a highly mobile form, i.e., in a form which, in cases of national

---

[57]Declaration made by Sir Benjamin Rudyard in the House of Commons in 1623. Cf. L. F. Stock, *Proceedings and Debates of the British Parliaments Respecting North America* (Washington, 1924), I, 62.

[58]Cf. J. W. Fortescue, *A History of the British Army* (London, 1899), I, 76 ff.; Hans Delbrück, *Geschichte der Kriegskunst* (Berlin, 1920), part IV.

[59]Viner, *Studies*, p. 25.

[60]J. Morini-Comby, *Mercantilisme et protectionisme* (Paris, 1930), p. 16; Gonnard, *Histoires des doctrines économiques*, p. 49.

emergency, could be quickly liquidated and effectively tapped through taxation and loans.⁶¹ Such a line of thought would lead to an identification of general prosperity with power. However, even in the case of such argumentation, it was not wealth as such which was usually wanted but wealth for the sake of power. The point of departure was not the consumer, i.e., the best possible satisfaction of his wants, but considerations of power.⁶² The wealthier a state, the more powerful it was politically and militarily. Hence, the mercantilist ideal of the powerful state was generally not that it should be wealthy but that it should be wealthier than any other state.⁶³

The mercantilists also advocated a number of specific means by which the state's power could be increased and sustained. Aid to the fishing industry was proposed in order to effect an increase of shipping and a multiplication of mariners. Also, England's mercantile marine was to be enlarged by fostering maritime trade and confining it as much as possible to English bottoms by the establishment and enforcement of navigation laws. In order to maximize the nation's employed manpower, various proposals were put forward designed to increase the volume of production.⁶⁴ The number of skilled artisans could be increased by encouraging the immigration of foreign and hindering the emigration of national artisans. England being a country without gold and silver mines within her national frontiers, an increased stock of treasure could be procured only by acquiring territories where such mines existed or could be built or through the mechanism of foreign trade. Indispensable raw materials which were not produced in Britain

⁶¹Heckscher, *Mercantilism*, II, 31.

⁶²This view is supported by Edmond Silberner, *La Guerre dans la pensée économique du XVIᵉ au XVIIIᵉ siècle* (Paris, 1939), p. 111; Heckscher, *Mercantilism*, I, 24; Morini-Comby, *Mercantilisme et protectionisme*, p. 72; Lipson, *Economic History of England*, III, 2.

⁶³This line of reasoning is also stressed by Heckscher, *Mercantilism*, II, 22. The tendency to think in terms of comparative loss or gain rather than in absolute loss or gain is frequently expressed in mercantilist literature. Erasmus Philips, to give an example, discussed the fact that of all the silver that had been imported into Europe since 1602, no less than 150 million pounds were "buried" in the East-Indies. "I shall not contend with those that say, that this Commerce [East-India trade] is not carried on without a Loss of Silver to us; but then it must be considered too that we only lose in Proportion to the rest of Europe, every Nation bearing some share in the general Loss, and ours perhaps less than any other" (*The State of the Nation with Respect to Its Trade, Debts, and Money* [1725], in *Miscellaneous Works* [London, 1751], p. 33).

⁶⁴The mercantilist theories underlying such proposals will be discussed below.

could be obtained only by artificially encouraging their production at home, by developing substitutes which could be produced domestically, by acquiring territories where such materials could be produced, or, again, through the mechanism of foreign trade. Thus, in the case of the precious metals as in that of indispensable raw materials, alternative methods existed for securing sufficient supplies. One of these alternatives, namely, the acquisition of additional territory under English sovereignty will be the subject of the next chapter. The other,[65] that of procuring treasure and vital raw materials through foreign trade, must be discussed at some length, although the mercantilist conception of international commerce will interest us only in so far as it throws light on the main subject matter of this study.

As regards the importation of bullion through the medium of foreign commerce, the mercantilists wanted to secure this by means of a "favourable" balance of payments mainly as a consequence of a favourable balance of trade, i.e., through an export surplus.[66] Malynes, for example, stated: "If the Natiue Commodities exported doe waigh downe and excede in value the forraine Commodities imported; it is a rule that neuer faile's, that then the Kingdom growe's rich, and prosper's in estate and stocke: because the ouerplus thereof must needs come in, in treasure."[67]

Belief in the balance-of-trade doctrine necessarily led to the demand that the volume of imports be reduced as far as possible by discouraging the importation of foreign "luxuries" and by encouraging the production of "necessaries" at home or in the colonies. Equal attention was paid to the possibility of expanding exports by furthering the domestic or colonial production of commodities for which a foreign market could be found. In turn, this consideration put a premium on a large working population and a low wage level.[68] The exclusive solicitude for the largest possible amount of exports is perfectly expressed by Giles Earle speaking in the House of Commons in 1732: "As the great advantage reaped by the nation, by any branch of its trade or manufacture, depends upon exportation; therefore when any matter of trade comes to be considered in this House, we ought to regard only

---

[65] The alternative of fostering the production of some materials at home will be disregarded as being immaterial to the purpose of this study.

[66] Viner, *Studies*, p. 15.

[67] Malynes, *Center of the Circle of Commerce* (1623), p. 117.

[68] Cf. Johnson, *Predecessors of Adam Smith*, pp. 238, 252.

those methods or means, which may tend towards the encouraging and promoting the exportation of any manufacture."[69]

Given the possibility of colonizing, it is easy to perceive that these fundamental considerations would lead to the quest for a colonial empire. Colonies would be expected to fulfil a double function: they would diminish Great Britain's dependence on foreign goods and they would produce commodities that would swell the volume of English exports.

It may be noted here that the mercantilists had but an extremely primitive notion of the principle of the international division of labour. Entirely disregarding the element of relative production cost, it was the dissimilarity of commodities resulting from differing natural resources in the various producing areas on which mercantilist belief in some form of division of labour among nations rested.[70] This line of thought again favoured the acquisition of sovereignty over areas endowed with a rich variety of physical resources.

Finally, it is very important to realize the political[71] and essentially bellicose conception of foreign commerce which was cultivated by the majority of mercantilist authors. This attitude resulted from the notion of a fixed quantity of trade available in the world for which the various nations had to compete. Any increase in one nation's share of exports was possible only at the expense of the volume of exports enjoyed by other nations.[72] Thus Bacon expounded: "It is likewise to be remembered that, foreasmuch as the increase of any estate must be upon the foreigner (for whatsoever is somewhere gotten is somewhere lost). . . ."[73] Hence there arose the idea that it was necessary to rob the foreigner of his trade and to outwit him. Elking wrote: "The Advancement of Trade

[69]Stock, *Proceedings and Debates*, IV, 144.

[70]Bonn, *Crumbling of Empire*, pp. 92 f.; Morini-Comby, *Mercantilisme et protectionisme*, pp. 53 ff.

[71]The adjective "political" is applied here because mercantilist theorizing in this respect seems closely related to the notions which were held regarding the balance of power. Power is something relative, i.e., at any one time there is only a fixed amount of power distributed throughout the world. Whenever one nation increases its share, some other power or powers are bound to lose *in toto* the same amount (cf. R. G. Hawtrey, *Economic Aspects of Sovereignty* [London, 1930], p. 27). The mercantilists were of the opinion that some such mechanism of distribution operated with respect to foreign trade.

[72]Cf. Heckscher, *Mercantilism*, II, 23 f.; Lipson, *Economic History of England*, III, 4.

[73]Bacon, "Of Seditions and Troubles," *Essays*, p. 45.

is the general Aim of all the Nations of Europe, and they seem to strive who shall out-wit one another therein."[74]

This doctrine of the necessarily antagonistic interests of different nations with regard to international commerce, introduced a significant element of bellicosity in considerations of foreign trade. The idea that augmenting the trade of one's own nation would hurt that of other nations was, of course, extremely welcome.[75] This attitude was liable to lead to statements as ridiculous as that made by W. Horsley who, advocating the raising of indigo in the West Indies because the French had done so in their islands, concludes that its cultivation, "if we get nothing by it, it would lessen the Gain of France, and that I conceive would be a real Profit to ourselves; since every thing we cause so bad a neighbour to lose, is in effect a gain to ourselves."[76]

On the other hand, since any trade increase achieved by other nations was presumably accomplished at the expense of the trade volume of one's own nation, a dense atmosphere of jealousy prevailed which is easily traceable in the mercantilist writings throughout the centuries.[77] This attitude of suspicious vigilance was strongly reinforced by the notion of the general inseparableness of power and trade politics.[78] The concept of economic rivalry reacted as a stimulus on that of political rivalry and *vice versa*.

In order to diminish the trade of a rival nation it was deemed necessary to reduce its power. But, *vice versa*, in order to reduce its power it was deemed necessary to diminish its trade. The latter idea was already voiced by Burghley who pleaded against the importation of French wines because "it enrycheth fraunce, whose power england ought not increase."[79] About the middle of the eighteenth century this idea was still much in evidence. Discussing the question of concluding peace with France, an anonymous writer declares himself against peace because "no peace can be solid to Us which is not founded on the reduction,

---

[74] Elking, *The Interest of England Considered* (1720), p. 22.

[75] For the same reason it was deemed desirable to reduce imports from foreign states in order to diminish their share of international trade.

[76] W. Horsley, *A Treatise on Maritime Affairs* (London, 1744), p. 28.

[77] Cf. Silberner, *La Guerre dans la pensée économique*, p. 116.

[78] This close interrelationship between power and trade is clearly revealed by James Whiston who dreamed of making England so powerful "that we may command the Trade of the World, the Riches of it, and consequently the World itself..." (*A Discourse of the Decay of Trade* [1693], pp. 2 f.).

[79] R. H. Tawney and E. Power (eds.), *Tudor Economic Documents* (London, 1924), II, 124.

at least of the French commerce...."⁸⁰ Bethel, also jealous of the French, remarked that "by taking away their trade, their power at Land will be taken away, the first being that which gives life to the latter...."⁸¹ When, in 1753, a bill prohibiting the wearing and importing of French textiles was debated in the House of Commons, Alderman Baker said, "I should rather chuse that the Germans should take 200,000 l. yearly from us for Dresden work, than that the French should take 100,000 l. yearly from us for cambrics and lawns...."⁸² Discussing the merits of an export bounty on British corn, Henry Home, as late as 1774, singled out as a distinct advantage the fact that such a bounty would hurt French agriculture and that therefore "this bounty ... is our palladium, which we ought religiously to guard, if we would avoid being a province of France."⁸³

The enlargement of foreign trade, it was believed, might serve as an effective weapon in the pursuit of power politics and some authors expressed a clear preference for trade war as distinguished from naval and military war. Thus, Yarranton, jealously discussing the power and wealth of the Dutch, suggested to "beat them without fighting; that being the best and justest way to subdue our Enemies."⁸⁴ Barbon thought that "Trade may be Assistant to the Inlarging of Empire; and if an Universal Empire, or Dominion of very Large Extent, can again be raised in the World, It seems more probable to be done by the Help of Trade; By the Increase of Ships at Sea, than by Arms at Land...."⁸⁵ Similarly Paterson wrote: "We ought not only to begin with trade, as the most fundamental to us in this Kingdom, and to which we have the plainest and clearest call, but as our part of a thing that at this day is capable of making greater alternation in the world than the sword, and may eneable us to strengthen the hands of our King in this dangerous time...."⁸⁶ And Sir Charles Whitworth quoted a

---

⁸⁰*Gentleman's Magazine*, XVIII (1748), 66.

⁸¹Slingsby Bethel, *The Interest of the Princes and States of Europe* (2nd ed.; London, 1681), p. 61.

⁸²Cobbett, *Parl. Hist.*, XV, c. 181.

⁸³Henry Home, *Sketches of the History of Man* (Edinburgh, 1774), I, 491 f.

⁸⁴Andrew Yarranton, *England's Improvement by Sea and Land* (London, 1677), I, The Epistle to the Reader.

⁸⁵Nicholas Barbon, *A Discourse of Trade* (1690), ed. J. H. Hollander (Baltimore, 1905), pp. 23 f.

⁸⁶William Paterson, *Proposals and Reasons for Constituting a Council of Trade* (1701), in S. Bannister (ed.), *The Writings of William Paterson* (2nd ed.; London, 1859), I, 103.

French writer in the preface of his work as follows: "It was a mistaken Notion which obtained almost to the present Times,— that War alone determined the superior Power of Nations. It is now more than Half a Century, that the Balance of Power has depended more upon Commerce, than on War."[87]

A large export surplus was also regarded as the principal means of augmenting the "general" wealth of the country and, again, comparison with the progress of other nations was considered the chief criterion of prosperity. This mercantilist emphasis on export trade as the source from which any increase in the wealth of a country is derived makes the above observations upon the mercantilist conception of foreign trade also applicable in this case. Some English writers said in effect that a favourable balance of trade would go far towards tipping the balance of power. Postlethwayt declared that it was necessary "to throw the balance of trade so effectually into the hands of Great Britain, as to put the constant balance of power in Europe into her hands."[88] The same idea was expressed by George Heathcote who wrote with regard to the peace negotiations between Britain and France: ". . . whichsoever of the two Nations, shall possess a Ballance of Trade in her Favour . . . and . . . a Right in that great Nursery of Seamen, must of Necessity become the most powerful, both in external and internal Strength; and that the weakest must fall a Victim to that State Power. . . . And that whoever shall, in making a Peace with France, make such Concessions to her, as shall turn that Balance and restore her naval Power, will infallibly raise the Greatness of France, out of the Ruins of Britain. . . ."[89]

The foregoing considerations explain why foreign commerce was held to be the most important agent in building up the "wealth" and, hence, the power of the state. The argumentative association of foreign trade, wealth, and power is an ever-recurring theme in the broad stream of the pertinent literature. Three additional quotations illustrate this point.

The great Source of our particular Opulence and Power, has hitherto been considered to arise from Trade; and it would be an unfortunate Effect of all our Bravery and Policy, if we had either fought or negotiated ourselves

---

[87]Sir Charles Whitworth, *State of the Trade of Great Britain in Its Imports and Exports* (London, 1776), p. 1.

[88]Malachy Postlethwayt, *Great Britain's Commercial Interest* (London, 1759), II, 551.

[89]George Heathcote, *A Letter to the Right Honourable the Lord Mayor* (2nd ed.; London, 1762), pp. 8 f.

out of our commercial Character. Advantages of a merely political Kind, will be always more or less problematical . . . but there is no Situation in which Wealth is not Strength, and in which Commerce is not Wealth.[90]

A Nation cannot be safe without Power; Power cannot be obtained without Riches; nor Riches without Trade.[91]

Trade is to the Body politick, as the Blood is to the human body; it . . . gives Life and Vigour to the whole; Without this, no Country can be happy within itself, or support herself without against the Attacks of a powerful Neighbour.[92]

The foregoing demonstrates that to the mercantilists, considerations of power were of the utmost importance whenever questions of policy were discussed. They realized that the original sources that fed Britain's power, in its entirety or in its various physical components, were partly located outside the British Isles. Two alternatives presented themselves for the procurement of non-domestic elements of power (or wealth in the sense of potential power): foreign trade and the acquisition of sovereignty over transmaritime sources of supply. The former was considered the more precarious, the latter the more dependable way. Hence, the more England's power would rest on colonies, and the less on foreign trade, the safer she could feel. The acquisition of colonial areas of supply would appear highly desirable even in case international commerce would be the cheaper means of procurement.

The same line of argumentation was applicable also to the objective of diminishing, as far as possible, the relative power of rival nations. The magnitude of their power appeared to depend in part on their share in the supposedly fixed volume of international exports. Hence, the more colonial supplies could be made to replace their exports, in the British as well as in the international market, the more would their relative power tend to decline. These broad considerations, then, are apt to illumine English ideas on the subject of empire-building.

One more phenomenon of a general character needs mentioning, namely, the firmly rooted belief in the utility and feasibility of state action for the purpose of regulating matters of national interest. This staunch faith in the efficacy of rational[93] statecraft

---

[90][William Burke], *An Examination of the Commercial Principles of the Late Negotiation between Great Britain and France in 1761* (London, 1762), p. 3.

[91]Sir William Mildmay, *The Laws and Policy of England Relating to Trade* (London, 1765), p. 3.

[92]Erasmus Philips, *The State of the Nation with Respect to Its Trade, Debts, and Money* (1725), in *Miscellaneous Works*, p. 29.

[93]The word "rationalism" is used here not in the epistemological sense but in that of planned activity.

was something essentially new.[94] It did not prevail during the Middle Ages. According to the medieval creed, states *grow* "as do the lilies in the field."[95] The new state was *made* in accord with a preconceived scheme. No doubt, the plans in question were often bad, short-sighted, and inconsistent. Frequently they were haphazardly pragmatical, devised opportunistically to solve some immediate problem.[96] The significant difference from medieval quietism[97] is to be seen in the ceaseless and ubiquitous attempts to subject particular problems to logical analysis in order to detect the causes of a supposed evil, followed by a deliberate search for a policy of public action which would remedy it.[98] It is perfectly correct to say that this new era inaugurated the age of "social engineering,"[99] although this trend started in the Tudor period. Such imposing structures as the Navigation Laws or the drafting of new "societies" overseas are excellent examples illustrating this spirit.[100]

Particular efforts were made in the sphere of national economy. Even a cursory perusal of mercantilist literature shows this clearly.[101] There was no belief in a God-ordained order or in a more anonymous "invisible hand" of Smithian implication. Trade, as a matter of fact, was much freer during the Middle Ages than during the sixteenth century.[102] The belief that the achievement of some particular objective depended only on the intelligence and power of the rulers was a product of the Renaissance in general, and of Machiavellism in particular.[103] Brentano, for this reason, identifies the mercantilist system with "economic Machiavellism."[104] By means of decrees and laws it was attempted to rectify the supposed non-coincidence of private interest and public good.[105] Mercan-

[94]Instances of utilitarian statecraft, of course, did occur during the Middle Ages. But their frequency and comprehensiveness grew towards the end of that historical period and became a dominating feature only at the beginning of what is called the Modern Era.
[95]Bonn, *Crumbling of Empire*, p. 19.
[96]Read, *Mercantilism*, p. 65.
[97]Johnson, *Predecessors of Adam Smith*, p. 24.
[98]*Ibid.* [99]Bonn, *Crumbling of Empire*, p. 19.
[100]See L. A. Harper, *The English Navigation Laws* (New York, 1939), p. 233.
[101]See the excellent study of P. W. Buck, *The Politics of Mercantilism* (New York, 1942).
[102]Cf. Morini-Comby, *Mercantilisme et protectionisme*, p. 11.
[103]Lujo Brentano, *Der wirtschaftende Mensch in der Geschichte* (Leipzig, 1923), p 57.
[104]*Ibid.*, p. 64. [105]Cf. Morini-Comby, *Mercantilisme et protectionisme*, p. 30.

tilism was indeed, as Gonnard remarks, "étatiste" in character.[106] Two representative quotations may be added here to illustrate the nucleus of mercantilist thinking on this subject. Hobbes, observing that the gain of the private trader may imply damage to the state, continues to say: "And therefore it belongeth to the Common-wealth, (that is, to the Soveraign only) to approve, or disapprove both of the places, and matter of forraign Traffique."[107] And Sir Francis Brewster speaks of trade and government as something essentially inseparable and scolds those "who would divide that Child of the Nation, Trade and Government, which I take to be but one United Body...."[108]

Obviously this belief in the efficacy and benefit of official intervention in matters of trade exerted a significant influence whenever the question of the utility or inutility of colonies was discussed. For, as will be shown below, it was through a controlled economic system that colonies were to be made an undertaking advantageous to the metropolis.[109]

[106] *Histoire des doctrines économiques*, p. 49.
[107] Hobbes, *Leviathan*, p. 132.
[108] Sir Francis Brewster, *New Essays on Trade* (London, 1702), Preface.
[109] The general *advantage* of a controlled economy being granted for a moment, the belief, during the period under discussion, in the *efficacy* of state action seems remarkable on account of the almost total lack of a trained civil service which could be entrusted with the enforcement of such action. Historically seen, on the other hand, this lack of a comprehensive civil service, and, hence, lack of consistent enforcement of laws, probably made the burden of legislative mercantilism relatively tolerable and considerably less pernicious. Deliberate non-enforcement of laws in the economic sphere was a not infrequent feature of public policy.

CHAPTER II

COLONIAL THEORIES: 1570-1660

THE discrepancies between the motivations that propelled individuals and groups toward colonial enterprise, on the one hand, and the theories on the utility of colonies, on the other, have been suggested in the preface. For example, the desire to own and cultivate a sufficient area of land operated as an extremely powerful motive in luring individual colonists across the Atlantic.[1] Yet, apart perhaps from Bacon's idea of planting little transmarine daughter-commonwealths,[2] this motive finds only *incidental* expression in colonial theories, and then only in relation to the products which might be raised in colonial settlements. It is necessary to keep this basic distinction in mind in order to arrive at a true appreciation of the theories.

It has likewise been pointed out that theories may and often do have a propagandist character. With regard to early English colonial theories this is a most important fact. Almost all of them betray a propagandist flavour and some are really nothing but advertisements put out by companies engaged in colonial enterprise. Yet in this respect, colonial theories only partake of a quality which characterizes the bulk of English mercantilist writings, and this fact can by no means disqualify such material as far as its theoretical content is concerned.

[1] C. M. Andrews, *The Colonial Period of American History* (New Haven, 1934), I, 54; W. Cunningham, *The Growth of English Industry and Commerce* (5th ed.; Cambridge, 1915), I, 119 f.

[2] As will be shown below, the English merchants stood most aggressively behind English colonial enterprise. Naturally, they were not interested in the welfare of the settlers. They were interested in goods and markets. Bacon's opinions of oversea plantations, on the other hand, betray a distinct anti-merchant prejudice. In his letter of advice addressed to the Duke of Buckingham (in James Spedding, *The Letters and the Life of Francis Bacon* [London, 1872], VI, 22), he demands that the trade with the colonies be regulated "in such a manner as some few merchants and tradesmen . . . may not grind them [the colonists], so as shall always keep them in poverty." In his essay "Of Plantations" (*Essays* [Everyman ed.; London, 1936], p. 104) he observes that "planting of countries is like planting of woods; for you must make account to loose almost twenty years' profit. . ." and he warns of "the base and hasty drawing of profit in the first years." This attitude is particularly revealing because Bacon, on other occasions, shows himself very much interested in the prosperity of the merchants.

Colonial theories, as has been stated, are composed of arguments regarding the respective advantages or disadvantages attending the foundation or maintenance of colonies. Viewed as an ensemble, it appears that among these arguments there are important and unimportant ones. Concerning the latter, some were of a subsidiary, marginal, or indeed insignificant nature from the very beginning of the formative period of English colonization, while others, deemed highly important at first, grew less and less important in the course of time. Completely insignificant advantages seen in the new colonies will, of course, be duly disregarded.[3] The remaining ones deserve discussion of varying length.

In a letter addressed to James I, written in 1608, George Popham comes out in favour of English colonies in America "since they seem to redound to the glory of God, the greatness of your Majesty, and the utility of the Britons."[4] In his time these phrases constituted a commonplace summary of the advantages which were expected to accrue to Britain from colonization. The glory which would redound to the king and the nation from such enterprise is duly mentioned in all the tracts discussing the subject. Although, for this reason, its presence in contemporary discussion cannot be denied, the elusiveness of this factor renders its appraisal rather difficult. German historians like Brie[5] and Schulze-Gaevernitz[6] have persisted in making much of it as a motive and as an element in English theorizing on the question of empire. Careful perusal of the literature and the annals of that period, however, leads to the inescapable conclusion that as far as theorizing is concerned, the actual weight of this factor was exceedingly small if not negligible. The very hackneyed cursoriness of its inclusion among a string of broadly discussed arguments proves that the overwhelming majority of writers had little confidence in its

[3]Thus some early writers, appealing to the sportsmen among the English gentry, pointed out the abundance of animal life which could be enjoyed by deer-minded gentlemen. Sir William Alexander (*An Encouragement to Colonies* [1624], in E. F. Slaffler [ed.], *Sir William Alexander and American Colonization* [Boston, 1873], p. 212) wrote: ". . . I might speak of the sport that may bee had by Hunting, Hawking, Fishing and Fowling, where all these creatures haue had so long a time for increase, without being destroyed or frighted. . . ."

[4]Alexander Brown (ed.), *The Genesis of the United States* (Boston, 1897), I, 145.

[5]Friedrich Brie, *Imperialistische Strömungen in der englischen Literatur* (Halle, 1928).

[6]G. v. Schulze-Gaevernitz, *Britischer Imperialismus und englischer Freihandel* (Leipzig, 1906).

appeal value. Evidently, its propagation was left to the more excitable poets. There is not one writer who advocates the establishment of colonies mainly for the glory of king or nation. If the prospective harvest would consist of something more tangible plus glory, the latter, too, would be quite welcome.

THE SPREADING OF THE GOSPEL

With regard to the glory supposedly acceptable to the Lord, there are even greater difficulties of evaluation. The argument that the English were called to colonize in order to propagate the Gospel played an important part during the first decades of British colonial enterprise. The frequency and insistence with which this point is discussed are truly amazing in the light of the subsequent absence of any noteworthy action in this respect. Thus, Edward Haie speaks approvingly of "Gods word and religion, which from the beginning hath moved from the East, towards, & at last unto the West, where it is like to end."[7] Hakluyt, in a preface attached to Sir Walter Raleigh's translation of René Laudonnierre's "Description of Florida," addresses the translator "I know you meane hereafter to sende some goode Churchmen thither, as may truely say with the Apostle to the Savages, Wee seeke not yours but you."[8]

The following quotations contain the same kind of argument:

Seeinge that the people of that parte of America ... are idolaters ... it remayneth to be thoroughly weyed and considered by what meanes and by whome this most godly and Christian work may be perfourmed of inlarginge the glorious gospell of Christe.... Nowe the Kinges and Queenes of England have the name of Defendours of the Faithe. By which title I thinke they are not onely chardged to mayneteyne and patronize the faithe of Christe, but also to inlarge and advaunce the same.[9]

So I wish and intreat all well affected subiects, some in their persons, others in their purses, cheerefully to aduenture, and ioyntly take in hand this high and acceptable worke, tending to aduance and spread the kingdome of God ... among so many millions of men and women, Sauage and blind.[10]

If hee haue any graine of faith or zeale in Religion, what can hee doe lesse hurtfull to any or more agreeable to God, then to seeke to conuert those poore Saluages to know Christe?[11]

---

[7] Richard Hakluyt, *The Principal Navigations* (Glasgow, 1904), I, 38.
[8] *Ibid.*, VIII, 443.
[9] Richard Hakluyt, *Discourse on Western Planting* (1584), in C. Deane (ed.), *Documentary History of the State of Maine* (Cambridge, 1877), II, 7 ff.
[10] Robert Johnson, *Nova Britannia* (1609), in Peter Force, *Tracts and Other Papers* (Washington, 1836), I, 6.
[11] John Smith, *A Description of New England* (1616), in Force, *Tracts*, II, 18.

That it is not enough to discover countries, and leave them without plantation . . . but it is the Part of Princes to see Plantations made, for two maine reasons, That is, to convert the inhabitants or neighbours to Christianity . . . .[12]

it is more honor to overcome paganism in one than to conquer a thousand pagans.[13]

In the face of the clamourous pathos of this apparently indomitable desire for diffusing Christianity in heathenish America, it seems hard to doubt the sincerity of such sermons. Spanish and Portuguese missionary enterprise as conducted by the Jesuits, Franciscans, and other Catholic orders in the New World certainly was serious in doctrine and action.[14] Potentially, religious proselytism was a quality inherent in Protestantism as well as in Catholicism. Yet, quite certainly, the British were not very zealous apostles of their religious faith. In his instructions to Cabot, Henry VII made the conversion of natives a duty attending on territorial acquisition and he sent at least one priest to Newfoundland.[15] The Letters Patent granted to the Virginia Company in 1606 expressed the hope that the colonization of Virginia would lead to the propagation of Christianity among the Indian tribes.[16] Similar interests are expressed in the early instructions of the trading companies to their governors. The Levant Company sent out chaplains to the Near East.[17] In 1600, the founders of the East India Company voiced their desire that the East Indians might be converted to Christianity and engaged the services of Patrick Copland for this purpose.[18] Between 1618 and 1620 four collections were held by royal order throughout the parishes of England to finance the education of native as well as white children in Virginia.[19]

All these activities, whether planned, preparatory, or executed, taken together were so meagre that they shrink to insignificance compared with the exploits of the Spaniards in America. If conceived in sincerity, the missionary intentions of the British

[12]Gerard Malynes, *Consuetudo* (London, 1656), p. 166.
[13]Thomas Fuller, *The Holy and Profane State* (1642) (Boston, 1865), p. 239.
[14]Cf. Georges Goyau, *Missions et missionaires* (Paris, 1931), pp. 27 ff.
[15]S. Bannister, *British Colonisation and Coloured Tribes* (London, 1838), p. 21.
[16]J. E. Gillespie, *The Influence of Oversea Expansion on England to 1700* (New York, 1920), p. 188.
[17]*Ibid.*, pp. 189 f.
[18]E. D. Neill, *The English Colonization of America* (London, 1871), pp. 105 f.
[19]Gillespie, *The Influence of Oversea Expansion on England*, p. 190.

were moribund from the moment of their conception. In the light of the following passages, however, it seems more likely that they were deficient in sincerity.

... this earth which is mans fee-simple by deede of gift fro God, is the greater part of it possessed and wrongfully vsurped by wild beasts, and vnreasonable creatures, or by brutish sauages, which by reason of their godles ignorance & blasphemous idolatrie, are worse than those beasts. ... So may man say to himselfe: The earth was mine, God gave it me, and my posteritie. ... we are warranted by this direction of Joshua, to destroy wilfull and cunuicted Idolaters, rather than to let them liue, if by no other meanes they can be reclaimed.[20]

... it shall fall out in proofe, that the Savages shall hereby have just cause to blesse the houre when this enterprize was undertaken. First and chiefly, in respect of the most happy and gladsome tidings of the most glorious Gospel of our Saviour Jesus Christ, whereby they may be brought from falsehood to trueth, from darknesse to light. ... And if in respect of all the commodities they can yeelde us (were they many more) that they should but receive this onely benefit of Christianity, they were more than fully recompenced ... we may say with S. Paul, If wee have sowen unto you heavenly things, doe you thinke it much that we should reape your carnall things? And with all, the workman is wirthy of his hire.[21]

... vs, who by way of marchandizing and trade, doe buy of them the pearles of earth, and sell to them the pearles of heauven. ...[22]

For the first how it may tend to aduance the kingdome of God, by reducing sauage people from their blind superstition to the light of Religion, when some obiect, we seek nothing lesse then the cause of God, beeing led on by our owne priuate ends, and secondly how we can warrant a supplantation of those Indians, or an inuasion into their right and possessions. ... To the first we say, as many actions both good in themselves, and in their successe, haue beane performed with badde intents: so in this case, howsouever our naughtiness of minde may sway very much, yet God may haue the honor. ...[23]

The commission for Raleigh's voyage was "to discover some commodities and marchandize profitable for the subjects of our kingdom ... whence may ensue, by commerce, some propagation of the Christian faith ... among those idolatrous people," and it authorizes the adventurers "to advance the conversion of savages, and increase traffic."[24]

[20]Robert Gray, *A Good Speed to Virginia* (1609), ed. W. F. Carven (New York, 1937), The Epistle Dedicatorie.

[21]Sir George Peckham, *A True Report of the Late Discoveries* (1583) in Hakluyt, *The Principal Navigations*, VIII, 119.

[22]*A Trve Declaration of the Estate of the Colonie of Virginia* (1610), in Force, *Tracts*, III, 6.

[23]R. Johnson, *Nova Britannia* (1609), I, 12.

[24]Cf. Bannister, *British Colonisation and Coloured Tribes*, p. 47.

What impresses the reader of these passages most is the close connection between missionary enterprise and trading. The English expected to trade with the natives. They also expected that the Indians would not be given a fair deal. To pacify their bad conscience they threw, in addition to glass beads, and liquor, a certain amount of Christianity into the bargain. Another reason is suggested by Bannister who points out that in the fifteenth and sixteenth centuries it was generally held that the discoverer of lands inhabited by pagans acquired lawful title to the soil and dominion over the natives only on condition that the heathens were converted to the Christian religion.[25] Both explanations suggest that these early writers were ultimately interested in justification and sanction rather than in missionary enterprise for its own sake. Jealousy over the missionary success of the Spaniards also may have played a part. Thus one writer remarks: "When therefore, it is a sweete smelling sacrifice, to propagate the name of Iesus Christ, when the Babylonish Inchantresse hath encompassed sea, and land, to make, sixe, eight, or ten millions, of Romish proselites."[26]

It may be concluded, therefore, that the call to evangelize the Indians was lip-service to a duty which was acknowledged but not performed.[27] This is the judgment passed by Bacon who wrote: "It cannot be affirmed, if we speak ingeniously that it was the propagation of the Christian faith that was the ... [motive] ... of the discovery, entry, and plantation of the new world; but gold and silver, and temporal profit and glory."[28] Similarly, William Castell in a petition to Parliament, signed by seventy-six ministers, accuses his nation of hypocrisy: "In a humble manner sheweth unto your approval wisedomes, the great and generall neglect of this Kingdome, in not propagating the glorious Gospel in America ... indeed the undertaking of the worke is (in the generall) acknowledged pious and charitable; but the small prosecution that hath hitherto beane made of it ... having (as yet) never beene

---

[25] *Ibid.*, pp. 18 f.

[26] *A Trve Declaration of the State of the Colonie of Virginia* (1610), p. 7; similarly: Richard Eburne, *Plaine Path-Way to Plantations* (London, 1624), p. 4.

[27] This opinion is supported by Sir Charles Lucas, *Religion, Colonising, and Trade* (London, 1930), pp. 10 f.; G. L. Beer, *The Origins of the British Colonial System* (New York, 1908), p. 29; E. A. J. Johnson, *American Economic Thought in the Seventeenth Century* (London, 1932), p. 62.

[28] Quoted in Bannister, *British Colonisation and Coloured Tribes*, p. 58.

generally undertaken in pitty to mens soules, but in hope to possesse the land of those infidels, or of gaine by commerce. . . ."[29]

It is not surprising that the English colonizers, a few exceptions in the New England colonies apart, have left traces of their missionary impulse in print only. The general attitude of the settlers is revealed in a report which the Virginian colonists sent to London after the massacre of 1622. They said that they were glad of the incident for "our hands, which before were tied with gentleness and fair usage, are now set at liberty by the treacherous violence of the savages" and "because the way of conquering them is much more easy than of civilizing them . . . ."[30] The much professed duty of Christianizing the American natives as an argument for colonization must be dismissed as being either spurious or extremely insignificant in comparison with other arguments.[31]

THE NORTHWEST PASSAGE

The search for a northwest passage to Asia and the South Sea was an integral part of English exploratory voyages and colonizing adventures as was its discussion in British theorizing on the merits of colonization. The discovery of the passage was an important weapon in the argumentative armory of writers and explorers. To be sure, the main objective, in this case, was not the founding of colonies but the establishment of trade connections with Far Eastern islands and countries of whose fabulous wealth the English merchants had a very high opinion.

More specifically, the British assumed that the opening of commercial contact with the Orient would provide a new market for the "uttering of our country commodities," and an abundant source of a variety of products such as gold, silver, precious stones, silk, and spices, for which there was a demand in Europe. In connection with the latter objective the *shortness* of the new route to be discovered was a most important aspect. Thus Gilbert

---

[29] Quoted in L. F. Stock, *Proceedings and Debates of the British Parliaments Respecting North America* (Washington, 1924), I, 129.

[30] Quoted in Bannister, *British Colonisation and Coloured Tribes*, pp. 50 f.

[31] It may be noted here that Hakluyt advocated large-scale missionary efforts because their consummation would mitigate religious strife at home. Thus he wrote, "but also many inconveniences and strife amongest ourselves at home, in matters of ceremonies, shalbe ended. For those of the clergye which by reason of idleness here at home are now alwayes coyninge of new opynions, havinge by this voyadge to set themselves on worke in reducinge the savages to the chefe principles of our faithe, will become less contentious. . ." (*Discourse on Western Planting* [1584], p. 12).

wrote: "For through the shortnesse of the voyage, we should be able to sell all maner of merchandize, brought from thence, farre better and cheape then either the Portugall or Spaniard doth or may do."[32] Edward D. Neill reports that in 1583 "one Apsley, an enterprising man, who dealt in beads, playing-cards, and gewgaws calculated to please the tastes of the Orientals, told a friend that he expected to live to see a letter dated at London, on the 1st of May, delivered in China before midsummer, by a short passage over the American Continent, between the forty-third and forty-sixth parallel of north latitude. . . ."[33]

The British search for the "routes de fortunes," as Rabelais called them,[34] antedated the initiation of English colonization. Of the "foure famous wayes" to the Orient which Richard Willes enumerated, the two southern ways around the Cape of Good Hope and through Magellan Strait had been discovered by Portuguese and Spanish navigators. These routes being pre-empted by the Iberian powers and, besides, extremely long, the British attempted the northern routes in order to find a "short cut" to the East. The expeditions of Cabot and the three Corte-Real brothers between 1497 and 1502 failed to show a passage in the westerly direction. After Robert Thorne's famous suggestion, to proceed via the North Pole, had been discarded, Willoughby, Chancellor, and Stephen Burrough, backed by the Muscovy Company, tried unsuccessfully to find a northeastern route to China. Eden, Frobisher, and Sir Humphrey Gilbert, in the meantime, had revived the project of finding a northwest passage and henceforth the English bent their efforts in that direction.[35]

These few historical data are important because they stress the fact that both the search for the Northwest Passage and the desire for founding colonies pushed the British towards the North American sub-continent.

In the literature, the connection between colonial expansion and the search for the famous passage appears to be twofold. On

[32]Sir Humphrey Gilbert, *A Discourse written to prove a Passage by the Northwest to Cathaia* (1576), in Hakluyt, *The Principal Navigations*, VII, 186.
[33]Neill, *English Colonization of America*, p. 104.
[34]A. Rein, *Die europäische Ausbreitung über die Erde* (Potsdam, 1931), p. 90.
[35]An excellent account of the early English search for the Northwest Passage is given in G. B. Manhart's "The English Search for a North-West Passage in the Time of Queen Elizabeth," in A. L. Rowland and G. B. Manhart, *Studies in English Commerce and Exploration in the Reign of Queen Elizabeth* (Philadelphia, 1924).

the one hand, it was assumed that the search for the backdoor to the Pacific might, incidentally, lead to colonization. Thus, Sir Humphrey Gilbert remarked: "Also we might inhabite some part of those countreys, and settle there such needy people of our countrey."[36] On the other hand, the planting of colonies might, incidentally, lead to the discovery of the Passage. Hakluyt pointed out, "that by these colonies the north west passage may easily, quickly, and perfectly be searched oute as well by river and overlande as by sea."[37]

Thus, the desire for finding "an easy and short passadge to the South Sea either by land or sea"[38] formed a subsidiary, but by no means unimportant argument for English colonization. Its relative significance is all the greater because the main effort exerted in the search for the Passage coincided with the initial establishment of the British oversea empire. The importance of the argument, of course, was destined to wane rapidly in consequence of successive failures. Yet throughout the reign of the first Stuarts the merchants of London and Bristol were found willing to finance new expeditions.[39] And even thereafter, almost dormant though it was for decades, again and again the argument was revived and then, for a short while, attracted the fancy of substantial numbers of people.[40]

AMERICAN GOLD AND SILVER

Towards the end of the Middle Ages the requirements of expanding commercial activity for sufficient stocks of precious

[36] Gilbert, *A Discourse* (1576), p. 186.
[37] Hakluyt, *Discourse on Western Planting* (1584), p. 108.
[38] Petition of the Virginia Company to Parliament in 1624. Cf. Stock, *Proceedings and Debates*, I, 65.
[39] C. M. MacInnes, *A Gateway of Empire* (Bristol, 1939), p. 108.
[40] In 1759, the writer of an article in the *Scots Magazine* remarks that "after finding out the Terra Australis, another discovery, quite opposite, would remain to be made in the northern seas; namely, that of a shorter passage to the Indies, than by doubling the southern points of Africa or America" ("Of Discoveries to be made in the Terra Australis," *Scots Magazine*, XXI [1759], p. 457). In 1791, there appeared an article in the *Gentleman's Magazine* (LXIX, 404-6) entitled: "North-West Passage to the Pacific Ocean Practicable." And as late as the second decade of the nineteenth century there appeared a crop of books and pamphlets which seriously tried to revive interest in the project. Cf. "Polar Ice, and a North-West Passage," *Edinburgh Review*, XXX (1818), 1-59. At that time, of course, the possibility of opening a Northwest Passage could not have been a factor favouring expansion. But, if really practicable, this argument might have played some role in the discussions of the question whether the colonies should be retained or allowed to drift away from the imperial connection.

metals could not be met satisfactorily by the small production of European mines and the thin trickle from the Levant. It was mainly the severely felt want of gold and silver which prompted the voyages of Columbus and other navigators. Spain succeeded in tapping and monopolizing the metallic wealth of Central and South America. Especially after the discovery of the mines of Potosi and Zacatecas in 1545,[41] the stream of treasure flowing across the Atlantic to Seville seemed inexhaustible and evoked in contemporary minds a quite exaggerated picture of the revenues which the King of Spain drew from his American empire.[42]

Under these circumstances it is quite conceivable that the English looked with envy upon their feared and powerful rival. There were no auriferous or argentiferous soils in England. The desire to gain access to such soils overseas operated as a powerful motive behind the activities of the early English explorers, buccaneers, and colonizers. Sir Walter Raleigh's expedition to Guiana to find a mythical Eldorado is well known. Less well known is the fact that this expedition was in large part financed by merchants.[43] The first Virginian settlers at Jamestown were so much more interested in mining than in the pursuit of agriculture that only the threat of impending starvation could prompt them to raise foodstuffs.[44]

Thus, it is not surprising to find the search for gold and silver and precious stones a powerful argument in the literature favouring colonization. Sir Humphrey Gilbert, for example, maintained that ". . . in the whole trace of that land, by the description of as many as have been there, great plenty of mineral matter of all sorts, and in very many places . . . are to be found."[45] However, Christopher Carlile very cautiously put forward the argument that "what Minerall may fall out to bee found, is a thing left in suspence, untill some better knowledge. . . ."[46] Hopes of discovering precious

[41]Henri Hauser, *La Préponderance espagnole* (Paris, 1933), p. 196.
[42]Cf. C. H. Haring, "American Gold and Silver Production in the First Half of the Sixteenth Century," *Quarterly Journal of Economics*, XXIX (1915), 434.
[43]Cf. W. R. Scott, *The Constitution and Finance of English, Scottish and Irish Joint-Stock Companies to 1720* (Cambridge, 1910), II, 245.
[44]Cf. E. R. Johnson et al., *History of the Domestic and Foreign Commerce of the United States* (Washington, 1922), I, 17.
[45]Sir Humphrey Gilbert, *A True Report of the Late Discoveries and Possession Taken in the Right of the Crown of England of the Newfound Landes* (1583), in A. E. Bland et al., *English Economic History, Select Documents* (London, 1914), p. 437.
[46]Christopher Carlile, *A Briefe and Summary Discourse upon the Intended Voyage to the Hithermost Parts of America* (1583), in Hakluyt, *The Principal Navigations*, VIII, 141.

metals lingered for some decades, but more and more people became ready to abandon the Project[47] and as an argument in favour of colonization it almost disappeared from the literature. Bacon exhorted his countrymen: "But moil not too much under ground; for the hope of mines is very uncertain, and useth to make the planters lazy in other things."[48] This quotation indicates that from the point of view of the colonizationist, interested in the steady growth of the plantations, the search for mines introduced a disturbing factor.

Under these circumstances, there remained to the English, aside from buccaneering activities, two alternatives to satisfy their thirst for treasure. One of these was the way of conquest by attacking the Spaniards in the West Indies. This policy was demanded by Sir Benjamin Rudyard in the House of Commons in 1623: "So we have no other way, but to endeavour to cut him [the Spanish King] up at root, and seek to impeach, or to supplant him in the West Indies."[49] Similarly, in 1640, John Pym exhorts the King to attack the Spanish West Indies because such undertaking would "easily make his majestie master of all that treasure . . . ."[50]

The other and, undoubtedly, less expensive method of acquiring treasure was through foreign trade. Owing to her continuously unfavourable balance of trade and the Hapsburg imperialism of Charles V, which involved her in endless wars, Spain, from the beginning of her American monopoly, succeeded against her will in distributing her accruing metallic wealth over Europe.[51] It was mainly this method of securing treasure through the medium of commerce to which the English had resort.

---

[47]David Macpherson reports (entered under the date of 1625) that "after the Virginia Company had, at sundry times, raised by subscriptions for their adventures a capital of no less than £200,000, still, in vain, hoping for gold and silver mines . . . many of them at length became weary of the charge. . ." (*Annals of Commerce* [London, 1805], II, 333).

[48]Bacon, "Of Plantations," *Essays*, p. 105. The power which the desire for treasure and mines exercised over the English mind is interestingly revealed in the following passage of Bacon's "Letter of Advice to the Duke of Buckingham" (p. 24): ". . . I beseech you to take into your serious consideration that Indian wealth, which this island and the seas thereof excel in, the hidden treasure of Fishing . . . half a day's sail with a good wind will shew the mineral, and the miners."

[49]Cf. Stock, *Proceedings and Debates*, I, 62.

[50]*Ibid.*, I, 98.

[51]Cf. Haring, "American Gold and Silver Production in the First Half of the Sixteenth Century," pp. 472 ff.

In summary it can be said safely that even during the very first phase of English colonizing, the search for oversea mines of gold and silver played only a subsidiary role and that from then on its importance decreased rapidly.[52]

STRATEGIC CONSIDERATIONS

According to contemporary English opinion Spain's power rested mainly on the metallic basis of the treasure she received from her American Empire. Hence, the English concluded that to cut this stream of wealth which constantly replenished her coffers, was to hit Spain in the most decisive spot.[53] Naval and military action against Spain would be made practicable by the possession of bases in America. From this train of thought sprang another argument in favour of oversea colonization. Already in 1584, Hakluyt had written:

> That thos voyadge will be a greate bridle to the Indies of the Kinge of Spaine . . . for wee shoulde not onely often tymes indaunger his flete in the returne thereof, but also in fewe yeres put him in hazarde in loosinge some parte of Nova Hispania.[54]

> And entringe into the consideration of the way how this Philippe may be abased, I meane firste to begynne with the West Indies, as there to laye a chefe foundation for his overthrowe.[55]

> If you touche him in the Indies, you touche the apple of his eye; for take away his treasure, which is his nervus belli. . . .[56]

In a petition to Parliament, in 1624, the Virginia Company enumerated several reasons for the planting of colonies in America. It was claimed that settlements there would be "An inestimable advantadge, that would be gayned to this state of England in case of warr both for the easie assaultinge of the Spanyards West Indies, from those parts, and for relievinge and succouringe of all shipps and men warr that should goe on reprysalls...."[57] However, the

[52]Cf. Johnson, *American Economic Thought in the Seventeenth Century*, p. 43.

[53]Thus, in 1624, on the renewal of war with Spain, a strong group in Parliament condemned "the diverting of his Majesty's course of wars from the West Indies, which was the most facile and hopeful way for this kingdom to prevail against the Spaniard, to an expenceful and successless attempt upon Cadiz" (quoted in J. Ewing, "The Constitution and the Empire," in J. Holland Rose *et al.* [eds.], *The Cambridge History of the British Empire* [London, 1929], I, 606).

[54]Hakluyt, *Discourse on Western Planting*, p. 45.

[55]*Ibid.*, p. 55. [56]*Ibid.*, p. 59.

[57]Cf. Stock, *Proceedings and Debates*, I, 65.

strategic argument, though not without influence, was decidedly of minor importance.[58]

GET THERE FIRST

An argument for colonial expansion which was to become of extraordinary importance during the scramble for colonies in the last quarter of the nineteenth century, was the demand for the immediate establishment of colonies in particular regions simply in order to prevent other powers from doing so. This consideration is also encountered at this early stage of English reasoning on the question of colonies. The following two sample citations illustrate this notion which also must be classified among arguments of secondary importance.

That spedie plantinge in divers fitt places is moste necessarie upon these laste luchye westerne discoveries, for feare of the danger of being prevented by other nations which have the like intention. . . .[59]

The apparent danger all the Colonies may be in if this is not possessed by the English, to prevent the Spaniard, who already has seated himself on the North of Florida, and on the back of Virginia in 34, where he is already possessed of rich silver Mines, and will no doubt vomit his fury and malice upon the neighbour Plantations, if a prehabitation anticipate not his intentions. . . .[60]

NURSERY OF SEAMEN

Because of Britain's insularity, naval strength constituted the mainstay of her external power. In order to further maritime strength, the English were keenly interested in possessing a large mercantile marine. As a matrix of sea power, the main function of the merchant marine was that of supplying a large number of skilled mariners.[61] The establishment of colonies would tend to create a new carrying trade and thus vastly increase the supply of sailors.[62]

[58]Cf. Beer, *Origins of the British Colonial System*, p. 27.
[59]Hakluyt, *Discourse on Western Planting* (1584), p. 95.
[60]Edward Williams, *Virginia* (2nd ed., 1650), in Force, *Tracts*, III, 7. This passage presents an early instance of the line of thought which argues for the expansion of existing colonies in order to prevent their being engulfed by the expansionist drive of another colonial power. This argument for colonial expansion is, of course, logically self-perpetuating until the last bit of colonizable area in any region is under the dominion of some power. Then the only road open is that of conquest of the colonial possessions of other nations.
[61]Ships as such were not unimportant in this connection; yet at this stage the differentiation between the man-of-war and the merchant vessel already made rapid progress.
[62]The problem of naval stores will be discussed in connection with the general question of colonies as sources of raw materials. Considerations re-

From this relationship between colonies and a sufficient supply of mariners arose the argument that it was worthwhile to have colonies for this particular purpose. Hence, English pamphleteers enlarging on the question of colonization spoke much of "skilfull marriners" necessary for manning "our wooden wals."[63] Hakluyt remarked that the establishment of oversea plantations "will be for the greate increase, maynteynaunce, and safetie of our navie, and especially of greate shippinge, which is the strengthe of our realme.... For it is the longe voyadges that harden seamen, and open unto them the secretes of navigation...."[64] Similarly, E. Williams stated that colonization "will to admiration increase the number of Ships and Seamen, (the brassen wall of this Nation) ...."[65] And Robert Johnson stressed the fact that in consequence of the carrying trade to the colonies "we shall not still betake our selues to small and little Shipping but shall reare againe such Marchants Shippes both tall and stout...."[66]

These few quotations may suffice in view of the simplicity of the argument. The main emphasis was that this new carrying trade as such would augment British shipping and the number of sailors. The very fact that the conduct of this carrying business necessitated the crossing of the Atlantic implied a large number of ships in proportion to any given quantity of freight. This long voyage was supposed to enhance the training to which the sailor was subjected in its course. These two characteristics distinguished the carrying trade with the colonies favourably from inter-European sea transport. That it could be pursued uninterruptedly throughout the seasons appeared as an advantage over the trade with the Baltic countries and Russia. Finally, the fact that, by navigation ordinances, foreign vessels could be effectively excluded from the freight business with the colonies, was regarded as another advantage over the inter-European carrying trade.

As regards the weight of the argument, it has to be noted that

---

garding colonial shipbuilding are almost absent at this stage of the discussion and were not to arise before the New England colonies were well on the way to becoming a major shipbuilding centre. Apart from the carrying trade, the most important activity which led to an enhancement of the number of ships and sailors was fishing. The establishment of transoceanic fisheries forms in itself part of the question of colonies and will be discussed below.

[63]*A Trve Declaration of the Estate of the Colonie of Virginia*, p. 25. Similarly, Sir Humphrey Gilbert, *A True Report of the Late Discoveries*, p. 435.
[64]Hakluyt, *Discourse on Western Planting*, pp. 91 f.
[65]*Virginia* (1650), p. 5.
[66]*Nova Britannia* (1609), p. 22.

it shared its persuasiveness with the encouragement given to the American fisheries. Uncomplicated as the argument was, it weighed heavily throughout the centuries to come. It became stereotype and intellectually uninteresting. Yet up to the repeal of the Navigation Acts, its presentation had telling effects.

THE TRANSATLANTIC FISHERIES

Notwithstanding earlier efforts of this kind, the systematic development of the fisheries as a mainstay of English maritime power started with the vigorous policy launched by Lord Burghley.[67] While he condemned the then existing Navigation Laws on a variety of grounds, he pushed the expansion of English fisheries. To be sure, the desire for an extensive fishing industry was based upon two considerations. On the one hand, it would render England independent of foreign fish. On the other hand, it would result in an increase of ships and sailors. As to the latter aspect the remarks made in the foregoing paragraphs are fully applicable in this case. The desire to render the English demand for fish independent of foreign supplies and, if possible, to create a surplus supply which could be sold abroad, is part of the general consideration of colonies as a new source of goods and will be discussed as part of that question.

Indeed, the establishment of North American fisheries formed an important argument favouring colonization.[68] A few pertinent passages follow:

And the chiefest cause why our English men do not go so far westerly as the especial fishing places do lie, both for plenty and greatness of fish is for that they have no succour and known safe harbour in those parts. But if our nation were once planted there or thereabouts, whereas they now fish but for two months in the year, they might then fish for so long as pleased themselves ... which being brought to pass shall increase the number of our ships and mariners....[69]

Now, a Colonie planted in New-England may be many wayes usefull to this State. As first, in furthering our fishing-voyages....[70]

---

[67]Cf. Cunningham, *Growth of English Industry and Commerce*, I, 63 ff.

[68]It also had some effect on the decision upon which regions the English would bestow their colonizing endeavours. While the desire to discover gold mines drew the English adventurers and colonizers towards the southern portions of the North American subcontinent, the project of establishing fisheries tended to push them towards its northern portions.

[69]Gilbert, *A True Report of the late Discoveries* (1583), p. 435.

[70]John White, *The Planters Plea* (1630), in Force, *Tracts*, II, 14.

The implication of this line of argument is obvious. In persuasiveness it ranked among the more important ones.[71]

OUTLET FOR SURPLUS POPULATION

The argument that through colonization the excess population of England would be effectively drained from the mother country was of utmost importance in the literature of the period under discussion. Contemporary writers devoted to its presentation a great deal of space and expository effort. It deserves a more lengthy discussion not only for this reason but also because it involves some difficulties of interpretation. George L. Beer,[72] for instance, examining the argument in a rather common-sense manner,[73] comes to the conclusion that up to about 1660 it was of outstanding weight. On the whole, this is today the text-book version of this matter. Professor Johnson,[74] probing considerably deeper, arrives at the conclusion that the interest in colonization professed during the period before 1660, cannot be explained in terms "of a fetish of over-population." Quoting John Hales who, as early as 1549, "decried any policy which might lead to depopulation," he asserts that in the period before the Civil War there already emerge ideas on the problem of population which are entirely consistent with the later mercantilist theories on the subject, theories which demanded the largest possible employed population.

Professor Johnson gives three reasons why the mercantilist argument for increasing the density of England's population did not appear as frequently before 1660 as it did thereafter. These three reasons, reducible to two, are: First, that the promoters of colonies for propagandist reasons had to demonstrate the utility of colonies. A sufficient supply of dependable colonists was the only limiting factor in the pursuit of expanding colonies, and they overstressed the excess-population argument in order to make

[71]For a discussion of Sir Fernando Gorges' project to base the English colonization of New England on the codfish, the staple product of that area, see R. A. Preston, "Fishing and Plantation," *American Historical Review*, XLV (1940), 29-43. The whole question of the reciprocal reaction of fisheries and colonization is excellently discussed in H. A. Innis, *The Cod Fisheries* (New Haven, 1940).

[72]Beer, *Origins of the British Colonial System*, pp. 32 ff.

[73]Broadly stated, he shows that the English thought of their country as overpopulated and, hence, welcomed relief of this population pressure through the outlet of colonies.

[74]Johnson, *American Economic Thought in the Seventeenth Century*, pp. 49 ff.

colonization popular. Secondly, that the mercantilist theory of population, though already traceable, was still in its beginnings and, therefore, its supporters were presumably unable to oppose the promoters with a fully-developed doctrine. Finally, Professor Johnson remarks that the arguments for colonization as a means of relieving the country of surplus population "centre around the expected decrease of domestic unemployment, the diminution of crime, lower cost of poor relief, and lower taxes."

While George L. Beer attributed too much weight to the surplus-population argument and also somewhat oversimplified it, the present writer intends to argue that he and the text-book version are substantially right, while Professor Johnson deserves due praise for having probed deeper than his predecessors did. In order to acquire a basis for further argumentation, a number of representative passages follow.

Besides this, it [colonization] will proove a generall benefit unto our countrey, that through this occasion, not onely a great number of men which do now live idlely at home, and are burthenous, chargeable, & unprofitable to this realme, shall hereby be set on worke, but also children of twelve or fourteene yeeres of age, or under, may bee kept from idleness, in making of a thousand kindes of trifling things, which wil be good merchandize for that countrey. And moreover, our idle women (which the Realme may well spare) shall also be imployed on plucking, dying, and sorting of feathers, in pulling, beating, and working of hempe, and in gathering of cotton, and divers things right necessary for dying.... And the men may imploy themselves in dragging for pearle, woorking for mines, and in matters of husbandry, and likewise in hunting the Whale for Trane ... besides in fishing for cod, salmon, and herring ... and felling of trees.... [75]

Truthe it is, that throughe our longe peace and seldome sickness wee are growen more populous than ever heretofore; so that now there are of every arte and science so many, that they can hardly lyve one by another, nay rather they are readie to eate upp one another; yea many thousandes of idle persons are within this realme, which, havinge no way to be sett on worke, be either mutinous and seeke alteration in the state, or at leaste very burdensome to the commonwealthe, and often fall to pilferinge and thevinge and other lewdness, whereby all the prisons of the lande are daily pestred and stuffed full of them ... these pety theves mighte be condempned for certen yeeres in the western partes.... [76]

.. it maie trulie bee verefied, that as the people thereof do in number so exeede, as if some speedie order be not taken for the removinge of the surplusage, or at least of the basest and poorest sorte of them into some forraigne place of habitation the Realme cannot possible long maintaine them.... [77]

---

[75]Peckham, *A True Report* (1583), p. 112.

[76]Hakluyt, *Discourse on Western Planting* (1584), pp. 36 f.

[77]Sir Henry Knyvett, *The Defence of the Realme* (1596), in new ed. (Oxford, 1906), p. 11.

There is nothing more daungerous for the estate of commonwealths, then when the people do increase to a greater multitude and number then may iustly parallel with the largnesse of the place and countrey: for hereupon comes oppression, and diuerse kinde of wrongs, mutinies, sedition, commotion, & rebellion, scarcitie, dearth, pouertie, and sundrie sorts of calamities. . . .

And herupon many statesmen haue thought nothing more profitable for populous common-wealths, then to haue foreigne and externe warres, to the ende that thereby the superfluous braunches might be cut off. . . . Our multitudes like too much bloud in the body, do infect our countrey with plague and pouertie, our land hath brought fwrth, but it hath not milke sufficient in the breast thereof to nourish all those children which it has brought forth . . . we are to note the direction of Iosua, vpon the aforesaid complaint to the children of Ioseph, which is to enlarge their territories, and dilate their borders, by destroying Gods enemies the Perizzites, and Giants,[78] which inhabited the valleyes, bordering vpon mount Ephraim. . . .[79]

Two things are especially required herein, people to make the plantation, and money. . . . For the first we neede no doubt, our land abounding with swarmes of idle persons, which hauing no meanes of labour to reeleue their misery, doe likewise swarme in lewd and naughtie practices, so that if we seeke not some waies for their forreine employment, wee must prouide shortly more prisons and corrections for their bad conditions . . . so that you see it no new thing, but moste profitable for our State, to rid our multitudes of such as lie at home, pestering the land with pestilence, and penury, and infecting one another with vice and villanie, worse than the plague it selfe.[80]

The author of a sermon preached at White-Chapel remarked that "the People blessed be God, doe swarme in the land, as young bees in a hive in June. . . ." and urged "the younger bees, to swarme and hive themselves elsewhere. Take the opportunity, good honest labourers, which indeed bring all the honey to the hive. . ."[81]
More quotations follow:

Secondly, to provide and build up for the publike Honour and Safety of our gratious King and his Estates some small Rampier of our owne . . . by transplanting the rancknesse and multitude of increase in our people; of which there is left no vent, but age. . . .[82]

. . . . for foreign Plantations and Colonies abroad, thats both honourable and profitable to disburthen the land of such inhabitants as may well be spared. . . .[83]

[78]The author refers here to the American Indians.
[79]Robert Gray, *A Good Speed to Virginia* (1609), The Epistle Dedicatorie.
[80]Johnson, *Nova Britannia* (1609), p. 19.
[81]William Symonds, *Virginia* (1609), in Brown, *Genesis of the United States*, I, 288 f.
[82]*A True and Sincere Declaration of the Purpose and Ends of the Plantation Begun in Virginia* (1610), in Brown, *Genesis of the United States*, I, 340.
[83]Francis Bacon, "A Letter of Advice Written to the Duke of Buckingham," in Spedding, *Letters and Life of Francis Bacon*, VI, 21.

Whereas our Land, at this present, by meanes of our long continued both Peace and Health, freed from any notable, either warre or Pestilence, the two great deuourers of mankinde . . . euen swarmeth with multitude and plentie of people, it is time, and high time . . . which if they were transported into other regions, might both richly increase their own estates, and notably ease and disburden ours.[84]

For unless the three Impostumes of the world, namely, Wars, Famine, and Pestilence, do purge that great Body; all Kingdomes and Countries become very populous, and men hardly can live in quiet, or without danger. Merchants therefore seeking to discover new Countries, are much to be commended and cherished. . . .[85]

It [colonization] will disburthen this Nation of many indigent persons, who having formerly perhaps enjoyed a fulnesse of abused or forfeyted plenty, & at present reduced to an inequality of such subsistence, are commonly prompted to their owne and other mens ruine by making the high wayes an ambuscado to innocent Travellers . . . and dayly examples informs us, that prisons at present are almost as full of criminall as indebted persons. . . . It will take off all Parish charges, in providing for destitute Minors and Orphans, whereof there are at present a burthensome multitude, whereby the Parishes so freed, may with greater alacrity and ability, part with contributory moneys to maintaine, recruite, and incourage your Armies and Navies. . . . The republic in its present constitution abounding with so dangerous a number of male contents, who commonly like shrubs under high and spreading Cedars, imagine the spacious height of others to be the cause of their owne lowness . . . and such men removing their discontents with their persons, will have a brave and ample theater to make their merits and abilities emergent. . . .[86]

. . . and send them for some of the new Plantations, all delinquents for matters which deserve not hanging, might bee served so too without sparing one of them . . . so should we not onely free the streetes and countrey of such rascals and vagrant people that swarme up and downe at present; but prevent many others, some whereof are successively borne and bred so the rest brought to the same begging lasie life by their ill example, and a great summe of money saved, which uses yearely to bee given to such vagabonds to no purpose but to make them worse. . . .[87]

Before entering into an analysis of the above statements, it may be remarked that for the purpose of this study it is unnecessary to establish whether or not England actually was over-populated during the period under discussion. That question is immaterial. Of importance is only whether or not the English observers of the time believed that their country suffered from demographic congestion.

[84] Eburne, *Plaine Path-Way to Plantations* (1624), p. 9. See also p. 12.
[85] Malynes, *Consuetudo* (1656), p. 164.
[86] Williams, *Virginia* (1650), pp. 4 f.
[87] Henry Robinson, *Englands Safety in Trades Encrease* (London, 1641), p. 13.

It is common knowledge today that owing to the large influx of American precious metals a marked rise occurred in the price level of European countries. England was not excluded from this experience. The lag in the adjustment of wage levels caused a great deal of misery among the labouring population. General distress was vastly heightened by the enclosure movement and the introduction of a new system of land economy which diminished the demand for agricultural labour. As a consequence, a considerable volume of unemployment was created and the readjustment of wage to price levels was still further retarded.[88]

A careful reading of the above-quoted passages will dispel any doubts that their authors were sincerely convinced of their country's overcrowded condition. Admittedly they had very crude notions as to the causes of the prevailing distress. Usually they attributed it to the non-occurrence of wars and decimating epidemics.[89] They also made no attempt at defining the term "surplus population" or whatever synonymous expression they employed.[90] Their test of demographic overcrowding amounted to the simple enumeration of such symptoms as widespread unemployment and its numerous social and political consequences like idleness, beggary, vagrancy, crime, vice, unhygienic conditions, social unrest, political discontent, etc. But it is quite clear that they attributed these various evil consequences to their responsible matrix: unemployment. Idleness, crime, and social unrest appeared as the most objectionable of these consequences.

As regards the horror of widespread idleness, there was, at least during the first quarter of the seventeenth century, as yet little of that tendency of mercantilist thought which regarded employment as an end in itself. The very fact that many members of the English clergy participated in the current discussion on unemployment and colonization indicates that this particular disgust with respect to idleness, apart from humane considerations, had important roots in religious concepts and the clergyman's abhorrence

[88]Cf. H. M. Robertson, *Aspects of the Rise of Economic Individualism* (Cambridge, 1935), pp. 182 f.

[89]Sir Thomas More ascribed the misery he observed to the change in the agricultural system. Writing at the beginning of the sixteenth century, i.e., long before the first English attempts at colonization, he did not discuss the establishment of plantations as a means of draining off England's excess population. Cf. Sir Thomas More, *Utopia* (1516) (Everyman ed.; London, 1937), pp. 23 ff.

[90]A failure which is all the more excusable as even modern experts are unable to agree on a satisfactory definition.

of the by-products of idleness in the form of vice (Puritanism!). As to the phenomenon of crime, these writers were less concerned with the removal of criminals by transportation than with the prevention of crime by removing the conditions conducive to its increased occurrence. In view of the riotous uprisings of 1549 in Cornwall, Devon, Oxfordshire, and other counties, the fear of resulting social and political discontent seems a quite natural concern. As Deloney put it "the poore hate the rich, because they will not set them on worke; and the rich hate the poore, because they seeme burdenous...."[91] And Bacon wrote: "The matter of seditions is of two kinds; much poverty and much discontentment.... And if this poverty and broken estate in the better sort be joined with want and necessity in the mean people, the danger is imminent and great. For the rebellions of the belly are the worst."[92]

These three phenomena of idleness, crime, and social unrest in themselves formed important subjects of discussion in the period after the Civil War when the notions of England's suitable density of population underwent a decisive change. The significant point is that in the period before the Civil War these phenomena are seen as causally connected with unemployment, and unemployment, in turn, with an undesirable density of population. Passages of the kind above simply do not occur in the literature produced after the Civil War. To the writers of the period under discussion, England appeared in an overcrowded condition and the removal of this condition was regarded as extremely desirable. Thus Bacon said: "Generally, it is to be foreseen that the population of a kingdom (especially if it be not mown down by wars) do not exceed the stock of the kingdom which would maintain them."[93] (This is already the notion of an increasing population pressing against the means of subsistence.)

In the search for remedies several alternatives were postulated. Bacon himself proposes: "The first remedy or prevention is to remove by all means possible that material cause of sedition whereof we spake; which is want and poverty in the estate. To which purpose serveth the opening and well-balancing of trade; the cherishing of manufactures; the banishment of idleness; the repressing of waste and excess by sumptuary laws; the regulating of prices of things vendible."[94] Eburne discusses the "restraint

[91]Quoted in Robertson, *Aspects of the Rise of Economic Individualism*, p. 184.
[92]Bacon, "Of Seditions and Troubles," *Essays*, p. 44.
[93]*Ibid.*, p. 45.   [94]*Ibid.*

of excessive rents," home colonization (i.e., the cultivation of waste lands), and public works. But he concludes that all these constitute "but an imperfect Cure" and suggests that "the true and sure remedie is, The diminution of the people. . . ."[95] The only "speedie" and "infallible remedie" is emigration to the colonies.[96] As appears from the passage quoted above,[97] Bacon likewise suggested emigration to the new plantations as an effective remedy. Thus, while the creation of a new market in the colonies appeared as an eligible alternative promising the elimination of unemployment,[98] these writers saw in the possibility of emigration to the colonies an effective remedy for England's congested condition.

It is quite true that during the period under discussion, the doctrine that a large population was indispensable to a powerful state, was already widely held. Yet this notion was not expressed as frequently as it was after the Civil War and, even at this stage, what was wanted was not sheer multitude of people but a multitude of *employed* people. Thus Hakluyt pointed out: "Salomon saieth, that the honour and strength of a prince consisteth in the multitude of people. And if this come aboute, that worke may be had for the multitude, where the realme hath nowe one thousande for the defence thereof, the same may have fyve thousande. For when the people knowe how to live, and how to mayntayne and feede their wyves and children, they will not abstaine from mariage as now they doe."[99]

Objections also were raised by some writers against the proposed emigration to the colonies and especially against the proposed emigration of skilled workers who were not unemployed. Eburne mentions the objection that "the remouing of so great a number, will be a great weakning and impouerishing to our land," but counters this argument by remarking: "No, none at all. For first, The strength of a Land, consisteth not so much in the number of people, as, in the aptnesse and ablenesse of them vnto seruice.... 2. If Number onely bee respected, it will no whit be empaired, but rather bettered, not diminished, but augmented, in that so great a Multitude of vs being planted otherwhere, shall become, as it were, another England, ready, and able vpon, all occasions, to ioyne with this."[100] Similarly, John White wrote: "First, I deny

---

[95]*Plaine Path-Way to Plantations* (1624), p. 10.
[96]*Ibid.*   [97]*Ibid.*, The Epistle.
[98]This point will be discussed below.
[99]Hakluyt, *Discourse on Western Planting* (1584), p. 43.
[100]*Plaine Path-Way to Plantations* (1624), p. 76.

that such as are gone out from the State, are cut off from the State .... Secondly, if some usefull men bee spared, to whom doe we spare them? is it not to a part of our owne body?"[101]

It may be safely concluded that, though not unopposed,[102] the argument favouring colonies as an outlet for an excess population carried great weight during the period under discussion.

THE TRANSPORTATION OF CRIMINALS AND UNDESIRABLES

In the literature written before 1660, the idea of colonies serving as a dumping-place for criminals and other undesirables is as yet not clearly distinguished from the argument which favours colonization and colonies because they seem to promise an outlet for surplus population. Yet the beginnings of the former notion as an independent argument are already vaguely traceable.

The early writers of this period were mainly concerned with the prevention of crime by means of removing those conditions which were conducive to its increased incidence. They saw in the fact of widespread unemployment the basic condition responsible for the multiplication of crime. Such a line of thought blamed circumstances rather than the individual criminal or potential criminal. The proper remedy was to reduce unemployment and thus to limit the human reservoir from which criminals were recruited. The transportation idea proper, however, springs from a different train of reasoning. It is less concerned with the social and economic conditions of crime. It proposes the removal of convicted criminals and, to a limited extent, of prospective criminals (i.e., beggars, vagrants, etc.) mainly for reasons of convenience.[103] Colonies were regarded as useful dumping-

[101]*The Planters Plea* (1630), p. 21.

[102]Such opposition is referred to and rebutted in the writings of some of the authors mentioned above. However, the present writer was unable to find anything to this effect in written form by the supporters of the opposition.

[103]No doubt, in an age and country which provided capital punishment for a large number of crimes, motives of humaneness were not absent in inducing some influential quarters to support the transportation system. The Act of the Privy Council of March 24, 1617, expressly mentions "clemencie and mercy" as a reason for instituting the system. On the other hand, the notorious lack of labour from which the development of many colonies suffered and the idea that felons, by partially satisfying this demand, would become useful to the interest of the realm, was another powerful factor. It is likewise mentioned in the preamble to the above-mentioned Act. Cf. Gillespie, *Influence of Oversea Expansion on England*, pp. 20 ff.; A. E. Smith, "The Transportation of Convicts to the American Colonies in the Seventeenth Century," *American Historical Review*, XXXIX (1934), 232-49.

grounds which enabled the mother country to rid itself of the sweepings of Bridewell and Newgate.

Some of the arguments presented above[104] may be interpreted as containing the first formulations of the idea of transportation.[105] However, during the earliest phase of the English discussion on colonies this argument met with violent opposition. Bacon wrote: "It is a shameful and unblessed thing to take the scum of the people with whom you plant: and not only so, but it spoileth the plantation; for they will ever live like rogues, and not fall to work . . . ."[106] On another occasion he remarked: "That if any transplant themselves into plantations abroad, who are known to be schismaticks, outlaws, or criminal persons, that they may be sent back upon first notice: such persons are not fit to lay the foundation of a new colony."[107] John White suggested: "It seems to be a common and grosse errour that Colonies ought to be Enunctories or sinckes of States to drayne away their filth: whence arise often murmurings at the removall of any men of State or worth. . . ."[108] And Thomas Fuller argued: "Let the planters be honest, skilful, and gainful people, For if they be such as leap thither from the gallows, can any hope for cream out of scum? . . . It is rather bitterly than falsely spoken concerning one of our western plantations, 'that it was very like unto England, as being spit out of the very mouth of it'."[109]

This opposition to the idea of recruiting colonists partly from the criminal dregs of the mother country originated in the peculiar conception of plantations of the above writers which differed largely from that of the majority of the English writers on colonies.[110] In a later chapter this majority conception of plantations will be examined. Here it may suffice to say that men like Bacon, White, and Fuller agreed that colonies should be useful to the metropolis, but they also had a vision of duplicating the society of the mother country in the colonies. What they had in mind were little

[104]*Supra*, pp. 42-4.
[105]It may be said that in these cases the idea of transportation was supplementary to the general idea of relieving the population pressure of the mother country. At any rate, the desire to send excess population to the American colonies would naturally particularize itself in the desire to get rid of the unemployed, the paupers and beggars, the criminals, etc.
[106]Bacon, "Of Plantations," *Essays*, p. 104.
[107]Bacon, "A Letter of Advice Written to the Duke of Buckingham," p. 21.
[108]*The Planters Plea* (1630), p. 19.
[109]*The Holy and Profane State*, pp. 237 f.
[110]The idea of transportation was almost generally conceded to be useful.

Englands strewn along the Atlantic seaboard of North America. In a rudimentary form, this was the idea of an empire as a congeries of nations.

During the period under discussion, the idea of transportation was, on the whole, subsidiary to the surplus-population argument. Only toward the end of the period did the transportation idea receive separate treatment. Judged by itself, it was distinctly second or third rate in importance but, although it came to be little discussed, its relative influence should not be underestimated.[111]

COLONIES AS SOURCES OF RAW MATERIALS

The expectation of finding new sources of supply in the colonies must be regarded as the most potent of all the arguments offered in favour of English colonization. During the period under discussion the English import trade, aside from the purchase of fish, was composed of three main branches.[112] First, the importation of naval stores and potash from the Baltic countries; secondly, the importation of salt, wines, fruit, silk, and, increasingly, sugar and tobacco from southern Europe; and thirdly, the importation of spices, dyestuffs, etc., from the Far East. Of these commodities wine, fruit, silk, sugar, and tobacco, were of the nature of luxuries. Their designation as luxuries implied that they could be dispensed with if need be, yet it is certain that influential groups in England had become habituated to their enjoyment and were not inclined to do without them. Of the other commodities, salt was indispensable to the fisheries, potash and dyestuffs to the woollen industry, and naval stores to shipbuilding. These products, therefore, were regarded as of vital importance to the nation and the very fact that their supply was under the control of foreign princes caused a feeling of uneasiness and insecurity.

At the time in question, the problem of important raw materials frequently carried great political significance.[113] Countries which possessed a quasi-monopoly of a particular produce or controlled

[111]Curiously enough, when, after the American Revolution, the American dumping-ground ceased to be available, the British, seriously at a loss, thought of founding a convict settlement in West Africa, but finally decided on Australia. It was to the idea of transportation that that continent owes its initial settlement by the British.

[112]Cf. Beer, *Origins of the British Colonial System*, p. 56.

[113]Cf. Henri Hauser's investigation into the political aspects of the European salt trade (*Les Origines historiques des problèmes économiques actuels* [Paris, 1930], pp. 17ff., 53-69).

the bulk of the world supply available to European nations, were often disposed to exploit that opportunity by boosting its price to foreign customers. Portugal, for example, after she acquired Brazil, controlled more than half of the world production of sugar and thus was in a position to manipulate its price.[114] Queen Christina of Sweden set up a joint-stock tar company in 1648 which, exploiting its monopolist position, charged exorbitant prices for pitch and tar.[115] There were still other causes which rendered supplies from foreign countries unduly expensive. Because of the necessity of bribing Russian officials, the expense of maintaining ambassadors, etc., the Russian trade had "a precarious bottom."[116] Again and again Macpherson reports English complaints that the King of Denmark exacted exorbitant tolls from the English vessels engaged in the Baltic trade.[117] But quite apart from this matter of prices and extra expenses, the monarch, controlling the supply of a particular product, frequently restricted or even stopped its exportation in order to exert political pressure on the importing country.[118] The frequent occurrence of wars often rendered the foreign supply of some merchandise precarious for a time. Finally, the more imports could be diminished, the more likely the achievement of a sizable export surplus.

In the light of these reasons, the acquisition of colonial areas which produced or might produce goods, hitherto drawn from foreign countries, appeared highly desirable. It was this outlook that prompted the formation of the East India Company and the colonization of North America.[119] English discoverers like Christopher Carlile still believed that many of the desired products could be supplied by the American natives and that the problem was one of erecting trading posts along the North American coast, a policy which the East India Company was to follow in India.[120] It soon became obvious, however, that such hopes were illusory and that in order to get the desired commodities, the English had to organize their production.

The first English writings on the colonial question are replete

---

[114]*Ibid.*, p. 15.   [115]Macpherson, *Annals*, II, 432.   [116]*Ibid.*, p. 172.

[117]*Ibid.*, pp. 172, 186, 213, 224 f., 228 f., 476 f.

[118]For example, when Henry VIII desired to put pressure on Charles V, he restricted and, finally, altogether interdicted the exportation of English wool to Antwerp. Similarly, the English stopped the exportation of coal to the Netherlands as a reprisal against the Dutch. Cf. Hauser, *Les Origines historiques des problèmes économiques actuels*, pp. 15, 20.

[119]Beer, *Origins of the British Colonial System*, pp. 57 f.   [120]*Ibid.*, pp. 65 f.

with exaggerated speculations on the kind and quantity of products which could be raised in America. In this respect the English were also inclined to pasture on illusions and, regarding some particular commodities, continued to do so for centuries. As will be seen from the quotations given below, the principal cause of the illusory nature of their excessive expectations is to be found in the fact that they thought simply in terms of geographical latitudes. They naïvely assumed that American areas situated in the same latitude as Portugal, North Africa, etc., could be expected to yield the same raw stuffs. Thus Christopher Carlile wrote:

> But when it is asked what may be hoped for from thence after some yeeres, it is first to be considered, that this situation in fourtie degrees, shall bee very apt to gather the commodities either of those parts which stand to the Southward of it, as those which are to be Northward. . . . In the Northerlie may be expected not onely as especiall good fishing for Salmon, Codde, and Whales, but also any other such commodities, as the Easterne Countryes doe yeeld us now; as Pitch, Tarre, Hempe, and thereof Cordage, Masts, . . . hides, rich Furres, and other such like without being in any such beholding to a king of Denmarke, or other prince or state that shall be in such sort able to command our shippes at their pleasure, as those doe at this day, by meanes of their straite passages and strong shipping. . . . As for those partes which lie West and to the Southwardes, it may well bee hoped they will yeeld Wines with a small helpe, . . . Olive being once planted, will yeelde the like Oyle as Spaine, Province and Italie. . . .[121]

Hakluyt points out the precariousness of the trade with Spain, Turkey, and Russia, complains of the "exactions of the King of Denmarke at our passage in and oute by the Sounde,"[122] and concludes: "Thus havinge regarde unto the premisses, yt behoveth us to seeke some newe and better trade, of lesse daunger and more securitie, of lesse damage, and of more advantage. . . ."[123] As to the kind of products to be expected from North America, he assumes:

> That this westerne voyage will yelde unto us all the commodities of Europe, Affrica and Asia. . . . The countries therefore of America where unto we have just title . . . from Florida northewarde to 67. degrees being answerable in clymate to Barbary, Egipte, Siria, Persia, Turky, Greece, all the islands of the Levant sea, Italie, Poringale, Fraunce, Flaunders, High Almayne, Denmarke, Estland, Poland, and Muscovye, may presently or within a shorte space afforde unto us, for little or nothinge, and with moche more safetie, eyther all or a greate parte of the commodities which the aforesaid countries do yelde us at a very dere hande and with manifolde daungers.[124]

---

[121] *A Briefe and Summary Discourse*, p. 139.
[122] Hakluyt, *Discourse on Western Planting* (1584), pp. 13 ff.
[123] *Ibid.*, pp. 16 f.   [124] *Ibid.*, p. 19.

Similarly, Sir Humphrey Gilbert expected that "within the degrees aforesaid is doubtless to be found the most wholesome and best temperature of air, fertility of soil, and every other commodity or merchandise, for which, with no small peril, we do travel into Barbary, Spain, Portugal, France, Italy, Muscovy, and Eastland ...."[125] An anonymous writer remarked: "... by recovering and possessing ... a fruitfull land, whence they [the colonizers] may furnish and provide this Kingdom, with all such necessities and defects under which we labour, and are now enforced to buy, and receive at the curtesie of other Princes, under the burthen of great Customs, and heavy impositions, and at so high rates in trafique...."[126] A similar line of thought is presented in the following statement: "The merchant knoweth, that through the troubles in Poland & Muscouy, (whose eternall warres are like the Antipathy of the Dragon & Elephants) all their traffique for Mastes, Deales, Pitch, Tarre, Flax, Hempe, and Cordage, are euery day more indaungered, and the woods of those countries are almost exhausted. All which are to be had in Virginia with farre lesse charge, and farre more safety."[127]

Robert Johnson, discussing the "many waies" in which the possession of American colonies would benefit the mother country, observed: "... if we consider what strength of shipping may be raysed and maintained thence, in furnishing our owne wants of sundrie kindes, and the wants of other Nations too...."[128] He assumed that the English would get timber there "50 per cent" cheaper than from Prussia or Poland, and would also get sufficient supplies of wine, raw silk, hemp, flax, pitch, tar, turpentine, "sope-ashes," etc.[129] Edward Williams thought that Virginia "dispences a moderate equality of heat and cold, between the two violent extreams thereof in Barbadoes and New England. It will admit of all things producible in any other part of the world, lying in the same Parallel with China, Persia, Japan, Cochinchina, Candia, Cyprus, Sicily...."[130] He likewise promised his readers that "all Materialls for shipping ... and what ever else we are necessitated to supply our wants with out of the Easterne Countries, who make

[125] *A True Report* (1583), p. 437.
[126] *A True and Sincere Declaration of the Purpose and Ends of the Plantation Begun in Virginia*, in Brown, *Genesis of the United States*, I, 340.
[127] *A Trve Declaration of the Estate of the Colonie of Virginia* (1610), p. 23.
[128] *Nova Britannia* (1609), II, 16.
[129] *Ibid.*, pp. 16 f.
[130] *Virginia* (1650), p. 8.

it not unusuall to take advantages of their neighbours necessity, and often times upon a pretence of difference or misintelligence betwixt us, embrace an occasion to over-rate or over-custome their commodities...."[131]

The tenor of all the passages quoted above is remarkably uniform. Generally, these writers held exaggerated opinions of the range and quantity of goods which England would be able to obtain from her American colonies, and generally they expected that the supply of goods from colonial sources would mean a *cheaper* and a more *dependable* supply as compared with purchase from foreign nations. How far these notions and hopes were part of a general craving for imperial self-sufficiency will be examined in a subsequent chapter. Here it may be added that a vague idea of imperial self-sufficiency as the basis of the nation's external power was not absent at the time under consideration. This becomes clear from the phrasing of the following citation.

That with all possible conveniency wee enlarge our Forraigne Plantations, and get farther footing in Barbarie, East and West Indies.... Not only that wee may be better provide our selves of Canvas for Sailes, Masts, Timber, with all other things necessary for Shipping within our own Dominions; but also in that a little spot of ground, as England is, with its Dominions, if it doe not enlarge them, in future generations, and feare me, will be found inconsiderable in respect of Spain, Portugall, the United Provinces, or any other European Nation, which shall have arrived to, and be armed with five or ten times a greater strength, power, and riches, either from their Asian, African, or American Dominions.[132]

On the other hand, it is surprising that of all the passages given above none expresses the idea that the substitution of colonial raw materials for products hitherto obtained from foreign nations, would reduce the total of English imports from abroad and, hence, result in a larger export surplus. Such considerations, too, were not entirely absent. Thus, Sir Edward Sandys, discussing, in 1624, Britain's trade with Spain, complained "that the importation of Spanish tobacco hindereth this kingdom 100,000 l. per annum, which else would have been imported." And he moved to petition the King "... to banish all foreign tobacco, not being of the growth of his Majesty's dominions."[133]

Similarly, of all the statements quoted above, none mentions the possibility that by producing in the colonies goods marketable

[131]*Ibid.*, p. 5.
[132]Henry Robinson, *Certain Proposalls* (London, 1652), p. 11.
[133]Cf. Stock, *Proceedings and Debates*, I, 69.

abroad, the English would be able to augment the total volume of their exports which, again, would have a desirable effect on England's balance of trade.[134] In the next chapter, it will be seen that English writers of the period after the Civil War paid a great deal of attention to the general effect of colonial exports on the English balance of trade.

The body of mercantilist thought of the period under discussion already contained that element of protectionism which demands the maximum substitution of domestic for foreign products in order to obtain a maximum of domestic employment.[135] This idea is clearly expressed by Bacon: "... let us advance the native commodities of our own kingdom, and employ our country-men before strangers: let us turn the wools of the land into cloaths and stuffs of our own growth, and the hemp and flax growing here into linen cloth and cordage; it would set many thousand hands on work...."[136]

Departing from this notion, it was logical to argue that instead of importing some goods in half-finished or finished state from foreign countries it might be possible to receive their constituent raw substances from the colonies. Thus Hakluyt pointed out: "... wee are to note, that all the comodities wee shall bringe thence, wee shall not bringe them wroughte, as we bringe now the comodities of Fraunce and Flaunders, &c., but shall receave them all substaunces unwroughte, to the ymployment of a wonderfull multitude of the poore subjectes of this realme in returne."[137]

In general, the writers of the period in question did not pay much attention to the problem of production difficulties and production costs in the colonies. When they did, their assumptions were usually of an extraordinarily naïve and optimistic character. Thus one author, apparently unaware of the capital outlay and the magnitude of labour costs involved, wrote: "When in Virginia there is nothing wanting, but onely mens labours, to furnish both Prince, State and merchant, without charge or difficulty."[138] Particularly strange are those projects which envisaged the stimulation of novel wants in the American Indians, and, through wants, of industry and industrial employability. Sir William Alexander,

---

[134]Only Robert Johnson (*supra*, p. 53) remarks that naval stores produced in the colonies might be sold abroad after England's needs had been satisfied.
[135]Cf. Viner, *Studies*, p. 73.
[136]Bacon, "A Letter of Advice Written to the Duke of Buckingham," p. 23.
[137]Hakluyt, *Discourse on Western Planting* (1584), p. 42.
[138]*A Trve Declaration of the Estate of the Colonie of Virginia* (1610), p. 42.

speculating on the possibility of utilizing native labour, wrote: "... for their ruine could giue to vs neither glory nor benefit, since ... it ... would defraud vs of many able bodies, that hereafter (besides the Christian duties in sauing their soules) ... may serue to many good vses, when by our meanes they shall learn lawful Trades and industries."[139]

Much more elaborate and rather ludicrous is Edward Williams's proposal to christianize the Indians with the help of the silk-worm. To have the natives produce raw silk is, of course, an integral part of this benevolent scheme.[140] Finally, it may be surmised that the damage to foreign producers resulting from the substitution of colonial products for foreign commodities was considered an extra-benefit.[141]

COLONIES AS MARKETS

In the foregoing section, passages have been cited which reveal much English anxiety about the precariousness of foreign trade prevalent at the time under consideration. This feeling of insecurity is demonstrated in the following statement: "It is publicly knowne that trafique with our neighbor Countries begin to be of small request, the game seldom answering the merchants adventure, and forraigne states either are already or at this presente are preparing to inrich themselves with woole and cloth of their owne which heertofore they borowed from us ... therefore we must of necessity foregoe our greate showing if we doe not wish prepare a place fit for the vent of our wares and so set our marriners on

[139] *An Encouragement to Colonies* (1624), p. 205.

[140] Williams suggested: "First, the Indian is naturally curious and very ingenious ... the only thing that frights them from bringing work to perfection, is the labour attending it. 2. But to feed his curiosity, there is nothing in the world more proper than this curious atome of Nature the Silkworme; to see this untaught Artist spin out his transparent bowels, labour such a monument out of his owne intralls ... and that those spirits whose thoughts are of a higher wing then ordinary, may bee convinced of a divine power of the hand of God in the Creation: which gayned upon him, it will not be impossible to drive him to an acknowledgement of Redemption.... In this curiosity there is little or no labour (a thing which they abhorre) their women and children will bee sufficient to goe through with it: and if they could but be brought to it, our Trade with them for silke would be of greater consequence then all their Furs or other commodities put together." Cf. *Virginia* (1650), p. 38.

[141] When in the nineties of the sixteenth century, the English undertook voyages to Newfoundland with the view of searching for new sources of train-oil, the mayor of Bristol declared in 1592: "If this train-oil would make good soap, the King of Spain may burn some of his olive trees" (quoted in MacInnes, *Gateway of Empire*, p. 89).

worke, who dayly run to serve forraigne nacons for wante of imployment. . . ."[142]

Indeed, the quest for export markets was as much a characteristic of this period as the search for new sources of raw stuffs.[143] From the beginning, the voyages of discovery were partly prompted by the desire for new export markets in the fabulous Orient. Among other things, the famous Treaty of Tordesillas embodied a partition of the world export market between Spain and Portugal[144] and soon the British, the French, and the Dutch were to clamour and fight for the largest possible share in this market. The need for the discovery of new markets was particularly pressing in the case of England[145] because her output of manufactures, especially in the expanding woollen industry, was rapidly increasing at a time when her old markets became increasingly precarious. This development was largely due to the disturbing and trade-dislocating influence of the Reformation which rent Europe not only religiously and politically but, to a considerable extent, also commercially.[146] The steady growth of hostility between Spain and England, furthermore, gave rise to the haunting fear that the Spaniards might be able to bring England to submission simply by hampering and cutting off her trade.[147]

In view of the notorious uncertainty of the European and Mediterranean trade, the possession of *dependable* markets, guaranteeing a certain volume of trade, was deemed very desirable.[148]

[142]*Reasons for Raising a Fund for the Support of a Colony at Virginia* (1607), in Brown, *Genesis of the United States*, I, 38.

[143]Cf. Hauser, *Les Origines historiques des problèmes économiques actuels*, chap. III.

[144]*Ibid.*, p. 24.   [145]*Ibid.*, pp. 25 f.

[146]Cf. MacInnes, *Gateway of Empire*, p. 50. Until Henry VIII severed England's connection with the Roman Catholic Church, English merchants enjoyed a lucrative and well-established trade with Spain and were even permitted to share generously in the Spanish trade with the Spanish West Indies (cf. *ibid.*, p. 34). After 1534, the Spaniards put increasing obstacles in the way of the English merchants. Thus, before being admitted to trade at any Spanish port, the English traders were required to take the oath, on the sign of the Holy Cross, that they faithfully adhered to the creed of the Roman Church. Cf. Professor Walter Raleigh, "The English Voyages of the Sixteenth Century," in Hakluyt, *The Principal Navigations*, XII, 33.

[147]Lipson, *Economic History of England*, II, 185.

[148]Cf. Auguste Deschamps, "Les Moyens de la politique de conquête commerciale des marchés étrangers au XVIIe et au XVIIIe siècles," *Revue d'Economie Politique*, XXXII (1918), 385.

Such markets should preferably be controlled[149] or "sole markets,"[150] and colonies would, of course, admirably fit that design.

English desires for an expanding and safe export market were strengthened by the realization that an increased industrial output would serve as an eligible alternative to emigration for the purpose of curbing the dreaded volume of unemployment.

Indeed, these two objectives, to secure a safe outlet for English manufactures, especially woollens, and to effect a reduction of unemployment through expanding foreign sales, form the basic themes of the contemporary discussion on colonies as markets for the mother country. This is clearly epitomized by an anonymous writer who, discussing the usefulness of colonies, puts the rhetorical question: ". . . whither shall wee transport our cloth, and how shall we sustaine our Artisans?"[151] Some representative quotations follow.

And seeinge the savages of the Graunde Baye . . . are greatly delighted with any cappe or garment made of course wollen clothe, their contrie beinge colde and sharpe in the winter, yt is manifeste wee shall finde great utteraunce of our clothes, especially of our coursest and basest northerne doosens.[152]

Moreover, it is well known that all savages . . . will take marvellous delight in any garment, be it never so simple, as a shirt, a blue, yellow, red, or green cassock, or cap, or such like, and will take incredible pains for such a trifle . . . which being so, what vent for our English cloths will thereby ensue, and how great benefit to all such persons and artificers. . . .[153]

. . . this want of cloth, must alwaies bee supplied from England, whereby when the Colony is thorowly increased, and the Indians brought to our Ciulitie (as they will in short time) it will cause a mighty vent of English clothes. . . .[154]

Edward Williams likewise speaks optimistically of the possibility "to fasten Cloaths" upon the Indians.[155] Again it is curious how much thought these English writers devoted to the idea that the stimulation of novel wants in the American natives would create a considerable demand for English goods. Eburne, however, discussing the profitableness and superior security of the colonial market, exhibited more advanced insight when he remarked that

---

[149] Johnson, *American Economic Thought in the Seventeenth Century*, pp. 47 f.
[150] J. E. T. Rogers, *The Economic Interpretation of History* (New York, 1889), p. 323.
[151] *A Trve Declaration of the Estate of the Colonie of Virginia* (1610), p. 25.
[152] Hakluyt, *Discourse on Western Planting* (1584), pp. 38 f.
[153] Gilbert, *A True Report* (1583), p. 435.
[154] Johnson, *Nova Britannia* (1609), p. 22.
[155] *Virginia* (1650), p. 38.

this trade "shall be exercised for the most part, betweene one and the same people, though distant in Region, yet vnited in Religion, in Nation, in Language and Dominion."[156]

In addition to the considerations already mentioned, the possession of a controlled market in the colonies was expected to prove advantageous as an outlet for low-grade commodities not in demand, at profitable prices, in a highly competitive foreign market. This argument, as will be seen below, was advanced again and again in support of colonization and colonies.

In evaluating the relative weight of the argument for establishment and maintenance of colonies as controlled markets for the mother country, it must be kept in mind that competent writers of the period did not devote to it as much space and argumentative efforts as to the appreciation of colonies as sources of raw stuffs. Nevertheless, the argument must be considered one of great importance.

THE AUGMENTATION OF REVENUES

The argument considered here does not refer to the expected increase of revenues derived indirectly from increased production and decreased unemployment due to the possession of colonies. The proposition that colonization would lead to enlarged revenues from export and import duties was of distinctly subordinate if not negligible significance. Indeed, it was mentioned only vaguely if at all and, on the whole, served merely to increase the number of arguments that could be cited in support of colonization. Hence, it is hardly necessary to give pertinent quotations from contemporary authors. Suffice it to say that from the very beginning of English colonization it was commonly taken for granted that the colonies would be outside the English customs area. From this assumption sprang the idea that increased custom revenues would be a welcome consequence of colonial expansion.[157]

THE OPPOSITION TO COLONIZATION

Modern students of the "Old Colonial System" usually refrain from reviewing the early opposition to the proponents of colonization.[158] There are very good reasons for this omission since, a few scanty remarks excepted, such objections are unavailable in

---

[156] *Plaine Path-Way to Plantations* (1624), p. 11.

[157] Cf. Beer, *Origins of the British Colonial System*, pp. 101 f.

[158] Cunningham acknowledges such opposition without giving any references (*Growth of English Industry and Commerce*, I, 333).

written form. Yet it is hard to believe that the stupendous obstacles and financial failures, involved in early colonization, would not have challenged some observers. On general grounds, the necessary diversion of capital and labour from other uses might also be expected to have elicited misgivings in some critical minds. This supposition is corroborated by the fact that the pertinent literature contains frequent references to such opponents and offers more or less ingenious rebuttals in answer to their criticisms.

Daniel Price, a chaplain, scolded those who opposed colonization as a vehicle of missionary activities and who "have injuriously vilified and traduced a great part of the Glory of God. . . . I mean the Plantation of Virginia."[159] One author wrote for the express purpose of redeeming "ourselves and so Noble an action, from the imputations and aspertions, with which ignorant rumor, virulent enemy, or impious subtilty, daily callumniateth our industries. . . ."[160]

John White mentions one objection which arose from the competitive requirements of Irish colonization. According to him, the objection took the following line: "But if we have any spare people, Ireland is a fitter place to receive them then New England. Being 1. Nearer. 2. Our owne. 3. Void in some parts. 4. Fruitfull. . . ."[161] Other criticisms mentioned by White are: "All experience is against the hope and good successe of Colonies; much money, and many mens lives have beene spent upon Virginia, St. Christophers, New-found-land, &c., with no proportionable successe. . . ."[162] "But the pretended end of winning the Heathen to the knowledge of God . . . is a meere fantasie, and a worke not onely of uncertaine but unlikely successe. . . ."[163]

White already mentions the fear of the colonists' inevitable desire to become eventually independent of the mother country: "Yea but if they do not separate, yet they dislike our discipline and ceremonies, and so they will prove themselves semi-separatists at least, and that is their intention in removing from us, that they

---

[159] Daniel Price, *Savles Prohibition Staide* (1609), in Brown, *Genesis of the United States*, I, 313.

[160] *A True and Sincere Declaration of the Purpose and Ends of the Plantation Begun in Virginia*, in Brown, *Genesis of the United States*, I, 339.

[161] *The Planters Plea* (1630), p. 15. White's rebuttal is that ". . . Ireland is well-nigh sufficiently peopled already" and that ". . . besides, this worke needs not hinder that. . ." (*ibid.*, p. 16).

[162] *Ibid.*, p. 27. White replied that one ". . . cannot expect gaine from them before they have taken roote. . ." (*ibid.*, p. 28).

[163] *Ibid.*, p. 29.

may free themselves from our government."[164] Robert Gray mentioned the objection

> that this age will see no profit of this plantatio. Which obiection admit it were true, yet it is too brutish, and berates their neglect and incurious respect of posteritie: we are not borne like beasts to our selues, ... posteritie and the age yet ensuing haue not the least part in our life & labours. ... We sow, we set, we plant, we build, not so much for our selues as for posteritie .... Others obiect to the continuall charges which prove in their opinion very heauie and burdensome.... But it is demonstratiuely proved in Noua Britannia, that the charges will be nothing, in comparison of the benefit that will grow thereof.[165]

Richard Eburne's entire pamphlet is written in the form of a dialogue between Respire, a farmer who puts forth objections, and Enrubie, a merchant who defends colonization and, who, in line with the author's conviction, carries the argument. Among the counter-arguments raised by Respire are: (1) that "the remouing of so great a number, will be a great weakning and impouerishing to our Land,"[166] (2) that "the revenues of the Crowne must needs be, by this meanes, extremely spent and diminished,"[167] (3) that "the countries are scarcely habitable, the soil thereof but barren and bad,"[168] and (4) that the profit is small "and little the good that is like to arise of so great dangers, labours, and expences."[169]

Sir William Monson's "Naval Tracts" contain a good many cautionary and deprecatory remarks about the colonization of America. Thus, he animadverted that

> many are ignorantly carried away with the name of Indies, and the spoil we shall there commit; thinking it will afford wealth and riches to the King and kingdom sufficient to maintain a war, and preferment and gain to the undertakers, not valuing nor esteeming the king of Spain's force in those part to resist us.[170] ... I observe in all the English and French plantations the hopes are alike. Sometimes they feed themselves with the conceit of a passage into the South Sea; other times with the riches of mines, and the commodities they produce....[171]

Sir William's sober cool-headedness, however, seems to have been fed only by geographical prejudices, for he himself suggested the English colonization of Madagascar because it seemed to him the most "convenient" and "profitable" place. To him it is "the greatest island in the world," because its climate is "healthy," the

---

[164]*Ibid.*, p. 34.
[165]*A Good Speed to Virginia* (1609), The Epistle Dedicatorie.
[166]*Plaine Path-Way to Plantations* (1624), p. 76.
[167]*Ibid.*, pp. 77 f.   [168]*Ibid.*, p. 21.   [169]*Ibid.*, p. 32.
[170]Sir William Monson, *Naval Tracts* (1624), in M. Oppenheim (ed.), *The Naval Tracts of Sir William Monson* (London, 1902-14), II, 135.
[171]*Ibid.*, IV, 432.

soil "fruitful to produce wealth," and because cattle would prosper there magnificently.[172]

Lewis Roberts also apparently had no great love of colonies. He stated that there are "three principall meanes, whereby a Kingdome may be inriched, the first whereof is by arms and conquest, but this way must be confessed to be, both chargeable, bloody, and hazardable. The second is, by planting of colonies . . . this is also accounted uncertain, chargeable, and tedious. But the third and last is by traffike, and forraigne Trade, which is held the most certain, easiest, and soonest way. . . ."[173] However, while he expressed a preference for international trade, he did not deny that colonization could be a means towards enriching the state and did not refrain from approving of "the inlargement of trade by any new Inventions, Plantations, or Discoveries of new traffikes," provided such was left to the guidance of "a qualified Merchant."[174]

There were also a few writers who warned lest England overreach herself by gathering colonial possessions of too large extension. Bacon remarked that "there are states great in territory, and yet not apt to enlarge and command,"[175] and James Harrington demanded that there "be a right balance between native and foreign parts of an Empire."[176] He also was apprehensive of future emancipation of the colonies: "For the Colonies in the Indies, they are yet babes that cannot live without sucking the breasts of their mother-Cities, but such as, I maistake, if when they caome of age they do not wean themselves: which causeth me to wonder at Princes that delight to be exhausted in that way."[177]

Interesting as they are when considered singly, viewed collectively all these counter-arguments and cautionary declarations, mostly of anonymous authorship, are intellectually of no more commanding calibre than the pro-arguments. For the most part they are simply assertions, guesses, and expressions of pessimism, sometimes drawn from individual and company-experience. Certainly there was no well-founded, comprehensive theory behind them. Equally certainly, they were offered by an unorganized minority-group for the arguments favouring colonization easily carried the day.

[172] *Ibid.*, pp. 434 ff.
[173] Lewis Roberts, *The Treasure of Traffike or Discourse of Forraigne Trade* (1641), in McCulloch, *Select Collection of Early English Tracts on Commerce*, p. 58.
[174] *Ibid.*, p. 95.
[175] Bacon, "Of the True Greatness of Kingdoms and Estates," *Essays*, p. 90.
[176] James Harrington, *The Commonwealth of Oceana* (London, 1656), pp. 8¾f.
[177] *Ibid.*, p. 9.

CHAPTER III

COLONIAL THEORIES: 1660-1776

IN so far as this chapter attempts to analyse the various arguments for and against colonies for the period from 1661 to 1775, it represents but a continuation of the preceding one. However, some of the arguments which played a role during the earlier period will not be taken up again for the simple reason that they were discarded or relegated to the position of a negligible quantity in the later period. To this group belong the search for precious metals, the Northwest Passage, and the Christianization of the natives.[1] The reaping of glory for King and nation likewise may safely be kept in the category of negligible arguments. If mentioned at all, this noble prospect served the function of embellishment or appeared as a stereotype in dedications.[2]

STRATEGIC AND NAVAL CONSIDERATIONS

Two other arguments—the one concerning strategic considerations and the one concerning the trade with the colonies as a nursery of seamen—lost nothing of their relative weight and were

---

[1] There were, however, notable exceptions to this general indifference. Edward Chamberlayne pleaded "for erecting in London a Colledge de propagande Fide for propagating the Christian Religion amongst the Americans bordering on the English Plantations, (where it is a shame to this nation, that so few in the space of so many years have been converted to Christianity..." (*England Wants* [London, 1685], p. 7).

Robert Mountgomry was of the opinion that plantations "are meritorious in a double Sense; Religiously, as they illuminate the Souls of Heathens through the Darkness of their Ignorance, and Politically, as they strengthen the Dominion, which sends out the Colony, and wonderfully more than any other Means enrich the Undertakers" (*A Discourse Concerning the design'd Establishment of a New Colony to the South of Caroulina* [1717], in Peter Force, *Tracts and other Papers* [Washington, 1836], I, 4).

Mention must be made also of Bishop Berkeley's well-known scheme of converting the American Indians to the Christian religion. See his *Proposal for the Better Supplying of Churches in Our Foreign Plantations* (1725), in A. C. Fraser (ed.), *The Works of George Berkeley* (Oxford, 1871), III, 215-25.

For a similar plan see Locke's *Fundamental Constitution of Carolina* in *The Works of John Locke* (12th ed.; London, 1824), IV, 194 f.

[2] This fact surely distinguished English literature from the bulk of French writings in a most pleasing manner.

faithfully acknowledged in the stream of books and pamphlets. But they were little discussed[3] because the point they raised seemed obvious. Their discussion in this chapter can, for the same good reason, be reduced to a minimum.

Strategical considerations were presented in four ways. First, it was thought desirable to retain a colony or acquire new colonial possessions in order to gain a foothold from which to attack the colony of some other power or to harass the colonial trade of an enemy nation in time of war. Thus Carew Reynell praised the possession of Jamaica because it "is situated so well for Trade, or conquest of the Main, if there be occasion . . . it being the key of the Indies . . . lying in the very Belly of all Commerce. . . ."[4] Secondly, colonies were welcomed because they seemed to convey on their possessor the mastery of the sea. For example, an anonymous author wrote: "Whoever holds possession of our colonies in America will keep the sovereignty of the Atlantic ocean, through which the homeward bound trade from the East and West Indies usually passes. . . ."[5]

Thirdly, it was deemed necessary to take precaution lest the colonial balance of power be shifted against one's own nation. Such a change was apt to affect the security of one's colonies and also to react adversely on the balance of power in Europe.[6] Thus, Postlethwayt, disliking the Northern American colonies on general grounds, advocated their retention only for one reason: ". . . if these colonies should ever fall into French hands, it will not be possible, I apprehend, to maintain a ballance of trade and power in America; and who will imagine that we can maintain them, after that, in Europe?"[7] The same author remarked: "If it be needful to maintain a balance of power in Europe, why not in Asia among

[3]Regarding the nursery-of-seamen argument it must be admitted that it elicited much discussion in connection with the Navigation Laws. These laws, however, were of the nature of a *means* designed *to ensure* the advantage supposedly accruing from the trade with the colonies. The general problem of the Navigation Laws will be discussed in the next chapter.

[4]Carew Reynell, *The True English Interest* (London, 1679), p. 89.

[5]*Gentleman's Magazine*, XXV (1755), 437.

[6]Even such a clear-sighted thinker as Bernard Mandeville recognized the paramount importance of these considerations. Prefatory to a discussion on the value of Gibraltar to Britain he remarked that "the Ballance of Power must ever be the Standard, that all Property and Possession . . . are to be weigh'd by . . ." (*Free Thought on Religion, the Church, and National Happiness* [London, 1720], p. 348).

[7]Malachy Postlethwayt, *The Universal Dictionary of Trade and Commerce* (4th ed.; London, 1774), I, "Colonies."

the European powers established there? Will not the rise or decline of their trade and power in the Indies effect that of their particular states in Europe?"[8]

Fourthly, there is the strategic consideration which demands colonial expansion in order to safeguard already existing colonial possessions. Even the staunchest proponent of colonial expansion would not argue that this "necessity" constituted one of the advantages of possessing colonies. Seen logically, this need for expansion was clearly a disadvantage which had to be contended with for the sake of retaining the advantages gained from the already existing colonies. However, this consideration appeared again and again as a defensive argument in favour of colonial expansion.

The implications of this argument can be clarified by presenting some quotations from the literature produced during the Seven Years' War. In 1755, William Shirley suggested the conquest of Nova Scotia because its reduction by the British would render innocuous French military and naval power in North America.[9] Another writer, incensed at alleged French encroachments and concerned with ways of securing the English colonies, suggested that the British acquire control of the "Dominion of the Lakes" in order to "render the French Project of a Junction between Louisiana, and Canada abortive. . . ."[10]

[8] Malachy Postlethwayt, *Great Britain's Commercial Interest* (London, 1759), II, 238.

For the sake of its speciousness mention may be made here of William Paterson's gigantic scheme to plant a colony in Darien. After having established an English colony on the isthmus of Central America, "which is the natural centre, not only of America but of the whole Indies, and the only place on earth most capable of being the common storehouse of the neighbouring oceans," the English would be able to penetrate gradually the Spanish and French colonial empires in America (William Paterson, *A Proposal to Plant a Colony in Darien* [1701], in S. Bannister, *The Writings of William Paterson* [2d ed.; London, 1859], I, 143 ff.). By permitting the people of all nations to trade with the English colonial possessions upon "easy terms," by admitting the nationals of all states to residence and naturalization there and, last not least, by the British command of the sea, Paterson believed, the English would be able to blast the colonial monopolies of other nations. But they would relinquish theirs too and open a universal colonial trade to all European nations (*ibid.*, pp. 148 ff.). According to Paterson's bold vision such a development would enable Great Britain "to give laws to both oceans," "to become arbitrators of the commercial world" (*ibid.*, p. 159) and to maintain "the balance and umpirage of Europe, and consequently of the world" (*ibid.*, p. 157).

[9] C. H. Lincoln (ed.), *Correspondence of William Shirley* (New York, 1912), II, 148 f.

[10] *A Letter from a Merchant of the City of London* (2d ed.; London, 1757), p. 26.

After the conquest of Canada popular clamour in favour of its retention was mainly based on the reason of removing the French threat to the American colonies. One author wrote: "And shall we now be so mad as to lay the foundations of a future war by yielding up our conquests at a peace? Our settlements cannot possibly be of half the value to us while another nation is in possession of the back country."[11] A similar idea is expressed in the following passage: ". . . we have now got possession of the vast, extensive and fruitful continent of America, by which we have a much fairer prospect for a perpetuity of peace in that part of the world than we could ever have expected. . . ."[12] John Douglas remarked that Canada had little intrinsic value but ". . . we can never consent to leave the French any Footing in Canada."[13] Henry M'Culloh, likewise having exclusively strategic considerations in mind, declared: ". . . if wee have Possession of the Lakes and the Territories belonging thereto, and also the whole Province of Acadia, the Remainder of Canada exclusive of the Fishery is not an Object of any great Moment to this Kingdom."[14]

Regarding the number of trained seamen from which the navy would be able to recruit its crews in time of war, the argument was presented much in the fashion outlined in the preceding chapter. Superior naval power was, of course, of paramount concern to England. As one writer expressed it: "One Day at Sea may determine the Fate of these Kingdoms."[15] Sir Francis Brewster remarked: "Our Naval Force is thought the Main Body and Strength of the Nation . . . yet there is something else wanting to make us formidable at Sea and that is Marine Trade and Navigation, which like Food to the Body must be dayly renewed, or else our Naval Strength will decay."[16]

It was mercantile navigation which lent sustenance to naval power. Some of the reasons which, in the eyes of contemporary theorists and politicians, made the trade with the colonies compare favourably with the trade with European nations, have been mentioned above.[17] In the case of trade with the colonies, it was

[11] *Considerations on the Expediency of a Spanish War* (London, 1761), p. 28.
[12] "An Impartial Examination of the Conduct of the Whigs and Tories," *Gentleman's Magazine*, XXXIII (1763), 404.
[13] [John Douglas], *A Letter Addressed to Two Great Men on the Prospect of Peace* (Dublin, 1760), p. 24.
[14] Henry M'Culloh, *Miscellaneous Representations Relative to Our Concerns in America* (1761), ed. W. A. Shaw (London, n.d.), p. 6.
[15] Sir Francis Brewster, *Essays on Trade and Navigation* (1695), pp. 5 f.
[16] *Ibid.*, p. 2.   [17] *Supra*, p. 38 f.

relatively easy to enforce a shipping monopoly.[18] The very remoteness of the colonies was considered to be an advantage from the point of view of training sailors[19] and so was the fact that colonial staple products were "bulky, and employ and maintain a great Number of Ships and Mariners . . . ."[20] The vital importance of a sufficient supply of skilled sailors[21] determined the English to let considerations of power over-ride considerations of profit. Thus Sir Francis Brewster wrote: ". . . other Countries may encourage Seamen for their advantage in Traffick, but we must enlarge and encourage Numbers for our Security. . . ."[22]

Two more pertinent considerations must be registered here. According to contemporary opinion, the African slave trade was one of the most valuable "nurseries of seamen."[23] Not only did this trade provide the occasion for the erection of a few British forts along the west coast of Africa. Much more important was the fact that it was largely dependent on the existence of the English colonies in the West Indies and the southern portion of North America.[24] This train of reasoning naturally prompted the English to attribute an enhanced value to their American colonial possessions.

Another factor to be mentioned is that the eighteenth century witnessed the development of a large ship-building centre in the New England provinces and of an extensive carrying trade based on the ports of the same colonies. While many Englishmen regarded this with considerable misgivings and complained that it

[18]Cf. John Campbell, *Considerations on the Nature of the Sugar Trade* (London, 1763), p. 21.
[19]Cf. Thomas Mun, *England's Treasure by Forraign Trade* (1664), p. 130.
[20]John Ashley, *Memoirs and Considerations* (London, 1740-3), II, 98. Similarly, Campbell, *Considerations on the Nature of the Sugar Trade* (1763), p. 24.
[21]Thus Oglethorp pointed out concisely: "Money will buy all naval stores except mariners. . ." (*A New and Accurate Account of the Provinces of South Carolina* [1733], in *Collections of the Georgia Historical Society* [Savannah, 1840], I, 73).
[22]Sir Francis Brewster, *Essays on Trade and Navigation* (1695), p. 80. Similarly, W. Wood, *A Survey of Trade* (London, 1718), p. 153.
[23]John Cary, *An Essay on the State of England in Relation to Its Trade* (London, 1695), p. 86; Malachy Postlethwayt, *The National and Private Advantages of the African Trade Considered* (London, 1746), p. 2; Sir Matthew Decker, *An Essay on the Causes of the Decline of Foreign Trade* (4th ed.; Dublin, 1751), p. 178.
[24]Thus, George Stepney wrote: "For every one knows that none can carry on a trade for Negroes but such as have a footing in America" (*An Essay upon the Present Interest of England* [London, 1701], p. 65).

meant an undesirable competition with the mother country, others welcomed it as an addition to the maritime and naval strength of the metropolis.[25]

The general conclusion which contemporary writers drew from all these considerations is obvious: other reasons apart, the colonies were highly valued because the trade connected with them was supposed to form a solid basis for British maritime and naval power. Thus, M'Culloh declared: ". . . the enlarging our Footing in distant Parts of the World will enlarge our Navigation. . . ."[26]

Finally, it may be mentioned that on the basis of the same reasoning it was considered good policy to prevent and curb as much as possible the colonial expansion of maritime rivals and to reduce their colonial trade by all possible means. As an example may be cited the frequent demands that the growth of the French sugar trade be prevented by all possible means because it was supposed to be an important nursery to the French Navy.[27]

THEORIES ON POPULATION AND THE COLONIES

During the pre-Civil War period of British colonization the bulk of influential public opinion saw in the colonies a welcome means for relieving England from demographic congestion. Throughout this time a minority opinion, as yet little articulate, regarded a large population as a major prop of the nation's strength. These dissenting theorists must be viewed as the precursors of that large body of mercantilists who emphasized the necessity of an abounding population for a variety of reasons and, at the same time, tirelessly deplored England's alleged want of populousness.

The revision of opinion on this subject was consummated roughly with the commencement of the post-Restoration period.[28]

[25]Cf. Joshua Gee, *The Trade and Navigation of Great Britain* (London, 1731), pp. 173 ff.; William Keith, *A Collection of Papers and Other Tracts* (London, 1740), p. 172; Arthur Young, *Political Essays Concerning the Present State of the British Empire* (London, 1772), p. 344.

[26]*Miscellaneous Representations Relative to Our Concerns in America* (1761), p. 10.

[27]Cf. John Ashley, *A Supplement to the Second Part of the Memoirs* (2d ed.; London, 1744), Preface. During the bitter discussion upon the peace concluding the Seven Years' War this argument was much presented by those who favoured the retention of Guadeloupe.

[28]E. Lipson, *The Economic History of England* (London, 1931), III, 164; C. M. MacInnes, *An Introduction to the Economic History of the British Empire* (London, 1935), p. 24.

Notable among the writers of the Commonwealth period is James Harring-

Because it threw an entirely different light on the subject of emigration, this revulsion of sentiment was bound to exert a profound influence on the valuation of colonies. Henceforth emigration to the colonies was considered by most writers as either a necessary or an unnecessary evil. Those who adhered to the latter point of view, i.e., those who denied the value of colonies to the mother country, will be discussed below. The majority of writers, however, admitted the undesirability of such emigration on general grounds, but pointed to the compensatory benefits which accrued from the possession of colonies or asserted that, in the long run, oversea plantations would tend to enlarge the metropolitan population.[29]

In order to understand fully the effect of this trend of thought on the shaping of colonial theories it is advisable to review the several intellectual ingredients of the mercantilist assumption that a numerous population constitutes a major source of wealth and power. The following are some representative citations.

... here in England is a false opinion, that our Country is fully peopled, ... and a mistake, that the greatness and glory of a Prince lyeth rather in the extent of his Territory, then in the number, art, and industry of his people ....[30]

Fewness of people, is real poverty; and a Nation wherein are Eight Millions of people, are more than twice as rich as the same scope of Land wherein are but Four....[31]

That a small Country and few People, may be equivalent in Wealth and Strength to a far greater People and Territory.[32]

A small countrey well peopled, will be able to effect things of more advantage and grandeur, than a great Dominion ill stocked.[33]

People are therefore in truth the chiefest, most fundamental, and pretious

---

ton. He did not dread the phenomenon of a growing population but, on the contrary, suggested devices by which the state could encourage marriage and, hence, accelerate demographic growth. See C. E. Stangeland, *Pre-Malthusian Doctrines of Population* (New York, 1904), pp. 116 f.; James Bonar, *Theories of Population from Raleigh to Arthur Young* (London, 1931), p. 53.

[29]A smaller group of writers, as will be shown below, belittled the number, or the character and hence the value, of the emigrants.

[30]Sir William Petty, *A Treatise of Taxes & Contributions* (1662), in C. H. Hull (ed.), *The Economic Writings of Sir William Petty* (Cambridge, 1899), I, 21 f.

[31]*Ibid.*, p. 34.

[32]Sir William Petty, *Political Arithmetick* (1690), in *Economic Writings*, I, 249.

[33]Slingsby Bethel, *An Account of the French Usurpation upon the Trade of England* (London, 1679), p. 15.

commodity, out of which may be derived all sorts of Manufactures, Navigation, Riches, Conquests, and solid Dominion. . . .[34]

First I agree, That Lands (though excellent) with out Hands proportionable will not enrich any Kingdom. 2. That whatever tends to the Depopulating of a Kingdom, tends to the Impoverishment of it. 3. That most Nations in the civilised Parts of the World, are more or less Rich or Poor proportionably to the Paucity or Plenty of their People, and not to the Sterility or Fruitfulness of their Lands.[35]

From Reason and Experience it is certain, that the Power and Riches of a Nation depend not upon it's having Mines of Gold and Silver, but upon it's having a numerous and industrious People.[36]

. . . the strength of a nation, all other things being the same, is in proportion to the number of its inhabitants. . . .   But if the increasing the populousness of a state by certain measures would render it more powerful in one respect, and yet reduce its strength, and make it more feeble in proportion in another, the populosity of the state ought to be sacrificed to its political strength and general safety: For people alone are no the strength of a state, or, it does not consist only in its numbers.   If this Kingdom were a nation of husbandmen without navigation or commerce, without arts and manufactures, whose wealth consisted only in corn and cattle, there is little reason to believe it would preserve its independence long. . . .[37]

. . . I allow . . . that People are the wealth of a Nation, yet it can only be so, where we find Imployment for them, otherwise they must be a Burthen to it.[38]

From these quotations it is quite apparent that their authors were not interested in mere numbers. On the one hand, they were thinking in terms of working people. Unemployed Englishmen were considered a weakening burden. On the other hand, some of the statements betray a particular liking for a maximum density of population. This preference for a dense rather than a large population must be interpreted in terms of the mercantilist predilection for industry and trade as against agriculture. Thus, one author offered as a "basic observation" the rule "that the Multiplicity of People increase Manufacture and Merchandize."[39] As the writers who clamoured for a large population were doubtless influenced by the superior numbers of England's chief rival, France, so those authors (notably Roger Coke and William Temple)

[34]*Britannia Languens* (1680), in J. R. McCulloch (ed.), *A Select Collection of Early English Tracts on Commerce* (London, 1856), p. 176.

[35]Sir Josiah Child, *A Discourse about Trade* (London, 1690), p. 165.

[36][David Bindon], *A Letter from a Merchant Who Has Left off Trade* (London, 1738), p. 4.

[37]William Temple, *A Vindication of Commerce and the Arts* (1743), in McCulloch, *Select Collection of Scarce and Valuable Tracts*, pp. 491 f.

[38]John Cary, *A Discourse on Trade* (London, 1745), p. 48.

[39]*A Discourse of the Nature, Use and Advantages of Trade* (London, 1693), p. 30.

who stressed density of population, were deeply impressed by the stupendous maritime, commercial, and industrial success of the Dutch. Deriving their peculiar notions from the study of this model country, they were inclined to assume that small extent of territory and a high density of population were prerequisites for industrial and commercial greatness. According to empirical observation, a dense population could not be a predominantly agricultural population.[40]

Still, the question why the mercantilists were obsessed with a desire for a large and dense population is rather difficult to answer. While they asserted almost unanimously that populousness meant power and wealth, they were markedly less voluble in particularizing these broad statements. Considerations of manpower, from which a large army could be recruited in time of war, certainly were unimportant in the case of England.[41] Power considerations, therefore, were largely identical with considerations of what the mercantilists conceived as national wealth. According to conventional mercantilism the wealth of the nation was augmented chiefly by a favourable balance of trade. The promotion of exports, in turn, would be facilitated by low wages[42] and the necessary increase of production could be ensured by a large number of workers. There can be no doubt that such lines of thought, based on a primitive theory of production (the "theory of constant returns"), were largely responsible for the desire for a numerous population.[43]

[40] Of course, there were other reasons of a re-enforcing nature pointing to the desirability of a dense population. Petty, for example, wrote: ". . . the same Governours which are the great charge, may serve near as well for the greater, as the lesser number" (*A Treatise of Taxes and Contributions* [1662], in *Economic Writings*, I, 34). Thus, the expense of government per capita (or per tax-payer) would diminish in proportion to increasing density of population. The wish for a high density of population was sometimes pushed to a ludicrous extreme. Oglethorp (*New and Accurate Account of the Province of South Carolina and Georgia*, p. 60) spoke of "one of the gentlemen would have Scotland, Ireland and Wales sunk under water, but all the people saved and settled in England. He certainly deceived himself with a view of the artificial strength of the Dutch."

[41] Cf. E. A. J. Johnson, *Predecessors of Adam Smith* (New York, 1937), pp. 247 f.

[42] See E. S. Furniss, *The Position of the Laborer in a System of Nationalism* (Boston, 1920); P. W. Buck, *The Politics of Mercantilism* (New York, 1942), p. 44.

[43] The desire for a large population arising from what Professor Heckscher called the "fear of goods" also constituted an important argument. Thus the author of *The Grand Concern of England Explained* (London, 1673), referring to the victims of wars and plagues, deplored the loss of those ". . . who, when they were living amongst us, did Eat our Provisions, Wore off our Manufactories; imployed themselves in some Calling. . ." (p. 13). In some cases, no doubt,

The mercantilist writers of the period in question were obsessed not only with the desire for a large and dense population, but some of them also expressed the fear that England's population, instead of increasing, was actually on the decrease. Lack of reliable data makes it impossible to estimate the precise character of the demographic development which took place in England between the Restoration and the War of Independence. Contemporary estimates are widely conflicting. Yet it is certain that the population of England did not decline but, on the contrary, underwent a slow but gradually increasing growth.[44]

Among the various reasons which contemporary writers held responsible for England's underpopulated condition, were voluntary emigration and compulsory transportation to the colonies and the loss of life in consequence of epidemics, the Civil War, and external wars. Thus one writer stated: "The two last great Plagues, the Civil Wars at Home, and the several wars with Holland, Spain, and France, have destroyed several hundred thousands of Men, which lived amongst us; besides, vast numbers have Transported themselves or been Transported into Ireland, and other our Foreign Plantations. . . ."[45] The same author also mentioned the spreading practice of birth control as one of the causes. "And many Marryed Women, by their lewd Conversations, prevent the bringing forth many Children, which otherwise they might have had, These Humours and Practices, if continued, will prove so mischievous . . . ."[46]

---

this desire for sufficient consumption flowed directly from the mercantilist preference for a large body of employment. Consumption and employment begot each other. Carew Reynell remarked: "The more Trade, Husbandries and Manufactures, there are in a Nation, the more people there will be, more employment for them, and more riches; everything again will vend the more one for another. . ." (*The True English Interest* [1679], p. 17). On the other hand, the landlord-interest favoured a large population not only because of the expectation of cheap agricultural labour, but also because a numerous population meant a large domestic market for corn. Thus, one writer stated: "First as employment lessens, the most industrious rather than starve here will fly to other countries, where trade can maintain them; so the consumption of these being taken away, the market at home must grow less, and of course rents must fall; yet the farmers' charges must grow greater, for the fewer hands, the higher the wages are" ([Mathew Decker], *An Essay on the Causes of the Decline of Trade* [1744], in McCulloch, *Select Collection of Scarce and Valuable Tracts*, p. 212).

It must be observed, however, that, with few exceptions, mercantilists did not think of consumption as an end in itself but as a means to some other object.

[44] Cf. Lipson, *Economic History of England*, III, 166.
[45] *The Grand Concern of England Explained*, p. 13.
[46] *Ibid.*, p. 14.

In this connection it has to be recalled that many mercantilists, in accordance with the dominant view on the subject of population, advocated the immigration of foreigners in order to accelerate the growth of the English people.[47] Hence, even those writers who dedicated themselves to the praise of the colonies, could hardly disregard the fact that a certain number of Englishmen actually did emigrate to the colonies.

There were some mercantilist writers who asserted that the colonies had depopulated or were depopulating the mother country and, far from granting any redeeming features, denied the value of plantations to the metropolis. The author of *Britannia Languens* even claimed that "our Plantation-Trade hath robbed and prevented us of some Millions of our People; amongst which very many being, or might have been Manufacturers, the Nation hath also lost more Millions of Pounds in the loss of their Manufactures."[48] Slingsby Bethel maintained: "I cannot observe, that it doth any ways comport with the interest of State, to suffer such multitudes of people to pass out of his Majesties Kingdoms unto other Princes Dominions, or the Western Plantations, thereby to disfurnish ourselves of people; the sad consequences and effects whereof, are too visible in the misfortune of Spain."[49] Other writers expressed particular displeasure because of the large number of skilled artisans and manufacturers who left England for the colonies. Thus an anonymous author stated: "The numbers of labouring people of all kinds in any country, are justly considered

[47]Cf. Samuel Fortrey, *England's Interest and Improvement* (4th ed.; London, 1744), p. 4; Charles Davenant, *Discourses on the Publick Revenues and the Trade of England* (London, 1698), II, 199; Bethel, *An Account of the French Usurpation upon the Trade of England* (1679), p. 15; *Britannia Languens* (1680), section VII. One writer even went so far as to demand the repeal of that part of the Navigation Act which stipulated that three-fourths of the mariners on English vessels be Englishmen, for the sole reason that "we want people, therefore we ought to invite more, not restrain any" (Thomas Sheridan, *A Discourse on the Rise and Power of Parliaments* [1677], in Saxe Bannister [ed.], *Some Revelations in Irish History* [London, 1870], p. 213).

[48]*Britannia Languens* (1680), p. 88.

[49]*An Account of the French Usurpation upon the Trade of England* (1679), p. 16. Furthermore, see Roger Coke, *A Treatise* (London, 1671), pp. 26, 33; Jacob Vanderlint, *Money Answers All Things* (1734), ed. J. H. Hollander (Baltimore, 1914), p. 129. However, it is interesting to note that Vanderlint who praises "Peace and Plenty" above everything else, holds an aggressive war justifiable if it means "fighting for Territory when we are over-peopled, and want Land for them, which our Neighbours have, but will not part with on amicable and reasonable Terms" (*ibid.*, p. 122).

to be the strength and riches of a state ... for with a transfer of arts and people, we make such a transfer of strength and property, as will soon throw out of our own hands all power and wealth."[50]

Against this type of argument the majority of mercantilist writers offered an imposing array of counter-arguments which questioned its truth or denied its implications. Some authors minimized the number of Englishmen who had emigrated to the colonies.[51] Davenant, for instance, averred: "'Tis evident that since we had these Plantations, England has rather increas'd than diminish'd in People ... which could not be, if the Plantations were such a drein of the People...."[52] Others asserted that those who had left England and proceeded to the colonies would have emigrated in any event and if Britain had been without colonies, they would have sought refuge in foreign countries. Sir Josiah Child admitted that many Englishmen repaired to the colonies but continued: "the first Question will be, Whether if England had no foreign Plantations for those People to be transported unto, they could or would have stayed and lived at home with us?—I am of Opinion that they neither would nor could."[53]
Davenant declared:

Such therefore as found themselves disturb'd, and uneasie at home, if they could have found no other Retreat, must have gone to the Hans Towns, Switzerland, Danemark, Sweeden, or Holland (as many did before our Plantations flourish'd, to our great detriment) and they who had thus retir'd to the European Countries, must have been for ever lost to England.... But, Providence, which contrives better for us, than we can do for ourselves, has offer'd in the new World, a Place of Refuge for these, peradventure mistaken and mislead People.... And as to the Malcontents in the State, perhaps it is for the Publick Safety, that there should always be such an Outlet, or Issue, for the ill Humours which from time to time are engender'd in the Body Politick.[54]

---

[50]*Gentleman's Magazine*, XXXV (1765), 7. However, this writer is not only concerned with the emigration of people, but also with the transfer of property, manufacturing skills, and managerial techniques. This transfer, he fears, would assist the colonists in setting up rival manufacturing industries.

[51]And it must be admitted that their estimates were considerably nearer to the truth than was the author of *Britannia Languens*.

[52]Davenant, *Discourses on the Publick Revenues and the Trade of England* (1698), II, 195 f.; similarly, Child, *A Discourse about Trade* (1690), pp. 165 f. Davenant estimated that no more than about 1,000 English persons emigrated to the colonies annually (*ibid.*, II, 196).

[53]*A Discourse about Trade* (1690), p. 169.

[54]Davenant, *Discourses on the Publick Revenues and the Trade of England* (1698), II, 200. William Wood, without acknowledgment, copied this passage almost verbatim. It is interesting to note that Davenant here makes out a case

Similarly John Campbell pointed out:

> ... the old objection ... that people going to our plantations weakened the mother country, is now ... incontestably obviated. For those who go thither, do it either from a principle of necessity, or with a view to the making their fortunes. In the first case they could not, and in the second they would not stay at home. So that when we consider attentively the consequences of their going thither, with respect to Britain; instead of looking upon such people as lost, we ought to consider them as preserved to this country, which but for our plantations they would not have been.[55]

Then he went on to remark that, had it not been for the colonies' these people would have either "supplied Sweden, France and Holland with soldiers, or stocked the wide Kingdom with peddlars."[56]

The argument brought forward by the above writers is self-explanatory. It is an early version of the later nineteenth- and twentieth-century argument which reasoned that an overpopulated nation for which emigration is a "necessity," needs pressure-relieving colonies so that the emigrating nationals will not be lost to the flag of their home country.

While these publicists for the most part referred to Englishmen who left their country in order to find a safe refuge from religious and political oppression or who were compulsorily transported for political reasons during the Civil War, other authors animadverted that those who had emigrated to the colonies were mostly beggars and paupers whose departure was a boon to the mother country. Sir Francis Brewster, for example, asserted: "It cannot be denied, however some may apprehend, but the Foreign Plantations add to the Strength and Treasure of the Nation, even in that of People, which is generally thought our Plantations abroad consume; but if it were considered, That by taking off one useless person, for such generally go abroad, we add Twenty Blacks in the Labour and Manufactories of this Nation, that Mistake would be removed."[57] Charles Davenant likewise stated that those who had emigrated were "generally of such sort of People, as their Crimes and Debaucheries would quickly destroy at home, or whome their Wants would confine in Prisons or force to beg, and so render them useless, and consequently, a Burthen to the

---

for colonies serving as a useful outlet for political and religious malcontents (*A Survey of Trade* [1718], pp. 133 f.).

[55] John Campbell, *Considerations on the Nature of the Sugar Trade* (London, 1763), p. 28.

[56] *Ibid.*

[57] *Essays on Trade and Navigation* (1695), p. 70.

Publick. . . . If the Majority of those who are thus transported, or transport themselves, consists of such as would perish here, or beg, it must certainly be advisable to transplant them to Places, where they may be of more use, or grow better by removal."[58]

Regarding the poor, the loafers, the criminals, and similar categories of people who could be designated as useless to the nation, the colonies continued to be valued as a convenient depository relieving the mother country of their onerous presence and promising their being put to some use which would ultimately redound to the advantage of the metropolis. Again and again it was urged that the poor be put to work in the colonies to raise raw materials which Great Britain needed and which she had to import from abroad. Joshua Gee, for example, said: "The First and greatest [benefit] will be in finding effectual ways for employing our poor, and putting all hands to work, either at home or in the plantations, who cannot support themselves."[59] When General Oglethorp was about to realize his project of founding the new colony of Georgia, this argument was assiduously exploited.[60] One writer maintained that "in America there are fertile lands sufficient to subsist all the useless Poor in England . . . yet Thousands starve for want of mere sustenance."[61]

Oglethorp himself expounded this point at great length and it is exceedingly interesting to note what types of people he had in mind. He wrote:

Let us in the mean time cast our eyes on the multitudes of unfortunate people in the kingdom of reputable families, and of liberal . . . education: some undone by guardians, some by law suits, some by accidents in commerce, some by stocks and bubbles, and some by suretyship. . . . These are the people that may relieve themselves and strengthen Georgia, by resorting thither, and Great Britain by their departure. Besides . . . there are others whom it may be proper to send abroad. . . . I think it may be laid down for a rule, that we may well spare all those, who having neither income, nor

---

[58]*Discourses on the Publick Revenues and the Trade of England* (1698), II, 196 f.

[59]*The Trade and Navigation of Great Britain* (1731), p. 71.

[60]There is no doubt that in this case Oglethorp needed a sufficient number of settlers and that the argument was therefore put to propagandist use. On the other hand, it cannot be denied that the Georgia project had an important root in Oglethorp's philanthropic ideas. It was to a large extent his wish to remedy the appalling situation of the poor which propelled him to embark upon the Georgia project. Cf. A. A. Ettinger, *James Edward Oglethorp, Imperial Idealist* (Oxford, 1936), p. 110.

[61]*A Brief Account of the Establishment of the Colony of Georgia* (1733), in Force, *Tracts*, I, 4.

industry, equal to their necessities, are forced to live upon the fortunes, or labors of others. . . .[62]

. . . some who mean very well to the public have fancied that our numbers absolutely taken, without a distinction, are real wealth to the nation. Upon a little examination this will appear to be a mistaken notion . . . when these great men esteem people as the wealth of a nation, surely they can only mean such as labor, and by their industry add yearly to the capital stock of their country . . . but is an infirmary of incurables wealth to a community? Or are hundreds of prisons filled with thousands of English debtors, are they a glory, or a reproach, a benefit, or a burthen to the nation?[63]

Whatever they consume more than they earn, must be furnished, first either by the bounty, or charity of others; or secondly, by frauds . . . or, thirdly, by what our laws call force and felony. . . . Behold then the benefit the common weal receives by relieving her famishing sons.[64]

Sir William Mildmay, couching the proposition in more abstract phrasing, likewise maintained: "But if the multiplicity of inhabitants should be greater than what their skill and labour, or the products of our country, can sustain; then it becomes a necessary policy . . . to plant Colonies in other soil and climates, lest our subjects should take refuge amongst our neighbours, and by adding an encrease of people to a foreign country, prove a double loss to our own."[65] Thus, it was deemed good policy to send those "many lusty poor"[66] to the colonies. An anonymous writer, who suggested the colonization of Tierra del Fuego, remarked: "If the Wisdom of our Parliaments should judge it proper to send thither all sturdy Beggars, and able Bodyed lazy and idle Persons of both sexes . . . it would deliver us of an unsufferable Plague. . . ."[67]

It has already been pointed out that some writers, in vindication

[62]Oglethorp, *New and Accurate Account of South Carolina and Georgia*, pp. 57 f. The idea that those, coming from the higher and middle strata of the British society, who are without means of livelihood might "subdue their pride and descend to mean employments" is discouraged by Oglethorp (*ibid.*, p. 57). He thought that even those "mean" occupations are already "overstocked" and that "it is too late for them to learn a trade." Indulging in the usual exaggerated opinion of the ease of working conditions for raw settlers in new-established American colonies, he remarked: "They have land there for nothing, and that land is so fertile that they receive an hundredfold increase for taking very little pains" (*ibid.*).

[63]*Ibid.*, p. 59. Considering the usual demographic notions of his age, Oglethorp's ideas on the value of population were founded on solid economic insights.

[64]*Ibid.*, pp. 61 f.

[65]*The Laws and Policy of England Relating to Trade* (London, 1765), p. 10.

[66]Reynell, *The True English Interest* (1679), Preface.

[67]*The Considerable Advantages of a South Sea Trade to Our English Nation* (London, n.d.), p. 13.

of colonies and emigration thereto, stressed the compensatory benefits accruing to the mother country. They put emphasis on the products which these emigrants would raise overseas[68] or underlined the fact that the colonies created employment at home by means of the export and the carrying trade to the colonies. John Cary, for example, stated: "... though I allow ... that People are the wealth of a Nation ... 'Tis my Opinion, that our Plantations are an Advantage to this Kingdom ... as they take off our Product and Manufactures, supply us with Commodities, which may be either wrought here, or exported again, or prevent fetching things of the same Nature, from other Places for our Home Consumption, employ our Poor, and encourage our Navigation ...."[69]

The employment argument[70] weighed more heavily in this respect than the raw-materials argument because many mercantilists assumed that the creation of additional employment in the mother country was not only of the nature of a compensation but would, in the long run, lead to an increase of the metropolitan working population. Thus, John Houghton pointed out:

That if an English-man be brought to Earn and Consume 10 l. a year more than he was wont ... then I say, if Interest wont lye, and profitable Imployments will draw people, our Populations in America have not prejudiced our Coasts ... for they have increast the profitable Imployments, not only by building of Ships, carrying our Manufactures and Products thither, but also by returning theirs hither to supply our selves, and also a great part of the rest of the World: And if it should be said that they might have consumed as much if they had staid here; yet it cannot be said that we should have employed so many men in building Ships, and carrying and recarrying, as we do: I am apt to think it might be made out, that it is a Wheel to set most of our other Trades a going.[71]

Brewster asserted that for each person going to the colonies "we add Twenty Blacks in the Labour and Manufactories of this

[68]This idea was so much cherished that even the emigration of skilled people was deemed warrantable by a few authors. One publicist, for example, demanded that people "of Skill and Capacity" be sent to the American plantations and to the East Indies in order to start the production of particularly desirable commodities like potash, etc. Cf. Fayne Hall, *The Importance of the British Plantations in America to This Kingdom* (London, 1731), p. 19.

[69]Cary, *A Discourse on Trade* (1745), pp. 48 f.

[70]The essence of the employment-argument will be discussed below.

[71]John Houghton, *A Collection of Letters for the Improvement of Husbandry and Trade* (London, 1681-3), pp. 36 f. Houghton was so much inspired by this train of thought that he went so far as to write: "I would advise, that One hundred thousand English should quickly be sent to Jamaica, foreseeing that others would supply them with Negro's, and other Servants and Slaves. . ." (*ibid.*, p. 37).

Nation...."[72] Similar ideas are expressed in the following statements:

I do not agree that our People in England, are in any considerable measure abated by reason of our Foreign Plantations; but propose to prove the contrary.[73]

... if it be considered that our Plantations spending mostly our English Manufactures, and those of all sorts almost imaginable, in egregious quantities; and employing near two thirds of all our English Shipping, do therein give a constant Sustenance to it, may be two hundred thousand Persons here at home; then I must needs conclude upon the whole matter, that we have not the fewer, but the more People in England, by reason of our English Plantations in America.[74]

For admit the American Colonies to contain not quite 200,000 Persons of English Parentage ... the Labour of such a Number of Men, reckon'd in the Mass, could by no means bring to the Nation 720,000 l. per Annum clear Profit. But in the Southward Parts, cultivating a plentiful Soil, productive of Commodities, not to be had elsewhere, and every Head, in the Islands, employing, peradventure, six Others, of Negroe Slaves, and European Strangers, they bring it to pass, that one Head there, is as profitable as seven Heads would be in England.[75]

... this mode of visiting our most distant territories, is so far from thinning the mother country from inhabitants, that it is one, and indeed the principal means of making us populous, by providing such a vast variety of methods for the commodious subsistence by labour and industry, in this country; as before we had these plantations were utterly unknown, and which are also continually increasing, as the commerce with our colonies is increased.[76]

The idea that, under the conditions envisaged by the above publicists, the work of a man is more profitable in the colonies than in the mother country, is a particularly interesting one. It derives from three main considerations: First, the exploitation of slave labour and quasi-slave labour (e.g., that of indentured and "spirited" servants and criminal transportees).[77] Secondly, the marketing of the staple products raised in the oversea colonies required a remote carrying trade which was regarded by most mercantilists not as an item of expense but as an additional advantage attending oversea production. Thirdly, these writers continually praised the bountiful fertility of soil and nature in the colonies. The entire frame of reference within which this phe-

---

[72]*Essays on Trade and Navigation* (1695), p. 70.

[73]Child, *A Discourse about Trade* (1690), p. 165.

[74]*Ibid.*, p. 176.

[75]Davenant, *Discourses on the Publick Revenues and the Trade of England* (1698), II, 224.

[76]Campbell, *Considerations on the Nature of the Sugar Trade* (1763), p. 29.

[77]This point will be further elaborated below.

nomenon was mentioned, suggests that some of them had a hazy notion of some law of diminishing returns which, applicable to agricultural pursuits, led them to the vague realization that a certain amount of labour spent on the virgin tropical and subtropical soils of the colonies yielded produce of a higher exchange value than the same amount of labour spent on the less fertile soils of England.

To summarize the arguments brought forward in connection with the problem of population: All the writers of the period believed that a large working population was an important source of national wealth and power and wished for an increase of the employed population of Great Britain. While some of them asserted that only undesirable elements of the English population emigrated to the colonies, the majority conceded that the colonies tended to depopulate the mother country. To a small minority, the realization of this process was the main reason for their outright denial of the value of colonies to the metropolis.

The majority, however, maintained that the loss of population involved (a sacrifice which most of them considered to be relatively small) was in the final analysis profitable to the mother country because the possession of colonies in the tropical and sub-tropical zone assured Great Britain of the supply of valuable raw materials, because the colonial population consumed English manufactures, and because the import and export trade between colonies and mother country gave rise to a large metropolitan carrying trade which, in turn, was regarded as a potent matrix of sea power. Export trade and carrying trade, moreover, created additional employment in England, which tended to augment the metropolitan working population in the long run. However, the emigration of people from the mother country being regarded as a sacrifice or an investment, the redeeming advantages or returns enumerated above would accrue, so the mercantilists thought, only if the metropolis was able to monopolize export, import, and carrying trade with the colonies. Thus, Child stated expressly that all the restrictions imposed on the colonies were just because they are being "supplied with People from their Mother Kingdoms,"[78] and on another occasion he remarked "that all Colonies or Plantations do endamage their Mother-Kingdoms, whereof the Trades

---

[78] *A Discourse about Trade* (1690), p. 184. The peculiar effect of this argument on the framing of imperial policy will be discussed below.

of such Plantations are not confined by severe Laws, and good executions of those Laws, to the Mother-Kingdom."[79]

COLONIES AS SOURCES OF RAW MATERIALS

As to the value of colonies as raw-materials-producing areas under the jurisdiction of the mother country, post-Civil-War argumentation did not differ materially from pre-Civil-War discussion. The various arguments, as examined above, were reiterated, confirmed, and, in some cases, amplified.

The same generous flight of imagination nurtured the belief that almost no product of the growth of this earth could not be profitably raised within the Empire. The same naïve speculation in terms of geographical latitude was indulged in and the same credulous confidence shown regarding the ease with which some desirable commodity or other might be produced in the colonies. Discussing the possibility of raising raw silk in the southern provinces of North America, Patrick Lindsay pointed out that "the Situation of those Settlements, with respect to Latitude, and their Vicinity to Sea, differs little from the coasting Provinces of China, India, Persia, Coast of Turkey, Sicily, Italy, Provence, Languedock . . . ."[80] Another author declared that several commodities, hitherto imported from European countries, might be produced "in his Majesty's Dominions of America, they being so extensive, that they take in all the Latitudes of Europe. . . ."[81] One writer, desirous of seeing the American colonies produce wines and fruits, asserted that "the principal objects of culture in America, between 30 and 40 degrees of Northern latitude should be, vines, almonds, raisins, currants, olives, and particularly . . . wines. . . ."[82]

William Penn suggested the growing of wine in Pennsylvania and expressed the hope that it would be "as good Wine as any European Countries of the same Latitude do yield."[83] The writer, mentioned above, who thought of the large-scale production of wines, raisins, olives, etc., maintained that all "these interesting advantages may be apparently acquired soon, even in five or ten

[79]*Ibid.*, p. 166. Similarly, Patrick Lindsay, *The Interest of Scotland Considered* (Edinburgh, 1733), p. 137.

[80]*The Interest of Scotland Considered*, pp. 133 ff.

[81]*An Enquiry into the Melancholy Circumstance of Great Britain* (London, ca. 1730), pp. 45 f.

[82]*Scots Magazine*, XXIX (1767), 148.

[83]William Penn, *Original Proposal and Plan for the Founding and Building of Philadelphia* (1683), reprinted by James Coleman (London, 1881), p. 4.

years, if our national administrators take reasonable and active measures immediately...."[84] The "reasonable" measure, he advocated, was that of making no grant of land in the colonies in question except on condition that the grantee devote a certain number of acres to the production of the mentioned goods.

Such proposals and such over-optimistic expectations were by no means unusual. Very typical is the following parliamentary discussion. On February 3, 1738, the House of Commons debated the question whether a regiment of troops should be sent to Georgia. Sir John Hynd Cotton opposed the proposed measure on account of the excessive expense involved. Sir John Selwyn objected strongly to this plea for economy: "I beg leave to inform the House ... that this money is the best employed of any money that ever the government laid out; because, in a short time, that colony will be able to produce as much raw silk as will save the nation upwards of 300,000 l. which is now yearly sent out of England to Italy and other countries, for that commodity...." Immediately following Sir John's speech George Heathcote declared: "... I own that till now I have not approved our laying out so much money as we have done on the settlement of Georgia, because I was of opinion, that if the hands we have sent thither had been duly employed in agriculture and manufactures here, they might have been useful to their native country. But the honourable gentleman who spoke last has entirely removed my scruples; for if what he says is truth, which I am far from disputing, it is like to prove the most beneficial colony that ever was sent from Britain both because it will save a great deal of money to the nation and as it will produce a larger revenue to the crown."[85] This example shows the astounding credulity even of important members of Parliament although, in this particular case, credulity was founded on nothing but a mere assertion regarding which not the slightest bit of evidence had been offered.

The mercantilist literature dealing with the question of territorial sources of raw materials, referred chiefly to commodities that England had to import from abroad. Such goods could, of course, not be procured from colonial instead of foreign sources of supply before their production in the colonies was sufficiently organized. Suggestions to substitute colonial for foreign materials, therefore, were suggestions to encourage their production in the

[84] *Scots Magazine*, XXIX (1767), 148.
[85] L. F. Stock, *Proceedings and Debates of the British Parliaments Respecting North America* (Washington, 1924), IV, 350 f.

American plantations. As to the benefits which would result from such a substitution, the various writers spoke of several. A few authors asserted that the colonial products would be of better quality than those of foreign nations.[86] Others advanced the argument that imported articles, hitherto regarded as "luxuries," might soon become goods of common usage.[87]

Often repeated was the expectation that colonial supplies would be cheaper than those bought from foreign countries. Thus, Governor Berkeley of Virginia declared that "those commodities wee were wont to purchase at great rates and hazards, wee now purchase at half the usuall prices."[88] Patrick Lindsay likewise claimed that raw silk, hemp, and flax might be furnished by the colonies "at easier Rates than they can be imported from foreign Parts...."[89] It was usually admitted, however, that the comparative cheapness of colonial products was contingent upon the new industry having passed through the stage of its infancy.[90] In the case of some materials, moreover, the expectation of relative cheapness of colonial supplies was not based on the assumption of

[86]Patrick Lindsay (*The Interest of Scotland Considered* [1733], p. 135), thought that the southern colonies in North America would be able to furnish England with "Flax of a finer Quality than any that grows in Europe." Needless to say, this claim was based not on experimentation but on sheer speculation. Similarly, *Gentleman's Magazine*, XXVI (1756), 162.

[87]The author of *An Enquiry into the Melancholy Circumstances of Great Britain* (p. 46) maintained that "then [i.e., when the colonies would supply the mother country] those things that are now luxuries would cease to be so, and become our common Commodities...." However, during the period of time in question the desires of the common consumer were of little concern to the ruling groups of the state. The enjoyment of "luxuries" was conceded to the rich and powerful (and sometimes even to them only grudgingly). Their enjoyment by the poor was deliberately discouraged. See Buck, *Politics of Mercantilism*, pp. 53-6; 88-101.

[88]Quoted in G. L. Beer, *The Old Colonial System* (New York, 1933), I, 39.

[89]*The Interest of Scotland Considered* (1733), p. 135.

[90]One writer, discussing the possibility of producing raw silk in North Carolina, Virginia, Maryland, and Pennsylvania, spoke of "a few years" which had to elapse before silk could be produced more cheaply in America than in Italy ("Interesting Observations on Raising Raw Silk," *Gentleman's Magazine*, XXVI [1756], 162). This author is one of the very few who made an attempt to investigate comparable production costs. He asserted "that very few places are agreeable to the silk-worm, and that none are more so than our colonies, as the goodness of the silk imported from thence has shown." Besides the silk-worm's preference for America, he pointed out that both land and labour (he refers to slave labour) were cheaper in America than in Italy (*ibid.*, p. 161).

lower production costs but inspired by the ever-present dread of foreign monopoly prices.[91]

However, the most important and most frequently presented consideration which determined these English writers to express such a decided partiality for colonial products, arose from a desire for safer and more dependable supplies of important raw materials in time of peace as well as in time of war. This is particularly true of naval stores. Brewster stated: "That there is nothing of greater consequence to a people that live by Trade, than to be makers of their own Tools by which they work, none will deny; now Shipping are the Tools and Utensils of the Nation; to fetch them from abroad is to Trade by Licence; whenever our Northern Neighbours please, we must lye still, or pay such rates as they please...."[92] William Wood observed: "Nor is it out of the way to observe, that our Shipping being our Security, and our Naval Stores so essentially necessary; our being obliged to fetch them from the East Country, may some time or other be of pernicious Consequence to the Kingdom, should the Balance of Power in the Baltick come so to alter, that a Prince, an Enemy to Great Britain, should be possessed of it."[93]

Sir Gilbert Heathcote, speaking in the House of Lords in 1721, declared: "That, besides, while we fetch'd our naval stores from Russia, it was in the power of the Czar, not only to set what price he pleas'd upon them, but even to prevent our having them at all.... That therefore since these commodities were so absolutely necessary for our navy, it was not fitting we should lie at the mercy of a foreign prince for them...."[94] Another writer likewise maintained that "the advantage accruing to a maritime power from having its naval stores supplied from its own dominions, is no less evident than important; they cannot then be withheld, in case of war, by the prohibition of any prince, in whose dominions they must be purchased."[95]

---

[91]The chronicler of the *Annual Register* (I [1758], 76), for example, applauding Admiral Keppel's reduction of French Goree, commented: "At present we are obliged to buy all our gum senega of the Dutch, who purchase it from the French; and they set what price they please on it. But as the trade to Africa is now open, by this important acquisition, the price of this valuable drug ... will be much reduced." Similarly, with respect to Russian tar, see Sir Gilbert Heathcote's speech in the House of Lords in 1721 (Stock, *Proceedings and Debates*, III, 446).

[92]*Essays on Trade and Navigation* (1695), p. 86.

[93]*A Survey of Trade* (1718), p. 152.

[94]Cf. Stock, *Proceedings and Debates*, III, 446.

[95]*Gentleman's Magazine*, XXV (1755), 437.

George Grenville also was in favour of encouraging the growth of hemp and flax in the northern American colonies in order to render Britain independent of the "precarious Supply" from other countries "who by some unexpected fluctuation in political Connections, may become adverse to these Kingdoms." It was necessary, he said, "to wrest . . . out of the hands of other States, be they ever so friendly, such an undue Influence over all our Operations. . . ."[96] Anderson likewise declared that "by the vast increase of the productions of our American plantations, we have got rid, for the most part, though not as yet entirely, of a precarious dependence on other nations. . . ."[97]

Indeed, this particular argument, for colonial as against foreign supplies, exercised a most potent influence on the valuation of the colonies as well as on the shaping of imperial policy. It must be admitted that these apprehensions with regard to the precariousness of foreign supplies were by no means absurd. England could never be sure of enjoying the naval mastery of the Baltic. The British had always to reckon with the possibility of finding themselves at war with Sweden or Russia or both, that is, with those countries who were in a position to control those areas which produced the bulk of the Northern and Eastern European naval stores.[98]

Weighty as this consideration was, the replacement of foreign by colonial supplies of vital raw materials appeared equally desirable on the ground that such substitution would diminish the dreaded outflow of bullion and improve the balance of trade. The following quotations express this line of thought.

The wealth resulting from colonies ought certainly to arise from the cultivation of staple commodities; that is from the production of those articles which a mother-country must purchase of foreigners, if her own settlements did not yield them. The difference between purchasing a commodity of a

---

[96]George Grenville, *The Regulations Lately Made Concerning the Colonies* (London, 1765), p. 55.

[97]Mr. Coombe (ed.), *Anderson's Origin of Commerce* (Dublin, 1790), I, Introduction, p. xxix.

[98]The alternative of *storing* a sufficient supply of these vital materials (and at that time they were as vital as oil is today) was not unknown. Bacon already suggested it (*A Letter of Advice written to the Duke of Buckingham*, in James Spedding, *The Life and Letters of Francis Bacon* [London, 1872], VI, 45) and William Wood (*A Survey of Trade* [1718], p. 152) criticized the responsible officials for being negligent in this respect. However, the techniques required for preserving the quality of such stores, especially timber, hemp, etc., were probably not advanced enough to allow their storage over a longer period of time. At any rate, storage was never considered to be a seriously eligible alternative.

foreign country, or of a colony, is immense: in the first case, it is paid for probably with cash; but in the latter, manufactures are exchanged for it; that is, the labour of our poor.... What a prodigious difference there is between paying to the French a million sterling for sugars, or exchanging a million's worth of our manufactures for the same commodity with our own colonists....[99]

... our naval Stores might, in great Measure, be supplied from New England, and we might save a great Part of four or five hundred thousand Pounds per Annum in these Commodities, which we bring from Denmark, Sweden, and the East Countries.[100]

It is a certain Truth that we might be Gainers by taking all our Lumber from our own Plantations ... in the case of our own Plantations and Shipping we do not advance one Penny in Cash; for whatever is sent abroad is our own Produce and Manufacture, whereas in the other Case 'tis thought that at least more than one third of the Whole is paid in Cash: In short, whatever we have from our own Plantations costs us nothing, but the Labour of manufacturing Goods for them, and that of bringing theirs here....[101]

Sir William Keith said once that the only reason for planting colonies was "to redress Balance of National Trade if it is turned against us."[102] On another occasion he demanded that naval stores, copper ore, pig and bar iron be drawn from the colonies "by means whereof the Ballance of Trade to Russia and the Baltick may be very much reduced in Favour of Great Britain."[103] An anonymous writer likewise pleaded for the encouragement of colonial naval stores "which, if duly cherished, may turn the current of that trade from a channel that annually drains wealth from England, in as lavish a manner as court whores ever did the King's coffers in the lascivious reign of Charles the second; for the deals and iron &c. imported from the Baltic and Norway, are mostly freighted on foreign bottoms, and paid for in specie, but our colonists are glad to take English manufactures in return for their outsets...."[104] Another author, previously mentioned, who advocated the growing of wine and fruit in America, pointed out that such a policy "will save and produce millions to the nation in a few years, now remitted to enrich some enemies, and to impoverish many subjects."[105]

[99] A. Young, *Political Essays* (1772), p. 329.
[100] Erasmus Philips, *Miscellaneous Works* (London, 1751), p. 36.
[101] Fayne Hall, *Importance of the British Plantations in America* (1731), p. 5.
[102] Sir William Keith, *The History of the British Plantations in America* (London, 1738), part I, p. 10.
[103] Keith, *A Collection of Papers* (London, 1740), p. 172.
[104] *Gentleman's Magazine*, XXXV (1765), 353.
[105] *Scots Magazine*, XXIX (1767), 148; similarly, *Anderson's Origin of Commerce*, Introduction, p. xxx; Brewster, *Essays on Trade and Navigation* (1695), p. 89.

The above quotations contain all the cruder elements of the conventional balance-of-trade doctrine. Britain, it was argued, had an unfavourable balance of trade with the Baltic countries, hence, the balance could only be redressed by the outflow of precious treasure. In conjunction with this notorious *over*-valuation of bullion, appears the equally erroneous *under*-valuation of exports in the form of manufactures. This combination of fallacies led to absurd statements such as that England would get raw materials from her colonies for "nothing" except the labour embodied in manufactures.[106]

Connected with this idea of preserving England's stock of bullion by substituting colonial for foreign products, was the idea of augmenting this precious stock by re-exporting to foreign countries that portion of colonial supplies that exceeded the needs of the mother country. Thus Brewster wrote: "As this Plantation [New England] may save the Nation the Expence they are now at in purchasing Naval Stores, so it will bring in considerable returns in Bullion for what they send into the Levant, Spain. . . ."[107] John Cary declared "when we consume their [the colonies'] Growth we do as it were spend the Fruits of our own Land, and what thereof we sell to our Neighbours for Bullion, or such Commodities as we must pay for therein, brings a second Profit to the Nation."[108]

One anonymous author likewise proposed that of the colonial supply of naval stores "we might sell some [naval stores] to other Nations, and inforce our Ballance and Trade with them."[109] This argument, of course, applied with full force to those colonial staples which were not produced within the confines of Europe. Sugar was the most important of these staples. The Earl of Sandwich, speaking in the House of Lords in 1671, demanded that England monopolize the European sugar market. He claimed "that, by encouraging the English sugar plantations, and making it a matter of state so to do, we might in short space of time engross that manufacture to ourselves, and serve the Straights and other coun-

---

[106]The implications of the so-called balance-of-employment doctrine probably also influenced these considerations.

It may be noted here that the procurement of raw materials from the colonies instead of from European states was expected not only to "improve" England's balance of trade, but at the same time to "worsen" that of the nations from whom Britain had purchased the commodities in question. Any gain tasted doubly sweet if at the same time it meant detriment to some other country.

[107]*Essays in Trade and Navigation* (1695), p. 89.
[108]Cary, *An Essay on the State of England* (1695), p. 67.
[109]*An Enquiry into the Melancholy Circumstances of Great Britain* (1730), p. 46.

tries therewith, to the advantage of doubling at least the balance of trade we now enjoy by the same...."[110]

It was less out of regard for the English consumer than to expand the re-export trade in colonial staples that such a "prodigious value"[111] was attributed to the sugar islands in the West Indies. William Burke, for example, stated this expressly: "Those [sugar islands] who supply the home Consumption purvey to our Luxury: those who supply the foreign Market administer to our Wealth and to our Power."[112] Erasmus Philips declared: "Tobacco, Cotton, Ginger, Sugars, Indigo, Rice, and the rest of the Plantation Goods have brought us (besides what was necessary for our Consumption) a Balance from France, Flanders, Hambrough, Holland, and the east Countries, of above six hundred thousand Pounds a Year."[113]

Another argument which induced the British to place colonial raw materials above those of foreign origin, rested on the fact that the former could be fetched in English bottoms while the navigation ordinances of other nations often did not allow this in the case of their exports. Sir Josiah Child, for example, pointed out: "If the Commodity should be somewhat dearer for the present [he referred to a colonial product], it would be no loss to the Nation in general, because all freight would be paid to English men; whereas the freight paid to Strangers is all clear loss to the Nation."[114] And Sir William Mildmay declared: "... we may now be supplied in a certain and beneficial manner from our own

[110]Stock, *Proceedings and Debates*, I, 383.
[111]Campbell, *Considerations on the Nature of the Sugar Trade* (1763), p. 26.
[112]William Burke, *Remarks on the Letter Address'd to Two Great Men* (3d ed.; London, n.d.), p. 32. Again it was considered good policy to prevent the French from engrossing too much of the European sugar market, a consideration which assumed great significance when the English had to determine the spoils of victory after a successful war with France or when the intricacies of imperial policies were under discussion. Joshua Gee, for example, was highly perturbed about the fact that the French "have of late years generally undersold us in the markets of Hambourg, Holland, Flanders, &c. which about 35 or 40 years ago, were chiefly supplied by us...." (*The Trade and Navigation of Great Britain* [1731], pp. 82 f.). He therefore exhorted his countrymen in the following manner: "As the declension of this trade is visible, and the danger of losing it too apparent, without some speedy care, I am humbly of opinion, there can be no other way to retrieve it, but by enlarging our plantations, and not only vye with the French in foreign markets, but, if possible, to beat them out, as we formerly did the Portuguese" (*ibid.*, p. 83).
[113]*Miscellaneous Works* (1751), p. 32.
[114]*A Discourse about Trade* (1690), p. 100.

dominions, with all these products, which, as one of our acts of parliament recites, 'were formerly brought mostly from foreign parts in foreign shipping, at exorbitant prices to the great prejudice of our Trade and Navigation.' "[115]

Thus, as compared with the acquisition of raw materials from the colonies, their purchase from foreign nations entailed disadvantages in two ways: First, in the same inane manner in which the export of bullion was dreaded as a painful loss to the nation while the loss of labour and other productive agents embodied in exported manufactures was counted lightly, so the employment of foreign shipping was considered extremely prejudicial to the nation while the employment of English shipping was supposed to cost "nothing." Secondly, importation of raw materials from foreign countries meant a deplorable loss of carrying business and, hence, was considered detrimental to British seapower.[116]

Finally, it has to be mentioned that, to some writers, the encouragement of the production of raw materials in the oversea colonies afforded a valuable weapon for reprisals against those nations on which Great Britain had hitherto been entirely or largely dependent for her supplies. Brewster suggested: "To give such Encouragement for raising Naval Commodities as Pitch, Tar, Hemp, &c. on our Foreign Plantations, as may advance that Trade to more than our Consumption; if this were done, it would make the Northern Princes abate their Impositions they have lately laid on their Commodities, and set them upon all ways of furnishing us so cheap, as might render our attempts of raising

[115] *The Laws and Policy of England* (1765), pp. 33 f. See also Cary, *A Discourse on Trade*, p. 84; Daniel Defoe, *A Plan for the English Commerce* (1728) in reprint (Oxford, 1927), p. 269.

[116] This consideration was, of course, reiterated with regard to all colonial staple products. William Wood (*A Survey of Trade* [1718], pp. 154 f.) wrote: "No trades deserve so much our care to procure and preserve, and Encouragement to prosecute, as those that employ the most Shipping; altho' the Commodities carry'd be of small Value in themselves, as a great Part of the Commodities from our Colonies are. For besides the Gain accruing by the Goods, the Freight in such Trades, often more than the Value of the Goods, is all Profit to the Nation; and they likewise bring with them a great Access of Power by the Encrease of Ships and Seamen, the proper Strength and Security of this Kingdom." Similarly, John Campbell (*Considerations on the Nature of the Sugar Trade* [1763], p. 21): ". . . its [the sugar trade] being confined to America, is the principal cause of its affording such a variety of advantages, and more especially of its contributing so highly to the support of navigation, and in consequence of that to the maintenance of naval power. . . ." For a lengthy enumeration of all the advantages in this respect see Young, *Political Essays* (1772), pp. 339 ff.

them ourselves unprofitable; and let it succeed to their expectation or not, the effect would be to our advantage...."[117] Oglethorp likewise thought that the colonial capacity to raise certain raw materials in the colonies conferred upon the mother country a weapon which might be used for retaliatory purposes: "If Muscovy supplies its own wollen goods, or is supplied by any other foreigner, it ought to make us resolve to bring our naval stores from North America; if Spain and Italy refuse our drapery, we may reject their silk, their raisins, oil, wine, olives, and divers other merchandizes, and be supplied from Carolina and Georgia."[118]

However, these two writers had two different purposes in mind. Sir Francis Brewster's idea was to reduce the quasi-monopoly which the Baltic states enjoyed with regard to naval stores. The very existence of other potential sources of supply, would sufficiently weaken the monopolist position of the Baltic countries. Oglethorp, on the other hand, thought of turning to new sources of supply as a threat against those countries that refused to accept a sufficient quantity of British exports. In both cases, the colonies, as raw-materials-producing areas, would serve a supposedly useful purpose.

Two more arguments may be mentioned briefly although they were of a distinctly marginal nature and played an insignificant role in the pertinent literature. Patrick Lindsay estimated that, once the colonies supplied Britain with cheaper raw materials, this would operate as a cost-decreasing factor in the production of manufactures for exportation.[119] Arthur Young considered it a distinct advantage that in the case of colonial materials the profits of primary cultivation would ultimately redound to the metropolis.[120] Although some publicists asserted that colonial products would eventually become less expensive than foreign ones, they sometimes admitted that, over an initial period of time, these products would be more expensive than those of foreign origin. However, in consideration of the manifold advantages to be derived from the substitution of colonial for foreign supplies, they were ready to accept higher prices and inferior quality as a factor of subordinate importance.[121]

[117] *Essays on Trade and Navigation* (1695), p. 87.
[118] *New and Accurate Account of South Carolina and Georgia*, pp. 76 f.
[119] *The Interest of Scotland Considered* (1733), p. 135.
[120] *Political Essays* (London, 1772), p. 329.
[121] Cf. Wood, *A Survey of Trade* (1718), p. 152; Child, *A Discourse about Trade* (1690), p. 100; *Scots Magazine*, XXIX (1767), 148; *Gentleman's Magazine*, XXXV (1765), 352. That informed officials were quite aware of higher production costs in the American colonies, is revealed in the report of Lord Dartmouth delivered

The arguments discussed so far centred around two main considerations: First, the substitution of colonial products for foreign commodities. Secondly, the creation of a large English re-export trade in colonial staples. However, some authors approached the entire problem of colonies as raw-stuff producing areas from a somewhat different point of view. In their minds, the patterns of imperial economic relations were to be fashioned on the basis of one fundamental ideal: the dissimilarity and, hence, the non-competitiveness of colonial and metropolitan production. In accordance with this notion, the metropolis was seen as the industrial centre of the Empire, providing the colonies with manufactured goods, whereas the colonies would serve the function of supplying the mother country with those raw materials which the metropolis could not raise at all or was unable to produce in sufficient quantity. This clear-cut division of economic functions between colonies and parent state was not merely regarded as an automatic outcome of natural conditions. Its strict and rigid maintenance, enforced with the help of legal regulations, was deemed imperative because—according to the prevalent doctrine of the value of plantations—the profits of Empire depended exactly on the perpetuation of this division of labour.

Speaking of the British West Indies, William Burke remarked: "The Trade we carry on with that Part of the World, is as happily circumstanced as Imagination could form it. The West India Islands lie in a Climate totally different from ours. The natural Produce therefore interferes in no respect with that of England."[122] Similarly, Mildmay stressed that Great Britain needed "dominions extending to different climates . . . which cultivate different productions from our own."[123]

In some colonies, however, natural conditions were not so accommodating to the wishes of the metropolis. In such cases, it was considered good policy to provide the desired stimulus in the form of restrictive laws or encouraging bounties. The direction of colonial production into definite channels, i.e., the encouragement of the production of certain raw materials, would serve to keep such colonies from establishing manufacturing industries of their own.

in the House of Lords in 1704 (cf. Stock, *Proceedings and Debates*, III, 71). This acknowledgment, however, did not restrain the Commissioners of Trade and Plantations from advocating the production of Naval Stores in the New England colonies (*ibid.*).

[122] *Remarks on the Letter Address'd to Two Great Men*, p. 47.
[123] *The Law and Policy of England* (1763), p. 33.

Thus, Lindsay pointed out: "But great Care must be taken to encourage them to imploy all their Hands in their own Trade, and to prevent their making of any manufactured Goods of their own. ... The only Way to prevent this, is to find them Business enough in their own Way, to enable them to purchase our Manufactures."[124] Similarly, George Grenville wrote: "I desired, for the sake of both the Mother Country and its Colonies, to turn their thoughts to Agriculture, and by that means to prevent their interfering with Great Britain in her manufactures, which I thought would be greatly prejudicial to both. That the wisest and most effectual method of accomplishing this would be to give all possible encouragement to the importation of their raw materials from the Colonies into Great Britain. ..."[125] To observers like Grenville, colonial specialization on primary production exclusively seemed desirable, less for the sake of the raw materials produced, than for the purpose of preserving the colonies as a market for English manufactures.

Similar in character was the plea for the encouragement of the production of raw materials in the colonies because their consequent dependence on the market of the mother country would keep them politically dependent.[126] Keith declared: "In order therefore to possess and retain the Inclinations and dutiful Obedience of the Subjects in the Plantations to the lawful Authority and Jurisdiction of Great-Britain over them, those restrictive Acts of Trade and Navigation, which are or may be found necessary to render the Plantations more useful, ought to be counterpoised with proper Encouragements for raising there, and importing from thence, all such Foreign Commodities, as Great-Britain desires and expects from them. ..."[127] Postlethwayt wrote: "But keeping our planters to the raising of such materials for our British manufactures, as we are necessitated to take at present from foreign nations and their colonies, will effectually prevent jealousies and misunderstandings between Britons and their American brethren, and give mutual strength, riches, and power."[128] Similarly, Hall stated: "Will it not appear much more reasonable to make them produce all the rough Materials we want, and which

---

[124] *The Interest of Scotland Considered* (1733), p. 137.

[125] Cf. William Knox, *Extra Official State Papers* (London, 1789), II, 16.

[126] Mercantilists held that a colony, bare of manufacturing industries, would not possess the wealth and power prerequisite to political independence.

[127] Keith, *The History of the British Plantations in America* (1738), p. 177.

[128] Postlethwayt, *Dictionary*, "Colonies."

they are certainly capable of. This alone, so long as the Navigation Act subsists, would effectually keep them dependent on us."[129]

The raising of large quantities of raw materials in the colonies, furthermore, would not only tend to keep them from setting up their own manufacturing industries, and thus to preserve them as a market for metropolitan manufactures. Increasing production of marketable rawstuffs would also expand their capacity to absorb British manufactured articles. Thus, George Grenville remarked that if the mother country would lend all possible encouragement to the importation of colonial raw materials, this "would enable the Americans to pay in that manner for a considerable part of the manufactures which they would take from hence. . . ."[130]

The northern American colonies presented a particularly vexing problem to the theorists on colonial questions. While the southern American plantations and the West Indian islands fitted perfectly into the imperial economic scheme, the northern colonies produced few raw materials which were non-competitive with those raised in Great Britain. Therefore they were regarded as of distinctly inferior utility to the mother country as compared with those colonies which raised valuable staples like sugar, tobacco, etc.[131] Projects, therefore, which envisaged the encouragement of the production of naval stores in the colonies received the willing support of those who demanded that the New England colonies be rendered more useful to the mother country. Sir Francis Brewster remarked that the execution of this policy "would make New England, of the most useless and unprofitable Plantation of this Nation, the best and most advantageous to this Nation. . . ."[132] William Wood nursed the same expectation: "But the Northern Colonies might be made more Advantageous to their Mother

[129]*The Importance of the British Plantations in America* (1731), p. 22. See also, Lindsay, *The Interest of Scotland Considered* (1733), p. 145; Burke, *Remarks on the Letter Address'd to Two Great Men*, p. 48.

[130]Cf. Knox, *Extra Official State Papers*, II, 16; similarly, Oglethorp, *New and Accurate Account of South Carolina and Georgia*, p. 69.

[131]Indeed, some writers regarded the northern colonies with such disfavour that they proposed to give them up. Carew Reynell, for example, wrote: "For our Northern Colonies, as those of New England, and the rest afford only such Commodities as we have our selves, and so breed no good Commerce" (*The True English Interest* [1679], p. 91). He concluded that it would be best to re-settle the colonists of New England in the southern part of the American continent (*ibid.*).

[132]*Essays on Trade and Navigation* (1695), p. 88.

Country than they have hitherto been, or otherwise can be, if all necessary Encouragement were given by this Kingdom for their supplying us with Naval Stores."[133]

Of the various raw materials and foodstuffs which Britain used to purchase from European nations and whose production in the colonies was proposed most frequently were, apart from fish, naval stores, raw silk, wines, fruit, and raw iron. The motives behind such plans have been examined. The means to this end will be discussed in one of the following chapters.

As mentioned before, the raising of colonial staples was not welcomed because their abundant production would redound to the benefit of the mass of the British population as consumers. Consumption as an end in itself usually was disparaged and discouraged by the mercantilists. Thrift and frugality were glorified as supreme virtues to which the mass of the people were asked to aspire.[134] However, there were a few notable exceptions to this rule.[135] Referring to sugar as a consumers' good, John Campbell wrote:

... we are but too apt to fancy that the nation can only gain by its foreign commerce and a balance of trade arising from thence; whereas nothing is more certain, than whatever enables men to support themselves in ease and independence, and repays their honest endeavours with a comfortable subsistence, is to them, as well as to their country, RICHES.... We formerly...consumed about a thousand hogsheads of sugar, and exported about twice that quantity.... We now consume about fourscore thousand hogsheads, and except in time of war export but very little.... But does it follow, because we consume fourscore thousand hogsheads... we gain so much less by it now than when we imported but half the quantity? No certainly, we pay for the sugar now as we did then, that is, we pay for it in our commodities, manufactures... and therefore it is twice as beneficial to us now as it was then; and if we consume it, this is owing to the increase of our industry, that is our affluence... this increase of our consumption is an indubitable proof of the increase of our riches... this affords the most convincing and conclusive demonstration of the benefits we have derived from them [the colonies]....[136]

Much more forcefully concerned with the interest of the average English consumer is the following statement by an anonymous writer:

[133] *A Survey of Trade* (1718), pp. 149 f.

[134] Cf. Jacob Viner, *Studies in the Theory of International Trade* (New York, 1937), pp. 26 ff., 55.

[135] Vanderlint is an outstanding example. Cf. Vanderlint, *Money Answers All Things* (1734). For further examples see Viner, *Studies,* pp. 90 f.; Buck, *Politics of Mercantilism,* pp. 63-72.

[136] *Considerations on the Nature of the Sugar Trade* (1763), pp. 30 ff.

It has been said, and I suppose may again, that Sugar is a Matter of Luxury: If it be so, it must be owing to the present extravagant Price of it; for when Moscovada Sugar was retailed at Three-pence Halfpenny per Pound, as it constantly used to be in Time of Peace, Farmers and Labouring People sweetened their Pyes and Puddings with it, and employed it in other Family Uses . . . and if this be deemed a Luxury by any, it is such a one that I hope our industrious People will never be deprived of. And, for God's Sake, why should they? only to fill the Pockets of People never deemed averse to Luxury, and enable them to indulge themselves in many Expences which are indisputably luxurious.[137]

Yet such consideration for the interests of the individual consumer was an exception during the period here under discussion. The following statement by Sir Francis Brewster is much more typical of the general trend of thought: ". . . the Product of our Foreign Plantations is in greatest part consumed in the Kingdom, and that adds nothing to the Riches of the Nation."[138]

COLONIES AS MARKETS

No English writer who looked with favour on the oversea plantations, omitted to mention the value of colonies as a market for metropolitan products. Passages like the two following ones appear in the pertinent literature with tedious frequency.

Our Trade to our Plantations or West-India Collonies takes off great quantities of our Products and Manufactures, as well as Provisions and Handicraft Wares. . . .[139]

The Colonies take off and consume above one sixth Part of the Woollen Manufactures exported from Britain, which is the chief Staple of England . . . . They take off and consume more than double that Value in Linen and Callicoes, which is either the Product of Britain and Ireland, or partly the profitable Returns made for that Product carried to foreign Countries. The Luxury of the Colonies, which increases daily, consumes great Quantities of English manufactured Silk, Haberdashery, Household Furniture, and Trinkets of all Sorts; also a very considerable Value in East-India Goods.[140]

The above citations reveal the principal types of goods which were marketed in the colonies. They were commodities of British and of foreign make, manufactured and unmanufactured articles. Those colonial imports which were of foreign origin and constituted English re-exports will be disregarded in the following, for, the

---

[137]*An Enquiry into the Causes of the Present High Price of Muscovada Sugars* (London, 1735), pp. 6 f.

[138]*Essays on Trade and Navigation* (1695), p. 71.

[139]John Pollexfen, *A Discourse of Trade, Coyn, and Paper Credit* (London, 1697), p. 86.

[140]Keith, *A Collection of Papers* (1740), pp. 171 f.

East India trade excepted, the very fact that there existed a colonial demand for foreign goods was frowned upon[141] as causing loss of foreign exchange or bullion rather than welcomed as giving rise to an English re-export trade. Nor does the export of British "provisions" to the colonies warrant much attention since the volume of these exports was relatively insignificant. This trade was seldom stressed by the publicists. Some writers, indeed, did not consider it particularly "profitable" to the mother country. They heartily approved of the fact that the northern American plantations rather than the mother country itself, provided the English West Indies increasingly with these goods. Wood, for example, stated "I am inclined to think, the present course most advantageous to this Kingdom, for this Reason, because the Provision we might send to Barbadoes, etc. would be unimproved Product of the Earth, as Grain of all kind, or such Product where there is little got by the Improvement, as Salt Beef, Pork, etc. but the Goods we send to the Northern Colonies, are such whose Improvements may be justly said, one with another, to be near Four Fifths of the Value of the whole Commodities, as Apparel, Household Furniture, and many other Things."[142] Postlethwayt, without acknowledgment, incorporated this passage verbatim into his article on colonies.[143]

Most writers who commented on the function of the colonies as markets of the metropolis, mentioned only manufactured articles. This particular emphasis on manufactured goods as against the "unimproved Product of the Earth" manifests a characteristic notion of mercantilist thought. Conventional mercantilist reasoning on exports was derived from the desire for effecting a favourable balance of trade which would result in an influx of precious bullion. However, this was not the only doctrine on foreign trade which occupied, or rather preoccupied, the mercantilist mind. Side by side[144] with it appeared the maxim according

[141]D. Bindon, *A Letter from a Merchant Who Has Left Off Trade* (1738), p. 27.
[142]*A Survey of Trade* (1718), p. 147.
[143]Postlethwayt, *Dictionary*, "Colonies."
[144]The expression "side by side" is used here in order to stress that the employment-argument did not suddenly make its appearance, as some writers assert, some time during the last quarter of the seventeenth century and then more or less displaced the balance-of-trade doctrine. Actually it can be traced back to the earliest mercantilist literature (cf. Viner, *Studies*, p. 52) and though it deprived the balance-of-trade concept of its exclusiveness, at no period of time did it displace the latter. True it is that the balance-of-labour doctrine was elaborated further in the later period and that it then gained more general

to which the largest possible volume of exports was appreciated less for the sake of preserving or augmenting the nation's stock of precious metals than that of increasing the country's volume of employment [by the means of large export industries]. In its most elaborate form, this "balance-of-employment" doctrine appraised exports in terms of labour embodied therein. If the amount of labour represented in the total of exports was in excess of the amount of labour embodied in the total of imports, then the nation supposedly had gained by the exchange.

It is not easy to discern what ultimate objective the mercantilists had in mind when they wanted the largest possible volume of employment. In spite of their exceedingly befuddled theories of values, it is safe to conclude that they did not think of employment as an end in itself. Very few of them regarded, even in a most nebulous manner, maximum consumption as the ultimate desideratum. The majority of mercantilist writers were obviously concerned with considerations of power and "wealth" in terms of "population" and "production."[145] To them, a larger volume of employment meant a larger volume of national output and a larger working population. In turn, the latter phenomenon was welcomed by the majority of theorists because the larger the number of employed, the lower the wage level, and the cheaper production for export. Thus, however twisted, the chain of reasoning seems closed.

The following contemporary statements may serve to illustrate this particular line of mercantilist ratiocination. Reyneld emphasized: ". . . manufactures must do the work, which will not only increase people, but also Trade, and advance it. It saves likewise mony in our purses by lessening importation, and brings many in by importation."[146] David Bindon stated similarly:

The chief Methods of gaining Riches by Industry are Agriculture, Fishery, and Manufacture; and of these, Manufacture is the most advantageous for a Nation; because whatever may be gained that way, will employ and maintain ten times the Number of People that can be employed and maintained, by gaining the same Sum to the Nation in either of the other Methods. Therefore, tho' every wise Nation will encourage Agriculture and Fishing as much as they can, yet they will always encourage both, rather with a View to render Provisions cheap among their Manufactures, than with a

---

recognition. Quite often however, mercantilist theorists argued, simultaneously or alternately, along both lines of thought.

[145]Cf. Br. Suviranta, *The Theory of the Balance of Trade in England* (Helsingfors, 1923), pp. 141, 152.

[146]Carew Reynell, *The True English Interest* (London, 1679), Preface.

View to get by Exporting the Produce of either to Foreign Nations; for the cheaper Provisions are in any Country, the more able will their Manufactures be to undersell Foreigners in every sort of Manufacture.[147]

Exquisitely confused but no less characteristic is the following passage by Malachy Postlethwayt: "Foreign Rivalship in the Trade of a Nation, consists in being able to sell abroad as much of the Productions of our Country's Lands and Industry as other Nations do; and in employing as many more as they, with the Money of Foreigners; that is to say, in respective Proportion to the Populousness, Capitals, Extent and Fruitfulness of each other's Lands .... The Balance of Trade, I cannot too often repeat it, is in Fact the Balance of Power."[148]

A subsidiary but still very powerful motive that prompted the mercantilist desire for an increased volume of employment was their profound disgust with idleness among the common people.[149] Apart from the reasons already discussed, the violence of this feeling must be attributed to the sustained influence of religious dogmas and of religious residues even in the case of those to whom religion was little more than lip-service. Thus, the economic theorist received on this score the full-hearted support of the moralist who wanted nothing more than to see every "lusty" idler and "sturdy" beggar put to work.

The implications of the balance-of-employment doctrine of foreign trade are simple. If the nation could manage to import largely raw materials and export largely manufactured articles, then its chances of effecting a large surplus of exported labour were excellent.[150] Hence the desire for expanding the export of manufactures and the attitude of belittling that of raw materials and "provisions."[151] Thus, by receiving raw materials from the colonies and sending them manufactures, the balance of labour

---

[147] *A Letter from a Merchant Who Has Left Off Trade* (1738), p. 5. A similar statement can be found in *Britannia Languens* (1680), p. 11.

[148] *Great Britain's True System* (London, 1757), p. 234.

[149] See Buck, *Politics of Mercantilism*, pp. 88-96.

[150] On this whole matter see Viner, *Studies*, pp. 52-7.

[151] With respect to the trade carried on with foreign nations this curious argument, of course, re-enforced the conventional mercantilist conception of the non-mutuality of benefits accruing from international commerce. The successful pursuit of this policy was only possible at the expense of the other nation and if the ultimate gain from this policy was supposed to be affluence of "wealth" and "power" (to use the terms of ambiguous reference cultivated by the mercantilists), their augmentation could only be realized by means which at the same time decreased the "wealth" and "power" of rival states.

would be clearly in favour of the mother country. This advantage to the metropolis was appreciated all the more because throughout the period under discussion, as during the period previously considered, the English complained of the precariousness of foreign markets. Indeed, protectionist devices, prompted by mercantilist theorizing, were as commonly adopted in the other Western European countries as they were in Great Britain herself.[152] The English were particularly concerned with finding a satisfactory vent for their expanding woollen industry.[153] It was, therefore, important to have a *dependable* market and in this respect the colonies were deemed extremely useful to the metropolis. Bolingbroke stressed this factor of security and dependability when he said:

Whoever will look into the present State of the British Commerce will find that the Ballance runs against us in many Branches; and that the most valuable (if not the only Remains, which are intrinsically so) are to our own Plantations.... They are likewise to be considered as intirely our own; and therefore it is highly our Interest to encourage and improve them, since they may be useful to us, and be a considerable Support to the Nation, when other Branches may possibly fail us, through the Designs and Contrivances of our Rivals in Trade....[154]

Similar ideas are expressed in the following citations:

... we are a trading Nation; and whatever affects our Trade is our nearest Concern.... Of all the Branches of our Commerce that to our own Colonies is the most valuable upon many Accounts. If I am rightly informed, it is by that alone we are enabled to carry on the rest, and therefore ought to be the most secure. Foreign markets may be lost or spoiled by various Acci-

---

[152]The majority of mercantilists found it quite compatible to complain bitterly of the protectionism practised by other nations while advocating the same policy for England. However, during the course of the eighteenth century, a growing group of dissenters like Paterson, the author of the *Considerations on the East India Trade*, Isaac Gervaise, etc., expressed anti-protectionist views (cf. Viner, *Studies*, pp. 91 ff.). Erasmus Philips (*Miscellaneous Works* [1751], p. 38), for example, pointed out the incompatibility of complaining of French duties on English exports while shutting off French goods by the same device when he declared: "But high Duties and Prohibitions on our Side beget high Duties and Prohibitions on theirs...."

[153]The woollen industry was regarded as England's most important manufacturing industry. One author, for example, wrote metaphorically: "I begin with this Trade [the woollen trade], because it is like the Water to the Mill that driveth Round the Wheel of all other Trades" (*The Ancient Trades Decayed, Repaired Again* [London, 1678], p. 2). Regarding the foreign markets of this industry there were perennial complaints of severe French and Dutch competition. Cf. *ibid.*, pp. 14 f.; Coombe, *Anderson's Origin of Commerce*, I, Introduction, p. xxix; Erasmus Philips, *Miscellaneous Works* (1751), pp. 34 f., 38 f.

[154]*The Craftsman* (London, 1731-7), IV, 53.

dents: other Nations may get in, and carry Commodities, that may be preferred to ours; or by working cheaper, may be able to undersell us there; But in our own Plantations nothing of this can happen.[155]

That from the nature of this [colonial] trade, consisting of British manufactures, and all of them tending to lessen our dependence on neighbouring states, it must be deemed of the highest importance in the commercial system of this nation.[156]

The view of trade in general, as well as of manufactures in particular, terminates in securing an extensive and permanent vent; or to speak more precisely, (in the same manner as shop-keeping does) in having many and good customers: the wisdom, therefore, of a trading nation, is to gain, and to create, as many as possible. Those whom we gain in foreign trade, we possess under restrictions and difficulties, and many lose in the rivalship of commerce: those that a trading nation can create within itself, it deals with under its own regulations, and makes its own, and cannot lose.[157]

General Oglethorp severely criticized reliance on precarious foreign markets:

Thus the British empire has a natural wealth in itself and its dependent members; but it has also for many years past enjoyed an adventitious, or artificial traffic. We have been employed by all the world in the wollen manufacture, but other nations have begun of late to clothe themselves and their neighbours too.... We feel this trade decreasing daily; and yet there are those among us who argue against demonstration. But when they hope, by any laws of Great Britain to hinder foreign nations from falling into the wollen manufacture, they may as well solicit an act of parliament to prevent their grass to grow, and to intercept their sunshine.[158]

Oglethorp expressed strong preference for the promising "natural" trade with the colonies as against the "artificial traffic" with foreign countries.[159] Defoe likewise was much in favour of safeguarding and expanding Britain's "sole markets" in the colonies. Pointing to the precariousness of foreign markets, he declared:

But that a full Answer may be given to all they can say of what Loss we yet suffer, and to all they can suggest of what we may suffer hereafter; this work is calculated, to shew how we may counteract it all at once: Namely, by improving and encreasing our Trade in other Places where those Prohibitions and Imitations cannot reach, and where, if half Europe should drop our Manufacture, ... we shall raise an equivalent Vent for our Goods, and make Markets of our own; in which the whole World could not supplant us, unless they could subdue us ... and we have Room enough: The World is wide: There are new Countries, and new Nations, who may be so planted, so

---

[155] *Gentleman's Magazine*, IX (1739), 32.

[156] "The History of Europe," *Annual Register*, IX (1766), 35.

[157] Thomas Pownall, *The Administration of the Colonies* (4th ed.; London, 1768), p. 38.

[158] *A New and Accurate Account of South Carolina and Georgia*, p. 76.

[159] *Ibid.*, pp. 76 f.

improv'd, and the People so manag'd, as to create a new Commerce; and Millions of People shall call for our Manufacture, who never call'd for it before.[160]

New planting Colonies then, and farther improving those already settled, will effectually encrease this Improvement.... Clothing new Nations cannot fail of encreasing the Demand of Goods, because it encreases the Consumption....[161]

The general tenor of the above passages is obvious. In consequence of keen competition and protectionist practices, European markets had become increasingly precarious and the mother country found in the "natural" market of the plantations (as contrasted with the "artificial" trade in Europe) a dependable and permanent outlet for its manufactures. There the metropolis would enjoy a monopolist position and could be without fear of being undersold by rival nations. Instead of competing in the contracting European market, England would "create" and "make" exclusive markets overseas and in order to get the business of "clothing new Nations" it would be expedient even to increase this colonial market by territorial expansion.

From this point of view the introduction of a large number of negro slaves into the American colonies was extremely welcome because, instead of their scanty African habiliments, they would be wearing cloths or rags of English make. Sir Matthew Decker, for example, pointed out: "... there must be a large Importation of Negroes to raise these Growths in our Plantations, and of our Cloathing accordingly ... may not this be said to be transplanting of Men for our Benefit, by taking them from one Climate, where by its heat they want no Cloathing, and carrying them to another where they cannot live without, nor be supplied by any but ourselves? and there is Land enough in our Plantations to employ a greater Number of Slaves, than we can supply with our Manufactures...."[162] Similarly Defoe remarked that "nothing is to me more evident, than that the civilising of Nations where we and other Europeans are already settled; bringing the naked Savages to Clothe, and instructing barbarous Nations how to live, has had a visible Effect already, in this very Article."[163] No matter whether the African was to be civilized or simply transported to American slave-owners, to cover his "barbarous" nakedness with English

[160]Daniel Defoe, *A Plan for the English Commerce*, Preface, p. xi.
[161]*Ibid.*, p. xii.
[162]*Essay on the Causes of the Decline of Foreign Trade* (1751), p. 178.
[163]*A Plan for the English Commerce*, Preface, p. xi.

cloth was regarded a lucrative business and seemed to promise lasting prosperity to the woollen industry.

The colonial market was highly valued also because the natural increase of the colonial population anticipated by the English promised an expanding future outlet for their manufactured articles. Wood remarked, "If we take care to preserve them from Foreign Insults and Invasions, They will, as They encrease in People, probably, consume much more of our Manufactures, than at present They do; tho' They now give Employment to many Thousands of Artificers at Home."[164] And Governor Wentworth congratulated Pitt on the conquest of Canada because it "must be of inestimable Value to Great Brittain, as the peopling of this Continent, cannot fail of Creating a full Employ for the Manufactures of our Mother Country...."[165]

That the mother country could find an outlet for inferior goods, not marketable in Europe was a minor argument, offered by a few writers. Pollexfen, referring to the African trade, which depended on the American colonies, pointed out that it "Carries for us great quantities of our Draperies made from our Coursest Wooll, which could not be vended elsewhere...."[166] Gee, speaking of the cloths exported to the New England colonies, likewise observed that "any ordinary sort sells with them; and when they are grown out of fashion with us, they are new fashioned enough there...."[167]

But English manufactures were sent to the colonies not only for reasons of profit. To provide them with a sufficient quantity of manufactures was also regarded necessary in order to keep them from setting up their own manufacturing industries. Some writers, therefore, suggested that the mother country had better not exploit its monopoly to the limit but keep the colonists supplied with plenty of cheap manufactured goods. Sir William Keith, for instance, remarked that the object of preventing the colonies from establishing manufacturing industries could not, in the long run, be achieved with the help of "Penal Laws, Prohibitions, and suchlike Severities" but rather by taking "due Care that the Colonies be always plentifully supply'd with British Cloths, and other European Commodities, at a much cheaper Rate than it is possible for them to raise and manufacture such Things within them-

[164] *A Survey of Trade* (1718), p. 132.
[165] Letter written to Pitt on October 19, 1760. Quoted in G. S. Kimball (ed.), *Correspondence of William Pitt with Colonial Governors* (New York, 1906), II, 343.
[166] *A Discourse of Trade, Coyn, and Paper Credit* (1697), p. 129.
[167] *The Trade and Navigation of Great Britain* (1731), p. 171.

selves."[168] Henry Home supported this idea of discouraging the establishment of colonial manufacturing industries by sending cheap supplies. He therefore opposed the imposition of export duties and advocated their replacement by export bounties: "The exportation of British manufactures to our American colonies ought to meet with such encouragement as to prevent them from rivalling us: it would be a gross blunder to encourage their manufactures, by imposing a duty on what we export to them. . . . We ought rather to give a bounty on exportation; which, by underselling them in their own markets, would quash every attempt to rivalship."[169]

However precarious these writers judged the foreign markets of Europe to be, it is notable that the majority exhibited much anxiety about safeguarding the security of the exclusive colonial market against encroachments by the colonists themselves. As demonstrated previously, colonies were expected to produce raw materials that otherwise would have to be imported from abroad. Yet in part they were given this assignment with the view of checking any colonial attempt at producing manufactures competitive with metropolitan commodities.[170] Every such attempt was regarded with jealous watchfulness. Colonies should have no "arts." Postlethwayt declared peremptorily that "it is a law founded on the very nature of colonies, that they ought to have no culture or arts."[171] In this respect, the Northern American plantations were viewed with a great deal of suspicion. It was apprehended that they might try not only to provide themselves with their own manufactured articles but also to rival the mother country in the other colonies. Thus, Davenant wrote: "'Tis true, if in New-England, or in other Parts there, they would pretend to set up Manufactures, and to cloath, as well as feed their Neighbours, their Nearness and low Price, would give 'em such Advantages over

[168]Keith, *The History of the British Plantations in America* (1738), p. 13.

[169]*Sketches of the History of Man* (Edinburgh, 1774), I, 492. To the knowledge of the present writer, this is the only instance of an English writer suggesting the safeguarding of the colonial market (which was supposed to be a highly profitable outlet for British manufactures) against possible interference on the part of colonial manufacturers by the grant of export bounties.

[170]Cf. *supra*, pp. 92-4.

[171]*Great Britain's Commercial Interest*, I, 153 f. See also, Gee, *The Trade and Navigation of Great Britain* (1731), p. 173; F. J. Hinkhouse, *The Preliminaries of the American Revolution as Seen in the English Press, 1763-1775* (New York, 1926), p. 102.

this Nation, as might prove of pernicious Consequence...."[172] It was partly owing to this deep-rooted fear that the emigration of artisans and manufacturers to the colonies was regarded with strong disapproval. In 1702, Lord Dartmouth, a Commissioner of Trade, delivering an account "of the state of the trade of this Kingdom," said:

We also observe of later years, great numbers of people are enticed over to her Majesty's northern colonies in America . . . which persons, while they were in England, did contribute to the consumption of our woollen manufacture, but, being entertained there, do with the rest of the inhabitants, clothe themselves, children and servants with the woollen manufacture of the product of those countries. And not only so, but divers manufacturers and workmen also are carried over upon specious pretences of a more easy livelihood in those parts. And in this manner those proprietaries do not only clothe themselves with woollen goods, but furnish the same commodity to the more southern plantations, notwithstanding the prohibition in the act of 10 and 11 of his late Majesty. And by their application to this sort of trade, instead of confining themselves to the production of such commodities as are agreeable to the true design and intention of their settlements, they have improved their skill to such an degree, that . . . as good druggets are made in those countries as any in England. . . .[173]

By way of summarizing the above considerations, it may be concluded that, quite apart from the profits exacted by the English trader, the colonies were highly appreciated as a market for British manufactures from which the competition of rival nations could be excluded by law. This outlet would secure to the mother nation an additional volume of employment which, in turn, would provide all the benefits expected therefrom by the mercantilists. Furthermore, it was by means of these exports that England would pay for the raw materials received from the colonies.

In weight this argument was second to none. Compared with the same line of thought expressed during the earlier period already

[172]*Discourses on the Publick Revenues and the Trade of England*, II, 226 f. Some writers were aware of the fact that, with regard to manufactures, production costs obtaining in the American colonies were substantially higher than in the home country. George Grenville, for example, enumerated the items of capital, experience, skill, and "science" and maintained that, in the case of each of these factors, the parent nation enjoyed a definite superiority over the colonies. He concluded: "The Manufactures therefore of Great Britain must on all these Accounts be superior in Quality, and lower in Price than those in America. And the necessary Consequence from the different Circumstances of the two Countries is, that neither can encroach upon the other in the Articles that are particularly adapted to each, without Prejudice to both" (*The Regulations Lately Made Concerning the Colonies* [1765], pp. 64 f.).

[173]Cf. Stock, *Proceedings and Debates*, III, 5. See also, Hinkhouse, *Preliminaries of the American Revolution*, p. 108.

examined,[174] there was no noteworthy modification of the fundamental idea involved. But it can well be argued that in the course of the later period it gained additional weight in the discussion on the utility of colonies.[175]

ANTI-COLONIAL ARGUMENTS, MISGIVINGS, AND DEPRECATIONS

As late as 1774, John Campbell stated with unruffled assuredness that "in our Days the Value, Utility, and Importance of the Colonies in respect to this Island have been by Evidence of Facts put beyond Dispute."[176] This was a masterpiece of over-statement for, although it expressed the conviction of the bulk of articulate public opinion, there existed, and had existed for a long period of time, a minority group holding exactly opposite views. While throughout the period here under consideration this group had been small numerically, after 1765 it was re-enforced by those whom the acrimonious dispute between the North American colonists and the home government had rendered increasingly weary and doubtful.

But apart from these two cross-currents of opinion and sentiment it is necessary to recall that many of those writers who came out in favour of colonies had arrived at their conclusion only after a careful weighing of the advantages and disadvantages incurred by the mother country in consequence of its colonial possessions. Recording assets and liabilities, these writers made up a balance sheet and came to the conclusion that the possession of colonies was good business to the metropolis.

As has been demonstrated before, the two principal debits entered by these authors were, first, that the emigration proceeding from the mother country to the colonies implied an unwelcome drain on the metropolitan population; and, secondly, that some

[174] Cf. *supra*, pp. 56-9.
[175] The present writer cannot confirm the thesis, advanced by G. L. Beer (*British Colonial Policy, 1754-1765* [New York, 1907], pp. 135 ff.), that a major shift in appraising the value of the colonies occurred approximately in the year 1745. While before that time, Professor Beer asserts, emphasis was put on the plantations as areas producing useful raw materials and colonial staples, thereafter they were mainly valued as markets for metropolitan manufactures. Professor Beer's conclusions are mainly based on a careful analysis of the debate preceding the Peace of Paris of 1763 (*ibid.*, pp. 139 ff.). The present writer is of the opinion that before and following 1745 the colonies were highly appreciated as outlets for British manufactures.
[176] John Campbell, *A Political Survey of Britain* (London, 1774), II, 565.

of the American colonies failed to fulfil their function of producing raw materials non-competitive with those raised in Great Britain. However, in each case these critics were able to point to compensating advantages of sufficient counterweight. Still they stood ready to admit that the steady influx of these countervailing benefits hinged squarely on the strict observance and maintenance of regulatory laws imposed by the mother country.[177] Charles Davenant, for example, said expressly: "'Tis true, if a Breach in the Navigation-Act be conniv'd at, even our own Plantations may become more profitable to our Neighbours, than to us...."[178] "Colonies are a Strength to their Mother Kingdom, while they are under good Discipline, while they are strictly made to observe the Fundamental Laws of their Original Country, and while they are kept dependent on it. But otherwise, they are worse than Members lopp'd from the Body Politick...."[179]

From the same premises derived reflections inimical to the expansion of the colonial empire or even favouring contraction of its territorial extent. Thus, Davenant observed:

It cannot be for the Publick Good of a Kingdom, to furnish Colonies out of it with People, when the Product of such Colonies, is the same with the Kingdom's, and so rivals the Kingdom.... It can hardly be the interest of a Country, to suffer it's People to make Settlements of several Plantations, that yield one and the same Commodity.... As many Empires have been ruin'd by too much enlarging their Dominions, and by grasping at too great an Extent of Territory, so our Interest in America may decay, by aiming at more Provinces, and a greater Tract of Land, than we can either cultivate or defend. Upon which Accompt, it may perhaps be sometime or other worth the Consideration of the State, whether a Way may not be proposed of collecting within a narrower Compass, the scatter'd Inhabitants of the Continent, by inviting some to cultivate the Islands where their Labour is certainly most profitable to this Kingdom, and by drawing the rest, if possible, to four or five of the Provinces best situate and most productive of Commodities, not to be had in Europe....[180]

Reynell likewise remarked: "Concerning our Plantations in America, the Southern Plantations are the most advantageous to us; and it were well hereafter we planted no more behither Jamaica, but settled and removed, if possible, rather our Northern Colonies

[177]The problem of the Navigation Laws will be discussed in the following chapter.

[178]*Discourses on the Publick Revenues and the Trade of England*, II, 204.

[179]*Ibid.*, II, 208; without acknowledgment, Postlethwayt copied this passage almost verbatim (*Dictionary*, "Colonies").

[180]*Ibid.*, II, 232 f.

more forward...."[181] "It concerns the English to Plant and fix Colonies, only in the chiefest and most considerable fastnesses for Trade and Design: and not waste men in large and unprofitable Territories...."[182] For the same reason Sir William Petty suggested the transport of the New Englanders to Ireland.[183] Oliver Goldsmith declared that "an acquisition of new colonies is useless, unless they are peopled."[184] Another writer asserted that "we have ... more territory than we can people."[185]

Some mercantilist writers also applied their notions of the desirability of a dense population rather than large extent of territory to the colonies. Postlethwayt, for example, argued that populous colonies are more valuable than extensive ones because "numbers of men are to be preferred to the largeness of dominions."[186]

The above declarations against excessive colonial expansion and demand for territorial contraction, coupled with the resettlement of colonists, were mainly prompted by the idea that the emigration of people to the colonies was justifiable only if the area of their destination ensured precisely those economic returns which were desired by the mother country. Some authors, in addition, mentioned the fact that the burden of imperial defence increases in direct proportion to the extent of colonial territory whereas it is diminished in inverse proportion to its populousness. Thus Davenant argued: "For Inhabitants thus dispers'd, are neither so useful to each other in time of Peace, nor strong enough to defend themselves in times of War: So that their Mother Kingdom is usually at a great Charge for their defence, whereas if they lay in a more compact, and less extended Territory, they could be more ready to give each other mutual Help, and not be expos'd,

[181]*The True English Interest* (1679), pp. 90 f.
[182]*Ibid.*, p. 88.
[183]*Political Arithmetick* (1690), in *Economic Writings*, I, 300 f.
[184]Oliver Goldsmith, "Thoughts upon the Present Situation of Affairs," in R. S. Crane (ed.), *New Essays by Oliver Goldsmith* (Chicago, 1927), p. 95.
[185]*Arguments against a Spanish War* (London, 1762), p. 35. See also [Cato], *Thoughts on a Question of Importance Proposed to the Public, Whether it is Probable that the Immense Extent of Territory Acquired by this Nation at the Late Peace, will Operate towards the Prosperity, or the Ruin of the Island of Great Britain?* (London, 1765), pp. 12-20.
[186]*Dictionary*, "Colonies." Some of the statements quoted on the preceding page must likewise be interpreted in this sense. Sir William Petty (*Political Arithmetick* [1690], pp. 300 f.) already anticipated Wakefield's principle of the concentration of colonial populations as such concentration would stimulate the building of roads, canals, schoolhouses, etc. W. Burke dismissed inland

as they are, to every little Strength, and Insult of an Invader."[187] Such considerations were bound to lead to the inference that "dominion often becomes more feeble as it grows more extensive."[188]

Owing to this hostility against unlimited expansion, many writers and statesmen abhorred the settlement of the vast hinterland of the North American plantations. Oliver Goldsmith wrote: ". . . but to people those desarts that lie behind our present colonies, would require multitudes from the mother-country; and I do not find that we are too populous at home. All that are willing or able to work in England . . . . can live happy, and those who are neither able nor willing, would starve on the banks of the Ohio, as well as in the streets of St. Giles's. . . ."[189] After the conclusion of the Seven Years' War the Earls of Shelburne[190] and Hillsborough[191] likewise proposed emphatically that the English refrain from settling the territories west of the Appalachian Mountains and confine themselves to the coastal regions.[192] Mildmay concurred in this opinion and mentioned as an additional reason for it that littoral colonies are on principle more valuable to the metropolis than inland settlements: ". . . the enlargement of our inland

---

expansion of the continental colonies as useless partly because increasing transportation cost would render anything but subsistence farming commercially unprofitable (*An Examination of the Commercial Principles of the Late Negotiation, between Great Britain and France in 1761* [London, 1762], p. 72). Similarly *Thoughts on a Question of Importance Proposed to the Public* (1765), pp. 16-21.

[187]Davenant, *Discourses on the Publick Revenues and the Trade of England*, II, 232 f.; similarly, Petty, *Political Arithmetick*, pp. 298 f.

[188]Oliver Goldsmith, in Crane, *New Essays by Oliver Goldsmith*, p. 92. Charles Davenant examined the phenomenon of immoderate expansion on general grounds ("An Essay upon Universal Monarchy," *Essays* [London, 1701]). This essay, it must be admitted, was directed against French expansionism. He fulminated against those "irregular and bad Appetites" that "know no End" (*ibid.*, p. 234), and against "desires to add Dominion to Dominion" (*ibid.*, p. 235). He claimed that "Commonwealths, well founded, would be Eternal, if they could contain themselves within a reasonable Extent of Territory" (*ibid.*). He deplored that "the Ambitious Part of Mankind have hunted after this Game for near four thousand years, with short Intermissions and breathing whiles" and held that this obnoxious drive was facilitated by the fact that people "have given wrong Names to Things, and have allotted to Vice the Stamps and Attributes of Virtue" (*ibid.*, p. 236).

[189]Oliver Goldsmith, in Crane, *New Essays by Oliver Goldsmith*, p. 95.

[190]Lord Edmund Fitzmaurice, *Life of William, Earl of Shelburne* (London, 1875), I, 261 f.

[191]W. Knox, *Extraofficial State Papers*, II, 43 f.

[192]Such restraint was strongly advocated by the great landowners in the colonies because the value of their unsettled lands could be expected to rise if the vast empty territories to the West would not be tapped. Cf. *ibid.*, p. 44.

acquisitions should be attended with an enlargement of our navigation, so much the less shall we be able to protect them, or they deserve our protection . . . after all, those continental acquisitions should not be so much the object of our conquest, as other maritime territories which may encrease our navigation as well as commerce. . . ."[193] Thomas Pownall, referring to projects of settling the American hinterland, even spoke of "this ambitious folly of dominion" and pointed out the "enormous endless expence" which such a policy would entail due to the necessity of maintaining forts and garrisons in those vast areas.[194] It must be inferred from all these statements that even those writers who, on the whole, praised the value of colonies to the mother country saw themselves obliged to insert certain qualifications and to caution against the drawbacks of over-expansion.

Israel Mauduit, discussing the much-vaunted advantages of colonies, said that "as Colonies increase, this Advantage must be increasing."[195] It must be emphasized, however, that statements connoting such unqualified optimism were relatively rare at this phase of the discussion on the utility of plantations. As a matter of fact, if the annals of the time from the middle of the eighteenth century to the end of the period here considered are carefully scanned, deprecatory expressions with regard to the English predilection for colonial conquest are frequently discovered.[196]

[193] *The Laws and Policy of England* (1765), p. 88.
[194] *The Administration of the Colonies* (1768), p. 265.
[195] Israel Mauduit, *Some Thoughts on the Method of Improving and Securing the Advantages which Accrue to Great-Britain from the Northern Colonies* (London, 1765), p. 11.
[196] To give a few examples: During the peace negotiations of 1761 the Duke of Bedford wrote to Pitt, urging him to desist from his endless plans of conquest: ". . . if we retain the greatest part of our conquests out of Europe we shall be in danger of Over-colonizing and undoing ourselves by them as the Spaniards have done" (quoted by W. E. H. Lecky, *A History of England in the Eighteenth Century* [new ed.; New York, 1892], III, 207). Rigby wrote similarly: "While we succeed . . . the fire is kept constantly fanned. For my own part I am so convinced of the destruction which must follow the continuance of the war, that I should not be sorry to hear that Martinico or the next windmill you attack should get the better of you" (quoted in *ibid.*, p. 208). Most characteristic of this attitude of mind is the following passage written by an anonymous author: "There is one thing, sirs . . . which your enemies have . . . taken care to forget. I mean the important conquest of the Isle of Aix; yes, sirs, I call it important, because we acquired by it not only an immense number of war-like stores; but, I am told, some household effects of the inhabitants; a part of the priest's library, and many, very many, bunches of grapes" (*A Consolatory Epistle to the Members of the Old Faction Occasioned by the Spanish War* [2d ed.; London, 1762], p. 41).

Of those mercantilists who thought the possession of colonies a disadvantage to the mother country, the author of *Britannia Languens* serves as an instructive example.[197] He was ready to blame on the plantations all the evils from which England suffered at the time: "Nay, these Plantations may be considered as the true Grounds and Causes of all our Present Mischiefs."[198] His foremost complaint was that they drained the population of Great Britain: "Our Plantation-Trade hath robbed and prevented us of some Millions of our People; amongst which very many being, or might have been Manufacturers, the Nation hath also lost more Millions of Pounds in the loss of their Manufactures."[199] Slingsby Bethel wrote: "Whereas England wanting neither Havens nor Ports, nor having an over-plus of people, it would be a damage to them in the loss of their inhabitants, and unprofitable Charge to maintain Foreign Colonies, where the Seas must be perpetually crossed for supplying them Men, Money, and necessaries...."[200] Similarly Roger Coke: "The peopling of the American Plantations subject to the Crown of England, hath diminished the strength of England...."[201] "The peopling ... and the re-peopling of Ireland, have endangered the Crown, Church, Wealth, Lands, Liberty, Trade, and Glory of England."[202]

Writers like Davenant had maintained that the "super-lucration" produced by emigrants put to work on the fertile soils of the colonies and employing slave labour would create a vent for English manufactures which would have been lacking, had they stayed at home.[203] The author of *Britannia Languens*, on the other hand, denied the truth of this supposition. He asserted:

Then for the supposed advantage we have in the Vent of our home-Commodities to the Plantations, 'tis plain they are but our own People; and it must be undeniable, that had the same People stayed in England, they would have taken off a far greater Quantity; for whereas we now furnish them with some small part of their Victuals, we should then have supplyed them with All, viz. with Bread, Flesh, Fish, Roots, &c. which now we do

---

[197]There were not many English writers during the period in question who straightforwardly discounted the value of colonies. Some like Dudley North and Jacob Vanderlint were clearly against colonies but did not discuss the subject (North's arguments against the Navigation Laws will be presented below). The last portion of this sub-chapter will be devoted to Josiah Tucker.

[198]*Britannia Languens* (1680), p. 132.   [199]*Ibid.*, p. 88.

[200]Slingsby Bethel, *The Interest of the Princes and States of Europe* (2d ed.; London, 1681), p. 70.

[201]Roger Coke, *A Treatise* (London, 1671), p. 26.

[202]*Ibid.*, p. 33.

[203]*Discourses on the Publick Revenues and the Trade of England*, II, 223 f.

not; and they would have taken off far more of our Butter, Cheese, Cloathing, Drink, and other home Commodities, when they had them at hand, and had been put to no other shifts. . . .²⁰⁴

Thus this author rejected the argument that the colonies provided the mother country with an additional market. Apparently making no distinction between manufactures and foodstuffs, the plantations had, in his reasoning, reduced the market for English goods. Equally negative was his opinion of the plantations as raw-materials-producing areas. He said:

All the Gain England can or ever could receive by this Trade, must be in the Return and Result of those Commodities we import from the Plantations, (viz. Sugars, Tobaccoes, Dying Stuffs, &c) in Exchange for so much of our Butter, Cheese, Woollen Cloaths, Hats, Shoes, Iron-work, and other home-Commodities as we Export thither,—Now that the Labours of the same People in Fishing or Manufactures at home did, and would have produced a greater Profit to the Nation than these Plantation-Commodities, I think no man, . . . can so much as make a question. In fact our Fishing for White Herring and Cod was deserted for this Trade, and the Continual transplanting of multitudes of our Manufacturers and other people, hath inevitably more and more sunk and disabled us in all Manufactures and home-Employments.²⁰⁵

Here he explained that, had the colonists stayed in England, they (and presumably their descendants) would have produced goods of greater value to Britain than they did in the oversea plantations. He maintained, therefore, that colonization had caused English productive capacity to be directed into channels of comparatively inferior profitableness to the nation.

The author of *Britannia Languens* held the existence of colonies responsible also for the extremely complicated system of duties and regulations under which England laboured: "Certainly it was very unfortunate for England, That when Sir Walter Raleigh wrote these . . . Observations on Trades, our Councels were under the earnest pursuit of the Plantation-Trade, on which great Customs were projected; for so it hath hapned, that whilst our Neighbour Nations have been vigilant to ease and Facilitate their ways of Trade, the Trade of England hath continued under the former disadvantage, and is incumbred with new charges and difficulties of later years. . . ."²⁰⁶ Nor would he grant that the plantation trade assisted England in securing a favourable balance of trade with foreign nations: ". . . nothing of this is to the present question, being only, whether it hath advantaged the Nation in its Annual

²⁰⁴*Britannia Languens*, pp. 130 f.   ²⁰⁵*Ibid.*, p. 130.
²⁰⁶*Ibid.*, p. 88.   Similarly, Coke, *A Treatise* (1671), pp. 36 ff., 87.

Gain of Treasure; which I conceive this Trade hath not, if ballanced with the losses the Nation hath received by it."[207]

Although this author admitted that "this Trade hath imployed a good number of Ships,"[208] he asserted on the other hand that, because of the plantations, the English lost part of their shipping engaged in the fisheries and complained that the colonial ship-builders and ship-owners competed with and reduced the business conducted by the metropolitan shipping industry. "I shall add, That we have little reason to boast of our Navigation in this Trade, when it was the occasion of the loss of a more certain and beneficial Nursery of Seamen and Shipping in our Fishery, when at the same time the Strength and Business of the Nation have been so much contracted by the loss of our People, when our Planters of New England having gotten a considerable Navigation of their own, do Trade from Port to Port in America, and have in a manner beaten us out of that kind of Imployment in those Parts. . . ."[209]

Finally, he mentioned a point which was to become of great importance in the early nineteenth-century argumentation against the value of colonies. He pointed out that in the case of the re-exportation of colonial goods a drawback of half the customs duty, collected on their importation into England, was granted and that, hence, ". . . the Dutch coming to be furnished with our Sugars and Dying Stuffs much cheaper than the English, have been by that means able to set up and beat us out of the Forreign Trade of baked Sugars, of which they bake and vend above 20 times the quantity the English do; so do they now use far the greatest part of our Dying Stuffs gaining near as much, if not more, by these Manufactures than the raw materials yield to the English."[210] Thus, the author of *Britannia Languens* deplored the fact that the colonial trade "makes such a great noise amongst us."[211] He was convinced that this trade "ought to be reckoned amongst the defalcations of our present Trade,"[212] and he crowned his gloomy analysis by predicting that it "must grow worse and worse Continually."[213]

Interestingly enough he did not say that England, without colonies of her own, would be able to purchase colonial products more cheaply than she could being in possession of plantations. This possibility was realized by Roger Coke who declared that the British could not expect "any great benefit from the Trade to our

[207] *Ibid.*, p. 130. [208] *Ibid.* [209] *Ibid.*, pp. 131 f.
[210] *Ibid.*, p. 131. [211] *Ibid.*, p. 130. [212] *Ibid.*, p. 131.
[213] *Ibid.*

Plantations for Tobaccoes and Sugars," as the Dutch would be able to furnish them with these commodities much more cheaply than the English colonists.[214]

One author perceived a disadvantage in the very fact that the colonial market was exclusively open to the mother country. He apprehended that this monopoly "will be, nay probably it has been, a Temptation to us not to make our Manufactures as good and as cheap as possible to procure voluntary Purchasers, because we think we can send them to those who are obliged to take them."[215] Hence, by discouraging efficiency in English export industries, Britain's competitive position in the international market was seriously impaired: ". . . if the Ballance be against us with other Nations, it is probable our Plantations themselves are the Cause of it, by shewing us an easy Way of making a considerable Profit, so that we are not at so great Pains to work as well and as cheap, and as much, as our Neighbours about us."[216]

Regarding the substitution of colonial for Baltic timber the English Navy Board exhibited a consistent antipathy to colonial supplies which they held to be of considerably inferior quality in comparison with English and Baltic materials.[217] In view of this, it is surprising that those writers, who looked with disfavour on colonies, should not have seized upon this opportunity to disparage one argument which was constantly used as a proof of the utility of plantations. Only Horsley, who otherwise praised the value of colonies, observed: ". . . tho I should be very cautious of hurting our own Plantation Produce, I am afraid our New England Masts are not so good as the Gottenburgh. . . ."[218]

Horsley also was outstanding in criticizing the idea that maritime commerce served as an all-important nursery of seamen. This expectation found expression in the imperial navigation system that regulated the water-borne trade between colonies and metropolis. Horsley, however, observed that "this odd Way of raising

[214]Coke, *A Treatise* (1671), p. 87.
[215]*Thoughts on a Question of Importance Proposed to the Public* (1765), p. 27.
[216]*Ibid.*, p. 29.
[217]Cf. R. G. Albion, *Forests and Sea Power* (Cambridge, Mass., 1926), pp. 39 ff., 95, 240 f. With very few exceptions, indeed, the Royal Navy made no use of colonial timber after the Seven Years' War (*ibid.*, p. 244).
[218]*A Treatise on Maritime Affairs* (London, 1744), p. 8. George Berkeley suggested that it would be "in vain" to expect sufficient supplies of hemp for the navy from the American colonies. However, he proposed that this product might be raised in Ireland instead (*The Querist* [1735-7], in A. C. Fraser [ed.], *The Works of George Berkeley* [Oxford, 1871], III, 262).

Seamen" was really hurtful to commerce and, besides, did by no means provide the Royal Navy with adequately trained crews.[219]

It is likewise surprising that during the period in question very few English writers criticized the appointments to colonial governorships and similar posts because these constituted a considerable volume of patronage at the disposal of the English ruling groups.[220]

It has been pointed out previously that, after the termination of the Seven Years' War, the incessant disputes between metropolitan authorities and the North American colonists evoked among many Englishmen serious misgivings and doubts in regard to the value of colonial possessions. This kind of reaction to the contumacious conduct of the colonists was apt to add to the incisiveness of anti-colonial arguments.[221]

This development deepened already existing apprehensions regarding the permanency of the imperial connection with the North American colonies. Davenant already had discussed this problem at some length. He thought that "Corrupt Governors, by oppressing the inhabitants, may hereafter provoke 'em [the plantations] to withdraw their Obedience, and by supine Negligence, or upon mistaken Measures, we may let 'em grow . . . in Naval Strength, and Power, which if suffer'd we cannot expect to hold 'em long in our Subjection."[222]

---

[219] He argued that this method only handicapped commerce because as soon as war started, indispensable sailors were requisitioned for the navy. On the other hand, he thought that the fighting value of the crews of naval vessels would be much more enhanced if men-of-war were partly manned by "well disciplin'd Land-men" who "make better Musqueteers than Seamen" do (*ibid.*, pp. 14 ff.). Thus Horsley realized the gradual development which changed the ratio between sailors and fighting technicians in favour of the latter.

[220] Sir William Keith once remarked that "the sending over of Men of high Rank and Quality to be Governors in the Plantations, in order chiefly to repair, in a short time, their broken and decay'd Fortunes, has often been attended with very bad Consequences..." (*The History of the British Plantations in America*, p. 184). Bolingbroke, no doubt for reasons of party polemics, made similar accusations (*The Craftsman*, IX, 264 ff.). Yet this argument was never, to the knowledge of the present writer, exploited by those authors who attacked the majority opinion on the utility of colonies.

[221] Cf. Hinkhouse, *Preliminaries of the American Revolution*, p. 104.

[222] *Discourses on the Publick Revenues and the Trade of England*, II, 204 f. Davenant recommended that the North American colonies be not permitted to build men-of-war: "... we may teach 'em an Art which will cost us some Blows to make 'em forget. Some such Courses may indeed drive 'em, or put in their Heads, to erect themselves into Independent Commonwealths" (*ibid.*, p. 205). "Wise Countries never teach their Colonies the Art of War..." (*ibid.*, p. 208).

Towards the end of the Seven Years' War, some writers, participating in the discussion on the preferableness of retaining either Canada or Guadeloupe, suggested that the major portion of Canada be handed back to the French because their menacing presence on the North American continent would keep the English colonists from striving for independence.[223] During the late sixties and seventies of the eighteenth century these fears spread considerably.[224] In 1768, a rumour circulated to the effect ". . . that a Negotiation is on the Tapis for Restoring Canada to France in return for one of their Sugar Islands, as the most effectual means of securing the Dependence of America on the Mother Country."[225] Some observers were alarmed by the rapid increase of the colonial population.[226] One writer was afraid of the colonial population surpassing in numbers that of the mother country and apprehended that some day New York might be to London what Byzantum had been to Rome.[227]

Another source of grief was represented by doubts whether the North American colonists could be kept from establishing manufacturing industries rivalling those of the mother country. Already in 1738 an anonymous writer had denied that the colonies could be forever kept in line with imperial policy in this respect.[228] During the years leading up to the American War of Independence, this feeling of jealousy became increasingly bitter.[229] One writer, in

[223]"The History of the Present War," *Annual Register*, V (1762), 58 f.
[224]See Hinkhouse, *Preliminaries of the American Revolution*, pp. 104 f.
[225]Quoted, *ibid.*, p. 105.   [226]*Ibid.*, p. 106.
[227]Cf. *ibid.*, p. 107. Another writer, convinced that England would be unable to hold the American colonies in subjection for any length of time suggested a very drastic solution to the problem. "Perhaps the true politicks of the time would be to dispeople Britain at one stroke, and send them over to America, with their arts, manufactures, agriculture, implements, riches, spirit, manners, and government . . . that the thing is possible cannot be doubted . . . a country where there is ten times more land than all could want, with a united people of twenty millions for employing arts, manufactures, and commerce, would in that country at once form an empire, very different from one consisting of ten on one side of the ocean, and ten on the other" ([Arthur Young], *Letters Concerning the Present State of England* [London, 1772], pp. 69 f.). As an alternative this writer proposed that the King reside "much in America, leaving a regency in England, and thereby draw over as many people as possible. . ." (*ibid.*, p. 70).
[228]*Reflections and Considerations Occasioned by the Petition Presented to the Honourable House of Commons, for Taking off the Drawback on Foreign Linens, &c.* (London, 1738), pp. 15 f.
[229]On expressions of this attitude, see Hinkhouse, *Preliminaries of the American Revolution*, p. 106.

the *St. James's Chronicle* of February 23, 1769, remarked that ". . . a Colony, incapable of producing any other commodities than those produced by its Mother Country, would be more dangerous than useful; it would be proper to call home its inhabitants and give it up. . . . This maxim cannot be contested."[230]

Considering this state of feeling it is not surprising that some of these disillusioned writers were prepared to give up the American colonies. In the *Public Advertiser* of September 17, 1768, appeared the suggestion to "cut America off."[231] Another paragrapher proposed to sell the colonies to France, the "Grand Turk," and the Dey of Algiers and "if his Infernal Highness the Devil would continue to exercise his Sovereign Power over the Bostonian Saints, to let him have them on his own terms."[232]

A few writers expected England to gain from cutting off the North American colonies. It was observed that the mother country would save in military expenditures and in bounties which would no longer have to be paid on colonial products.[233] Others pointed out that the benefits accruing to England from the possession of colonies would survive separation. Thus, one writer declared in the *St. James's Chronicle* of November 12, 1774: "Every commercial advantage to both countries may be much better secured by treaty under such separation, than by dragooning the colonists into subjection."[234]

[230]Quoted, *ibid.*, p. 102.
[231]*Ibid.*, p. 114.
[232]Quoted, *ibid.*, p. 105.
[233]Cf. *ibid.*, p. 114.
[234]Quoted, *ibid.*, p. 115. David Hume likewise thought that the English "should preserve the greater part of this Trade even if the Ports of America were open to all Nations. . ." (Letter to Strahan of October 26, 1775. Cf. J. Y. T. Greig [ed.], *The Letters of David Hume* [Oxford, 1932], II, 300). In the same letter Hume welcomed a rumour according to which the Fleet and Army would be withdrawn from America. He wrote, "I wish I had been a Member of His Majesty's Cabinet Council, that I might have seconded this Opinion. I should have said, that this Measure only anticipates the necessary Course of Events a few Years; that a forced and every day more precarious Monopoly of about 6 or 700,000 Pounds a year of Manufactures, was not worth contending for. . ." (*ibid.*). Hume saw the coming of the American Revolution. If he was opposed to any attempt at coercing the Americans into submission and even welcomed separation, he was not only inspired by his superior insight into the economic relations between colonies and mother country. Already on July 22, 1768, he had written to Sir Gilbert Elliot: "There are fine doings in America. O, how I long to see America and the East Indies revolted, totally and finally; in the revenue reduced to half,—public credit fully discredited by bankruptcy,—the third of London in ruins, and the rascally mob subdued" (*ibid.*, II, 184). There is no doubt that expressions like these were dictated by Hume's at times profound hatred of "the barbarians who inhabit the banks of the Thames" (*ibid.*, I, 436).

It must be recognized, however, that a great many of these gloomy considerations were the consequence of resignation and despair over dealing with a refractory people, rather than the fruit of dispassionate reasoning. Furthermore, it is important to note that even during the last years anterior to the outbreak of the American War of Independence, the described current of metropolitan opinion, although gaining in breadth, represented a decidedly small minority.[235]

This review of expressions of disbelief in the value of a colonial empire to the mother country may be closed with quoting a remark of George Blewitt. He sharply censured the worship of expanding dominions and utterly denied that such expansion could in any respect augment the happiness of the individual in the parent state.

... the Happiness of a Community is nothing but the Happiness of the private Individuals who compose it. ... If we are to judge by this Test of the Use that new Acquisitions of Territories are to a Society, they will be far from serving the Purposes of the Author. Are private Men the more happy or the more wealthy, because their Sovereign has the Glory to be a Conqueror? It is not the Grandeur of the Prince, that makes them rich. New Provinces may be brought or added every Year, and yet the Estates of private Men be not at all enlarg'd by it. ... 'Tis highly absurd to call a Nation happy and flourishing, only because it makes a Figure abroad, and is a Terrour to its Neighbours.[236]

JOSIAH TUCKER AND THE COLONIES

Among those English writers who denied the value of colonies to the mother country, Dean Tucker is singled out for separate treatment because he was the most voluble and most consistent advocate of separation among those who witnessed the preliminaries to and the eventual consummation of American independence. Tucker's views on problems of foreign trade bear the characteristic imprints of the intellectual controversialism of an age of transition. He discarded many of the hackneyed doctrines of mercantilist thought. In 1761, he wrote in a letter to Lord Kames that "war, conquests and colonies are our present system, and mine is just the opposite."[237] He bitterly denounced those whose attitude towards foreign commerce was permeated by a deep-seated feeling of jeal-

[235] The majority of those Englishmen who were in favour of appeasing the American colonists were well convinced of the advantages of a colonial empire to the metropolis. They favoured conciliation because they did not want this empire to be lost.

[236] George Blewitt, *An Enquiry whether a General Practice of Virtue Tends to the Wealth or Poverty, Benefit or Disadvantage of a People?* (London, 1725), pp. 19 f.

[237] Quoted in W. E. Clark, *Josiah Tucker, Economist* (New York, 1903), p. 64.

ousy.[238] Incessantly he claimed that the conduct of international trade was mutually beneficial to all the nations involved.[239] And yet, in other respects, he failed to strip off the shackles of mercantilist reasoning. He remained a believer in the merits of state regulation and intervention in matters of trade and a staunch supporter of protectionism in the form of import duties.[240] It is, therefore, quite correct to say that he was, at bottom, a mercantilist.[241]

In his early days as a pamphleteer, Josiah Tucker upheld the dominant view of the usefulness of colonies to the mother country.[242] The reasons he advanced in support of this opinion were the customary ones. He proposed that naval stores be imported from the American dependencies rather than from foreign countries in order to reduce British dependence "upon the Will and Pleasure of Foreign Courts," and because Britain's "Balance to all these Countries [Sweden, Denmark, Russia] is considerably against us." Hence, "common Prudence will suggest, that we ought to turn it in our Favour if we can. Now this we shall be able to do if we can purchase the same Commodities in our own Plantations."[243] He also appeared very anxious for the preservation of the colonies as a market exclusively open to the mother country[244] and he summed up his conclusions by remarking that "the Trade to our Colonies and Plantations, must appear to be of the utmost Consequence to the Power, Strength, and Prosperity of Great Britain."[245]

Dean Tucker's next tract, privately printed in 1755, already shows a remarkable change of opinion.[246] There he fully endorsed that current of mercantilist theorizing which regarded populousness

---

[238] Josiah Tucker, *Four Tracts* (Glocester, 1774), p. 82.

[239] *Ibid.*, p. 75.

[240] In respect to these doctrinal items he was, indeed, much less advanced than many of his predecessors and contemporaries.

[241] This conclusion is sustained by Clark, *Josiah Tucker, Economist*, pp. 156 ff., 174 f.; and by R. L. Schuyler, *Josiah Tucker* (New York, 1931), p. 13.

[242] Josiah Tucker, *Brief Essay on the Advantages and Disadvantages which respectively attend France and Great Britain with regard to Trade* (2d ed.; London, 1750).

[243] *Ibid.*, p. 93.   [244] *Ibid.*, p. 94.   [245] *Ibid.*, p. 96.

[246] Josiah Tucker, *The Elements of Commerce and Theory of Taxes* (1755), reprinted in Schuyler, *Josiah Tucker*, pp. 55-219. Clark (*Josiah Tucker, Economist*, p. 184) maintained that the ever-increasing controversies between mother country and colonies were instrumental in bringing about Tucker's change of attitude. This was certainly an important contributory factor. However, as evidenced by the above-mentioned book, this change was at least partly the result of insights arrived at quite independently from these bitter disputes.

as the major source of national wealth and power.[247] "Considering the Property of the Marriage Bed, as the Foundation of Civil Society,"[248] he supported various devices designed to increase England's population. It is, therefore, not surprising to find him arguing, in this connection, that "our numerous Colonies . . . are great and continual Drains upon us."[249] In the same work, Tucker also assailed the custom of maintaining fortified trading posts along the coasts of distant countries. He stated: "To what Commercial Uses are these Forts to be applied? If they are in order to plant a colony;—then the having a few Forts, without making farther Settlements, is only being a continual Expence to answer no End. If they are to awe and bridle Natives, It would be difficult to shew, what Advantage can accrue to Trade by insulting and disobliging the People you trade with: And sure I am, that that Shopkeeper would be deemed a strange kind of Creature, who would go and bully all his Customers, in order to bring Custom to his Shop."[250]

In the meantime he had also abandoned the conventional balance-of-trade doctrine,[251] a change which implied the abandonment of the argument that raw materials should be purchased in the colonies rather than in foreign countries in order to improve England's national balance of payments. And yet, the same study contains a great many residues typical of his earlier attitude towards the colonies.[252]

[247]Thus he wrote: "Where a Country is thinly peopled, it is impossible to promote a brisk and general Circulation of Industry and Labour, by reason of the Distance and Dispersion of the People for each other, and the Consequence of that, their Want of Rivalship and Emulation. . . ." (*ibid.*, p. 63).

[248]*Ibid.*, p. 68. [249]*Ibid.*, p. 67.

[250]*Ibid.*, p. 141. He also denied that such forts secured trade against similar activities of rival nations. "Do these Forts prevent other Nations . . . from trading, if they have a mind to trade? Do the English Forts, for Example, prevent the French, or the French the English from trading to India? Not at all. Nay, those European Nations which have not one Fort, find the way to trade as well as others. . . . Moreover, the English themselves have no Forts in China. . ." (*ibid.*).

[251]"If this Bullion, or Coin, is carried out to purchase Raw Materials, for the Imployment of our People, the Trade is good and beneficial to the State, because it creates Industry, and promotes Labour. For Industry and Labour are the only real Riches. Money being merely a Ticket or Sign belonging to them. . ." (*ibid.*, p. 146). This passage reveals that Tucker had switched over from the balance-of-trade doctrine to the balance-of-employment doctrine.

[252]Contrary to later utterances as to his statements on the subject of population, he speaks of Canada as a "Country extremely proper for settling a Colony" (*ibid.*, p. 170) to which the Scottish highlanders might be sent (*ibid.*, p. 172).

Tucker's writings published after the Seven Years' War reveal that his change of mind on the question of colonies had become complete. Henceforth he was untiring in pointing out the disutility of colonial possessions to the metropolis and straightforwardly advocated a policy of separation. Reference to the fact that the plantations supposedly tended to depopulate the mother country remained a stock argument among the various reasons he offered in support of his suggestion. Thus, he stated that "a disjunction from the Northern Colonies would effectually put a Stop in our present Emigrations."[253] He denied that colonies are valuable as exclusive markets to the metropolis. He belittled the quantitative importance of the export trade carried on with the plantations as compared with that carried on with European states.[254] He pointed out that the relative cheapness and the superior quality of British manufactures would secure to them a market in the colonies even after separation from the parent state. Thus, he wrote:

Let us now consider their Imports. And here one Thing is very clear and certain. That whatever Goods ... the Merchants of Great-Britain can sell to the rest of Europe, they might sell the same to the Colonies, if wanted: Because it is evident, that the Colonies could not purchase such Goods, at a cheaper Rate at any European Market.[255]

The very best System (best I mean in Behalf of England) would have been, To have thrown up all foreign Dominions at once;—and to have trusted solely to the Goodness and Cheapness of our Manufacture, and to the long Credit we can give, for procuring them a Vent in these (abdicated) Governments. . . .[256]

The Dean thought that "the Planting of Colonies for a monopolising, or exclusive Trade" is nothing but a "cheat," a "Self-Deception, which poor, short-sighted Mortals ever put upon them-

---

He writes of policies for "improving our Colonies, and extending the Trade between them and the Mother Country to their mutual Advantage" (*ibid.*, p. 214) and he gives a classic formulation of the transportation argument: "The British Nation are in great want of such a Country as Hudson's Bay, for the purpose of disposing of their numerous Convicts and Malefactors in a proper Manner. For this Country ... would effectually answer the same Ends to us, which Siberia does to the Russians..." (*ibid.*, p. 174).

[253] Josiah Tucker, *The True Interest of Great-Britain Set Forth* (1744), in Schuyler, *Josiah Tucker*, p. 214.

[254] Josiah Tucker, *A Letter to Edmund Burke* (1775), reprinted in Schuyler, *Josiah Tucker*, p. 385.

[255] Tucker, *Four Tracts*, p. 216.

[256] Josiah Tucker, *Cui Bono?* (Glocester, 1782), p. 129.

selves."[257] He had no fear that the American colonists might establish manufacturing industries of their own rivalling those of Great Britain.[258] And even if they would actually succeed in producing some manufactures themselves, such would not be detrimental to England. "Daily Experience proves beyond Contradiction, that we do actually send vast Quantities of British Manufactures to Spain, to Italy, Germany, Russia, Holland, and even to France:—Though each of these Countries have long established similar Manufactures of their own, and have laid discouraging Duties on ours."[259]

Josiah Tucker held similarly intelligent views regarding the raw-materials argument. The objection that the loss of the northern American dependencies would entail the loss of a vital source of naval-store supplies, he countered by arguing, first, that the American colonists would be dependent on the British market for these very articles; and secondly that the French, the Dutch, and the Spaniards also had to import these materials and did not possess any "Northern Colonies." "Yet these Nations are supplied with all these Articles at a moderate Price, and without Bounties. What therefore should prevent the English from being supplied from the same Source, and on as good Terms."[260]

[257]Josiah Tucker, *Four Letters on Important National Subjects* (Glocester, 1783), p. 10. However, he added significantly: ". . . at least in a national View: . . . For I am not here considering, and never will consider, the Interests of Individuals, when they are sacrificing the Public Good to their own private Emolument. . ." (*ibid.*).

[258]"In regard to the Capabilities of America to rival Great-Britain in the Cheapness and Goodness of Manufactures . . . be it observed that America naturally labours under many capital Defects respecting Manufactures" (Josiah Tucker, *A Series of Answers to Certain Popular Objections against Separating from the Rebellious Colonies* [Glocester, 1776], pp. 42 ff.).

[259]*Ibid.*, p. 41. As a minor argument Tucker pointed out: "When we are no longer connected with the Colonies by the imaginary Tie of an Identity of Government, then our Merchant Exporters and Manufacturers will have a better Chance of having their Debts paid, than they have at present: For as Matters now stand, the Colonists chuse to carry their ready Cash to other Nations, while they are contracting Debts with their Mother-Country; with whom they think they can take greater Liberties" (Tucker, *Four Tracts*, p. 217). Due to these excessive credits, Tucker said, the trade to these colonies accounted for more bankruptcies and ruined more exporters than "almost every other Export-Trade besides" (Tucker, *A Letter to Edmund Burke*, pp. 386 f.).

[260]Tucker, *A Series of Answers*, p. 32. He also pointed out that "The English Navy receives much greater, and more necessary supplies from the Northern States of Europe than from the Northern Colonies of America" (*ibid.*, p. 33).

With respect to colonial staples, opponents to Tucker's scheme of separation queried: "In Case of a Separation, from whence shall we produce Rice and Tobacco?" The Dean replied with poignancy: "This Objection turns on two Suppositions, viz. I. That after a Separation the Virginians and Carolinians will not sell Tobacco and Rice to English Merchants for a good Price, and ready Money: ....And, 2dly, that Tobacco and Rice can grow in no Part of the Globe, but in Virginia and Carolina. Will any Man in his Senses dare to affirm either of these Things?"[261] This argument would also apply in the case of the West Indian possessions being lost or given up: "... what would be the Consequence?—Nothing but this, that the British Merchants would in that Case buy Sugars, Rum, Ginger, Cotton, &c. &c. just as they now buy Wines, Fruit, Oils, Coffee, Chocolate, &c. &c.; that is, at the best and cheapest Market. And it is a fact well known in the commercial World, that were we permitted to enjoy the like liberty at present, we might purchase Sugars and Rum almost Cent. per Cent. cheaper than we now do, by being confined to the Market of our Sugar Planters.[262]

Thus, Josiah Tucker underlined the self-evident fact that the possession of colonies coupled with the regulations of the "Old Colonial System" had the effect of preventing the mother country from procuring raw materials from the cheapest market. On the other hand, Tucker argued that the encouragement of the production of certain goods in the colonies (by means of bounties, a monopoly in the metropolitan market, or even the prohibition of domestic production) had checked the development of a metropolitan industry in the case of these products. As examples he mentioned tobacco and hemp.[263]

The Dean, moreover, did not refrain from investigating the expenses which the mother country incurred in consequence of maintaining its colonial empire. Thus, he remarked: "Another great Advantage to be derived from a Separation is, that we shall

[261] *Ibid.*, p. 38.

[262] *Ibid.*, p. 20. And he added significantly: "It would also be possible, then, to champion the anti-slavery cause" (*ibid.*, pp. 20 f.).

[263] *Ibid.*, pp. 47 ff. In "A Letter to Edmund Burke" (*ibid.*, p. 393) he wrote: "Two words more about Spain. . . . The first is, that before the Discovery of America, there were upwards of 30,000 Hogsheads of Sugar raised in the Kingdom of Granada; and all raised by free People. . . . Whereas at present there are hardly any. Why? Because Spain has now Sugar Colonies in America. . . . We have, I think, made no less than six Acts of Parliament here in England, on a similar Plan, to prevent the Cultivation of Tobacco, in order to favour the Colony of Virginia."

then save between 3 and 400,000 1. a Year, by being discharged from the Payment of any civil or military Establishments belonging to the Colonies:—For which generous Benefaction we receive at present no other Return than Invectives and Reproachments. . . ."[264] The ceasing of the Payment of Bounties on certain Colony Productions will be another great saving; perhaps not less than 200,000 l. a Year. . . ."[265] He was quite aware of the fact that, to meet these expenses, the metropolis was being taxed for the sake of maintaining an Empire. ". . . if we shall still submit to be fleeced, taxed, and insulted by them, instead of throwing them off, and declaring ourselves to be unconnected with, and independent of them, we shall become (and indeed we are now becoming) a Monument of the Greatest Infatuation."[266] The main items of expense to which Josiah Tucker referred were bounties, defence, and the administrative and governing costs not defrayed by the colonists themselves. With regard to the last item he pointed out the problem of patronage. He observed that part of the national revenue "is, in a Manner, swallowed up in Governments, Guards, and Garrisons, in Salaries and Pensions, and all the consuming Perquisites and Expences attendant on distant Provinces."[267]

Opponents of separation used to ask: "Will not a Separation from the Northern Colonies greatly decrease the Number of our Seamen?" Tucker parried this objection by observing that it cannot be proved "that a Separation will necessarily decrease the Shipping and Navigation belonging to the Ports of Great-Britain and Ireland."[268] In addition, he pointed out that the Navigation Acts, if maintained after separation, would automatically exclude North American shipping from carrying colonial products to Great Britain and Ireland.[269] His best counter-argument, however, was his observation that even if Britain should suffer, "some small Diminution in the Number of its Sailors: Still, even on this Supposition, it doth by no Means follow, that we shall have fewer Ships, or fewer Sailors, than we have at present, for the Defence of our central Territories, Great-Britain and Ireland. On the contrary,

[264]Tucker, *The True Interest of Great-Britain*, p. 216.

[265]*Ibid.*, pp. 216 f.

[266]Josiah Tucker, *The Respective Pleas and Arguments of the Mother Country and of the Colonies* (London, 1775), p. 51.

[267]Tucker, *Four Tracts*, p. 65. For similar statements see Tucker, *The Elements of Commerce*, pp. 142, 175. The political aspect of this problem will be discussed below.

[268]Tucker, *A Series of Answers*, p. 46.

[269]*Ibid.*, pp. 46 f.

when we shall have a less extended Coast to guard by almost 1500 Miles (and this Coast actually at Home, in the very Centre of our Empire, instead of being 3000 Miles distant from it) it is evident to common Sense, that we shall be better able to defend our Channel and narrow Seas. . . ."[270]

Dean Tucker also must be considered one of the first theorists who found fault with the colonial attachment because of its adverse effects on interior politics in the parent state. On the one hand, he envisaged the danger of growing tyranny at home due to increasing metropolitan tyranny in the plantations resulting from a policy of stern suppression of colonial recalcitrance. He commented: "What baneful Influence this Government à la Prusse would have on every other Part of the British Empire. England free, and America in Chains! And how soon would the enslaved Part of the Constitution, and perhaps the greater, contaminate the free and lesser."[271]

The phenomenon of patronage filled him with similar apprehensions:

. . . and as the Mock-Patriots and Republicans are in full Cry, that the Crown hath too much Power already by the Disposal of so many Places; I ask, With what Face can these Men oppose a Separation, if they really think what they say? The Places in North-America lately in the Disposal of the Crown (or if you please, of the Ministry), were (great and small) some Hundreds. . . . You who desire to counter-act the Influence of the Crown by legal and constitutional Means, wish nevertheless to retain dear America withall its evil Appendages of Places, Pensions, Sine-Cures, Contracts, Jobs, etc.[272]

On the other hand—and this, no doubt, disturbed his paternalist mind considerably more than the peril of tyranny—Tucker showed himself much concerned about the wave of republicanism and democratism which rolled across the Atlantic. To him American constitutional projects were of a "mob-cratic" nature.[273] Thus he asserted: "As long as ever North-America shall remain connected with Great-Britain, under any Mode whatever; the republican Party among us will find an Asylum for sheltering themselves under that Connection. . . ."[274] In a Word, nothing short of a total Separation, can prevent the spreading, or can radically cure the Contagion of Republicanism."[275]

[270] *Ibid.*, p. 52.
[271] Tucker, *The True Interest of Great-Britain*, p. 198.
[272] Tucker, *A Series of Answers*, p. 61.
[273] Tucker, *A Letter to Edmund Burke*, p. 379.
[274] Tucker, *A Series of Answers*, pp. 61 f.   [275] *Ibid.*, pp. 73 f.

It is almost needless to say that Tucker was convinced of the parent state's inability to keep the North American colonists from achieving independence in the long run. ". . . it is the Nature of them all to aspire after Independence, and to set up for themselves as soon as ever they find that they are able to subsist, without being beholden to the Mother-Country."[276]

Thus, on the basis of all the arguments considered above, he demanded immediate and complete separation as the only feasible and sound policy. It was Dean Tucker, not Disraeli, to whom this statement is generally attributed, who for the first time spoke allegorically of the colonies or, rather, of America as having been "a Milstone hanging about the Neck of this Country, to weigh it down."[277] Separation having taken place, in 1783, he remarked with gleeful irony: ". . . as we·ourselves had not the Wisdom to cut the Rope, and to let the Burthen fall off, the Americans have kindly done it for us."[278]

[276] Tucker, *The True Interest of Great-Britain*, pp. 161 f. Even if the British should be able, for the moment, to subdue the colonists, "it doth by no Means follow, that they could be able to maintain a Superiority in it afterwards for any Length of Time" (*ibid.*, p. 197). Besides, such a success would be bought altogether too dearly. "Victory alone is but a poor Compensation for all the Blood and Treasure which must be spilt on such an Occasion" (*ibid.*, pp. 196 f.).

[277] *Four Letters on Important National Subjects*, p. 7.

[278] *Ibid.*, pp. 7 f.

CHAPTER IV

THE OLD COLONIAL SYSTEM
BASIC OBJECTIVES, CONCEPTIONS, POLICIES

THE diverse reasons which determined Englishmen to establish, maintain, and expand oversea dependencies, have been enumerated in the preceding chapters. While the Old Colonial System reigned supreme, i.e., between 1660 and 1775, trade was the main objective pursued through colonization and colonies. Sir William Keith pronounced that redressing the "Balance of National Trade if it is turned against us," was the only adequate objective for planting colonies.[1] In the course of the Canada-Guadeloupe controversy, William Burke admonished his countrymen to let their policy be guided by considerations of commerce only.[2] In 1774, John Campbell stated: "There are certain Principles so clear and self-evident.... To this we may attribute the Idea of fixing Settlements in distant Countries for the Sake of Commerce."[3]

These citations could be easily multiplied. What England primarily looked for in the colonies was neither extension of territory *per se* nor oversea aggregations of Englishmen, but goods and markets. Trade, of course, can be obtained and increased by means of exchange operations between nations and, as such, has no territorial aspects in the sense of necessitating acquisition of sovereignty over areas lying beyond the national frontiers. In the case of colonization the idea of a territorial basis of trade was introduced due to three considerations. Speaking, in 1774, about Britain's colonial enterprise, Edmund Burke remarked: "You not only acquired commerce, but you actually created the very objects of commerce; and by that creation you raised the trade of this

---

[1] *The History of the British Plantations in America* (London, 1738), part I, p. 10.

[2] He said: "... it would be an unfortunate Effect of all our Bravery and Policy, if we had either fought or negotiated ourselves out of our commercial Character. Advantages of a merely political kind, will be always more or less problematical" (*An Examination of the Commercial Principles of the Late Negotiations between Great Britain and France in 1761* [London, 1762], p. 3).

[3] *A Political Survey of Britain* (London, 1774), II, 561.

Kingdom at least four-fold."⁴ Thus, colonization had virtually created markets and sources of goods where there had been none before, and, in this sense, it had certainly increased the total of the world's trade.⁵ The planting of agents of production and consumption in hitherto commercially unexploited and, for all practical purposes, unsettled regions, lent to this new trade a territorial basis which, in conjunction with other considerations, would lead to the demand for acquiring dominion over the distant areas involved.

Another consideration stimulating the desire for territorial acquisitions was that concerned with the establishment of bases for the undisturbed conduct of exchange operations. Such bases, or trading posts, would serve the purpose of organizing a local mart and of lending armed protection and shelter to the merchant vessels engaged in distant trades. Of such a nature were the trading posts, forts, and naval bases erected in the Mediterranean, in Africa, and in Asia.⁶

Bryan Edwards, one of the first historians of the English West Indies, observed that "commercial monopoly ... is the leading principle of colonial intercourse."⁷ This objective of initiating and maintaining a closed system of commercial monopoly, indeed,

⁴William Cobbett, *The Parliamentary History of England* (London, n.d.), XVII, c. 1236.

⁵None of the critics of English colonization, as will be seen later, denied that Europe, as a whole, benefited from the colonization of the Americas. The question whether it was profitable for a particular nation to participate, by colonization, in the creation of this trade rather than, by foreign trade, to acquire only a share in the additional volume of trade created, cannot be a matter of discussion at this point.

⁶The author of *The Considerable Advantages of a South Sea Trade to our English Nation* (London, n.d.), pp. 7 f. who proposed the foundation of English colonies "about Rio de la Plata," "about the Streights of Magellan," etc., gave the following reasons for his suggestion: "Now for the better caring of this gainful Trade, it is absolutely needful that we should have two, three or more Colonies at such convenient Distance and near our Business, with such Fortifications that we may be Masters, and be able to Defend ourselves, and command a Trade if denyed. For if it be precarious, infallibly the Priests and Roman Bigottry will prevent and stop it, with all such Heretics as we are said to be.... But if we have one Settlement or more in those Parts, we can have our Ships there at hand to force them either by fair means or by foul to yield to us.... And this being so long a Voyage, it is convenient that in our way thither we should have some Colonies of English to recruit and refresh our Men, and to supply them with things wanting."

⁷Bryan Edwards, *The History Civil and Commercial of the British West Indies* [1793], 5 vols. (5th ed.; London, 1819), II, 443.

is the third and most important consideration suggesting the acquisition of sovereignty over distant areas, for only through sovereignty would the colonizing nation be enabled to exclude the foreigner from participation in colonial trade.

Indeed, monopoly and complementarity of economic functions were the salient features of the Old Colonial System. With regard to either trait, the colonies were resolutely relegated to a position of subservience to the supposed interests of the mother country.

It has been demonstrated above that the desire for a trading monopoly of the metropolis in the colonies sprang directly from the fallacious mercantilist conceptions of international trade. In matters of navigation and the colonial markets this monopolist system was most complete. In the case of colonial productions it found expression in those Acts which provided that the so-called "Enumerated Articles" be shipped to the mother country for purposes of metropolitan consumption or re-exportation.[8]

The idea of the complementarity of economic functions as between mother country and colonies likewise has been explained in the previous chapter. The colonies, according to this point of view, were supposed to specialize in the production of raw materials which in no way interfered with the productions and the trade of the metropolis. Such a course of economic development would base the Colonial System on a beneficial mutuality of interests between colonies and metropolis.[9] The Empire was visualized

[8] The Enumeration Act was supposed to render Britain "the Grand Market of the Universe" (James Whiston, *A Discourse of the Decay of Trade* [London, 1693], p. 3). This idea of England destined to become Europe's chief market for colonial staples was already fondly expressed by Robert Johnson who dreamt of making "this little Northerne corner of the world, to be in short time the richest Storehouse and Staple for marchandize in all Europe" (*Nova Britannia* [1609], in Peter Force, *Tracts and other Papers* [Washington, 1836], II, 23).

[9] It has been observed above that the different degrees to which the various colonies fitted into this scheme provided metropolitan writers with a canon by which they estimated the relative value of the various plantations to the parent state. It was on the basis of such standards that Arthur Young listed the British colonies in the following sequence of diminishing utility to the mother country: (1) the West Indian islands, (2) the Southern colonies, (3) the tobacco plantations, (4) the Northern colonies. He concluded: "It appears from the preceding accounts that, in respect of consumption of British commodities, every soul in the West Indies is worth better than fifty-eight in the northern colonies, eighteen in the tobacco, and rather better than one and a half in the southern ones" (*Political Essays Concerning the Present State of the British Empire* [London, 1772], pp. 337 f.).

However, many writers saw the utility of the Northern American plantations enhanced by the complementarity of economic functions between them and the English West Indian islands.

as a large commercial unit consisting of England, Scotland, Ireland, and the plantations as separate but co-operative complements. Their commercial relations were to be strictly of a complementary, not of a competitive character.[10]

Complementarity of economic functions and mutuality of interests as between parent state and filial dependencies are, of course, notions which are ingredients of any system of planned self-sufficiency. In the previous chapter quotations have been given that convey the significance which many writers attributed to the acquisition and preservation of dependable markets and sources of supplies. There can be no doubt that the idea of a self-sufficient Empire occupied the minds of some theorists and statesmen. Already in 1607 an anonymous writer declared:

That Realme is most compleet and wealthie which either hath sufficient to serve itselfe or can finde the meanes to exporte of the naturall comodities then [if] it hath occasion necessarily to importe, consequently it muste insue that by a publique consent, a Collony transported into a good and plentiful climate able to furnish our wantes, our monies and wares that nowe run into the handes of our adversaries or cowld frendes shall pass unto our frendes and naturall kinsmen and from them likewise we shall receive such things as shalbe most available to our necessaties, which intercourse of trade maye rather be called a home bread trafique than a forraigne exchange.[11]

Similar ideas showing a tendency to rely on intra-imperial autarky even in the matter of markets for metropolitan goods were uttered by Daniel Defoe and General Oglethorp.[12] However, in the case of most writers, notions of imperial self-sufficiency were limited to Britain's needs for raw materials. Even in this respect there appear hardly any statements voicing the desire of seeing the

[10]This aversion to intra-imperial competition is well expressed by Postlethwayt (*Great Britain's Commercial Interest* [London, 1759], I 56 f.): "However great some may conceive the advantage to be that England has over its other territories, wherewith it is united and connected; yet when duly considered, they will be found to be less considerable than what may be too generally apprehended. For Scotland as well as Ireland, and the British Northern colonies do all, more or less interfere with England in her native produce, and in some of her staple manufactures; and these distinct parts of the British empire do also greatly interfere in their produce and fabrics with each other; which can be no such advantage to either, nor to the whole kingdom, as if the commercial circumstances of the several parts of the kingdom did in no respect clash and interfere with each other; it would certainly prove more for the general interest of the State, that the constituent territories of the British nation, should interfere in their trade only with foreign rivals, and not with that of England, or with that of each other."

[11]*Reasons for Raising a Fund for the Support of a Colony at Virginia*, in Alexander Brown (ed.), *The Genesis of the United States* (Boston, 1897), I, 39.

[12]Cf. *supra*, pp. 100-1.

mother country *completely* independent from foreign supplies. On the other hand, it was never suggested that the metropolis limit its output to the demands of the Empire. On the contrary, the largest possible expansion of sales abroad was generally desired for metropolitan as well as for colonial products.[13]

The colonies' absolute subservience to the interests of the mother country was commonly accepted as a matter of course by metropolitan politicians and theorists. Robert Richardson wrote in the *London Chronicle* of July 31, 1764: "The colonies were acquired with no other view than to be a convenience to us; and therefore it can never be imagined that we are to consult their interests preferably to our own."[14] Similarly, in 1774, Lord Carmarthen declared in the House of Commons: "For what purpose were they [the colonists] suffered to go to that country, unless the profit of their labour should return to their masters here? I think the policy of colonization is highly culpable, if the advantages of it should not redound to the interests of Great Britain."[15]

In this connection metropolitan writers were not at all unmindful of the expense which colonization and colonies had imposed on the mother country. Postlethwayt said: "Certain it is, that the crown of England has not hitherto been sparing in expence to cherish those important plantations in order to raise them to the height to which they have arrived. . . ."[16] The parent state had given men, in the form of emigrants, and money, mainly for defence, to the colonies. It expected not only to be reimbursed but also to receive an adequate profit on the outlay involved. Many writers, indeed, regarded the colonies as nothing but a business enterprise undertaken by the mother country. As one anonymous writer put it in the *London Packet* (January 4, 1775): "I have always considered the Colonies as the great farms of the public and the Colonists as our tenants. . . it is time to look about us, and keep them to the terms of their leases. . . ."[17]

This almost exclusive regard for the tangible economic utility of the colonies had two interesting consequences: On the one hand,

---

[13]Cf. for confirmatory view, M. J. Bonn, *The Crumbling of Empire* (London, 1938), pp. 86, 90 f.

[14]Quoted in F. J. Hinkhouse, *The Preliminaries of the American Revolution as Seen in the English Press, 1763-1775* (New York, 1926), p. 100.

[15]Cobbett, *Parl. Hist.*, XVII, c. 1208 f.

[16]Postlethwayt, *Great Britain's Commercial Interest* (1759), I, 439.

[17]Quoted in Hinkhouse, *Preliminaries of the American Revolution*, p. 102.

an authoritarian home government granted to the colonists a remarkable degree of political freedom in all matters which were unrelated to the economic purposes of the Old Colonial System; on the other hand, there was an almost complete absence of that sentimental imperial-brotherhood idea which was to play such an important role after the collapse of Little-Englandism.

The Empire was not regarded as a confederacy of English nations, nor were the colonists considered to be fellow-citizens.[18] The colonies were thought to be possessions and not an extension of England. Allan Ramsay admitted that the American was "not completely a foreigner," but he was incensed at the fact that the American colonists "have artfully persuaded the people of England that they are fellow-citizens, and Englishmen like ourselves. . . . But this is altogether a fallacy. . . ."[19]

Thomas Pownall, Chatham, Edmund Burke, and Adam Smith[20] usually are singled out among notable Englishmen who, anterior to the American War of Independence, uttered opinions precursory to the later evolution of the idea of a British Commonwealth of Nations. Added to this list must be General Oglethorp. Addressing the House of Commons in 1732 he demanded that "in all cases that come before this House, where there seems to be a clashing of interests between one set of people and another, we ought to have no regard to the particular interest of any country or any set of people; the good of the whole is what we ought only to have under our consideration: our colonies are all a part of our own dominions; the people in every one of them are our own people, and we ought to shew an equal respect to all."[21] This utterance, indeed, was remarkably at variance with the broad stream of influential opinion of the time. While writers and orators were fond of pointing out that Britain's imperial system rested on a basis of mutual benefit, most of them admitted readily that in the case of a conflict of interests between parent state and colony, the interest of the latter had to be subordinate to that of the former. Oglethorp's statement that colony and metropolis deserve equal regard if their interests clash, is the only one of the kind the present writer could find in the records of the period under discussion.

[18]For citations see *ibid.*, pp. 100, 103.

[19]Allan Ramsay, *Letters on the Present Disturbances in Great Britain and Her American Provinces* (London, 1777), pp. 20 f. (This collection of letters is a reprint of articles originally written in 1775.)

[20]Adam Smith's opinions will be discussed in the following chapter.

[21]Quoted in A. A. Ettinger, *James Edward Oglethorp, Imperial Idealist* (Oxford, 1936), p. 101.

Pownall considered the Old Colonial System to be sorely obsolete and wanted to see the Navigation Acts discarded. He dreamt of a future British empire in which "Great Britain may be no more considered as the kingdom of this Isle only, with many appendages of provinces, colonies, settlements, and other extraneous parts, but as A Grand Marine Dominion Consisting Of Our Possessions in The Atlantic And In America United Into One Empire. . . ."[22] He agreed that in the near future Great Britain would form the commercial and political centre of this "one Empire," but he added that "the center of power, instead of remaining fixed as it now is in Great Britain, will, as the magnitude of the power and interest of the Colonies increases, be drawn out from the island. . . ."[23]

Chatham's case is vastly different from that of Oglethorp or Pownall. He assailed the attempt to impose taxation on the American colonists and persisted in advocating a policy of reconciliation even during the first years of the American War of Independence. He wanted to keep the Old Empire intact. But regarding the commercial or constitutional aspects of imperial policy he was no more liberal than the large majority of his contemporaries. Speaking in the House of Commons in January, 1775, he exclaimed: "I shall ever contend, that the Americans justly owe obedience to us in a limited degree—they owe obedience to our ordinances of trade and navigation . . . let the sacredness of their property remain inviolate; let it be taxable only by their own consent. . . . As to the metaphysical refinements, attempting to shew that the Americans are equally free from obedience and commercial restraints, as from taxation for revenue, as being unrepresented here, I pronounce them futile, frivolous, and groundless."[24] In the course of the same speech, Chatham declared that if it were true that the Americans intended also to attack the Navigation Laws, there would be no one readier than he "to resist and crush any attempt of that nature. . . ."[25]

Burke likewise was against taxing the Americans without their consent. He also proposed reconciliation as the only wise policy to be pursued. In matters of political, constitutional, and economic theory he was by far superior to the narrow-minded Chatham. Yet, apart from the issues referred to above, his attitude was one of ambiguity. He realized precisely the function of the Navi-

---

[22]Thomas Pownall, *The Administration of the Colonies* (4th ed.; London, 1768), pp. 9 f.

[23]*Ibid.*, p. 37. [24]Cobbett, *Parl. Hist.*, XVIII, c. 150 f.

[25]*Ibid.*, c. 165.

gation Laws,[26] but he did not advocate their repeal or even their modification. Regarding the political rights of the colonists, Burke held views which the politicians of his day were unable to follow because they were beyond the range of their petty conceptions. He denied the unlimited omnipotence of Parliament in matters of colonial legislation. Yet he declared: "I have held, and ever shall maintain to the best of my power, unimpaired and undiminished, the just, wise and necessary constitutional superiority of Great Britain. . . . To reconcile British superiority with American liberty shall be my great object. . . ."[27]

Burke was aware that the American colonists had outgrown the stage of their political childhood. He knew that if the British insisted on treating them like political children, they might "as well think of rocking a grown man in the cradle of an infant."[28] But he did not command the vision to imagine a system of Imperial Federation or of a British Commonwealth of Nations. What Chatham and Burke had in common was that they offered their nation a wise policy designed to prevent the break-up of the Old Empire. Neither of them had drawn up the "blueprint" of a new empire.

Entirely different again was the case of the English Dissenters.[29] To them the colonists were not just customers but so many "congregations of brethren beyond the seas."[30] They knew that the collapse of the Old British Empire would be a disaster to British dissent and to the cause of British democracy.[31] This realization

[26]In April, 1774, Burke said in the House of Commons: "Permit me . . . to lead your attention . . . back to the Act of Navigation, the corner-stone of the policy of this country with regard to its colonies. Sir, that policy was, from the beginning, purely commercial; and the commercial system was wholly restrictive. It was the system of a monopoly. No trade was let loose from that constraint, but merely to enable the colonists to dispose of what, in the course of your trade, you could not take,—or to enable them to dispose of such articles as we forced upon them, and for which, without some degree of liberty, they could not pay. Hence all your specific and detailed enumerations; hence the inumerable checks and counterchecks hence that infinite variety of paper chains by which you bind together this complicated system of the colonies" (Edmund Burke, *The Works* [9th ed.; Boston, 1889], II, 30 f.).

[27]Speech to the electors of Bristol in October, 1774. See John Almon, *Biographical, Literary, and Political Anecdotes* (London, 1797), III, 400 f.

[28]Burke, *Works*, II, 232.

[29]The views of Price and Priestley will be discussed in a later chapter.

[30]L. B. Namier, *England in the Age of the American Revolution* (London, 1930), p. 44.

[31]*Ibid.*, pp. 44 f. On early projects for imperial federation see E. A. Smillie, *Historical Origins of Imperial Federation* (Montreal, 1910), pp. 13-29; G. B. Hertz, *The Old Colonial System* (Manchester, 1905), pp. 93-153.

marks the greatness as well as the limitation of their vision. They saw in the revolting Americans not so much colonists fighting for their rights and interests against the mother country, as fellow-democrats struggling against tyrannical class rule.

However, all these men and little groups represented minority opinions. Until the disruption of the first British Empire the overwhelming bulk of metropolitan opinion upheld the Old Colonial System. No advantage was seen in extent of territory as such. The colonist was not a fellow-citizen but a customer or a producer of goods. Of a feeling of sentimental affinity there was none. It is quite remarkable that the sequence of disturbances leading up to the American Revolution did not perturb this smug righteousness and incredible unimaginativeness of metropolitan thinking. But the age was that of George III and Lord North rather than of Burke and Shelburne, of Sir Robert Filmer and Samuel Johnson rather than of Price and Priestley, of Hutchinson rather than of Pownall, and of Postlethwayt rather than of Adam Smith.

The various devices by which the policies underlying the Old Colonial System were implemented need not be described here.[32] Nor is it necessary to review their general effects on the economy of the mother country for such a study would only anticipate the strictures advanced by the later critics of the Old Colonial System. It is revealing, however, to examine some objections raised by

[32] There are a good many excellent descriptive accounts of these devices. In addition to the works of G. L. Beer and the *Cambridge History of the British Empire* (London, 1929), vol. I, the following books can be recommended: E. Lipson, *The Economic History of England* (London, 1931), III, 116-37, 169-92; Hertz, *The Old Colonial System*, pp. 38-68; H. E. Egerton, *A Short History of British Colonial Policy* (London, 1897); C. M. MacInnes, *An Introduction to the Economic History of the British Empire* (London, 1935); E. R. Johnson et al., *History of the Domestic and Foreign Commerce of the United States* (Washington, 1922), vol. I; David Macpherson, *Annals of Commerce* (London, 1805); L. A. Harper, *The English Navigation Laws* (New York, 1939); Eleanor L. Lord, *Industrial Experiments in the British Colonies of North America* (Baltimore, 1896); M. P. Ashley, *Financial and Commercial Policy under the Cromwellian Protectorate* (Oxford, 1934). Of course, there are numerous additional items, reference to which will be found in the bibliographical notes attached to the above-mentioned studies.

Regarding the subject of special encouragement afforded to colonial production, there is one minor item which should not be overlooked. The Royal Society of Arts, since its foundation in 1754, had made great efforts to encourage the development of resources in the British colonies by the offer of prizes and premiums to be awarded to the production of particular commodities. For a general account of these endeavours see Sir H. T. Wood, *A History of the Royal Society of Arts* (London, 1913), especially pp. 83-112.

contemporaries against the establishment and maintenance of particular policies and institutional devices. The Navigation Acts, passed between 1650 and 1660, may serve as an interesting example.

Some critics opposed these laws on the general ground that trade had better be left to itself and not unnecessarily encumbered by state regulations. Thus, Sir Dudley North declared "that no Laws can set Prizes in Trade, the Rates of which, must and will make themselves: But when such Laws do happen to lay any hold, it is so much Impediment to Trade, and therefore prejudicial."[33] The following statement by another writer contains one of the earliest and clearest expressions of laissez-faire views: "I am persuaded it is scarcely possible to make any Law on the Subject of Trade, but what shall do more harm than good, excepting those which are directly intended for preventing Fraud."[34]

These writers recognized the Navigation Laws as constituting a monopoly which, like all monopolies, operated to the benefit of some special interest-groups but to the disadvantage of the country as a whole. Sir Matthew Decker wrote: "For a Law that confines, in any degree, our Imports or Exports to particular Ships or Men, gives a Monopoly to those for whose Benefit the Restraint is framed . . . ."[35] Another writer asked: "Have not most Laws been made to satisfy the interested Demands of particular Persons, Classes and Counties?"[36] Indeed, this author emphasized that the maintenance of colonies and of laws regulating colonial trade was profitable not to England but to English sectional interests. ". . . one Thing is certain; that the Basis of all Deliberations on our Connection with the Colonies abroad, ought to be NOT—how will they bring the greatest immediate Wealth into the Coffers of a few Merchants? Or how will they bring the greatest immediate Splendor to the City of London?—But how will they continue to

---

[33]Sir Dudley North, *Discourses upon Trade* (London, 1691), reprint (Edinburgh, 1822), preface. Similarly, Roger Coke, *A Treatise* (London, 1671), p. 87.

[34]*Thoughts on a Question of Importance Proposed to the Public, Whether it is Probable that the Immense Extent of Territory Acquired by this Nation at the Late Peace, will operate towards the Prosperity, or the Ruin of the Island of Great Britain?* (London, 1765), p. 39. This author's objection to state planning in matters of trade was based on the realization that governments do not command the wisdom and justice necessary for making laws in the true interest of the nation as a whole (*ibid.*, pp. 34 ff.).

[35]*An Essay on the Causes of the Decline of Foreign Trade* (4th ed.; Dublin, 1751), p. 53.

[36]*Thoughts on a Question of Importance Proposed to the Public* (1765), pp. 36 f.

promote the Population of the Island, and the Industry of the People of Great Britain?"[37]

As regards specific objections directed against these regulations, it was pointed out that they had the effect of raising the wages of sailors[38] and of increasing the cost of ship-building.[39] As a consequence, sea transportation was more expensive to the English foreign trader than it would have been in the absence of the Navigation Laws. Decker concluded: ". . . this Monopoly is very prejudicial to our Manufacture, for it is enacting that several Necessities and Materials of Manufacture shall not be imported by the cheapest Navigation, but by a dear one, and of course they shall pay dear Freights, which must raise their Prices. . . ."[40] Roger Coke argued: "From hence it is, viz. the dearness of our Navigation, principally that we have upon the matter, Lost our Trade to Muscovy, and all the Kingdoms and Countries within the Sound, with our Woollen and other Manufactures, and upon that account the Dutch drive tenfold more Trades to Turkey, Italy, Spain, Portugal, the East-Indies and Africk. . . ."[41]

According to these critics, dearer transportation resulted (1) in higher prices of imported articles to the English consumer, and (2) in higher prices of British export articles. Also the British objective of making the United Kingdom a major *entrepôt* was frustrated because, as Roger Coke stated: ". . . the Act of Navigation debars of us the greatest part of the World from Trading with us, whereby it excludes multitudes and concourse of Men and Traders. . . ."[42] Thus, in the eyes of these authors, the Navigation Laws injured the interests of the English consumer and the English export trade while conferring on English shipping a benefit which they regarded as doubtful or wholly illusory.[43]

It is a well-known fact that the proponents of the Act envisaged it as a deadly blow to the maritime superiority of the Dutch. Interestingly enough, its opponents likewise were inspired by the

[37]*Ibid.*, preface, vi-vii.
[38]R. Coke, *A Treatise* (1671), p. 48.
[39]*Ibid.*, see also, *Britannia Languens* (1680) in J. R. MacCulloch, *A Select Collection of Early English Tracts on Commerce* (London, 1856), pp. 45 f.
[40]*Essay on the Causes of the Decline of Foreign Trade* (1751), p. 53.
[41]R[oger] C[oke], *A Treatise Concerning the Regulation of the Coyn of England* (London, 1696), p. 27.
[42]Roger Coke, *A Treatise wherein is demonstrated that the Church and State of England are in Equal Danger with the Trade of it* (London, 1761), p. 36.
[43]Coke declared that the Act "hath diminished the Shipping of England" and that it "hath hindered the Navigation of England" (*ibid.*, pp. 47 f.).

remarkable success of the Dutch. In their opinion the Dutch should be rivalled not by means of a monopoly basically inimical to trade but by employing the very means to which Holland owed her enviable success: cheapness of transportation, e.g., "by finding a cheaper way of building and sailing our Trading-Ships."[44]

The above-mentioned strictures on the Navigation Laws referred to their function with regard to colonial trade only by implication. Their adverse effect on the economic development of the colonies and, hence, on their usefulness to the mother country, was singled out for consideration in John Bland's noteworthy petition against the Navigation Laws which predicted "the inevitable destruction" of the colonies if these acts were not dispensed with.[45] Bland began his animadversion by asserting that "a few covetous and interested men" had procured this legislation because

... they would keep still in their own hands that Trade which they had ingrossed, and have no body come there to hinder them, and that for the following reasons. First, That for whatever goods they carried out of England to those Plantations, the inhabitants should pay them what prices and rates they please to require.... Secondly, To force the Planters to deliver them such Tobaccos, which by the labour and sweat of their browes they have made, at the rates they themselves trading thither would have it.... By which I hope it's apparent, that it was nor is not theire love to the Plantations, the commerce or to encrease the Duties in England, that caused them to seek the Hollanders prohibition from Virginia and Mariland, but their own private interests.[46]

---

[44]*Britannia Languens* (1680), p. 48. Defenders of the Navigation Laws like Brewster and Sir Josiah Child conceded most of the points raised against them by the above-mentioned critics. Brewster, for example, did not deny that these regulations had rendered English shipping dearer to the merchant. But he argued that the merchants would not be damaged thereby, "for Merchants will rate their Goods according to their Charge; and it is the Consumer, not Importer, that pays it..." (*Essays on Trade and Navigation* [1695], p. 98). To these writers these Acts were promotive of English naval strength, a national interest which was entitled to furtherance even if other interests were injured thereby. Child wrote: "Some will confess that as to Merchants and Owners of Ships the Act of Navigation is eminently beneficial, but say, that Merchants and Owners are but an inconsiderable number of men in respect of the whole Nation, and that Interest of the greater number.... My answer is, That I cannot deny that this may be true, if the present profit of the generality be barely and singly considered; but this Kingdom being an Island, the defence whereof hath always been our Shiping and Sea-men, it seems to me absolutely necessary that Profit and Power ought joyntly to be considered..." (*A Discourse about Trade* [London, 1690], p. 93).

[45]Bland was an English merchant engaged in the trade with the tobacco plantations in which he had invested a great deal of capital. His memorial, written in 1660, has been reprinted in the *Virginia Magazine of History and Biography*, I (1893-4), 141-55.   [46]*Ibid.*, pp. 144 f.

As to the effects of these regulations on the colonial trade he remarked:

> Seeing what the commodities of Virginia and Mariland are is it not a great advantage to those Colonies to have them by every body fetched thence? ... If therefore then we debar the Hollanders from going thither, see the inconveniences that will arise thereby. The Hollanders began to plant Tobacco in his own Territories, as soon as the Act for their prohibition from Virginia and Mariland in the long Parliament was obtained, will he not proceed to plant greater quantities, and so totally supply himself by his own labour? do we not force him to this ourselves, and so thereby cut off our own trade?[47]

The reason for this action on the part of "the Dutch" is explained when Bland put the rhetorical question:

> ... will he ever buy that of us, when by passing so many hands, and so much charge contracted thereon, is made so dear, that he can have it cheaper in his own Territories? .... Therefore it clearly appears, that being so, of necessity we must lose that Trade and Commerce.[48]

> Will not this contract a great deal of needless commodities as Virginia and Mariland affoard, which will not keep in long and tedious voyages? doth it not hereby then appear to be an absolute hindrance of trade and commerce, not onely to those places but to ourselves here in England?[49]

The principal objection raised by John Bland was that the Navigation Acts led to a contraction of the market for the products of the colonies and, therefore, meant an impediment to colonial production itself. Other critics showed that the same regulations would render provisions dearer to the colonists and thus entail increased production costs in respect of colonial staples.[50]

Regarding the colonies, the main objects of the Navigation Laws were: (1) to confine all transportation connected with the plantations to English shipping, and (2) to ensure that the benefits to be derived from colonial establishments fall exclusively to the mother country.[51] The latter consideration, curiously enough,

---

[47]*Ibid.*, p. 147. Bland also pointed out that the French likewise followed the example of the Dutch (*ibid.*, p. 150).

[48]*Ibid.*, p. 147.   [49]*Ibid.*, p. 149.

[50]Lord Willoughby wrote in 1666: "Free Trade is the life of all Colonies, but such is the condition of the Caribbean Islands that they have not clothes sufficient to hide their nakedness, or food to fill their bellies. Whoever he be that advised his Majesty to restrain and tie up his Colonies in points of trade is more a merchant than a good subject, and would have his Majesty's Island be nursed up to work for him and such men" (quoted in Egerton, *Short History of British Colonial Policy*, pp. 76 f. See also statements by Sir T. Lynch and Sir J. Atkins, quoted, *ibid.*, p. 77).

[51]Several of the writers quoted above asserted that sectional interests had procured the passage of the Acts or, at any rate, were their obvious beneficiaries. The latter fact is incontestable. The question whether the enactment of these

was prompted by the recognition of the cost involved in colonization and the maintenance of colonies, however vague and sometimes erroneous these notions were. Sir Josiah Child gave clear expression to this apprehension: "If they [the colonies] were not kept to the Rules of the Act of Navigation, the consequence would be, that in a few Years the benefit of them would be wholly lost to the Nation . . . the Dutch, who as I have said, are Masters of the Field in Trade, would carry away the greatest of advantage by the Plantations, of all the Princes in Christendom leaving us and others only the trouble of breeding men, and sending them abroad to cultivate the Ground, and have Bread for their Industry."[52]

Throughout the period during which the Navigation Laws served as the pre-eminent instrument for regulating the commerce of and with the British colonies, proposals for modifications of some of the rules were being made and sometimes accepted. One series of such suggestions was concerned with the English sugar colonies. During the first quarter of the eighteenth century it became obvious that the French sugar islands could and did produce cheaper sugar than their English rivals. The French were able to capture the larger part of the European market of which the English formerly had enjoyed a major share. The English sugar merchants and a great many of the West Indian planters assumed an indifferent attitude toward this situation. They commanded a monopoly in the home market which they exploited with alacrity. British politicians and writers were less concerned with the latter aspect

---

regulations was motivated by national or selfish group interests permits of no precise answer. No doubt motivation was of a multiple kind. For years shipowners and mariners had been complaining of the keen competition of the Dutch. Harper (*English Navigation Laws*, pp. 39 ff.) arrives at the conclusion that powerful corporate interests engaged in the East India, the Levant, and the Eastland Trade secured the enactment of the laws. These merchant companies, of course, were hardly interested in driving Dutch shipping out of the colonial trade in America. Indeed, it seems that merchant pressure groups interested in the trade with the English colonies were not very vociferous at that time in demanding an English shipping monopoly. The Bristol merchants, for example, as the majority of English merchants outside the large companies mentioned, were at first decidedly hostile to the Acts. However, as soon as they realized the opportunities for monopoly profits offered by these laws, they became their staunchest supporters and tolerated no exceptions to the regulations enacted unless they worked to their particular benefit. On this see C. M. MacInnes, *Gateway of Empire* (Bristol, 1939), pp. 218 f., 226 f.

[52]Child, *A Discourse about Trade* (1690), pp. 94 f.

of the question[53] than with the competitive weakness of English sugar in foreign markets. But they looked with envy upon the French success and were eager to recapture a leading position in the European sugar market. There were six different ways of increasing and cheapening British sugar production: (1) by reducing the duties on sugar; (2) by throwing the English West Indies open to supplies of provisions and raw materials; (3) by permitting the refining of sugar in the plantations; (4) by conquering or settling additional sugar islands; (5) by preventing the colonists of the North American plantations from supplying the French planters with provisions and timber; and (6) by removing sugar from the list of enumerated commodities.

The government never relished the first possibility as it might have led to a fiscal loss to the Exchequer.[54] The second possibility would have antagonized the Northern American plantations. The third proposal encountered the violent and successful opposition of the metropolitan sugar refiners. The alternative of conquest and additional colonization was supported by several writers.[55] A great many pamphleteers demanded that the North American colonists discontinue the export of provisions and raw materials to the French islands.[56] It was the proposal to remove sugar from

[53]There were of course some exceptions, the most noteworthy of which is the author of *An Enquiry into the Causes of the Present High Price of Muscovado Sugars* (London, 1735). The fact that the West Indian sugar interests were abusing their monopoly position in the metropolitan market was fully realized and frowned upon by some observers. One writer, though not at all solicitous of the English consumers' interest, even suggested "to give a liberty to import Muscovado Sugars (paying the same Duty with our own) even from whencesoever we can get them cheapest . . . this would immediately reduce our Planters to the necessity of lowering their prices and using us better . . ." (*A Short Answer to an Elaborate Pamphlet, Entitled, The Importance of Our Sugar Plantations, &c.* [London, 1731], pp. 21 f.).

[54]The Act of 1733 indeed granted to the English planters a drawback on the entire duty on sugar in the case of re-exportation from England within a year of its importation. It also provided for a sizable increase of the bounty on refined sugar exported from the mother country. See on this, J. F. Rees, "Mercantilism and the Colonies," *Cambridge History of the British Empire*, I, 584.

[55]One writer declared that this evil could be remedied "by settling more Sugar Colonies, which the Government ought to have at heart, and to set about with vigour" (*A Short Answer to an Elaborate Pamphlet* [1731], p. 21). John Bennet also demanded that "we must plant more fertile and cheaper lands. . ." (*The National Merchant* [1736], p. 137). This alternative was also discussed in the course of the Guadeloupe-Canada controversy.

[56]For example, W. Perrin, *The Present State of the Sugar Colonies* (London, 1740), p. 2; L. F. Stock, *Proceedings and Debates of the British Parliaments Re-*

the list of enumerated articles which aroused most interest and which was finally carried out by the Act of 1739 which secured to the English sugar planters the privilege of exporting raw sugar directly to continental ports.[57] The purpose of this provision was to save the extra expense incurred by the circuitous transportation imposed by the Navigation Law of 1660.[58]

The discussion leading up to the adoption of this new policy is worthwhile reviewing in rough outlines. It is important to realize that before the passage of the Navigation Laws the English sugar islands, especially Barbados, enjoyed almost unlimited freedom of trade and, for this reason, achieved a state of flourishing prosperity.[59] The enactment of the Navigation Acts meant a severe blow to this affluence. The sugar colonies' case was well formulated by Edward Littleton:

In former times we accounted our selves as part of England: and the Trade and Entercourse was open accordingly. . . . But upon the King's Restauration we were in effect made Forainers and Aliens: a Custom being laid upon our Sugars amongst other Forain Commodities.[60]

Heretofore we might send our Commodities to any part of the World. But now we must send them to England, and to no Place else. By which means the whole Trade of Sugars to the Streights, (to say nothing of other places), is lost both to Us and to the English Nation. For by multiplying our Charge, others can under-sell us.[61]

As for confining the Plantation Trade to English Ships and English Men, though it be to our particular Loss; yet we took it in good part, in regard our great and dear Mother of England hath by it such vast Advantages. But

---

specting North America (Washington, 1924), IV, 137. Such suggestions provoked the counter-arguments that the French would get their supplies elsewhere and that the trade of the North American colonists with the French islands could not be prevented (*A Short Answer to an Elaborate Pamphlet* [1731], pp. 11, 14).

The Molasses Act of 1733, passed in the interest of the English sugar planters, was meant to check the flourishing trade between the Northern colonies and the French West Indies. Its main purpose, however, was to prevent the importation of French products into British North America.

[57] In order to safeguard the British shipping interest, all boats carrying sugar to European ports north of Cape Finisterre were required to touch a British port before proceeding to their port of destination. Ships bound to ports south of Cape Finisterre were permitted to proceed there directly but were required to call at an English port on their return voyage.

[58] It may be remarked here that this Act fell far short of achieving its purpose. Relatively little direct trade ensued as English sugar remained unable to compete with the cheaper sugars of non-English origin.

[59] Edwards, *History of the British West Indies*, I, 327.

[60] Edward Littleton, *The Groans of the Plantations* (London, 1698), p. 1.

[61] *Ibid.*, pp. 4 f.

that English Ships and English Men should not be permitted to trade to their best convenience and profit, is a thing we cannot understand."[62]

This statement may be taken as representative of the opinion of those English planters who desired an expansion of their market in Europe. They never ceased to demand deliverance from the fetters of the Navigation Laws.[63]

It was not until the seventeen-thirties that metropolitan writers took up the subject seriously and suggested modifications of the Navigation Acts in order to strengthen the competitive capacity of English sugar. Patrick Lindsay claimed: ". . . if the Enumeration Act was in Part repealed, and some Alterations made in the Laws for regulating the Plantation Trade, our Navigation might be greatly increased by it. Their Materials for Home-Manufacture ought to be imported directly to Britain. . . , and the Remainder they might carry directly to any foreign Market, where they could draw the highest Price for them. . . ."[64] An anonymous writer actually anticipated the provisions of the Act of 1739. He said: "And therefore to put our own Colonies upon an equal Foot with the French, I think that they ought to be permitted to carry their clay'd Sugar directly to any part of Europe to the Southward of Cape Finisterre. . . ."[65] He deplored the fact that "we still continue to restrain our own People from enlarging and extending our Trade. . . ."[66] Adoption of his proposal would mean that ". . . we shall in all Respects be Carriers of the same Quantities we now are, and there will be gained or saved to this Kingdom just so much as the Freight from England to Spain, or Italy, at least. This I conceive will put our Sugar Colonies upon a Par with the French. . . ."[67]

[62] *Ibid.*, p. 5.

[63] William Perrin, after the passage of the Act of 1739, continued to bemoan the obstacles presented to the English planter by metropolitan restrictions which were "so many Cramps on the Sugar Trade." He exclaimed "that no Endeavours, no Laws whatsoever can be expected to produce the desired Effect, unless they tend to enable the Planter and Merchant to afford our Growths and Manufactures at as low a Rate in foreign Markets as the French can do theirs"(*The Present State of the Sugar Colonies* [1740], p. 3). He suggested that American vessels be allowed to carry English raw sugar to all foreign ports directly (*ibid.*, p. 13).

[64] Patrick Lindsay, *The Interest of Scotland Considered* (Edinburgh, 1733), pp. 140 f.

[65] *Remarks upon a Book, Entituled, The Present State of the Sugar Colonies Considered* (London, 1731), p. 7.

[66] *Ibid.*, p. 9.   [67] *Ibid.*, pp. 9 f.

When the Bill of 1739 was discussed in the House of Commons, Alderman Perry stated the case for the opposition. The main arguments of his speech are worthy of citation because they furnish a lucid example of the narrow-minded selfishness which determined the attitude of English politicians. Perry declared that, in his opinion, "it would be madness in us to give up any of the advantages we enjoy by means of these regulations, without apparent necessity."[68] What he considered these precious advantages to be appears from the following quotation:

As the law now stands, their sugars must be all landed in Great Britain, and as soon as they are landed, the ship is generally put into some of our docks to refit, the seamen are paid their wages and discharged, and the freight is divided among the owners. . . . By this means our people here at home have the advantage of refitting the ships, and furnishing the seamen with every thing they stand in need of upon their landing; so that not only the freight, but also the seamens wages are wholly laid out in this kingdom. Then, upon the ship's clearing out for a new voyage, a fresh advantage accrues to our people here at home, from furnishing the ship and seamen with everything they want upon their out-set. . . . These are advantages, Sir, that arise from the sugar's being unloaded in Great Britain; and then, if it is to be reloaded for exportation, our people have an advantage of a double commission, and by the rent for warehouse room while it is here. . . . But the great advantage we reap by our sugar's passing thro this island to foreign parts, is that of its being manufactured and refined by our people here at home, and thereby made to sell for a much higher price at every foreign market. It is chiefly owing to this, that the sugar-baking trade has been for so many years a thriving trade in this nation, a trade by which some gentlemen have got large fortunes, and many of our poor a considerable subsistence.[69]

Sir John Barnard, speaking in favour of the bill, declared:

The navigation acts . . . have certainly been of great benefit to this nation. They were certainly right at the time they were enacted; and if circumstances were now the same, I should be against altering them in any part. . . . When those laws were passed, we had a monopoly of the trade. . . . But the case is now very different: we have now a rival, and a dangerous rival in the sugar trade; and if we do not allow foreigners to have our sugars, at least as cheap as they can have the same sort of commodity from our rival, they will have none of ours. . . . If we had been as wise and vigilant as we ought to have been, we might have . . . ruined the French sugar trade in its infancy, by taking off all those unnecessary charges that enhanced the price of our sugars at the foreign market. . . . The dispute therefore, Sir, is not, upon this occasion, between our planters in the West-Indies and our own people here at home: the question is, whether we shall encourage and entirely establish the French sugar trade, by giving them all foreign markets for sugar?[70]

---

[68]Stock, *Proceedings and Debates*, IV, 814.   [69]*Ibid.*, p. 815.

[70]*Ibid.*, p. 181. It is interesting to note that Barnard was more concerned about the French success than the English failure.

Thus the whole controversy centred around the amount of money the English exporter of sugar had to spend on extra-charges and costs necessitated by the circuitous route prescribed by the Navigation Act of 1660. The discussion is indicative of the impediments to any change away from the policy of the Navigation Acts, impediments created by ignorance of economic laws, by lack of imagination, and by the stubborn opposition of vested interests whose growth these Acts had encouraged.

Another vexing problem which disturbed the minds of metropolitan politicians and writers was that of providing sufficient export markets to the Northern American plantations.[71] Neither the mother country nor the southern and West Indian dependencies of England offered markets of sufficient capacity for the products these possessions raised. The question was whether they should be given freedom to trade directly with European countries and with non-English colonies in the Caribbean. Some representative statements will be cited which approved of such a policy in the interest of the mother country.

Thomas Pownall stated the case of the Northern American plantations as follows:

... it is the singular disadvantage of the Northern British colonies, that, while they stand in need of vast quantities of the manufactures of Great Britain, the country is productive of very little which affords a direct remittance thither in payment; and that from necessity therefore, the inhabitants have been driven to seek a market for their produce, where it could be vended, and, by a course of traffic, to acquire either money or such merchandize as would answer the purpose of a remittance, and enable them to sustain their credit with the mother country.[72]

To provide a solution for this predicament Matthew Decker proposed "to encourage our Plantations in raising Growths by permitting their Exportation to any Part of Europe."[73] He asserted: "Our Colonies in America ... might be made ten times more advantageous to us than they now are, by consuming most of our Manufactures, and turning the general Ballance of Trade with

---

[71] It will be recalled from foregoing discussions that this problem demanded a solution for two important reasons: first, the productions of these colonies were largely not complementary to those of the mother country and Ireland. Their capacity for importing metropolitan manufactures, therefore, was greatly reduced due to the lack of purchasing power. Secondly, if these colonies could not be provided with markets for the rawstuffs they raised, they would, it was feared, turn to setting up manufacturing industries of their own.

[72] *The Administration of the Colonies* (1768), p. 285.

[73] *An Essay on the Cause of the Decline of Foreign Trade* (1751), p. 176.

Europe greatly in favour of their Mother-Country, and be fixed on a Basis that will prevent their manufacturing or rebelling for Ages to come...."⁷⁴ Israel Mauduit even suggested that the Northern colonists be allowed to export grain to the Iberian Peninsula in exchange for wines. He said:

> It is a Quere, whether our Remittances might not also be encreased by allowing us to bring directly from Spain and Portugal, Wines, paying a Duty; for this would enable us to supply those Countries with Wheat, for which we often want a Market: But to supply them, and return with Vessels entirely empty, will seldom answer. It is true, this Method would interfere with the British Market for that Commodity: But sound Policy will teach us, that Britain ought never to fear a Competition between her and her Colonies in Trade; because . . . all the Acquirements of her Colonies, in the End, must be remitted to Britain.⁷⁵

The same argument was used by writers who approved of the trade conducted by the Northern American colonists with non-English Caribbean islands. Sir William Keith stated that "the Profits arising to British subjects in America, from their exchanging Lumber, &c. with the Product of foreign Plantations, either to be used in America, or returned to Europe for British Account, must terminate in the Advantage of Great Britain; who thereby reaps a certain Gain from the Labour of Foreigners, as well as from that of her own Subjects, besides engrossing a larger Share of such Commodities as the better enables her to govern the European Market."⁷⁶

Another author, applauding the repeal of the Sugar Act of 1764, advised the government to follow a general policy of extending the commercial freedom of the colonies "by striking off those shackles that have unfortunately been put on through false principle, clogging and retarding its progress and extension, contrary to all

---

⁷⁴*Ibid.*

⁷⁵Israel Mauduit, *Some Thoughts on the Method of Improving and Securing the Advantages Which Accrue to Great-Britain from the Northern Colonies* (London, 1765), p. 19.

⁷⁶*The History of the British Plantations* (1738), I, 12. The interesting point of this statement is that Keith not only appreciated the fact that, by trading with the French sugar islands, the Northern colonists were able to obtain purchasing power for their imports from the mother country, but also welcomed the nature of the returns they received from their French customers. Obviously he did not only refer to molasses and rum but also to French sugar and other indigenous products. The ability to dispose of an additional share of the West Indian sugar output would help the British to crowd the French out of the European market. The West Indian sugar interest, of course, was stoutly opposed to such a policy. Perrin, for example, deplored "the pernicious Practice

sound policy, and the true interest of these Kingdoms."⁷⁷ He declared:

> The complaints of our northern colonies are the want of markets for vending their several productions, and a channel for receiving returns, which have a natural tendency to encrease commerce, shipping, seamen, and treasure, that in due time will find its way home to the mother country; for this purpose, the exportation of every natural production of North-America, to every part of the West Indies should be encouraged, and permission given to import from all parts of the West-Indies into North-America every kind of produce whatsoever . . . by which means to become the general carriers for all nations as much as we be. . . .⁷⁸

Israel Mauduit supported this point of view. He also advocated the admission of French sugars into the North American continent. ". . . for if our own Islands do furnish a sufficient Quantity of Sugars, whatever we procure more will be exported, and bring a Gain to the Nation in Proportion to its Value. . . . Even Money sent to the French Islanders can be no Injury to the Nation, since, by purchasing their Produce at the first Hand, we shall acquire all the Profits of transporting it to foreign Parts."⁷⁹

Mauduit's proposal to permit the Northern colonists the import of French colonial products in exchange for "Money," frankly expressed the desirability of such imports even if they competed with British goods. Earlier, Keith had approved of the nature of

---

of introducing French Sugars into our Northern Colonies . . . which has been but too long carried on under the Denomination of English Produce" (*The Present State of the Sugar Colonies* [1740], p. 2).

The Molasses Act of 1733 was passed in order to put a stop to this importation of French products. Placing prohibitive duties on rum, molasses, and sugars of non-British origin, it proved ineffectual since the colonists did not abide by it. Grenville's Sugar Act of 1764 reduced the duties on colonial imports of foreign molasses to a revenue basis, retained the duty on foreign sugar and altogether forbade the importation of foreign rum. However, the most important part of this novel policy was that it envisaged the creation of administrative machinery capable of enforcing this new legislation. Because of the violent opposition of the Northern colonists the Act of 1764 was repealed in 1766 along with the Stamp Act.

⁷⁷S.F.V., "On the British Colonies Trade and Commerce" (written on March 5, 1766), reprinted in John Almon, *A New and Impartial Collection of Interesting Letters from the Public Papers* (London, 1767), II, 140.

⁷⁸*Ibid.* This writer, however, disapproved of the free importation of sugar which "is the great article that is essentially exceptionable" (*ibid.*). He thought that the French could and did raise sugar at half the cost of the English planters. If the French would find a vent for that article on the continent of North America, they would expand their production and become "rich" and "strong" at the expense of the English sugar islands (*ibid.*, pp. 140 f.).

⁷⁹*Some Thoughts* (1765), p. 18.

the returns obtained by the Northern colonists from their trade with the non-British Caribbean islands. He had also spoken of the fact that England would thereby "reap a certain Gain from the Labour of Foreigners."[80] If pursued to its logical conclusion, this line of thought would have forced these imperialist writers to realize that non-possession of colonies might mean an economic advantage. For, given the possibility of importing products from French colonies, the English might acquire these goods at lower cost than the French themselves who had to bear the expense of governing and protecting their plantations. William Wood indeed, came close to this realization. He wrote:

But by insisting that no Breach in the Navigation Act be connived at, I would not have it inferred, that I am against permitting the Inhabitants of our Colonies and Plantations to trade with, or sell their Product one among another; or that they should be prohibited to Trade to the Colonies or Plantations of any Foreign Nation ... altho' in return they should not bring Gold or Silver, but the Product of that Country they shall trade to; and altho' such Product interfere with, or be of the same Species with any of our Colonies of Plantations Produce. This may not perhaps be relished by our Planters; but if they will not allow it to be for their Interest in particular, I am sure they can't dispute its being for the Interest of Great Britain in General. For by this means we render Foreign Colonies and Plantations, to be in effect, the Colonies and Plantations of Great-Britain. And this brings me to say, That all Laws in our Southern Plantations, which lay great Duties on Sugar, Indico, Ginger, and other West-India Commodities, imported into them, will be found, when fully and impartially considered, not only prejudicial to them, but to the Trade and Navigation of this Kingdom.... For the Inhabitants, by carrying on a Trade with their Foreign Neighbours, do not only occasion a greater Quantity of Goods and Merchandize of Europe being sent from hence to them, and a greater quantity of the Product of America, to be sent from them hither, which would otherwise be carried from, and brought to Europe by Foreigners; but an Encrease of the Seafaring Men....[81]

This whole question of a direct trade between English and foreign colonies in America was broached again in connection with the erection of free ports in the British West Indies. The arguments used for and against such institutions were the same

[80] *Ibid.*

[81] *A Survey of Trade* (London, 1718), pp. 136 ff. Another advantage seen by Wood in the adoption of such a policy was that of transporting French sugars from America to Europe in English rather than in French bottoms.

But Wood spoke sharply against the Northern colonists purchasing manufactures in the foreign West Indian islands (*ibid.*, p. 141).

Postlethwayt copied the above-quoted passage and incorporated it into his article on Colonies in his *Universal Dictionary of Trade and Commerce* (4th ed.; London, 1774).

as those examined above. A lengthy discussion of the problem was given by Joshua Gee.[82] The two main arguments in favour of this "novel arrangement" were that it would secure an additional volume of raw materials and provide an additional outlet for British manufactures.[83] The main argument against it was that it was supposed to operate to the detriment of English navigation.[84] S.F.V. succinctly stated this early attack on the integrity of the Navigation Acts when he remarked that it meant "the extension of British trade and sale of manufactures beyond the bounds of our own settlements."[85]

In spite of English and Spanish imperial regulations forbidding such intercourse, a profitable, illicit trade had been carried on between the English and Spanish Central American colonies with the connivance of the authorities.[86] The Grenville administration, in line with its general fiscal and colonial policy, instructed colonial governors in 1765 henceforth to enforce the Navigation Law with thorough strictness. The result was that British exports to Jamaica alone declined by one-fourth between 1763 and 1765. Due to the pressure exerted by interested merchants, the Free Port Law of 1766 was passed which constituted one of the earliest relaxations of the British Navigation Laws. The West Indian planters, of course, did not like this foreign competition with their own products and were therefore sharply opposed to the renewal of the Act. In 1774, however, the Act was renewed and it is interesting to note that at this time not only the merchants were responsible for its passage but that, for the first time, the Lancashire cotton manufacturers found it to their advantage to advocate the relaxation of the Navigation Acts. Because of the insufficiency of British colonial production they had to buy cotton and indigo from foreign sources of supply and through the West Indian free ports they were able to import these materials at a price 30 per cent lower than by roundabout imports via France.[87]

[82]*The Trade and Navigation of Great Britain Considered* (London, 1731), p. 190 ff.   [83]*Ibid.*, pp. 191 ff.   [84]*Ibid.*

[85]S.F.V., "On the British Colonies Trade and Commerce" (1766) in Almon, *A New and Impartial Collection of Interesting Letters* (1767), II, 148.

[86]A circular letter directed Colonial Governors in 1685 not to enforce the Navigation Laws against ships coming to Jamaica and Barbados with the produce of the Spanish West Indies. This arrangement was highly appreciated by the English slave traders (S. H. N. Iddesleigh, *A Short Review of the History of the Navigation Laws of England* [London, 1849], p. 18).

[87]*Ibid.*, p. 19; Arthur Redfield, *Manchester Merchants and Foreign Trade 1794-1858* (Manchester, 1934), p. 3. Edwards, *History of the British West Indies*, I, 288 ff.

Little can be said here on the question of the social genesis of the whole array of British arguments on the utility of colonization and colonies to the metropolis. Even a very detailed study would have only corroborative value. In broad outline the facts are obvious. It has been shown that up to the American War of Independence the overwhelming majority of influential public opinion favoured the establishment and retention of colonies in the supposed interest of the mother country. Of the literature examined in the course of the present study, the larger part was written by mercantilists who were merchants or who represented the merchants' point of view.[88] But, as between writers who can be identified with the merchants' interest and those that cannot, there appears no appreciable difference in the basic approach to important questions of imperial theory and policy. Nor is it possible to detect any noteworthy disagreement between Whigs and Tories. As a whole, the influential in England stood for Empire as a good business proposition and for laws that, in their eyes, appeared to make this business as profitable and secure as possible. What anti-imperial criticism there was came from a very small minority of men who had no stake in the profits of Empire but subscribed to more advanced ideas on the nature of the public good than their contemporaries.

At the beginning of English trans-Atlantic colonization many different social groups took a lively interest in this expansionist movement. In addition to the persecuted elements of the population who sought refuge across the ocean, the monarch, statesmen, courtiers, officials, soldiers, navigators, adventurers, the clergy, the business promoter, and the landed gentry, all these various sections contributed men, money, ships, and propaganda for this novel undertaking.[89] Yet from the beginning English merchants were the principal agents of colonization,[90] and it is safe to say that they

[88]If the overwhelming majority of the English merchants engaged in seaborne commerce were in favour of colonization and colonies, the specific interests of particular merchant groups were, of course, often conflicting. This led them to adopt different opinions as to the virtue of particular imperial regulations.

[89]See Walter Raleigh, *The English Voyages of the Sixteenth Century*, in Hakluyt, *The Principal Navigations* (Glasgow, 1904), XII, 1-120; W. Cunningham, *The Growth of English Industry and Commerce* (5th ed., Cambridge, 1915), I, 119 f.; H. M. Robertson, *Aspects of the Rise of Economic Individualism* (Cambridge, 1935), pp. 188 ff.; W. R. Scott, *The Constitution and Finance of English, Scottish, and Irish Joint-Stock Companies to 1720* (Cambridge, 1910), I, passim.

[90]Eburne's pamphlet, which is, at bottom, nothing but a propaganda sheet in favour of English colonization, expressly refrained from addressing the mer-

assumed this role increasingly in the course of the centuries. Throughout the period ending with the disruption of the first British Empire, merchants were the main force behind colonial expansion[91] and behind legislation dealing with colonial trade. Merchants were interested in the suppression of tobacco growing in England which gave the colonists a monopoly of the metropolitan market.[92] Merchants proposed the colonization of the American hinterland as early as 1689.[93] Merchants had been instrumental in the establishment of the Navigation Acts.[94] Merchants favoured the granting of bounties for the production of naval stores in America.[95]

Indeed, these examples could be easily multiplied. Anyone who reads the records of the British Parliament, and especially those of the House of Commons, is impressed by the ubiquity and the influence of the merchant-interest in all matters relating to the colonies.[96] There is little, if any, exaggeration in the judgment

chants. He said: "But . . . I need speake little of the Merchants good, as . . . doe so well know it of themselues and thereupon affect the enterprise so much, that if other mens desires and endeuours were correspondent, it would take both speedy and condigne effect" (*Plaine Path-Way to Plantations* [London, 1624], p. 11).

[91]On the expansionist attitude of the merchants during the Seven Years' War see Kate Hotblack, *Chatham's Colonial Policy* (London, 1917); [Richard Glover], *Memoirs by a Celebrated Literary and Political Character* (London, 1814), pp. 59 f.; John Almon *Review of Pitt's Administration* (London, 1763), pp. 12 f.; Stock, *Proceedings and Debates*, II, 24, 26.

[92]*Ibid.*, II, 106.

[93]G. H. Guttridge, *The Colonial Policy of William III* (Cambridge, England, 1922), p. 173.

[94]Cf. *supra*, p. 156.

[95]H. L. Osgood, *The American Colonies in the Eighteenth Century* (New York, 1924), I, 497 ff.

[96]On the parliamentary influence of the merchants see Namier, *England in the Age of the American Revolution*, pp. 263-327; Witt Bowden, *Industrial Society in England towards the End of the Eighteenth Century* (New York, 1925), pp. 1-6; Ashley, *Financial and Commercial Policy under the Cromwellian Protectorate*, pp. 4 ff., 61, 132 ff., 153 ff.; G. N. Clark, *The Later Stuarts* (Oxford, 1934), pp. 42-9.

The influence of the merchants in parliament was, of course, not of equal strength with regard to all matters of public interest. They were more influential in matters relating to trade than in those relating to non-commercial subjects and it appears that they were more influential in matters relating to colonial trade than in matters of trade in general.

The notorious corruptness of English parliamentary politics in the eighteenth century lent additional weight to the political influence wielded by the merchants. An excellent account of political corruption in the second half of the eighteenth century is found in Allan Ramsay, *A Letter to Edmund Burke* (London, 1780).

of Adam Smith who declared: "Of the greater part of the regulations concerning the colony trade, the merchants who carry it on, it must be observed, have been the principal advisers. We must not wonder, therefore, if, in the greater part of them, their interest has been more considered than either that of the colonies or that of the mother country."[97]

[97]Adam Smith, *An Inquiry into the Nature and Causes of the Wealth of Nations*, ed. Edwin Cannan, reprinted by the Modern Library (New York, 1937), p. 550.

PART II

CHAPTER V

INTRODUCTION

THE last quarter of the eighteenth century in England was replete with events that heralded the approach of a new era. This period witnessed the collapse of the Old British Empire, an event that inaugurated the gradual decolonization of the Americas but was followed shortly by the establishment of a new Anglo-Saxon empire in Africa, Asia, and the Antipodes. There occurred a remarkable acceleration of that process of technological progress which is called the Industrial Revolution. A predominantly industrial age was to succeed a predominantly mercantile age. This development was to render the United Kingdom the "industrial workshop" of the world. It also brought about a vast redistribution of economic power which, in turn, called for a redistribution of political influence and social prestige.

This gradual transformation of the political, economic, and social organization of Britain was accompanied by important changes in the sphere of ideas, sentiments, and values. The beginnings of Philosophical Radicalism and the strengthening of the Evangelical revival were two manifestations of this change of spirit which were to leave a distinct imprint on British imperial thinking.

The publication of Adam Smith's *An Inquiry into the Nature and Causes of the Wealth of Nations* in 1776 was another event of epochal importance within the realm of ideas. This book owed its eminent significance to two principal reasons. On the one hand, it contained the first systematic assault on mercantilism as a system of doctrinal elements and of policies implemented by the state. On the other hand, it initiated economics as an academic science.

Obviously Adam Smith's accomplishments in both respects produced far-reaching and revolutionizing repercussions on English patterns of theorizing on the subject of colonies. Before resuming the examination of colonial theories it seems advisable, therefore, to review briefly the main features of this change in economic thinking.

It is the final verdict of modern students of the history of economic theories that Adam Smith was not an original, but an eclectic thinker.[1] His great merit lies in systematizing the findings of his predecessors, in showing to his contemporaries the existence of certain laws inherent in social phenomena, in demonstrating that, through the application of these laws to economic reality, it was possible to penetrate logically even the most complicated interplay of economic forces. With the help of the abstract analytical tools he created, the totality of economic life could be subjected to critical examination.

The foundation of economics as an academic science carried two significant implications for imperial theorizing. By laying bare the principles underlying the working of any economic system, Adam Smith had lent autonomy to the science of economics. No matter what spiritual, political, or social changes may occur in the environment of a nation, they cannot invalidate the findings of the economist. He is not competent to determine ends but he is qualified to examine the suitability of means in the economic sphere. The scientific technique of the economist could claim universal applicability whenever and wherever a problem posed specifically economic questions. Consequently, in so far as the governing body of an imperial power cared to consider the possession of colonies from an intelligently economic point of view, it had to resort to the expert economist and to accept his findings as binding.

Quite aside from Adam Smith's methodological achievements, it seems useful, at this point, to mention the fundamental concepts with which he tore apart the decaying tissue of mercantilist reasoning. The Old Colonial System was part of the Mercantile System and the intimate connection between mercantilist conceptions of foreign trade and opinions on the utility of the colonies has been demonstrated. The refutation of these mercantilist notions, therefore, whether originally presented or only systematized and popularized by Adam Smith, had an important bearing on the question of the usefulness of imperial connections.

The fallaciousness of the customary mercantilist balance-of-trade doctrine had been exposed before by David Hume's elucidation of the theory of the automatic mechanism of international specie distribution.[2] Indeed the balance-of-trade doctrine is the

[1] Jacob Viner, "Adam Smith and Laissez Faire," in J. M. Clark et al., *Adam Smith, 1776-1926* (Chicago, 1928), p. 117.

[2] On the historical development of this theory see Jacob Viner, *Studies in the Theory of International Trade* (New York, 1937), pp. 74-87. Note that Adam

only element of mercantilist reasoning which was so completely effaced from the public mind of the following generations that it does not reappear in English speculation on the utility of colonies.

Much more prodigious in its ultimate consequences was the evolution of the concept of the international division of labour. Here also, theorists like the author of *Considerations on the East-India Trade*, Isaac Gervaise, and others, had anticipated the essence of the new principle.[3] Explaining this concept, Adam Smith started by pointing out that division of labour "occasions, in every art, a proportionable increase in the productive powers of labour."[4] The benefits of increased productivity were obvious.

Division of labour is stimulated by "the propensity to truck, barter, and exchange one thing for another."[5] If the implementation of this principle, therefore, is based on the exchange of goods, then, the actual extent of division of labour is only limited by the extent of the market.[6] Hence, the function of foreign trade is to widen the market and thus to insure the widest possible operation of the principle. "By means of it, the narrowness of the home market does not hinder the division of labour. . . ."[7] In this manner, foreign commerce encourages labour "to improve its productive powers, and to augment its annual produce to the utmost, and thereby to increase the real revenue and wealth of the society."[8]

This change in the conception of the utility of international trade was of incalculable portent. While the typical mercantilist theorist saw the usefulness of foreign commerce as flowing from the God-ordained differences in the natural resources of different areas of production, henceforth this notion was replaced by the principle of comparative production cost.

The implications of this change of view were immense. As long as the attention of theorists and politicians was largely focused on the different physical resources with which different areas of production were endowed, there was always the possibility of doing without foreign trade by acquiring such areas as complemented the natural resources of one's own country. The view of

---

Smith did not incorporate this theory into the *Wealth of Nations* (*ibid.*, p. 87). He pronounced the balance-of-trade theory absurd on the ground that treasure is only a commodity as any other (*An Inquiry into the Nature and Causes of the Wealth of Nations*, ed. Edwin Cannan [New York, 1937], pp. 406, 408 f., 415).

[3]Viner, *Studies in the Theory of International Trade*, pp. 104-10.
[4]*Wealth of Nations*, p. 5. [5]*Ibid.*, p. 13.
[6]*Ibid.*, p. 17.   [7]*Ibid.*, p. 415.   [8]*Ibid.*

international commerce based on division of labour, occasioned by differences in production cost, lent to the wealth to be derived from it a basis which partook only incidentally of a territorial nature. Trade beyond the national frontier was dependent on exchange, not on dominion.[9]

Political frontiers marking the fact of dominion, if identical with customs barriers, would have the effect of limiting international division of labour by impeding or deflecting the natural flow of goods. The effectuation of Free Trade, by obliterating these barriers, would result in the augmentation of all those benefits which unfettered division of labour promised to afford. The implementation of free trade, consequently, seemed to render the possession of territorial empire unprofitable in matters of trade. Also, territorial expansion and conquest appeared incapable of increasing the gains to be derived from trade.[10] The "trade empire" was to be based on the free international exchange of goods.[11] Unless fostered on account of non-economic objectives, the notion of self-sufficiency lost even the semblance of a national advantage. The trend of free-trade considerations as such was definitely away from appraising economic advantages in terms of nations. Its ultimate implication was world economic unity based on the most economical distribution of production. Utmost competition, unrestricted by national considerations, alone assured the fullest effect of the principle of economy of production.

The conception of a fixed total of foreign trade for the largest comparative share of which the various nations had to struggle, was another notion which had confused the minds of mercantilists as to the true benefits to be reaped from international commerce. The classical economists proved the fallaciousness of this notion and established that foreign trade was of mutual, if not of exactly equal, benefit to all nations engaged in it.[12] Here again Adam

[9]See on this, M. J. Bonn, *The Crumbling of Empire* (London, 1938), p. 92.

[10]It was for this reason that the Physiocrats spoke of "la folie des conquêtes" and "la fureur de s'étendre" (Adolf Rein, *Die europäische Ausbreitung über die Erde* [Potsdam, 1931], p. 320).

[11]Bonn, *Crumbling of Empire*, pp. 88 f., 94. It is interesting to note that the phrase, the "trade empire," was already used by Joseph Addison at the beginning of the eighteenth century. He wrote: "Trade, without enlarging the British territories, has given us a sort of additional empire; it has multiplied the number of the rich, made our landed estates infinitely more valuable than they were formerly, and added to them the accession of other estates as valuable as the lands themselves" (Thomas Arnold [ed.], *Addison* [Oxford, 1891], p. 118).

[12]Smith, *Wealth of Nations*, pp. 415, 456.

Smith had numerous predecessors, even among the mercantilists themselves.[13] This novel concept, of course, rendered any feeling of jealousy in matters of foreign trade superfluous as long as that trade was approached on a rational basis. It also made the intelligent observer aware of the fact that the wealth of foreign nations only enhanced their capacity as customers and suppliers of goods.[14]

Regard for the consumers' interest signified another change of view which profoundly affected English theorizing on the utility of empire. The mercantilists, as has been pointed out, cared, on the whole, very little about the large mass of the people as consumers. This attitude was almost reversed by the classical economists. Henceforth cheapness of consumers' goods, whether produced at home or imported from abroad, was regarded as the main objective of economic activity. Thus, Adam Smith stated that it was one object of political economy "to provide a plentiful revenue or subsistence for the people. . . ."[15]

It is the greatest multiplication of the productions of all the different arts, in consequence of the division of labour, which occasions in a well-governed society, that universal opulence which extends itself to the lowest rank of the people.[16]

Consumption is the sole end and purpose of all production; and the interest of the producer ought to be attended to, only so far as it may be necessary for promoting that of the consumer. The maxim is so perfectly self-evident, that it would be absurd to attempt to prove it. But in the mercantile system, the interest of the consumer is almost constantly sacrificed to that of the producer; and it seems to consider production, and not consumption, as the ultimate end and object of all industry and commerce.[17]

World-wide division of labour, implemented by the unhindered flow of international trade, would tend to put capital and labour to optimum use and would thereby maximize production and consumption.[18]

To the mercantilist faith in the efficacy and benefit of state action in matters of trade and production, Adam Smith and his fellow economists opposed the idea of laissez-faire.[19] Smith

[13]For example, Josiah Tucker, *Four Tracts* (Glocester, 1774), pp. 75, 96 f.

[14]Smith, *Wealth of Nations*, p. 461. Also David Hume's essay "Of the Jealousy of Trade," *The Philosophical Works* (Edinburgh, 1826), part II, pp. 768 ff.; Tucker, *Four Tracts*, p. 82; Tucker, *Cui Bono?* (Glocester, 1782), pp. 32, 46, 65.

[15]*Wealth of Nations*, p. 397.

[16]*Ibid.*, p. 11.   [17]*Ibid.*, p. 625.   [18]*Ibid.*, p. 424.

[19]On the English forerunners of Smith in this respect see Viner, *Studies in the Theory of International Trade*, pp. 91-103.

postulated that it is the individual, selfishly striving for the greatest possible personal gain, who will employ his capital in a manner most advantageous not only for himself but also for society as a whole. The more productive the use to which he will put his capital, the greater his profit and the greater the benefit of society. Running a personal risk he also will be disposed to judge the value of his investment with more foresight than the statesman or legislator.[20] The extent to which this new doctrine is based on the belief in a predetermined harmony inherent in the nature of economic forces is immaterial to the purposes of the present study.[21] It found considerable support inspired by the empirical insight into the defects of state action in the economic sphere.[22] The significant content of this doctrine was that, in the realm of business, the activity of man, even though selfish in nature, providentially results in a neutral good, namely the free-market price. And even if later economists, like Malthus and Ricardo, detected certain flaws and perceived a certain amount of disharmony in the unrestricted working of economic forces, they remained convinced that government interference in general could not result in improvement and that the defects attending a system of laissez-faire were still by far the smaller evil if contrasted with a system of state regulation.[23]

The implications of the doctrine of laissez-faire were indeed so important for British conceptions of the utility of colonial trade, that it seems advisable to present, in the following, some of Adam Smith's major conclusions on systems of restraints and encouragements:

> It is thus that every system which endeavours, either, by extraordinary encouragements, to draw towards a particular species of industry a greater share of the capital of the society than what would naturally go to; or, by

---

[20] *Wealth of Nations*, pp. 422 f.

[21] See on this, Viner, "Adam Smith and Laissez Faire," pp. 127 ff. For a view that denies Adam Smith's belief in a natural-law order, see H. J. Bitterman, "Adam Smith's Empiricism and the Law of Nature," *Journal of Political Economy*, XLVIII (1940), 487-520, 703-34.

[22] As a liberalist creed the new belief in laissez-faire had also political-philosophical roots. Due to the evolution of Locke's concept of the right of private property it was assumed that the owner of property as a producer has the right to sell his goods in the widest and most promising market, while the owner of property as a consumer has the right to buy where he receives most for his money. See on this, Guido Ruggiero, *The History of European Liberalism* (Oxford, 1927), pp. 32 ff.

[23] See E. Heckscher, *Mercantilism* (London, 1935), II, 317; Viner, *Studies in the Theory of International Trade*, p. 93.

extraordinary restraints, to force from a particular species of industry some share of the capital which would otherwise be employed in it; it is in reality subversive of the great purpose which it means to promote. It retards, instead of accelerating, the progress of society towards real wealth and greatness; and diminishes, instead of increasing, the real value of the annual produce of its land and labour. All systems either of preference or of restraint, therefore, being thus completely taken away, the obvious and simple system of natural liberty establishes itself of its own accord. Every man, as long as he does not violate the laws of justice, is left perfectly free to pursue his own interest his own way, and to bring both his industry and capital into competition with those of any other man, or order of men. The sovereign is completely discharged from a duty, in the attempting to perform which he must always be exposed to innumerable delusions, and for the proper performance of which no human wisdom or knowledge could ever be sufficient...."[24]

Similarly his verdict on bounties and monopolies in foreign trade: "A trade which is forced by means of bounties and monopolies, may be, and commonly is disadvantageous to the country in whose favour it is meant to be established.... But that trade which, without force or constraint, is naturally and regularly carried on between any two places, is always advantageous...."[25]

Organization in contradistinction to laissez-faire is, according to the classical economists, not only as a rule disadvantageous to society because the individual if "left perfectly free to pursue his own interests his own way" is achieving a public good which government, even if possessed of "wisdom" and "knowledge," cannot bring about to the same extent. Organization also is ever an evil because by its very nature it breeds monopolies and unfair practices.

In addition to all his other accomplishments, Adam Smith, in his *Wealth of Nations*, performed the useful function of the muckraker. Relentlessly he exposed the crafty and vicious activities

---

[24] *Wealth of Nations*, pp. 650 f. The following is a quotation from a contemporaneous statement of the doctrine. Comparing the principles of government with the principles of commerce, Allan Ramsay concludes that they are "opposite" to one another. "The principle of Government is ... arising from supreme command and subordination, to provide, upon maxims general and extensive, for the order and safety of the whole; whereas the interest of commerce is best promoted, when each private merchant, without any extensive view of commerce in general, and without concerning himself about the interest of his neighbour, or the interest of the State, quietly employs his industry in his own branch of business for his own private emolument" (*Letters on the Present Disturbances in Great Britain and her American Provinces* [1775] [London, 1777], pp. 31 f.).

[25] *Wealth of Nations*, p. 456.

of people possessed of "vested interests." He showed that the Mercantile System was the deliberate creation of influential sectional interests which exploited its concomitant monopolies.[26] He spoke contemptuously of "the sneaking arts of underling tradesmen" which were "erected into political maxims for the conduct of a great empire,"[27] and of "the mean rapacity, the monopolizing spirit of merchants and manufacturers, who neither are, nor ought to be, the rulers of mankind."[28] ". . . The interested sophistry of merchants and manufacturers confounded the common sense of mankind. Their interest is, in this respect, directly opposite to that of the great body of the people."[29] No doubt, Smith's low opinion of the actual working of the British system of government[30] only re-enforced his aversion to any sort of government control of business. The portent of these accusations by Adam Smith and, later, by the Benthamites and other reformist groups, can hardly be over-estimated. They contributed greatly to the success of the cause of liberalism in general and had, as will be seen below, a notable effect on the question of empire.

Finally, it is necessary to mention briefly the problem of power and wealth. The mercantilists had spoken profusely of the promotion of "wealth" and "power" as seemingly inter-related, if not identical, objectives of policy. All their utterances on this inter-relationship are of such impenetrable vagueness that even the most painstaking research fails to yield any definite conclusions as to the meaning they attributed to these terms. The mercantilist theorists appear to have assumed that wealth and power beget each other and that any measure promotive of one is presumably also promotive of the other.

To this subject, too, Adam Smith made a noteworthy and fertile contribution. As Cunningham observed, he isolated the subject of wealth for purposes of economic investigation and treated it apart from other political and social phenomena.[31] He lent to the terms "wealth," "riches," and "opulence" an abstract meaning quite distinct from such concrete things as treasure, ships, and manpower which to many mercantilists seemed to be the direct constituents of wealth.[32] Never did he talk loosely about

[26]*Ibid.*, pp. 402 f.   [27]*Ibid.*, p. 460.   [28]*Ibid.*
[29]*Ibid.*, p. 461. For similar references see *ibid.*, pp. 437 f., 460 f., 545, 549, 580, 608 f., 616.
[30]He spoke of "the great lottery of British politics" (*ibid.*, p. 587).
[31]W. Cunningham, *Richard Cobden and Adam Smith* (London, 1904), p. 32.
[32]See on this, Emanuel Leser, *Der Begriff des Reichthums bei Adam Smith* (Heidelberg, 1874), pp. 4 ff.

"wealth" and "power" as fundamentally conjoint phenomena. While to many mercantilist writers power was an end in itself, there can be no doubt that Adam Smith recognized the necessity for state power only for one purpose: that of defence against aggression. He lived in an age in which international organization for the elimination of war was a definitely Utopian affair. A nation's capacity for defence rested entirely on its ability to inspire fear by the mobilization of a sufficient aggregate of force.[33] Yet it is quite clear that the author of *The Wealth of Nations* conceived of wealth and power as conflicting ends of policy. He approved of the Navigation Acts and of certain bounties as conducive to the defensive strength of the nation although he disapproved of them as means to the attainment of national wealth.[34] In his introduction to Book IV he wrote: "Political economy, considered as a branch of the science of a statesman or legislator, proposes two distinct objects: first, to provide a *plentiful* revenue or subsistence for the people, or more properly to enable them to provide such revenue or subsistence for themselves; and secondly, to supply the state or commonwealth with a revenue *sufficient* for the public services."[35] As the task of defence is one of the public services, this passage reveals unambiguously that public consideration of power is an objective definitely limited to the point at which preparedness has reached a "sufficient" state, while considerations of plenty should be pursued without limitations once the requirements of defence are satisfied.

Mercantilist writers assumed that wealth bred power and that power bred wealth. Adam Smith, as has been shown, perceived

[33] *Wealth of Nations*, p. 591.

[34] Smith wrote: "The act of navigation is not favourable to foreign commerce or the growth of that opulence which can arise from it. . . . As defence, however, is of much more importance than opulence, the act of navigation is, perhaps, the wisest of all the commercial regulations of England" (*ibid.*, p. 431).

Of the basic conflict between a policy of power and a policy of plenty David Hume gave an interesting formulation: "Here . . . seems to be a kind of opposition between the greatness of the state and the happiness of the subject. A state is never greater than when all its superfluous hands are employed in the service of the public. The ease and convenience of private persons require that these hands should be employed in their service. The one can never be satisfied but at the expense of the other. As the ambition of the sovereign must entrench on the luxury of individuals, so the luxury of individuals must diminish the force, and check the ambition of the sovereign." This is a passage of Hume's essay, "Of Commerce," see *Philosophical Works*, III, 289.

[35] *Wealth of Nations*, p. 397. See on this, Theodor Pütz, *Wirtschaftslehre und Weltanschauung bei Adam Smith* (München, 1932), pp. 108 f.

a definite conflict between policies aiming at wealth and those aiming at power. He realized that the creation and maintenance of power was economically costly. He agreed that wealth was productive of power[36] but there is no reason to conclude that he conceived of power as being conducive to wealth.[37]

To the extent that these ideas were squarely in conflict with corresponding mercantilist opinions it must, of course, not be assumed that, in the public mind, the latter were ever completely superseded by the former. It took a long struggle before the free-trade and laissez-faire theories achieved their temporary triumph in Britain. As will be seen in the course of the following examination of English colonial theories, mercantilist notions, with the exception of the old balance-of-trade doctrine, continued to be extremely potent and lingered on for more than half a century after the publication of *The Wealth of the Nations*. Never were they completely routed.

In the introductory chapter to this study an attempt was made

[36] See *Wealth of Nations*, pp. 668 f. There Adam Smith notes that the expensiveness of foreign wars gives an advantage to the "opulent" over the "poor" nation. See also *ibid.*, pp. 410-14.

[37] Adam Smith apparently assumed that to the selfish supporters of the Mercantile System the external power of the state was a means to the attainment of "wealth" for themselves. Discussing the Old Colonial System he wrote: "... a nation whose government is influenced by shopkeepers ... will find some advantage in employing the blood and treasure of their fellow-citizens, to found and maintain such an empire" (*Wealth of Nations*, p. 579). Following this statement, Smith intimated that the Seven Years' War and the war of 1739 were caused by exactly such considerations (*ibid.*, p. 581). No doubt, his exhortation that merchants be not allowed to become or to influence rulers was determined by his suspicion that such interest-groups might find it convenient to utilize the power of the state for the furtherance of their own selfish business interests. It is interesting to note that Allan Ramsay likewise deplored "a friendly alliance between the camp and the counting-house" for exactly the same reasons (*Letters on the Present Disturbances*, p. 34). Ramsay maintained that of the evil consequences of such alliance "the two last wars carried on by England against France and Spain, furnish a most melancholy illustration. To obtain the sole and exclusive commerce of the western world, in which the French and Spaniards were their rivals, was the modest wish of our merchants, in conjunction with our Americans. The fair, and truly commercial, method of effecting this would have been, by superior skill, industry and frugality, to have undersold their rivals at market: but that method appearing slow and troublesome to a luxurious people, whose extraordinary expences required extraordinary profits, a more expeditious one was devised; which was that of driving their rivals entirely out of the seas, and preventing them from bringing their goods at all to market. For this purpose, not having any fleets or armies of their own, the powers of the State were found necessary, and they applied them accordingly" (*ibid.*, pp. 32 f.).

to analyse the effect of contemporary conceptions of international relations on those of economic policies in general and those of the utility of empire in particular. Indeed, the conceptions which ruling groups cultivate with regard to the exigencies of present and future interstate relations have always influenced their approach to economic policies and colonies.

Following the disintegration of the First Empire, English opinions of the value of colonial possessions were decisively affected by the progress of the free-trade cause. The abolition of imperial tariff preferences and the repeal of the Navigation Laws were bound to follow the final repeal of the Corn Laws. The movement which effected this portentous change of policies was actually one and the same. Although the main struggle was spectacularly fought over the Corn Laws, the fundamental question at issue was free trade in general and free trade in colonial products and in navigation was as logical an application of the principle involved as free trade in corn.

Undoubtedly, the argumentative armory of the Free Traders was supplied by the classical economists and their case was scientifically sound. But it can hardly be denied that the free-trade politicians' conception of the trend of international relations had a definite bearing upon their attitude toward the cause they fought for. Contemporary thought as to the present and future trend of international politics always has a bearing on contemporary colonial theories. No doubt, in the case here under consideration, the traditional approach to the country's external environment, in terms of balance-of-power diplomacy, remained a powerful factor in the first half of the nineteenth century. But this traditional approach was increasingly rivalled by a school of thought bent upon a lasting pacification of international relations that would render superfluous many of the paraphernalia and drawbacks of power politics. It is for this reason that, in the following, this novel conception of foreign politics will be examined in the light of the extremist views of the Manchester School.[38]

[38]However, one important fact must be recognized. After the collapse of the Napoleonic régime on the continent the United Kingdom enjoyed, for many generations, a relative power position which practically promised immunity from physical attack by any European aggressor. England, therefore, was able to play the game of international power-diplomacy at leisure. Whether it was to be engagement or aloofness, the decision was up to her. It was due to this position of safety that she was enabled to follow an intermittent policy of interventionism on behalf of classical Greece or Polish nobility, of the Turks or Don Pacifio.

The attitude of the Manchester School towards problems of foreign politics at no stage represented more than a minority opinion. The traditional formulae and conceptions in this sphere lost little of their persuasiveness and usefulness. Yet they were forcefully challenged by a small but vocal minority which declined to accept any such formula or tradition unless it proved its unquestionable utility in the present and for the concrete case at issue. The utterances of the Manchester reformers, moreover, contain plenty of evidence to the effect that the basic issues involved in the struggle for free trade as in that for a saner conduct of foreign affairs was essentially a class struggle. In each case, the ascending middle class, then at the height of its virility and political acumen, had to fight the tenacious resistance of deeply entrenched aristocratic class interests.[39]

Frequently the prominent spokesmen of the Manchester School, Cobden and Bright, have been accused of being pacifists, appeasers, and cosmopolitan internationalists. Yet neither of these ready-made labels is applicable to them. That they lacked a good measure of intelligently subdued patriotism will be asserted by no one who reads not only their public speeches but also their private letters and diaries.[40] Proud of their people's virtues and their country's greatness, they differed from the majority of their fellow-citizens only in their estimation of the nature of these virtues and of what had made their country great and could keep it so.[41]

Advocating the solution of international conflicts by arbitration Cobden declared in 1849: "It is not necessary that any one in this House, or out of it, who accedes to this motion, should be of opinion that we are not justified, under any circumstances, in resorting to war, even in self-defence. It is only necessary that

[39] Regarding most of their major tenets, the leaders of the Manchester School were intellectually indebted to the economists and the Philosophical Radicals. However, instead of tracing origin and evolution of the various constituent ideas it seems more fertile to study their combined and consistent dissemination by a group of politicians who set out to find for them that mass-basis which they had formerly lacked.

[40] Cobden was exceedingly distrustful of the more common form of patriotism. Once he observed: "Patriotism or nationality is an instinctive virtue, that sometimes burns the lightest in the rudest and least reasoning minds; and its manifestation bears no proportion to the value of possessions defended and the object to be gained" (Quoted in J. A. Hobson, *Richard Cobden, The International Man* [New York, 1919], p. 33).

[41] John Morley, *The Life of Richard Cobden* (new ed.; London, 1883), p. 128.

you should be agreed that war is a great calamity, which it is desirable we should avoid, if possible. . . . I assume that every one in this House would only sanction war, in case it was imperatively demanded on our part, in defence of our honour, or our just interests."[42] Nor were these men averse to a reasonable amount of military preparedness. In 1860, Cobden wrote in a letter to Lord John Russell: "So far am I from wishing that 'we should be unarmed,' and so little am I disposed to 'place my country at the mercy of France, that I would, if necessary, spend one hundred millions sterling to maintain an irresistible superiority over France at sea'."[43]

Yet while the Manchester party approved of defensive war and a reasonable state of military preparedness, they well knew the disastrous consequences of war and, therefore, were ever active to prevent unnecessary resort to it. The deleterious effects of war, they feared, were mainly the following: Firstly, war is incompatible with, and obstructs the progress of, political freedom and reform

[42] John Bright and J. E. T. Rogers (eds.), *Speeches on Questions of Public Policy by Richard Cobden* (London, 1870), II, 161. (This book will be referred to, in the following, as *Cobden, Speeches.*)

For Bright's attitude upon this question see George Macaulay Trevelyan, *The Life of John Bright* (6th ed.; London, 1913), p. 218.

Goldwin Smith wrote: "Nor, it is hoped, is any language used which can impugn the duty incumbent upon England not only of placing her own shores beyond the ignominious danger of attack and maintaining her own honour on every just occasion, but of using the strength which Providence has given her to vindicate the violated rights of nations and to defend the oppressed against the oppressor" (*The Empire*, Preface, p. ix).

In contradistinction to the policy of "splendid isolation" as advocated by Bright and Cobden, Goldwin Smith defended the use of armed force also for a policy of active intervention on behalf of undemocratically-governed nations.

[43] Morley, *Cobden*, p. 501.

The Manchester School's concern about Britain's "potentiel de guerre" is also evidenced by their assertion that for purposes of defence the Empire did not strengthen but weaken the mother country. This argument will be further examined below.

The Manchester reformers were fully aware of England's immense potential power which, they thought, was capable of speedy mobilization for the conduct of war. Cobden wrote: "The manufacturing districts alone—even the four counties of . . . Lancashire, Yorkshire, Cheshire, and Staffordshire—could, at any moment, by means of wealth drawn, by the skill and industry of its population, from the natural resources of this comparative speck of territory, combat with success the whole Russian Empire" (*The Political Writings of Richard Cobden* [London, 1867], I, 194 [this work will be referred to in the following as *Cobden, Pol. Writings*]).

and renders impossible the rational enjoyment of such freedom.[44] It demoralizes those who are engaged in its conduct, it corrupts society[45] and "throws power into the hands of the most worthless of the class of statesmen."[46] Secondly, apart from casualties, war and preparations for war are enormously expensive and therefore sap the wealth of the national community.[47] Thirdly, war and the possibility of war impede the causes of free trade.[48]

[44]Cobden maintained: "For let it never be forgotten, that it is not by means of war that states are rendered fit for the enjoyment of constitutional freedom; on the contrary, whilst terror and bloodshed reign in the land, involving men's minds in the extremities of hopes and fears, there can be no process of thought, no education going on, by which alone can a people be prepared for the enjoyment of rational liberty" (*ibid.*, pp. 44 f.).

[45]See Morley, *Cobden*, p. 264; also, James E. Thorold Rogers, *Cobden and Modern Political Opinion* (London, 1873), p. 119.

[46]Trevelyan, *Life of Bright*, p. 249.

[47]Regarding the cost of armaments Bright remarked in 1878: "The situation of Europe at this moment is deplorable; its nations are groaning under the weight of enormous armies and burdensome taxation" (H. J. Leech [ed.], *The Public Letters of John Bright* [2d ed.; London, 1895], p. 38).

Cobden stated: ". . . war itself, owing to the application of greater science to the process of human destruction, has become a much more costly pursuit" (*Pol. Writings*, I, 463 f.).

And again: "So true is the saying of Bastiat, that 'the ogre, war, costs as much for his digestion as for his meals'" (*ibid.*, II, 271).

[48]It must be admitted that earlier in their careers the spokesmen of the Manchester School usually argued the other way round. Later, however, they realized that peace was as much a condition of free trade as free trade was a condition of peace. Thus, Bright wrote in 1878: "To abolish tariffs is the only way which leads to the abolition of great armies. Free Trade between nations would give the nations peace; but war, anxieties, and menaced conflicts make it impossible for the nations calmly to consider their true interests" (Leech, *Public Letters of Bright*, p. 37).

Goldwin Smith wrote in 1879: "The Cobden Club will find out some day that to get free trade they must have peace" (Arnold Haultain [ed.], *Goldwin Smith's Correspondence* [New York, 1913], p. 83).

It may be added here that the Manchester politicians denied emphatically that a nation could gain anything by having recourse to aggression. In particular they scoffed at the idea that a nation's commerce could be furthered by the decision of battle. They even refused to believe that power and prestige could have an advantageous effect on a nation's volume of foreign trade. Thus Cobden declared: "The foreign customers who visit our markets are not brought hither through fears of the power and influence of British diplomatists: they are not captured by our fleets and armies: and as little are they attracted by feelings of love for us. . . . It is solely from the promptings of self-interest." "England owes to the peaceful exploits of Watt and Arkwright, and not to the deeds of Nelson and Wellington, her commerce, which now extends to every corner of the earth. . . ." (*Pol. Writings*, I, 46, 192 f.).

The Manchester School distinguished between economic, psychological, and socio-political causes of war. Broadly speaking, they recognized only one economic cause of war: the absence of free trade. They were so convinced of this fact that they speculated very little about it. On the other hand, they did not overestimate the importance of the economic causation of war.[49] Measured by the standards of their time, Cobden, Bright, and Goldwin Smith had a remarkably profound insight into the psychological causation of war.[50] Most significant, however, for the purpose of this study, are their reasonings on the political and social causes.

Cobden, for example, realized that a variety of interest groups might conceive of war and armaments as yielding lucrative profits. There was the agriculturist who might "be interested in that state of things which yielded an augmentation of prices for his produce."[51] "A very small number of shipowners . . . entertains an indistinct kind of hope that hostilities would, by putting down competition, again restore to them a monopoly of the ocean."[52] There were certain "young" trading houses which might promise themselves extraordinary profits from little and distant wars.[53] However, the most dangerous of these groups was that which controlled the funds allotted for defence purposes and the "jobs" available in the "Services." Cobden observed: "We cannot disguise from ourselves that the military spirit pervades the higher and more influential classes of this country; and that the Court, aristocracy, and all that is aping the tone of the latter, believe that their interests, privileges, and even their very security are bound up in the maintenance of the "Horse Guards."[54]

A foreign policy involving the constant risk of war and rendering military preparedness an imperative necessity, and even a policy of deliberate resort to war served two important purposes from the standpoint of this ruling interest group. First, the obtaining of such material profits as mentioned above and, secondly, the diversion of public opinion from the need for political, social, and commercial reforms in Britain and Ireland.

[49] In this respect friends and critics of these men have been almost equally unjust in appraising the political acumen of the leading Manchester politicians.
[50] Their opinions on this subject will be discussed in connection with their views on the general prospects of peace.
[51] Cobden, *Pol. Writings*, I, 324.
[52] *Ibid.*, p. 327.
[53] Morley, *Cobden*, pp. 545 f.
[54] *Ibid.*, p. 391.

While negotiating the famous trade agreement with France, Cobden wrote to Henry Ashworth (August 27, 1860):

> Unfortunately, we have a class—and that the most influential one—which makes money out of these distant wars, or these home panics about a French invasion. How could your aristocracy endure without this expenditure for wars and armaments? Could not a less ... inhuman method of supporting them be hit upon? When talking over the reduction of duties with M. Rouher, and we come to some small industry employing a few hands and a little capital, which has put in its claim for high protection, I am in the habit of suggesting to him rather than interfere with the trade of the country for the purpose of feeding and clothing these small protected interests, he had better withdraw the parties from their unprofitable occupations, take some handsome apartments for them in the Louvre Hotel, and feast them on venison and champagne at the country's expense for the rest of their days. Might not a similar compromise be entered into with the younger sons of our aristocracy, instead of supporting them by the most costly of all processes, that of war or preparation of war?[55]

As to the purpose of diverting the people's attention from the necessity of internal reforms by the concoction of war scares, Bright wrote in 1859: "The Reform question here is an ugly one for our oligarchy. A war with France would, in their eyes, be a cheap price to pay for a few years' respite only from the hated Reform. . . . I presume they want a war with France, and as the former one was so successful, postponing Reform for forty years, they think the experiment worth trying again."[56]

The means by which the aristocratic ruling group kept its pernicious control over the conduct of foreign affairs and by which it succeeded in swaying public opinion into supporting their devious manœuvres were held to be mainly two: first, by monopolizing the Foreign Office and the Foreign Service, and, secondly, by influencing public opinion and fostering a nationalistic and warlike spirit in

---

[55] *Ibid.*, pp. 532 f. In 1849, Cobden asked his audience: "Now, does that look as if you had been wisely spending in fortifying yourselves, and keeping up your enormous standing armaments, because certain parties, who are interested in clothing regiments, or being admirals, with nothing to do, choose to tell you that the French people are a mighty hobgoblin, ready to come over and devour you some morning?" (Cobden, *Speeches*, I, 480 f.).

[56] Trevelyan, *Life of Bright*, pp. 285 f. Denouncing Palmerston's interventionist policy Cobden declared in 1850: "It was part of the policy of the noble Lord, which has always been a 'sensation' policy, the object being to govern the country by constantly diverting its attention from home affairs to matters abroad" (Cobden, *Speeches*, II, 272).

For an even more radical exposition of this motive of aristocratic class politics see T. Perronet Thompson, *Exercises, Political and Others* (London, 1842), V, 166 *passim*.

the nation through the media of education and propaganda. Bright wrote in 1876: "You should condemn this foolish and wicked jealousy of Russia, which springs from ignorance among our people, and is fostered by writers in the press. It suits those who live out of the 25,000,000 l. spent annually, and for the most part wasted on our monstrous armaments, to keep up this feeling, and the influential among them are constantly acting on the proprietors, editors, and writers of the London newspapers."[57]

Another means of confusing public opinion and disguising their real designs was the cultivation of traditional forms of diplomatic procedures[58] (e.g., secret diplomacy) and the skilful use of such formulae as the balance of power. To the Manchester reformers balance-of-power diplomacy was nothing but a dangerous figment. Thus, Cobden maintained: ". . . the balance of power is a chimera. It is not a fallacy, a mistake, an imposture—it is an undescribed, indescribable, incomprehensible nothing. . . . So far . . . as we can understand the subject, the theory of the balance of power is . . . a creation of the politician's brain—a phantasm, without definite form or tangible existence—a mere conjunction of syllables, forming words which convey no sound meaning."[59] Similarly Bright: "This whole notion of 'the balance of power' is a mischievous delusion which has come down to us from past times; we ought to drive it from our minds, and to consider the solemn question of peace or war on more clear, more definite, and on far higher principles than any that are involved in the phrase 'balance of power.'"[60]

The leaders of the Manchester party were not content with offering criticism. They also proposed definite measures and policies designed to introduce a saner spirit into international relations. Apart from the obvious remedy of re-educating the

[57]Leech, *Public Letters of Bright*, pp. 18 f.

[58]Cobden declared: "I have always had an instinctive monomania against this system of foreign interference, protocolling, diplomatizing, etc. . . ." (Morley, *Cobden*, p. 304).

[59]Cobden, *Pol. Writings*, I, 258, 263.

[60]Bright, *Speeches*, I, 459. On another occasion Bright remarked that the theory of the balance of power "rises up before me when I think of it as a ghastly phantom which during one hundred and seventy years, whilst it has been worshipped in this country, has loaded the nation with debt and with taxes, has sacrificed the lives of hundreds of thousands of Englishmen, has desolated the homes of millions of families, and has left us, as the great result of the profligate expenditure which it has caused, a doubled peerage at one end of the social scale, and far more than a doubled pauperism at the other" (*ibid.*, II, 108).

public and countering nationalistic propaganda by exposing its fallacies and actual motives, they suggested the abolition of secret diplomacy[61] and the "democratization" of the conduct of foreign affairs. In 1851, still optimistic as to the prospects of peace, Cobden wrote: "My own opinion is that we are on the eve of a revolution in the diplomatic world; that the old régime of mystification and innuendo and intrigue cannot survive the growth of the democratic principle; that diplomacy must be a public and responsible organization. . . ."[62] In large measure the introduction of a more "democratic" spirit into the Foreign Office depended on the progress of political reform.[63]

Apart from these remedies to be effectuated at home, there were others to be introduced on an international scale. The institutionalization of international arbitration was one of them.[64] Much more important, however, seemed the world-wide acceptance of free trade. Apart from the economic principle involved, Manchesterism advocated free trade also because its universal application seemed to promote the cause of peace. Thus, Cobden expounded:

But, besides dictating the disuse of warlike establishments, free trade arms its votaries by its own pacific nature, in that eternal truth—the more any nation trafficks abroad upon free and honest principles, the less it will be in danger of wars.[65]

[61]Goldwin Smith declared hopefully: "There is nothing chimerical either . . . in the hope that from the progress of reason and still more from the progress of liberty, open dealing between nations will at no distant time supersede secret diplomacy, and put an end to the existence of the brotherhood of intriguers whom secret diplomacy harbours. . ." (*The Empire*, Preface, p. xvi).

[62]Morley, *Cobden*, p. 365. See also Hobson, *Richard Cobden*, pp. 10 ff., 34.

[63]In his later years Cobden, as we shall see, became rather doubtful whether the widening of the franchise would have this desirable effect.

[64]See Cobden, *Speeches*, II, 161-74. It is interesting to note that Cobden did by no means nurse any Utopian expectations regarding the efficacy of international arbitration of conflicts. Against the doubts professed by his critics he denied "that, as a rule, treaties are violated." "I may be told that, even if you make treaties of this kind, you cannot enforce the award. I admit it. . . . I have no plan for compelling the fulfilment of treaties of arbitration. . . . What I say, however, is, if you make a treaty with another country, binding it to refer any dispute to arbitration, and if that country violates that treaty, when the dispute arises, then you will place it in a worse position before the world. . ." (*ibid.*, p. 174).

He was against the collective enforcement of arbitrational awards by an international institution. He said: "I am no party to the plan . . . of having a Congress of Nations, with a code of law —a supreme court of appeal, with an army to support its decision. I am no party to any such plan. I believe it might lead to more armed interference than takes place at present" (*ibid.*).

[65]Cobden, *Pol. Writings*, I, 292.

And if such is the character of free trade, that it unites, by the strongest motives of which our nature is susceptible, two remote communities, rendering the interest of the one the only true policy of the other, and making each equally anxious for the prosperity and happiness of both; and if, moreover, every addition to the amount of traffic between two independent states, forges fresh fetters, which rivet more securely these amicable bonds—how can the extension of our commerce call for an increase in our armaments.[66]

Universal adoption of free trade also would lead to "the increase of all those feelings of sociability and good-will which commercial intercourse produces among nations."[67] Free trade, in other words, would eradicate the economic causes of war, whether real or imaginary. It would induce every nation to be interested in the material prosperity of every other nation. By increasing industrial specialization it would render the conduct of war more difficult and more costly for all nations. And by multiplying social contacts between the nationals of the different powers it would engender a wholesome spirit of goodwill.

Undoubtedly, the Manchester School was over-optimistic as to the efficacy of some of these methods of stabilizing peace. In the case of others they greatly over-estimated their chances of being put into practice.[68] And yet, all of these men, in their later years, realized the tremendous difficulties in the way of the momentous changes they worked and hoped for. In the late seventies Bright and Goldwin Smith took an increasingly gloomy view of the future success of the free-trade principle. In the sphere of domestic politics all of them complained that the upper middle classes were rapidly discarding their reformist zeal and eagerly accommodated themselves to habits, manners, and opinions of the aristocracy.[69] Most of all they despaired of overcoming, in the

[66]*Ibid.*, p. 295.
[67]Goldwin Smith, *The Empire*, preface, p. xx.
[68]This was particularly true of their anticipation of a universal free-trade victory.
[69]Cobden, to quote an example, wrote in 1849: "For we cannot shut our eyes to the fact that our law or rather custom, of primogeniture, has its roots in the prejudices of the upper portion of the middle class as well as in the privileges of the aristocracy. The snobbishness of the moneyed classes in the great seats of commerce and manufactures is a fearful obstacle to any effectual change of the system" (Morley, *Cobden*, p. 330).
   In 1874, Goldwin Smith wrote in a letter to William Rathbone: "I am afraid in England you, and men like you, are the survivors of a more public-spirited generation. It seems to be that in the former generation public spirit was almost dead and that the universal cry was, Leave us alone to make money and enjoy it. That plutocracy would reign till it rotted, was the conviction with which I left the country. It was not that Conservative principles had triumphed,

near future, the deeply-ingrained prejudices and the dark psychological forces conducive to war which they perceived manifest in all strata of British society.[70]

So much for the attitude of the Manchester School toward the basic problems of interstate relationships. It is hoped that this somewhat sketchy analysis of their views on these problems indicates the new intellectual temper and frame of mind with which an eminent portion of the rising middle class approached questions of public policy which, as experience shows, react to and are affected by the question of the utility of empire. But it must never be forgotten that, although of eminent importance, the ideas of these groups represented only one trend of English public opinion parallelled and opposed by various other currents of ideas and sentiments.

---

but that reform, and movement of every kind were voted bores" (Haultain, *Goldwin Smith's Correspondence*, p. 53).

[70]The spokesmen of the Manchester School fully realized the significance of the psychological causes of war. They spent a great deal of thought on the "combativeness"; and the "pugnaciousness" of man. They knew that, beside education, it was necessary to find more innocuous outlets for these instinctive forces. Cobden remarked: "Far from wishing to destroy the energy, or even the combativeness, which has made us such fit instruments for the battle-field, we shall require these qualities for abating the spirit of war, and correcting the numberless moral evils from which society is suffering" (*Pol. Writings*, I, 494).

Goldwin Smith was aware of the fact that the effects of the Industrial Revolution had even strengthened the force of the combative instinct. He maintained the "progress of civilisation" had resulted in a new cause of war. "It arises from a re-action of the adventurous and self devoting spirit of man, against the dull prosaic tenor of peaceful society and of commercial and industrial life. It will not be allayed by the acquisition of wealth, nor by the increase of material enjoyments. It will be allayed only when the chivalrous instincts of mankind find some better satisfaction than that which is afforded by the romance, the peril, and the pageantry of war" (*The Empire*, preface, pp. xiv-xv).

The Manchester reformers expressly denied that they had ever predicted the abolition of war and the "millenium" if their proposals were followed (see Cobden, *Speeches*, I, 471; Cobden, *Writings*, I, 459). Cobden, as a matter of fact, became increasingly pessimistic in this respect. He lamented that "there is no out-of-doors support for the party of peace. . ." (Morley, *Cobden*, p. 409). He saw that "the evil" was deeply rooted "in the pugnacious, energetic, self-sufficient, foreigner-despising and pitying character of that noble insular creature, John Bull. . ." (*ibid.*, pp. 304 f.). And in a letter to George Combe he admitted sadly: ". . . I do not look for very great advances in our social state during our generation . . . . I am afraid the animal is yet too predominant in the nature of Englishmen, and of man generally. . . . I have always had one test of the tendency of the world: what is its estimate of war and warriors, and on what do nations rely for their mutual security? Brute force is, I fear, as much worshipped now, in the statues of Wellington and the peerage to Gough, as they were two thousand years ago in the colossal proportions of Hercules or Jupiter" (*ibid.*, p. 264).

CHAPTER VI

ADAM SMITH AND THE DISSENTERS

1. Adam Smith and the Empire[1]

IN *The Wealth of Nations* Adam Smith started his chapter "Of Colonies" by discussing the motives for establishing colonies and arrived at the conclusion that "though the utility which has resulted from them [the European colonies in America] has been very great, it is not altogether so clear and evident. It was not understood at their first establishment . . . and the nature, extent, and limits of that utility are not, perhaps, well understood at this day."[2]

As has become sufficiently evident from the review of British colonial theories in Part I of the present study, Smith's conclusion that the utility of colonization and colonies was not well understood in his time, was certainly not an over-statement. Indeed, his treatment of the subject doubtless constituted so much of an improvement over previous English theorizing, that, in respect to this subject, his work may be called truly revolutionary. While, in the field of economic theory and general commercial policies, numerous predecessors had anticipated his contributions, in the field of colonial theories, i.e., in the application of the principles of theoretical economics to the subject of colonial trade, he had virtually none. In this specific field, too, all that was left to his successors was to expand, elaborate, qualify, and, above all, disseminate his conclusions. On the subject of colonies, then, *The Wealth of Nations* marks the most revolutionary advance in the evolution of British thought.

---

[1] Adam Smith's views on the utility of colonies referred only to the European colonies in America. In line with the plan of the present study, Smith's statements on India will be disregarded. He approved of the maintenance of fortified trading posts on the western coast of Africa (*An Inquiry into the Nature and Causes of the Wealth of Nations*, ed. Edwin Cannan [New York, 1937], p. 690). This approval, however, did not contain any imperial intentions. Along with British ministers and consuls in foreign countries, he viewed these trading posts as "public works" designed to "facilitate commerce" (*ibid.*). Their only function was to protect the "ordinary store or counting-house" from interference by barbarous natives. Territorial ambitions *per se* were not involved in these considerations.

[2] *Wealth of Nations*, p. 525.

In the third part of his chapter on colonies, Smith analysed the advantages which had accrued to Europe from the discovery of America. He divided these advantages, first, "into the general advantages which Europe, considered as one great country, has derived from those great events," and secondly, "into the particular advantages which each colonizing country has derived from the colonies which particularly belong to it, in consequence of the authority or dominion which it exercises over them."[3]

That Europe as a whole, including all those countries which never had possessed any colonies, had derived great material gain from the colonization of America, he considered obvious. This gain consisted in the use and enjoyment of various articles which otherwise the European consumer would not have obtained at all or not in the same quantity.[4] Furthermore, by offering "new values, new equivalents" for exchange, the colonization of America had added considerably to the total market available to European commodities and thereby had greatly "contributed to augment the industry" of European countries.[5] "The mass of commodities annually thrown into the great circle of European commerce, and by its various revolutions annually distributed among all the different nations comprehended within it, must have been augmented by the whole surplus produce of America. A greater share of this greater mass, therefore, is likely to have fallen to each of those nations, to have increased their enjoyments, and augmented their industry."[6] In describing these general advantages Adam Smith emphasized that they had accrued to nations "which may never, perhaps, have sent a single commodity of their own produce to America"[7] and even to such countries, "which, not only never sent any commodities to America, but never received any from it."[8]

[3]*Ibid.*, p. 557.   [4]*Ibid.*   [5]*Ibid.*, pp. 557 f.

[6]*Ibid.*, p. 558. Because the truth of the general benefit derived by Europe as a whole from colonization is incontestable, the reiteration of this statement will not be pursued through the subsequent literature. The important question was, of course, whether a nation had to possess colonies of its own in order to receive a larger share from the total of benefits obtained or whether it could let other nations shoulder the burdens of empire without thereby diminishing its share in the benefits.

[7]"Some part of the produce of America is consumed in Hungary and Poland, and there is some demand there for the sugar, chocolate, and tobacco, of that new quarter of the world. But those commodities must be purchased with something which is either the produce of the industry of Hungary and Poland, or with something which had been purchased with some part of that produce" (*ibid.*, p. 558).

[8]"Even such countries may have received a greater abundance of other commodities from countries of which the surplus produce had been augmented

The total amount of the advantages reaped by Europe, "considered as one country," from oversea colonization was, of course, substantially affected by the imperial trade policies framed and enforced by the countries in possession of the colonies. If this benefit depended upon the quantity of "new equivalents" raised in the colonies in anticipation of exchange for European goods, then any policy restricting the freedom of this exchange correspondingly diminished the benefit derived by Europe as a whole from the existence of colonies. Thus, Adam Smith declared:

The exclusive trade of the mother countries tends to diminish, or, at least, to keep down below what they would otherwise rise to, both the enjoyments and industry of all those nations in general, and of the American colonies in particular. It is a dead weight upon the action of one of the great springs which puts into motion a great part of the business of mankind. By rendering the colony produce dearer in all other countries, it lessens its consumption, and thereby cramps the industry of the colonies, and both the enjoyments and the industry of all other countries which both enjoy less when they pay more for what they enjoy, and produce less when they get less for what they produce.[9]

Hence, this exclusive trade policy of the mother countries appeared as nothing but "a clog which, for the supposed benefit of some particular countries, embarrasses the pleasures, and encumbers the industry of all other countries; but of the colonies more than of any other."[10]

In addition to its share in the general advantages which accrued to Europe as a whole from the colonization of America, what were the particular profits which arose to the colonizing country in consequence of the sovereignty it wielded over its colonies? In preparing an answer to this question Adam Smith distinguished between "those common advantages which every empire derives from the provinces subject to its dominion" and the peculiar gains supposedly resulting from these provinces as European colonies in America.[11]

On general grounds "the common advantages" secured by an empire from provinces subject to its dominion are two: the military force which they contribute to its defence, and, the revenue they furnish for the support of its civil government.[12] On each score, Adam Smith maintained, the colonies of European states contributed nothing to their mother countries. He stated:

---

by means of the American trade. This greater abundance, as it must necessarily have increased their enjoyments, so it must likewise have augmented their industry" (*ibid.*).

[9]*Ibid.*, pp. 558 f.   [10]*Ibid.*, p. 559.
[11]*Ibid.*   [12]*Ibid.*

The European colonies of America have never yet furnished any military force for the defence of the mother country. Their military force has never yet been sufficient for their own defence; and in the different wars in which the mother countries have been engaged, the defence of their colonies has generally occasioned a very considerable distraction of the military force of those countries. In this respect, therefore, all the European colonies have, without exception, been a cause rather of weakness than of strength to their respective mother countries.[13] The taxes which have been levied upon those [colonies] of other European nations, upon those of England in particular, have seldom been equal to the expence laid out upon them in time of peace, and never sufficient to defray that which they occasioned in time of war. Such colonies, therefore, have been a source of expence and not of revenue to their respective mother countries.[14]

In regard to power as well as in regard to revenue, colonies were a drain on the resources of the mother countries.[15] Therefore, if any exclusive benefit accrued to the metropolis from the possession of colonies, such gain must be obtained from the exclusive trade it conducted with its oversea dependencies. In order to examine this phase, Adam Smith investigated the case of the Enumerated Articles as provided for by the British Navigation Acts. He observed[16] that these commodities, since other countries could purchase them only from Britain, would be cheaper to the English than to the non-English consumer. For the same reason, this arrangement would also "encourage England's industry more than that of other nations because her manufactures would exchange for the colonial produce at a more favorable rate than would the manufactures of non-British countries."[17] Consequently, by cur-

[13]*Ibid.*, pp. 559 f.   [14]*Ibid.*, p. 560.
[15]With the exception of the Spanish and Portuguese colonies in the matter of revenue.
[16]Adam Smith here assumed that a demand existed in Europe for these enumerated articles. If this demand could be satisfied by an alternative source of supply, as in the case of sugar, then his conclusions would have to be qualified accordingly. Again, collection of customs duties on these goods when entering Britain coupled with a provision for drawbacks in the case of re-exportation would render Smith's assumptions inconclusive.
[17]"For all those parts of her own surplus produce which England exchanges for those enumerated commodities, she must get a better price than any other countries can get for the like parts of theirs, when they exchange them for the same commodities. The manufactures of England, for example, will purchase a greater quantity of the sugar and tobacco of her own colonies, than the like manufactures of other countries can purchase of that sugar and tobacco. So far, therefore, as the manufactures of England and those of other countries are both to be exchanged for the sugar and tobacco of the English colonies, this superiority of price gives an encouragement to the former, beyond what the latter can in these circumstances enjoy" (*ibid.*).

tailing the advantages flowing to other nations, England enjoyed "an evident advantage" over them.[18]

But just because this advantage is gained "by depressing the industry and produce of other countries" rather than by raising her own "above what they would naturally rise to in the case of a free trade," this gain is not an absolute but a relative one.[19] Furthermore, other burdens of empire apart, this comparative advantage reaped by the metropolis was attained at the cost of forgoing a higher absolute gain. Had other European nations been allowed a free trade with British plantations, the export produce of the latter would have been imported at a cheaper price not only by these non-British countries but also by England herself.[20] But Great Britain would then not have enjoyed any advantage over other countries. "She might, perhaps, have gained an absolute, but she would certainly have lost a relative advantage."[21]

Yet, "in order to execute this invidious and malignant project of excluding as much as possible other nations from any share" in the colony trade, Adam Smith argued, "England, there are very probable reasons for believing, has not only sacrificed a part of the absolute advantage which she, as well as every other nation, might have derived from that trade, but has subjected herself both to an absolute and to a relative disadvantage in almost every other branch of trade."[22]

What is this absolute and relative disadvantage England incurred by embarking upon a monopolistic policy in the colony trade? Owing to the establishment of this monopoly, foreign capital which previously had been invested in this trade, was necessarily withdrawn. English capital available for its replacement, having been insufficient at first, yielded higher than average profits and, consequently, drew additional capital from other branches of English trade. This "revulsion of capital," gradually increasing the competition of capitals in the colony trade, correspondingly diminished that competition in all the other branches of trade, the

[18]*Ibid.*, pp. 560 f.
[19]*Ibid.*, p. 561. Adam Smith wrote that this advantage would "perhaps" be found a relative rather than an absolute one. His exposition is proverbial for the ubiquity of qualifications which he attached to the pronouncement of a principle or an observation. Even such unspecified qualifications as the insertion of "perhaps" are excessively numerous. Though in many cases not unjustified, this academic prudence may have had the character of a rather indiscriminatory habit in other instances. To the present writer the use of the phrase "perhaps" in the present instance seems "perhaps" to fall within that category.
[20]*Wealth of Nations*, p. 561. [21]*Ibid.* [22]*Ibid.*, pp. 561 f.

ultimate effect being a generally higher level of profits in all sections of the British economy.[23] This effect, Adam Smith observed, had been sustained "ever since" because the colony trade increased faster than the total amount of British capital.[24] Higher interest rates, in turn, had impaired the competitive capacity of English export industries and, thus, resulted in the general and persistent decay of the country's foreign trade.[25] The colonial monopoly, therefore, did not occasion an addition to the trade Britain had enjoyed before, but merely caused a shift in the direction of her trade.

> ... whatever raises in any country the ordinary rate of profit higher than it otherwise would be, necessarily subjects that country both to an absolute and a relative advantage in every branch of trade of which she has not the monopoly. It subjects her to an absolute disadvantage: because in such branches of trade her merchants cannot get this higher profit, without selling dearer than they otherwise would do both the goods of foreign countries which they import into their own, and the goods of their own country which they export to foreign countries. Their own country must buy dearer and sell dearer; must both buy less and sell less; must both enjoy less and produce less, than she otherwise would do.[26]

---

[23] *Ibid.*, p. 562.   [24] *Ibid.*

[25] "Since the establishment of the act of navigation ... the colony trade has been continually increasing, while many other branches of foreign trade, particularly of that to other parts of Europe, have been continually decaying. Our manufactures for foreign sale, instead of being suited, as before the act of navigation, to the neighbouring market of Europe ... have, the greater part of them, been accommodated to the still more distant one of the colonies, to the market in which they have the monopoly, rather than to that in which they have many competitors" (*ibid.*, p. 563).

[26] *Ibid.*, p. 565. The reasons (and they contain certain residues of the mercantilist reasoning manifest in the balance-of-employment doctrine) are the following: "The most advantageous employment of any capital to the country to which it belongs, is that which maintains there the greatest quantity of productive labour, and increases the most the annual produce of the land and labour of that country. But the quantity of productive labour which any capital employed in the foreign trade of consumption can maintain, is exactly in proportion ... to the frequency of its returns" (*ibid.*, pp. 566 f.). Now, Smith thought that the frequency of these returns diminished with the distance of the country with which foreign trade was conducted and with the degree of "indirectness" with which it was carried on. The colonial trade, however, was a distant and round-about trade as compared with that engaged in with European countries (*ibid.*, p. 567). Curiously enough, it was for these reasons that Smith assumed that Britain's trade with France, if not shackled by restrictions, would be more advantageous to her than that carried on with any other country, especially with one situated at such a distance as America. It was because "France is the nearest neighbour to Great Britain" (*ibid.*, p. 462).

It subjects her to a relative disadvantage; because in such branches of trade it sets other countries which are not subject to the same absolute disadvantage, either more above her or less below her than they otherwise would be. It enables them both to enjoy more and to produce more in proportion to what she enjoys and produces. It renders their superiority greater or their inferiority less than it otherwise would be.

However, heavily as they weighed, these were not the only disadvantages Britain had taken upon herself by establishing and maintaining a monopoly of the colony trade. Mercantilist theorists, it will be recalled, used to argue that colonial markets and colonial sources of supplies were preferable to foreign markets and foreign sources of supply because trade relations with the colonies were less precarious and less subject to the illwill or the caprice of foreign rulers. In order to enjoy a more secure trade they were even willing to accept definite drawbacks attending the colony trade as compared with foreign trade.[27] Adam Smith, on the other hand, entirely reversed this argument. In his opinion Britain's far-going reliance on the colony trade introduced an element of insecurity rather than security into her commercial system.

The monopoly of the colony trade besides, by forcing towards it a much greater proportion of the capital of Great Britain than would naturally have gone to it, seems to have broken altogether that natural balance which would otherwise have taken place among the different branches of British industry. The industry of Great Britain, instead of being accomodated to a great number of small markets, has been principally suited to one great market. Her commerce, instead of running in a great number of small channels, has been taught to run principally in one great channel. But the whole system of her industry and commerce has thereby been rendered less secure; the whole state of her body politic less healthful, than it otherwise would have been.[28]

It was exactly for this reason that an imminent rupture with the American colonies seemed to forbode disaster to British merchants and manufacturers.

The expectation of a rupture with the colonies, accordingly, has struck the people of Great Britain with more terror than they ever felt for a Spanish armada, or a French invasion. It was this terror, whether well or ill grounded, which rendered the repeal of the stamp act, among the merchants

---

[27]For example: higher cost of colonial raw materials.

[28]*Ibid.*, pp. 570 f. Smith continued: "In her present condition, Great Britain resembles one of those unwholesome bodies in which some of the vital parts are overgrown, and which, upon that account are liable to many dangerous disorders scarce incident to those in which all the parts are more properly proportioned" (*ibid.*, p. 571).

at least, a popular measure. In the total exclusion from the colony market, was it to last only for a few years, the greater part of our merchants used to fancy that they foresaw an entire stop to their trade; the greater part of our master manufacturers, the entire ruin to their business; and the greater part of our workmen, an end of their employment."[29]

Still another disadvantage inherent in the monopoly of the colony trade, as indeed in any monopoly, is that it is not easily capable of reform. "Such are the unfortunate effects of all the regulations of the mercantile system. They not only introduce very dangerous disorders into the state of the body politic, but disorders which it is often difficult to remedy, without occasioning for a time at least, still greater disorders."[30]

Having thus analysed the vicious consequences of the metropolitan monopoly of the colony trade, Adam Smith made a statement which lent itself to misinterpretation. He said: "The natural good effects of the colony trade, however, more than counterbalance to Great Britain the bad effects of the monopoly, so that, monopoly and all together, that trade, even as it is carried on at present, is not only advantageous, but greatly advantageous."[31]

What Smith wanted to point out here was simply that the general benefits of the colonization of America derived by Great

[29] *Ibid.*, p. 571. Smith went on to observe: "A rupture with any of our neighbours upon the continent, though likely too, to occasion some stop or interruption in the employments of some of all these different orders of people, is foreseen, however, without any such general emotion. The blood, of which the circulation is stopt in some of the smaller vessels, easily disgorges itself into the greater, without occasioning any dangerous disorder; but, when it is stopt in any of the greater vessels, convulsions, apoplexy, or death, are the immediate and unavoidable consequences. If but one of those overgrown manufactures, which by means either of bounties or of the monopoly of the home and colony markets, have been artificially raised up to an unnatural height, finds some small stop or interruption in its employment, it frequently occasions a mutiny and disorder alarming to government, and embarassing even to the deliberations of the legislature. How great, therefore, would be the disorder and confusion ... which must necessarily be occasioned by a sudden and entire stop in the employment of so great a proportion of our principle manufactures?" (*ibid.*).

[30] *Ibid.*, p. 572.

[31] *Ibid.*, pp. 574 f. Smith continued: "The new markets and the new employment which are opened by the colony trade, are of much greater extent than that portion of the old market and of the old employment which is lost by the monopoly. The new produce and the new capital which has been created, if one may say so, by the colony trade, maintain in Great Britain a greater quantity of productive labour, than what can have been thrown out of employment by the revulsion of capital from other trades of which the returns are more frequent" (*ibid.*, p. 575).

Britain as a European nation more than outweighed the disadvantages resulting from the monopoly of the colony trade. "If the colony trade," Smith remarked, "even as it is carried on at present, is advantageous to Great Britain, it is not by means of the monopoly, but in spite of it."[32] However, that the English colonies, despite the injurious effects of the monopoly system, were of benefit to the parent state, is a conclusion which Smith does not logically justify. The important point is that Adam Smith in this passage of his work discussed only the utility of the trade to which the colonization of America gave rise. He did not discuss the utility to the mother country of the maintenance of colonies under its dominion. If the costs of imperial defence and civil administration were added to the disadvantages of the monopoly system, then it might yet appear that the possession of colonies constituted a total loss to Great Britain. It is this line of reasoning which Adam Smith pursued. For, after having further examined the financial burdens of empire, he concluded succinctly that "under the present system of management . . . Great Britain derives nothing but loss from the dominion which she assumes over her colonies."[33]

As to the expense of empire, it has already been stated that according to Adam Smith's sober judgment the mother country was financially sapped by the colonies which she had to govern and to defend. In the following quotation he particularized the item of defence.

The expence of the ordinary peace establishment of the colonies amounted, before the commencement of the present disturbances, to the pay of twenty regiments of food; to the expence of the artillery, stores, and extraordinary provisions with which it was necessary to supply them; and to the expence of a very considerable naval force which was constantly kept up, in order to guard from the smuggling vessels of other nations, the immense coast of North America, and that of our West Indian islands. The whole expence of this peace establishment was a charge upon the revenue of Great Britain, and was, at the same time, the smallest part of what the dominion of the colonies has cost the mother country. If we would know the amount of the whole, we must add to the annual expence of this peace establishment the interest of the sums which, in consequence of her considering her colonies as provinces subject to her dominion, Great Britain has upon different occasions laid out upon their defence. We must add to it, in particular, the whole expence of the late war, and a great part of that of the war which preceded it.[34]

Perhaps scarcely less important than Adam Smith's appraisal of the economic value of colonies and the colony trade was his

[32]*Ibid.*   [33]*Ibid.*, p. 581.   [34]*Ibid.*, pp. 580 f.

investigation into the social genesis of the ideas according to which Britain's Old Colonial System had been fashioned. To the conclusions of the economist he added those of the political scientist and historian. The foundation of a great empire "for the sole purpose of raising up a people of customers," he argued, was a project "extremely fit for a nation whose government is influenced by shopkeepers."[35]

England purchased for some of her subjects, who found themselves uneasy at home, a great estate in a distant country. The price, indeed, was very small.... The land was good and of great extent, and the cultivators having plenty of good ground to work upon, and being for some time at liberty to sell their produce where they pleased, became in the course of little more than thirty or forty years so numerous and thriving a people, that the shopkeepers and other traders of England wished to secure to themselves the monopoly of their custom. Without pretending, therefore, that they had paid any part, either of the original purchase-money, or of the subsequent expence of improvement,[36] they petitioned the parliament that the cultivators of America might for the future be confined to their shop; first for buying all the goods which they wanted from Europe; and, secondly, for selling all such parts of their own produce as those traders might find it convenient to buy.[37]

The maintenance of this monopoly for the sake of the "shopkeeper" was "the principal, or more properly perhaps the sole end and purpose of the dominion which Great Britain assumes over her colonies.... Whatever expence Great Britain has hitherto laid out in maintaining this dependency, has really been laid out

[35] *Ibid.*, p. 579. Smith continued to remark: "Say to a shopkeeper, Buy me a good estate, and I shall always buy my clothes at your shop, even though I should pay somewhat dearer than what I can have them for at other shops; and you will not find him very forward to embrace your proposal. But should any other person buy you such an estate, the shopkeeper would be much obliged to your benefactor if he would enjoin you to buy all your clothes at his shop" (*ibid.*, pp. 579 f.).

[36] This statement is, of course, not correct. English merchants had, from the beginning of British colonization, fitted out expeditions and invested money in colonial companies, money, moreover, which during the first phase of English colonization they usually lost.

[37] *Ibid.*, p. 580. This passage continues as follows: "For they did not find it convenient to buy every part of it. Some parts of it imported into England might have interfered with some of the trades which they themselves carried on at home. Those particular parts of it, therefore, they were willing that the colonists should sell where they could; the farther off the better; and upon that account proposed that their market should be confined to the countries south of Cape Finisterre. A clause in the famous act of navigation established this truly shopkeeper proposal into a law" (*ibid.*).

in order to support this monopoly."³⁸ The following is Adam Smith's final summary:

After all the unjust attempts ... of every country in Europe to engross to itself the whole advantage of the trade of its own colonies, no country has yet been able to engross to itself any thing but the expence of supporting in time of peace and of defending in time of war the oppressive authority which it assumes over them. The inconveniences resulting from the possession of its colonies, every country has engrossed to herself completely. The advantages resulting from their trade it has been obliged to share with many other countries.³⁹

At first sight, no doubt, the monopoly of the great commerce of America, naturally seems to be an acquisition of the highest value. To the undiscerning eye of giddy ambition, it naturally presents itself amidst the confused scramble of politics and war, as a very dazzling object to fight for. The dazzling splendour of the object, however, the immense greatness of the commerce, is the very quality which renders the monopoly of it hurtful. . . .⁴⁰

What were the remedies Adam Smith proposed? Theoretically, he had brilliantly exposed the indisputable inutility of the Old Colonial System and shown the profitability of a system of colonial free trade. Was he prepared to let practice unreservedly follow the guidance of theory? Adam Smith did not offer an answer of unmistakable clearness. Indeed, up to the very present he has been cited with apparently equal assuredness and alacrity alternately by imperialists and anti-imperialists, colonial protectionists and free traders. One recent reviewer remarked that in his discussion of imperial questions Adam Smith was somewhat like the man who mounted his horse and rode off in opposite directions.⁴¹ Yet, though there is a real problem of interpretation, this phrase seems hardly apposite.

In the first place, Adam Smith proposed the gradual relaxation of the metropolitan monopoly of the colony trade. He wrote:

Some moderate and gradual relaxation of the laws which give to Great Britain the exclusive trade to the colonies, till it is rendered in a great measure free, seems to be the only expedient which can, in all future times, deliver her from this danger. . . . To open the colony trade all at once to all nations, might not only occasion some transitory inconveniency, but a

---

³⁸*Ibid.*

³⁹Smith maintained that there are cases in which "even the regulations by which each nation endeavours to secure to itself the exclusive trade of its own colonies, are frequently more hurtful to the countries in favour of which they are established than to those against which they are established" (*ibid.*, p. 592).

⁴⁰*Ibid.*, pp. 592 f.

⁴¹Donald O. Wagner, "British Economists and the Empire," *Political Science Review*, XLVII (1932), 74.

great permanent loss to the greater part of those whose industry or capital is at present engaged in it.... In what manner, therefore, the colony trade ought gradually to be opened; what are the restraints which ought first, and what are those which ought last to be taken away; or in what manner the natural system of perfect liberty and justice ought gradually be restored, we must leave to the wisdom of future statesmen and legislators to determine.[42]

From this passage it appears beyond doubt that the object of the author's proposal was the ultimate establishment of colonial free trade.[43] Since the machinery by which the monopoly of the colony trade was maintained, had been incorporated into the Navigation Act of 1660 and numerous subsequent amendments, the abolition of the one would have involved the partial repeal of the other. Yet although denouncing the Navigation Act on economic grounds, Adam Smith approved of it in the following passage of his book: "As defence, however, is of much more importance than opulence, the act of navigation is, perhaps, the wisest of all the commercial regulations of England."[44]

The question is whether Smith conceived of the monopoly of the colony trade as one of the cases in which considerations of defence might legitimately over-ride considerations of plenty. It is the present writer's opinion that such was not the case. In the first place, it may almost be taken for granted that an author so prone to insert qualifications when submitting major principles, would probably have done so in the case under consideration. Furthermore, the British Navigation Law was a complicated structure of diverse enactments. It dealt with foreign trade as well as with the colony trade and regarding the latter it consisted of provisions dealing with navigation proper as well as with the maintenance of the colonial-trade monopoly. The Navigation Act, therefore, was separable into its constituent elements for purposes of examination as well as for the purpose of their modification or repeal. When he approved of this Act as a measure promotive

[42] *Wealth of Nations*, pp. 571 f.
[43] As established by the events subsequent to the publication of *The Wealth of Nations*, an immediate extinction of the monopoly would not have occasioned losses to a disastrous extent because it would not have led to a considerable shrinkage of the volume of Britain's trade with her colonies in the New World. But Smith was probably aware of the fact that the prejudices of the merchants could not have been removed by mere argument. It took the event of the American War of Independence and the trend of Anglo-American trade thereafter to impress the more enlightened of the English merchants with the superfluity of the colonial monopoly system.
[44] *Ibid.*, p. 431.

of English sea power, it is certain that Adam Smith thought merely of that portion of it which regulated Britain's foreign as distinct from her colonial trade. Discussing the effects which the Navigation Law presumably had had on the development of British maritime strength, he remarked that even without the monopoly of the colony trade a large share of that trade would have fallen to England while she would not have lost a large part of her foreign trade.[45] Moreover, as has been stated already in the foregoing, Adam Smith was firmly convinced that regarding the matter of defence, the colonies had always been a source of weakness and not a source of strength to the mother country.[46] If he was of the opinion that the principle of the superior importance of defence as against opulence had a claim to universal applicability, it is quite certain that he wanted it applied only in the most intelligent and consistent manner.

In addition to exposing the fallacies of the monopoly of the colony trade, as embodied in the Old Colonial System, Adam Smith questioned the value of empire as such and declared that, up to the time of his writing, Great Britain had incurred a total loss on account of her colonial possessions. Obviously, this evil could be remedied only in two ways. Sovereignty over the colonies could be renounced or a novel imperial arrangement might be devised by which the colonies would take upon themselves the burden of their defence and the cost of their civil administration. Adam Smith discussed both alternatives but failed to make clear which one he would have preferred to see adopted. It is this part of his analysis of the problem of empire as it confronted Britain which up to the present has remained a controversial issue. Most of his more recent reviewers agree that Adam Smith rejected separation in favour of a thoroughgoing reconstruction of the Empire on the basis of free trade and federation. To these writers Adam Smith appeared as a "liberal imperialist."[47]

[45]*Ibid.*, p. 564.
[46]For a confirmatory view see J. Shield Nicholson, *A Project of Empire* (London, 1910), p. 15.
[47]Smith was called a "liberal imperialist" and an imperialist "of cosmopolitan vision" by C. R. Fay, *Great Britain from Adam Smith to the Present Day* (New York, 1928), p. 3.

The following opinion was advanced by Rae, Smith's biographer: "Smith followed the struggle [the American War of Independence], as we see from many evidences in the concluding portion of the Wealth of Nations, with the most patriotic interest and anxiety.... Hume was in favour of separation.... But Smith ... held that there need never be any occasion for separation ...

The respective amounts of space devoted by Adam Smith to his discussion of the two alternative solutions of Britain's imperial problem are exceedingly unequal. This in itself, of course, is in no way indicative of his own preference. If the best solution was separation, there was not much to be said about it. If it was imperial reform, then it was necessary to show what kind of reorganization would remedy the detrimental effects of the existing system and how the proposed reform might be implemented.

The following quotation contains Adam Smith's opinions on the alternative of separation.

To propose that Great Britain should voluntarily give up all authority over her colonies, and leave them to elect their own magistrates, to enact their own laws, and to make peace and war as they might think proper, would be to propose such a measure as never was, and never will be adopted, by any nation in the world. No nation ever voluntarily gave up the dominion of any province, how troublesome soever the revenue which it afforded might be in proportion to the expence which it occasioned. Such sacrifices, though they might frequently be agreeable to the interests, are always mortifying to the pride of every nation, and what is perhaps of still greater consequence, they are always contrary to the private interest of the governing part of it, who would thereby be deprived of the disposal of many places of trust and profit, of many opportunities of acquiring wealth and distinction, which the possession of the most turbulent, and, to the great body of the people, the most unprofitable province seldom fails to afford. . . . If it [such a measure] was adopted, however, Great Britain would not only be immediately freed

and that the sound policy to adopt was really the policy of closer union—of imperial federation, as we call it. . . . He would not say, 'Perish dependencies,' but 'Incorporate them'." (John Rae, *Life of Adam Smith* [London, 1895], pp. 281 f. Similarly, W. Cunningham, *Richard Cobden and Adam Smith* [London, 1904].)

W. A. S. Hewins maintained: ". . . it is not clear that Adam Smith was contemplating the final and complete separation of the colonies. That would scarcely be a reasonable interpretation in view of his subsequent discussion of imperial federation. He was really arguing against the 'dominion' of the mother country and the 'monopoly' of the merchants" (W. A. S. Hewins, "The Fiscal Policy of the Empire," *The Times*, June 5, 1903, p. 14).

Another author who interpreted the chapter on the colonies in *The Wealth of Nations* as the project of a new Empire is J. Shield Nicholson, *A Project of Empire* (London, 1910).

It is to be noted that Rae, Cunningham, Hewins, and Nicholson wrote at a time when Britain had taken renewed interest in her Empire. All these authors denied that Adam Smith seriously contemplated separation as an alternative to reform.

In the opinion of Donald O. Wagner ("British Economists and the Empire," *Political Science Quarterly* (1931), 253), Smith did contemplate the separation of the colonies and proposed federation simply as an alternative. Which alternative he preferred, Wagner concluded, remains obscure.

from the whole annual expence of the peace establishment of the colonies, but might settle with them such a treaty of commerce as would effectually secure to her a free trade, more advantageous to the great body of the people, though less so to the merchants, than the monopoly which she at present enjoys. By thus parting good friends, the natural affection of the colonies to the mother country, which, perhaps, our late disensions have well nigh extinguished, would quickly revive. It might dispose them not only to respect, for whole centuries together, that treaty of commerce which they had concluded with us at parting, but to favour us in war as well as in trade, and, instead of turbulent and factious subjects, to become our most faithful, affectionate, and generous allies. . . .[48]

One inference can be safely drawn from the above passage, namely, that, as far as Great Britain as a whole was concerned, voluntary separation would be unattended by any drawback whatsoever. To be sure, sectional interests would be sacrificed by the adoption of such a course of action. The ruling class would lose lucrative patronage and an opportunity of obtaining glory and thus exacting additional deference from the masses of the people. The merchants, in particular, would be deprived of a profitable monopoly. But the great body of the people as taxpayers would be delivered from onerous taxation and as consumers they could enjoy the benefits of a freer trade with the former colonies. There can be no doubt that Adam Smith would not have preferred the protection of the vested interests at the cost of disregarding that interest of the whole community which throughout *The Wealth of Nations* he proposed to regard as the supreme objective of national policy.

Yet, although the solution of voluntary separation seemed entirely satisfactory from the point of view which dictated his approach to the problem, Adam Smith did not offer this step as an alternative which he expected to be seriously considered. It is exactly from this point that confusion, misunderstanding, and disagreement among his interpreters take their departure. For example, Nicholson, discussing Adam Smith's exposition of the case for voluntary separation, reasoned: "He shows that this alternative has certain advantages, even from the point of view of national power and wealth. But the idea is dismissed as not even worthy of practical consideration."[49]

The first sentence of this statement already contains an entirely unwarrantable misrepresentation of Adam Smith's arguments. To say that, in his opinion, separation had "certain" advantages "even" from the point of view of national power and wealth, is perfectly

[48] *Wealth of Nations*, pp. 581 f.
[49] Nicholson, *Project of Empire*, p. 21.

absurd; for this misinterpretation implies that the dismemberment of the colonial Empire would have entailed disadvantages—to national power and wealth, or to a category of national advantages ranking superior to power and wealth?—outweighing those "certain advantages" which would have resulted from such a step. That Adam Smith was convinced of the economic advantages following a friendly negotiation of separation is conceded by Nicholson.[50] But, according to his view Smith rejected this solution not as impracticable but as undesirable. Nicholson asserted that "confronted with this alternative of abandonment or organization Adam Smith had no hesitation . . . this alternative of separation is rejected by Adam Smith at once on the grounds of national sentiment."[51]

Thus Nicholson attempts to convey the impression that Adam Smith, because he was a nationalist patriot, rejected "without hesitation" the alternative of separation in spite of the obvious gain that would accrue to the wealth and the power of Great Britain in consequence of this policy. Nicholson, in other words, imputed to Adam Smith a type of patriotism that is willing to forgo important and clearly definable national advantages for the sake of enjoying the pride of empire or of exercising a self-imposed duty to people and civilize the world.[52]

It seems to the present writer that Adam Smith was, to a large and decisive extent, a thinker who subscribed to the ideas and sentiments of eighteenth-century enlightenment. His main work, indeed, breathes the same air of cool rationality which is characteristic of the literary production of that philosophical movement. And even if the exact wording of Smith's passage, dealing with the alternative of separation, is subjected to the most exhaustive and unbiased analysis, no evidence can be adduced that would support the interpretation of Nicholson and like-minded critics. Adam Smith simply stated that no nation had ever voluntarily relinquished dominion over a burdensome province because such a measure would be "mortifying" to national pride and prejudicial to the special interests of the ruling group. (To the latter circumstance, incidentally, he ascribed the greater weight.) In the absence of subsequent qualifications, the very fact that he grouped together these two insuperable obstacles to sane action excludes

[50]*Ibid.*, p. 212.   [51]*Ibid.*, p. 207.
[52]Nicholson refrained from defining or even describing Adam Smith's nationalist attitude. See also, *ibid.*, pp. 5-15.

the possibility that he approved of the former while disapproving of the latter.

In judging human nature Adam Smith was by no means an optimist. *The Wealth of Nations* is full of statements in which he trenchantly exposed the unscrupulous greed of men and their willingness to "conspire" against the public good. Less outspokenly, its underlying laissez-faire philosophy is based on the conviction not only that government, even if operating with the optimum of intelligence, falls short of the wisdom necessary for a wise regulation of human affairs, but also on his suspicion of governments being too susceptible to the desires of influential interest groups. There is hardly any important case in which he was over-optimistic in appraising the chances of sane principles being put into practice. On the contrary, he was rather inclined to be over-pessimistic in this respect. When discussing the prospect of setting up a system of free trade, he remarked gloomily: "To expect, indeed, that the freedom of trade should ever be entirely restored in Great Britain, is as absurd as to expect that an Oceana or Utopia should ever be established in it. Not only the prejudices of the public, but what is much more unconquerable, the private interests of many individuals, irresistibly oppose it."[53]

The line of argumentation followed by Adam Smith in this case as in that regarding the feasibility of separation is essentially the same. In each case he intimated that it would be folly to expect that the measure in question would be readily adopted and in each case he named the same powerful obstacles which stood in the way of such adoption: popular prejudice and selfish group-interests. Now, it certainly cannot be argued that Adam Smith did not want the adoption of a complete free-trade policy just because he thought that it would never be adopted. Hence, it seems safe to conclude that Nicholson's interpretation is erroneous. Adam Smith did not, without hesitation, reject separation because he thought that measure undesirable. He only rejected it, unhesitatingly, because he was a shrewd observer of mankind in general and his countrymen in particular. He realized immediately that the scheme was completely impracticable. Therefore he said that "the most visionary enthusiast would scarce be capable of proposing such a measure, with any serious hopes at least of its ever being adopted."[54]

Smith's imperial reform project was a substitute proposal. If executed precisely along the lines he suggested, this solution would

[53] *Wealth of Nations*, pp. 437 f.
[54] *Ibid.*, p. 582.

have been as satisfactory, from his point of view, as the alternative of dismembering the Empire. The important point is that his programme of imperial reform deals fundamentally only with fiscal considerations. The question of trade relations aside, the British colonies were a drain on the wealth and the power of their mother state. Hence, Smith suggested, the alternative to separation would be to let the colonies assume a proportionate share of the cost of imperial government and defence. "In order to render any province advantageous to the empire to which it belongs, it ought to afford, in time of peace, a revenue to the public sufficient not only for defraying the whole expence of its own peace establishment, but for contributing its proportion to the support of the general government of the empire."[55]

Direct taxation, Adam Smith continued to argue, is the only satisfactory source from which this financial contribution of the colonies can be derived. "The colonies may be taxed either by their own assemblies, or by the parliament of Great Britain."[56] The former possibility he rejected because colonial assemblies could never be induced to impose upon their constituents a sufficient amount of taxes, a predisposition which seemed re-enforced by their ignorance of what is required from the point of view of the Empire as a whole.[57] On the other hand, due to the lack of sufficient authority, Great Britain appeared unable to tax the colonies by requisition.[58] Smith, therefore, proposed colonial representation in parliament in proportion to taxation.

The parliament of Great Britain insists upon taxing the colonies; and they refuse to be taxed by a parliament in which they are not represented. If to each colony ... Great Britain should allow such a number of representatives as suited the proportion of what it contributed to the public revenue of the empire, in consequence of its being subjected to the same taxes, and in compensation admitted to the same freedom of trade with its fellow-subjects at home; the number of its representatives to be augmented as the proportion of its contribution might afterwards augment; a new method of acquiring importance, a new and more dazzling object of ambition would be presented to the leading men of each colony.[59]

[55] *Ibid.*   [56] *Ibid.*, p. 583.
[57] *Ibid.*, pp. 583 f.   [58] *Ibid.*, pp. 584 ff.
[59] *Ibid.*, p. 587. The last part of this passage betrays Adam Smith's deep insight into the real causes of the American War of Independence. He realized that formulae like the "rights of man" were merely symbols in the hands of an ascending colonial *élite* which desired to replace the local representatives of the English ruling groups. Therefore he suggested that his scheme would present to these colonial ruling groups "a new method of acquiring importance, a new and more dazzling object of ambition." For he recognized that the satisfaction

The above are virtually all the considerations which compose Smith's project of imperial reform. There is not the slightest flavour of that sentimental "imperialism" that can be found in the utterances of earlier and later imperial federationists. It is nothing but a scheme designed to render the colonies willing to assume the full costs of their own defence and government.

Nicholson averred that Adam Smith looked at the Empire not merely from an economic standpoint.[60] As the sole evidence supporting this statement he pointed to Smith's plan for the parliamentary representation of the colonists in an imperial union—"an Imperial Parliament based on taxation."[61] But even the most painstaking scrutiny of the text reveals nothing more than that Adam Smith thought of his Imperial Parliament as a machinery devised for the purpose of exacting adequate taxes from the colonists. If he had the vision of a British Commonwealth of Nations,[62] as projected and shaped by a later age, he certainly

of these ambitious groups was the indispensable condition of any enduring settlement of the disputes between mother country and colonies. Thus he declared: "Instead of piddling for the little prizes which are to be found in what may be called the paltry raffle of colony faction; they might then hope . . . to draw some of the great prizes which sometimes come from the wheel of the great state lottery of British politics. Unless this or some other method is fallen upon . . . of preserving the importance and of gratifying the ambition of the leading men of America, it is not very probable that they will ever voluntarily submit to us. . ." (*ibid.*).

This shrewd observation was, of course, all the more true after the formation of the Continental Congress. Adam Smith wrote: "Five hundred different people, perhaps, who in different ways act immediately under the continental congress; and five hundred thousand, perhaps, who act under those five hundred, all feel in the same manner a proportionable rise in their own importance. Almost every individual of the governing party in America, fills, at present in his own fancy, a station superior, not only to what he had ever filled before, but to what he had ever expected to fill; and unless some new object of ambition is presented either to him or to his leaders, if he has the ordinary spirit of a man, he will die in defence of that station" (*ibid.*, p. 588).

[60]Nicholson, *Project of Empire*, p. 213. [61]*Ibid.*, p. 215.

[62]It is true, Adam Smith envisaged the possibility that in the more distant future the imperial centre of gravity would move across the Atlantic. "Such has hitherto been the rapid progress of that country [North America] in wealth, population and improvement, that in the course of little more than a century, perhaps, the produce of America might exceed that of British taxation. The seat of the empire would then naturally remove itself to that part of the empire which contributed most to the general defence and support of the whole" (*Wealth of Nations*, p. 590). This, however, is nothing but a factual observation based on the mechanics of parliamentary representation according to the amount of revenue contributed.

refrained from committing this vision to paper. It is more likely that what he had in mind was less an imperial parliament based on taxation than an imperial parliament designed for the procurement of imperial revenue. His imperial parliament, in other words, was the means to an end rather than an end in itself.

Adam Smith did not fail to realize the difficulties to be overcome if his project was to be put into practice. "That this union, however, could be easily effectuated, or that difficulties and great difficulties might not occur in the execution, I do not pretend. I have yet heard of none, however, which appear insurmountable. The principal perhaps arise not from the nature of things, but from the prejudices and opinions of the people both on this and on the other side of the Atlantic."[63] Thus, he deemed the extent of the difficulties less formidable in this case than in that of the resolute dismembering of the Empire. It was to him the more feasible rather than the more desirable solution.

In the closing paragraphs of *The Wealth of Nations* Adam Smith once more took up the subject of empire. Again he confined himself to a discussion of the financial burden which the colonies imposed upon their parent state. Again he stressed the imperative necessity of reform.

But countries which contribute neither revenue nor military force towards the support of the empire, cannot be considered as provinces. They may perhaps be considered as appendages, as a sort of splendid and showy equipage of the empire. But if the empire can no longer support the expence of keeping up this equipage, it ought certainly to lay it down; and if it cannot raise its revenue in proportion to its expence, it ought, at least, to accomodate its expence to its revenue. If the colonies, notwithstanding their refusal to submit to British taxes, are still to be considered as provinces of the British empire, their defence in some future war may cost Great Britain as great an expence as it ever has done in any former war. The rulers of Great Britain have, for more than a century past, amused the people with the imagination that they possessed a great empire on the west side of the Atlantic. This empire, however, has hitherto existed in imagination only. It has hitherto been, not an empire, but the project of an empire; not a gold mine, but the project of a gold mine; a project which has cost, which continues to cost, and

---

[63] *Ibid.*, p. 589. Fear of the influx of democratic ideas from the colonies appeared to Adam Smith as one of the major prejudices prevailing in Britain. But in this respect he allayed the suspicions of his countrymen. "But if the number of American representatives were to be in proportion to the produce of American taxation, the number of people to be managed would increase exactly in proportion to the means of managing them; and the means of managing, to the number of people to be managed. The monarchical and democratical parts of the constitution would, after the union, stand exactly in the same degree of relative force with regard to one another as they had done before" (*ibid.*).

which, if pursued in the same way as it has been hitherto, is likely to cost, immense expence, without being likely to bring any profit. . . . It is surely now time that our rulers should either realize this golden dream, in which they have been indulging themselves, perhaps, as well as the people; or, that they should awake from it themselves, and endeavour to awaken the people. If the project cannot be completed, it ought to be given up.[64]

In spite of Adam Smith's anxious exhortations, neither the rulers of Great Britain nor their people awoke from this golden dream. The "project" was not completed. Three-quarters of a century after the publication of *The Wealth of Nations* we shall find the Manchester School vigorously engaged in the task of dispelling the roseate clouds which obscured the realities of empire from the people of Great Britain. Adam Smith's phrase of the "appendage," of the "splendid and showy equipage" of empire will be found an every recurrent theme in their untiring denunciation of their country's "project of empire."[65]

2. The Dissenters and the American War of Independence

Having reviewed, at some length, the negative attitudes of Josiah Tucker, the Tory, and Adam Smith, the economist and Whig, toward the British Empire, a brief discussion of the Dissenters' opinion seems called for. This discussion will be confined to the views of Richard Price and Joseph Priestley. The liberal dissenters did not single out the problem of empire *per se*, but in the

[64]*Ibid.*, pp. 899 f. In the above passage Smith, apparently contrasted the "empire"—i.e., an empire of which the constituent portions contributed to the cost of governing and defending the whole in proportion to their income—with the "project of empire,"—i.e., an empire in which such a just distribution of the expense did not obtain.

[65]After Cornwallis's defeat at Yorktown, Adam Smith wrote a letter to Sir John Sinclair (October 14, 1782) that contains a vigorous statement on the uselessness of colonial dependencies to the metropolis. This letter is particularly interesting as it includes such an important naval station as Gibraltar in its depreciation of oversea possessions. Adam Smith wrote: "The real futility of all distant dominions, of which the defence is necessarily most expensive, and which contributes nothing, either by revenue or military force, to the general defence of the empire, and very little even to their own particular defence, is, I think, the subject on which the public prejudices of Europe require most to be set right. In order to defend the barren rock of Gibraltar (to the possession of which we owe the union of France and Spain, contrary to the natural interests and inveterate prejudices of both countries, the important enmity of Spain and the futile and expensive friendship of Portugal) we have left our own coasts defenceless. . ." (quoted in Rae, *Life of Adam Smith*, pp. 382 f.).

course of their diverse writings they touched upon this problem from various points of view and in the outbreak and issue of the American War of Independence they found a distinct stake of their own.

Neither Price nor Priestley were economists. Indeed, if compared with the accomplishments of David Hume, Adam Smith, and others, they lagged considerably behind the standard of their time. In one respect their conception of foreign trade is of interest. Like Tucker and Adam Smith they deplored the existence of a deeply-ingrained sentiment of jealousy in the attitude of nations towards international commerce.[66] Indeed, in line with their anti-nationalistic disposition, they hoped that the universal expansion of foreign trade, if carried on in the right spirit, would result in a corresponding spread of cosmopolitanism. Thus, Price observed: "Foreign Trade has, in some respects, the most useful tendency. By creating an intercourse between distant kingdoms, it extends benevolence, removes local prejudices, leads every man to consider himself more a citizen of the world than of any particular State, and, consequently, checks the excesses of that 'Love of our Country' which has been applauded as one of the noblest, but which, really, is one of the most destructive principles in human nature."[67]

This aversion to parochialism and emotional patriotism is highly significant in itself. The dissenters did not think of nations as inevitably pursuing antagonistic interests.[68] They rather thought in terms of a fundamental community of peoples as aggregates of individuals striving for their personal happiness.[69] All these considerations influenced the attitude of Price and Priestley

[66]Priestley wrote: "Many of the received maxims of commerce have for their object the enriching of one nation at the expense of others, arising from national jealousy, as if the gain of one must necessarily be the loss of the other. But the maxim is by no means true...." "The happiness of all nations... as one great community, will be the best promoted by laying aside all national jealousy of trade..." (Joseph Priestley, *Lectures on History and General Policy* [Birmingham, 1788], pp. 379, 398).

[67]Richard Price, *Observations on the Importance of the American Revolution* (London, 1785), pp. 74 f.

[68]Price welcomed the idea of trade producing among nations "a sense of mutual dependence" (*ibid.*, p. 75).

[69]Their abhorrence of war led this group to search for effective means for its suppression. Price had a bold vision of a union of states to which the various constituent nations would delegate their sovereign rights in all matters outside domestic affairs. "Let every state with respect to all its internal concerns, be continued independent of all the rest; and let a general confederacy be formed by the appointment of a Senate consisting of Representatives from all the dif-

toward the problem of colonies in general and of the English dispute with the North American colonists in particular. Still more important in this respect, as will be seen, was their fight for political liberalism and democracy.

The opinions of Price and Priestley on the utility of colonies to the parent state, were somewhat at variance. Priestley was fully aware of the disadvantages attending the possession of oversea dependencies. He pointed to the financial burden involved[70] and asserted that the maintenance of a colonial empire not only did not add to the military strength of the parent state but was in itself a frequent cause of wars.[71] Both, Priestley and Price, were afraid of the internal political effects of conquest and expansion because they were convinced that the extension of empire was, at bottom, incompatible with the freedom of the citizen.[72] Price, in contrast to Priestley,[73] conceived of real benefits flowing from the trade with affiliated colonies.[74]

---

ferent states. Let this Senate possess the power of managing all the common concerns of the United States, and of judging and deciding between them, as a common Arbiter or Umpire, in all disputes; having, at the same time, under its direction, the common force of the states to support its decisions" (Richard Price, *Observations on the Nature of Civil Liberty, the Principles of Government, and the Justice and Policy of the War with America* (London, 1776), pp. 8 f.

[70]Priestley stated: "Little did Great-Britain think of the price they were to pay for their foreign colonies in North America. For to this account must be put, besides the expense of planting them, both the expense of defending them, and that of the war in which we lost them" (*Lectures*, p. 403).

[71]"It may be said that a nation must be stronger by the addition of the power of foreign dominions. But in proportion as any nation becomes powerful, it excites the jealousy of other nations, and thereby has much more powerful enemies to contend with.... Had England nothing to do with the East or West Indies, America, or Gibraltar, it would have fewer wars, and would, no doubt, be much more wealthy (as its industry would, by one means or other, find a market) and if it was invaded, would have much greater resources for defending itself" (*ibid.*, p. 498).

[72]Discussing the rise and decline of the Roman Empire, Priestley remarked that "no history furnishes so striking an example how incompatible extensive empire is with political liberty" (*ibid.*, p. 257).

Price wrote: "Montesquieu has observed, that England, in planting colonies, should have commerce, not dominion, in view; the increase of dominion being incompatible with the security of public liberty" (Richard Price, *Additional Observations on the Nature of Civil Liberty* [London, 1777], p. 76).

[73]In a pamphlet, written in 1774, Priestley anticipated with regret the loss of the American colonies. This regret, however, was caused by the impending loss of British fellow-fighters for the cause of democracy rather than by economic considerations. See Joseph Priestley, *An Address to Protestant Dissenters of All Denominations* (London, 1774), *passim*.

[74]In his *Observations on the Nature of Civil Liberty* (pp. 72 ff.) Price spoke in

But throughout the course of the American War of Independence the attitude of the dissenters was preponderantly determined by purely political considerations. They did not come out in favour of a policy of separation. On the contrary, from the beginning of the dispute and even during the war itself they demanded that the American colonists be appeased by the offer of reasonable concessions.[75] To this group of thinkers, the Americans did not fight primarily for independence but for their political freedom from metropolitan tyranny. Basically, they fought for the same objectives for which the dissenters battled at home. Thus, Price declared that the American revolt was "a revolution by which the Britons themselves will be the greatest gainers, if wise enough to improve properly the check that has been given to the despotism of their ministers, and to catch the flame of virtuous liberty which has saved their American brethren."[76] Priestley similarly declared:

Do you imagine, my fellow-citizens, that we can sit still, and be the idle spectators of the chains which are forging for our brethren in America, with safety to ourselves? Let us suppose America to be completely enslaved, in consequence of which the English court can command all the money, and all the force of that country; will they like to be so arbitrary abroad, and have their power confined at home? especially as troops in abundance can be transported in a few weeks from America to England; where, with the present standing army, they may instantly reduce us to what they please.[77]

---

exalted words of the metropolitan trade with the colonies. "This trade, it should be considered, was not only ... an increasing trade; but it was a trade in which we had no rivals; a trade certain, constant, and uninterrupted; and which, by the shipping employed in it, contributed greatly to the support of that navy which is our chief national strength ... upon the whole, it is undeniable, that it has been one of the main springs of our opulence and splendour; and that we have, in a great measure, been indebted to it for our ability to bear a debt so much heavier, than that which, fifty years ago, the wisest men thought would necessarily sink us." This is, of course, all along the mercantilist line of argumentation. The question, however, is whether Price did not stress these advantages in order to induce his countrymen to agree to a peaceful conciliation of their quarrel with the American colonists.

On another occasion Price observed: "With the colonies united to us, we might be the greatest and happiest nation that ever existed. But with the colonies separated from us, and in alliance with France and Spain, we are no more a people. They appear, therefore, to be indeed worth any price. Our existence depends on keeping them" (*Additional Observations*, p. 73).

[75]See Roland Thomas, *Richard Price* (London, 1924), p. 69.
[76]*Observations on the Importance of the American Revolution*, p. 2.
[77]*Address to Protestant Dissenters*, p. 14.

Price, indeed, exclaimed: "With heart-felt satisfaction, I see the revolution in favour of universal liberty which has taken place in America,—a revolution which opens a new prospect in human affairs...."[78]

What Price had in mind and what he wished to see set up on the North American continent was "an Empire of Freemen" in contradistinction to "an Empire of Slaves."[79]

An Empire is a collection of states or communities united by some common bond.... If these states have each of them free constitutions... and, with respect to taxation and internal legislation, are independent of the other states, but united by compacts, or alliances, or subjection to a Great Council, representing the whole, or to one Monarch entrusted with the supreme executive power: In these circumstances, the Empire will be an Empire of Freemen.... If, on the contrary... none of the states possess an independent legislative authority; but are all subject to an absolute monarch, whose will is their law; then is the Empire an Empire of Slaves.[80]

The liberal dissenters were ever inclined to be jealous of any augmentation of the state's power.[81] The determination of the English ruling group to coerce the American democrats into submission threatened immensely to increase the power at the disposal of the King and the "King's Friends." Therefore, the dissenters struggled against this evil war with manful courage.

But even apart from this purely political issue, they criticized the policy of the government because even a successful war would earn the mother country nothing but losses in men and money and further troubles. "America recovered by the sword must be kept by the sword, and forts and garrisons must be maintained in every province to awe the wretched inhabitants.... This will create another addition of expence.... The colonies, desolated and impoverished, will yield no revenue."[82]

Concern with the rapid increase of the public debt and the passion for financial economy were other considerations that in-

[78]*Observations on the Importance of the American Revolution*, pp. 1 f.

[79]This vision sprang directly from Price's political philosophy: "From the nature and principles of Civil Liberty..., it is an immediate and necessary inference that no one community can have power over the property or legislation of another community, that is not incorporated with it by a just and adequate representation" (*Observations on the Nature of Civil Liberty*, p. 19).

[80]*Ibid.*, pp. 28 f.

[81]Price declared: "There is nothing that requires more to be watched than power. There is nothing that ought to be opposed with more determined resolution than its encroachments. Sleep in a state, as Montesquieu says, is always followed by slavery" (*ibid.*, p. 18).

[82]*Additional Observations*, pp. 73 f.

fluenced the attitude of the dissenters.[83] It was mainly these aspects which finally reconciled this group to the loss of the North American colonies. Shortly before the Peace of Paris was concluded, Price wrote: "Happily for the kingdom, a peace must be obtained; and had the terms on which it has been obtained brought us more within the limits of this island, and eased us more of the expence of foreign dominion, I should have thought it only more a blessing to us and to mankind . . . let us turn our thoughts another way, and recollect, that the loss of Minorca and the liberation of America have already produced great savings. . . ."[84]

As the above review of dissentient thought shows, the liberal Nonconformists had no comprehensive theory of empire. Their principal interest, moreover, was focused on the political and constitutional rather than on the economic issues involved. Yet it seemed justifiable to devote to the discussion of their views more than only a few sentences because, as a social class, they were to become increasingly influential as the process of the Industrial Revolution gathered momentum. Even their purely political philosophy,[85]—their hostility toward the traditionalism of the Tories or of Burke and like-minded Whigs, their constant demand for the complete secularization of politics, and their laissez-faire ideals—especially as expressed in Philosophical Radicalism and Manchesterism[86]—were to exert considerable influence on the shaping of English colonial theories.

[83] As shall be seen in the following chapters, the passion for economy became, in Great Britain, a consideration which increasingly affected the attitude of the middle class towards the problem of empire.

[84] Richard Price, *The State of the Public Debts and Finances* (London, 1783), p. 20.

[85] See on this, Anthony Lincoln, *Some Political and Social Ideas of English Dissent, 1763-1800* (Cambridge, England, 1938).

[86] Bright and Cobden were Dissenters.

CHAPTER VII

COLONIAL THEORIES: 1776-1815

I

1776-1782

IN the preceding chapters British theories, attitudes, and sentiments in relation to the usefulness of colonial possessions have been presented, roughly, up to the outbreak of the American War of Independence. Conventional and unconventional mercantilist theorizing, the new conceptions of the first classical economists, early projects of imperial federation, and the ideas of the English Dissenters were recorded. All these different currents of opinion were represented in the stream of public comment that accompanied the events of the war. However, the years from 1776 to 1783 were, of course, not conducive to judicious discussion of the problems of empire.

There were gloomy pessimists like the Earl of Shelburne[1] who assumed that "the moment that the independence of America is agreed to by our government, the sun of Great Britain is set, and we shall no longer be a powerful or respectable people."[2] Then there were a few resolute anti-imperialists like Dean Tucker. A group of appeasers propagated a policy of conciliation; this school was composed of men like Chatham[3] and Burke, the Dissenters and large numbers of merchants.[4] The dreadful spectre of war

[1] In October, 1775, Shelburne had written to Richard Price: "What a dreadful crisis are our publick affairs reduc'd to? I look upon the Colonies as lost, no exertions can prevent it, and the consequence will be, that he will be the happiest who can live upon the least" (Massachusetts Historical Society, *Letters to and from Richard Price, 1767-1790* [Cambridge, Mass., 1903], p. 47).

[2] Lord Fitzmaurice, *Life of William, Earl of Shelburne* (London, 1912), II, 14. Shelburne's melancholy sentiment at that time is sharply at variance with his cool approval of the final loss of the colonies (in the meantime he had read the *Wealth of Nations* and met its author). Such reversals of opinion were quite frequent among writers and politicians during these hectic years.

[3] Pitt, however, was one of the first to change his mind and to endorse the war policy of the government. On April 7, 1778, delivering his last speech before his impending death he said: "Shall we tarnish the lustre of this nation by an ignominious surrender of its rights and fairest possessions? Shall this great kingdom . . . fall prostrate before the House of Bourbon?" (William Cobbett, *The Parliamentary History of England*, XIX, 1023).

[4] The merchants feared interruption and loss of their profitable American trade and were extremely anxious about their outstanding credits oversea. For

naturally led to further proposals for a federative empire or an imperial union.[5] But the bulk of influential groups were, of course,

petitions of the merchants of London, Bristol, Glasgow, and Birmingham for reconciliation with America (1775) see Cobbett, *Parl. Hist.*, XVIII, 168-71, 179-81, 194-5; G. H. Guttridge (ed.), "The American Correspondence of a Bristol Merchant, 1766-1776," *University of California Publications in History*, XXII (1934), no. 1.

After the surrender of General Burgoyne, Israel Mauduit advocated immediate recognition of American independence in order to save Britain's trade with the colonists. He wrote: "The Americans will then have full liberty to trade with which nations they please; they will like best to trade with both [Britain and France], and we shall have our full share. Their manners, habits and clothing is now English; if we instantly declare their independence, they will continue so; but if we continue a long war with them, and oblige them to receive all things from France, they will in time be totally Gallicized, and estranged from us, and prefer French manufactures of all kinds to ours" (*A Hand Bill Advocating American Independence* [1778], republished by P. L. Ford [ed.] [Brooklyn, 1890], p. 17).

The unanimity, determination, and even the sincerity of merchant opinion should not, however, be over-estimated. The accelerated pace of the Industrial Revolution was already having considerable effect on English business and business sentiment. On August 8, 1775, Samuel Curwen wrote in a letter: "It is a capital mistake of our American friends to expect insurrections here.... The manufactories are in full employ, and one of the warmest of the friends of America told me that letters from Manchester expressed joy that no American orders had been sent, otherwise there must have been disappointment somewhere." William Lee wrote on March 10, 1775: "... the Ministry knew well enough the merchants, except 2 or 3 of us, were not at all serious; hence it is, that our petitions are almost all ... little else than milk and water. The Glasgow merchants played the same game with less trouble, they sent a strong petition to the House of Commons in favour of America, but at the same time gave Lord North to understand by their Member, Lord F. Campbell, that they did not mean any opposition, but to gain credit in America, and thereby more easily collect their debts" (L. B. Namier, *England in the Age of the American Revolution* [London, 1930], p. 296).

[5]Thus, William Pulteney suggested a Union under the same king, American representation in Parliament, and inter-imperial free trade. In that manner, Pulteney argued, Great Britain would find relief from expenses for imperial defence and administration. Then "the prosperity of America would be more than ever, the interest and the wish of this country" (William Pulteney, *Considerations on the Present State of Public Affairs* [3d ed.; London, 1779], p. 13).

David Hartley declared in 1778: "I would seek the alliance and friendship of America. I would cement the two countries together by a mutual naturalization, in all rights and franchises to the fullest extent. We are derived from the same stock; we have the same religion, the same manners, the same language, the same love of liberty and of independence; and if we must be seemingly divided, let there be at least a union in that partition" (Cobbett, *Parl. Hist.*, XIX, 1077. See also David Hartley, *Letters on the American War* [1778] [6th ed.; London, 1779], pp. 4, 13 ff., 93 ff.). It is interesting that Hartley confessed in his *Letters*

in favour of forcing the rebellious colonists into subordination to the metropolis. The large majority of the Tories, the King and his friends, the Established Church, and the Armed Services did, on the whole, adhere to this attitude.[6] This was quite natural since the majority opinion was still fully convinced of the utility of the colonies and of the virtues of the Old Colonial System. Moreover, in its strictly legal aspects the British case was strong and the metropolitan demand for a colonial contribution to the expense of governing and defending the Empire was just. Their case had just one defect: it was inexpedient and the attempt to enforce its principles by an appeal to armed force was unwise and futile.[7]

Before the war in America looked entirely hopeless from the English standpoint, proposals were brought forward which contemplated the possibility of saving at least part of the North American Empire in addition to Canada. William Knox, for example, approached the Government with a plan that envisaged, somewhat immediately, "the establishment of a port on the Chesapeak, and ... expeditions for the recovery of Georgia and South Carolina; ... the retaining them, with the islands of New York, Statin, Long Island, Canada, and Nova Scotia, would ... secure to this country all the trade of America which was worth having, at a much less charge to the Nation, than we had hitherto been at for that country."[8]

Shortly before the end of the war, Sir John Sinclair wrote a pamphlet which suggested several alternatives to the "total" abandonment of the North American colonies. One of them contemplated the retention of "some posts on the continent." Charleston, he thought, might be rendered impregnable against the

that the Navigation Act "is the only British interest in America, which I ever took to my heart" (*ibid.*, p. 112).

Joseph Galloway also presented a "plan of a proposed Union between Great Britain and the Colonies" (Joseph Galloway, *A Candid Examination of the Mutual Claims of Great Britain and the Colonies* [London, 1780], pp. 65 ff.).

[6]The following quotation may be taken as an expression of opinion typical of the war party: "Britain, like the pelican, has fed her young with her blood; grown strong, they rise up to prey upon her vitals. Every principle of reason, justice, and policy, require that she should exert her force, and establish her just supremacy.... Whatever America gains, independence, commerce, dominion, glory, so much does Britain lose..." ([M. J. Home], *A Letter from an Officer Retired to His Son in Parliament* [London, 1776], pp. 12 f.).

[7]See on this question, Bernard Holland, *Imperium et Libertas* (London, 1901), p. 28.

[8]*Extra Official State Papers* (London, 1789), I, 27.

American armies. It would "insure to us some of the most lucrative branches of the American trade" and, besides, would serve as an "asylum" for "the unfortunate loyalists."[9] As another alternative Sinclair suggested the abandonment of the North American continent followed by a determined attack on the French West Indies. These colonies would not be able

to resist the efforts of a spirited attack; and, heavy as the charges of the war have been, there is every reason to believe that we could conquer possessions from that nation, whose value would nearly repay the expences we have been put to: or, if France is thought to be an enemy whose colonies cannot easily be mastered, we are likely to find the continental possessions of Spain a very easy acquisition. ... The possession of almost any province in that part of the world, would enable us to acquire the greatest part of the trade of Spanish America, and would amply compensate for the treasure we have lost.[10]

These various proposals, however, by no means exhausted the inventive imagination of Sir John Sinclair. He offered a final alternative proposing as a convenient sequel to the disruption of the British Empire, the general emancipation of European colonies in America.

But there is one plan, which, though we were reduced to a state ever so desperate, it will always be in our power to pursue; and that is, to support, in conjunction with the other powers of Europe, and in particular with the armed neutrality, a system of a general colonial emancipation. If the colonies of France, and more especially of those of Spain, were open to our manufactures, we should have the greatest reason to rejoice at the independence of America. ... Indeed a general colonial emancipation would be a fortunate conclusion of the present war, both for this country, and for mankind: those rich and fertile provinces, which South America contains, have too long groaned under the dominion of the proud and sluggish Spaniard, and might soon wear a new face, were they opened to the exertions and industry of this country, and of Europe. ... To question whether the different powers of the European continent would support such a system, is to doubt of their being possessed of common ambition, or indeed of common sense: for were the House of Bourbon to retain its colonies entire, whilst Great Britain lost hers, every one must perceive, that the safety and independence of Europe in general would be greatly endangered.[11]

---

[9] Sir John Sinclair, *Thoughts on the Naval Strength of the British Empire* [1782] (2d ed.; London, 1795), pp. 67 ff.

[10] *Ibid.*, pp. 73 f.

[11] *Ibid.*, pp. 74 f. In order to induce the Powers of the Armed Neutrality to help Britain force upon France and Spain the emancipation of their colonies, Sinclair suggested with sly naïveté to offer to the "Neutral Powers" the dominion of some of the islands to be conquered from the French and the Spaniards. Sinclair sent his pamphlet to Adam Smith who gave the following reply: "I have read your pamphlet. ... As to what effect it might produce if translated upon

Yet the course of events that forced the British to accept defeat, destroyed whatever hopes there might have been of retaining, besides Canada, a portion of the American continental empire. Instead of hopes there was defeatism and resignation.[12] Not a few, some sincerely and some in a rather forced manner—the grapes had turned sour—,[13] expressed their acceptance of the loss. Thus, the Earl of Stair, "the Cassandra of the State," ever mindful of the need for strictest economy and horrified at mounting public debts, said: "Having profited so little by our foreign Excursions, let us turn Homewards, and try what Precedent and Experience will do for us there."[14]

A review of the typical arguments used by those who perceived advantages in what appeared an irreparable loss to the majority of the nation, reveals some interesting points.[15] First, it was agreed among this school of thought that the subject of the utility of colonies required much more analytical effort than had been bestowed upon it hitherto. James Anderson declared: "It has appeared to me not a little extraordinary, that among the many treatises which have been written of late, in consequence of the dispute between Great Britain and her colonies, no attempt should have been made to ascertain with some degree of precision wherein

the Powers concerned in the Armed Neutrality, I am a little doubtful. It is too plainly partial to England. It proposes that the force of the Armed Neutrality should be employed in recovering to England the islands she lost, and the compensation which it is proposed England should give for this service is the islands which they may conquer for themselves . . . from France and Spain. There seems to me besides to be some inconsistency in the argument. If it be just to emancipate the continent of America from the dominion of every European power, how can it be just to subject the islands to such dominion? . . . The real futility of all distant dominions . . . is, I think, the subject on which the public prejudices of Europe require most to be set right" (quoted in John Rae, *Life of Adam Smith* [London, 1895], p. 382).

[12]Lord North, tormented by the difficulties arising from the war, lamented the success with which Columbus had discovered America, contending, "that Europe would have gone on much better without that discovery" (*The Correspondence of John Sinclair* [London, 1831], I, 74).

[13]The following statement made by William Knox may be taken as an example of this type of reaction. Knox remarked "That the separation of the thirteen American Colonies from the Government of Great Britain, is not so great an evil to this country as would have been their continuance under it for half a century longer" (*Extra Official State Papers*, II, 28).

[14]John Earl of Stair, *Facts and Their Consequences* (London, 1782), p. 19.

[15]That these arguments betray the growing influence of Adam Smith and Josiah Tucker, then more widely read than before, is not surprising. The French Physiocrats also had found a considerable English following.

consist the advantages that have accrued to the mother country, or the disadvantages that may be expected to be felt by her in consequence of her connection with the American colonies."[16]

While the supposed profitability of the metropolitan monopoly of the colony trade had formed the centre of mercantilist reasoning on the usefulness of colonies and the *raison d'être* of the Old Colonial System, the writers here considered viewed the loss of this monopoly from two different standpoints. The reaction of one group was influenced by conceptions which belittled the importance and utility of any trade carried on beyond the national frontiers and advised concentration on agriculture and the cultivation of the home market. Other writers, on the other hand, came to the conclusion, soon to be substantiated by experience, that the loss of the colonies would not materially diminish the flow of this trade. The Earl of Stair remarked: "Whenever the war ceases, it is highly probable that much of the antient Intercourse betwixt this Country and her American Brethren will be renewed, perhaps on a Footing not much less advantageous than formerly...."[17]

Henceforth the fact, realized by a great many people, that Great Britain had been able to keep a large share of American foreign trade, that the mother country had lost nothing "except the barren honour of sovereignty,"[18] was exploited both by the critics of the Old Colonial System and by the anti-imperialists. The same experience, however, furnished the basis for a stock-argument with those expansionist imperialists who had discarded the out-worn principles underlying the monopolist system. Later

[16]James Anderson, *The Interest of Great Britain with Regard to Her American Colonies, Considered* (London, 1782), p. 1.

[17]*Facts and Their Consequences* (1782), p. 35. Throughout the following decades the truth of such predictions was confirmed by various writers. Chalmers stated: "... by comparing the exports to the discontented colonies, before the war began, with the exports to the United States, after the admission of their independence it will appear ... that we now supply them with manufactures to a greater amount, than even in the most prosperous times" (George Chalmers, *An Estimate of the Comparative Strength of Great-Britain* [1782] [new ed.; London, 1802], pp. 166 f.).

Another writer commented: "The apprehension of ruin from this separation soon subsided in the discovery of our error. It was seen that natural causes had operated by force what we had neglected to do from foresight; that in giving up, though involuntarily, the narrow minded monopoly of the colonial system, we still retained that which resulted from our being in every thing but Government the same people" (Alexander Baring, *An Inquiry into the Causes and Consequences of the Orders in Council* [London, 1808], p. 17).

[18]*Ibid.*, p. 20.

they were to point out that there are "invisible and more pleasing ties of similar habits, laws, and, above all, language," which produce a natural "monopoly" bare of any kind of metropolitan "compulsion."[19]

Many writers acknowledged that the emancipation of the Northern American colonies had relieved the United Kingdom of a considerable financial burden. Macpherson, for example, affirmed that "relief from the expense of governing and protecting them" was one of the beneficial consequences of American independence.[20] "Among the lesser advantages may be reckoned the relief from the payment of bounties, which had been very liberally granted for the encouragement of many articles of American cultivation, that can now be imported without taxing the people of this country for the benefit of the American planters."[21] Chalmers likewise concluded that "while this nation has saved the annual expence of great military and civil establishments, it can hardly be said to have lost any commercial profits."[22] He also pointed out that Great Britain had gained in power by the emancipation of the colonies.

I have long thought, what I now think, that those colonies, from the peace of 1763 to the epoch of their revolt, formed balances to the power, rather than buttresses to the strength of Great Britain. Experience has evinced, what Tucker had taught, that we should derive, from the independence of those colonies, all the advantages of their trade, without the vexations, and weaknesses, of their government. . . . If it be true, then, that our resources, and strength, lie in the People of the United Kingdom, what do we lose, by the several relinquishments of the Preliminary Treaty? Do we lose men? No. Do we lose money? No. Would they have been expensive establishments, during peace? Yes. Would they have been a still greater source of weakness, in war? Yes.[23]

---

[19] *Ibid.*, pp. 17 f.
[20] *Annals of Commerce* (London, 1805), IV, 10.
[21] *Ibid.*
[22] *Estimate of the Comparative Strength of Great-Britain* (1782), p. 173.

[23] *Ibid.*, pp. 371 f. In examining these questions some writers proceeded to deplore, in retrospect, the expansion of British colonies resulting from the Seven Years' War. Chalmers called it "a war, glorious, but unprofitable. Upwards of fifty-eight millions had been added to our funded debts, before we began to negociate for peace in 1762. . . . But, the acquisitions of peace proved, unhappily, more embarrassing to the . . . nation, than the imposts, which were constantly collected, for paying the interest of debts, and the charges of government" (*ibid.*, pp. 139 ff.). ". . . the true objection to the peace of 1763 was not, that we had retained too little, but that we had retained too much" (*ibid.*, p. 143).

Another writer observed that the "terms of the peace [of 1763] were universally abused, though I think it would be difficult to show what greater advan-

One advantage which some writers attributed to American independence was seen in connection with the monopoly enjoyed by British shipping. It is remarkable that the same authors who applauded the loss of the monopoly of the colony trade, saw a gain in the fact that American shipping could now be excluded from Britain's imperial trade. Consideration of English maritime power was, of course, the reason for this attitude. Macpherson stated: ". . . a very important advantage was the recovery of the valuable trade of ship-building, which had in great measure been, very impolitically, sacrificed to the zeal for promoting the prosperity of the colonies, insomuch that, notwithstanding the very great inferiority of the greatest part of the American oak, a large portion of the vessels belonging to the different ports of Great Britain were built in America."[24] Chalmers concluded that the loss of the colonies had conferred "a real advantage" on Great Britain. "It is, indeed, fortunate for us, that the French were so much blinded, by the splendour of giving independence to the British colonies, as not to see distinctly how much their interposition and their aid promoted the real advantage of Great Britain. . . . And they have even conferred on the people, whom they wished to depress, actual strength, by restoring, unconsciously, the ship-building, the freights, and the fisheries; of which the colonists had too much partaken . . . ."[25]

As for that part of the Empire which was left intact in 1783, some observers regretted that the Canadas had not been relinquished too. John Nicholls, for example, held that it would be very difficult to defend these provinces against the United States, that Upper Canada was likely to desire incorporation into the Union and that Lower Canada was without value to Britain.[26]

---

tages could have been obtained; every thing which we did retain, was either injurious or of little benefit" (John Nicholls, *Recollections and Reflections* (2d ed.; [London, 1822], I, 9 f.). A similar opinion is stated by Anderson, *Interest of Great Britain . . . Considered* (1782), p. 33.

[24]*Annals of Commerce* (1805), IV, 10 f. Similarly, George Chalmers, *Opinions on Interesting Subjects of Public Law and Commercial Policy* (London, 1784), pp. 108 ff.

[25]*Estimate of the Comparative Strength of Great-Britain* (1782), p. 171.

[26]*Recollections and Reflections* (1822), II, 86 f. Canadian timber, Nicholls asserted, was definitely inferior to Norwegian wood and its fur trade "may be profitable to the North-West Company, which possesses the exclusive commerce . . . ." Its value to Great Britain certainly was entirely out of proportion to the expense occasioned by the possession of the colony (*ibid.*, pp. 87 f.).

Replying to members of the House of Lords who had censored the relinquishment of part of the fur trade to the United States, Shelburne declared

"What have we not already expended on these provinces? and if they are to be defended, what sum is not probable that we shall waste before we get rid of them?"[27] James Anderson, on the other hand, subscribing to the thought of the inevitability of the ultimate colonial emancipation, remarked:

... in examining the power or the riches of the British empire ... we must consider Britain by herself, as the fundamental state, and regard America as an extraneous appendage, not necessarily connected with her. We must view it as an accidental acquisition which may be lost. Our aim, therefore, should be to preserve the vigour of the parent state independent of its colonies. To avail ourselves to the utmost of the benefits that may be derived from them, but not for a moment to forget, that they can never be connected with Britain into one compacted uniform empire; that sooner or later they must be separated from her, and that she must so act as to be prepared for that event.[28]

The foregoing review of a sample of British reactions to the emancipation of the American colonies poses these important questions: to what extent did these views represent metropolitan opinion as a whole? What was the general trend of British thought after the independence of the United States had become an irrevocable fact and the first British Empire had collapsed in a most spectacular fashion?

There is no ready and unambiguous answer to these questions.

---

in February, 1783: "Suppose the entire fur trade sunk into the sea, where is the detriment to this country? Is 50,000 l. a year imported in that article any object for Great Britain to continue a war of which the people of England ... have declared their abhorrence? Surely it is not. But much less must this appear in our sight, when I tell parliament, and the whole kingdom, that for many years past, one year with another, the preservation of this annual import of 50,000 l. has cost this country, on an average, 800,000 l. I have the vouchers in my pocket, should your lordships be inclined to examine the fact" (Cobbett, *Parl. Hist.*, XXIII, c. 409).

On the loss of Tobago, Shelburne observed: "With respect to Tobago, it is said, the cession of that island will ruin our cotton manufacture.... We have been long in possession of that great branch of trade, consequently we can afford to give a greater price for cotton than our neighbours. Cotton, therefore, be it in the hands of friends or foes, will always find its way to our door, in preference to that of those who cannot meet it with such a purse. But I know a few over-grown monopolisers of that article, or selfish proprietors, would see the nation steeped in blood, sooner than they would forfeit, by the peace, one farthing of that emolument which they used to make when Tobago was in our hands" (*ibid.*, XXIII, c. 415).

[27]*Recollections and Reflections* (1822), II, 87. Pulteney even suggested that Canada, Nova Scotia, and the West Indies be given up because the defence and government of these possessions would be too expensive to the mother country (*Considerations of the Present State of Public Affairs* [1779], p. 14).

[28]*Interest of Great Britain ... Considered* (1782), p. 39.

The Empire had been disrupted beyond apparent prospect of repair and the very process of its disruption had occasioned formidable losses in men, money, and prestige. All the mercantilist arguments, supposedly showing the utility of colonies under the Old Colonial System, had been theoretically exploded. Novel doctrines of foreign trade and of economic activity in general had introduced new conceptions that were bound to influence any serious consideration of the value of colonial dependencies whether under a closed or a free trade system.

In view of these facts the relatively small number of those who advocated an anti-imperialist programme is amazing. It may be true that the English people "fell into a kind of disgust with colonial matters"[29] and that the nation was filled with "confusion" and "lethargy" as regards colonial affairs.[30] Yet mingled with disgust and confusion was the dogged determination to hold fast to the possession and exploitation of the remnants of the Old Empire. For a long time to come, this attitude had, at bottom, little to do with the contents of different colonial theories. It was not susceptible to intellectual arguments. Indeed, the colonial theories brought forward by the classical economists and the Philosophical Radicals were never refuted on an intellectually creditable level of reasoning. No matter how often and how brilliantly the out-worn arguments of the mercantilists were disproved, they were advanced again and again with tedious monotony. Any study of influential opinion on the colonial question during the half-century following the defection of the United States requires frequent indication of the relative weight which the various arguments carried with the general public.

Before 1783, the opinions of the intellectual leaders of public opinion were, on the whole, in line with that of the bulk of influential groups. After 1783 a situation arose in which the intellectual *élite* of Great Britain, eminently articulate on the colonial question, was opposed by the broad mass of influential groups which were rather inarticulate and chary of expressing reasoned opinions on the subject. Nevertheless this majority seemed to know exactly what they wanted and were apparently unperturbed by the argumentative "broadsides" of their intellectually superior opponents.[31]

[29] Bernard Holland, *Imperium and Libertas* (London, 1901), p. 95.

[30] H. E. Egerton, *A Short History of British Colonial Policy* (London, 1897), p. 258.

[31] This view of the subject is affirmed by Helen Taft Manning, *British Colonial Government after the American Revolution, 1782-1820* (New Haven, 1933), pp. 3 ff.

This fact is clearly revealed by a perusal of parliamentary records. Quantitatively the speeches delivered by the contending groups appear about evenly balanced; qualitatively, the arguments of the minority seem, to the objective observer, far superior to those advanced by the majority. But, almost invariably, what really mattered was the list of division.

It is by no means difficult to account for the conditions that brought about this situation. Public opinion, on any matter and at any time, is determined by an incredibly confused maze of thoughts and sentiments, prejudices and traditions, more or less closely related to the supposed interests of the specific carrier of opinion. To disentangle, weigh, and label these various constituent elements with precision in any concrete case defies the analytical tools at the disposal of the observer. Yet, in the special case here under consideration, the following rough conclusions may be hazarded without too much risk: In the spheres of traditionalism and of national pride of empire the attachment of large influential groups to the symbols of empire remained impervious to intellectual arguments. Large sections, no doubt, were prevented from grasping these arguments because they were intellectually too lazy, incapable, or unschooled. Most important, however, was that a great many interest-groups, who had a selfish stake in the preservation of the old system, wielded a disproportionate influence in politics.

It is certain that the American War of Independence did not lead to any widespread indifference toward the remainder of the Empire.[32] Indeed, it may be said that the fall of the first Empire was accompanied by the birth of the second. When following Cornwallis's surrender at Yorktown, in April, 1782, Rodney defeated the French fleet in the Battle of the Saints, the British recovered their undisputed command of the seas and made the establishment of the second Empire not only possible but, in view of the attitude of the English ruling groups, almost inevitable.

[32]Even the fear that all settlement colonies ultimately would aspire to and achieve independence did not become popular immediately after the loss of the American plantations. Later it received fresh affirmation by the revolt of the Spanish and Portuguese South American colonies and was most widely accepted in the thirties, forties, and fifties of the nineteenth century when the Canadian rebellion, the Indian mutiny, and the plodding struggle for self-government of the Canadians, Australians, and New Zealanders seemed to confirm earlier experiences.

Immediately after the Peace of Paris the centre of imperial interest shifted to Canada in the West[33] and to India in the East.[34]

That the revolt of the American colonists taught the imperial ruling groups in England a lesson in how to govern colonies wisely is nothing but a legend. Constitutionally and politically, imperial rule was not relaxed but tightened. The rebellious Americans, as has been pointed out, had enjoyed a great deal of freedom in political respect. Hence, when these colonies revolted while Canada remained loyal, it seemed to the majority of the metropolitan ruling group that this large amount of political freedom had fostered a spirit of democracy and independence which, in turn, had caused the revolution. It was for this reason that the government, determined to keep what was left of the Empire, now embarked upon a reactionary course and imposed upon its old and

[33] See John Davidson, *Commercial Federation and Colonial Trade Policy* (London, 1900), pp. 9 f. The shift of interest to Canada rather than to the West Indies which, during the ante-Revolution period, had attracted so much attention was, at that time, mainly due to the fact that Canada and Nova Scotia had become the haven of the Loyalist refugees. See Knox, *Extra Official State Papers*, II, Appendix, 47 f.; Manning, *British Colonial Government after the American Revolution*, pp. 34-9.

[34] See R. Coupland, *The American Revolution and the British Empire* (London, 1930), pp. 203-9. Undoubtedly, it was no accident that, immediately after the loss of America, Parliament bestowed so much of its attention and energy on the affairs of the East India Company (the attack on the "Nabobs," the trial of Warren Hastings, Fox's and Pitt's India Bill, etc.). Throughout the decades following the Peace of Paris, this interest in India continued to grow. In 1804, one influential writer suggested that Britain give up her Northern American colonies, Botany Bay, Gibraltar, and other naval stations, but keep India. "Of all the resources which this country may boast of, none can equal its possessions in the East, for pecuniary advantages; and thence alone a treasure might be drawn, sufficient in itself to discharge the incumbrances of the nation" (Sir John Sinclair, *The History of the Public Revenue of the British Empire* [London, 1804], III, 220 f., 303).

Another writer called India "not only the brightest jewel in the British Crown, but the fairest portion of the British Empire" (Charles Maclean, "A View of the Consequences of Laying Open the Trade to India," *The Pamphleteer*, I [1813], 194).

This increased interest in the exploitation of India was, however, from the beginning opposed by a small minority of sober-minded observers. One of them declared: "The East-Indies will prove a millstone round the neck of England..." (John King, *Thoughts on the Difficulties and Distresses in Which the Peace of 1783 Has Involved the People of England* [5th ed.; London, 1783], p. 27). Similarly, Thomas Coutts, the banker, wrote in 1787: "I always thought this country was ruined by getting the Eastern Empire, and I continue to fear our ruin will one day be completed by losing it" (Ernest H. Coleridge, *The Life of Thomas Coutts, Banker* [London, 1920], I, p. 232). See also, *ibid.*, p. 305.

new colonies a system of centralized supervision and control that was to be maintained for more than half a century.[35]

On the other hand, in regard to economic colonial policies, the former system of mutual preferences and monopolies was retained to be sure, but soon this arrangement began to operate almost entirely in favour of the colonies (excepting the West Indies). This was the result, not only of new preferences granted to the colonies, but also of the increase of Britain's capacity to produce manufactures more cheaply than her European rivals and of her growing capacity to consume colonial articles.[36] Thus, while during the ante-revolution period the imperial régime had been restrictive of the economic development of the colonies but rather liberal in the sphere of politics, this situation was, as Davidson observed,[37] almost reversed after 1783: the colonies were to exploit the mother country commercially while the latter ruled her dependencies in a stern and, sometimes, despotic fashion.

What led, in the final analysis, to a gradual liberalization of the political imperial régime, to the abolition of the system of imperial monopolies and preferences, and even to a widespread indifference toward the colonies, was not the experience of the American War of Independence but the effect of the rapid progress of the Industrial Revolution in England.[38]

II

1783: THE AMERICAN INTERCOURSE BILL

Under the auspices of the Old Colonial System, an important triangular trade had developed between Great Britain, the English West Indies, and the Northern American colonies. Owing to their economic complementarity, this trade had become a vital part of the commercial organization of the sugar islands and the northern continental plantations.[39] When in 1783 the thirteen colonies placed themselves outside Britain's imperial system, so

[35]See on this development the excellent account of Davidson, *Commercial Federation and Colonial Trade Policy*, pp. 5 ff. Vincent Harlow, "The New Imperial System, 1783-1815," *Cambridge History of the British Empire*, II, 129, 187.

[36]This was, however, not true of the protection of metropolitan shipping monopoly in the colony trade which continued to act as a burden on the colonies.

[37]*Commercial Federation and Colonial Trade Policy*, pp. 5 ff.

[38]This conclusion is confirmed by Namier, *England in the Age of the American Revolution*, p. 296; Manning, *British Colonial Government after the American Revolution*, p. 5.

[39]The northern colonies provided the West Indies mainly with provisions, horses, and lumber, and took sugar products in return.

tightly enclosed by the Navigation Laws, the important question arose whether the Navigation Act should be preserved in its entirety or partially relaxed in order to allow for the continuation of this trade.

At first it seemed as if the latter course would be adopted. Adam Smith and the principles and spirit of *The Wealth of Nations* had made converts as important politically as the younger Pitt, Shelburne, and Burke. In February, 1783, Shelburne had told the House of Lords: "I avow that monopoly is always unwise; but if there is any nation to reject monopoly, it is the English. Situated as we are between the old world and the new, and between the southern and northern Europe, all that we ought to covet upon earth is free trade, and fair equality. With more industry, with more enterprize, with more capital than any trading nation upon earth, it ought to be our constant cry, let every market be open, let us meet our rivals fairly, and we ask no more."[40] "This seems to be the aera of protestantism in trade," Shelburne declared.[41] For a short time, the old commercial policy of restriction seemed discredited. Part of the "City," English merchants formerly engaged in the trade with the colonies now incorporated in the American Union, demanded that Anglo-American commerce be put on a free basis.[42] The West India interest and, of course, the Americans themselves pressed for the continuation of unrestricted commercial intercourse between the sugar islands and the United States. On March 3, 1783, Pitt, firmly convinced that Britain would gain rather than lose by liberal concessions, introduced the American Intercourse Bill enabling the American states to retain their former commercial privileges within the Empire. Macpherson commented:

With respect to the political arrangements for the commercial intercourse, many people in their zeal of their renewed friendship for America, went so far as to propose, that the Americans . . . should be admitted to the commercial privileges of British subjects, and that the Navigation act, so long esteemed the Palladium of the naval power of Britain, should be infringed by a free admission of their vessels into the ports of our West-India islands. The press teemed with pamphlets written in support of these new maxims of commercial policy . . . even the government was like to be carried away with the stream, and on the point of confirming by law those concessions with respect to the commerce of the West-Indies . . . when Lord Sheffield published his "Observations on the commerce of the American states. . . ."[43]

[40]Cobbett, *Parl. Hist.*, XXIII, c. 409 f. [41]*Ibid.*, c. 409.
[42]See Manning, *British Colonial Government after the American Revolution*, p.165.
[43]*Annals of Commerce* (1805), IV, 18 f. William Eden, in great doubts as to the wisdom of Pitt's bill, asked Adam Smith for his opinion. Smith wrote to

Indeed, Sheffield's book, soon followed by publications manifesting the same trend of thought, marked the turn of the tide. In the following the arguments of the Sheffield school will be presented at some length because they throw a great deal of light on the motivation of those who clung tenaciously to the supposed virtues of the Old System.

Sheffield exhorted his countrymen to abide by a traditional policy, tested by experience, and not to embrace novel principles of the "wildest" imagination. "As a sudden revolution, an unprecedented case, a momentous change, the independence of America, has bewildered our reason, and encouraged the wildest sallies of imagination, systems have been preferred to experience, rash theory to successful practice, and the Navigation Act itself, the guardian of the prosperity of Britain, has been almost abandoned by . . . levity or ignorance. . . ."[44]

Preservation of the Navigation Act, as the matrix of British sea power, was the main consideration of the Sheffield school. They assumed that it was the monopoly of the carrying trade that rendered the maintenance of a colonial empire valuable to the mother country.

The Navigation act prevented the Dutch from being the carriers of our trade. The violation or relaxation of that act in favour of the West Indian Islands, or of the American States, will give that advantage to the New-Englanders. The bill, in its present state, allowing an open trade between the American states and our islands relinquishes the only use and advantage of colonies or West India Islands, and for which alone it would be worth while to incur the vast expence of their maintenance and protection, viz. The monopoly of their consumption; and of the carriage of their produce. . . .[45]

---

him: "What degree of connection we should allow between the remaining colonies, whether in North America or the West Indies, and the United States may to some people appear a more difficult question. My own opinion is that it should be allowed to go on as before, and whatever inconveniences result from this freedom may be remedied as they occur. The lumber and provisions of the United States are more necessary to our West India Islands than the rum and sugar of the latter are to the former. Any interruption or restraint of commerce would hurt our loyal much more than our revolted subjects" (quoted in Rae, *Life of Adam Smith*, p. 385). However, Eden, who later became famous on account of his negotiation of the Anglo-French commercial treaty of 1786, did not heed this advice. Indeed, he became one of the foremost opponents of Pitt's bill.

[44]John, First Earl of Sheffield, *Observations on the Commerce of the United States* (1st ed.; London, 1783), p. 1.

[45]*Ibid.*, p. 45. William Knox (*Extra Official State Papers*, II, 53 f.) reported: "When Lord North received the deals of Secretary of State for the home department, in the year 1783, my assistance was desired in framing regulations for our remaining Colonies, and for the intercourse between the United States and

It is true that at first I did not see, at least to the extent I do after a minute and full investigation, that Britain will be highly benefited by the separation from the United States; that she may be stronger in future, and greater in all respects . . . our marine will be highly benefited; the business of shipbuilding will be greatly increased in the British dominions; the multitude of artificers employed in it will be kept at home; they will be doubled in number, and both will be ready on the emergency of war; all this, however, absolutely depends on the support of our navigation laws. If those laws should be relaxed, the reverse will be our fate. . . ."[46]

George Chalmers, whose book forcefully seconded Sheffield's findings, also supported this view: "The profit of freights is of greater importance to Britain than the mines of Potosi are to Spain, because the one strengthens while the others enfeeble the unhappy nation to which they belong. Whence may we infer of how much advantage it is to preserve and extend the navigation to the West-Indies. . . ."[47] William Eden declared that, if Pitt's bill were passed, it was to be feared "that we should totally lose the carrying trade; for as the Americans were to be permitted, under this Bill, to bring the West India commodities to Europe, so he feared that the 600 ships of this country, which that trade employed at present, would become useless, not only to the great decrease of our revenue, but the absolute destruction of our navy. . . ."[48] Even Burke, free of all monopolist and protectionist prejudices, came out against the bill for the same reason. "At all events, it would not be improper to let the ministers know the country expected the principle of the Navigation Acts should be kept entire; the country was as tenacious of the principle of that Act as it possibly could be of the principle of the Magna Charta. The ministers should understand that the carrying trade must not be given up; they must reserve to our remaining dominions the exclusive trade to the West

---

them. . . . But before I entered upon the business, I desired to know if the Administration concurred with me in the principle I meant to found the regulations upon, which was, that it was better to have no colonies at all, than not to have them subservient to the maritime strength and commercial interests of Great Britain." Knox, regarding the Navigation Laws as the true foundation of British maritime power, then drew up a paper on the future intercourse between the United States and the British colonies framing the regulations "so as utterly to exclude . . . American shipping" (*ibid.*, pp. 54 ff.).

[46]John Lord Sheffield, *Observations on the Commerce of the American States* (6th ed.; London, 1784), Introduction, pp. xxxvii f.

[47]George Chalmers, *Opinions on Interesting Subjects of Public Law and Commercial Policy*, p. 127. See also *ibid.*, pp. 108 ff., and Grace A. Cockroft, *The Public Life of George Chalmers* (New York, 1939), pp. 72 f.

[48]Cobbett, *Parl. Hist.*, XXIII, c. 604.

India islands, otherwise the only use of them would be lost. . . ."[49] Other reasons advanced by this school against Pitt's bill were subsidiary to their principal argument that, for reasons of security, the integrity of the Navigation Act should be preserved under all circumstances.

Sheffield concluded that ". . . it is in the light of a foreign country that America must henceforward be viewed."[50] He did not expect that the implementation of his policy would arouse the irritation of the United States. Nor did he assume that British manufactures needed any preferential treatment in the American market.[51] "The demand for our manufactures will continually encrease with the population of America."[52]

Sheffield also denied that the sugar islands were dependent on open trade with the United States for he seemed fully convinced that the British colonies in North America would be capable of providing them with sufficient provisions and timber at a reasonable price.[53] A final motive behind the programme of the Sheffield school was their high estimation of the importance of Canada to Great Britain.[54] As far as this motive operated for the rejection of Pitt's bill, the West India interest was consciously sacrificed for the benefit of Canada, a policy which was to be pursued by Britain for more than half a century.[55]

The spokesmen of the sugar interest, of course, fought with great determination for Pitt's bill. They pointed out that the British West Indies were much more valuable to the mother country than the Northern colonies.[56] They denied that the latter would be able to supply the sugar islands with cheap provisions and timber.

[49] *Ibid.*, cs. 763 f.
[50] Sheffield, *Observations* (1st ed.), p. 2.   [51] *Ibid.*, p. 5.
[52] *Ibid.*, p. 63.
[53] *Ibid.*, pp. 49 f. Chalmers went so far as to say: "If an accidental scarcity should induce the West Indians to apply to the neutral islands in their neighbourhood, for what they want; if avarice should induce them, to continue a practice, which accident began; Great Britain would thereby be driven to the dilemma of either depriving the West Indies of vessels proper for such traffic; or of declaring them independent. If the West Indies expect protection from Great Britain, they must study to be useful to them" (*Opinions*, p. 120). In effect, Chalmers here threatened the sugar colonies with independence if they should be unwilling to subordinate their own interests to those of the mother country.
[54] Sheffield, *Observations* (1st ed.), pp. 56 ff.
[55] See on this the excellent study of Davidson, *Commercial Federation and Colonial Trade Policy*, pp. 9 ff.
[56] [Edward Long], *A Free and Candid Review of a Tract, Entitled "Observations on the Commerce of the United States"* (London, 1779), pp. 9 ff.

"It is impossible that this great manufacture of sugar can be carried on, any more than others, where the food of the manufacturers, and the necessaries required for it, are irregularly, dearly, precariously, and improperly supplied."[57] They declared further that a diminution of the consumption of British manufactures in the West Indies would be one of the consequences of prohibiting their trade with the United States.[58]

Metropolitan faith in the Navigation Act stood firmly in the way of their suggestions. They could not frankly advocate its emasculation. Thus, this group began to propagate an idea that was to become of great importance in the hands of later Free Traders. They maintained that, if navigation was the matrix of British seapower, then it was extensive trade which gave rise to British navigation. "But navigation and naval power are among the happy fruits, not the parents of commerce.... The carrying trade is of great importance, but it is of greater importance still to have trade to carry."[59] "Navigation and naval power are the children, not the parents, of commerce."[60]

Also written in opposition to Sheffield's famous *Observations* was a book by Richard Champion representing the views of those merchants who demanded that the former trade between Great Britain and the United States be restored as fully as possible.[61] Throughout his book Champion stressed the importance of the United States as a market for British manufactures.[62] He deprecated the value of the remaining British colonies on the North American continent[63] while he praised that of the West Indies in glowing terms.[64] On the basis of these considerations and prefer-

[57]*Ibid.*, p. 8. Similarly, Bryan Edwards, *Thoughts on the Late Proceedings of Government* (London, 1784), pp. 7 f., 11, 42 ff. James Allen, *Considerations on the Present State of the Intercourse between His Majesty's Sugar Colonies and the Dominions of the United States of America* (London, 1784). The Northern colonies were at that time hardly able to victual themselves. See the interesting observations of Macpherson, *Annals of Commerce* (1805), IV, 70 f.

[58]Long, *Free and Candid Review*, pp. 7 f.

[59]Allen, *Considerations*, p. 37.

[60]Bryan Edwards, *History of the British West Indies* (London, 1819), II, 456.

[61]Richard Champion, *Considerations on the Present Situation of Great Britain and the United States of North America* (London, 1784), p. 7.

[62]"It would be prudent to bid even high for such industrous consumers of our manufactures..." (*ibid.*, p. 37).

[63]Indeed, he advised that they be given up because they would be a very expensive "appendage" to the mother country and because, in the end, they would be certain to enter the American Union (*ibid.*, pp. 73-84).

[64]*Ibid.*, pp. 85 ff.

ences Champion was prepared to scrap the Navigation Law. "The greatest bar to the settlement of the American trade . . . is the attachment of this country to the Act of Navigation . . . the Maritime Charta. . . ."[65] He proposed such a step not only with the view of facilitating Anglo-American commerce but also because British traders were in need of cheaper American-built ships in order to preserve Britain's carrying trade.[66] Like the spokesmen of the sugar interest he pleaded that only through the expansion of commerce could Britain safeguard her naval superiority.[67] If his suggestions were acted upon, Champion promised, England was bound to become the "entrepot for American commodities."[68]

If we recur to our experience, to the amazing growth of our power and riches, which kept an even pace with the growth of our Colonies, it would certainly point out to us the superior wisdom of endeavouring to recover what is gone astray from us, rather than in a fit of puerile and fruitless resentment, to turn Knights Errant in search of new consumers of our manufactures. A country, where agriculture or fishery is the staple, and where great plenty of unoccupied and fertile lands prevent the settlements of manufactures, will prove better and more certain customers, than settled nations, whose principle is to encourage manufactures of their own.[69]

Neither the selfish proposals of the sugar planters and merchants and of the English trading houses engaged in the trade with the United States, nor the consistent reasoning of the Pitts and Shelburnes were able to overcome the united opposition of all those who had a stake in the preservation of the old mercantilist system (mainly the ship-owners) and those who, with or without re-examining its principles, regarded the Navigation Act as the inviolable foundation of Britain's seapower and security. The arguments of the Sheffield school achieved a striking victory and Pitt's bill was rejected. The first attempt to unfetter Britain's trade had failed as had those groups who wished to draw the United States back into the orbit of the British Empire.[70]

III

1784-1815:[71] POPULATION AND EMIGRATION

The mercantilists had regarded a large and, particularly, a dense population as a *sine qua non* of national wealth and power, what-

[65] *Ibid.*, p. 9.   [66] *Ibid.*, pp. 12-19.   [67] *Ibid.*, p. 147.
[68] *Ibid.*, p. 128.   [69] *Ibid.*, pp. 128 f.

[70] In the latter respect the prevalent attitude was one of petulant resignation. "For God's sake! let us stand on the ground of the advantages we possess, and leave the Americans to the blessings of independence!" (*A Brief and Impartial Review of the State of Great Britain* [3d ed.; London, 1783], p. 13.)

[71] In the following part of this study (even more so than in the first it is possible to discuss only representative opinions. The volume of available source

ever they meant by these terms. On the basis of this dogma they had either frowned upon colonies as tending to depopulate the mother country, or welcomed them because of their tendency to provide the parent state with an increased volume of employment which, in turn, had a stimulating effect on the growth of the metropolitan population.

Regarding the period from 1784 to 1815 any marked change in English sentiment and thought on the subject of population before the turn of the century, i.e., before the publication of Malthus' *Essay* in 1798[72] and before the first British Census of 1801 could hardly be expected.

Regarding the desirability of a large and dense population, William Paley, a thorough pre-Benthamite utilitarian, wrote: ". . . the quantity of happiness in a given district, although it is possible it may be increased, the number of inhabitants remaining the same, is chiefly the most naturally affected by alteration of the numbers: that, consequently, the decay of population is the greatest evil that a state can suffer; and the improvement of it the object which ought, in all countries, to be aimed at in preference to every other political purpose whatsoever."[73] Similarly, James Anderson pronounced: "It is universally admitted, that the real strength of a kingdom consists in the number of its inhabitants, and

---

material, in the form of books, pamphlets, articles, parliamentary debates, etc., becomes increasingly copious as the reviewer turns to the last quarter of the eighteenth and, then, to the nineteenth century. For this reason, and also in order to avoid excessive repetition, he is forced to have increasing recourse to a selective method of presenting the development of ideas.

It is also impossible to adhere strictly to the limits of the period of time mentioned above. Some statements will have to be examined which were uttered before 1783 or after 1815.

[72]It is, of course, true that Malthus' contribution was not in any strict sense an original one. That the growth of population is limited by the means of subsistence was an idea already accepted by such thinkers as David Hume, Robert Wallace, Sir James Steuart, Adam Smith, etc. Even the theorem that population tends to increase at a geometric ratio while the means of subsistence tend to increase at a slower pace, can be found in the studies of Graunt and Petty. See on this, C. E. Stangeland, *Pre-Malthusian Doctrines of Population* (New York, 1904), pp. 308, 338 ff., 353 ff.

Yet these writers saw no reason why they should apply this doctrine to the particular case of Great Britain. Neither of them was alarmed at the rate of demographic growth in their country and most of them favoured a further increase in the population of Britain.

[73]Alexander Chalmers (ed.), *The Works of William Paley* (new ed.; London, 1821), II, 61. This and the following quotations from Paley are taken from his *Moral and Political Philosophy* which was first published in 1785.

that its riches will be in proportion to the industry of its people . . . it is also admitted, that of two countries which contain an equal number of inhabitants, that whose territory is least extensive, will be the most powerful. This arises not only from the greater difficulty of defending a large territory than one of smaller extent, but also from several other causes. . . ."[74] Like the mercantilist theorists, these writers thought, of course, only in terms of an employed population.[75]

Thus, though departing from the same basic idea, Paley and Anderson, arrived at exactly opposite conclusions about the effect of colonial dependencies on the volume of population in the parent state. Anderson maintained that the American colonies had deprived the mother country of a great number of its valuable inhabitants.[76] In his opinion, the consumption of these emigrants, had they remained at home, would have amounted to many times the exports to the colonies which their emigration occasioned.[77] "From these considerations I am compelled to draw this general conclusion. That our American colonies, instead of augmenting the trade and industry of Britain, have tended greatly to diminish them both."[78]

Anderson also pointed out that it is not the paupers but the most valuable members of society which the colonies draw from

[74]*Interest of Great Britain . . . Considered* (1782), pp. 24 f.

[75]Richard Price, although admitting that "numbers" are "power," introduced several qualifying considerations. He estimated that England and Wales had fewer than five million inhabitants as compared with 4.3 in the kingdom of Naples and 25.7 in France. He concluded: "These facts show, in a striking light, the superiority which arts, commerce, science, industry and liberty give to a people. England does not consist of many more inhabitants than the kingdom of Naples; but in respect of dignity, weight and force, the kingdom of Naples, compared with it, is nothing" (*An Essay on the Population of England* [London, 1780], pp. 14 ff.

[76]*Interest of Great Britain . . . Considered* (1782), pp. 80 ff. Among many other causes of Britain's progressive depopulation, Price likewise listed "the migrations to our settlements abroad. . ." (*Essay on the Population of England* [1780], p. 29). Still in 1776 Price had written to Josiah Tucker that he did not think that the colonies "have any great tendency to produce depopulation. When a number of people quit a country there is more employment and greater plenty of the means of subsistence left for those who remain; and the vacancy is soon filled up" (quoted in James Bonar, *Theories of Population from Raleigh to Arthur Young* [London, 1931], pp. 204 f.). Thus within a period of four years, Price completely reversed his opinion on this subject.

[77]*Interest of Great Britain . . . Considered*, pp. 94 ff.

[78]*Ibid.*, p. 96.

the metropolis.[79] Paley, on the other hand, believed that emigration to the colonies tended to augment the population of the parent state. The colonists, he assumed, would confine their economic activity to the production of foodstuffs and other raw materials. "The mother-country . . . derives from this connexion an increase both of provision and employment. It promotes at once the two great requisites upon which the facility of subsistence, and by consequence the state of population depend . . . and this in a manner the most direct and beneficial."[80]

Paley, too, is typical of those writers who had realized that population may grow faster than the means of subsistence. But he still discussed such a possibility as an entirely academic contingency.[81] In the eighties and nineties of the eighteenth century most English writers expressed a desire to see Britain's population multiplied. Richard Price, who was considered an expert on population problems, even assumed that Britain's population was and had been decreasing, since the Revolution, by a quarter of a million.[82] It should not be forgotten that even after the publication of Malthus' *Essay* and the Census of 1801 the change of sentiment, especially in respect of emigration to the colonies, was by no means immediate. It took the obvious evidence of widespread and increasing unemployment and pauperism after the termination of the Napoleonic Wars, to give rise to sustained agitation over the surplus population of Great Britain. Thus, authors who immediately after the turn of the century had advocated emigration to the colonies as a remedy for the redundant population of the

---

[79] *Ibid.*, pp. 127 ff. He remarked: ". . . there is not a single instance to be found of one person who ever came upon the parish funds in England, having voluntarily gone over to America with a view to better his condition. It is the young, the active members of society that transport themselves thither, and not the aged and infirm. Instead therefore of relieving the pressure of the poor laws, these emigrations rather tend to augment them" (*ibid.*, p. 128).

[80] *Works*, II, 87 f.

Similarly, William Eden remarked: ". . . many who emigrate, would have perished unproductive in the parent soil, though they prosper with little exertion in another country, and become sources of new commerce, wealth, and population to the world. . . . And with respect to emigrations, we are assured, that those provinces in Spain, which send the largest numbers of their people to South America, continue the most populous. . ." (*A Fifth Letter to the Earl of Carlisle* [London, 1780], p. 13).

[81] *Works*, II, 86.

[82] *Essay on the Population of England* (1780), pp. 17 ff. However, this opinion was by no means generally accepted. Anderson, for example, held an opposite view (*Interest of Great Britain . . . Considered*, pp. 7 ff.).

country, were still on the defensive and took great pains to explain that the drawbacks of such a movement, feared by earlier theorists, would not materialize.[83]

The accelerated pace of the Industrial Revolution seemed to some writers to promise an unlimited expansion of the means of subsistence. Anderson, for example, denied "that when a country becomes too full of inhabitants so that they are straightened for room, and do not find means of subsistence, it becomes necessary to drive away a part of the people, that the remainder may be enabled to live."[84] He believed that "industry and commerce can supply every defect, even where the very surface of the earth is wanting."[85] "Hence it follows," he concluded, "that no commercial country can be too fully peopled where industry abounds."[86] Another author was likewise of the opinion that increasing means of subsistence for an increasing population "is chiefly to be found in the extension of the manufacturing principle, which will furnish employment for thousands of those whose labours are not required by the agricultural interest."[87] In contrast with Anderson's standpoint, however, this writer assumed that "the extension of the manufacturing principle" was dependent on the extension of dependable colonial markets. "It is this consideration which renders foreign possessions so extremely valuable, nay even necessary, to the well-being of states yielding an increase of population."[88]

The Earl of Selkirk, having read Malthus' *Essay* and observed the crowded demographic condition of Scotland, was one of the first to advocate emigration to the colonies as an outlet for the excess population of the mother country. He wrote:

... the difficulty of procuring either land or employment would almost amount to an impossibility; and if the people should escape famine, few would be inclined in such circumstances to undertake the burthen of rearing a family, or would venture on marriage. The misery of the people would thus in time produce the effect which emigration is now working, and reduce

---

[83]As examples may be named: Thomas Mortimer, *Lectures on the Elements of Commerce, Politics, and Finances* (London, 1801); The Earl of Selkirk, *Observations on the Present State of the Highlands of Scotland* (2d ed.; Edinburgh, 1806).
[84]*Interest of Great Britain ... Considered* (1782), p. 133.
[85]*Ibid.*, p. 134.   [86]*Ibid.*, p. 135.
[87]*Considerations on Colonial Policy* (London, 1813), p. 2.
[88]*Ibid.*, pp. 2 f. This writer was fully convinced of the difficulty and even the impossibility of counteracting the natural tendency of colonies to strive for and achieve emancipation from the dominion of the mother country. Yet in order to safeguard their markets for an expanding metropolitan manufacturing industry, he advised that the colonies be kept in subjection at any cost and as long as possible (*ibid.*, pp. 5 ff., *passim*).

their numbers to a due proportion with the employment that can be given them. On the other hand, if a number of people, who are under no absolute necessity, should emigrate, those who remain behind will find it so much easier to procure employment and subsistence that marriages will more readily take place, and the natural increase of population will proceed with more rapidity, till every blank is filled up.[89]

This statement contains two interesting points. First, emigration is accepted as the more humane method of achieving a sound balance between the means of subsistence and the growing size of the population than the alternative of want and starvation. Secondly, in order to overcome deeply-ingrained prejudices of mercantilist origin, Selkirk found it necessary to persuade his readers that, in the course of time, the "blanks," created by emigration, would be filled up again. Emigration also appeared to him as an effective outlet for social and political discontent engendered by the miseries attending over-population.[90]

Emigration, of course, is not necessarily dependent on the possession of colonies. But Selkirk, like a great many writers of his time, stressed that emigrants should be directed to the British colonies rather than be allowed to proceed to foreign countries.[91] Thus, he argued, if the colonies were to be retained at all, then "it cannot surely admit of a doubt, that it is better the overflowings of our population should contribute to their improvement, than to that of a country with which we are unconnected, and which may become hostile to us. It is besides of no small importance, that our own colonies should be peopled by men, whose manners and principles are consonant to our own government."[92] Colquhoun contrasted the case of Great Britain with that of Switzerland "where for want of colonies the labour of the people is lost to the Parent State."[93] Thomas Mortimer also argued that there was bound to be some emigration even if Great Britain had no colonial possessions, in which case "we should have lost so many subjects . . . by their flying to the dominions of foreign princes."[94] Brougham, finally, pointed out that emigration to the colonies facilitated the egress of surplus population because emigration to foreign countries involved such obstacles as differences in language, government, etc.[95]

[89]*Observations* (1806), pp. 115 f.   [90]*Ibid.*, pp. 123 ff.
[91]*Ibid.*, p. 164.   [92]*Ibid.*, pp. 164 f.
[93]Patrick Colquhoun, *A Treatise on the Wealth, Power, and Resources of the British Empire*, 2d ed. (London, 1815), p. 4.   [94]*Lectures* (1801), p. 127.
[95]Henry Brougham, *An Inquiry into the Colonial Policy of the European Powers* (Edinburgh, 1803), I, 166.

Malthus' views on the subjects of population and emigration merit more detailed discussion. The gist of his arguments can be summarized easily enough. He postulated the existence of a natural law whereby population tends to increase faster than the means of subsistence. While the former increases with geometrical progression, the latter increases only with arithmetical progression. In the first edition of his *Essay* (1798), Malthus asserted that this constant pressure of population against the means of subsistence was subdued and lessened only by two checks: an increase in the death-rate (which he called "positive") due to such phenomena as war, epidemics and other diseases, famine, infanticide, cannibalism, etc.; and a decrease in the birth-rate (called "preventive") mainly brought about by sexual impotence caused by over-indulgence in various vices.

Since both checks on the growth of population were evils in themselves, insurmountable obstacles to progressive wealth and happiness seemed to exist. In the second edition of his *Essay* (1803) Malthus modified his arguments to the extent of introducing man's reasoning faculty as a third possible check on the pressure of population against the means of subsistence. This check was that of "moral restraint," i.e., control of the birth-rate by the exercise of self-imposed celibacy and postponement of marriage.

It has been stated previously that none of the intellectual ingredients that make up Malthus' doctrine represented an original contribution to the knowledge already assembled by his various predecessors.[96] Still, his *Essay* figures as a truly epoch-making

---

[96]Furthermore, as irrefutable as the Malthusian theory appeared to some contemporary readers, it contained fallacies because it was based on imperfect observation and, therefore, erroneous premises. For the same reason, it distorted the apparently insoluble demographic problem, with which Britain was confronted.

In the first place, Malthus and the Malthusians were wrong in assuming that the extraordinary growth of British population was caused by reckless procreation. Actually this increase is now believed to have been due to a remarkable decline in the death-rate and not to a sudden swelling of the birth-rate (see J. H. Clapham, *An Economic History of Modern Britain* [Cambridge, England, 1926], I, 54 f.). Also, the Malthusians did not foresee the future multiplication of the means of subsistence through the discovery of new production techniques and the spreading international division of labour. They failed to realize that Britain's demographic problem was substantially a transitory one and that it originated in economic and social dislocations caused by the Industrial Revolution, the Napoleonic Wars, etc., and was unnecessarily aggravated by the commercial policies of a selfish and reactionary ruling class.

Finally, Malthus, biased by the inhibitions of his profession and social

event in the history of modern England. This prodigious effect was due to several circumstances. First, Malthus' diagnosis of Great Britain's over-populated condition was shortly to be confirmed by the results of the Census and by the appearance of numerous symptoms of demographic congestion.[97] Great Britain's population (England, Scotland, Wales) was reported to be 10,943,000 in 1801, 12,597,000 in 1811, 14,392,000 in 1821, and 16,529,000 in 1831.[98] This rapid increase plus the unmistakable augmentation of unemployment and pauperism was a terrible shock to public opinion.

Secondly, this effect was only re-enforced by the dismal gloom of Malthus' conclusions. He stated his doctrine in the form of an immutable and inexorable law of nature. His "positive" as well as his "preventive" checks were of a depressing character and even "moral self-restraint" meant nothing but a demand on the poor to forgo marriage. To the Malthusian the evil was formidable indeed and satisfactory remedies were non-existent. Thirdly, Malthus' opinion that the size of population depends upon prosperity, was strictly in opposition to the mercantilist assumption that prosperity was largely dependent on a large and dense population.

All these factors led to a striking reversal of British sentiment and thought on the subject of population. The evident prostration of large masses of the British people took on such distressing proportions that the problem of the country's excess population became one of the most discussed questions of the day and remained so for many decades to come.

The assumption that wretchedness and suffering were essentially the unavoidable concomitants of a superabundant population, assuaged the conscience of many a politician and writer. Indeed, the swelling cry for a rule of laissez-faire only sustained this reaction. Not all were content with accepting the miserable living conditions of a large portion of the people as an unavoidable and irremediable necessity. Yet the search for a satisfactory remedy was pursued within narrow confines. One year before Malthus' *Essay* appeared, Bentham called the attention of the public for the first time, to

---

milieu, anticipated neither the future spread of contraceptive techniques nor the incentives which led to their utilization.

[97] Richard Price, as has been shown, estimated the population of England and Wales at about five millions. Until the turn of the century there was a general inclination to under-estimate the populousness of the country. It is now estimated that Great Britain's population amounted to about 7,250,000 in 1751 and 9,250,000 in 1781. Cf. Clapham, *Economic History of Modern Britain*, I, 53.

[98] *Ibid.*, pp. 53 f.

the possibility of controlling reproduction by the use of contraceptives.[99] Francis Place took up the propagation of this remedy with great zeal but in view of the hostility of a prudish and prejudiced ruling class[100] and the uneducated state of the masses, its initial spread was bound to be extremely slow.

It was quite natural, therefore, that the alternative of emigration began to attract increasing attention. Malthus himself discussed it. He did not entirely deny its usefulness but he claimed that instead of an adequate remedy it was only a "slight" palliative. He wrote: ". . . as it is not probable that human industry should begin to receive its best direction throughout all the nations of the earth at the same time, it may be said that in the case of a redundant population in the more cultivated parts of the world, the natural and obvious remedy which presents itself is emigration to those parts that are uncultivated . . . but when we advert to experience and the actual state of the uncivilised parts of the globe, instead of anything like an adequate remedy it will appear but a slight palliative."[101]

Malthus was led to these conclusions by several considerations. He pointed out that "the class of people on whom the distress arising from a too rapidly increasing population would principally fall, could not possibly begin a new colony in a distant country" because "they must necessarily be deficient in those resources, which alone could insure success."[102] Even in the case of already securely established colonies, Malthus argued, this want of resources would place formidable obstacles in the way of large-scale emigration. Broaching the question of government assistance, Malthus, the economist and believer in laissez-faire, remarked: "How far it is incumbent upon a government to furnish these resources may be a question; but whatever be its duty in this

[99]"Situation and Relief of the Poor," *Annals of Agriculture*, XXIX (1797), 393-426. See also, N. E. Himes, "Jeremy Bentham and the Genesis of Neo-Malthusianism," *Economic History*, February, 1936, pp. 267-76.

[100]Malthus himself was strongly opposed to the use of contraceptives. He declared: "I have never adverted to the check suggested by Condorcet without the most marked disapprobation. Indeed I should always particularly reprobate any artificial or unnatural modes of checking population, both on account of their immorality and their tendency to remove a necessary stimulus to industry" (quoted in G. T. Griffith, *Population Problems of the Age of Malthus* [Cambridge, 1926], p. 94).

[101]T. R. Malthus, *An Essay on the Principle of Population* (9th ed.; London, 1888), p. 287.

[102]*Ibid.*, p. 290.

particular, perhaps it is too much to expect that, except where any particular colonial advantages are proposed, emigration should be actively assisted."[103]

In the "natural unwillingness of people to desert their native country," Malthus saw a further reason that made him doubt the adequacy of emigration as a means of relieving population pressure in the mother country. "The vis inertiae of the great body of the people, and their attachment to their homes, are qualities so strong and general that we may rest assured they will not emigrate unless, from political discontents or extreme poverty, they are in such a state as will make it as much for the advantage of their country as of themselves that they should go out of it."[104] Yet in spite of these doubts Malthus did advocate emigration to the colonies as a means of obtaining "temporary relief." He observed that "in all countries great variations may take place at different times in the rate at which wealth increases, and in the demand for labour. But though the progress of population is mainly regulated by the effective demand for labour, it is obvious that the number of people cannot conform itself immediately to the state of this demand."[105] "It is precisely under these circumstances that emigration is most useful as a temporary relief. . . ."[106] Malthus, therefore, concluded that "the subject at the present moment is well worthy the attention of the government, both as a matter of humanity and policy."[107]

COLONIES AS MARKETS

The period here considered saw little literary production on the merits of colonies as markets and sources of raw materials that could match Adam Smith's discourse.[108] Some writers upheld the

---

[103]*Ibid.* This statement is interesting also because it shows that the contemplation of government-assisted emigration naturally led to the search for other arguments which would make colonization appear as an enterprise profitable to the nation as a whole.

[104]*Ibid.*, p. 293. This passage was intended to dispel the fears of those who still adhered to the belief that emigration would tend to depopulate the country, and, still more important, the apprehensions of those employers who expected rising wage rates as a consequence of large-scale emigration.

Besides attachment to their home country, Malthus also mentioned "doubts and uncertainty" as to the fate that awaited them oversea as a factor tending to operate against the emigration of the poor (*ibid.*, p. 291).

[105]*Ibid.*, p. 293. [106]*Ibid.* [107]*Ibid.*

[108]The early contributions of Bentham and James Mill will be studied in the following chapter.

utility of colonies as markets and some denied it. Anderson, for example, followed closely in the footsteps of Adam Smith. In the introduction to his plan for a general pacification of the European colonies in America,[109] he agreed that "it is the interest of Great Britain to promote her own manufactures and commerce to the utmost of her power,"[110] and that she should therefore try to secure to herself "as much of the American trade as possible."[111] On the other hand, he argued that it was not in Great Britain's interest to continue to defend and protect the American colonies.[112] If his plan were followed, Britain would lose nothing by the discontinuation of the colonial trade monopoly. "The export trade of manufactures from this country, it is highly probable, would even increase," for manufacturers would become more "careful" and their goods "somewhat better" and cheaper than formerly.[113]

Playfair, on the other hand, while not denying the intrinsic value of the colony trade as then regulated, maintained that the possession of colonial markets caused the envy of other nations and, hence, tended to embroil the country in international quarrels and wars.[114] In the sphere of foreign trade, therefore, he suggested that Britain rely on the inventiveness of her technicians and her ability to extend liberal commercial credits.[115]

The opposite view is represented by Brougham. Even if the mother country possessed no monopoly of the colony trade, he pointed out, the commerce with the colonies was preferable to foreign trade because it partook of the nature of a "home trade." "The commerce which a country carries on with its colonies, is, in every respect, a home trade. The stock and the industry engaged in it, are employed for the purpose of circulating the surplus produce of the different parts of the same extensive empire, subject to one government, inhabited by the same people, and ruled, in general, by the same system of laws."[116]

While the first advantage mentioned in this passage may be passed over as the intellectual relic of a line of argumentation no

[109]*Interest of Great Britain . . . Considered* (1782), Appendix. Anderson suggested that, by international agreement and guarantee, the American colonies of the various powers be placed under uniform regulations providing, above all, for a demonopolization of the colony trade.

[110]*Ibid.*, Appendix, p. 2.   [111]*Ibid.*   [112]*Ibid.*
[113]*Ibid.*, Appendix, pp. 12 f.
[114]William Playfair, *An Inquiry into the Permanent Causes of the Decline and Fall of Powerful and Wealthy Nations* (London, 1805), pp. 199 f.
[115]*Ibid.*, p. 200.
[116]*Inquiry into the Colonial Policy of the European Powers* (1803), I, 148 f.

longer appreciated,[117] the second was to become of great significance in the future discussion on the value of colonial markets. According to this argument, identity of language, customs, and, above all, law, in mother country and colony, bestowed a valuable advantage over foreign competitors upon the exporting industries of the mother country. ". . . all traders find it more agreeable and advantageous to deal with a state inhabited by the same people, and subject to the same laws: they are better acquainted with the character, manners, and language of their customers: they have a greater confidence in their debtors; and can more certainly obtain justice, when injured. . . . Speculations can . . . be undertaken with greater safety, and capital invested in a colonial trade with much less danger. . . ."[118]

COLONIES AS SOURCES OF RAW MATERIALS

The appreciation of colonial dependencies as sources of raw materials declined rapidly during the period here considered. Of course, some writers still adhered to the old mercantilist line of reasoning. Thus, Bosanquet, spokesman of the West India interest, declared: "The commerce with the West is not only carried with people amongst whom are no manufacturers, but it is domestic commerce; both ends are British, and all the profits accruing, on all transactions, centre in Great Britain . . . the whole importation is profit, which having revolved and circulated through our fields, our manufactures, our shops, and our warehouses, is at last swallowed up in the vortex of the British Treasury."[119] But a more typical note is struck by Arthur Young. He denied the value of colonies as sources of raw materials. Nations, in his opinion, did not plant colonies in order to obtain coffee or sugar. ". . . they are sure of those, and of any other commodities, if they

[117]Brougham went on to say: "Every operation of this traffic replaces two capitals, the employment and distribution of which, puts in motion, and supports the labour of the different members of the same state. The trade of London, or Liverpool, with the countries round the Baltic and Mediterranean, replaces, indeed, two capitals; but one of these only is British: the other puts in motion the industry of foreigners. . ." (*ibid.*, p. 149).

Another writer argued similarly: "The colonies are foreign but in name—the trade is domestic; both ends are British—all the produce appertains to British subjects, and all remains in Great Britain" (Charles Bosanquet, *Thoughts on the Value to Great Britain of Commerce in General* [London, 1808?], p. 41). Similarly, *Emancipation in Disguise* (London, 1807), p. 92.

[118]*Inquiry into the Colonial Policy of the European Powers* (1803), I, 162.

[119]*Thoughts on the Value to Great Britain of Commerce in General*, p. 5.

be rich enough to pay for them; a Russian, or Pole, is as certain of commanding sugar as a Frenchman, or an Englishman; and the governments of those countries may raise as great a revenue on the import, as the governments that possess the islands."[120]

But if it was the trend of articulate opinion to deprecate the value of colonial possessions as sources of primary commodities, the opinion of the British legislature lagged far behind. This body continued to uphold unflinchingly the preferential treatment granted to British colonial timber and sugar.[121] However, among the arguments advanced in support of such a policy, a distinct shift of emphasis took place. Compared with former times the self-sufficiency argument was mentioned only infrequently. Proponents still called attention to the preference enjoyed by metropolitan exporters in the colonies. But, as the sale of metropolitan goods became increasingly independent of this privilege, the advantages granted to colonial articles were defended more and more on the general and unspecified ground that the colonies as dependencies were entitled to special considerations. Most important, however, was the argument that only in the case of staples procured from the colonies, could British shipping be provided with a monopoly.

Demanding the imposition of higher duties on Baltic than on Canadian timber, George Rose, in 1810, declared that the disadvantage attending the trade with the Baltic countries was "that ... the timber was brought to us, not by British but by foreign ships, and this to such a degree, that he believed there was paid last year between 2 and 3 millions to foreigners alone for freightage of timber imported, to the amount of 358,000 tons.... The system now in use encouraged not only the building of foreign ships, but the formation of foreign sailors...."[122] Similarly, when it was proposed in 1813 to increase the tariff preference granted to West Indian over East Indian sugar, Alderman Atkins declared "that the permission to import East India sugar would materially affect and injure the shipping interest, by the great encouragement that it would afford to India-built shipping."[123]

However, another important change occurring in connection with the problem of colonial supplies was that, henceforth, no

[120]Arthur Young, *Travels* (Dublin, 1793), II, 426.
[121]Such privileges were, of course, granted to many additional colonial products. However, sugar and timber were and remained by far the most important ones.
[122]*Hansard*, first ser., XVII, 164.   [123]*Ibid.*, XXVII, 202.

parliamentary discussion on this question took place without some members defending the interest of the consumer against special producers' or merchants' interests. In the course of the above mentioned debate on the proposed change of the sugar duties, W. Smith pleaded:

> ... that although he would be one of the last to recommend any proceeding likely to produce a convulsion in trade, or a serious injury to any class of merchants, the main object of legislative consideration being the interest of the public, he could see no objection to the revision of any commercial system to effect that object ... it would appear, that the whole produce of the West India colonies was a forced cultivation, kept up for some sinister purpose, merely to answer the ends of individuals, but by no means with the view to cheapen the price to the consumer—to answer the interest of the public.[124]

Yet it could hardly be expected that regard for the consumers' interest would lead to a change in the outlook of the rulers of Parliament. It was the manufacturer of English export articles who, particularly after the turn of the century, began to pay attention to those artificial shackles of trade which prevented him from procuring cheap raw materials and from extending his foreign markets. Since the end of the American War of Independence, the English cotton industry in particular had experienced a remarkable expansion of output.[125] Formerly, the cotton manufacturer and the "Manchester politician" had asked for the encouragement of cotton plantations in the British West Indies.[126] When the inventions of Watt, Hargreaves, Arkwright, Cartwright, etc., were exploited, the cotton industry witnessed such an enormous growth[127] that in the matter of markets as in that of raw-stuff sources, the bounds of the British Empire became wholly inadequate for its

---

[124] *Ibid.*, p. 204.

[125] Interestingly this expansion took place in defiance of the unpopularity with which it was regarded by many politicians. It violated the sentiments of those whose attitude was determined by the objective of self-sufficiency. The raw material of the woollen industry was produced in England (although there, too, a change was to take place at the beginning of the nineteenth century). Raw cotton, on the other hand, had to be obtained from abroad and, therefore, involved a precarious dependence on foreign sources of supply. See G. B. Hertz, *The Manchester Politician, 1750-1912* (London, 1912), pp. 14 f.

[126] *Ibid.*, pp. 15 ff.

[127] A contemporary observer had written as early as 1789: "... all ranks in the Community beheld, with wonder and astonishment, the sudden and unexampled increase of this branch of national industry. . ." (Patrick Colquhoun, *A Representation of Facts Relative to the Rise and Progress of the Cotton Manufacture in Great Britain* [London, 1789], p. 3).

needs.[128] In the eyes of the industrialists, merchants, and politicians of Lancashire, the former imperial ideals became increasingly discredited. Economically, the Empire appeared to them a financial burden and a barrier to progress. All they wanted was unrestricted commercial access to ever-expanding markets and sources of rawstuffs. Indeed, the conversion of this group to new economic principles was to become an event of truly revolutionary magnitude both as regards public policy toward international trade and the evaluation of colonies.

COLONIES AS OUTLETS FOR SURPLUS CAPITAL

Adam Smith, it will be recalled, had denounced the metropolitan monopoly of the colony trade because it had led to an undesirable scarcity of capital in the parent state. Indeed, since Britain, at the time, did not suffer from a superabundance of capital, no writer had yet advanced the argument that the possession of colonies benefited the mother country because excess capital could be most safely and advantageously invested there.

Brougham, it appears, was the first one to introduce this argument. He maintained that "the colonial trade has all the advantages of a home trade, except the quickness of returns."[129] However, in his opinion, the latter circumstance was by no means objectionable. "Long credits, in fact, and slow returns, like small profits and slow accumulation of stock, are the necessary consequences of a great national wealth. A colonial trade ought not surely to excite discontent on this account, any more than a great capital ought to be deemed a national misfortune."[130] "The capital thus withdrawn," Brougham argued, "and invested in colonial speculation, is chiefly a part which cannot find profitable employment at home."[131]

When a nation has so greatly increased in wealth and industry, that its trading profits are extremely small, its capital will seek every sort of outlet, in order to pursue more profitable employments. It will first go to foreign trades of slow returns; then to the loans required by the colonies; then to the immediate cultivation of the colonies, by the emigration of its proprietors: and, if the state possesses no such colonies, this capital will overflow into

---

[128]Hertz, *Manchester Politician*, p. 27. By 1801 it had become clear that Empire-grown cotton, could satisfy only a fraction of the supply demanded by Lancashire, while the cotton output of the United States increased with rapid strides (*ibid.*). See also, Arthur Redfield, *Manchester Merchants and Foreign Trade, 1794-1858* (Manchester, 1934), pp. 25 ff.

[129]*Inquiry into the Colonial Policy of the European Powers* (1803), I, 168.

[130]*Ibid.*, p. 172.   [131]*Ibid.*, pp. 214 f.

foreign colonies, by loan or emigration. . . . A country in this situation can evidently receive no benefit from wanting colonial establishments; on the contrary, its stock will be transferred to enrich foreign nations: and, surely, the security of a capital employed in colonial speculation, is infinitely greater than that of a capital lent to the merchants or princes of foreign states."[132]

Brougham was firmly convinced that a country can suffer from both surplus population and surplus capital.[133] Some outlet would have to be found in such a case for the pressure of these surpluses would become so insistent that in the absence of colonies ". . . an outlet would still be found, less advantageous to the emigrants and stockholders, and more dangerous to the state, in the territories of its hostile or rival neighbours."[134]

THE FINANCIAL BURDEN OF EMPIRE

After Adam Smith's performance little additional light could be thrown on the expense of empire. Still, an increasing number of writers and politicians paid attention to this particular corollary of empire. With men like the Earl of Stair,[135] George Tierney,[136] and James Currie,[137] their incessant condemnation of the expense of empire became a passion if not an obsession. But many others also showed that the matter of imperial expense figured, to a considerable extent, in their thoughts on the subject of colonies. In 1780, in the speech on his "Plan for Economical Reform," Edmund Burke remarked: "The province of Nova Scotia was the youngest and the favorite child of the Board [of Trade and Plantations]. Good God! what sums the nursing of that ill-thriven, hard-visaged, and ill-favored brat has cost to this wittol nation! Sir, this colony has stood us in a sum of not less than seven hundred thousand pounds. To this day it has made no repayment,—it does not even support those offices of expense which are miscalled its government; the whole of that job still lies upon the patient, callous shoulders of the people of England."[138] Another writer

---

[132] *Ibid.*, p. 214.

[133] *Ibid.*, p. 218. Brougham mentioned low or no profit on invested capital and a decreasing standard of living as the consequences of a condition of excess capital (*ibid.*, p. 219).

[134] *Ibid.*, p. 222.

[135] Cf. John Earl of Stair, *State of the Public Debt* (2d ed.; London, 1783), and *Advice and Expostulation with the People* (London, 1784).

[136] Cf. George Tierney, *A Letter to the Right Honourable Henry Dundas* (London, 1791).

[137] James Currie, *A Letter, Commercial and Political* (2d ed.; London, 1793).

[138] *Works* (Boston, 1889), II, 345. Burke, incidentally, had assumed an anti-expansionist attitude. During the debates over the Nootka Sound Affair in

asserted that Great Britain "was involving herself in inextricable debts to raise herself to a pitch of grandeur...."[139] James Anderson stated: "Had our people instead of being enticed to go to America, been kept at home ... we should have been at once freed of all the expence that has been laid out in the settlement and defence of that country.... In that case, our whole taxes, instead of forty-four shillings and five-pence, would have amounted to no more than seven shillings and six-pence a head. I leave any one to judge what encouragement our manufactures would receive, were such an abatement of our taxes at present to take place...."[140] The objection that the magnitude of Britain's debt, accumulated in founding, defending, and ruling an empire, formed a serious handicap to the competition of British goods in foreign markets, will be frequently found in the future discussion of the utility of colonial possessions.

In yet another respect was Adam Smith's condemnation of the cost of empire followed up by later observers. Not only was a part of the country's wealth wasted upon its imperial connections, but this expenditure was controlled, directed, and voted for by a relatively small group of people who paid only a small part of the taxes exacted from the nation for this purpose. James Currie complained that, owing to the ignorance of the ruling class "we find them in all ages wasting the little hoards of property acquired by private industry, in projects of foolish vanity."[141] To add selfishness to ignorance was only one more step in this direction and Cobbett and his disciples assailed the entire system of extravagance, sinecures, and pensions that made Great Britain a paradise for the "tax-eaters."[142]

Brougham held the opposite view. He envisaged the Empire as a political union, in which no basic difference existed between Suffolk and a British colony oversea except that the former was

---

1790 he declared: "Besides what had we to contend for? Extent of dominion would do us no good; on the contrary, if all the territories of Spain abroad were thrown into the scale of England, he did not think it an object for a wise man to desire. The effect would prove to us, what it was at the moment to Spain; we should be the weaker for our accumulation of distant dominion" (Cobbett, *Parl. Hist.*, XXVIII, c. 781).

[139]Nathaniel Buckington, *Serious Considerations on the Political Conduct of Lord North* (London, 1783), p. 32.

[140]*Interest of Great Britain . . . Considered* (1782), p. 109.

[141]*A Letter* (1792), p. 10.

[142]See Clapham, *Economic History of Modern Britain*, I, 311.

geographically contiguous to the home country while the latter was a distant "province." Thus, he argued that

> the provinces of a state that lye contiguous, do by no means furnish supplies, either of men or money, in proportion to the benefits of defence and security which they receive from the government.... It is impossible to distribute the burden of the national expence, with such equality, among the different parts of the community, that each shall bear exactly the share determined by its interest in the purposes for which the whole supplies are required. One part of the state always contributes more than its protection costs: the surplus goes to protect another part, which contributes less.[143]

Furthermore, Brougham asserted that colonies generally contributed their share to the burden of imperial defence.[144]

THE ENGLISH "PHYSIOCRATS"

England never produced a physiocratic school comparable in public importance and intellectual ability to the French *économistes*. Yet during the half-century, roughly between 1775 and 1825, a great many English writers endorsed some of the fundamental ideas of Physiocracy, and principally that of the paramount importance of agriculture as a source of national wealth. To some extent this shift of emphasis represented a reaction to the over-emphasis placed by mercantilism on the manufacturing industries and commerce, particularly foreign commerce. As this anti-mercantilist movement—sharply distinguished from that of the classical economists—set in at a time when the Industrial Revolution progressed at an unexampled pace, it was foredoomed to a short-lived existence and never became more than a relatively unimportant adjunct to the evolution of economic ideas in the period mentioned. Indeed, most of the statements and principles advanced by this school of thought were of a decidedly anachronistic nature considering that their propagation coincided with Great Britain's rapid transformation into an industrial and commercial nation *par excellence*. Nevertheless for some length of time this movement received strong support from the intellectually susceptible portion of the British agriculturist interest on the one hand (particularly from those groups who embraced the cause of scientific agriculture), and from Cobbettism, on the other.

Physiocracy regarded the earth as the sole source from which wealth can be drawn and therefore considered only agriculture and mining as truly productive of wealth. The physiocrats put agri-

---
[143]*Inquiry into the Colonial Policy of the European Powers* (1803), I, 108 f.
[144]*Ibid.*, pp. 133 f.

culture above industries and trade and demanded an increased application of capital to the cultivation of the soil. English writers accepted this idea with varying degrees of completeness. Some, indeed, were content with merely stressing the importance of agriculture and betraying toward it a certain partiality as compared with industry and trade.[145] Others went so far as to deny the utility of commerce altogether. William Spence is representative of these extremists. In his pamphlet *Britain Independent of Commerce* (1807) he asserted that England's wealth and greatness were totally independent of foreign trade.[146] "It appears, then," he concluded, "in whatever point of view we regard commerce, that Britain is wholly independent of it. It contributes not a sixpence to her wealth."[147] Spence advocated high prices for agricultural produce,[148] the large-scale cultivation of waste lands,[149] and the closest possible approximation of national self-sufficiency.[150]

Cobbett, in express agreement with Spence, stated that "England has long groaned under a commercial system,"[151] and that "the commercial tribe, with Pitt at their head, have so long and so impudently assumed, that it is commerce that 'supports the nation' . . . ."[152] He, too, saw England's salvation in reliance on agriculture.[153]

[145] Adam Smith belonged to this group.

[146] He stated naïvely: "Whatever a nation imports, it pays an equivalent for, to the country of which it is purchased: whence, then, say the economists, springs any wealth from this branch of commerce?" (William Spence, *Tracts on Political Economy* [London, 1822], p. 11). (This book contains the above-mentioned pamphlet in a revised edition.)

[147] *Ibid.*, p. 71. [148] *Ibid.*, Prefatory Remarks, p. xv. [149] *Ibid.*, p. 24.

[150] *Ibid.*, pp. 5 f. Spence denied that a large proportion of British imports were absolutely necessary to the nation. "This may appear, at the first glance, to be the case; but if any one will examine a list of our imports, he will be surprised to find how few of the articles we get from other countries are necessary even to comfortable and luxurious existence" (*ibid.*, p. 67).

[151] *Cobbett's Political Register*, XII (London, 1807), c. 824.

[152] *Ibid.*, c. 822.

[153] The following quotation may be given as a sample of Cobbett's way of reasoning. Contemplating the possible loss of the British market for woollens in the United States he declared: ". . . how would it injure us? The consequence would be, that cloth would be cheaper in England; the consequence of that would be, that sheep would be less valuable; the consequence of that would be, that less of them would be raised. But, the feed which now goes to the keeping of part of our sheep, would go to the keeping of something else, and the labour now bestowed upon part of our woollen cloths, would be bestowed upon something else; in all probability upon the land, which always calls for labour, and which never fails to yield a grateful return" (*ibid.*, cs. 820 f.).

Beside Spence and Cobbett,[154] there were many English authors who did not deny the value of commerce but minimized it in comparison with that of agriculture.[155] In regard to the question of the utility of imperial connections, this pro-agriculturist school was split into two groups. Most of them pursued a definitely anti-imperialist line of argumentation, while some expressed a preference for the colony trade over foreign trade, to the extent that self-sufficiency seemed impossible of achievement.

Those physiocratically-minded English writers who opposed colonization and deprecated the value of empire, were convinced that the colony trade only diverted the attention of the nation from agriculture, its true concern. However, what they denounced most bitterly was the diversion of capital from domestic employment to oversea employment. Thus, Arthur Young wrote: "When the present rage for monopoly (the true characteristic of the com-

[154]Against the confused fulminations of these two authors James Mill wrote his *Commerce Defended* (London, 1808). Though advocating free trade, Mill agreed that the value of foreign trade was generally over-rated (*ibid.*, pp. 106 ff.). *Sketches on Political Economy* (London, 1809) is a rejoinder to Mill's pamphlet. The author of the *Sketches*, upholding Spence's views against Mill's, saw in foreign commerce the direct cause of Britain's over-population and her involvement in frequent wars (*ibid.*, p. 106).

[155]Arthur Young, assailing the "spirit of the counter-house," stated "that too much national attention cannot be given to agriculture..." (*A Tour in Ireland* [2d ed.; London, 1780], Preface, p. vii). Thomas Mortimer spoke of agriculture as the "fountainhead of national wealth," the "parent of all other arts, and the source of the natural riches of any nation.... Husbandry being the only sure dependence of any nation for its subsistence..." (*Lectures* [1801], pp. 25 f.).

William Paley wrote: "Let it be remembered, then, that agriculture is the immediate source of human provision; that trade conduces to the production of provision only as it promotes agriculture; that the whole system of commerce, vast and various as it is, hath no other public importance than its subserviency to this end" (*Works*, II, 83). George Chalmers maintained that "our resources arose then, as they arise now, from the land and labour of this island alone" (*Estimate of the Comparative Strength of Great-Britain* [1802], p. 61). Patrick Colquhoun declared: "It is by the labour of the people alone, and by means of the property created yearly by that labour that all empires, kingdoms, and states, are supported, whether employed in agriculture (which is the best of all) or in manufactures, commerce, or any other sources of productive industry" (*A Treatise* [1815], p. 4). The writings of Sir John Sinclair, the untiring advocate of the landed interest, are replete with similar statements.

Among writers who, apart from James Mill, defended the utility of commerce against that of agriculture see: Bosanquet, *Thoughts on the Value to Great Britain of Commerce in General*; James Currie, *A Letter, Commercial and Political*; Brougham, *Inquiry into the Colonial Policy of the European Powers*, I, 141 ff.

mercial system) has half beggared Europe with the thirst of wealth; and that nations have grown wiser by experience, they will, it is to be hoped, found their greatness in the full cultivation of their territories; the wealth resulting from that exertion, will remain at home, and be secure...."[156] On another occasion he declared:

One great deviation of French capital has been in the sugar islands, which according to the produce, cannot have a less capital employed in them than fifty millions sterling. The royal navy of France has been, and is now, a favourite object, chiefly for the sake of defending and securing these colonies; let us take but twenty-five years expence of the navy, at two millions sterling, and here are fifty other millions; in these two alone ... there are one hundred millions sterling ... which, under a different policy, might have been invested in agriculture.... Now what comparison can there be in the wealth, prosperity, power, or resources, between the import of five or six millions sterling in West Indian commodities, and the production of ten times that amount in the native soil of France? Yet this wretched commercial policy is now continuing....[157]

Admonishing his country to reverse its imperialist policy, John Cartwright said: "It is time she sought to know, in what the natural, solid, well-wearing strength of a nation depends. It is time she thought of employing more capital on the cultivation of her native soil, and less on that of distant countries."[158] Others demanded the cultivation of waste lands, interior colonization in contrast to oversea colonization. Buckingham wrote: "The cultivation of our waste lands will add to the number of our peoples five millions ... as to colonising, I hope we have had enough of it; let us colonise at home...."[159]

Another group of this school of writers, realizing that their demand for far-going elimination of Britain's foreign commerce was patently impracticable owing to her lack of self-sufficiency, reluctantly approved of the colonies as rawstuff-producing areas. When discussing his country's dependence on foreign supplies for some of these goods, William Spence argued: "It should be considered, too, that of the most important of these essential articles, our colonies and possessions in different parts of the world offer us an abundant supply. The forests of Canada, as well as those of India, abound in timber necessary for our ships of war; and from the former, tar and turpentine might be procured in any quantity."[160] However, this author thought only of such indispensable

[156] *Tour in Ireland* (1780), Preface, p. xi. [157] *Travels* (1793), II, 304 f.
[158] John Cartwright, *The Commonwealth in Danger* (London, 1795), p. 43.
[159] *Serious Considerations* (1783), p. 75. See also, Cartwright, *Commonwealth in Danger* (1793), pp. 43 f.; Young, *Tour in Ireland* (1780), Preface, p. vii.
[160] *Tracts on Political Economy* (1822), p. 67.

commodities as naval stores,[161] and even their supply by the colonies he regarded as a necessary evil. Basically, the colony trade was no better source of wealth than foreign commerce.

... in every point of view, it appears, that this nation derives no wealth from its colonial commerce, any more than from any other branch of commerce; and hence although there is certainly no reason why we should give up our colonies, so long as we can preserve them without enormous expense, yet we may dismiss from our minds, all fear and anxiety as to our future possession of them. If we are deprived of them by the occurrence of events, out of our power to control, we have, for our consolation, the reflection, that they are by no means essential to our well-being.[162]

Sir John Sinclair, on the other hand, thought in terms of imperial self-sufficiency. Attacking the "fashionable doctrine" of free trade, he wanted Britain to become a great "agricultural Empire."[163] In 1813, he advocated the retention of the Cape of Good Hope where the British might raise wine so that the mother country would "become independent of France for that great article of consumption." If grain were grown there, Britain would "have a store of wheat so accessible as at the Cape, ready to be imported in case of scarcity."[164] He also thought of introducing scientific agriculture in India, of procuring from India "the seeds of such articles as might be cultivated in this country," and of "transferring such East Indian productions to our West Indian colonies, as are likely to thrive there. . . ."[165]

[161] He did not think of such colonial staples as sugar. ". . . no increase of national wealth or revenue is derived from the home consumption of sugar and rum. . ." (William Spence, *The Radical Cause of the Present Distresses of the West India Planters* [2d ed.; London, 1808], p. 103).

He did not even value sugar as an article of consumption. "It may be asked . . . where is the difference between the wealth which all allow is brought into existence by the growth of corn, and that which is brought into existence by the growth of sugar? . . . The simple reason why the production of sugar and rum has not the same title to be regarded as an increase of national wealth with that of wheat and potatoes, is, that the latter serve as the food of man, and that by performing this valuable service they may be transmuted into the most valuable wealth; whereas the former merely serve as a temporary gratification of the palate, and leave no trace of their existence when consumed" (*ibid.*, p. 96).

[162] *Tracts on Political Economy*, pp. 91 f.

[163] *The Correspondence of Sir John Sinclair* (London, 1831), I, 322 f.

[164] John Sinclair, "A Collection of Papers on Political Subjects," *The Pamphleteer*, XXV (1818), 244.

[165] John Sinclair, "A Collection of Papers on Political Subjects," *The Pamphleteer*, XXVI (1819), 368.

AVERSION TO EMPIRE, IMPERIAL EXPANSION, AND IMPERIAL WARS

All the writers, reviewed so far in this chapter, who denied the value of the colony trade, deplored also the financial burden of empire, and were suspicious of the permanency of imperial connections. Hence, they assumed a strongly anti-imperialist attitude. Their most pungent argument was that the whole system of foreign and colonial commerce was obnoxious because it tended to breed international conflicts and wars.

As early as 1780, Arthur Young claimed that "the present rage for monopoly" constantly kindled the jealousy of other powers.[166] "It was the commercial system that founded those colonies—commercial profits reared them—commercial avarice monopolized them—and commercial ignorance now wars to recover the possession of what is not intrinsically worth the powder and ball that are shot away in the quarrel."[167] Anderson complained that the possession of empire constituted a "temptation" to frequent wars which were destructive of population and wealth and opened a wide door "for accumulated frauds and abuses."[168] John Nicholls recognized the vicious tendency of colonial expansionism to become self-perpetuating. "Every acquisition renders it more necessary for us to extend our conquests. . . ."[169]

Combined with this deep-seated aversion to imperial wars was the recognition that this whole "system," while yielding profits to some sections of the nation, weighed heavily on the people as a whole. Anderson stated: ". . . the idle and needy dependents on the court . . . look forward with pleasure to the approach of war: monied men behold it with equal joy. . . . From the influence of these two powerful classes of men, aided by the national folly, which ever grasps at extended dominion, a wise and good minister, were he willing, dares hardly listen to terms of accommodation. . . ."[170]

Arthur Young, beholding "the gloomy eye of the Financier rolling with baleful vigilance in search of new ways and means" of obtaining extraordinary profits, foresaw with anxiety the approach of another war with France.

. . . suppose the greatest to be imagined—suppose more sugar islands acquired in one hemisphere, and richer fields, to fatten Nabobbs, in another

---

[166] *Tour in Ireland*, Preface, p. xi.   [167] *Ibid.*, p. xiii.
[168] *Interest of Great Britain . . . Considered* (1782), p. 102.
[169] *Recollections and Reflections* (1822), I, 247.
[170] *Interest of Great Britain . . . Considered*, pp. 103 f.

... of what difference [is it] to me when I pay the malt and beer duty to be told, that it produced victories and the acquisition of Canada in 60 ... and when I pay for my horses, house, and windows, that they produced defeats and the loss of America in 80;—victory and defeat, conquest and loss end exactly the same—in taxation. Will the debility of France pay us for the miseries of England?[171]

Charles Hall denied that the discovery of America had benefited the people of England.[172] Denouncing Sir Home Popham's expedition to the Argentines, Cobbett wrote:

No man has, that I know of, attempted to shew, that the possession of Buenos Ayres would have been of any advantage to this country; except, indeed, by Sir Home Popham, in his congratulatory letters to the traffick-men at the Change, and the knife grinders at Birmingham. To them and to him the adventure might be advantageous; but, to the nation, who had to furnish twenty thousand men to defend the colony, and, perhaps, a million of pounds sterling a year to defray the expence of it, no advantage could ... possibly arise. The troops and the ships will come home; and, I should think, that the rage of colonial conquest will be a little abated.[173]

Thus, the driving force behind imperial expansion was thought to be the consequence of a particular socio-political structure at home. To Adam Smith's "shopkeeper" are added "the idle and needy dependents on the court," the "traffick-men at the Change," the "monied men," the "Financier," and the "knife grinders at Birmingham." They feared indeed that extended empire endangered the preservation of political liberty at home. "Where there are large dominions many are the places of profit that come to be in the disposal of government...."[174] Every circumstance "which tends to facilitate the sudden acquisition of money by court favour, should be guarded against with care, as endangering the liberty of the state. In this sense, extended empire must ever prove pernicious."[175]

Added weight was given to the anti-imperialism of these writers by their lack of any real hope that sovereignty over fully-developed settlement colonies could be retained in the long run. The wealth

[171] *Travels* (1793), I, 680 f.
[172] Charles Hall, *The Effects of Civilization on the People in European States* (London, 1805), pp. 79, 306.
[173] *Cobbett's Political Register*, XII (1807), c. 423.
[174] Anderson, *Interest of Great Britain ... Considered*, p. 100.
[175] *Ibid.*, p. 102. Anderson, indeed, arrived at the conclusion that the smaller country is happier than the powerful one. "The only states in which the felicity of the people has been considerable, and of long duration, have been those whose want of power precluded any idea of conquest" (*ibid.*, pp. 32 f.).

which the mother country invested in its oversea dependencies seemed to rest on a precarious basis. Discussing the potentialities of Britain's new colony of New South Wales, Sydney Smith remarked: "It may be a curious consideration, to reflect, what we are to do when it comes to years of discretion. Are we to spend another hundred millions of money in discovering its strength, and to humble ourselves again before a fresh set of Washingtons and Franklins? The moment after we have suffered such serious mischief from the escape of the old tiger, we are breeding up a young cub, whom we cannot render less ferocious, or more secure."[176] He was enough of a sceptic to be quite certain that such warnings would not be heeded. "... we confess ourselves not to be so sanguine as to suppose, that a spirited and a commercial people would, in spite of the example of America, ever consent to abandon their sovereignty over an important colony, without a struggle. Endless blood and treasure will be exhausted to support a tax on kangaroos' skins; faithful Commons will go on voting fresh supplies to support a just and necessary war...."[177]

Against the background of these pessimistic views of the anti-imperialist school, Brougham set his counter-arguments. He denied that the colonies involved the mother country in wars and that the cost of their defence was disadvantageous to her. Refurbishing earlier theories he saw several Colonial Balances of Power in conjunction with the European Balance of Power.[178] Fully convinced of the efficacy and utility of balance-of-power diplomacy,[179] Brougham perceived of its extension oversea as an advantage to Great Britain. The very fact that European wars spread to the colonies of the belligerents involved, served to deflect fighting from the centres of civilization to areas less vulnerable. "How many fair portions of the globe might have been deluged in blood, instead of some hundred sailors fighting harmlessly on the barren plains of the ocean, and some thousands of soldiers carrying on a scientific, and regular, and quiet system of warfare, in countries set apart for the purpose, and resorted to as the arena where the

[176]"Collin's Account of New South Wales," *Edinburgh Review*, II (1803), 32.
[177]*Ibid.*, pp. 32 f.
[178]*Inquiry into the Colonial Policy of the European States* (1803), II, 2. "Thus, there is such a system in the Asiatic, and another in the American settlements of the European powers" (*ibid.*, p. 3).
[179]"... had it not been for that wholesome jealousy of rival neighbours, how many conquests and changes of dominion would have taken place, instead of wars, in which a few useless lives were lost, and some superfluous millions were squandered?" (*ibid.*, pp. 197 ff.).

disputes of nations may be determined."[180] Colonies, moreover, were valuable in Brougham's judgment because they could be relinquished after defeat in war.

> It does indeed almost always happen ... that when any necessity for reparation of injuries, or any change in the balance of power, is attended with a transference of dominion in consequence of a decisive war, the territories given up as indemnities obtained by right of conquest, are taken from the colonial establishments, of the humbled nation, because every state naturally wishes to retain, first of all, its contiguous provinces, and to make both the calamities and the effects of war fall as much as possible on the remote districts, which, from their distance, are too much undervalued.[181]

THE EMPIRE AS THE BASIS OF SEAPOWER

As shown above, the Sheffield school of thought defeated Pitt's American Intercourse Bill mainly on the issue of the navigation system as the foundation of British seapower. It was exactly the same issue that twenty-five years later decided the division of the House of Commons with regard to a new edition of the same bill. The ship-owners and ship-builders of England sharply remonstrated against any relaxation of the Navigation Laws in the case of the West Indies. Lord Sheffield, G. H. Rose, Lord Hawkesbury, Lord Mulgrave, and Lord Castlereagh deemed the preservation of British maritime power of paramount interest. Lord Hawkesbury declared: "... that our navigation was a paramount consideration, and that if the necessity should arise, partial sacrifices of our commerce ought to be made, to ensure the continuance of that system of navigation from whence had arisen all our maritime superiority."[182] Lord Castlereagh stated that he "was glad that they [the ministers] had not urged such a monstrous proposition as that we ought to repeal our Navigation laws."[183]

---

[180] *Ibid.*, p. 198.

[181] *Ibid.*, pp. 315 f. Brougham continued to remark: "It would, however, be extremely erroneous to conclude from thence, that the acquisition of those dominions was the object of the war on the one side, or their defence the motive of resistance on the other." This statement is interesting in so far as it contains one of the elements that gave rise to the later absence-of-mind theory of the gradual accretion of the British Empire.

The beginnings of that theory, however, date back further. James Anderson already remarked: "Thus, from accident rather than from preconcerted design, was formed a species of colonies, altogether different from any that had ever been known in Europe" (*Interest of Great Britain ... Considered* [1782], pp. 19 f.).

[182] *Hansard*, first series, VI, c. 1038.

[183] *Ibid.*, VII, c. 345.

Brougham likewise saw in the colony trade, as organized under the navigation system, a potent matrix of British maritime strength. He praised the nursery-value of the long voyages necessitated by the mother country's intercourse with its colonies overseas[184] and pointed to the fact that "the sailors it employs are seldom or never in a foreign port," a circumstance that counteracted the danger of desertion in times of war.[185]

Some of the opponents of empire ventured so far as to contest even this consideration. Anderson reasoned that since seapower is the consequence of extensive maritime trade and since "that trade is not necessarily connected with colonies . . . neither can naval power be necessarily dependent on them. In fact, Britain possessed the superiority at sea before she had any colonies at all. Spain never enjoyed it. . . ."[186] Discussing the same problem in the case of France, Arthur Young flayed that policy which is "going eternally in this vicious circle; planting American wastes on account of the navy, and keeping up the navy because these wastes are planted. . . ."[187]

But in spite of such criticism it is safe to conclude that around the turn of the century the seapower-argument had become more powerful than any other argument favouring the maintenance of imperial connections and the preservation of the navigation system.[188] The equation of colonies with ships and naval power

[184]*Inquiry into the Colonial Policy of the European Powers*, I, 174 f., 180 f., 187 f.
[185]*Ibid.*, p. 189.
[186]*Interest of Great Britain . . . Considered*, p. 123.
[187]*Travels*, II, 305.
[188]This modification of attitude is clearly demonstrated in Lord Sheffield, *Strictures on the Necessity of Inviolably Maintaining the Navigation and Colonial System of Great Britain* (2d ed.; London, 1806).

Sheffield deplored that the followers of Adam Smith diverted the attention of their readers "from fact to theory," that they involved the "legitimate" doctrine of colonial policy "in metaphysical discussion" and proposed "false and hasty" policies with regard to the Navigation Laws (*ibid.*, Preface, p. ix; p. 4).

The whole book constitutes a staunch defence of the navigation system as it then stood. Indeed, Lord Sheffield suggested that it was only for the furtherance of British shipping that the retention of the colonies was worthwhile. He declared: ". . . I maintain, not only that on no other principles are they [the colonies] worth the holding, but that, on any other, they must directly encumber and enfeeble the state to which they belong" (*ibid.*, p. 64).

Though exhibiting much inconsistency of argumentation on this point, he concluded that the colony trade was "infinitely" more valuable to the colonies than to the mother country and that British exports to her oversea dependencies "are of much less value than is generally supposed" (*ibid.*, pp. 132 f.). As regards imports from the colonies he remarked: "The same articles which they furnish,

was deeply embedded in the minds of the British ruling class. It was on account of this predisposition that the shipping interest was able to defeat any attempt to relax the system of imperial Navigation Laws.

THE MISSION OF EMPIRE

The development of the notion of Britain's supreme mission to civilize the world by means of her far-flung Empire began with the downfall of the first Empire. That may have been a pure coincidence. But it was probably less coincidental that this new line of argumentation made rapid headway at a time when many of the economic arguments in favour of colonization and colonies were being torn to shreds by the economists.[189]

It was in connection with the Eastern, not with the Western part of the Empire that this sentimental inflammation was kindled. The parliamentary debates during the trial of Hastings and the subsequent investigations into the affairs of the East India Company, and especially the speeches of the younger Pitt, Burke, and Sheridan, give ample proof of the sudden emergence of imperial missionarism and the dominant refrain of the white man's burden.[190]

It would be wrong to assume that this new phenomenon owed its existence to the crafty propagandist effort of an imperial class that observed the emergence of social and economic forces with inherent anti-imperial tendencies. The evolution of this new sentiment was intimately connected with the general development of a powerful humanitarian current in the spiritual life of the English people.[191] From its very beginning the manifestations of

---

might be purchased at least twenty per cent. cheaper at other markets, and the same revenue would arise from them, if they came through the Dutch, the Danes, or the French" (*ibid.*, p. 132).

Yet, in Sheffield's opinion, all these obvious disadvantages were compensated for by the benefit derived by the mother country in respect of her maritime strength. He maintained, therefore, that: "The production of a navy, to an insular power, is the best criterion of the value of the trade. . ." (*ibid.*, p. 230). In effect, Sheffield claimed that the value of Empire and Navigation Laws should not be assessed on the basis of economic considerations at all.

[189]Certain it is that this new argument lent itself to effective exploitation by those interest-groups who were interested in the maintenance and extension of the Empire and eager to make use of every argument by which the public could be persuaded to endorse their policy.

[190]See E. Wingfield-Stratford, *The Foundations of British Patriotism* (London, 1939), pp. 258 ff. The emergence of this new imperial force was already noticed by the Earl of Stair (*A Defense of the Earl of Shelburne* [7th ed.; London, 1783], p. 27).

[191]Such important components of this novel movement as the initiation of

this new imperial sentimentalism revealed the existence of genuine feeling of concern for the lot of the coloured peoples and a deep sense of duty. This strange union of imperial expansionism and trusteeship is clearly revealed in the activities and writings of Sir Stamford Raffles.[192] But from its beginning this movement betrayed the qualities of insincerity and arrogance as well. The following quotation may serve as an illustration. Having depicted the enormous material profit Britain would derive from improving the economic organization of India, the author concluded by observing:

This comprizes no presumptuous view of our character; it is Britain that now gives to the world the standard of all that is excellent—it is to British manners and customs that all nations now conform themselves—Britain leads the fashion and gives the law, not merely in the tinsel of dress, but in the whole frame of social acquirements.[193]

It appears to me that there is something in our national character and condition that fits us for this exalted station. I think too, that there is a kind of destination of this character and condition to these services. It was the privilege of Britain to receive the first and the purest beams of the reformed religion. . . .[194]

Quotations such as these could be easily multiplied. Suffice it to say that the idea of the providential destiny of Great Britain to carry the white man's burden was to grow into an extremely powerful movement in the course of the nineteenth century. That the argumentative exposition of this imperial motive was most frequently coupled with an enumeration of the material advantages Great Britain would derive from performing this duty to herself and to the world, may or may not be an indication of insincerity. A general conclusion cannot be drawn. Sydney Smith, with his suave irony, once observed: "To introduce a European population, and consequently the arts and civilization of Europe, into such an untrodden country as New Holland, is to confer a lasting and important blessing upon the world. . . . The savage no sooner becomes ashamed of his nakedness, than the loom is ready to clothe him. . . ."[195]

---

widespread religious missionarism and the forces behind the abolitionist movement that fought for the suppression of the slave trade and the outlawry of slavery, will be discussed in separate chapters.

[192]See R. Coupland, *Raffles* (Oxford, 1926).
[193]David Laurie, *Hints Regarding the East India Monopoly* (Glasgow, 1813), p. 5.
[194]*Ibid.*, p. 51.
[195]"Collin's Account of New South Wales," pp. 30 f.

SUMMARY

During the period under consideration, the most important feature of the public discussion of the utility of colonies and of the system of imperial management to which they were subjected, is to be seen in the fact that those theorists and politicians who questioned or refuted the usefulness of colonies and the navigation system, though representing a minority only, were incomparably more articulate than their opponents. Whether it was due to intellectual inertia, narrow-mindedness, sectional selfishness, misconceived patriotism, or simply antipathy against the spirit of innovation as such, the proponents of monopolist empire seemed firmly convinced of the virtues of their conclusions. They were little susceptible to the force and truth of counter-arguments and were not overly eager to discuss the subject at all. But unfailingly their parliamentary representatives voted for the preservation of empire and the navigation system. In so far as they did attempt to deploy arguments in support of their position they reiterated the old arguments in the traditional fashion, except for the fact that the nursery-of-seapower argument was pushed into the foreground of the debate, sometimes, as in the case of Lord Sheffield, even to the exclusion of all other arguments. The idea of colonies as a convenient outlet for surplus population also was refurbished and gained increasing strength. Only one argument[196] was added to their array of considerations: that of Great Britain's providential mission to spread order, civilization, and prosperity over the world.

The opponents of the pro-imperial school were divided into several groups of which the economists and the English "Physiocrats" were the most important ones. They, too, pursued different objectives. Some of them argued in favour of outright separation from the colonies and would have welcomed the complete disintegration of the Empire. Others, and they constituted the majority, either were opposed to any further expansion or suggested a contraction of the Empire. Almost all of them argued against the maintenance of the navigation system and the monopoly of the colony trade.

Intellectually their arguments did not, on the whole, constitute an advance over those formulated by Adam Smith.[197] Particularly

---

[196]Brougham's idea of the colonies as dependable outlets for excess capital also constituted a novel argument. But it did not gain popularity until much later.

[197]Indeed, in many cases, their arguments were crude as compared with those advanced by Adam Smith.

strong emphasis was given to the financial burden of the Empire. Among a large group of the English "Physiocrats," anti-imperial sentiment was condensed into an attitude of Little-Englandism. Pro-agriculturist, anti-commercial, they professed a profound hatred for what they regarded as a system of colonial monopolies, foreign trade, and wars. Hence they advocated a system of Stay-at-home, Cultivate-the-native-soil, and Self-sufficiency. Among the anti-imperialist school there was a good deal of uncertainty and doubt whether, as a rule, it was not the natural desire of grown-up colonies to emancipate themselves from the dominion and guardianship of the metropolis.

Owing to the rapid progress of the Industrial Revolution, the period in question witnessed the gradual rise of a new middle-class, a class of manufacturers to whom the bounds of mother country and empire appeared too narrow and the protectionist commercial system of the country too obstructive. Although they were disinclined to take the broad and systematic view of the theorists, it was among this class that the spokesmen of anti-imperialism and laissez-faire were to recruit a mass-basis for many of their leading ideas.

Finally, it is necessary to mention the shock with which the nation received the unmistakable symptoms of over-population and the gloomy doctrine of Malthusianism. Indeed, it was this violent reaction that made the retention and even the extension of empire palatable to many of the economists and the Benthamites who had at first assumed a definitely anti-imperial attitude.

The fact that the bulk of influential opinion favoured the preservation of the Empire and the traditional system of imperial government helps to explain why, so shortly after the collapse of the first Empire, Great Britain was again well on the way to founding a new empire that was to rival and surpass the first in magnitude. To be sure, during the period under consideration, there were very few voices clamouring for imperial expansion. Indeed, Parliament passed a law forbidding the East India Company to advance the boundaries of its Eastern empire. And yet, the same period witnessed the unexampled expansion of British India, the beginning of the colonization of Australia, the acquisition of Cape Colony and other naval stations, and the foundation of a colony in tropical West Africa.

However, this large-scale extension of empire was only to a small degree the outcome of deliberate design. The Cape of Good Hope was acquired less as a future settlement colony than as a naval station. Other acquisitions of the peace treaties of 1802 and 1814 likewise were secured as naval bases designed to improve the defensibility of the existing Empire. Even in the case of these acquisitions it is difficult to say how much imperial expansion was merely the casual fruit of British naval superiority. Australia was settled for the simple reason that the authorities at home did not know what to do with the growing number of convicts that accumulated in the mother country after the American War of Independence had stopped transportation to America. New South Wales was founded as a convict settlement.[198] The colony of Sierra Leone was founded almost exclusively for humanitarian reasons. Expansion in India and in the East Indies was largely the work of local officers who wanted to "pacify" the frontiers and of individual statesmen like Dundas, Wellesley, Lord Minto, and Raffles, who deliberately planned and executed an extension of empire.

Thus, during the period from the Peace of Paris of 1783 to the peace settlements of 1814 there is much truth in Seeley's contention that the British "have conquered and peopled half the world in a fit of absence of mind."[199]

[198] There were some people who argued for its settlement for other reasons. But their project would not have moved the government to embark upon the adventure.

[199] Sir John Seeley, *Expansion of England* (London, 1883), p. 8.

CHAPTER VIII

BENTHAM, JAMES MILL, AND RICARDO[1]

CLASSICAL economics, as a science, made little, if any, progress in England during the period between Adam Smith and Ricardo. The first generation of Benthamites, as represented by Jeremy Bentham and James Mill, subscribed, in the sphere of economics, to the teachings of Adam Smith. As far as they were economists—and neither of them can be regarded as an outstanding economist—they were pre-Ricardian economists.

THE COLONY TRADE

James Mill opened one of his discussions of the colony trade by stating: "Among the expedients which have been made use of, to force into particular channels a greater quantity of the means of production, than would have flowed into them of their own accord; colonies are a subject of sufficient importance to require a particular consideration.... And the question is, whether any peculiar advantage may be derived from it."[2]

To Mill and Bentham, as to Adam Smith, the problem of the forced distribution of capital was the central problem of the colony trade.[3] Both writers, and especially Bentham, over-simplified the problem involved. Bentham postulated:

I will tell you a great and important, though too much neglected truth—
TRADE IS THE CHILD OF CAPITAL: In proportion to the quantity of capital

---

[1] In order to avoid excessive repetition, the following survey of colonial theories will be confined to the salient arguments of the writers mentioned. Much investigation into details and much illustrative material presented by them, will be omitted.

David Ricardo's direct contribution to English thought on the subject of colonies was a relatively small and insignificant one. He contented himself with analysing a few problems involved in the metropolitan monopoly of the colony trade and their consequences. Ricardo's general contribution to economic theory and especially his restatement of the economic principles of international trade (the doctrine of comparative cost of production) had indirectly a considerable influence on English theorizing on the subject of colonial dependencies.

[2] James Mill, *Elements of Political Economy* (London, 1821), p. 167.

[3] They discussed the colony trade exclusively as a monopoly trade. Mill remarked: "It is needless to consider the case of free trade with a colony, because that falls under the case of trade with any foreign country" (*ibid.*, p. 168).

a country has at its disposal, will, in every country, be the quantity of its trade. While you have no more capital employed in trade than you have, all the power upon earth cannot prevent your having the trade you have. It may take one shape or another shape; it may give you more foreign goods to consume, or more home goods; it may give you more of one sort of goods, or more of another; but the quantity and value of the goods of all sorts it gives you will always be the same, without any difference which it is possible to ascertain, or worth while to think about.[4]

On another occasion Bentham wrote: "Suppose that the inhabitants of St. Domingo, in place of buying their corn in France, were to buy it in England; France would lose nothing, because, on the whole, the consumption of corn would not be less: England having supplied St. Domingo, would not be able to supply other countries, which would be obliged to supply themselves from France."[5] Even if a country lost its foreign markets altogether, no harm would arise. "If, article after article, you were driven out of every article of your foreign trade, the worst that could happen to you would be the being reduced to lay out so much more than otherwise you would have laid out in the improvement of your land. The supposition is imaginary and impossible, but if it were true, is there any thing in it so horrible?"[6]

Thus, in Bentham's opinion, capital automatically created trade and the quantity of trade was limited only by the quantity of capital available. He simply denied that there existed such a thing as the problem of markets. "Yes; it is the quantity of capital, not extent of market, that determines the quantity of trade. Open a new market, you do not, unless by accident, increase the sum of trade. Shut up an old market, you do not, unless by accident, or for the moment, diminish the sum of trade."[7] In the eyes of these writers, therefore, the very non-existence of the problem of markets rendered the possession or non-possession of colonial markets inconsequential.[8] Bentham argued: "The quantity of profitable industry that can be carried on in a country being limited by that of the capital which the country can command, it

[4] Jeremy Bentham, *Emancipate Your Colonies* (written in 1793), in John Bowring (ed.), *The Works of Jeremy Bentham* (Edinburgh, 1837), IV, 411.

[5] Jeremy Bentham, *A Manual of Political Economy* (written in 1798), in *Works*, IX, 54.

[6] *Emancipate Your Colonies*, p. 411.

[7] *Ibid.*; similarly, Mill, *Elements*, p. 170.

[8] The argument that fundamentally there is no difference between the employment of capital in production for foreign trade and for domestic trade exclusively, disregards the advantages flowing from the extension of the division of labour.

follows that no part of that quantity can be bestowed upon any one branch, but it must be withdrawn from all the others."⁹ Hence, any encouragement extended to any particular branch of trade would mean a corresponding discouragement of all other branches.¹⁰

According to Bentham's judgment, there was only one case in which the opening of a new market would increase the sum of trade, namely, "if the rate of clear profit upon the capital employed in the new trade is greater than it would have been in the old one, and not otherwise."¹¹ He denied that this held true of the colony trade, except "by accident." ". . . the existence of this extra profit is always taken for granted, never proved. It may indeed be true by accident."¹²

Investigating the supposed benefits accruing to the mother country from its monopoly of the colony trade, Bentham distinguished between two possibilities. First: "In the articles which you can make better and cheaper than foreigners can . . . not a penny do you get in consequence of the monopoly, more than you would without it. . . . Your own people, then, have still the faculty of underselling one another without stint, and they have the same inducement to exercise that faculty under the monopoly, as they would have without it. It is still the competition that sets the price. In this case as in the other, the monopoly is a chip in the porridge. . . ."¹³ Secondly: "In the instance of such articles as you can not make better or cheaper than foreigners can . . . it is still the same illusion. . . . Not a penny does the nation get . . . by this preference of bad articles to good ones, more than it would otherwise. . . . All that results from the monopoly you thus give yourselves of the custom of your colonies is, that goods of all sorts are somewhat worse for the money all over the world than they would be otherwise."¹⁴ In this case, it followed "that a species of industry will be cultivated among you, which does not

⁹Jeremy Bentham, *Principles of International Law* (written in 1786-9), in *Works*, VIII, 547.

¹⁰*Ibid*. As a matter of principle Bentham and Mill were opposed to any such encouragement of a particular branch of trade. However, if there was a case warranting such interference with the natural distribution of capital, "it would unquestionably be the improvement and cultivation of land" (*ibid.*).

¹¹*Emancipate Your Colonies*, p. 411.
¹²*Ibid*.
¹³*Ibid*.   ¹⁴*Ibid*., pp. 412 f.

naturally suit you; that bad commodities will be produced, and bad manufactures carried on."[15]

Analysing the same problem, James Mill introduced another distinction. "The monopoly which a mother country may reserve to herself, of the trade with her colonies, is of two sorts. First of all, she may trade with her colonies by means of an exclusive company.[16] In this hypothetical case, he agreed that the monopoly of the colony trade would yield a special advantage to the mother country. For "the company ... can make her [the colony] buy, as dear as it pleases, the goods which the mother country sends to her, and sell, as cheap as it pleases, the goods which she sends to the mother country. In other words, the colony may, in these circumstances, be obliged to give for the produce of a certain quantity of the labour of the mother country, a much greater quantity of goods than the mother country could obtain, with the same quantity, from any other country, or from the colony in a state of freedom."[17] On the other hand, if the colony trade is open to all merchants of the mother country, but closed to the competition of foreign trade, then

the competition of the merchants in the mother country reduces the price of all the articles received by the colony, as low as they can be afforded—in other words, as low as in the mother country itself, allowance being made for the expense of carrying them.... There is, therefore, no advantage whatsoever derived under freedom of competition, from that part of the trade with a colony which consists in supplying it with goods, since no more is gained by it, than such ordinary profits of stock as would have been gained if no such trade had existed.[18]

The only advantage that, according to James Mill's views, could arise to the mother country from the monopoly of the colony trade "must be derived from the cheapness of the goods which the colony

[15] *Manual of Political Economy*, p. 55. Similarly, James Mill, *Essays* (reprints from the *Supplement* to the *Encyclopedia Britannica*) (London, n.d.), pp. 20 ff.

[16] *Elements*, p. 168.

[17] *Ibid*. In this event, the terms of trade would be more favourable to the mother country than they would be otherwise. Such an arrangement, while utterly disregarding the interest of the colonists, would redound to the benefit of the metropolitan consumer only if the colonies would be able to satisfy the demand of the mother country and if the exclusive company would sell the colonial produce as cheaply as possible.

Apart from political considerations, the extent of this metropolitan exploitation of the colonists would be limited, of course, in so far as the mother country would not be interested in lessening the productive capacity of the colonies (*ibid.*, p. 170).

[18] *Ibid.*, pp. 170 f.

supplies to the mother country."¹⁹ "It is evident, that if the quantity of goods, sugar, for example, which the colony sends to the mother country, is so great as to glut the mother country; that is, to supply its demand beyond the measure of other countries, and make the price of them in the mother country lower than it is in other countries, the mother country profits by compelling the colony to bring its goods exclusively to her market. . . . This advantage, if drawn by the mother country, would be drawn at the expense of the colony."²⁰

Ricardo agreed that Adam Smith had "shown most satisfactorily the advantages of a free trade, and the injustice suffered by the colonies, in being prevented by their mother country from selling their produce in the dearest market, and buying their manufactures and stores at the cheapest."[21] But, in contradiction to Adam Smith, he doubted "whether a mother country may not sometimes be benefited by the restraints to which she subjects her colonial possessions."[22] "Who can doubt, for example, that if England were the colony of France, the latter country would be benefited by a heavy bounty paid by England on the exportation of corn, cloth, or any other commodity?"[23] France, in this case, would benefit from the loss sustained by England. The same effect could be realized by metropolitan management of the colony trade.

If it would suit the interests of Jamaica and Holland to make an exchange of the commodities which they respectively produce, without the intervention of England, it is quite certain that, by their being prevented from so doing, the interest of Holland and Jamaica would suffer; but if Jamaica is obliged to send her goods to England, and there exchange them for Dutch goods, an English capital, or English agency, will be employed in a trade in which it would not otherwise be engaged. It is allured thither by a bounty, not paid by England, but by Holland and Jamaica.[24]

Ricardo pointed out that, generally, "the loss sustained through a disadvantageous distribution of labour in two countries may be beneficial to one of them." In this way, "a measure which may be greatly hurtful to a colony may be partially beneficial to the mother country."[25] As compared with free trade "it is evident . . . that the trade with a colony may be so regulated, that it shall at the same

[19] *Ibid.*, p. 171.

[20] *Ibid.* Similarly, Bentham, *Emancipate Your Colonies*, p. 412.

[21] David Ricardo, *The Principles of Political Economy and Taxation* (1817), in J. R. MacCulloch (ed.), *The Works of David Ricardo* (new ed.; London, 1888), p. 204.

[22] *Ibid.* [23] *Ibid.* [24] *Ibid.*, p. 205. [25] *Ibid.*

time be less beneficial to the colony and more beneficial to the mother country. . . . As it is disadvantageous to a single consumer to be restricted in his dealings to one particular shop, so it is disadvantageous for a nation of consumers to be obliged to purchase of any particular country."[26]

While affirming the possibility of profits to the mother country through a judicious arrangement of the colony trade, Ricardo was by no means of the opinion that such benefits were reaped gratuitously. In continuation of the above statement he pointed out that "the shop, or the selling country, might lose by the change of employments."[27] The general benefit "is never so fully secured as by the most productive distribution of the general capital; that is to say, by a universally free trade."[28] "I allow that the monopoly of the colony trade will change, and often prejudicially, the direction of capital. . . . The injury suffered will be what I have just described; there will be a worse distribution of the general capital and industry, and, therefore, less will be produced."[29]

Thus, these writers conceived of particular cases in which, by a monopoly arrangement, the mother country would be in a position to benefit economically at the expense of the colonist and/or of other countries desirous of purchasing the products of the colonists. These cases, however, were of a purely hypothetical nature. For reasons of political expediency, such exploitation was hardly possible of achievement in the case of the English colonies. Furthermore, even from an exclusively economical point of view, the apparent profit would be exacted at a heavy price. It was the general tenor of the writings of James Mill, Bentham, and Ricardo that the monopolist management of the colony trade was fundamentally pernicious and that it should give way to a system of universal free trade.

THE COLONIAL EMPIRE AS A SOURCE OF POWER

In his "plan for a universal and perpetual peace," Bentham laid down the following propositions: "That it is not in the interest of Great Britain to keep up any naval force beyond what may be sufficient to defend its commerce against pirates. That it is not the interest of Great Britain to keep on foot any regulations whatsoever of distant preparation for the augmentation or maintenance of its naval force; such as the Navigation Act, bounties on the Greenland trade, and other trades regarded as nurseries for seamen."[30]

[26] *Ibid.*, p. 207.   [27] *Ibid.*   [28] *Ibid.*   [29] *Ibid.*, pp. 208 f.
[30] *Principles of International Law*, p. 546.

These statements are characteristic of the early Benthamites' attitude towards the question of defence. Not that they were opposed to adequate preparation for defence as long as a plan for universal and durable peace could not be implemented. But they were utterly suspicious of the unreasoning attitude with which the nation approached this subject of public policy. James Mill observed acidly: "Nothing is worthy of more attention, in tracing the causes of political evil than the facility with which mankind are governed by fears; and the degree of constancy with which, under the influence of that passion, they are governed wrong. The fear of Englishmen to see an enemy in their country has made them do an infinite number of things, which had a much greater tendency to bring enemies into their country than to keep them away."[31] Provision for defence should always be kept down "to the lowest possible, rather than always raised to the highest possible terms.... At the highest possible terms, the provision for defence really does all the mischief to a community which a foreign enemy could do."[32]

Excessive preparation for defence produces still another evil. "It enfeebles, by impoverishing the nation, and by degrading with poverty and slavery the minds of those from whom its defence must ultimately proceed. It makes the country, in this manner, a much easier prey to a powerful enemy, than if it had been allowed to gather strength by the accumulation of its wealth, and by that energy in the defence of their country which the people of a well-governed country alone can evince."[33] Thus, Mill pointed out: "A navy is useful for the defence of Great Britain. But a navy of what extent?... There is... a line to be drawn; a line between that extent of navy which contributes to strength, and that extent which... produces weakness.... As the passion of England has always been to have too great a navy; a navy which, by its undue expence, contributed to weakness; so it has been its passion to have too many sailors for the supply of that navy."[34] A navy of "a certain extent" requires a maritime trade of "only a certain extent." On the basis of these premises Mill criticized the argument that saw in imperial, colony-sustained navigation an indispensable nursery of seamen: "What reason has ever been assigned to prove, that the maritime traffic of Great Britain would not, without the monopoly of the colonies, afford a sufficient supply of sailors to a sufficient navy? None, whatsoever."[35]

[31]*Essays*, p. 28. [32]*Ibid*.
[33]*Ibid*. [34]*Ibid*.
[35]*Ibid*., p. 29.

Bentham ridiculed those who asserted that the colonies formed a main prop of metropolitan power. "Say rather, the whole of your weakness. In your own natural body, you are impregnable; in those unnatural excrescencies, you are vulnerable?... Are they attacked? They draw upon you for fleets and armies."[36] Besides, Bentham maintained, the bulk of the navy serves the function of protecting the colonies.[37] In the eyes of the navy-enthusiasts, navigation is "considered as an end, rather than as a means: or if as a means, as a means with reference to colonies."[38] "Here again comes in the ancient and favourite circle: a circle by which, in defiance of logic and mathematics, political conduct is squared, and wars generated. What are colonies good for? for nursing so vast a navy. What is so vast a navy good for? for keeping and conquering colonies."[39]

PENAL SETTLEMENTS

The Philosophical Radicals were the first to launch a systematic attack against the British system of the transportation of convicts to penal colonies. James Mill observed: "The brilliant idea of a colony for the sake of getting rid of a delinquent population, if not peculiar to English policy, is, at any rate, a much more remarkable part of the policy of England, than that of any other country."[40]

In his *Panopticon Versus New South Wales*, Bentham contrasted the virtues of his own project of a penitentiary-system with the alleged advantages of the British penal settlement in Australia. He averred that, in contrast to "Panopticon," his model penitentiary, the system of colonial convict settlements defeated the true objects of penal justice.[41] Then he compared the cost of the two methods and estimated the "rate of expense of the colonial establishment to the penitentiary establishment—in round numbers, from somewhat more than two to one, to somewhat less than four to one."[42] Similarly, James Mill held:

[36] *Emancipate Your Colonies*, p. 414.
[37] *Ibid.*, p. 415.
[38] Jeremy Bentham, *Panopticon Versus New South Wales* (written in 1802), in *Works*, III, 209.
[39] *Ibid.* [40] *Essays*, p. 14.
[41] See *Panopticon Versus New South Wales*, in *Works*, III, 173 f., 174-200. Similarly, Mill, *Essays*, pp. 14 f.
[42] *Panopticon Versus New South Wales*, p. 201. Condemned as a penal settlement, Bentham saw no other reason for retaining New South Wales. He concluded with pungent sarcasm: "In what then consists the real acquisition, the real advantage derived from the plan of colonizing the antipodes—colonizing

So much, then, with regard to the reformation of the individual and security from his crimes, neither of which is attained. But, even on the supposition that both were ever so completely attained, there would still be a question of great importance; viz. whether the same effects could not be attained at a smaller expense.... In this respect also, the policy of the New South Wales establishment is faulty beyond endurance. The cost of disposing in this way of a delinquent population is prodigious. We have no room for details, and there is no occasion for proof; the fact is notorious: . . .[43]

COLONIES AS A SOURCE OF WARS

"War is mischief upon the largest scale,"[44] was the dictum of Bentham. In advancing his "plan for a universal and perpetual peace," he laid down two fundamental propositions, the acceptance of which he regarded as the indispensable prerequisite for the prevention of war. First, "the reduction and fixation of the force of the several nations that compose the European system," and, secondly, "the emancipation of the distant dependencies of each state."[45] On the basis of these considerations Bentham suggested that, quite apart from their material unprofitability to the mother country, "it is not the interest of Great Britain to have any foreign dependencies whatsoever" because "distant dependencies increase the chances of war."[46] This proposition was true, Bentham maintained, because distant dependencies increase the number of possible subjects of dispute, because of the "natural" obscurity of title in case of new settlements and discoveries, and because men are less anxious to avoid wars when the theatre of war is remote, than when it is nearer to home.[47]

In addition to the constant danger of becoming involved in wars with other nations on account of colonial possessions, Bentham also pointed to the possibility of intra-imperial wars necessitated by the metropolitan determination to enforce the obedience of recalcitrant colonies.[48]

James Mill likewise averred that "colonies are a grand source of wars"[49] and observed "that the colonies multiply exceedingly the causes and pretext of war. . . ."[50]

---

them with settlers selected for their unfitness for colonization? . . . Two hundred and fifty plants, or thereabouts—two hundred and fifty new discovered plants—composed the amount of the stock of vegetable curiosities that had been imported from thence in 1796 . . . by Lieutenant-Colonel Paterson. . . . But plants, my Lords, as well as gold, may be bought too dear. . ." (*ibid.*, pp. 210 f.).

[43] *Essays*, pp. 15 f.
[44] *Principles of International Law*, p. 544.
[45] *Ibid.*, p. 546.   [46] *Ibid.*, p. 547.   [47] *Ibid.*
[48] *Ibid.*, p. 548.   [49] *Essays*, p. 32.   [50] *Ibid.*, p. 33.

THE FINANCES OF EMPIRE

Revenues.[51] Investigating the question of colonial tributes exacted by the metropolis, James Mill observed that Great Britain never had received any tributary contributions from her oversea dependencies. In regard to the West Indies and North America, he said, exaction of a tribute was never contemplated.[52] "With regard to the East Indies, we believe, there exists more or less of prejudice. Under the ignorance in which Englishmen have remained of East India affairs, it floats in the minds of a great many persons, that, somehow or other, a tribute, or what is equivalent to a tribute, does come from the East Indies. Never did an opinion exist, more completely without evidence, contrary to evidence. . . ."[53] Hence, Mill advanced the general proposition, deduced "from the experienced laws of human society, that there is, if not an absolute, at least, a moral impossibility, that a colony should ever benefit the mother country, by yielding it a permanent tribute."[54]

A large part of the British public had always assumed that, through the duties levied by the mother country on colonial produce, the colonies contributed prodigiously to the revenues of Great Britain. As numerous writers had done before, Bentham pointed out that "your taxes upon the articles of their production, and upon those of your importation from the colonies, are taxes of which you pay every farthing yourself. . . ."[55] If for fiscal reasons, the imposition of import duties on colonial articles was considered desirable, no case for the maintenance of a colonial empire could be based on such a policy. "The taxes levied upon the commerce with the colonies may produce a considerable amount. But if they were free, would they carry on no commerce? Could not this commerce be taxed?. . . The possession of colonies is not

---

[51]The following arguments are not concerned with local colonial revenues designed to defray part of the local cost of government and administration.

[52]*Ibid.*, p. 17.   [53]*Ibid.*

[54]*Ibid.*, p. 18. Mill argued as follows: ". . . the colonies must be governed . . . . No proposition in regard to government is more universal . . . than this, that a government always spends as much as it finds it possible or safe to extract from the people. . . . The government of the mother country itself cannot keep its expences within bounds. . . . The government of the colonies, managed by delegates from home, is sure to be worse . . . than the government at home; and, as expence is one of the shapes in which the badness of government is most prone to manifest itself, it is sure above all things, to be in proportion to its resources more expensive" (*ibid.*).

[55]*Manual of Political Economy*, p. 55.

necessary to the levying of taxes upon the commerce carried on with them."⁵⁶ The case of customs duties levied on imports into the colonies is, of course, entirely different. Bentham wrote: "I will show you how you may get revenue out of them: . . . Tax none of their produce, tax none of your imports from them; of all such taxes, every penny is paid by yourselves. Tax your exports to them: tax all your exports to them: tax them as high as smuggling will permit: of all such taxes, every penny is paid by them."⁵⁷

Yet in addition to the adverse effects of such a regulation on the productivity of the colonies and the political impracticability of subjecting the colonies to such exploitative procedure, the cost of enforcing and administering such a scheme would be prodigious. Therefore, Bentham argued: "An advantage, however, of this nature can only be deceptive. When you have made a prison of your colonies, it is necessary to keep all the doors carefully shut: you have to strive against the Proteus of smuggling; fleets are necessary to blockade their ports, armies to restrain a discontented people, courts of justice to punish the refractory. How enormous are the expenses to be deducted, before this forced commerce will yield a net revenue."⁵⁸

Expense. To the Benthamites, excessive government expenditure was objectionable not only because it denoted a spirit of wastefulness. Necessitating heavy taxation, unwarranted expenditure enabled the Few to exploit the Many and constituted an unjustifiable infringement on the liberty of the individual citizen by restricting his freedom to dispose of his property. Thus, their objections to excessive revenues and expenditure were part of their desire and struggle for a liberal and utilitarian system of government. In this sense, James Mill declared: "It never ought to be forgotten, that society is injured by every particle of unnecessary expense; that one of the most remarkable of all the points of bad government, is, that of rendering the services of government at a greater than the smallest possible expence; and that one of the most remarkable of all the points of good government is, that of rendering every service which it is called upon to render at the smallest possible expense."⁵⁹

⁵⁶*Ibid.*   ⁵⁷*Emancipate Your Colonies*, p. 414.
⁵⁸*Manual of Political Economy*, p. 55.
⁵⁹*Essays*, p. 15. Similarly, Ricardo wrote in 1818: "I am as great a friend to economy in Government as you can wish me to be; every guinea that is spent unnecessarily I think is a public wrong. . ." (J. H. Hollander [ed.], *Letters of David Ricardo to John Ramsay McCulloch* [New York, 1895], p. 11).

Bentham's and James Mill's views on the direct costs of imperial government and defence were virtually identical with those offered by earlier economy-minded writers.[60] In addition, Bentham underlined the cost of the colonial counter-monopoly to the metropolitan consumer of colonial products.

All this while, is not the monopoly against the colonists clogged with a counter-monopoly? To make amends to the colonists for their being excluded from other markets, are not the people in France forbidden to take colony produce from other colonies, though they could get it ever so much cheaper? If so, would not the benefit of France, if there were any, from the supposed gainful monopoly, be outweighed by the burthen of that which is acknowledged to be burthensome? Yes—the benefit is imaginary, and it is clogged with a burthen which is real.[61]

THE INTEREST OF THE FEW VERSUS THAT OF THE MANY

Having demonstrated the inutility of colonies to the mother country, Bentham and James Mill suggested that their retention was only in the interest of the Few who, through the colonies among other things, were able to exploit the Many. Their train of reasoning can be studied in the following quotation from Mill's essay on colonies.

If colonies are so little calculated to yield any advantage to the countries that hold them, a very important question suggests itself. What is the reason that nations, the nations of modern Europe, at least, discover so great an affection for them. Is this affection to be wholly ascribed to mistaken views of their utility, or partly to other causes?... It never ought to be forgotten, that, in every country, there is "a Few," and there is "a Many"; that in all countries in which the government is not very good, the interest of "the Few" prevails over the interest of "the Many," and is promoted at their expence. "The Few" is the part that governs; "the Many" the part that is governed. It is according to the interest of "the Few" that colonies should be cultivated.[62]

What is the stake of the Few in the maintenance of a colonial empire? "'The Few,' in some countries, find in colonies a thing which is very dear to them;... the one, the precious matter by which they augment their power; the other, the precious matter by which they augment their riches. Both portions of the ruling 'Few,' therefore, find their account to the possession of colonies."[63] Most important of all is the "job"-motive.

[60]See Bentham, *Emancipate Your Colonies*, pp. 415 f.; James Mill, *Essays*, pp. 18 f.
[61]*Emancipate Your Colonies*, p. 413.
[62]*Essays*, p. 31.   [63]*Ibid.*, pp. 31 f.

There is not one of the colonies but what augments the number of places. There are Governorships and judgeships, and a long train of et ceteras; and above all, there is not one of them but what requires an additional number of troops and an additional portion of the navy. In every additional portion of army and navy, beside the glory of the thing, there are generalships, and colonelships, and captainships, and lieutenantships, and in the equipping and supplying of additional portions of army and navy, there are always gains, which may be thrown in the way of a friend. All this is enough to account for a very considerable quantity of affection maintained towards colonies.[64]

Bentham adhered to the same point of view. Discussing the supposed value of the English colonies, he remarked: "Is it a secret to you any more than to ourselves, that they cost us much, that they yield us nothing—that our government makes us pay them for suffering it to govern them—and that all the use or purpose of this compact is to make places, and wars that breed more places?"[65]

The profiteers of monopoly arrangements (e.g., the shipping interest), influential as they were politically, must, of course, be added to that portion of the Few who, through the imperial connections, were enabled to augment their "riches" at the expense of the Many.[66] Colonies were "a cover for tyranny and peculation."[67]

[64]*Ibid.*, p. 32. Mill argued that, in this sense, the colonies become even more valuable to the Few because they are a "grand" source of wars. "There is nothing in the world, where a government is, in any degree, limited and restrained, so useful for getting rid of all limit and restraint, as wars. The power of almost all governments is greater during war than during peace. But in the case of limited governments, it is so, in a very remarkable degree.... Nothing augments so much the quantity of that portion of the national wealth which is placed at the command of the government, as war.... Whenever a war breaks out, additional troops, and an additional portion of the navy, are always required for the protection of the colonies" (*ibid.*, pp. 32 f.).

Thus, the colonies, by involving the parent state in wars, help the Few to augment their political power and put at their disposal more "Jobs" in the Armed Services, more ordnance business, more pensions, more social prestige, and so forth.

[65]*Emancipate Your Colonies*, p. 416.

[66]Analysing the reasons why under a protectionist economic system the producers' interest of the Few so easily overrides the consumers' interest of the Many, Bentham remarked: "Of these opposite interests, it is the lesser interest that always operates ... with peculiar force—with a force which is peculiar to every particular interest, as contra-distinguished from and opposed to the greater, universal interest. The individuals who compose the particular interest always are, or at least may be ... a compact harmonizing body—a chain of iron; the individuals making the universal interest are on every such occasion an unorganized, uncombined body—a rope of sand. Of the partakers in the universal interest, the proportion of interest centred in one individual is too small to afford sufficient inducement to apply his exertions to the support of his trifling

Their government helped the ruling Few to usurp more power to themselves than they possessed under the constitution. This usurpation of additional power was obtained mainly through "the means of corruption afforded by the patronage."[68] The rule of autocracy as set up in the colonies had a distinctly deteriorating effect on the constitutional government of the metropolis.[69]

Finally, Bentham conceived of two additional evils that emanated from the colonial empire and system. First, "bad government results to the mother country from the complication of interests, the indistinct views, and the consumption of time, occasioned by the load of distant dependencies."[70] Secondly, by the skilful manipulation of imperial symbols, the ruling Few, intent on the maintenance of the colonial Empire, were able to keep the people from realizing the fundamental inutility of colonies to Britain. "The stock of national intelligence is deteriorated by the false notions which must be kept up, in order to prevent the nation from opening its eyes and insisting upon the enfranchisement of the colonies."[71]

POPULATION, EMIGRATION, AND COLONIES

Nearly all English observers of the time interpreted the widespread unemployment and impoverishment among the population of England, Scotland and, especially, Ireland, as unmistakable signs of demographic congestion. The magnitude of the problem and its gloomy interpretation by Malthus and his followers, made

---

share in the common interest. Add to which the difficulty, the impossibility, of confederacy to any such extent as should enable the exertions of the confederates fairly to represent the amount of the general interest—that general interest embracing, with few exceptions, the whole mass of society. . . . Much greater, however, is the advantage which the lesser sinister interest possesses over the great common interest, as far as secret influence is concerned" (Jeremy Bentham, *Observations on the Restrictive and Prohibitory Commercial System* [written in 1821], in *Works*, IX, 98).

[67]Bentham, *Emancipate Your Colonies*, p. 416.

[68]Bentham, *Principles of International Law*, p. 548.

[69]See Jeremy Bentham, *A Plea for the Constitution* (written in 1803), in *Works*, III, 251-4. In this essay Bentham called the colony of New South Wales a "nursery of martial law" (*ibid.*, p. 252).

[70]*Principles of International Law*, p. 548. The relinquishment of the colonies would, therefore, have the result of "simplifying the whole frame of government, and thereby rendering a competent skill in the business of government more attainable—1. To the members of the administration; 2. To the people" (*ibid.*).

[71]*Ibid.*

many Englishmen turn to the colonies as welcome outlets for "superabundant" population at home. This was true of a great many statesmen and authors who otherwise were inclined to look upon the colonies with disfavour. To some extent, Bentham and James Mill shared in this reaction. Bentham declared:

Ought we not to form any colonial establishment? Certainly not with the intention of enriching the mother-country: it is always a certain expense, for a contingent and far distant profit. But we have seen that, as a means of relieving the population—of preventing its excess, by providing a vent for those who find themselves over-burthened upon their native soil, colonization offers an advantageous resource; and when it is well conducted, and free from any regulations which may hinder its prosperity, there may result from it a new people, with whom we shall possess all the connexions of language, of social habits, and of natural and political ties.[72]

Discussing the possibility of relieving population pressure in the mother country by means of colonization, James Mill observed: "In certain circumstances, this is a better resource than any scheme for diminishing the rate of population. So long as the earth is not peopled to that state of fulness which is most conducive to human happiness, it contributes to that important effect."[73] However, Mill advocated the removal of a body of people from one country for the purpose of colonizing another only under certain definite circumstances.

In the first place, it is necessary that the land which they are about to occupy, should be capable of yielding a greater return to their labour than the land which they leave; otherwise, though relief is given to the population they leave behind, their own circumstances are not better than they would have been had they remained. Another condition is, that the expense of removal from the mother country to the colonized country, should not be too great . . . . If the expense is too great, the population which remains behind in

---

[72] *Manual of Political Economy*, p. 56. This study was written in the seventeen-nineties, so that Bentham still discussed the question whether emigration might be of disadvantage to a state. He said: "Yes, if the emigrants could have found employment at home;—no, if they could not. But it is not natural that labourers should exile themselves, if they could live at home. However, if they desire so to do, ought they to be prevented? Cases must be distinguished. It is possible that this desire may have been produced by some momentary distaste, by some false idea, some whim, which may mislead a multitude of men before they have leisure to undeceive themselves. I will not therefore affirm, that circumstances may not happen in which emigration may not be forbidden by a law of short duration. . ." (*ibid.*, p. 74). Apart from such exceptional cases, however, Bentham favoured neither restrictive nor promotive action on the part of the government. "On the subject of emigration, the wisest part . . . is to do nothing" (*ibid.*, p. 75).

[73] *Essays*, p. 13.

the mother country, may suffer more from the loss of capital, than it gains by the diminution of numbers.[74]

THE QUESTION OF SEPARATION

There can be no doubt as to Bentham's and Mill's attitude toward the colonial system. They flatly demanded its elimination. To the question whether Great Britain ought to relinquish its colonies, the Benthamites failed to offer a clear answer. The general tenor of their statements seems to suggest that they would have welcomed such a step. In his *Emancipate Your Colonies* and in his *Principles of International Law*, Bentham exhorted his countrymen as well as the French to accept such a solution to the imperial problem. In his later years, however, he seems to have changed his mind. Yet, at no time did either Bentham or Mill alter their views with regard to the expense and the general economic inutility of empire. Halévy, therefore, concluded that "colonization is a fact before which their logic capitulated."[75]

Halévy suggested that the first generation of Philosophic Radicals did not flatly demand the abandonment of the colonies for two reasons. The first of these is well expressed in the following quotation.

Ought colonies already possessed to be emancipated? Yes, certainly; if we only consider the saving of the expenses of their government, and the superior advantages of a free commerce. But it is necessary to examine what is due to colonial establishments. Can they maintain themselves? Will not their internal tranquillity be interrupted? Will not one class of the inhabitants be sacrificed to another? for example, the free men to the slaves, or the slaves to the free men? Is it not necessary that they should be protected and directed, in their condition of comparative weakness and ignorance? Is not their present state of dependence their safeguard against anarchy, murder, and pillage? Such are the points of view under which this question ought to be considered. When we shall have ceased to consider colonies with the greedy eyes of fiscality, the greater number of these inconveniences will cease of themselves. Let governments lay aside all false mercantile notions, and all jealousy of their subjects, and everything which renders their yoke burthensome will fall at once; there will no longer be any reason to fear hostile dispositions and wars for independence. If wisdom alone were listened to, the ordinary object of contention would be reversed—the mother-country would desire to see her children powerful, that they might become free, and the colonies would fear the loss of that tutelary authority which gave them internal tranquillity and security against external foes.[76]

---

[74]*Ibid.* This opinion was based on the postulate of a direct and exclusive relationship between the volume of employment and the fund of capital available in a country.

[75]Elie Halévy, *The Growth of Philosophic Radicalism* (London, 1928), p. 510.

[76]Bentham, *Manual of Political Economy*, pp. 56 f.

This is an important statement. When, following the abandonment of the navigation system and the implementation of free trade, liberal opponents of separation, such as Earl Grey, advanced arguments to justify the maintenance of the Empire, they did so exactly in the terms used by Bentham. Their conception of empire and that of Bentham, half a century earlier, were largely identical. The strength of conviction with which Bentham supported the tutelage-argument is amazing. If this attitude is viewed in conjunction with James Mill's work in the East India Company, Halévy seems justified in presuming that the Radicals were "tempted to consider the colonial empire as a vast field for experiments in philanthropy and reform."[77]

Another reason, already mentioned, that determined the Benthamites, like many economists, reluctant to advise the abandonment of the colonies, was their grave concern over Great Britain's surplus population. In this respect, too, Bentham argued that colonies ought not to be established with the intention of enriching the mother country, but agreed that colonization might afford a means of relieving metropolitan population pressure.[78] This problem became ever more acute in the first half of the nineteenth century. When Wakefield had worked out his project of systematic colonization, whereby the parent state would be enabled to rid itself of its excess population, the majority of the Benthamites, especially such important followers as John Stuart Mill, Molesworth, and Grote, became zealous advocates of the new colonization movement.[79]

UTILITARIANISM AS A TEMPER OF THOUGHT

Bentham's and James Mill's statements on the subject of colonies may have exerted scant influence on the thinking of their contemporaries. Indeed, apart from their relentless exposure of "interest-begotten" prejudices, their arguments did not at all constitute an advance over those of previous writers. But philosophical radicalism as a mode of thought was bound to affect

[77] Halévy, *Growth of Philosophic Radicalism*, p. 510. In June, 1829, when James Mill had become an important official in the East India Company, Bentham added the following postscript to his *Emancipate Your Colonies:* "I shall be the dead legislative of British India. Twenty years after I am dead, I shall be a despot" (quoted *ibid.*).

[78] *Manual of Political Philosophy*, p. 56.

[79] Approached by Wakefield in 1831, through Francis Place as intermediary, Bentham himself drew up a scheme for the formation of a joint-stock colonization society. See Halévy, *Growth of Philosophic Radicalism*, pp. 510 f.

English theorizing on the pros and cons of empire to a truly prodigious degree. In this sense Bentham's *Book of Fallacies*[80] was of much greater significance than his *Emancipate Your Colonies*. It is true that the writings of the Radicals were not widely read. Yet, as John Stuart Mill put it, "they have been the teachers of the teachers."[81]

There is no need here to discuss utilitarianism as a system of philosophy. For the purpose of the present study it is sufficient to remark with the younger Mill "that to Bentham more than to any other source might be traced the questioning spirit, the disposition to demand the why of everything."[82] Bentham, indeed, was to his age and country "the great questioner of things established."[83]

His tireless refutation of illogical and sophistic arguments, his determined refusal to take any assertion for granted without sufficient proof on the one hand; and his suspicion of the fallacies inherent in generalizations and his painstaking insistence on precision of thought and language in political reasoning on the other hand, made Bentham perhaps the most influential Englishman in the first half of the nineteenth century. Regarding English theorizing on the questions of colonies and of the colonial system, there can be no doubt that the fundamentally anti-traditionalist outlook of the Benthamites, their unflinching campaign against the supposed virtue of long-established arguments and their firm insistence on judging institutions exclusively by their results, i.e., by their utility, exerted a profound influence.

[80] *Works*, vol. VIII.
[81] J. W. M. Gibbs (ed.), *Early Essays by John Stuart Mill* (London, 1897), p. 328.
[82] *Ibid.*, p. 329.   [83] *Ibid.*

CHAPTER IX

EMIGRATION AND COLONIZATION
1815-1850

"THE SHOVELLING OUT OF PAUPERS"

FOLLOWING the termination of the Napoleonic Wars, statistical certainty of a fast growing population on the one hand, and widespread unemployment and pauperism, large numbers of disbanded soldiers, the disorganization of commercial conditions and the wide acceptance of Malthus' pessimistic and seemingly irrefutable thesis on the other hand, drew the attention of English writers and politicians increasingly to the depressing subject of excess population. From the beginning emigration commanded the chief interest of those who searched for adequate remedies.

In 1816, the War Office decided on experimentation with the settlement of veterans in Canada.[1] In the early twenties the government and Parliament devoted increasing attention to the facilitation and regulation of emigration.[2] The appointment of the select committees of 1826 and 1827 mark the determination of government and Parliament to acquire a sound factual basis for the formulation of a broad and consistent policy.

Theoretical discussion of the subjects of pauperism, surplus population, emigration, and colonization was prolific throughout the period from 1815 to 1850. Considering the principal currents of thought on these subjects, this time span may be divided into two sub-periods. From 1815 to the early thirties the main consideration was that of the "shovelling out of paupers," as Charles Buller remarked. Great Britain, it was agreed, suffered from a plethora of labourers. The distressing consequences were low wage rates, numerous unemployed, and a staggering financial burden on account of poor relief. The remedy proposed was the removal

---

[1]Under the supervision of Lieut. Cockburn demobilized soldiers were settled in Canada. However, the experiment was a failure. On this and other government-sponsored projects see Fred H. Hitchins, *The Colonial Land and Emigration Commission* (Philadelphia, 1931), pp. 3 f.

[2]See on this, *ibid.*, pp. 4 f.; Stanley C. Johnson, *A History of Emigration from the United Kingdom to North America, 1763-1912* (New York, 1912), pp. 16 ff.

by emigration of a sufficiently large number of paupers, preferably to the British colonies. Sir H. Wilmot Horton can be considered as the typical representative of this school of thought.[3]

From the early thirties to the end of the period here considered, the predominant idea was that of systematic colonization. Great Britain was thought to be suffering both from demographic crowdedness and a superabundance of capital. Population pressure was considered responsible for distress not only among the lowest strata of society but among all other classes as well. The remedy was seen not simply in "shovelling out paupers" but in the transfer to the colonies of capital and of Englishmen from all social strata. The object was not simply that of getting rid of excessive capital and population but also of creating new producing areas and markets oversea. Edward Gibbon Wakefield was the foremost representative of this new colonization movement.

Before discussing the elements of the Hortonian school of thought[4] it must be emphasized that the participants in the debate spoke without experience. By necessity they had to rely on theoretical assumptions and conclusions. As late as 1841 Herman Merivale remarked: "In considering the question thus raised, of the applicability of emigration on a large scale to a country circumstanced like our own, with a view to relieving its supposed redundancy of labouring people, it must be remembered, in the first place, that we are utterly unable to submit our speculations to any test of experience."[5]

During the period here considered there was, on the whole, general agreement on the basic nature of Britain's plight. The third report of the Select House Committee on Emigration of 1827, predominantly influenced by Horton and Malthus, posed the problems as follows: "The first and main principle is, that Labour,

[3]In 1822, Horton became Under-Secretary of State for war and colonies. He became one of the leading figures in the emigration movement and was chairman of the Parliamentary Emigration committees of 1826 and 1827.

[4]In the following discussion the time limit suggested by the above-mentioned subdivision of the period from 1815 to 1850 will not be strictly observed. The Hortonian trend of thought, of course, was not completely displaced by the Wakefield school. It was partly absorbed by the latter and to some extent the two schools of reasoning co-existed in the second sub-period. The second part of this chapter, therefore, will be devoted exclusively to those features of the Wakefield system that were peculiar to it alone. All other aspects of the problem will be examined in the first portion of the present chapter.

[5]Herman Merivale, *Lectures on Colonization and Colonies* (London, 1841), I, 141.

which is the commodity of the poor man, partakes strictly, as far as its value is concerned, of the circumstances incident to other commodities; and that its price is diminished in proportion to the excess of supply as compared with the demand. . . . If this proposition be admitted, it follows that if the supply of labour be permanently in excess, as compared with the demand, the condition of the lower classes must be permanently depressed. . . ."[6]

Virtually all writers agreed that in Great Britain the supply of labour was in excess of demand. The consequences of this situation were self-evident. It led to a state of affairs "which is incompatible with the prosperity of a great proportion of the population, and equally so with the general interests of the country, which are involved in the equalization of national prosperity. . . ."[7] Apart from being exposed to the constant sight of widespread suffering, the non-pauper population had to shoulder the financial burden of poor relief[8] and was kept in a state of anxiety over the latent threat of social and political unrest, the augmentation of crime, etc.

To Malthusians and doctrinaire adherents to the tenets of laissez-faire any system of poor relief appeared theoretically un-

[6] Great Britain Parliament, House of Commons, Select Committee on Emigration, *Second and Third Reports from the Select Committee on Emigration from the United Kingdom: 1827* (London, 1828), p. 15.

Horton, the chairman of the committee, asked Malthus: "Are you of opinion . . . that that law which applies to commodities, and which is a matter of notoriety in every market in the country, namely, that a small excess of supply deteriorates the value of an article, applies completely and conclusively to labour, which is the article a poor man has to bring to market?" Malthus replied: "Certainly it does" (*ibid.*, p. 315).

The report pronounced: "It is not to be expected that the capitalist will purchase the commodity, labour, which he requires, at a higher price than the market price" (*ibid.*, p. 15).

[7] *Ibid.*

[8] Major Torrens declared in 1817: "That the poor rate in England, advancing as it does, at a perpetually accelerating pace, and threatening in its ultimate progress, to absorb the whole rental of the country, is an enormous and insupportable evil, seems now to be universally acknowledged" ("A Paper on the Means of Reducing the Poor Rates," *Pamphleteer*, X [1817], 510).

Another writer maintained: "It must also be borne in mind, that if no efforts be made to subvert the present allowance system, by providing an outlet for the surplus labourers, the charge on their account will, from the natural progress of the evil, go on regularly increasing, until it swallows up the whole net revenue of the country" ("Causes and Cures of Disturbances and Pauperism," *Edinburgh Review*, LIII [1831], 55).

G. Poulett Scrope similarly spoke of the "madness of continuing to support these persons in idleness. . ." (*Principles of Political Economy* [London, 1833], p. 334).

sound and practically mischievous. They thought that poverty is the inevitable consequence of demographic growth. Any system of doling out relief only served to prevent the establishment of a state of equilibrium between population and means of subsistence, and thus perpetuated pauperism.[9] Moreover, as experience had proved, the particular features of the English system of poor relief had occasioned the increasing pauperization of rural England.[10]

Bad as conditions were in England and Scotland, they were considerably worse in Ireland, even though Irish emigration to England had a tendency to equalize conditions in both countries. Asked by Horton what he considered to be the effect of the rapid increase of the Irish people on the condition of the English working class, Malthus replied: "I think that the effect will be most fatal to the happiness of the labouring classes in England, because there will be a constant and increasing emigration from Ireland to England, which will tend to lower wages of labour in England, and to prevent the good effects arising from the superior prudence of the labouring classes in this country."[11] This realization explains why English writers were concerned equally over the plight of Ireland and England.

The pressing character of the problem naturally led to a feverish, and sometimes frantic,[12] search for adequate remedies. Few advocated a policy of complete laissez-faire.[13] To the majority of

[9] In the course of the hearings of the House Committee on Emigration Horton asked Malthus: "If a system of emigration could be adopted . . . do you think that it might justify the enactment of a positive law, removing all claim upon the part of an able-bodied pauper for assistance. . .?" Malthus replied: "As I should say so independently of the question of emigration, I must say so still more strongly when coupled with the remedy proposed" (*Second and Third Reports from the Select Committee on Emigration*, p. 315). See also, Malthus' opposition to the introduction of a system of poor relief into Ireland (*ibid.*, p. 313).

[10] Between 1795 and 1834 the system of English poor relief was that of the Speenhamland Act which provided for the famous poor-rate in aid of wages paid out of parish rates. Aside from its other undesirable effects it accelerated the appalling increase of English population. See on this, G. M. Trevelyan, *British History in the Nineteenth Century* (4th ed.; London, 1923), pp. 148 ff.

[11] *Second and Third Reports from the Select Committee on Emigration*, p. 312.

[12] Some people apparently even discussed the virtues of infanticide as a means of diminishing the birth-rate. See Francis Place, *Illustrations and Proofs of the Principles of Population* (London, 1822), p. 173.

[13] Thomas Chalmers may be named as an example. He opposed emigration, home colonization, and poor law alike as only serving to multiply population and misery. While it is the task of government to administer justice, he thought, humanitarianism was outside its province of action (*Christian and Economic*

observers and reformers, the basic approach to the problem seemed plain. Horton declared "that, to remedy such evils, either more labour must be demanded, or less labour supplied; and that, unless one or other of these conditions can be satisfied, the evil is without remedy."[14] It seemed obvious "that there do not appear to be any natural and unforced means of profitably increasing the demand for labour in the United Kingdom to such an extent as to absorb the existing redundancy of the supply of labour."[15]

Some proposals were designed to effect, ultimately, a reduction of the supply of labour by a diminution of the birth-rate. Francis Place and a few intrepid reformers advocated the practice of birth-control by means of contraceptives.[16] But, for reasons already explained, this suggestion was ill-received and its adoption would have necessitated an educational campaign of no mean proportions. Much more popular, among the advisers, was the Malthusian proposal of exhorting the pauper population to exercise "moral restraint." However, while some authors condemned this suggestion outright,[17] the majority of writers agreed that, though fundamentally desirable and beneficent, this method was bound to work very slowly and that its spread presupposed a much higher standard of living than that prevailing among the poor of Great Britain. Thus, in the case of Ireland, Malthus himself admitted that this solution "would be a work of great time, and probably of great suffering, if it were accomplished," and he remarked that he "should not expect it to be accomplished without emigration."[18]

Polity [London, 1821], Preface, p. viii). For a censure of such extreme views see John Wade, *History of the Middle and Working Classes* (2d ed.; London, 1834).

[14]Sir R. W. Horton, *Lectures on Statistics and Political Economy* (London, 1832), Correspondence, pp. 10 f.

[15]*Ibid.*, p. 11.

[16]Place, *Illustrations and Proofs of the Principles of Population* (1822), p. 165.

[17]One writer asked indignantly: ". . . are we to suppose that the Almighty, whose arrangements excite our utter astonishment and unbounded admiration . . . are we to suppose, I ask, that the incomprehensible Author of all these wonders has erred in that law by which the world is peopled?" (Colonel Charles J. Napier, *Colonization* [London, 1835], p. 9).

Another author observed: ". . . that when prudent marriages commonly mean marriages unnaturally deferred, society must be in a state not favourable to virtue or to happiness. . . . The amount of the evil is itself one reason why it cannot thus alone be remedied" ("Colonization," *Edinburgh Review*, XCI [1850], 8).

[18]*Second and Third Reports from the Select Committee on Emigration*, p. 319. Similarly: "It may be right to say, that prudence is the only remedy for an excessive population. . . . We believe that these precepts have begun to have

Malthus also agreed that in order to make the poor susceptible to this argument, it was necessary to raise "their respectability" and to inspire "them with a taste for comforts for a short time by the removal of the redundant population."[19] Another author confirmed this observation: "This is an important truth ... that a certain degree of advancement in physical comfort, a clear separation from the confines of penury, is a necessary condition of that exercise of moral restraint, which is the only ultimate security for a more happy state of human society."[20] Similarly: "The prudential check, as recommended, supposes a high standard of life: while one effect of our large population is, that we sink to a low one."[21]

If the prudential check could work but slowly and if its widespread practice presupposed a higher standard of living, then this method could at best be a subsidiary one. Also, once a sound equilibrium of productive resources and population had been achieved in some other way, at least temporarily, the prudential check could be hoped to perpetuate the balance. Malthus, therefore, advocated emigration as an immediate and preliminary remedy.

Other writers rejected the method of the prudential check altogether because emigration appeared to them as a fully adequate solution. Patrick Matthews wrote: "The prudential check, from which so much has been expected, is but an irksome and unnatural palliative, scarcely preferable to the natural destructive check in itself. While two-thirds of the world are lying waste, and the other third very imperfectly cultivated, it is yet rather premature to speak of preventive or destructive checks—wars, nunneries, infanticide, single blessedness—the latter recommended as preferable by political economists, may be left to their own especial practice."[22]

One further alternative created much agitation. Instead of reducing the redundancy of the labouring population through the indirect means of diminishing the birth-rate, other proposals

---

some influence, and they will ultimately produce more and more benefit: but it is perfectly certain that they have not hitherto been nearly effective enough to promise immediate relief...." ("Third Emigration Report," *Westminster Review*, IX [1827-8], 116 f.).

[19]*Ibid.*, p. 325.
[20]"Third Emigration Report," p. 118.
[21]"Colonization," p. 8.
[22]Patrick Matthews, *Emigration Fields* (London, 1839), p. 7. Similarly, Scrope, *Principles of Political Economy* (1833), pp. 269 ff.

envisaged the possibility of providing work for the unemployed in Great Britain. The most important one of these demanded extensive projects for home colonization or a land reform for the purpose of breaking up the large landed estates. The following is a typical proposal of the former kind. "What is the remedy? Emigration—emigration to the uncultivated wastes and unreclaimed bogs of Great Britain and Ireland. This is the species of emigration which we think it necessary at present to advocate. Here is an inexhaustible field—here Nature offers us, at our own doors, a mine of wealth which, if properly worked, would furnish profitable employment for millions."[23] James Gratton said in the House of Commons in 1828: "If proper means were taken, there would not be a man too many in Ireland. While in that country there were three millions of acres of reclaimable land, it was too much to be told that there was a superabundant population. The true way to benefit Ireland was, to compel the landlords to improve the condition of the tenantry."[24]

However, the majority of writers, not to speak of Parliament, were opposed to such projects. Thus, the *Report of the Select Committee on Emigration* of 1827 stated:

Your Committee are fully aware that if it could be demonstrated ... that £1.140.000, or any greater or less sum, could be employed in any part of the mother country, with the presumption of an equal amount of wealth being produced ... as in the case of Emigration ... a very strong argument might be raised against the expediency of Emigration. But the opinions to be derived from the very extensive evidence taken before your Committee, in which the subject of cultivating the waste lands of the mother country has been fully considered, are conclusively in favour of the profit to be

---

[23]"Cultivation of Waste Lands," *Quarterly Review*, XXXVIII (1828), 411. In continuation of his proposal the writer of this article denounced the "whimsical theories" of those political economists "of the Cockney school" who asserted that it would be uneconomical to cultivate Britain's waste lands. He also belittled the alleged fertility of the soil in the colonies. Cf. *ibid.*, pp. 416, 435 ff.

[24]*Hansard*, sec. ser., XIX, c. 1510. In the late forties demands for land reform became particularly persistent. According to the general tenor of these demands the country would be benefited generally and labour redundance decimated by creating a nation of independent yeomen. For a critical discussion of these projects see "Freehold Assurance and Colonisation," *Westminster and Foreign Quarterly Review*, LI (1849), 408-19; "Colonization," p. 9.

See also the sweeping proposal advanced by Sidney Smith, *The Mother Country* (London, 1849), pp. 5 ff., *passim*. Smith asserted that "there are no fewer than 15,000,000 acres capable of improvement, which are at present lying about waste" (*ibid.*, p. 5). He wanted a people of free peasant proprietors and thought that his plan could be easily realized by instituting complete "free trade in the soil" (*ibid.*, pp. 34, 47).

derived from the employment of capital in the cultivation of the fertile lands of the Colonies, as compared with the unproductive appropriation of capital at home in the employment of these paupers.[25]

In agreement with Ricardo's theory of differential rent (law of diminishing returns), political economists held that progressively less fertile lands were being cultivated in Britain as the population and the demand for foodstuffs increased. Discussing the proposal for domestic colonization, one writer stated succinctly: "The answer is—That by an excess of population in any country, is meant, not an excess relatively to land, but an excess relatively to the means of productive employment. . . . By this test, although it be true that there is much land within this empire which remains uncultivated, it is as unquestionably true, that the population is excessive."[26] The effectuation of free trade was suggested as another alternative to emigration with the view of solving the "condition-of-England question." This proposal will be discussed later for it was only in the late thirties that it came to be propagated with vigour and success.

Obviously, to a nation possessing vast and expanding colonies, the idea of transferring the demographic "surplus" to an underpopulated part of the Empire must have appeared particularly intriguing. It appealed to the common sense of at least those who were not themselves prospective emigrants. It seemed a "natural" solution. The huge tracts of uncultivated or little-cultivated lands in the colonies seemed to beckon the "able-bodied pauper" in the mother country. Indeed, these areas appeared as the preserves provided by the Lord for the suffering peoples of Great Britain.

The following quotations are given as samples of this attitude. Grahame wrote: "Emigration . . . is the natural vent and remedy of redundance of population in the early stages of society, and indeed in every period, until the whole habitable world be fully peopled and cultivated. A remedy somewhat different might be

[25] *Second and Third Reports from the Select Committee on Emigration*, p. 40. Similarly, Horton, *Lectures* (1832), IV, 16 f.

[26] "Emigration Report," *Westminster Review*, VI (1826), 342. Torrens said in the House of Commons in 1827: "He need not remind any hon. gentleman who was conversant with these matters, that when double capital was applied to land, it would not always give a double result. There was a point at which, after repeated applications of capital to a farm, any succeeding applications of capital could not be successfully made. . ." (*Hansard*, sec. ser., XVI, c. 493. See also, R. Torrens, *Colonization of South Australia* [2d ed.; London, 1836], pp. 249 ff.; Arthur Mills, *Systematic Colonization* [London, 1847], pp. 8 f.).

necessary when the ultimate period of the total replenishment and complete cultivation of the earth had arrived."[27] Similarly, Lord Durham stated in his famous report: "The . . . country which has founded and maintained these Colonies at a vast expense of blood and treasure, may justly expect its compensation in turning their unappropriated resources to the account of its own redundant population; they are the rightful patrimony of the English people, ample appanage which God and Nature have set aside in the New World for those whose lot has assigned them but insufficient portions in the Old."[28] Extolling the advantages of emigration, Laing remarked: "Nor can it be well doubted that it is in a wise co-operation with these great designs of Providence that we are most likely to find a solution of our social difficulties, and relief from the evils which oppress us."[29]

Before discussing the various arguments brought forward in support of emigration, it is necessary to point to a contemporary ambiguity of language-usage. Theoretically speaking, there is of course a fundamental difference between emigration and colonization. Some English theorists and politicians, as will be seen, advocated emigration to the exclusion of colonization while others were opposed to emigration except to the British colonies. The majority of them, however, used the two terms interchangeably or spoke of emigration when they actually meant colonization.[30] It may be said that during the period characterized by the Hortonist trend of thought, the use of the word "emigration" covered both emigration to the United States and emigration to the British colonies. As long as the chief objective was simply that of ridding the country of its redundant labour, the destination of the emigrants did not make much difference. It should be added, however, that the majority of writers and politicians had a more or less definite preference for emigration to the colonies.

In its most simple form the case for emigration was put as follows: "Whenever population is redundant and the wages of labour depressed, every facility ought to be given to emigration.

[27]James Grahame, *An Inquiry into the Principle of Population* (Edinburgh, 1816), p. 104.

[28]Sir C. P. Lucas (ed.), *Lord Durham's Report on the Affairs of British North America* (Oxford, 1912), II, 13.

[29]Samuel Laing, *National Distress* (London, 1844), p. 121.

[30]John Wade, for example, wrote: "I shall submit a few brief observations on each [objection], bearing in mind that a systematic plan of colonization is meant, though the term emigration is used" (*History of the Middle and Working Classes* [1834], p. 340).

Were it carried to a considerable extent, it would have the effect, by lessening the supply of labour in the market, to raise the rate of wages, and to improve the condition of the labourers who remain at home."[31] In summary, the thesis of this school ran as follows: Britain (including Ireland) is over-populated; hence the supply of labour is in excess of demand and low wage rates and pauperism are the consequences. The colonies and the United States, on the other hand, are under-populated; there demand for labour is in excess of supply; hence wages are high and the people prosperous. Disregarding the cost of transferring labour from where it is superabundant to where it is relatively scarce, such a transfer will be advantageous to both the emigrants and to those remaining in the over-populated country as long as wage rates in the two areas are not equal. Thus, Scrope expounded that "the comparative rate of wages is the true test of the advantages of Emigration, and the expediency of giving that direction to our efforts for the relief of the poor."[32]

According to the Horton school of thought, the diminution of the supply of labour by means of emigration "upon an extended scale, to our colonial possessions, if regulated and assisted . . . presents an immediate, certain, humane, and specific remedy for the evil in question."[33] Horton was strictly opposed to the emigration of skilled workers unless, due to the introduction of machinery, their skill had become useless.[34] The subjects of emigration were supposed to be paupers.

To raise wage rates and to remove pauperism were the principal but not the only benefits expected from emigration. Aside from some minor expectations,[35] it was hoped that by solving, through

---

[31]"Restraints on Emigration, &c.," *Edinburgh Review*, XXXIX (1823-4), 342.

[32]G. Poulett Scrope, *Extracts of Letters from Persons Who Emigrated Last Year to Canada and the United States* (2d ed.; London, 1832), Preface, p. v.

[33]Horton, *Lectures* (1832), Correspondence, p. 11.

[34]*Ibid.*, II, 12.

[35]For example, large-scale emigration to Canada was favoured by some observers because they assumed that an influx of Englishmen into those colonies would constitute a safeguard against their being engulfed by the United States. In 1827, Henry Bright said in the House of Commons: "He thought Canada one of the bulwarks of the empire, and it was of the greatest possible moment that she should be adequately colonized and supported, if we meant to protect ourselves in our American possessions, or wished to defend them from encroachment" (*Hansard*, sec. ser., XVI, c. 496). Similarly, Lord Elgin wrote to Grey in 1848: "Climate and contiguity point out Canada as the most natural resort for the surplus population of England and Ireland, and I am convinced that filling up the back settlements of the Province with resident agriculturists

emigration, the condition-of-England question, the dangers of social unrest, political discontentment, and national disintegration would be minimized. In this sense, emigration was supposed to serve as a political safety-valve for the nation. Torrens wrote as early as 1817:

For the immediate relief of actual distress there remains no remedy, except an extension of colonization. . . . While the glut of hands was thus removed from the labour market, and while those who remained received, in consequence, a rate of wages adequate to their support, want would cease to engender the desire of change; the ideas of relief and of revolution would lose their fatal connexion in the minds of the multitude . . . a well-regulated system of colonization acts as a safety-valve to the political machine, and allows the expanding vapour to escape, before it is heated to explosion.[36]

With the growing power of Chartism, the fear of revolutionary upheavals mounted and became an increasingly powerful incentive to the promotion of the cause of emigration and colonization. William S. O'Brien told the House of Commons in 1840: "that, inasmuch as popular discontents have, at all times, and among all nations, originated, for the most part, in the physical privations of the mass of population; in so far as we are enabled, by colonisation, to diminish and mitigate these privations, to such an extent do we obtain a new guarantee for the preservation of peace and order in the community."[37] Charles Buller maintained that it was the constant swelling of population "up to the very brim of the cup that is the permanent cause of uneasiness and danger in this country."[38] "If you mean to uphold and transmit to your children those institutions through which you have enjoyed at once the blessings of freedom and order: if you hope to escape the tremendous wrath of a people whom force will vainly attempt to restrain," Buller asserted, then colonization is the only adequate remedy.[39]

furnishes the only possible chance of preventing Canada from becoming a State of the Union" (Sir A. G. Doughty [ed.], *The Elgin-Grey Papers, 1846-1852* [Ottawa, 1937], I, 183).

Others opposed this idea. One writer remarked: "We lay little stress on political influence, because the idea of balancing the power of the United States by a thread of population stretched along the immense Canadian frontier, can scarcely be seriously maintained. The growing circle of American Independence must speedily include every relic of European power in the Transatlantic hemisphere" ("Emigration," *Edinburgh Review*, XLVII [1828], 206).

[36]"A Paper on the Means of Reducing the Poor Rates," p. 524; similarly, N. W. Senior, *Remarks on Emigration* (London, 1831), pp. 4 f.

[37]*Hansard*, third ser., LIV, cs. 833 f.

[38]Speech in the House of Commons in April, 1843, reprinted in Edward Gibbon Wakefield, *A View of the Art of Colonization* (London, 1849), p. 465.

[39]*Ibid.*, pp. 470 f. Similarly, Wakefield, *Art of Colonization*, pp. 68-73.

In 1850, i.e., after the repeal of the Corn Laws and obviously under the influence of the revolutions of 1848-9 on the Continent, the *Edinburgh Review* attributed the ubiquity of political unrest and revolutionary movements in Western Europe to the evils arising from demographic congestion: "But it is not only when we contemplate English and Irish pauperism, that we are reminded of the dangers arising from the pressure of population on the means of subsistence. Those dangers are illustrated by the condition of half Europe at the present day."[40] The reviewer did not deny the existence of other causes.

But all other evil influences assuredly were aggravated by that chronic discontent which gives plausibility even to such agitators as the Red Republicans of Paris, and to such philosophers as her Socialists. . . . For so terrible an excitement there must have been predisposing causes; and the chief, we may assume, was the galling uneasiness which frets a population too closely packed to find an easy subsistence. In the United States and in Russia, two countries with few points of resemblance, there is one thing in common— a territory sufficient for all; and in each there is a common absence of those signs which forbode a social war.[41]

Filled with Malthusian pessimism this author noted a direct relationship between demographic density and political and social unrest. Excessive population, in making pauperism inevitable, was viewed as a disintegrative factor operating within the social body.

We have remarked that, in comparison with yet greater calamities, a disproportionate importance has sometimes been attached to the political evils of pauperism. And yet the most important of them has seldom been regarded. We allude to the decay of Patriotism. Insubordination and discontent are dangers which at least admit of being distinctly scanned, if not permanently repressed. A decline in the patriotic sentiment is an injury more dangerous because more insidious. . . . Morally, a man is attached to his country by the benefits she has conferred on him . . . and by the fact, that it is in and through her that Providence has bestowed upon him his place in universal being, here and hereafter. But what benefit has his country bestowed on the Pauper? She feeds him,—and loathes him. . . . What cause has he to be grateful to her for the part which she has given him in existence?[42]

Emigration and colonization also would lessen the frequent perpetration of crimes in the home country.[43] Finally, some

---

[40]"Colonization," p. 3.
[41]*Ibid.* [42]*Ibid.*, pp. 6 f.
[43]One writer stated: "In a moral point of view let us look at emigration as a means to prevent or lessen crime. It is a truth that no one will attempt to deny, that poverty tempts a man to do that which in its absence he would not dream of doing. . ." (C. H., *Letters on Emigration* [London, 1841], p. 21).

writers who were opposed to the adoption of such an alternative measure as the introduction of free trade, claimed that emigration was a remedy that benefited everyone and hurt no one.[44]

It has been shown what general benefits were expected from emigration. Some writers praised it as a perfect panacea.[45] Many claimed that it would afford relief immediately. Torrens asserted: "For the immediate relief of actual distress there remains no remedy, except an extension of colonization. This would produce an instantaneous and almost magical effect. . . ."[46] Similarly, the Bishop of Limerick said in 1826: "The evil is pressing and immediate. It calls, therefore, for an immediate remedy. Take a system of home relief, it must be gradual in its operation. . . . Now, Emigration is an instantaneous relief, it is what bleeding would be to an apoplectic patient."[47] Because emigration was supposed to result in immediate relief, some writers, especially in the forties, accepted this remedy as a short-run policy, designed to serve as a palliative in the case of transient business depressions. G. R. Porter, for instance, wrote: "In every country which is making any considerable progress in the arts of life, changes will from time to time occur in the sources of employment for particular classes of people, which must be felt as a hardship by individuals, although to the country at large they are productive of great and permanent good. . . . It can scarcely be doubted that in this and similar cases, a well-digested plan of emigration . . . might be rendered efficacious to palliate the evil."[48]

[44]"In almost every proposition for establishing a change, no matter what the object be, there is almost sure to be found some class interest—a seed ever sure to bring forth opposition. With emigration it is far different. Where is the interest to be affected by establishing a system of emigration? There is no agricultural interest likely to be destroyed as in the Corn Law question. No West Indian possession to be perilled, as by the Sugar Duties question. No Colonial interest to be sacrificed, as in the Timber Duties question. Look at it on all points, and the question of Emigration is one, that if adopted, will raise less class interested opponents than any other" (*ibid.*, p. 20).

[45]For such a view see, for example, "The Cape of Good Hope," *Quarterly Review*, XXII (1819-20), 203 f. In a speech addressed to the first colonists who left England for New Zealand in 1839, Archibald Alison said: ". . . in the steady considerations of these, and the persevering encouragement of enterprises such as the present, is to be found the means of obviating all our difficulties,—the sheet-anchor of the British Empire" (Archibald Alison, *Essays, Political, Historical, and Miscellaneous* [Edinburgh, 1850], II, 660).

[46]"A Paper on the Means of Reducing the Poor Rates," p. 524.

[47]Quoted in Johnson, *History of Emigration from the United Kingdom to North America*, p. 17.

[48]G. R. Porter, *The Progress of the Nation* (London, 1851), p. 127.

The value of emigration as a means of relieving Britain of her surplus population was questioned by many competent observers. Nassau Senior remarked:

> If any European nation could hope to make emigration a complete substitute for prudence, that hope might be entertained by the inhabitants of the British Islands. We have the command of unoccupied continents in each hemisphere, the largest navy that the world ever saw to convey us to them, the largest capital that ever has been accumulated, to defray the expense, and a population remarkable not merely for enterprise, but for enterprise of this particular description. These advantages we have enjoyed for centuries. . . . And yet during this long period how little effect has emigration produced on our numbers! The swarms which we have sent out, and which we now send out, seem to be instantaneously replaced.[49]

At the end of this passage Senior alluded to what might be called the "vacuum-theory" of emigration. Indeed, this theory proved to be one of the strongest counter-arguments advanced against the proponents of emigration. According to this point of view, any gap created by emigration only acted as a stimulus to further population growth and was thus effaced again in short order. Laing said: "Even supposing emigration on a large scale to be practicable, it is certain that, unless combined with other measures by which the standard of the home population was permanently raised, the vacuum created would be speedily filled up, and the redundancy of unemployed labour be as great as ever."[50] Joseph Hume was of the opinion that the "void" created by the volume of emigration in one year "would be made up in three years."[51] Merivale concluded:

> The truth then appears to be this, that in a natural state of the things, and leaving wholly out of view any excess of population above the means of employment which bad laws or political circumstances may produce, emigration is no remedy for over-population unless it be continually repeated; which, on a really great scale, is scarcely likely to happen in any country. Any single emigration, however large, can have no permanent effect in checking the undue increase of numbers unless it be followed either by increased forethought, or by an increase in the productiveness of labour. . . .[52]

Thus, Merivale pointed out that if large-scale emigration does not take place continually, it will have no permanent effect unless,

[49] N. W. Senior, *An Outline of the Science of Political Economy* (Library of Economics no. 1; London, 1938), p. 41. Senior supported emigration but held that it would operate in itself neither as an adequate nor as a complete check to population growth (*ibid.*).

[50] *National Distress* (1844), p. 130.

[51] *Hansard*, sec. ser., XVI, c. 509.

[52] *Lectures* (1841), p. 140.

during the period elapsing between the creation and the absorption of the vacuum, other means or events have begun to exert a restraining influence on population growth. Malthus apparently hoped that the intervening period would be long enough to give an opportunity to prudential restraint as a check on the birth-rate. Malthus also proposed a method by which the filling up of the void could be prevented. During the hearings held by the Emigration Committee in 1827, Horton asked him: "Supposing that by any system of emigration an immediate reduction of the population of Ireland to the extent of half a million could be effected, do you not think that there is in the existing order of things in that country a tendency immediately to fill up that vacuum?"[53] Malthus replied: "There is always a natural tendency towards the filling up of a vacuum; but if the landlords in Ireland were making a change in the management of their estates, and were altering the distribution of their land, I think it is possible that the vacuum might not be filled up, because those miserable hovels that had been deserted might be pulled down and not be replaced."[54] Horton propagated this proposal and advised in the case of Ireland, "the destruction of the cottages when the parties were removed from them."[55] Other observers parried the argument of the vacuum-theory by pointing out that this theory was hardly applicable if the emigrants left their country at an early age. Thus, William S. O'Brien, Irish M.P., declared in 1840: "But it is not, even theoretically, true, that the vacuum created by the annual removal of a given number of the population, would, of necessity, be speedily filled up. The correctness of this position depends entirely upon the age of the persons who emigrate."[56]

Another argument brought forward against emigration was that either quantitatively or qualitatively that policy deprived the home country of valuable portions of its population. There were few who stressed the quantitative aspect, but many asserted that the emigrants were either small capital-owners or, on the

[53] *Second and Third Reports from the Select Committee on Emigration* (1828), p. 313.

[54] *Ibid.* See also, *ibid.*, p. 315.

[55] *Hansard*, sec. ser., XVIII, c. 1550. Similarly, Robert Torrens, *The Budget* (London, 1841), pp. 125 f. For a statement, by G. Knight, to the effect that the intervening period would raise the living standard of the people remaining in Ireland enough to make them realize the benefits of "foresight or providence," see *Hansard*, third ser., LXVIII, cs. 540 f.

[56] *Hansard*, third ser., LIV, c. 851.

average, physically more fit and occupationally more skilled than those who remained behind. Laing maintained:

Even if the amount of emigration under the system of private enterprise was vastly greater, it would still be of very limited use as a means of relieving the mother country, for this obvious reason, that the class of emigrants will always be taken from the very part of the population whom it would be desirable to retain.... Under the present system, the bulk of the emigrants proceeding to Australia, and a large portion of those going to Canada, will always be persons possessing some capital, or capable of earning higher wages if they had remained at home.... It is even a serious question, whether the rapid increase in the relative amount of destitution, during the last ten or fifteen years, may not have been partly occasioned by the constant drain of the best and most energetic portion of the population....[57]

Merivale likewise stated: "Another reason against the practicability of very extensive emigration is to be found in the fact that those persons who are desirable as emigrants, are precisely those best able to find employment at home in difficult times—the young, industrious and well-conducted."[58] S. Crawford, Irish M.P., declared in 1843: "It was said, that young men and women were wanted abroad. Why, that was just the class we required at home. If the young and industrious were taken away, what was to become of those who were left behind? For his part, he should be by no means obliged to the hon. Member [Buller] for introducing a system of colonization which left us only the idle and infirm. Let it be remembered, that for every strong man we expatriated, we expatriated so much national wealth."[59]

No doubt, the strongest argument against any scheme of large-scale emigration related to the expense and to the outflow of capital that its execution necessitated. Regarding the item of expense, Merivale wrote:

There is no reasonable probability of this country ever submitting—as no country has ever yet submitted—to the enormous expense which would be required to carry any really great experiment of emigration into effect.

---

[57] *National Distress* (1844), p. 127.

[58] *Lectures* (1841), I, 152.

[59] *Hansard*, third ser., LXVIII, cs. 537 f. The three sample statements presented above were all uttered in the forties. This is quite natural because they were largely based on observations derived from experience. Horton and Malthus had thought in terms of able-bodied paupers when they propagated the cause of emigration, but their arguments were based on the assumption of a state-directed policy of emigration. Even in the twenties there were many observers who advanced the argument presently under consideration. See, for example, the parliamentary debate on Horton's scheme in June, 1828: *ibid.*, sec. ser., cs. 1510-12.

And, as I have noticed on a former occasion, the cost of extensive emigration is by no means fairly estimated by merely multiplying the expense now incurred in conveying small parties by the proposed number of emigrants. The expense of shipping, of seamen, of location in the colony, all these, and probably many other items, must, it should seem, of necessity augment in a greater ratio, in consequence of the greatly augmented demand.[60]

As to the loss of capital involved in emigration and colonization, Joseph Hume said:

... that to employ 20,000,000l. in carrying to a foreign country one out of every eighteen members of our population, was a wasteful employment of the public capital. ... The practical result of this project might be, to send away beggars from England, to make beggars of those who remained behind; for what other result could follow from sending 20,000,000l. out of the country, which, if left in, would be expended in some way or other among the working classes? Employment must always be in proportion to capital, and when so much floating capital was withdrawn from circulation, a proportionate quantity of employment must be withdrawn from the labouring part of the community. From all the information which he had been able to obtain, he was convinced that this project would, both immediately and ultimately, be a losing concern to the country.[61]

Accepted by many political economists of the time, this argument was based on the assumption that volume of employment and rates of wages progressed with the increasing accumulation of capital, and *vice versa*.

What were the rebuttals of the proponents of emigration? As regards the expense incurred by the government if it embarked upon a policy of large-scale emigration, the Hortonists, in the first place, proposed that the government or the local parishes, as the case might be, only advance funds which the emigrants would later on repay. Furthermore, they argued that the paupers, if they stayed at home, would have to be supported by the parishes through poor relief. By advancing money to the emigrants, it

[60]*Lectures* (1841), I, 153. Some observers, indeed, suggested that the government might as well give the money to the paupers while they remained in the country. James Gratton declared in 1827: "... that the expense of such a proceeding made it impossible for the country to execute it to any considerable extent. We were called upon to lay out enormous sums for the purpose of sending our population abroad. Would it not be better, in the first instance, to try the cheaper experiment, of making them comfortable at home?" (*Hansard*, sec. ser., XVI, c. 490).

Similarly, Joseph Hume said in 1826: "It never would answer for them to incur the expense of 100 l. for sending a poor man and his family from Ireland to the Canadas. Give the poor man the 100 l., and he would establish himself as comfortable in Ireland as any where else" (*ibid.*, XIV, c. 1364).

[61]*Ibid.*, XVI, cs. 509 f.

was claimed, the parish would be spared future outlays for relief. Thus, Horton explained: "The chief objection was, that any plan of emigration would be expensive, and that the finances of the country were not in a condition to bear the advances necessary for that purpose. He denied it would cost anything; for he considered it would cost nothing, if it involved the repayment of the advance.... He undertook to prove, that the maintenance of the labourers and their families, whose labour was not in demand in this country, was a direct tax on the community at large."[62] Archbishop Whately wrote: "... there are cases in which that mode of relief might be suggested by the wisest economy, even when the immediate support of the individuals in question might cost less at home: if, at a somewhat heavier expense, we have a fair prospect of getting rid of a permanent, and perhaps a growing burden...."[63] John Wade remarked: "... as to expense. To advance twenty or thirty pounds to remove an unemployed labourer, looks a great sum, but what is it to the expense of his permanent maintenance."[64] Another writer stated: "What price ... would be considered too great for it? Millions might be well laid out in its purchase; since, viewed only in a pecuniary light, the increased trade and business of all kinds that would follow from it, and the savings it would occasion in poor-rate, in the cost of crime, and in the cost of police armed and unarmed, would be worth many and many a million to the nation."[65]

Apart from arguments such as that emigration even on a large scale was a paying proposition or involved nothing but a lending-transaction, other writers maintained that the magnitude of destitution and distress among the pauperized population justified pecuniary sacrifices. Malthus said that emigration was "one of the cases in which ... a government is called upon to make a great pecuniary sacrifice."[66] Poulett Scrope complained: "While twenty millions are unhesitatingly offered for the promised redemption from slavery of the West Indian negroes, it is pitiable to see the same government scruple to lay out as many thousands in

[62]*Hansard*, sec. ser., XVIII, cs. 1549 f. See also, Torrens, "A Paper on the Means of Reducing the Poor Rates," p. 521.

[63]Richard Whately, "Emigration to Canada," *Quarterly Review*, XXIII (1820), 388.

[64]*History of the Middle and Working Classes* (1834), p. 342.

[65]"Emigration—Letters from Canada," *Quarterly Review*, LIV (1835), 418.

[66]*Second and Third Reports from the Select Committee on Emigration* (1828), p. 319.

promoting the liberation of the native poor of this island from a state of degradation and wretchedness, little, if at all, inferior to that of the slaves themselves."[67] Torrens claimed: "Let us consider for a moment the value of the benefits which Emigration is calculated to confer, and the magnitude of the evil which it would effectually remove. The condition of Ireland is appalling. Will any one venture to name the sum which, in his estimation, it would be inexpedient to expend in effectually relieving this frightful misery...."[68] And Arthur Mills argued:

... I am nevertheless assured that, if the only object of Great Britain were to rid herself of burdensome responsibilities at the lightest possible rate of cost, and to accept the lowest tender which the philanthropist or the political economist could offer for her relief, systematic colonization would win the preference of those whose first object is retrenchment; and that no schemes ... which shall have for their professed object the palliation of our social evils, or the enduring interests of the labouring classes, and which shall choose for their scene of action public undertakings at home of admitted importance, or the morasses and inferior soils of the British Islands, will ever accomplish, at lower cost, happier results than may be reasonably anticipated from a well-ordered system of colonization.[69]

Horton agreed with the position taken by the majority of economists as to the apprehensions over the outflow of capital occasioned by large-scale emigration. He claimed

that, looking at the proposed remedy simply as a measure of national policy, it would be objectionable, unless it could be satisfactorily proved, that the total expense of removing the redundant labourers by Emigration would be less than the expense which must inevitably be incurred for maintaining them at home at the cheapest possible rate.... That, were not this the case, the funds for the employment of labour, upon which the prosperity of the labouring classes so much depends, would be diminished by the application of the proposed remedy. In reference, therefore, to National Wealth, if the expense of Emigration be less than the expense of Home-maintenance, there would be a decided economy, instead of an apparent expense, in the application of National Capital to the purposes of regulated and assisted Emigration.[70]

Thus, whether emigration would drain the capital fund of the home country did not involve a question of principle but of fact.

Other proponents of emigration, for example, Archbishop Whately, maintained that:

[67] *Principles of Political Economy* (1833), p. 337.
[68] *The Budget* (1841), p. 132.
[69] *Systematic Colonization* (1847), p. 7.
[70] *Lectures* (1832), pp. 11 f.

As for the apprehensions of impoverishment to this country by the transfer of her capital to the other side of the Atlantic, we are convinced that they are altogether visionary . . . whatever opinion may be entertained respecting this loss of capital, it is quite certain that men will transfer it from one country, or one employment, to another, when they find their advantage in so doing, it should be the object of the politician to direct that stream which it would not be possible, even were it desirable, to dam up. We would be the last to encourage an illiberal jealousy of the United States, or to grudge them the advantages they may derive from this country; but it is not going too far to feel a preference, at least, for our own colonies. . . .[71]

Whately here came rather close to saying that Great Britain possessed excess capital which could not be prevented from flowing to investment-areas where more remunerative returns could be expected than at home, and that, under these circumstances, it would be desirable to canalize this natural flow into the direction of the colonies. Whately also presented a third argument that was to become very potent in the thirties and forties. "Lastly, it should be remembered that a commercial country, like this, should not consider all the capital carried out of it as so much loss: the market for our commodities, which is afforded by a flourishing and increasing colony, is a source of wealth to the mother country far exceeding probably what would have been produced by the amount of capital bestowed on it, if retained at home."[72]

The question of expense and capital drain assumed an entirely different complexion after Wakefield had worked out his plan of scientific colonization. As will be described later, this scheme put large-scale emigration and colonization on a self-supporting basis involving only loans on the part of the government.[73] Furthermore, the Wakefield group of colonial reformers maintained that Great Britain suffered not only from a redundancy of population but also from a plethora of capital. The existence of this state of affairs being granted, the diminution of the country's capital fund through emigration became an advantage in itself.

As regards the role which the state was supposed to play in support of emigration schemes, there were few people who advocated compulsory emigration.[74] On the other hand, only extreme

[71]"Emigration to Canada," pp. 388 f.
[72]Ibid., p. 389.
[73]See Charles Buller's Speech of 1843 in Wakefield, Art of Colonization, pp. 482 ff.; Torrens, The Budget (1841), pp. 133 ff.; John Stuart Mill, Principles of Political Economy, ed. Sir W. J. Ashley (new impression; London, 1936), pp. 740 f., 970 f.
[74]Having offered his plan of emigration, Major Torrens wrote: "It is very unlikely that an offer of this kind would be rejected by persons reduced to a degrading and miserable dependence upon parish support. If, however, the

apostles of laissez-faire and a small minority, utterly suspicious of the intentions of the English governments on political principles, disapproved of state-action in the case of voluntary emigration.[75] Even in the area of voluntary emigration the agenda of state-action might cover a vast multiplicity of points. In the case of emigration proper, the government might disseminate information, arrange for investigatory committees, provide for official supervision of embarkation and sea-voyage, induce parishes to put up the money necessary for the cost of emigration, or themselves allocate funds for that purpose, etc. In the case of colonization in British colonies, the government might enlarge the areas available for settlements, administer the system of land sales, supervise relations between colonists and natives, advance loans to colonial companies, grant tariff preferences for the goods of the colonists, etc. For the purpose of the present study it is hardly necessary to quote contemporaneous statements containing demands for different combinations of all these various forms of government intervention. Suffice it to say that the proponents of large-scale emigration and colonization requested the assistance of the government in a variety of forms[76] and that, by and large, governments and Parliament were utterly reluctant to provide for more than a minimum amount of official assistance.

On the whole the pertinent literature on the subject does not exhibit much solicitude for the lot of the emigrant as an individual. Most writers spoke in an abstract manner of wage rates, excess population, pauperism, etc. Proponents of colonization usually depicted the future habitat and life of the emigrant in the most

---

number of voluntary emigrants should be insufficient to remove the redundant supply of labour, then the legislature might interfere, and enact, that all who married after a given time, and who subsequently, in consequence of the labour market being overstocked, became incapable of maintaining their families at home, should no longer be entitled to parish aid, but in lieu of it, should receive grants of colonial land..." ("A Paper on the Means of Reducing the Poor Rates," p. 521). In July, 1819, Hume remarked in the House of Commons: "Parishes having able-bodied men willing to work, chargeable on them, ought to be called on to subscribe sums towards removing a part of them to this or some other settlement, where their industry might provide them with a comfortable subsistence. He thought that if men under such circumstances were unwilling to emigrate, it might even be advisable to transport them without their consent" (*Hansard*, first ser., XL, c. 1550).

[75]For a representative of the latter group see Archibald Prentice, *A Tour in the United States* (2d ed.; London, 1849), pp. 214 ff.

[76]Some of these solicitations of state-action will be discussed in connection with the Wakefield scheme.

glowing colours. The following is an extreme case of misrepresentation of the colonist's future. "On the Australian cattle runs, in the New Zealand valley, on the Tasmanian green hill, common life is found to be equal in ease, comfort, and enjoyment, to that of the idle rich in the mother country. All are land holders; all may hunt, and shoot, and fish; all may take the world at their leisure, and subsist without effort or anxiety, and live amid the beauties, the bounties, the enjoyment of nature, as only the privileged few can do in Europe."[77] Especially the colonial reformers, few of whom had been to the colonies, surrounded colonization with a halo of romanticism and heroism. Statements to the contrary, such as the following, were relatively rare.

In all cases, under all circumstances, to whatever country, emigration is an immediate and positive evil. . . . It is unnecessary to dwell on the separation, probably for ever, from their nearest relations, and their most valued and affectionate friends. . . . But, besides these, there is the total or partial dislocation of long-established associations and habits. . . . He must expect to live for years, crowded and incommoded, if he has a family, in a very small and inconvenient log-house. . . . These, with bad roads, alike unfavorable to social communication and to traffic; no returns, at first, from the hardest and most incessant labours, not even the plainest necessaries of life. . . .[78]

Another writer warned: "young gentlemen of education and refined tastes, large or moderate fortune, from being induced to settle in any colony by the romantic reasoning of the crimps of systematic colonization, who conjure up a phantasmagoria of 'Greek colonies and sacred fires'. . . . Colonization in the present day is as heroic in its immediate results as cultivating a farm or curing a fever, and that is saying enough."[79]

When the destination of future emigrants was discussed,— the United States or the British colonies—, few writers were prepared to consider their personal happiness.[80] Most publicists were interested in the welfare of Britain, not in that of her emigrating sons. Those authors who were inclined to place the personal interest of the emigrant above that of Great Britain often maintained that his destination should be determined solely on the basis of his individual happiness. Thus, considering the

[77]Sidney Smith, *Whether To Go, and Whither?* (London, 1849), Introduction, p. xiv.
[78]"On Emigration," *Westminster Review*, III (1825), 452 ff.
[79]Samuel Sidney, *The Three Colonies of Australia* (London, 1852), p. 227.
[80]Such, however, was the opinion of Prentice, *A Tour in the United States* (1849), p. 206.

proposition that emigrants ought not to proceed to the United States because, though to their personal advantage, they would become inhabitants of a country rivalling Britain commercially, one writer remarked: "The reply is direct, simple, and conclusive: my sole consideration ought to be my own real interest...."[81] That place ought to be preferred which unites in itself the fewest evils, the shortest duration of those evils, the greatest number of compensations and advantages, and the quickest arrival of those advantages."[82]

Authors who believed that dominion over oversea settlements did not confer any benefit upon the mother country likewise preferred not to have the egress of emigrants directed towards the British colonies as a matter of principle.

The first question is, whether, in the choice of a country, English possessions, merely as such, are entitled to a decided preference? This is, in fact, merely to return to the question of dominion. If colonies, in the modern sense of the word, offer no advantage there exists no reason for increasing their population or number. Thus patriotism and self-interest will not be found to range themselves under different banners. It may, however, happen that these possessions offer advantages in other points of view worthy of consideration, and something also must be allowed to political facilities.[83]

When it became increasingly clear that the majority of British emigrants preferred to go to the United States and found a ready welcome there, some writers argued that an over-populated country did not need colonies for the purpose of providing an outlet for its emigrating nationals.

The boasted advantages of Canada for emigration, hardly deserve a serious refutation. As long as England is over-peopled and Canada under-peopled; —as long as there is too little land in the one, and too much in the other;— emigration is sure to go on with a steady pace, and would go on tomorrow just as rapidly as it has gone on for the last five years, though Canada were an independent country. The only difference would be, that it would then go on without expense to the mother country. In this manner emigration is now going on, and has been going on from the United Kingdom to the United Republics of North America for fifty years.[84]

Similarly:

It appears ... from experience, that dependencies are not necessary to emigration, and it seems doubtful whether they materially promote it. No country possesses dependencies so extensive, and so thinly peopled, as those of England. No country so systematically encourages emigration to those

---

[81]"On Emigration," p. 450.
[82]*Ibid.*, pp. 457 f.
[83]"Emigration," p. 206.
[84]"Affairs of Canada," *Westminster Review*, XXIII (1835), 237.

dependencies. Yet of the 93,501 persons who left the British Islands in 1845, 53,538 emigrated to the United States. There seems no reason for supposing that, if our American and Australian colonies were independent, they would offer less facilities to emigration than they do now.[85]

Sir George Cornewall Lewis pointed out that even the implementation of the Wakefield scheme by no means depended upon the maintenance of British sovereignty over colonial settlement areas. He declared: "The system of defraying the expenses of the emigrants from the proceeds of the sale of public lands in the colony, does not necessarily suppose that the new settlement is a dependency of the country which sends out the emigrants. If it were advantageous for a new settlement to employ a portion of its public revenues in procuring immigrants, its government would naturally devote a portion of its revenues to this purpose, whether the settlement were dependent or independent."[86]

Most writers, however, preferred to see the main flow of emigrants proceed to the British colonies. Relatively few advised their countrymen to choose the United States for their future home-country,[87] while a much larger number deplored the fact that such a great proportion emigrated to the United States.[88]

Finally, it may be mentioned that some foes of emigration alleged that the British ruling classes favoured a policy of emigration in order to be relieved of the necessity of reforming the political, social, and economic organization of the United Kingdom. Defending the cause of the "underdogs," these writers usually denied the validity of the Malthusian doctrine and claimed that

[85]"Lewis on the Government of Dependencies," *Edinburgh Review*, LXXXIII (1846), 550 f.; see also pp. 551 f.

[86]Sir George Cornewall Lewis, *An Essay on the Government of Dependencies* [1841], ed. C. P. Lucas (Oxford, 1891), pp. 226 f.

[87]For examples, see Prentice, *A Tour in the United States* (1849), pp. 198 ff.; William Cobbett, *The Emigrant's Guide* (new ed., London, 1830), pp. 39 ff.

[88]One writer, for example, reflected with sorrow "on the numbers of persons who are yearly quitting these shores, weakening the strength of the empire, to add to the population of countries that may unfortunately at some future time employ them or their descendants in shedding British blood. . ." (W. J. Burchell, "Hints on Emigration to the Cape of Good Hope," *Pamphleteer*, XVII [1820], 98).

Similarly, "Pity it is: that many hundreds of thousands of good colonists have meanwhile carried their industry and their savings to enrich a foreign country—possibly to aggrandize a hostile power. Where the emigration to Australia may be told by tens, that to the United States must be counted by thousands" (G. C. Mundy, *Our Antipodes* [2d ed.; London, 1852!, III, 83). See also, Richard Whately, *Miscellaneous Lectures and Reviews* (London, 1861), p. 231.

over-population was not a natural phenomenon at all but the sorry result of selfish class-government. Mainly concerned over the destitution prevailing in Ireland, Colonel Napier remarked: "In fact then, over-population is a wrong term: the proper term is over-bad government, and the remedy consists neither in 'moral restraint' nor emigration; which last takes away our best men. . . . Emigration is a bending and shrinking from the evil, instead of meeting it boldly. The same energies which are roused within men to make them emigrate, would, if well and constitutionally directed, expose and consequently remove the evils which produce the wish to emigrate."[89]

While these men proposed free trade (mainly the repeal of the Corn Laws) and land reform as the better alternatives to emigration, they declared that these proposals were disregarded because the vested interests of the ruling classes stood firmly in the way of such reforms. Such evils as unemployment, low wage rates, and pauperism, were continuously re-created and sustained because selfish group-interests obstructed reformist legislation. Theorists who abetted this policy and advocated emigration were accused of having invented the myth of over-population. Actually Britain's paupers were persuaded and forced to emigrate only because the real evil was not eradicated at its source. Only on the surface, therefore, was emigration consummated on a voluntary basis. In reality it was nothing but the transportation of paupers. Crawford asserted:

The hon. and learned Member [Charles Buller] said, he objected to forced emigration; but it must be forced if the Legislature refused to give those measures which were necessary to provide employment and food for the people. He perceived, that in the present state of society there was a continual accumulation of wealth on the one hand in the possession of a few, while, on the other, the great mass of the people were growing poorer till they reached actual starvation. That was one great symptom of the evils the country was suffering. He did not approve, therefore, of an address to her Majesty which would deceive her if it represented that the distress of the people were to be relieved by emigration; and which was, in fact, but an apology for bad measures, and an excuse for the continuation of bad legislation.[90]

---

[89] *Colonization* (1835), p. 8. Notwithstanding this view Napier advocated colonization for other reasons.

Commenting upon Buller's famous speech for systematic colonization in April, 1843, S. Crawford said "that he believed the present proposition had sprung from the most hateful doctrine, the Malthusian doctrine. . ." (*Hansard*, third ser., LXVIII, c. 532).

[90] *Ibid.*

Hence, emigration amounted to "nothing less than transportation."[91] Perronet Thompson likewise maintained: "No class of men have a right to make a country untenable, and then take the credit to themselves for offering the means of transportation to the inhabitants."[92] Reviewing the monopolies sustained by the Corn Laws and the Colonial System, Thompson said that "they are only so many 'plants' (as the police phrase appears to be), of thieves too big to be hanged,—national larcencies,—picking of pockets by Act of Parliament, 'higher-class' frauds, founded always on the pillage of the humbler."[93] Archibald Prentice, too, stated that the various colonization schemes "had been formed merely to divert the attention of the people from other subjects with which they did not want them to interfere. . . . At present, there was no encouragement to go out under government auspices; there were things in which we did not wish them to meddle; rather let them leave us alone—not tax us so much—allow us to keep the money in our pockets—give us free trade, open ports, a fair field and no favour, and this was all we asked."[94]

SYSTEMATIC COLONIZATION

"Talk of negroes and galley slaves: American slaves, or convicts in New South Wales, are fat and happy compared with very many free-born Englishmen."[95] Thus, Edward Gibbon Wakefield, too, based his proposition on the condition-of-England question. But, in contrast to Hortonism, he and his followers set out to solve more problems than only that of pauperism. Britain, as they analysed the situation, suffered from congestion in *all* classes of her population; her commercial development, furthermore, was arrested by superabundance of capital and lack of markets.

[91] *Ibid.*, cs. 531 f.

[92] T. P. Thompson, *Exercises, Political and Others* (London, 1842), V, 22.

[93] *Ibid.*, pp. 22 f. Thompson exhorted the working population to refuse emigration: "Once more; stay here if you are wise. The time cannot be far off, when industry shall be free, and the man who works shall be allowed to sell the fruits of his labour, without going to the colonies for leave" (*ibid.*, p. 23).

[94] *A Tour in the United States* (1849), pp. 214 f.

Horton criticized these objections to emigration. He stated: ". . . I wish to meet an objection which may be made, that what is called surplus population is only the effect of the peculiar political institutions of this country, and that a reform of those institutions would render any other remedy unnecessary." His counter-argument consisted of pointing to the instance of Switzerland where, in his opinion, the demographic congestion existed in spite of democratic institutions (*Lectures* [1832], Lecture IV, p. 10).

[95] Edward Gibbon Wakefield, *England and America* (New York, 1834), p. 48.

As to the first of these points, emigration in the age of Wakefield ceased to be a device for shovelling out paupers. "Recently the spirit of colonization, under a new impulse, has acquired an entirely new character. Emigration is no longer confined to the most wretched portion of the population—to the mere labouring masses . . . colonization has taken the place of mere emigration: the removal of society, not that of mere masses. . . . A complete revolution in the state of opinion respecting emigration has in fact taken place."[96] Momentous as contemporaries viewed it, this change was seen as resulting from want of employment in all walks of life. Charles Buller declared in 1843:

No one will question the fact that there is a most severe competition among labourers; that from the highest to the lowest occupation of human industry, almost every one is habitually overstocked; . . . The liberal professions are more overstocked than any others. Gentlemen of the first station and fortune find a difficulty in knowing what to do with their younger sons; and you hear every day of the sons of gentlemen entering into occupations from which their pride in former times debarred them. Among the middle classes you hear the same complaints. There is the same intense competition amongst tradesmen, and notoriously a most severe competition amongst farmers.[97]

Wakefield likewise stated that there was "want of room for people of all classes."[98] ". . . in Great Britain all classes suffer from the want of room; the labourers, the small and great capitalists, the professional classes, and even the landed and mined aristocracy. . . ."[99] What did Wakefield mean by "want of room"? "By want of room, I mean a want of the means of a comfortable subsistence according to the respective standards of living established amongst the classes. . . . Whatever the fund for the maintenance of any of the classes, it is divided amongst too many people; there are too many competitors for a limited fund of enjoyment."[100] He pointed out that congestive conditions in the middle and upper classes had become noticeable since about 1830. "Since 1830, this

[96]"Emigration: Comparative Prospects of Our New Colonies," *Westminster Review*, XXXV (1841), 132. Similarly Gladstone said in 1855: "The change in the quality [of emigration] is still more worthy of your notice. Because, for a long time, emigration was nothing but the resort of the most necessitous; but now, on the contrary, in a great many cases . . . it is not the needy and the necessitous, but it is the most adventurous, the most enterprising, the most intelligent man . . . who goes to seek his fortune in those distant lands" (Speech reprinted in Paul Knaplund, *Gladstone and Britain's Imperial Policy* [New York, 1927], p. 188).

[97]Wakefield, *Art of Colonization* (1849), p. 464.
[98]*Ibid.*, p. 65.   [99]*Ibid.*   [100]*Ibid.*, p. 66.

competition of capital with capital, of education with education, and of place-hunting with place-hunting, has been continually on the increase."[101] In 1850, another writer observed: "The difficulty of earning a subsistence by trade increases each year. Every day it becomes more common for young men of good families to speak of marriage as a lot forbidden to them. . . ."[102]

Analysing the condition-of-England question from this point of view, Charles Buller distinguished between temporary and "permanent causes of distress," and concluded with regard to the latter: "I think . . . that we cannot contemplate the condition of this country without coming to the conclusion that there is a permanent cause of suffering in the constant accumulation of capital, and the constant increase of population within the same restricted field of employment. . . . This fresh amount both of capital and population have to be employed; and if no further space for their employment be provided, they must compete for a share of the previous amount of profits and wages."[103]

SURPLUS CAPITAL AND SURPLUS LABOUR

The Wakefieldian theory of colonization rested on the assumption that the mother country suffered from an excess of capital as well as from an excess of labour. The very concept of the co-existence of excessive labour and capital was in sharp opposition to the wage-fund theory developed by the classical economists. Adam Smith, James Mill, Bentham, and Ricardo, among others, endorsed this latter doctrine. Discussing the problem of emigration, James Mill wrote:

It has been enough . . . explained, that it is only capital which gives employment to labour; we may, therefore, take it as a postulate. A certain quantity of capital, then, is necessary to give employment to the population which any removal for the sake of colonization may leave behind. But if, to afford the expence of that removal, so much is taken from the capital of the country, that the remainder is not sufficient for the employment of the remaining population, there is, in that case, a redundancy of population, and all the evils which it brings.[104]

McCulloch stated the wage-fund theory as follows:

It is therefore apparent, that no country can ever reach the stationary state, as long as she continues to accumulate additional capital. While she does this, she will always have a constantly increasing demand for labour. . . .

---

[101] *Ibid.*   [102] "Colonization," p. 31.
[103] In Wakefield, *Art of Colonization*, p. 462.
[104] *Essays*, p. 13.

EMIGRATION AND COLONIZATION

But with every diminution of the rate at which capital has been previously accumulating, the demand for labour will decline.... And should the national capital diminish, the condition of the great body of the people would deteriorate; the wages of labour would be reduced; and pauperism, with its attendant train of vice, misery, and crime, would spread its ravages throughout society.[105]

In short, the wage-fund theory was based on the notion that in each country existed a definite fund for wage payments. Any improvement in wage rates depended on an increase in the demand for labour which, in turn, could only be created by further accumulation of capital.[106] Ricardo and his school believed that this fund could be augmented indefinitely without giving rise to difficulties in finding employment for increasing capital funds. If wage rates depended on the ratio of capital to population (i.e., wage-earners), then any diminution of the capital stock of a country tended to increase competition among wage-earners, and to lead to low wages, unemployment, and pauperism. How the case for emigration was limited by these considerations has been shown above.

Wakefield contradicted "these political economists who worship capital."

Speak of emigration to one ... and he will claim, "The question deserves profound regard; but as employment for labour is in proportion to capital, as emigration would cost money and diminish capital, therefore it would diminish employment for labour, and do more harm than good." ... Now upon what rests this assumption? It rests upon two ... assumptions, one of which is true, the other false; first, that no labour is employed save by capital; secondly, that all capital employs labour. If it were true that every increase of capital necessarily gave employment to more labour ... then it might be assumed that colonization would, on account of its expenses, do more harm than good. But it is not true that all capital employs labour.[107]

Similarly, Torrens, influenced by Wakefield, declared: "The objection, that the abstraction of labour and capital, in establishing new colonies, checks prosperity, and diminishes employment in the mother country, is not a deduction derived from experience, but an inference drawn from the assumed principle, that the increase of capital is, in itself, sufficient to increase the field of employment, and the demand for labour. This assumed principle is erroneous."[108]

---

[105] J. R. McCulloch, *The Principles of Political Economy* (2d ed.; London, 1830), p. 105; see also pp. 377 f. *Vide* a similar statement made by J. Hume and quoted p. 285.

[106] This, in turn, depended, of course, on the increased productivity of labour.

[107] *England and America* (1834), pp. 249 f.

[108] *The Budget* (1841-4), p. 85.

It was from "experience" that the Wakefield school inferred that Britain suffered from a superabundance of capital. Thus, Charles Buller observed:

> In this country, since the peace, there has been an immense accumulation of capital, of which a great part has, no doubt, been turned to excellent account in extending our trade and manufactures; in improving our agriculture; in covering the country with public works and private dwellings.... But, over and above this, there has been a further accumulation of capital for which no profitable employment could be found; and which consequently has been thrown away in the most unsafe investments lent to every government that chose to ask us for loans—sunk in South American mines, or fooled away in the bubble speculations of the day.[109]

The core of this argument against the Ricardian wage-fund theory was that capital did not find employment automatically. Lack of profitable employment for capital constituted Great Britain's surplus-capital problem. Malthus had stated earlier that "in supposing that accumulation ensures effectual demand," Say, Mill, and Ricardo had fallen into a fundamental error.[110] Torrens declared that, contrary to some political economists "who assume, that capital possesses some occult property or influence, by which it creates for itself the field in which it is employed, and renders demands co-extensive with supply ... capital cannot create for itself the field of profitable employment."[111] Hence there may be a "glut of capital." Examining the condition of England in particular, Torrens explained:

> ... in a manufacturing and commercial country, importing raw produce, the field of employment, and the demand for labour, cannot be determined by the amount of capital ready to be invested in manufactures and commerce. In a country thus circumstanced, employment and wages will depend, not so much upon the amount of commercial and manufacturing capital, as upon the extent of the foreign market.... If the foreign market

---

[109]In Wakefield, *Art of Colonization*, p. 463. In addition to investments abroad and "bubble speculations," capital excess manifested itself in a continually decreasing rate of profit (Merivale, *Lectures* [1841], I, 173 ff.). See also Thomas Tooke, *A History of Prices* (London, 1838-48), II, 145, 148, 159. Wakefield, *England and America* (1834), pp. 23 ff., 70 ff.

There is plenty of secondary material on this subject. See Paul Leroy-Beaulieu, *De la Colonisation chez les Peuples Modernes* (4th ed.; Paris, 1891), pp. 697-703; L. H. Jenks, *The Migration of British Capital to 1875* (New York, 1927), pp. 22 f., 29 ff., 52, 81 ff.

[110]Rev. T. R. Malthus, *Principles of Economy* (London, 1820), pp. 354, 359. "To justify the employment of capital, there must be a demand for the produce of it, beyond that which may be created by the demand of the workmen employed" (*ibid.*, p. 349).

[111]R. Torrens, *A Letter to Sir Robert Peel on the Condition of England* (London, 1843), pp. 14 f.

does not extend, no increase of manufacturing capital can cause a beneficial increase of production, or a permanent advance of wages. Indeed, an increase of manufacturing and commercial capital, unaccompanied by a proportional extension of the foreign market, instead of proving beneficial, might have a necessary tendency to lower the profits of trade, and to reduce the wages of labour.[112]

THE PROBLEM OF OVER-PRODUCTION

As has been shown above, the supporters of the wage-fund theory welcomed any increase in capital accumulation because of the resultant augmentation of the wage-fund. Ricardo had accepted Say's "théorie des débouchées" according to which excess capital and general over-production could never develop because every commodity automatically creates its own demand. Supply and demand being mutually creative, the occurrence of general over-production or a general glut of commodities seemed impossible. Only a temporary disequilibrium of supply and demand of particular goods could develop and such a short-run dislocation would rectify itself automatically. If this theory was true, then accumulation of capital could never be in excess of possibilities of its employment.[113]

[112]*The Budget* (1841), pp. 85 ff. For a detailed analysis of the problem, see *ibid.*, pp. 86-89.

Wakefield, indeed, regarded the existence of surplus capital in England as the principal cause of the condition-of-England question. He wrote: "With regard to the competition of capital with capital, I would only explain further, that it appears to be the immediate cause of all the other competitions. Our power of increasing capital seems to be unlimited. If the continually-increasing capital of Great Britain could be continually invested so as to yield high profits, the labourers' competition would cease, because there would be ample employment at good wages for the whole class. Trade of every kind would present an unlimited field of employment for all classes above the common people..." (*Art of Colonization* [1849], pp. 75 f.).

To find employment for Britain's redundant capital, therefore, was a prerequisite to the solution of all other problems that constituted the condition-of-England question.

[113]McCulloch stated this position as follows: "Suppose ... that the productive powers of industry are doubled; nay, suppose they are increased ten or ten thousand times, and that they are exerted to the utmost, it would not occasion any lasting glut of the market. It is true, that those individuals who are most industrious may produce commodities which those who are less industrious ... may not have the means of purchasing.... But the glut arising from such a contingency must speedily disappear.... A universal glut of all sorts of commodities is impossible; any excess in one class must be compensated by an equal deficiency in some other class" (*Principles of Political Economy* [1830], pp. 183 f., 201).

In this respect, the theories of Sismondi and Malthus were opposed to those of Say and Ricardo. The Wakefield school fully accepted the proposition of the former. Major Torrens, for example, asserted "that in a country depending upon foreign commerce, and importing raw produce, there may be a redundancy, a general glut of capital, occasioning over-trading, and a consequent fall of profits and of wages throughout all the branches of industry engaged in supplying the foreign market."[114] John Stuart Mill endorsed Wakefield's proposition as follows:

> Mr. Wakefield's explanation of the fall of profits is briefly this. Production is limited not solely by the quantity of capital and of labour, but also by the extent of the "field of employment." The field of employment for capital is two-fold; the land of the country, and the capacity of foreign markets to take its manufactured commodities. On a limited extent of land, only a limited quantity of capital can find employment at profit. As the quantity of capital approaches this limit, profit falls; when the limit is attained, profit is annihilated; and can only be restored through an extension of the field of employment, either by the acquisition of fertile land, or by opening new markets in foreign countries, from which food and materials can be purchased with the products of domestic capital. These propositions are in my opinion substantially true....[115]

If the accumulation of capital in Great Britain was in excess of the existing possibilities of profitable employment, if her "powers of production" had "outgrown the field of employment,"[116] then the extension of the field of employment was the only adequate remedy. "The one thing needful for all society is more room for the profitable employment of capital."[117]

FOREIGN TRADE OR COLONIZATION

> But now comes the more interesting case of a society, which, stimulated by the extension of its markets, has cultivated all that part of its territory which is fit for cultivation; a society in which the utmost skill in the application of capital and labour to agriculture is counteracted by the necessity of cultivating inferior land; a society, consequently, in which food is dear, and in which there exist the strongest motives for importing food from other countries by means of manufactures and exchange; a society, in short, which requires new markets in which to purchase the staff of life.[118]

"This," Wakefield said, "is preëminently the case of England."[119]

---

[114]*Colonization of South Australia* (1836), p. 242.
[115]*Principles of Political Economy* (1852), p. 293.
[116]Torrens, *Letter to Robert Peel* (1843), p. 17.
[117]Wakefield, *Art of Colonization* (1849), p. 76.
[118]Wakefield, *England and America* (1834), p. 244.
[119]*Ibid.*

Since additional application of capital to domestic land was rejected as unprofitable, there remained, in the eyes of contemporary observers, only two possibilities for obtaining foodstuffs, for expanding the field of employment for Great Britain's redundant capital, and, generally, for remedying the condition of the poorer classes in England: colonization and/or free trade. Indeed, during the thirties and forties a lively discussion took place upon the merits of these two means to the desired end. Some favoured free trade, others colonization, and still others regarded the two programmes as complementary. The alternatives were clearly stated in the following quotation: "There remains, therefore, this alternative—to employ these persons the [paupers] here in making articles to exchange for food, or to send them abroad to grow food by a more direct process;—to bring the food to them, or to send them to the food. In short, we must organize an emigration to the amount of 230,000 souls yearly; or we must extend our manufacturing industry every year sufficiently to absorb that number; or we must pursue both ends conjointly."[120]

The Case for Free Trade.[121] The following quotations represent writers who recommended free trade rather than colonization.

They [the colonies] do not even afford any advantage, as some persons suppose, by enlarging the field for the employment of capital; for there are still means enough for employing capital with profit at home; and if new means were wanting, they would be more effectually obtained by removing restrictions on trade and revising the taxes, than by increased trade with the Colonies.[122]

Perfect freedom of interchange . . . —willing and unburdened admission of the products of other countries,—must form the sole basis of our future prosperity, because it is the sole condition on which we can obtain extended markets for our goods, and increased employment for our people.[123]

They say that the people are impoverished; that a greater supply of food is required for them; and they seek to improve their condition either by foreign colonization or home colonization. . . . I do not impugn the motives of these persons: I believe that they are all animated by a desire to relieve the destitution that they hear of or that they witness. But I cannot help observing to them that since they acknowledge the condition of our people to be that of wanting food and that of procuring it, they should be heard on

---

[120] "Resources of an Increasing Population: Emigration or Manufactures," *Westminster Review*, XL (1843), 105.

[121] The case for free trade will be examined here solely in relation to the specific question under consideration.

[122] Henry Parnell, *On Financial Reform* (2d ed.; London, 1830), p. 239.

[123] W. R. Greg, *Not Over-Production, But Deficient Consumption the Source of Our Sufferings* (London, 1842), p. 26.

this occasion calling loudly for the repeal of the Laws that exist only to prevent food entering this country.... They say that we want new markets; that we want to employ our redundant people; and for this their plan is to colonize them. Our plan, on the other hand, is to suffer them to work at home for food which those who take their work would give them in exchange, but which these laws deprive them of. For if the food that is kept out of the country by the Corn Laws were to come in, it could only be received in exchange for articles that would be produced by our people with a view to such trade.[124]

These statements could be easily multiplied. To the supporter of free trade in preference to, or to the exclusion of, colonization, the repeal of the Corn and Navigation Laws, and the removal of other barriers to international trade appeared as an adequate and complete solution to the condition-of-England question.

The Case for Colonization Coupled with Free Trade. Adam Smith had analysed the benefits that accrued to Europe as a whole from the colonization of the Americas. In short, he pointed out that European trade and industry had been greatly stimulated and increased through the creation of "new equivalents." The Wakefieldians seized upon this idea and made it a cornerstone of their theory of colonization.

The basic consideration underlying the Wakefield system was that Great Britain suffered from a redundancy of capital and labour and from a scarcity of good land. In settlement colonies, on the other hand, rich land was abundant while labour and capital were scarce. Hence, in the mother country as well as in the colonies a sound balance of capital, land, and labour could be effected if the surplus capital and population of the metropolis were transferred to the virgin soils of the oversea settlements. Charles Buller expressed this idea as follows:

Here we have capital that can obtain no profitable employment; labour equally kept out of employment by the competition of labour sufficient for the existing demand.... In your colonies, on the other hand, you have vast tracts of the most fertile land wanting only capital and labour to cover them with abundant harvests; and, from want of that capital and labour, wasting their productive energies in nourishing weeds, or, at best, in giving shelter and sustenance to beasts. When I ask you to colonize, what do I ask you to do but to carry the superfluity of one part of our country to repair the deficiency of the other ... in one simple word, to convey the plough to the field, the workman to his work, the hungry to his food?[125]

---

[124]*The Free Trade Speeches of the Right Hon. Charles Pelham Villiers* (London, 1883), II, 23 ff. The above statement was made in a speech delivered in May, 1843.

[125]In Wakefield, *Art of Colonization*, p. 474.

Similarly, Wakefield stated: "Colonies are of value simply because they enlarge the productive territory of the nation that plants them; thus adding directly to the means of support at its command, and opening a wider field for its energies, as well by the advantages they hold out to the settlers who resort to them, as by the markets they create for the various industrial products which the manufacturing and commercial capacities of the old country furnish."[126]

Thus, the Wakefield school proposed to find additional outlets for capital and labour surplus in additional new land.[127] The advocates of maximum foreign commerce retorted that in a country that pursued a free-trade policy, redundant capital would not be applied to inferior land because required foodstuffs and raw materials could be more cheaply obtained abroad.[128] Maximum exchange between nations would permit increasing investment in British manufacturing industries. Supporters of the Wakefield theory of colonization questioned the truth of this argument. Torrens, for example, declared: "When, in England, the capital employed in preparing cotton fabrics for the foreign market increases faster than the capital employed in foreign countries in raising the raw materials, by the expenditure of which cotton fabrics are produced; then, in conformity with the universal law of supply and demand . . . the value of cotton fabrics will decline in relation to the elementary cost of their production, and, in the cotton trade, profits, or wages, or both, must come down."[129] ". . . the home capital employed in preparing woollen goods may increase faster than the foreign capital employed in producing equivalents for their purchase."[130]

Because of differences in the rate of capital accumulation, those countries endowed with less capital than Great Britain did not produce sufficient equivalents for trade with Britain. Owing to the law of supply and exchange, therefore, the terms of trade turned against England and prices of British export articles would tend to be low as compared with the prices of goods imported into the country. "The result would be, that English labour and skill

[126]Edward Gibbon Wakefield, "Sir Charles Metcalfe in Canada," [1844], article reprinted in E. M. Wrong, *Charles Buller and Responsible Government* (Oxford, 1926), pp. 348 f.

[127]See also Torrens, *Letter to Sir Robert Peel* (1843), pp. 63-77; *The Budget* (1841), p. 133.

[128]Merivale, *Lectures*, I, 174.

[129]*A Letter to Sir Robert Peel* (1843), p. 16.

[130]*Ibid.*, pp. 16 f. Merivale accepted this proposition: *Lectures* (1841), I, 175 f.

would command less return in the foreign market: they would produce less exchangeable value: the mass of commodities, the amount of comforts and conveniences of life enjoyed in England would diminish...."[131]

Wakefield and most of his followers were not opposed to the extension of foreign trade but asserted that the implementation of such a policy was not enough. They accepted the free-trade doctrines but, broadly speaking, they wanted to widen the area of profitable free trade by augmenting the equivalents available abroad for exchange with Britain's export articles. This could be brought to pass by stimulating an expansion of the world supply of foodstuffs and industrial raw materials which England, the industrialized country *par excellence* could import in exchange for her manufactures. Wakefield said:

It is not want of more acres, but of more capacity for production, whether by means of more acres, more fertility in the acres we have, or more skill for making those acres yield more.... It is not the land that we want, but the use of it. The use of land may be got elsewhere. It may be got by means of exchange. If, without any increase of capital or people, we could purchase with manufactured goods twice as much food as we obtain now by various means, everybody here would enjoy ... the same prosperity as if our land were doubled.... Every fresh importation of food by means of exporting more manufactured goods, is an enlargement of the field of production ... and has a tendency to abolish and prevent injurious competition. This was the best argument for the repeal of our Corn-Laws.

The question remains, however, whether the importation of food can outrun the increase of people. It never has done so yet; and apparently, it never can do so in the present state of the world. For to every importation there are two parties; the buyer and the seller of the thing imported. We could make goods for exportation much faster than population can possibly increase; but where would be the buyers? We could buy the food; but who would have it to sell? It is not manufactured goods only that we want to increase rapidly, but also customers who would buy them with food. Now, in countries where food can only be increased by agricultural improvements, the increase of food is very slow, like the advance of those improvements.... A great many such countries, besides, almost exclude our manufactured goods by means of hostile tariffs.... There remain countries where food is

---

[131] *Ibid.*, p. 176. Under conditions of a free movement of capital, differences in the interest rates obtaining in different areas would, of course, produce capital migrations which would tend to remedy the situation described by Wakefield. The latter, however, approached the problem from an empirical point of view. As will be seen, he noted that sufficient amounts of capital would not move to areas where fertile land was abundant unless there existed also an adequate supply of labour, cheaper than in such thinly populated countries like the United States and the British colonies, and more skilled than in more densely populated ones like Argentina.

increased by taking fresh land into cultivation; new countries; North America and the British colonies. There, the power of increasing food is practically unlimited; and the pace at which food is increased in such countries might be very much accelerated.[132]

In short, instead of relying exclusively on the benefits to be expected from the extension of foreign trade, the forceful prosecution of colonization would insure to Great Britain a more favourable exchange of her export commodities for foodstuffs and other raw materials and, at the same time, would drain the supposed superabundance of labour and capital in the mother country. "The objects of an old society in promoting colonization seem to be three: first, the extension of the market for disposing of their own surplus produce; secondly, relief from excessive numbers; thirdly, an enlargement of the field for employing capital ... these three objects may come under one head; namely, an enlargement of the field for employing capital and labour."[133] John Stuart Mill accepted Wakefield's thesis.

To appreciate the benefits of colonization, it should be considered in its relation, not to a single country, but to the collective economical interest of the human race. The question is in general treated too exclusively as one of distribution; of relieving one labour-market and supplying another. It is this, but it is also a question of production, and of the most efficient employment of the productive resources of the world. Much has been said of the good economy of importing commodities from the place where they can be bought cheapest; while the good economy of producing them where they can be produced cheapest, is comparatively little thought of. If to carry consumable goods from the places where they are superabundant to those where they are scarce, is a good pecuniary speculation, is it not an equally good speculation to do the same thing with regard to labour and instruments? The exportation of labourers and capital from old to new countries, from a place where their productive power is less, to a place where it is greater, increases by so much the aggregate produce of the labour and capital of the world. It adds to the joint wealth of the old and the new country, what amounts in a short period to many times the mere cost of effecting the transport. There needs to be no hesitation affirming that Colonization, in the present state of the world, is the best affair of business, in which the capital of an old and wealthy country can engage.[134]

There was one additional reason that determined the Wakefield school not to rely over-much upon the promises of free trade. This was the fear that other countries might not follow Great Britain's free-trade policy. Charles Buller, for example, declared:

[132]*Art of Colonization* (1849), pp. 88 ff. Similarly, *England and America* (1834), pp. 245 ff.
[133]*Ibid.*, p. 242.
[134]*Principles of Political Economy*, pp. 970 f.

I must not be understood to propose colonization as a substitute for free trade. I do not vaunt its efficacy as superior; indeed I admit that its effect in extending employment must be slower. But, on the other hand, it will probably be surer; and will be liable to no such interruptions from the caprice of others, as trade with foreign nations must always be subject to. . . . The commerce of the world is narrowed now not only by our own legislation, but by that of other powers; the influence of restrictive views is extending and acquiring strength among them. . . . I say, then, that in the present day the restrictive policy of other nations must enter into our consideration as an element, and no unimportant element, of commercial policy.[135]

In this respect, the special advantages of colonization over foreign trade were, first, that new settlement colonies naturally were food exporting communities, raising raw materials in exchange for manufactures;[136] and, secondly, that the colonizing country was able to control the foreign-trade policy of the colonies.[137]

Some of those who wanted to combine free trade with colonization considered the implementation of the former as a measure subsidiary to the implementation of the latter. Others took the opposite point of view. Again, some supported colonization as a short-run policy but predicted that the increasing extension of foreign trade would, in the course of time, render the extension of colonization unnecessary.[138]

Travers Twiss' opinion on the subject of colonization is interesting. He dismissed it curtly as a remedy for draining the population surplus of the mother country,[139] but advocated it as a method for the industrial conquest of the globe. ". . . the effects of colonisation, as distinguished from emigration, may not be disadvantageous where its direction is judicious . . . if colonisation be regarded as a system of industrial conquest, by which the waste

[135] In Wakefield, *Art of Colonization*, p. 473.

[136] This point was greatly stressed by the Wakefield school. Among others see Buller, *ibid.*, pp. 475 ff.; Wakefield, *ibid.*, pp. 83, 92; R. Torrens had stressed this point already in the early twenties (*An Essay on the Production of Wealth* [London, 1821], p. 230).

[137] Thus, Charles Buller remarked in his speech of 1843: "But of the legislation of your own colonies—of the fiscal policy of the different portions of your own empire you can always make sure, and may rely upon being met by no hostile tariffs on their part" (Wakefield, *Art of Colonization*, p. 473).

[138] As early as 1824, this view was taken by John Rooke, *An Inquiry into the Principles of National Wealth* (Edinburgh, 1824), pp. 362, 372 f. Similarly Senior, *Remarks on Emigration* (1831), pp. 6 f.

[139] He maintained that colonization "will in one sense rather act as a stimulus to population, for it will create a demand for labour, and thus must be cautiously and sparingly pursued, or it may over-stimulate population. . ." (Travers Twiss, *View of the Progress of Political Economy in Europe* [London, 1847], p. 220).

spots of the earth's surface are to be occupied and cultivated, and by which the commerce of a great race is to be extended, and greater scope given to its productive power, there is no doubt that such results will attend it, where the mother country does not tie up the hands of the colonists."[140]

The Case for Colonization without Free Trade. Major Torrens, perhaps, can be regarded as the intellectually most respectable representative of those writers and politicians who wanted Britain to embark upon a policy of large-scale colonization but were highly critical of the free-trade programme. He emphasized the security and the lack of hostile tariff regulations that characterized colonial as against foreign markets.

... the colonial resembles the home trade ... in the security and permanence which it possesses ... when we exchange our commodities with an independent state, the beneficial divisions of employment to which this traffic gives occasion, are liable to be suspended by a declaration of hostilities, or by the enacting of those restrictions and prohibitions which commercial rivalry is perpetually suggesting. But when a mother country and her colonies, particularly if they possess a commanding marine, interchange their surplus products, nothing short of a dismemberment of the empire can suspend their intercourse....[141]

In the early forties Torrens was also opposed to the repeal of the Corn Laws because he anticipated that such a step, though extremely favourable to the manufacturing industries, would destroy British agriculture. "Master manufacturers, in their increased prosperity, might have an increased demand for villas, for horses, and for ornamental domains; operatives, in full employment at ample wages, might consume increased quantities of animal food .... But when the corn fields of England should have been converted into parks and meadows, what would become of the peasant...?"[142] The introduction of free trade in corn, therefore, would force Great Britain to resort to emigration and colonization "on a gigantic scale in order to preserve masses of the rural population ... from perishing from the face of the earth."[143]

In the long run, Torrens thought, reliance on the benefits of an

[140] *Ibid.* In the last part of the above sentence, Twiss referred to the fact that the benefits attending colonization were contingent on the parent state's willingness "to admit without restriction the raw produce of the colony into the home market" (*ibid.*).

[141] *Essay on the Production of Wealth* (1821), pp. 231 f.; also, *Colonization of South Australia* (1836), pp. 246 f.

[142] *The Budget* (1841), pp. 82 f.   [143] *Ibid.*, p. 83.

extension of foreign trade was particularly precarious because foreign countries increasingly rivalled the industrial efficiency of England.

... the duty which devolves upon the statesman of the present day is, to save the industrious millions from the effects of a transition partly resulting from the progress of knowledge, and of improvement in other countries, and partly created by the tariff war, waged universally against British commerce .... We must ascertain the character of the disease, before we can apply an appropriate remedy.... The superior advantages which have hitherto rendered the produce of a given quantity of English labour, more valuable than the produce of the same quantity of foreign labour, and which have consequently enabled the English to command higher wages than the continental operative, are, mechanical inventions, manual dexterity, and productive coal mines. Now, ever since the termination of the wars of the French revolution, foreign countries have been approaching nearer and nearer to an equality with England, with regard to these advantages; and the consequence has been, that the value of the products of foreign industry has been gradually rising in relation to the products of British industry....[144]

Thus, voicing the apprehensions of a later generation of British statesmen and writers, Torrens became one of the early preachers of a British Zollverein. "The prosperity of the country cannot be arrested by the hostile tariffs of foreign rivals, if England will establish throughout her wide-spread empire a British commercial league—a colonial Zollverein."[145]

A number of writers adopted a similar outlook, of which the following samples give evidence.

In 1830 our manufactures were far superior to our foreign neighbours, they could not compete with us then; hence arose the fact of their buying of us our manufactures; since 1830 those foreign neighbours have perfected themselves in manufacture, and can produce themselves in 1840 what in 1830 they were obliged to buy of us.... Now, supposing the abolition of the Corn Laws had taken place in 1830, would those foreign countries have stopped their growing improvements in manufacture merely to have sent us their corn, and taken our manufactures? undoubtedly not....[146]

Let us calmly inquire whether, amidst the many resources of this highly-favoured country, Providence may not have reserved some safe and not uncertain mode by which to relieve ourselves ... from so many besetting difficulties.... The populous states of Europe, in ceasing to be consumers of our manufactures, may err, according to the theory of economists; but experience unhappily proves, that it is not by wisdom that the affairs of

---

[144] *A Letter to Sir Robert Peel* (1843), pp. 10 f.

[145] *The Budget* (1841), p. 102.

[146] C. H., *Letters on Emigration* (1841), p. 8; see also, Scrope, *Principles of Political Economy* (1833), pp. 372 f., 381 f. Richard Whately, "Emigration to Canada," pp. 389 f.

mankind are always regulated. Instead, therefore, of repining at that which is irretrievable, let us hasten, while the season is yet propitious to promote emigration to our colonies, and by means of the energies of our own subjects, create for ourselves better and more stable markets than foreign states have ever proved or will ever become.[147]

THE MAIN PRINCIPLES OF THE WAKEFIELD SYSTEM OF COLONIZATION

There is no need here to describe Wakefield's theory of systematic colonization in detail.[148] Its fundamental principles are quite simple, and have been stated by Merivale as follows:

1. That the prosperity of new colonies mainly depends upon the abundance of available labour at the command of capitalists, in proportion to the extent of territory occupied.

2. That this abundance is to be secured by introducing labourers from the mother-country, and other well-peopled regions, and taking measures to keep them in the condition of labourers living by wages for some considerable time; at least two or three years, according to the suggestion of Col. Torrens.

3. That the revenue derived from the sale of new land is the fund out of which the cost of introducing them is best defrayed.

4. That the most convenient way of preventing them from rising too rapidly from the condition of labourers into that of independent landowners is to sell the land at a sufficiently high price.

5. That the entire proceeds of the land sales ought to be devoted to the purpose of obtaining emigrants; and that only by devoting the whole, and not any portion, will the exact equilibrium between land, labour, and capital be secured.

6. That the sale of land should be at an uniform price per acre for all qualities and all situations, and not by auction.

7. That this system will lead to concentrate the population, and check that inconvenient dispersion which is apt to take place in new colonies.[149]

---

[147]Major Macarthur, *Colonial Policy of 1840 and 1841* (London, 1841), p. 72.

[148]See Edward Gibbon Wakefield, *A Letter from Sydney* (1829), partly reprinted in A. J. Harrop, *The Amazing Career of Edward Gibbon Wakefield* (London, 1928), pp. 217-37; *England and America* (1834), pp. 263-331.

For critical and disapproving reviews, see "New South Australian Company," *Westminster Review*, XXI (1834), 441-76; Merivale, *Lectures* (1841), I, 155; Laing, *National Distress* (1844), pp. 121-6; Samuel Sidney, *The Three Colonies of Australia* (1852), pp. 132-5, 180 ff.; Leroy-Beaulieu, *De la Colonisation*, p. 682.

For a description of the system in practice, see A. Grenfell Price, "Experiments in Colonization," *Cambridge History of the British Empire*, VII, Part I, 213-41.

[149]*Lectures* (1841), II, 42.

Thus, in contrast to the emigration scheme of Horton who wanted to make landowners out of inexperienced paupers immediately, the core of Wakefield's system was the disposal of waste lands in the colonies. By its sale at a fixed and sufficiently high price, immigrant-colonists would be barred from acquiring land immediately upon their arrival. They would work as labourers for several years. Thus, by means of Wakefield's land system "the purchasers of colonial land would not merely purchase a certain number of acres, but would indirectly buy the services of a number of labourers proportioned to the amount of land bought."[150] Through this device, it was hoped, British capitalists would be induced to invest capital in the colonies.

It has been said that the various elements that make up Wakefield's system of colonization were not original contributions.[151] That may be true. But to combine these elements into a consistent system of colonization may merit a claim to originality in itself. More important, however, than this moot question of the origins of the system, is the fact that, as a whole, it was never given a real trial. Those principles that were applied in Australia and New Zealand failed to produce the anticipated results. Whether their implementation was badly executed or whether they were inherently impracticable, is another moot question. From the point of view of the present study it must be sufficient to state that the above-enumerated principles of Wakefield's system were of incomparably lesser importance in the history of British imperial thought than his incessant and effective propagation of the cause of colonization as such.

THE MULTIPLICATION OF LITTLE ENGLANDS AND COLONIZATION BY ORDER OF PROVIDENCE[152]

Addressing the House of Commons in 1848 William Molesworth remarked: "But to colonise beneficially it is necessary that the

[150] H. E. Egerton (ed.), *Selected Speeches of Sir William Molesworth on Questions Relating to Colonial Policy* (London, 1903), p. 56.

[151] The sale of public lands to capitalists was already proposed by Joseph Pinsent, *Letters Addressed to the Earl of Liverpool* (London, 1820), p. 23. The disadvantages attendant on a system that permits the wide dispersal of settlers had already been pointed out by Adam Smith, *The Wealth of Nations*, pp. 539 f.

On this question see also Wagner, "British Economists and the Empire," *Political Science Review*, XLVI (1931), 262.

[152] Throughout the thirties and forties the ancient Greek idea and practice of colonization exerted a growing influence on the shaping of British colonial ideas. Such writers as Adam Smith and Dean Tucker had also studied Greek

higher and richer, as well as the poorer classes, that the employers of labour as well as the employed, that all classes of society should emigrate together, forming new communities, analogous to that of the parent state."[153] Before the same audience, Sir R. H. Inglis said in 1843:

Nothing ... could deserve the name of a colony of Great Britain, which did not represent all the interests, civil and religious, of the mother country, which was not, in fact, a miniature representation of England, complete in every part, according to its proportions. It was not merely the sending of a hundred thousand emigrants, without reference to their qualifications or fitness to bear their part in a civilised community.... It was the exercise of skill and statesmanlike principles in guiding and molding the masses whom they sent out that was required to justify a Government in transferring a large portion of the community to distant lands. He held, that they were not entitled to expatriate any portion of the people of this country unless they were also prepared to give those persons the benefit of all those institutions to which they were entitled at home.[154]

No doubt, it was not only the reminiscence of Greek colonization and the benign intention of conferring upon the British emigrant the blessings of a nobleman and a parson that motivated the above statements.[155] Archbishop Whately presented other reasons for this new conception of colonization. Whately compared English colonization of the past with Greek colonization:

The main cause of this difference may be stated in few words. We sent out colonies of the limbs, without the belly and head;—of needy persons, many of them mere paupers, or even criminals; colonies made up of a single class of persons in the community, and that the most helpless, and the most unfit

---

colonization but it was not until the period indicated above that the references to ancient Greek colonization were made with amazing frequency by a large number of English politicians and writers. In general, the purpose of these references was to show that the art of colonization consisted of sending out not merely paupers, the refuse of society, but daughter-societies well-proportioned in their social stratification, which in foreign areas became flourishing carriers of the mother-country's civilization. This influence of the Greek ideal of colonization was particularly strong with such men as Whately, Wakefield, Molesworth, Grote, Gladstone, etc., many of whom were classical scholars.

[153] *Selected Speeches*, pp. 212 f.

[154] *Hansard*, third ser., LXVIII, c. 577. See also, Wakefield, *Art of Colonization* (1849), p. 135.

[155] *The Labour League* wrote on Sept. 2, 1848: "The beau ideal of the 'systematic colonizers' is the British Constitution, their highest aim is to reproduce in the new settlements they advocate a facsimile of English society, with its classifications of landlords, parsons, lawyers, doctors, capitalists, and labourers.... Now we think that the creation of bishoprics and rectories, rich idlers and poor labourers in the 'bush' is not in itself a very desirable thing..." (quoted in S. Maccoby, *English Radicalism 1832-1852* [London, 1935], p. 349).

to perpetuate our national character, and to become the fathers of a race whose habits of thinking and feeling shall correspond to those which, in the mean time, we are cherishing at home. The ancients, on the contrary, sent out a representation of the parent state—colonists from all ranks.[156]

It seemed to this author that ancient Greek practice had two distinct advantages over English colonization. First, due to the expectation of becoming a member of a miniature Athens in the colony, "the lowest class again followed with alacrity, because they found themselves moving with, and not away from the state of society in which they had been living."[157] While in the case of England "those who do go, have, for the most part, made a reluctant choice between starvation and exile."[158] Arriving in the colony, the emigrant finds himself in alien surroundings. "His eye and his heart miss in all directions objects of social interest, on the influence of which he never speculated; but which he nevertheless felt, and must crave after. He has been accustomed, perhaps, to see the squire's house and park. . . . He has been used to go to his church. . . . He has children old enough for school. . . . He needs religious comfort or instruction, or advice in the conduct of his life. . . ."[159] Therefore, to provide the colonist with his familiar social environment means to make him happier than he would be otherwise; and this promise of greater happiness will ensure a large stream of emigrants to the colonies. The lower ranks need the leadership to which they have become habituated. Thus, Wakefield observed:

> The most respectable emigrants, more especially if they have a good deal of property, and are well connected in this country, lead and govern the emigration of the other classes. These are the emigrants whose presence in a colony most beneficially affects its standard of morals and manners. . . . If you can induce many of this class to settle in a colony, the other classes, whether capitalists or labourers, are sure to settle there in abundance: for a combination of honour, virtue, intelligence, and property, is respected even by those who do not possess it. . . .[160]

Secondly, by providing the emigrants of the lower classes with the supposed benefits of a miniature England in the colonies, they would form integral parts of a body that is the heir and carrier of English civilization, political institutions, and customs. Political conservatives (not in the party sense) also assumed that such

---

[156] Richard Whately, *Thoughts on Secondary Punishment* (London, 1832), p. 190.
[157] *Ibid.*, p. 191.   [158] *Ibid.*, p. 192.
[159] *Ibid.*, p. 193.
[160] *Art of Colonization* (1849), p. 136.

colonists would not as easily fall prey to democratization and plebeianization as happened in the case of the United States. Hence, the existence of a strong and lasting link between mother country and daughter colonies could be insured with a minimum of compulsion and supervision on the part of the metropolis. Whately wrote:

Nor is this defect in our system of colonization, one that merely affects the happiness of the emigrant-colonist, by adding to the strangeness of his condition.... He was a member of a community made up of various orders; he was a wheel in a machine of a totally different construction; it is a chance if he answers under circumstances so different. He must adapt his habits of thinking and acting to the change; and doing this he ceases to be an Englishman.... Witness the United States.... Is it we that taunt them with becoming a money-making, trafficking people? We severed the humble from the nobles of our land, and formed the embryo of a plebeian nation. Is it we that should find fault with their extravagant abhorrence of rank, or their want of the high breeding and gentle blood which we so sparingly bestowed on them?[161]

Whately, therefore, pondered on ways and means by which British aristocrats could be induced to go to the colonies. "But what is to be done? Are we to force our nobles and gentry to join the herd of emigrants? They have no need to go; and why should they go? What inducement can we hold out sufficient to allure them? They may, I conceive, be bribed to go; but not by pounds, shillings, and pence. Honour, and rank, and power, are less ruinous bribes than money ... offer him [the English gentleman] a patent of nobility for himself and his heirs,—offer him a hereditary station in the government of the future community; and there will be some chance of his acceding to the proposal."[162] If this policy were adopted and successful, then "a colony so formed would fairly represent English society, and every new comer would have his own class to fall into."[163]

[161] *Thoughts on Secondary Punishment*, pp. 194 f.

[162] *Ibid.*, pp. 196 f. Lalor, a Carlylean, observed: "... in England the honours at the disposal of the Crown have still power to accomplish much that cannot be accomplished by money. If successful leadership in colonial enterprises came to be regarded as a better title to peerages and blue ribands than such diplomatic exploits as are wont to be performed in the saloons of Berlin and Vienna, there would still be hope that the glories of the Ionic cities might be outdone, and that the English aristocracy ... would yet become the architects of a great colonial civilization, richer and more fruitful in benefit to man than any social achievement of the ancient world" (John Lalor, *Money and Morals* [London, 1852], p. 179).

[163] Whately, *Thoughts on Secondary Punishment*, p. 197.

Such a colony ... will be united to us by ties to which one of a different constitution must be a stranger. It will have received from us, and will always trace to us, all its social ingredients. Its highest class will be ours,—its gentry ours,—its clergy ours,—its lower and its lowest rank all ours; all corresponding and congenial to our manners, institutions, and even our prejudices.... Certain it is that our colonies prove enormously expensive to us: such a system promises an earlier maturity to them, and consequently a speedier release from the cost of assisting them.... It contemplates a colony in short, that shall be an entire British community, and not merely one formed of British materials.[164]

The belief, expressed in some of the statements quoted above, in the unquestionable benefit to Great Britain and, presumably, to the world at large, of having centres of English civilization scattered over the globe reached, in the case of a fairly large number of writers, the intense certainty that the British had been chosen by Providence for such an undertaking and that it was their obvious duty to follow this lofty call. This belief in the cultural mission of British colonization was expressed by Wakefieldians and other writers, by Tories, Whigs, and Radicals. Colonel Napier contented himself with pointing out that colonization was simply "grand." Having rejected as false all arguments that saw the benefits from colonization in relief from population pressure, in commercial advantages, etc., he exclaimed: "'But,' I shall be asked, 'are we not to colonize?' I answer yes; colonize by all means; only state the true and not the false inducements to a noble exploit. Let us not seek puerile excuses for doing that which is, in itself, grand. Why should we seek apologies for colonizing, as if we were about to commit a crime?"[165] Cooke spoke of "such a glorious and philanthropic undertaking as the furtherance of colonization, and the foundation of future empires?"[166] "Let the sons of Albion carry civilization to these distant shores, and a future age will applaud their enterprize. Providence has been bountiful in her gifts of territory to this happy country; should we neglect her favours?"[167]

William S. O'Brien declared: "There is no more legitimate kind of national pride than that which exults in viewing our country as the parent of many nations, whose future greatness is destined to bear witness to the wisdom and the energy of the people who founded them."[168] Laing remarked:

[164] *Ibid.*, pp. 199 f. See also Buller's speech in Wakefield, *Art of Colonization*, p. 492.
[165] *Colonization* (1835), pp. 10 f.
[166] W. B. Cooke, *Colonial Policy* (London, 1835), p. 26.   [167] *Ibid.*
[168] *Hansard*, third ser., LIV, c. 833.

When we consider the question of emigration in a general point of view, it must be evident that it is, of all others, the most important, and most intimately connected with the destinies of the English nation. The appointed mission of this nation evidently is to people the boundless regions of America and Australia with a race of men professing the purest religion, inheriting the richest literature and proudest history, and endowed by nature with the largest share of personal energy, perseverance, moral courage, self-command, habits of order and industry, and, in a word, possessing the highest degree or aptitude for practical civilization of any race the world has yet seen.[169]

Similarly, Archibald Alison:

... we behold the British race peopling alike the western and the southern hemispheres, and can already anticipate the time when two hundred millions of men on the shores of the Atlantic, and in the isles of the Pacific, will be speaking our language, reading our authors, glorying in our descent. Who is there that does not see in these marvellous events the finger of Providence; or can avoid the conclusion that the British race is indeed the chosen instrument for mighty things, and that to it is given to spread the blessings of civilization, and the light of religion, as far as the waters of the ocean extend?[170]

To consider themselves the chosen people, to spread civilization over the earth, to follow the beckoning finger of Providence, all these notions were to receive increasing currency in the following decades. It would be wrong to assume that these arguments for colonization were in all cases slyly invented to replace older arguments that had outlived their usefulness. In the majority of cases the authors of such phrases were probably quite sincere. Merivale, more discerning and more reflective than most of his contemporaries, remarked:

It is a sort of instinctive feeling to us all, that the destiny of our name and nation is not here, in the narrow island which we occupy; that the spirit of England is volatile, not fixed; that it lives in our language, our commerce, our industry, in all those channels of inter-communication by which we embrace and connect the vast multitude of states, both civilized and uncivilized, throughout the world. No circumstance, in my view, affords at once such a proof of our vocation to this great end, and such an augury of our success in the pursuit of it, as the peculiar and (in a certain sense of the word) unselfish interest with which schemes of colonization are regarded by almost all classes of society: the sanguine hopes we are apt to entertain of their success, the sacrifices we are willing to make for their promotion, even with little or no regard to the manner in which they may affect our economical prosperity at home.[171]

Without going into the question of its merits, the existence of this spirit must be conceded.

[169] *National Distress* (1844), pp. 120 f.
[170] Quoted from a speech delivered in 1839 (*Essays*, II, 659).
[171] *Lectures* (1841), I, 134.

CHAPTER X

THE FALL OF THE OLD COLONIAL SYSTEM

HUSKISSON'S CHANGES IN THE COLONIAL SYSTEM[1]

THE famous free-trade petition of the London merchants in 1820 heralded a change in Britain's commercial policy toward her colonies as well as toward the rest of the world. Her industrialists' quest for wider markets and confidence in their productive efficiency made them ever more averse to the restrictions of an outmoded commercial system. To some extent the government yielded to this pressure and became amenable to bargaining for concessions with other countries. This and the trade policy of the United States rendered possible the reforms of Thomas Wallace and William Huskisson. In 1821, the duties on Baltic timber were reduced. In 1822, Wallace revised the Navigation Laws and between 1823 and 1825, Huskisson initiated Britain's commercial policy of reciprocity.

Huskisson was neither an anti-imperialist nor a Free Trader in the strict sense. But he favoured freer trade and confined his reformatory work to what he deemed practicable proportions. His Navigation Act of 1825 codified the laws relating to shipping and relaxed the navigation system considerably, but it did not abandon its fundamental principles. After 1825, the main features of the navigation and colonial system stood as follows: (1) All intercourse between colonies and mother country, whether direct or circuitous, was considered as coast-wise trade and, therefore, reserved to British shipping. (2) Foreign goods were permitted to enter the colonies in British or in foreign vessels belonging to the producing country provided the foreign country in question accorded reciprocal privileges to Great Britain. (3) Foreign ships were allowed to carry colonial produce anywhere provided, again, that the country whose flag the vessel carried, granted reciprocity

---

[1]See C. R. Fay, "The Movement towards Free Trade," *Cambridge History of the British Empire*, vol. II, chap. XI; J. H. Clapham, *An Economic History of Modern Britain* (Cambridge, England, 1926), pp. 331-4; J. H. Clapham, "The Last Years of the Navigation Acts," *English Historical Review*, XXV (1910), 480-4.

of treatment to Britain.[2] (4) The obsolete list of enumerated articles was discarded.[3] (5) British goods received preferential treatment in the colonies.

Thus, through Huskisson's reforms, the colonial system was transformed from a monopolist into a preferential system. Fundamental as this change may appear in form, in substance it was by no means prodigious.

THE PROBLEM OF THE SUGAR DUTIES[4]

In the middle of the eighteenth century the West Indian sugar planters were among the richest men in the Empire; from that time on, however, dates the continuous decay of these Caribbean Island economies.[5] The main reasons for this development were: the proverbial backwardness of production methods as compared with other sugar-producing areas, the trade barriers maintained between the West Indies and the United States between 1783 and 1822,

[2] As some important countries were unwilling to grant such reciprocal privileges, the relaxation of the system appeared greater on paper than it was in reality. France and Spain enjoyed only very limited trading rights in the British colonies while Holland, Belgium, and Sardinia enjoyed none at all.

[3] However, the tariff preferences accorded to many important colonial products when imported to the mother country served to direct the main flow of these goods to the metropolis.

[4] The advocates of free trade in Great Britain concentrated their attack against the protectionist system primarily on the Corn Laws. Next in importance were the sugar and timber duties both of which involved a discussion of the colonial and navigation system. In the following the arguments used in the course of these debates will be studied.

Throughout the period here under discussion these debates took place in the House of Commons at frequent intervals and a vast literature of articles, pamphlets, and books accompanying these discussions is available. There was exceedingly little change in the arguments utilized by the opposed camps and it is, therefore, possible to cite literally dozens of statements reiterating the same argument. Hence, it is superfluous to present more than one or two wordings of the same argument.

That the following examination is confined to the cases of the sugar and the timber duties does, of course, not mean that there were not other commodities which received similar preferences in the metropolitan market. But the arguments utilized against or in favour of the retention of tariff preferences for colonial coffee or wines, etc., are in no way different from those used in the cases of timber and sugar except for the fact that the case of the timber duties involved, more than that of other preferential duties, the issue of protection to British shipping while the case of the sugar duties was complicated on account of the distinction between slave-grown and free-grown produce.

[5] See L. J. Ragatz, *The Fall of the Planter Class in the British Caribbean, 1763-1833* (New York, 1928).

and the successive abolition of the slave trade and slavery in the British possessions.

Before entering into an examination of the debate on the sugar duties it is necessary to note that up to the emancipation of the slaves, the English demand for sugar at the price then prevailing fell short of the West Indian supply. As a consequence, approximately one-fifth of their output had to be sold on the continent and the price received in the European market determined the price realized by the sugar planter.[6] Following the emancipation of the slaves in 1834, the sugar output in the English West Indian colonies dwindled to such an extent that it was utterly insufficient to supply the English demand. The tariff preference accorded to English West Indian sugar then acted as a subsidy to the planters.[7]

In the first place, the opponents of the preferential treatment granted to West Indian sugar pointed to the material loss which this arrangement inflicted on the metropolitan consumer. By preventing him from buying sugar at the cheapest source, the duty operated as a tax out of which the "aristocracy of the sugar hogshead"[8] was paid a subsidy. Taking the period from 1835 to 1841, Buchanan computed the difference between what the English people had been obliged to pay at the home-market price, and what they would have had to pay at the world-market price as about £5,537,140 annually. "Such has been, for some years past, the annual expense to Great Britain of the West India monopoly of sugar. It is one of the heaviest taxes which this narrow policy imposes on the country.... It thus abridges the comforts of the people...."[9] Similarly, Dunckley stated:

In 1846, West Indian sugar, the growth of our own colonies, was admitted to consumption on paying a duty of rather more than twenty-five shillings per cwt., while the produce of Cuba and Brazil was kept out by a duty of sixty shillings per cwt. The cost of the quantity of sugar retained for consumption that year, exclusive of duty, was £9,156,872. The cost of a like quantity of Brazil or Cuba sugar, of the same quality, would have been £4,141,181. For the benefit of our colonial planters this cheaper sugar was

---

[6] See John Davidson, *Commercial Federation and Colonial Trade Policy* (London, 1900), p. 51.

[7] Herman Merivale, *Lectures on Colonization and Colonies* (London, 1841), I, 201 f.; David Buchanan, *Inquiry into the Taxation and Commercial Policy of Great Britain* (Edinburgh, 1844), p. 150.

[8] John Bright and J. E. T. Rogers (eds.), *Speeches on Questions of Public Policy by Richard Cobden* (London, 1870), I, 84.

[9] *Inquiry into the Taxation and Commercial Policy of Great Britain* (1844), pp. 150 f.

kept out by law, and we had to pay £5,015,691 more than any other nation in Europe would have had to pay for the same quantity.[10]

These figures looked all the more stupendous if compared with the volume of British exports to the West Indies.

... It is shown that we paid for the same quantity of sugar used in 1840 more than 5,000,000l. sterling beyond what would have been paid for the same quantity, irrespective of duties, by any other people in Europe. The total value of our manufactures exported in that year to our sugar colonies was under 4,000,000l., so that the nation would have gained a million of money in that one year by following the true principle of buying in the cheapest market, even though we had made the sugar-growers a present of all the goods which they took from us.[11]

For a long series of years the West Indies were a positive drain upon the industrial resources of this country; the manufactures they purchased were less in point of aggregate value than the sum of which we were annually robbed for their maintenance; if all the goods which left our ports for the West Indies had been carted to the edge of Dover Cliffs and sunk in the Channel, the nation would have sustained no loss, if, as a compensation, it had merely received permission to purchase its sugar in the cheapest market.[12]

Another reason brought forward against the continuation of the West Indian monopoly was that it hindered the exporting industries in expanding their markets in Brazil. Thus, W. Ewart told the House of Commons in 1839: "The House might probably be aware that petitions had been presented to that House from the large commercial communities of Liverpool, Glasgow, and other places, in favour of that reduction [of the preference accorded to the Engl. West Indian sugar producers]. Our exports to Brazil were of very large amount, and our imports thence were very limited."[13]

These were the main[14] arguments raised against the retention

[10] Henry Dunckley, *The Charter of Nations* (London, 1854), pp. 255 f.
[11] G. R. Porter, *The Progress of the Nation* (London, 1851), pp. 723 f.
[12] Dunckley, *Charter of Nations* (1854), p. 256.
[13] *Hansard*, third ser., XLII, c. 1021; see also *The Political Writings of Richard Cobden* (London, 1867), I, 26 f.
[14] One interesting argument of lesser importance was that cheaper imports of sugar and coffee would curb the consumption of alcoholic beverages in Great Britain. "A still greater evil of the monopoly is, that in raising the price of sugar, it discourages the consumption of those articles, a taste of which is highly favourable both to health and morale, superseding, as they [coffee and tea] do, the use of ardent spirits, that never-failing source of vice and misery. Numerous houses have been, of late years, established in London and other places.... Such establishments are extremely favourable to regular and sober habits. They are schools of temperance, where the doctrine is not preached but practised..." (Buchanan, *Inquiry into the Taxation and Commercial Policy of Great Britain* [1844], pp. 154 f.). This view was shared by J. D. Hume; see Charles Badham, *The Life of James Deacon Hume* (London, 1859), pp. 270 ff.

of the preferential treatment of West Indian sugar. They were weighty reasons and they could hardly be proved incorrect. Even the argument that Great Britain enjoyed a preferential and, hence, safe market in the West Indies was advanced very infrequently. Perhaps the most important counter-argument of the West Indians and their metropolitan abettors was that the sugar planters had a just if not legal claim for such preferential treatment. Zachary Macaulay singled out several of the arguments on which the West Indians based their claim. "A preference, they say, has been granted for a very great length of time to West-Indian sugars: they possess, by prescription, an exclusive right to the supply of the home market, which it would be unjust to disturb."[15] "Great Britain has encouraged the cultivation of sugar in the West Indies . . . the faith of Parliament has been pledged for their protection . . . ."[16]

Metropolitan defenders of the monopoly arrangement pursued much the same line of argumentation. They said that justice did not allow the mother country to discuss the matter "in reference only to the question of supply and demand."[17] Charles Ellis argued in 1825: "that a solemn compact had been entered into between the mother country and her colonies; the former having stipulated to grant every protection to the latter. That compact ought never to be lost sight of."[18] More specifically, it was pointed out that the plight of the West Indian planter was due mainly to the abolition of slavery and that the £20,000,000 compensation paid by the government did not make up for the loss sustained.[19]

[15] Zachary Macaulay, *East and West India Sugar* (London, 1823), p. 10.

[16] *Ibid.*, p. 23. Mr. James, a sugar planter, told the House of Commons in 1844: "He was, unfortunately, one of those persons called West India proprietors, and he was not so through a fault of his own. He was a West India proprietor because, somewhere about a century since, an ancestor of his, relying on the faith of the Government of that day, did invest a considerable amount of capital in the purchase of a West India estate in the island of Jamaica; and he did so, perhaps, under the impression that future Governments would not interfere to injure, much less to utterly destroy, the value of that property" (*Hansard*, third ser., LXXV, cs. 423 f.).

[17] Cf. speech by T. S. Rice in the House of Commons in 1839 (*Hansard*, third ser., XLIII, c. 1024).

[18] *Ibid.*, sec. ser., XII, c. 1085.

[19] Thus, Viscount Sandon said in 1844: "Compensation, to be compensation, must leave parties where it finds them—must replace parties in their original position. Have the twenty millions done that? Did they not know that the West India proprietors who received that money have been ruined since its receipt?" (*ibid.*, LXXV, c. 464). Similarly, "The Foreign Slave Trade," *Quarterly Review*, LV (1835-6), 272 f.

Some pointed out, somewhat incautiously, that the mother country enjoyed preferential treatment in the colonies and that the same treatment was accorded the West Indians only by way of compensation.[20] Others asserted quite boldly that "everybody else" received protection, so why should not the West Indian planters? "The agricultural and manufacturing interests of Great Britain are both protected. The West Indian planters contribute to that protection ... and, therefore, they have a just claim to protection in their turn."[21] The representatives of the consumers' interest were told that "it was the duty of the House, when reduction of taxes was proposed, to look at the different classes of the community ...."[22] Similarly, H. Goulborn, then Chancellor of the Exchequer, said in 1844: "the object which I have in view is to reconcile very conflicting points which arise out of a consideration of the question of the Sugar Duties."[23]

The proponents of repeal rejected any compromise solution. In reply to these devious arguments they claimed that they did not see why the sugar interest should be supported at the expense of the much larger consumers- and manufacturing-interest of Great Britain.[24] Cobden asked: "The right hon. Gentleman said, that the claim of the West Indians to this monopoly rested upon the ground, that they had always enjoyed it without opposition. Why, if they were to go to such an argument as this, there was no existing monopoly, or abuse of any kind, which might not be defended with equal reason."[25]

Finally, this school of thought maintained that the sugar monopoly, though profitable to a handful of individuals, could never ensure the enduring prosperity of the West Indies; that, on the contrary, it would rather perpetuate their economic distress.

They [the West Indians] have wasted their energies in futile attempts unnaturally to raise prices, and to bolster up their own interests.... Foreign competition has continued to press them closer every day; and, since they are wholly without the means of sheltering themselves from its effects, would

---

[20]Cf. speech of Henry Bright in 1829 (*Hansard*, sec. ser., XXI, c. 1571).

[21]John Marryat, *A Reply to the Arguments* ... (London, 1823), p. 108. Similarly, Charles Ellis said in the House of Commons in 1825: "Every species of British manufacture was protected against competition ... why should not the same protection be afforded to our colonial produce?" (*Hansard*, sec. ser., XII, c. 1086.)

[22]*Ibid.*, X, c. 784 (speech of Alexander Baring in 1824).

[23]*Hansard*, third ser., LXXV, c. 155.

[24]See speech of Milner Gibson in 1844 (*ibid.*, c. 435).

[25]*Ibid.*, c. 445.

they not do well to set about trying to prepare for withstanding its keen but invigorating breeze? This is the course that common sense would point out. . . .[26]

It must be idle to suppose that colonists depend for their existence and progress upon such preferences. Unless prevented through the interference of legislative restrictions, they will certainly be able to apply their industry in some profitable channel. The very fact of their existence indicates that the inhabitants of colonies are in possession of advantages, whether of soil or climate, greater than are afforded by the country whence they have emigrated; and it must be reckoned among the evils produced by differential or protective duties, that they divert capital and industry from more profitable into less profitable, and sometimes even into hurtful, branches of employment.[27]

Thus, the promoters of free trade argued that the extinction of the preferential system would benefit the sugar colonies by, firstly, exposing the planters to the "invigorating breeze" of competition, and, secondly, by redirecting capital from less profitable into more profitable channels. Furthermore, it was claimed that under a preferential set-up the colony ran the risk implied in the fact that "the continuance of such a monopoly must always depend upon the good pleasure of the mother country."[28]

Another point raised frequently, especially during the twenties and thirties, by the opponents of repeal was that the state could not afford a reduction of duties in general as such a measure would entail a sizable fiscal loss. It must be kept in mind that in 1816 the commercial and industrial interests of the country had secured the abolition of the income tax while the public debt had been greatly multiplied during the wars with France. The Treasury, therefore, was compelled to raise a large revenue by indirect taxation. In the late twenties and early thirties statesmen like Lord Althorp and Huskisson assumed that a reduction of import duties of any kind was conditional upon the re-introduction of the income tax, but the ruling classes at that time were hostile to any such form of direct taxation.[29] Thus, when the House of Commons debated the issue of the sugar duties in 1828, the Chancellor of the

[26]"Colonial Policy—West Indian Distress," *Edinburgh Review*, LIV (1831), 334.

[27]Porter, *Progress of the Nation* (1851), p. 724. See also, C. P. Villier's speech in the House in 1844 (*Hansard*, third ser., LXXV, c. 438); Henry Parnell, *On Financial Reform* (2d ed.; London, 1830), pp. 231 ff.; Earl Grey, *The Colonial Policy of Lord John Russell's Administration* (London, 1853), II, 51 ff.

[28]Edward Gibbon Wakefield, *England and America* (New York, 1834), p. 331.

[29]See Sir Denis Le Marchant, *Memoirs of John Charles Viscount Althorp* (London, 1876), pp. 273 f., 284 ff. In 1842, Peel was able to re-introduce direct taxation as a prerequisite to the introduction of free trade.

Exchequer declared that "he rose for the purpose of moving for the continuance of the existing Duties on Sugar for another year. . . . It was unnecessary for him to enter into details of the various plans which were proposed to effect this object; but, as they went to produce a material reduction of duty, and as none of the arrangements held out the slightest expectation of repairing, until a distant period, the great loss which the revenue was likely to sustain, under these circumstances, he had deemed it most prudent to propose the continuance of the large revenue derived from sugar . . . ."[30]

In 1829, again discussing the question of the sugar duties, Alexander Baring likewise expressed his apprehension of hazarding the experiment "in the present state of the revenue."[31] In the course of these debates men like Joseph Hume and Charles Grant maintained that a reduction of sugar duties in general and of the preference accorded to the West Indian planters in particular would not be injurious to the revenue because of the increased consumption that would result from lower duties.[32] In the course of a House debate on the sugar duties in 1846, Lord John Russell said that the fiscus was a "very considerable sufferer" because of the high sugar duties necessitated by the preferential arrangement.[33]

Apart from the controversial issue of whether East Indian sugar should be granted the preferential treatment accorded to West Indian sugar,[34] the question here discussed was complicated by the problem of slave-grown sugar. In his paper *On the Maintenance of a Differential Duty in Favour of Colonial Sugar*, Major Torrens gave a lucid statement of the argument. In the first place, he observed, the admission at equal rates of cheaper Brazilian and Cuban sugars, both slave-grown, would replace free-grown West Indian sugar in the British market. By this step, therefore, the nation would practically reverse its policy regarding the slave trade. By making the consumer pay, the encouragement of free-grown

[30] *Hansard*, sec. ser., XIX, c. 1206.
[31] *Ibid.*, XXI, c. 1577.
[32] *Ibid.*, XIX, c. 1210; *ibid.*, XXI, c. 1566.
[33] *Ibid.*, third ser., LXXXVII, c. 1304.
[34] Faced with frustration of their efforts, the representatives of the East Indian sugar interest sometimes joined the ranks of the free-trade forces. For a discussion favourable to the East India sugar interest, see Zachary Macaulay, *East and West India Sugar* (1823); James Cropper, *Letters Addressed to William Wilberforce* (Liverpool, 1822), pp. 37-8, *passim;* for the opposite view see Marryat, *A Reply to Arguments* (1823), pp. 93 ff., *passim;* "The Foreign Slave Trade," p. 278.

sugar, it was claimed, would equally distribute the burden of atonement that the English nation had taken upon itself for having encouraged and legalized slave-trade and slavery in earlier centuries.[35] Throughout the thirties and forties the potency of this argument can hardly be over-rated, for the nation, as a whole, supported the anti-slavery campaign with rare determination. Thus the abettors of the West Indian sugar monopoly were not only able to make use of a very effective argument in their struggle against the Free Traders, but also received on this issue the support of men who favoured free trade otherwise but belonged to or approved of Exeter Hall.

However, the "repealers" had one unanswerable counter-argument at their disposal. In 1845, Macaulay said in the House of Commons:

... the Ministers of the Crown call upon us to sacrifice great pecuniary advantages and great commercial facilities, for the purpose of maintaining a moral principle.... I deny that we are under any moral obligation to turn our fiscal code into a penal code, for the purpose of correcting vices in the institutions of independent states.... I say, if such a moral obligation exists, our financial legislation is one mass of injustice and inhumanity.... The Statute Book swarms with enactments directly opposed to the rule which they profess to respect.... Take the article of tobacco. Not only do you admit the tobacco of the United States which is grown by slaves; not only do you admit the tobacco of Cuba which is grown by slaves ... but you actually interdict the free labourer of the United Kingdom from growing tobacco.[36]

The same thing, of course, was true of cotton which was mostly imported from the United States. "I affirm, then, that there exists in the United States a slave trade, not less odious or demoralising ... than that which is carried on between Africa and Brazil. North Carolina and Virginia are to Louisiana and Alabama what

[35]R. Torrens, *Tracts on Finance and Trade, No. 1* (London, 1852), pp. 31-8. Similarly, *The Times* wrote on May 7, 1841: "To extirpate the practical evils of slavery the people of this country consented, at the instigation of the Whigs, to make the enormous sacrifice of twenty millions sterling; and at length, when our national finances have become considerably embarrassed in consequence of that arrangement, we are gravely told by these same Whigs, that, in order to make up the deficit, it is now necessary to encourage the importation of slave-grown sugar at a suitable duty, and thus draw from the slave produce of foreign colonies the fiscal resources that may pay for its suppression in our own."

[36]Lady Trevelyan (ed.), *The Works of Lord Macaulay* (London, 1873), VIII, 284 f.

Congo is to Rio de Janeiro."³⁷ Cobden knew another, even more trenchant argument.

We send our manufactures to Brazil, as it is; we bring back Brazilian sugar; that sugar is refined in this country—refined in bonded warehouses . . . and it is then sent abroad by our merchants, by those very men who are now preaching against the consumption of slave-grown sugar . . . those very men and their connections who are loudest in their appeals against slave-grown sugar have bonded warehouses in Liverpool and London, and send this sugar to Russia, to China, to Turkey, to Poland, to Egypt; in short, to any country under the sun; to countries, too, having a population of 500,000,000; and yet these men will not allow you to have slave-grown sugar here. And why is this so? Because the 27,000,000 of people here are what the 500,000,000 of people of whom I have spoken are not—the slaves of this sugar oligarchy. Because over you they possess a power which they do not over others.³⁸

THE PROBLEM OF THE TIMBER DUTIES

In 1822, Sir I. Coffin declared in the House of Commons that "it would have been a good thing for this country, if Canada had been sunk to the bottom of the sea. It cost this country 500,000 l. per annum, and did not make a return to it of 500 pence. The Canadians, by the timber trade, had been in the habit of cheating this country out of 300,000 l. yearly. . . . The sooner the governor was called home, and the sooner the assembly and colony were suffered to go, he should be sorry to say au Diable, the better."³⁹ Six years later, the 300,000 pounds that had turned the wrath of Sir I. Coffin on the Canadians, had increased considerably. Senior stated: "We submit to a loss, exceeding probably a million sterling every year, occasioned by the restriction on the importation of Baltic timber; and voluntarily inoculate our houses with dry rot, lest saw mills in Canada, and ships in the North American timber trade, the aggregate value of which does not amount to a million sterling, should become less productive to their owners."⁴⁰

The differential duties on timber, favouring Canadian over Baltic supplies, owed their origin to the exigencies of the Napoleonic

---

³⁷*Ibid.*, p. 289. Macaulay continued to observe: "I see that the persons who now show so much zeal against slavery in foreign countries, are the same persons who formerly countenanced slavery in the British Colonies. They go round the whole compass, and yet to one point they steadfastly adhere; and that point is the interest of the West Indian proprietors" (*ibid.*, p. 302). See also Lord John Russell's speech in 1846 (*Hansard*, third ser., LXXXVII, c. 1310).

³⁸*Speeches*, I, 85 f.

³⁹*Hansard*, sec. ser., VI, c. 1076.

⁴⁰N. W. Senior, *Three Lectures on the Transmission of the Precious Metals* (London, 1828), p. 46.

wars that had severed Great Britain temporarily from the Baltic source of supply. The preferential arrangement was retained after the conclusion of the wars.[41] In 1840, for example, Canadian timber paid a customs duty of 10s. a load as compared with 45s. a load in the case of the Baltic material.[42] In spite of this ample difference in customs dues, Great Britain imported approximately two-fifths of her timber from the Baltic countries since for many purposes most kinds of Canadian timber were vastly inferior in quality to similar kinds of Baltic timber.[43] The timber duties, therefore, were doubly obnoxious because they resulted in the "forced consumption"[44] of a vastly dearer and vastly inferior product, a material, moreover, that had to be used in the production of innumerable goods.[45]

Nevertheless, the fight for the repeal of the differential in the case of the timber duties was considerably harder than that for the repeal of the tariff preference accorded to West Indian sugar. In the first place Canada seemed of much greater importance as a British colony than the sugar islands. Here the defenders of the system were able to assert that the abolition of the preference would amount to hazarding British shipping engaged in the trade[46] and,

[41] On the history of British legislation regarding lumber imports, see Henry Bliss, *On the Timber Trade* (London, 1831), pp. 5-15.

[42] Officially this arrangement was justified on the ground that the differential equalized transportation costs between the two areas of supply. This equalization of shipping costs did not prevent the fact that Baltic timber, quite frequently, was shipped to England via Canada in order to be imported as a North American product. See Merivale, *Lectures* (1841), I, 202 f.; Bliss, *On the Timber Trade* (1831), p. 25.

[43] Sir Robert Sepping declared in 1831 that frigates built of Canadian lumber possessed, on the average, only half the life-expectancy of those built of the Baltic material and that the Royal Navy, therefore, had discontinued the use of American timber. See Merivale, *Lectures*, I, 203. Another writer pointed to similar conclusions with regard to the building of houses (*Hints on the Subject of the Timber Duties* [London, 1821], pp. 14 f.).

[44] Merivale, *Lectures* (1841), I, 202; similarly, Sir Alexander Malet, *The Canadas* (London, 1831), p. 12.

[45] "Timber is not only a necessary of life, but, directly or indirectly, the raw material of every manufacture. In a country thickly peopled like ours, where the land is of high value, and considering that no good timber can on an average be grown under a century, it is a most inordinate folly to make a necessary of life, and the raw material of manufacture, the object of an oppressive monopoly, and impolitic to make it a subject of taxation at all" ("The Colonial Expenditure," *Westminster Review*, XXIV [1836], 10).

[46] As Baltic shipping operated at lower freight rates than English shipping, it was feared that the latter would be unable to hold its own in the Baltic timber trade.

therefore, endangering the naval superiority of the country. "The subject has been so much obscured by popular prejudices, and the judgement of the public has been so much biased by their naturally generous feelings, which have been industriously worked upon by interested persons, that cool and serious reflection is required, in order to arrive at correct and safe conclusions upon it."[47] Indeed, as soon as an argument touched the question of English maritime power, Englishmen were singularly insusceptible to logical reasoning. In 1821, Daniel Sykes said in the House of Commons that "he looked at the interests of the ship-owners as bound up with the general interests of the country. . . . The American timber trade was carried on by British shipping, but three-fourths of the Norway timber trade was carried on by foreign ships, and the other quarter by British. Even if all British ships, were employed in the Norway trade, it would be carried on by one-third of the numbers of ships employed in the American."[48]

In the course of the same debate Frederick Robinson declared: "As to the shipping interest, he trusted parliament and the country would never be so ungrateful as to forget that to it we owed the glory of that navy

"Whose flag had brav'd a thousand years
The battle and the breeze."[49]

Henry Bliss wrote: "Is it not lamentable to find the great interests of navigation thus lightly assailed, with so little pains apparently taken to inquire, compute, and reflect, upon circumstances and consequences? Some vague surmises, some loose and puerile conjectures, resting only on the confidence with which they are asserted, are thought sufficient grounds for perilling millions of capital, and even the maritime ascendancy of the British Empire."[50]

The opponents of the preference accorded to Canadian timber suggested that shipping should not be regarded exclusively as a nursery of naval power but also as a means of transportation and that in this latter function it ought to be viewed as any other branch of business. "Ships, in as far as regards the wealth of the community, must be considered merely as machines used for the transportation of commodities; machines of the same class with waggons and wheelbarrows. . . . The amount of capital expended

[47] *Hints on the Subject of the Timber Duties* (1821), pp. 10 f.
[48] *Hansard*, sec. ser., V, c. 54.
[49] *Ibid.*, c. 55.
[50] *On the Timber Trade* (1831), p. 90. See also *ibid.*, p. 3.

in these machines should, as regards the public wealth, be as small as possible; as thereby the commodities transported by them would be cheap, and the enjoyment of the community increased...."[51] As far as shipping as a nursery of trained seamen was concerned, it had never been shown that an appreciable diminution of British shipping would result from the discontinuation of the preference arrangement or, if that should be the consequence, that a smaller volume of British shipping would not be sufficient for the purpose under consideration. "It has never, however, been satisfactorily shown that there would be any material diminution of the shipping of Great Britain upon an alteration of the present law; nor that a larger mercantile marine is required than would be maintained by an unrestricted trade."[52]

C. P. Villiers maintained that "there is nothing of which I venture to speak with more confidence than that the British navy is in no way dependent for its efficacy upon that part of the mercantile marine which is employed in the timber trade."[53] It was also pointed out in this connection that only obsolete vessels, useless for any other purpose, were employed in this trade.[54] Furthermore, even if the Royal Navy needed a vast reservoir of experienced sailors to draw upon in time of war, it was questioned whether the maintenance of the intra-imperial timber trade was not a shockingly wasteful way to maintain the personnel-basis of British maritime power. David Ricardo intimated that in this respect the existing arrangement was in no way superior to one whereby "the ships engaged in the coasting trade should be obliged to sail round the island in order to give employment to a greater number" of sailors.[55] Hence, one writer proposed that it would be far more economical to pay for the training of a sufficiently large number of seamen by way of a direct tax.[56]

[51]"Timber Trade," *Westminster Review*, VII (1826-7), 142.

[52]*Ibid*. The question whether British shipping was really in need of protection will be further discussed in connection with the debate on the inexpediency of the Navigation Laws. At the present point this study is mainly concerned with the special arguments connected with the timber trade.

[53]*Hansard*, third ser., XL, c. 94.

[54]"Of the value of such shipping, we need say very little to anyone at all conversant with the timber trade. Until ships are unfit for any other business, they are seldom used for the transportation of timber..." ("Timber Trade," *Westminster Review*, VII [1826-7], 144).

[55]*Hansard*, sec. ser., V, c. 58.

[56]"Timber Trade," p. 145. Similarly, Ricardo's speech of 1821 (*Hansard*, sec. ser., V, c. 58).

The argument that the state owed continued protection to such important interests as British shipping and the Canadian timber business[57] was countered by the explanation that it was unsound, on general grounds, to support particular interests that were opposed to the general interest of the national community.[58] Thus, in 1821, David Ricardo opposed the view "that the interest of the producer ought to be looked to, as well as that of the consumer, in legislative principles. But the fact was, that in attending to the interest of the consumer, protection was at the same time extended to all other classes. The true way of encouraging production was to discover and open facilities to consumption."[59] Ricardo, in short, defended the virtues of the laissez-faire system according to which a consumer-oriented economy determined best how the available factors of production are used most economically.

Furthermore, it was argued that, although existing legislation on the subject was highly gratifying to the ship-owners, it was obvious from any but a short-sighted point of view that British shipping would greatly benefit from the abolition of the preferential timber duties, because it was largely owing to the dearness and inferior quality of the timber used in ship-building and ship-repairing that British shipping operated on a higher-cost basis compared with American or Scandinavian shipping.[60]

The supporters of the existing system also argued that it was the duty of the mother country to be mindful of the vested interests of the colonists engaged in the timber business. Bliss declared: "But, above all, what is to become of the capital invested in the Colonies in the conduct and advancement of this trade? Invested too, not merely on the tacit faith and encouragement of repeated

[57]See the speech of T. Wallace in 1821 (*ibid.*, cs. 50 f.).
[58]See Villier's speech in 1839 (*ibid.*, third ser., XL, c. 89).
[59]*Hansard*, sec. ser., V, c. 271. In the course of the same debate Ricardo declared: "In this, as in all other branches of commercial policy it was useless to urge partial views in behalf of one set of men or another. That House ought not to look to the right or left, but consider merely how the people of England, as a body, could best employ their capital and labour" (*ibid.*, c. 58). See also, speech by Henry Grey Bennet (*ibid.*, c. 52), and the speech by Dr. Bowring in 1835 (*ibid.*, third ser., XXVII, c. 217).
[60]"It must be evident to every rational mind, that the interests of the ship-owners would be considerably promoted by the importation of cheaper timber. If timber were cheaper, ships could be built at a smaller expense; if ships could be built at smaller expense, freights would be lower, and the British shipowner might then successfully compete for the carrying-trade of the world with the shipowners of other countries" ("Timber Trade," p. 144). Similarly, C. P. Villier's speech in 1839 (*Hansard*, third ser., XL, c. 99).

Acts of Parliament. but after the express invitation, the anxious solicitation, of the ministers, when by the hostilities of Europe this country was in danger of utter destitution."[61]

As in the case of the West Indian sugar monopoly, the Free Traders argued that because of the encouragement of uneconomic capital investment, the colonists were not all gainers by the present system. Thus, C. P. Villiers stated that the colonists "have been seriously injured by being tempted to divert their capital and industry from their natural channels of employment."[62] Moreover, it was explained that the British nation paid much more than the Canadians apparently gained. Computing the loss sustained by the British nation at approximately one million pounds per annum, one author stated: "The whole sum given by us in exchange for this timber is not gained by the colonies, but only so much of it as exceeds the cost of producing the timber and bringing it to the market; this surplus being by competition reduced to the usual profits of stock."[63] If the existing law were altered the Canadian capital invested in the timber industry would find a more profitable field of employment. "This, to a certain extent, might be an injury; it might depreciate the value of saw-mills which cut timber for exportation, and there the injury would stop. . . ."[64] But it would be much more economical if Great Britain, upon changing the preferential arrangement of the timber trade, "were to buy this property at the present price."[65]

Among arguments of marginal importance advanced in favour of the preferential system were, firstly, that it would be dangerous for Great Britain to be dependent on one source of supply only and that foreigners would raise their price as soon as the laws on the timber trade were repealed;[66] and, secondly, that, as a market,

[61]*On the Timber Trade* (1831), p. 42.
[62]*Hansard*, third ser., XL, c. 94.
[63]"Timber Trade," p. 135. [64]*Ibid.*, p. 136.
[65]*Ibid.*, p. 137. If, after the abandonment of the preferential system, Britain would sell the property, "she should not lose by the purchase more than 150,000 l., while we should gain by the alteration of the law more than quadruple that amount" (*ibid.*).
Another writer remarked: "That bounty is surely ill bestowed which costs the donor ten fold more than it contributes to its object; and it would be wise to withdraw it, even although he should feel himself called upon to recompense the party to the full extent of the benefit he had formerly derived from the bounty" (*Hints on the Subject of the Timber Duties* [1821], p. 16).
[66]See the Report of the Committee on Foreign Trade of March 9, 1821 (William Small, *Economic Annals of the Nineteenth Century* [London, 1910-18], II, 25 f.).

Canada, was much more dependable and, hence, much more valuable to Great Britain than the Baltic countries.[67] These arguments were easily disposed of by the opposition. "It is urged by the friends of restriction, that, the moment we equalize these duties, foreigners, being relieved from the competition of the colonies, will raise their prices. We answer, that competition will exist in the North of Europe to an extent and of a nature to render combination for the purpose of keeping up prices impossible. There will be competition, not only of individual dealers, but of three or four nations."[68] As to the market-argument the same writer remarked: "In showing that the colonists have other means of employing their capital and labour, independent of the timber trade, and that consequently the value of their exports would, except during the process of transfer and adjustment, remain undiminished, we, in effect, settled the question as to the unimpaired power of the North-American colonies to purchase our manufactures after their timber trade has been annihilated . . . and our manufacturers will, in addition, have all the benefit of any new demand which may spring up in consequence of the increased power of the North of Europe to purchase. . . ."[69] Thus, by directing Canadian capital employed in the timber trade into different channels Canadian production and foreign trade would expand and Great Britain would share in the increased total volume of trade. Another author, ignoring this point, countered the market-argument by maintaining: "The next argument in favour of the trade is, that it enables the Canadians to take our manufactures to a large amount; but it is manifestly impossible, that this branch of their trade can enable them to take a larger value of British goods, than the timber they export amounts to; and it is no less certain, that from whatever country we get our supply of timber, it must directly, or indirectly, be paid for in goods; and the less the proportion of the cost that consists in freights (if imported in British ships), the greater will be the return in goods."[70]

[67]See Bliss, *On the Timber Trade* (1831), pp. 53-8; and James Marryat's speech in 1921 (*Hansard*, sec. ser., V, cs. 58 ff.).

[68]"The Timber Monopoly," *London and Westminster Review*, XXVI (1836-7), 114.

[69]*Ibid.*, p. 126.

[70]*Hints on the Subject of the Timber Duties* (1821), p. 12. This writer, of course, ignored the terms-of-trade problem.

TRADE AND EMPIRE

For the period from 1815 to 1850, various arguments as to the merits or demerits of the preferential organization of intra-imperial commerce, and the importance or unimportance of colonies as markets or sources of goods have been presented. In the following the two opposing systems of thought will be surveyed as a whole.

Among the protectionists there prevailed a general tendency to belittle or question the benefits of trade with independent foreign countries as compared with those derived from trade with the colonies. This trend of thought was commonly expressed in the following fashion:

> Thus circumstanced, what is to her [Great Britain], after all, the real importance of trade with foreign nations? It is not necessary she should reject it; but why should she court it as indispensable? Above all, why should she, by discouraging her colonies for its sake, and thus depriving them of the means of being consumers of her exports, check their advancement, and place herself in dangerous dependence, for the supply of her own wants, and for a market for her manufactures, on nations which caprice, or jealousy, or cupidity, or prejudice, may render unwilling, or poverty or political distractions unable, either to supply her necessities or consume her productions?[71]

Similarly, John Marryat declared in the House of Commons in 1821: "Our trade with our own colonies and in our own ships, we can always call our own, because we hold it independent of the will of foreign powers; but in trading with foreign nations we are leaning on a broken reed. Have we already forgotten the continental system?..."[72]

This is, of course, the old self-sufficiency conception of the benefits of empire, the very core of which is dependability of markets and dependability of sources of supplies. To this bent of mind the free-trade doctrine appeared as nothing but pernicious irresponsibility or illusion.

> ... I ask, can that be a wise and prudent, or even a cautious policy, which renders the success of every interest in this country dependent on visitations and accidents of not infrequent occurrence—such as a famine at home—a revolution in France—an insurrection in Italy—distractions in Germany—commercial blindness in Spanish, or Dutch, or Belgian statesmen—or even on a presidential election in America? Does not common sense, if we would but listen to its dictates, impress on us the conviction that a policy subject to so many deranging influences cannot be wise?... Were the advantages of the course we have pursued under the guidance of ultra free-trade princi-

---

[71] G. F. Young, *Free-Trade and the Navigation Laws* (London, 1849), pp. 4 f.
[72] *Hansard*, sec. ser., V, cs. 58 f.

ples ten times greater than is presented, the very precariousness of the tenure on which they must be held would suffice to condemn the system. . . . Certainly, stability—the very elements of commercial prosperity must ever be wanting in a commerce exposed to constant and inevitable interruptions."[73]

According to this school of thought, then, the dependability of external sales and purchases was more important than their volume or, presumably, the more favourable terms of exchange obtainable in dealings with foreign nations. Concern over secure sources of supply was felt much less deeply than concern over secure markets.[74] Intellectually the arguments used were much the same as those advanced in earlier periods, arguments that led James Marryat to declare in 1820, that "the transfer of any branch of trade . . . from our colonies to foreign nations, is an act of the highest impolicy."[75] As compared with colonial markets, foreign markets were precarious and were becoming so more and more. Indeed, it is interesting to observe that the fear of foreign competition which was so characteristic of the imperialist wave of the last quarter of the century, made its appearance as early as the thirties and forties. Englishmen observed with anxiety the growing

[73] Young, *Free-Trade and Navigation Laws* (1849), pp. 5 ff.

[74] Young, indeed, denounced the illusions of free trade in compliance with which "instead of encouraging the growth of cotton in India and the West Indies, by the retention of a moderate differential duty . . . we have given the monopoly of supply of the raw material for our staple manufacture to our most jealous manufacturing rival;—receiving with extraordinary inconsistency, annually, 500 millions of pounds of that material duty free. . ." (*ibid.*, p. 5).

Dependability of foreign sources of supplies is a consequence of a multiplicity of sources of supplies. In this respect, indeed, the dependence of Great Britain on the cotton production of the United States loomed ominously in the mind of many an English observer. Lalor, for example, wrote: "If by any chance a Toussaint L'Ouverture should make his appearance in Alabama or Carolina . . . where would Manchester turn herself for a new supply of cotton?" (*Money and Morals* [London, 1852], p. 185).

For similar arguments with respect to wool, see Thomas Southey, *The Rise, Progress, and Present State of Colonial Wools* (London, 1848), pp. 2, 25. Southey wrote: "Our commercial greatness comes from our industry, to support which we require raw materials and outlets; but the records of our history tell us that events, over which we have no control, sometimes regulate the movements in trade. By sacrifices, we have been taught the value of self-reliance and mutual cooperation with our Colonies, more especially as regards the production of wool; and the important point of a steady and independent supply of this article being once gained, the advantages ought to be followed up, encouraged, and protected" (*ibid.*, p. 2).

[75] *Hansard*, sec. ser., I, c. 1182; see also the speech of Sir Howard Douglas in 1843, *Hansard*, third ser., LXVIII, cs. 588 f.; and Lord Stanley in 1842, *ibid.*, LXIII, cs. 532 ff.

industrialization of Western and Central Europe. Archibald Alison, arch-alarmist of the imperial-minded Tories, said in 1839:

> It is evidently owing to the fact, that these old States are in the same state of civilisation with ourselves, and therefore they are actuated by a natural desire to deal in the same articles, and to manufacture the same produce as ourselves. Are we Cotton Spinners?—so are they. Are we Iron Masters?—so are they. Are we Silk Manufacturers?—so are they. Are we Cutlery and Hardware Merchants?—so are they.... There is no branch of industry in which we excel, in which they are not all making the greatest and most strenuous, and sometimes successful, efforts to rival and outstrip us.[76]

Universal free trade was deemed an impracticable proposition by this school of thought. Alison, therefore, declared "Let us ... no longer strain after the impracticable attempt to disarm the commercial jealousy of the European States, and, boldly looking our situation in the face, direct our main efforts to the strengthening, conciliating, and increasing of our Colonial Empire. There is to be found the bone of our bone, and the flesh of our flesh."[77]

It would be wrong, however, to assume that only the Alisons felt inclined to speculate along these lines. Urging increased colonization, Sir William Molesworth stated in 1839: "I am profoundly convinced that the southern regions of the globe, Australia, New Zealand, and the Myriads of islands in the Polynesian Sea, might ere long form the most important markets for the productions of the industry of Great Britain, and amply compensate for those markets which we are on the eve of losing in the old world; provided those fair and fertile portions of the earth's surface were peopled with men of the British race...."[78] In 1855, Gladstone declared:

> If employment and trade with foreign countries are increased, you get the profit of the trade. But then you are undoubtedly liable to this disadvantage that the passing of unwise and bad laws in these foreign countries may greatly restrict and hamper the extension of your trade. Thus you are exposed to the utmost disadvantage, not because a proceeding of this kind makes the trade with foreign countries less lucrative than the trade with the colonies .... But the difference is this, in the case of a foreign country your trade often may be injuriously crippled and kept down so as to suffer by the bad laws of the country with which you are trading, while with respect to the colony you have no such danger ... so that when you found colonies, and

---

[76] *Essays, Political, Historical, and Miscellaneous* (Edinburgh, 1850), II, 667.
[77] *Ibid.*, p. 668.
[78] H. E. Egerton (ed.), *Selected Speeches of Sir William Molesworth on Questions relating to Colonial Policy* (London, 1903), pp. 81 f.

trade with them, you are practically sure that that trade will have fair play. . . .[79]

Thus, the Gladstones and Molesworths shared the suspicions and apprehensions of the Alisons but, in contrast to the latter, they were not protectionists and did not defend the kind of colonial system Alison upheld.

It is understandable that those who considered a free-trade policy impracticable and were apprehensive about the commercial future of Great Britain, were inclined to think along lines of an Imperial Zollverein. Major Torrens was the outstanding theorist of this school of thought before the country decided on adopting a policy of free trade.[80] He favoured the establishment of a mutually beneficent division of labour between mother country and colonies.[81]

A colonial trade may, at all times, be made a free trade. Here we can completely remove all those restrictions and prohibitions which prevent or obstruct that territorial division of employment which multiplies the power of production. Here no hostile tariff can cause the produce of a given quantity of British labour to exchange for the produce of a less quantity of foreign labour. . . . It is by extension of our colonial system, and by the expansion of colonial markets, we can most effectually sustain the prosperity of the country against the rivalry of Europe, and create new worlds to adjust the balance of the old.[82]

Torrens wanted the country to adopt a policy of strict reciprocity with foreign nations and a policy of absolute free trade within the Empire. He was, therefore, opposed to the retention of even preferential duties on British colonial produce. The colonies should be regarded as integral portions of the United Kingdom[83] and intra-imperial trade placed "upon the footing of a HOME TRADE."[84] Young supported the Zollverein-idea: "Unaffected by wars, uninterrupted by revolutions, undisturbed by political distractions, the pursuits of a commerce really free among ourselves would exhibit active importations of colonial products

[79] In Paul Knaplund, *Gladstone and Britain's Imperial Policy* (New York, 1927), p. 200.
[80] See above, pp. 344 ff.
[81] *An Essay on the Production of Wealth* (London, 1821), p. 229.
[82] Torrens, *The Budget* (London, 1841), pp. 65 f.
[83] *Ibid.*, p. 174.
[84] *Ibid.*, p. 176. In 1852, he warned of the consequences that might follow Great Britain's free-trade policy. "Let us not close our eyes against inevitable results. If, in our commercial dealings with our colonies, we treat them as foreign countries, foreign countries they will speedily become" (*Tracts on Finance and Trade*, No. 1 [1852], p. 40).

into our ports, and busy employment for our mills for the supply of colonial wants. This, I maintain, is the policy that practical wisdom would prescribe for such a country as England."[85] In 1848, Lord Elgin wrote to Earl Grey: "There is something captivating in the project of forming all the parts of this vast British Empire into one huge Zollverein with free interchange of commodities between its members, and uniform duties against the World without. Though perhaps without some federal legislation it might have been impossible to carry it out. Undoubtedly under such a system the component parts of the Empire would have been united by bonds which cannot be supplied under that on which we are now entering."[86]

Distrust of a universal trend towards world-wide free trade also led some free traders to conclude that the possession of colonies under a metropolitan free-trade régime guaranteed to the mother country absence of hostile tariffs in her oversea dependencies. Lord John Russell wrote to Earl Grey in 1849: "Even in his [Cobden's] own narrow view I wonder he does not see that the imposition of a duty of from 30 to 40 per cent. on British manufactured goods from the Mississippi to the St. Lawrence could be a great blow to Manchester and Leeds."[87] Similarly, Sir George Cornewall Lewis wrote: "The most plausible opinion respecting the commercial advantages derivable from dependencies seems to be, that the dominant country, by securing to itself an unrestricted trade with them, can prevent them from establishing the protecting and prohibitory duties which, if they were independent states, they would probably impose upon imports."[88]

Those Englishmen who supported free trade and colonization and yet were often concerned about protectionist trends in foreign countries, perceived three distinct advantages in the preservation and extension of the Empire. First, they expected that the

[85] *Free-Trade and Navigation Laws* (1849), p. 6. See also, *ibid.*, p. 4.

[86] Sir A. G. Doughty (ed.), *The Elgin-Grey Papers 1846-1852* (Ottawa, 1937), I, 181.

[87] Quoted in W. P. Morrell, *British Colonial Policy in the Age of Peel and Russell* (Oxford, 1930), p. 208.

[88] *An Essay on the Government of Dependencies* (1841), ed. C. P. Lucas (Oxford, 1891), p. 222. "If, however, the governments of civilised nations could once acquire so much reliance on the moderation and enlightenment of the governments of other civilised nations as to expect that the latter would allow an unrestricted trade with their own subjects, the motive for the acquisition and possession of dependencies, which is founded on the assumed folly of all governments, would no longer exist" (*ibid.*, pp. 223 f.).

colonies would adhere to the free-trade policy of the metropolis. Secondly, they desired to extend the area under free trade by creating new economies and markets overseas.[89] Thirdly, they assumed that the colonies would remain good customers of the parent state even in the absence of imperial tariff preferences on account of similarity or identity of language, political, social, and legal institutions, customs, tastes, etc., between the metropolitan and the colonial populations.[90] Thus, Molesworth declared in 1838: "Are we to regret that the more northern deserts of the American continent, which constitute her Majesty's possessions in that quarter of the globe, are in the course of being reclaimed, cultivated, and filled with inhabitants of our race, whose industry finds an ample reward, and who, having wants like our own, require objects that are produced here, and thus furnish us with continually increasing markets in which to sell the produce of our domestic industry?"[91] Whether the status of the colonies remained one of dependence seemed immaterial to some of these writers because they did not expect such a change to affect the validity of their argument.[92]

[89] Commenting on Parnell's free-trade programme, exclusive of colonization, Molesworth said in 1838: "The doctrine of the right hon. baronet rests on the assumption that the world abounds in independent States, able and willing to purchase British goods, and that whatever may be the increase of domestic capital and production requiring new markets, such markets will spring up, just at the moment we want them, in the form of independent States. Has that assumption any foundation in fact or reason? I cannot help thinking that it has none—that at all events it is greatly to the advantage of a country like this to plant colonies and thereby create markets where none exist. . ." (*Selected Speeches*, p. 7).

[90] This advantage, of course, was also pointed out by old-fashioned imperialists and by those Free-Traders who were indifferent or opposed to colonization. For example, see "New Colony on Swan River," *Quarterly Review*, XXXIX (1829), 340 ("The colonies that speak the language of Old England—that preserve her manners and her habits—will always be her best customers. . . "); J. R. McCulloch, *A Dictionary of Commerce and Commercial Navigation* (Philadelphia, 1840), p. 408.

[91] *Selected Speeches*, pp. 2 f.; similarly, J. A. Roebuck, *The Colonies of England* (London, 1849), pp. 11, 14.

[92] Critics pointed out that, although there was a core of truth in this argument, the benefits expected from a similarity of tastes and habits could be easily exaggerated. Merivale wrote: "It is undoubtedly true, that even under a system of free competition, the mother country will long retain an advantage in the market of her colony from the durability of national tastes and habits. . . . And a greater and more permanent advantage will result from that identity of language and customs which attracts to each other the traders of kindred nations, and modifies even the instincts of gain. But such exceptions to the general rule

Anti-protectionists, opposed to the imperial system of tariff preferences, belonged to the general free-trade movement. On principle they were determined to extinguish the last vestiges of the mercantilist system in Great Britain.[93] They utterly scorned the programme of national or imperial self-sufficiency. Senior, for example, remarked:

> Another most efficient fallacy consists in the use of the word "independent." To be independent of foreign supply, in consequence of the abundance of our own, is unquestionably a benefit. . . . The independence of the mercantile system is accompanied not by abundance, but by privation; it arises not from the extent, but from the mismanagement of our resources; not from our riches, but from self-inflicted poverty . . . it seems forgotten that dependence, as well as independence, must be mutual; that we cannot be habitually dependent on another nation for a large portion of our annual supplies without that nation's being equally dependent upon us.[94]

> . . . both natural causes and the course of events, while they have admirably fitted Great Britain for extensive commerce, have rendered her totally dependent on it.[95]

> We are dependent on foreign countries, not merely for what is agreeable, but for what custom has rendered necessary. Do I regret this dependence? Far from it, for it is the necessary consequence of two great benefits, the increase of our numbers and the increase of our wealth. It is the necessary dependence of the rich on the poor, of a metropolis on the surrounding

---

are comparatively slight and transitory. It has, therefore, been the favourite object of European governments . . . to confine the inhabitants of their colonies as far as possible to the use of articles produced in the mother country by legislative enactment" (*Lectures* [1841], I, 186).

McCulloch likewise was of the opinion that the similarity of habits and tastes tends to modify "the instinct of gain" only slightly. He wrote: "Owing to the identity of language, manners, and religion, the merchants of the mother country must always have very great advantages in the colony markets; and if the commodities which they have to sell be about as suitable for them, and as low priced, as those of others, none else will be imported into them; . ." (*Dictionary of Commerce and Commercial Navigation* [1840], I, 408).

The following deviation from the argument presented above is interesting. "Whether foreign nations be of our race or not, and whether they be dependent on us or not, are questions of no moment in the absolute value of our commerce with them—their energy and activity are the qualities that will make them valuable to us. We know that these are qualities eminently possessed by our own citizens; and therefore it is a common belief among us that the more thickly the same race is spread over the world, the better will it be for the commercial success of the empire" (J. H. Burton, *Political and Social Economy* [Edinburgh, 1849], p. 336).

[93] Senior's *Three Lectures on the Transmission of the Precious Metals* (1828) may be regarded as the most systematic attack on mercantilism since Adam Smith.

[94] *Ibid.*, pp. 48 ff.   [95] *Ibid.*, p. 91.

country. The half-naked subjects of Caractacus were doubtless independent of foreign supplies. . . .[96]

As demonstrated by their attitude toward the sugar and timber question, the anti-protectionists considered the system of imperial tariff preferences utterly obnoxious because it forced upon the metropolitan consumer goods which he could get much more cheaply in the world market.

The anti-protectionists also chided the general prejudice and ignorance manifest in the almost exclusive concern with exports and markets.[97] Merivale stated: "It is very true that our colonies are our best customers, and, if the value of our trade is to be reckoned by the consumption of our produce, by far our best customers."[98] Yet "our best customers are not those who take most of our produce, but those who give us the greatest amount of value in exchange."[99] This the colonies obviously did not do under the preferential system.[100]

Moreover, it was realized that, on the whole, the export of British manufactures to the colonies was not dependent on tariff preferences. "That England, which boasts of its power of competing successfully with the whole world in so many branches of manufacture, should have thought it necessary to force her goods by fiscal regulations upon people who had already the strongest inducements to trade with her, seems such an absurdity that one is at a loss to imagine how it could ever have been conceived."[101] The preferential system, therefore, was favourable only to the colonies and a total loss to the mother country.

. . . mutual restrictions, such as those imposed by the ancient system on the producers of the mother-country and the colony, for the supposed benefit of each other, have now become very little more than restrictions on one of the contracting parties only. We might draw many articles of raw produce cheaper and better from other countries than from our colonies. . . . But it may be questioned, whether any of the commodities they require from Europe, except some few articles which we do not and cannot produce, could

---

[96]*Ibid.*, p. 95.
[97]Merivale, *Lectures* (1841), I, 183 f.
[98]*Ibid.*, p. 224.   [99]*Ibid.*, p. 185.
[100]The chief pretext for the cost to which we are put by them [the colonies], is that they are a valuable market for British produce and manufactures; the fact that stares us in the face all the time, being, that with our British produce and manufactures we could buy better and cheaper pepper, &c., elsewhere. They consent to take more of our produce and manufactures for a pound of pepper, than another people would; this is the extent of our obligation" ("The Colonial Expenditure," p. 6).
[101]Porter, *Progress of the Nation* (1851), p. 724.

be obtained by them cheaper or better from any other source than from ourselves.[102]

Hence, Merivale concluded: "We give them commercial advantages, and tax ourselves for their benefit, in order to give them an interest in remaining under our supremacy, that we may have the pleasure of governing them."[103]

The Manchester School, which may be regarded as representative of Britain's exporting industries, scorned the idea of the English manufactures' dependence on "protection" of any kind. Cobden wrote in 1836 that the old motto "Ships, Colonies, Commerce". . . .

must now be dismissed, like many other equally glittering but false adages of our forefathers, and in its place we must substitute the more homely but enduring maxim—Cheapness, which will command commerce. . . .[104]

Provided our manufactures be cheaper than those of our rivals, we shall command the custom of these colonies by the same motives of self-interest which bring the Peruvians, the Brazilians, or the natives of North America, to clothe themselves with the products of our industry; and, on the other hand, they will gladly sell to us their commodities through the same all-powerful impulse, provided we offer for them a more tempting price than they will command in other markets.[105]

If it was cheapness of British export commodities that the country should rely on in the future as it did in the present, then it became imperative to erase every bit of British commercial legislation that tended to increase production costs by rendering raw materials and foodstuffs dearer and taxation heavier than they would be under a free-trade régime.

Some of the anti-protectionists stressed the fact that profitable international trade did not at all depend upon the economic complementarity of nations.[106] A number of them shared the belief that there existed a universal trend towards free trade. "The expectation that civilised nations may become, in no long time, sufficiently enlightened to understand the advantages of free trade is not visionary."[107] This expectation played an important part because these Englishmen were conscious of the fact that, following English leadership and example, other nations would

---

[102]Merivale, *Lectures* (1841), I, 72.
[103]*Ibid.*, p. 73. Similarly, Porter, *Progress of the Nation*, pp. 721 ff.
[104]*Political Writings*, I, 290. [105]*Ibid.*, p. 30.
[106]That part of our commerce which, being carried on with the rich and civilised inhabitants of European nations, should present the greatest field for extension. . ." (Porter, *Progress of the Nation* [1851], p. 361).
[107]Lewis, *Government of Dependencies* (1841), pp. 222 f.

adopt non-mercantilist policies. But England, and with her the Empire, would have to scrap restrictive tariff devices first.

In 1853, Earl Grey remarked that the initiation of a free-trade policy in Great Britain, including the open door in the colonies, amounted "to nothing less than a revolution in an established system of policy...."[108] Indeed, the change was of truly revolutionary proportions. Adam Smith's pessimism regarding the free-trade cause will be recalled. Senior, writing in 1828, had reason to be more confident. "The question of free trade," he wrote, "is, next to the Reformation, next to the question of free religion, the most momentous that has ever been submitted to human decision.... Slowly and reluctantly, and as if parting from our dearest friend, we have begun to withdraw from the restrictive system."[109] If considered on a rational basis, the free-trade case was not too difficult to be grasped. It was much more difficult to remove prejudices and the influence of group-interests. As late as 1841, Merivale observed the tenacity of the old monopolist persuasion. He spoke "of those very narrow views of commercial policy, which have become so inveterate by long indulgence, that even those who are convinced of their futility can scarcely shake off the prejudices produced by them ... we constantly under-rate those commercial benefits which are common to us with all the world.... To suit our contracted notions of economic gain to a particular country, the gain in question must be something exclusive and monopolized."[110]

The worst obstacle in the way of progress was what Bentham had termed "interest-begotten prejudice." Thus, the anti-protectionists had to combine the tasks of the teacher and the political reformer with that of the muckraker. Relentlessly, they had to expose the fallacies and the malignity of the monopolist system, the system which "is robbing Peter to pay Paul."[111] "The strange thing about the matter is always, that it should have been so long and so quietly taken for granted, that all that was got by robbery was public gain;—that it was gained by the robbers, and lost by nobody.... Public wealth was to be made, by one man taking

[108]*Colonial Policy of Lord J. Russell's Administration* (1853), I, 6. This question will be further discussed in a subsequent chapter on the Manchester School.
[109]*Three Lectures on the Transmission of the Precious Metals* (1828), pp. 88 f.
[110]*Lectures*, I, 184.
[111]*Morning Journal*, Jan. 5, 1830; quoted in Henry Bliss, *On Colonial Intercourse* (London, 1830), p. 105.

from another."[112] "All monopoly," Dunckley declared bluntly, "rests, in the last analysis, on the same basis as simple fraud."[113] "The Colonial System in general is only a mode of supporting the oligarchy at the expense of the community, by a process like cutting boots into shoes."[114] "The colonial system, like every other system of the kind, was constructed with a view to the present gain of particular classes...."[115]

Thus, as Adam Smith and the Benthamites had done before, these men showed that the existing system served the purpose of enriching the Few at the expense of the Many. And like their predecessors they demanded that the interests of the Few should be bent to the interest of the community. "I defend free trade, solely on public grounds.... For what is the end of government but to promote the happiness of the whole by forcing the interests of individuals to bend to those of the community?—the few to submit to the many?"[116] If the vested interests of the Few should suffer as they must from such a change of policy, that could not be helped. "To perpetuate the old system, because, whenever it is abandoned particular interests must suffer, is a principle which, if fairly applied, would lead to the suppression of every improvement whatever. No improvement can possibly be made which shall not be immediately injurious to somebody. Printing ruined the copyists; and the Turks, to protect their interests, prohibited it."[117]

THE END OF THE NAVIGATION SYSTEM

At first sight it may seem astounding that a relatively small group-interest like that of the British ship-owners and ship-builders was able to protract the debate on the merits and demerits of the Navigation Laws over such a long period of time. The fact that this interest-group received the support of other groups equally interested in the retention of protectionism and that the shipping-interest had organized an efficient and exceedingly influential "lobby"[118] cannot sufficiently explain its successful resistance to

[112]T. P. Thompson, *Exercises* (London, 1842), VI, 196.
[113]*Charter of Nations* (1854), p. 254.
[114]Thompson, *Exercises* (1842), V, 22.
[115]Merivale, *Lectures* (1841), I, 229. Similarly, McCulloch, *Dictionary of Commerce* (1840), I, 408.
[116]Senior, *Three Lectures* (1828), p. 60.
[117]*Ibid.*, p. 56; similarly, Dunckley, *Charter of Nations*, p. 254.
[118]Porter wrote: "There is not any class of persons in this country, with the exception perhaps of the landowners, which has made such loud and continued

the forces of Laissez-Faire. The most important factor, as mentioned before, was the apparently unshakable belief of the public in the close connection between British shipping and British seapower. The British shipping-interest exploited this belief to the utmost.

The arguments used for that purpose were the same as those advanced in earlier periods. The Navigation Laws were considered "the very basis of maritime strength and political ascendancy of this great empire."[119] The intelligent opponents of repeal frankly admitted that considerations of wealth alone would justify the scrapping of the navigation system. Thus, John Marryat declared: "It is certainly not favourable to the growth of our foreign commerce, or of that opulence which arises out of it; but while it makes commercial profit a subordinate object, it lays the foundation of naval power...."[120] Then as before the colony trade was regarded as the mainstay of British shipping and, from the point of view considered here, it seemed absurd to give up a colony "even if its products were somewhat more expensive than might be supplied from a foreign market...."[121] "We need not here enter into a proof of the fact that colonies are the nursery of a navy, and that the expense of colonies is part of the price which we pay for being mistress of the seas. Those who look at our colonies as a mere debtor and creditor account in the budget are very short-sighted politicians...."[122]

According to this school of thought Britain's shipping needed

---

complaints of distress as the shipowners have done since the peace in 1815. These gentlemen form a numerous, wealthy, and influential body, and acting as they do, in concert, have always been able to command attention to their representations..." (*Progress of the Nation* [1851], p. 390).

J. L. Ricardo observed that ship-owning was only one of the protected trades that "make it part of their business to remind Parliament of their existence. They have a committee constantly on the look for fresh privileges, and to resist invasions of the old; to give note of any pause in the progress or diminution of their profits; and whenever the trade looks down . . . to run to the ministry of the day, and get a Parliamentary committee appointed to hunt up some fresh means of help" (*Anatomy of the Navigation Laws* [1847], p. 44).

[119] *Memoir on the Spirit and Reason of the Navigation Acts* (1817), p. 7. Similarly, G. F. Young, *Letters on the Navigation Laws* (London, 1848), p. 22; Alison, *Essays*, I, 302; "Freedom of Commerce," *Quarterly Review*, XXIV (1820-1), 298.

[120] *Hansard*, sec. ser., X, c. 1300.

[121] "Political Importance of Our American Colonies," *Quarterly Review*, XXXIII (1825-6), 415.

[122] "The Australian Colonies," *Quarterly Review*, LXVIII (1841), 91. See also, "Parliamentary Prospects," *Quarterly Review*, LXXXI (1847), 571.

protection because the cost of building, repairing, and operating ships was higher in Great Britain than in a number of other countries.[123] Therefore, to expose British shipping to the full competition of foreign shipping meant to jeopardize the matrix of the country's maritime power.[124] And this was what the Free Traders apparently proposed to do. "In evil hour, the frenzied agency of free trade, having trampled under foot every other interest, has been brought to bear against this cherished policy."[125]

The supporters of the shipping-interest did not fail to make frequent reference to Adam Smith's dictum on the relative importance of "defense" and "opulence." Indeed, until the late forties, the Free Traders themselves were rather hesitant as regards their case against the Navigation system.[126] When, in 1845, the Navigation Laws were codified for the last time, the bill passed both houses without debate. In contrast to the cases of grain, timber, and sugar, no Free Trader apparently saw fit to attack the act as

[123] See G. F. Young, *Shipping Interest* (London, 1834), p. 18; "Parliamentary Prospects," p. 572.

[124] This higher cost level was largely a direct result of the protection accorded to other producing and trading interests and to the provisions of the Navigation Laws themselves. Before protectionist legislation was repealed generally, the shipping interest had a strong claim to equal consideration. In 1834, Young declared: "In all, the capital, the skill, the enterprise, the industry of British proprietors and artisans are protected, save only in the article of freight, of which, as an aggravation of the injustice, you have compulsorily and greatly raised the cost, by regulations supposed to be for the general benefit of the community, but onerous and expensive to the proprietor of shipping. . . . For the benefit of the British landowner, you drive us by duties on foreign timber to build our ships of British-grown timber, and to feed our seamen with British bread. To encourage the manufacturer, you impose heavy duties on the importation of every article requisite for the equipment of our ships. For the protection of the artisans, you expose our property to the penalty of confiscation, if we expend more than 20s. per ton for repairs in a foreign country. . . . For the support of your naval power, you oblige us to man our ships with British sailors, costing us 50s. per month, when we could obtain foreign seamen at 25s. per month. And thus burthened, shackled and incapacitated, you cooly tell us we must compete with foreign ship-owners. Sir, we cannot" (*Shipping Interest*, p. 21).

[125] Young, *Letters on the Navigation Laws* (1848), p. 24. Lord George Bentinck castigated the irresponsible language of the repealers according to which "the shipping interest and the commercial navy of England may be compared to pedlars and packhorses. . ." (*Hansard*, third ser., LXXXIX, c. 1044).

[126] In 1840, J. D. Hume told a parliamentary committee that certain matters fell outside the bounds of the free-trade principle and listed among these matters of power. See Clapham, "The Last Years of the Navigation Acts," p. 689.

a matter of principle.[127] Clapham observed that the navigation system might have been maintained indefinitely if positive proof had been forthcoming to the effect that British naval strength actually depended on the retention of protection.[128]

The anti-protectionists relied mainly on four arguments. First, that the Navigation Laws destroyed commerce; secondly, that the mercantile marine as a nursery of sea-power had considerably lost in importance; thirdly, that British shipping, if unshackled, would be able to hold its own against foreign shipping; and, fourthly, that Britain's protectionist legislation provoked retaliation on the part of other nations.

The argument of the declining importance of the mercantile marine as a nursery of trained seamen was based on the consideration that the Royal Navy was training an increasing number of sailors and that the proportion of sailors in the crews of men-of-war had decreased substantially.[129]

The Navigation Laws were said to "destroy" commerce in diverse ways. Often they caused a circuitous conveyance of cargoes, rendering transportation more expensive than it would have been otherwise. Since foreign ships were not allowed to carry colonial produce to England, the frequency of sailings from colonial ports to the mother country was much reduced.[130]

The ability of the British merchant marine to compete successfully with foreign shipping usually was asserted as a mere assumption. Thus, James Deacon Hume maintained: "I conceive that British shipping, if relieved from all those disadvantages which I attribute to our protective system would be able to compete with

[127] *Ibid.*, p. 692.   [128] *Ibid.*, p. 689.

[129] Sir J. Stirling stated: "It is a great mistake to suppose that the navy, at the present moment, desires any considerable number of seamen from the merchant service . . . there are not above a thousand men in the royal navy who have been brought up in the merchant service, the rest are trained in the navy itself . . ." (quoted in Ricardo, *Anatomy of the Navigation Laws* [1847], pp. 48 f.).

Another expert declared: "The navy is a composite force, of which not more than one-fourth are seamen, and of that number not above one-tenth part have been brought up in the merchant service; the men we get from the merchant service are not of the best description; we are not particularly desirous, indeed, of obtaining such as come to us" (quoted *ibid.*, p. 105).

[130] For many examples of this kind see *ibid.*, pp. 112-35. Ricardo concluded: "Turn to whatever quarter of the world we may, we find the Navigation Laws at war with trade" (*ibid.*, p. 156). See also, "Navigation Laws," *Edinburgh Review*, XXXVIII (1823), 484; S. H. N. Iddesleigh, *A Short Review of the Navigation Laws of England* (London, 1849), p. 59.

most parts of the globe."[131] It was pointed out that the strength of England's mercantile marine was not derived from protection but "from the capital of our merchants, the skill and industry of our manufactures, and the enterprise of our seamen."[132] Both camps regarded the effects of Huskisson's relaxation of the Navigation Acts as a test case and both camps concluded that the test had borne out their arguments. Stafford Northcote wrote in 1849: "The case of the free traders is that our shipping has increased to an enormous extent since the measures of 1824 ... the case of the shipowners is that, though the increase in British shipping has been great, the proportionate increase in foreign shipping is still greater."[133] Yet though this contention of the ship-owners was correct as far as it went, the Free Traders were able to show that British shipping had decreased in the protected and greatly increased in the unprotected trades.

British vessels are and have been the principal carriers between the ports in South America and from the ports of South America to the Mediterranean and the Baltic.[134]

... on the very showing of the Cornhill shipowners, it appears that in reciprocity trades British tonnage has increased 109 per cent., and foreign tonnage only 65 per cent.... The inference is inevitable whether it be that the activity and energy of our own traders are aroused by competition, or that protection is a weapon the foreigner is able to wield more successfully than ourselves.[135]

Finally, there was the well-grounded fear of retaliatory measures on the part of foreign governments. "By pertinaciously

[131]Quoted in Badham, *Life of J. D. Hume*, p. 265. Another author remarked: "There is something ludicrous in the idea of England fearing the competition of foreigners upon that element, of which it has always been our boast that it is eminently our own. But nothing is so unreasoning as fear" ("Navigation Laws," p. 280). See also Merivale, *Lectures* (1841), I, 215 f.

[132]Speech of E. Baines in 1838 (*Hansard*, third ser., XL, c. 511).

[133]Quoted in Clapham, "The Last Years of the Navigation Acts," p. 687.

[134]"The Navigation Laws," *Westminster Review*, XV (1831), 182.

[135]"Shipowners," *Westminster Review*, XLIII (1845), 150. Evidence was also brought forward to the effect that, in spite of their higher wages, British sailors were able to hold their own against foreign seamen. "The Navigation Laws allow every British vessel ... to have one-fourth of her crew foreigners; in other words compel her only to have three-fourths of her crew English. If, therefore, foreign sailors could be had at lower wages, or were better at the same wages, we should find advantage taken to the full extent of this limited number, and every British vessel would possess a crew one-fourth foreign seamen. To those who are acquainted with shipping it is well known that there are not twenty-five per cent of foreigners amongst the seamen of our commercial navy, nor even five per cent" ("Navigation Laws," *Westminster Review*, pp. 192 f.).

THE FALL OF THE OLD COLONIAL SYSTEM 347

adhering to our code of restrictions, we practically recommend them [other states] to pursue the same course."[136] Several writers contended that, as regards shipping, Great Britain in 1850 was in the position Holland had been in two hundred years earlier. "We were, in fact, in a position very analogous to that of Holland in 1650. Then, we had taken the aggressive against her; it was now to be apprehended that other countries might take the aggressive against us."[137]

So much for a summary of the battle of arguments. Britain's momentous decision, in 1849, to repeal the Navigation Acts was facilitated by the propagandist endeavours of the free-trade school. But to a large extent the fall of the navigation system was a logical sequence to the fall of the Corn Laws.[138] Pressure on the part of foreign powers, especially Prussia,[139] the potato famine in Ireland,[140] and the dissatisfaction of the colonies[141] acted as subsidiary causes.

THE SIGNIFICANCE OF ECONOMIC THEORY

As the arguments presented in this chapter show, the conclusions of economic theory proved an effective weapon in the hands of the anti-protectionists. It would be grossly exaggerated to infer that the change in Great Britain's commercial policies was largely an outcome of the development of economics as a science. Yet it would be equally erroneous to assume that the progress in economic theory had no influence upon this decision. The exceedingly numerous and bitter attacks against the "dismal science" bear out this latter assumption.

As long as increase of material wealth was regarded as the primary objective of British society and the contestants agreed to debate the issue on a rational basis, the anti-protectionists were bound to silence their opponents. Hence, the protectionists fre-

---

[136]"Navigation Laws," *Edinburgh Review*, p. 303; see also pp. 303 ff.

[137]Iddesleigh, *Review of the History of the Navigation Laws* (1849), p. 36. Similarly, "Navigation Laws," *Edinburgh Review*, XXXVIII (1823), 484.

[138]Clapham, "The Last Years of the Navigation Acts," p. 480.

[139]*Ibid.*, pp. 692 ff.

[140]*Ibid.*, p. 695. In January, 1847, Irish distress forced the Cabinet to suspend Corn Law and Navigation Acts in order to facilitate the import of foodstuffs.

[141]In June, 1848, Lord Elgin wrote to Earl Grey: "A rumour has reached us that the House of Lords may perhaps throw out the navigation measure. This would be a most untoward act—almost fatal I fear, in so far as this Colony [Canada] is concerned" (Doughty, *Elgin-Grey Papers*, I, 182 f.). See also Ricardo, *Anatomy of the Navigation Laws* (1847), pp. 134 f.

quently discredited the premise that the augmentation of material wealth ought to be the primary object of society,[142] and assailed the type of argument and the analytic approach of the economists by confronting their supposedly unrealistic speculations with the proved observations of the "practical" man. "The advocates of commercial protection have always shown themselves unwilling to meet their opponents in the field of argument;—they prefer denouncing them as theorists."[143] Thus, one protectionist declared:

> Within the last fifty years, Great Britain has become a theatre where the most astounding acts have been performed for the admiration and instruction of surrounding nations; opinions, the fruit of ages of experience, have been derided as puerile and barbarous; and a section of the people, monopolizing all the wisdom of the United Kingdom, have contrived to set that kingdom in a blaze. . . .[144]

> Our colonies are consigned to destruction . . . as useless lumber, no longer ministering to the wants of a starving people, because a new principle has been evoked, that a discontented population must be conciliated with preternaturally cheap sugar. Free Trade is the new dodge. Verily it is a perfect Goliath, with a face of brass, and a heart of adamant.[145]

Another writer argued: "Questions of commercial policy have been lately treated in so abstract a manner that their connection with common life and practice seems to be entirely forgotten. Speculative writers send forth from their closets general propositions and paradoxical dogmas upon matters relative to the common intercourse of the world, with the most confident affirmation of their universal applicability."[146] Censures of this kind, and the general denunciation of the "Free-trade mania,"[147] and the "metaphysical nonsense"[148] of the theorists, were extremely frequent.[149] The

---

[142] Attacking the economic theory of the free traders, one writer remarked that, apart from its fundamental unsoundness, "it would be even an easier task to prove its pernicious moral tendencies. It is in its very essence a mercenary, unsocial, demoralizing system, opposed to all generous actions, all kindly feelings. Based on selfishness . . . it directs that impulse into the lowest of all channels, the mere, sordid pursuit of wealth . . . wealth is its end and aim, the Mammon its divinity" ("Free Trade," *Quarterly Review*, LXXXVI [1849], 183). This type of criticism will be discussed further in a subsequent chapter.

[143] "Navigation Laws," *Edinburgh Review*, LXXXVI (1847), 278.

[144] Thomas Jelly, *A Cursory Glance at the Past and Present Condition of Great Britain* (London, 1848), p. 4.

[145] *Ibid.*, p. 68.

[146] "Freedom of Commerce," p. 281.

[147] "Parliamentary Prospects," p. 571.

[148] "New Colony on Swan River," p. 339.

[149] Not only the spirit of innovation was subjected to severe criticism. The spirit of inquiry, too, was declared objectionable. For example, when, in 1847,

theorists, however, knew how to strike back, as the following quotation shows.

A reasoner must be hard pressed, when he is driven to quote practical men in aid of his conclusions. There cannot be a worse authority, in any branch of political science, than that of merely practical men. They are always the most obstinate and presumptuous of all theorists. Their theories, which they call practice, and affirm to be the legitimate results of experience, are built upon a superficial view of the small number of facts which come within the narrow circle of their immediate observation; and are usually in direct contradiction to those principles which are deduced from a general and enlarged experience. Such men are the most unsafe of all guides, even in matters of fact. More bigoted to their own theories than the most visionary speculator, because they believe them to have the warrant of past experience; they have their eyes open to such facts alone as square with those theories. They are constantly confounding facts with inferences, and when they see a little, supply the remainder from their own imaginations.[150]

J. L. Ricardo opened the attack on the Navigation Acts by moving for a parliamentary inquiry into their workings and effects, Disraeli declared that he and his friends would vote against this not so much to defend the navigation system as to oppose the inquiry as such. "That appeared to him a very novel and dangerous proposition; as it seemed to him, that though investigation might be necessary in some cases, it was not a matter that should be morbidly encouraged on all occasions" (*Hansard*, third ser., LXXXIX, c. 1052).

[150]John Stuart Mill, "War Expenditure," *Westminster Review*, II (1824), 45.

CHAPTER XI

SOME ADDITIONAL ITEMS IN THE BALANCE-SHEET OF IMPERIALISM

EXPENSE

AS long as Great Britain upheld the Navigation Laws and the intra-imperial system of tariff preferences, part of the cost of empire to the British people was paid by the consumer in the form of high prices for sugar, timber, coffee, etc.[1] The financial burden of governing and protecting the Empire was carried by the British taxpayer.

The unwillingness to carry this onerous burden increased throughout the period under consideration. At various points in the course of this study, it has been noted that among liberals and radicals the fight against heavy taxation was a corollary of the fight against aristocratic class-rule and excessive government-interference.[2] Most representative of this attitude was the utilitarian Joseph Hume whose passion for economy in government sometimes bordered on the ridiculous and who, throughout his long and extremely active parliamentary career (especially between 1820 and 1850), let slip by hardly any opportunity of attempting to pare down public expenditure.

The Manchester School added to this disposition the grave concern of the entrepreneur over a tax-load that tended to raise production costs and constitute a handicap in foreign markets.[3]

---

[1]For a computation of these costs see "The Colonial Expenditure," *Westminster Review*, XXIV (1836), 1-19.

[2]"A government that would form its resolutions upon the plain exigencies of the public service, and not on the conveniences or the sufferings, the anticipated complaints, or the probable calumnies of individuals enjoying the emoluments or the patronage of office.... The abolition of useless and sinecure offices; the cutting down of all salaries, pensions, and allowances; the sacrifice of patronage; the temporary surrender even of revenue, and the resistance to old mercantile notions; are become indispensably necessary" ("Finance," *Edinburgh Review*, XXXIII [1820], 69).

[3]Cobden wrote in 1835: "... no person possessing sound reason will deny that we, who find it necessary to levy upwards of thirty millions annually upon the necessaries of life, must be burdened with grievous disadvantages, when brought into commercial competition with the untaxed labour of the inhabitants

Frowning upon this "universal and almost invincible repugnance to assessments," Archibald Alison called his the "tax-hating age." ". . . if there is any one peculiarity more than another by which this generation is distinguished, it is aversion to assessment. People may differ in other respects as to the designation by which the age should be characterised; but we believe all will agree that it is a tax-hating age."[4]

As to the financial burden arising from the possession of oversea dependencies, Sir George Cornewall Lewis stated: ". . . the dominant country can rarely succeed in compelling or inducing a dependency to contribute to the expenses of the supreme government; and, consequently, the dominant country generally defrays from its own resources the expenses caused by the protection of the dependency in peace and war. . . . It may be added, that the possession of a dependency often proves a powerful incentive to improvident and useless expenditure on the part of the supreme government. . . ."[5] There is no need here to go into the various and widely differing estimates of what the colonies cost the mother country during any specific period of time.[6] Aside from the difficulty of determining what part of the expenditure on army, navy, and general government should be attributed to the colonies, the annual government outlay on account of the dependencies was shrouded in darkness because these cost items were not separated in the budget. Thus, Hume pointed out in 1819 that "from the

---

of America" (*The Political Writings of Richard Cobden* [London, 1867], I, 105).

"Thus, it appears, that our gross expenditure under the United Service heads, is in the ratio of six and a-half to one, as compared with that of America;— a country, be it repeated, whose population, trade, and registered tonnage, are more than the half of our own—a country, too, whose public debt is cancelled, whilst ours amounts to nearly eight hundred millions" (*ibid.*, p. 109). In Cobden's opinion, the larger part of British public expenditure "under the United Service heads" was incurred on account of the dependencies. "We believe it might be shewn, that the dependencies of Great Britain are, at this moment, and, in future, are destined still more to be, the source of a considerable amount of taxation and pecuniary loss to the mother country" (*ibid.*).

[4]*Essays, Political, Historical, and Miscellaneous* (Edinburgh, 1850), I, 548.

[5]*An Essay on the Government of Dependencies* (1841), ed. C. P. Lucas (Oxford, 1891), p. 241.

[6]In 1836, one writer figured the total annual expenditure of the metropolis on account of its colonies at £8,525,210 (thereof £5,007,234 for government and defence and £2,718,976 for the cost of the colonial monopolies). Expenditures on account of that portion of the national debt that was incurred when the colonies were acquired or defended in time of war, are not included in this estimate ("The Colonial Expenditure," pp. 18 f.).

peculiar manner in which the accounts respecting the colonies were kept, it was almost impossible for any individual to know what they cost."[7] Parnell, therefore, demanded that "a Colonial Budget should be stated in the House of Commons every session by the Chancellor of the Exchequer, and all Colonial expenses should be voted on a distinct estimate."[8] Yet, even though the exact size of the financial burden could not be determined, it was felt to lie heavily on the British taxpayer. Some, indeed, ventured to say that the metropolitan taxpayer was worse off than the colonial taxpayer and that through the imperial connection, therefore, the colonists were actually exploiting the mother country.[9]

How could the financial burden of empire be eased? One solution, suggested by a small minority only, was that of giving up the colonial empire.[10] The vast majority of the economy-minded, however, proposed a more or less drastic reduction of the expense.[11] Thus, Parnell declared:

The past extravagance of our expenditure in the Colonies . . . renders it highly probable, that if a wise system of management were introduced, a

---

[7] *Hansard*, first ser., XL, c. 1078.

[8] *On Financial Reform* (2d ed.; London, 1830), p. 225.

[9] Cobden said in 1848: "The inhabitants of these colonies are a great deal better off than the mass of the people of England—they are in possession of a vast deal more of the comforts of life than the bulk of those paying taxes here" (John Bright and James E. Thorold Rogers (ed.), *Speeches on Questions of Public Policy by Richard Cobden* [London, 1870], II, 486). Similarly, James Mill, "State of the Nation," *London Review* (*Westminster Review*), I (XXIX) (1835), 24.

[10] Cobden wrote in 1835: ". . . we know nothing that would be so likely to conduce a diminution of our burdens, by reducing the charges of the army, navy, and ordinance (amounting to fourteen millions annually) as a proper understanding of our relative position with respect to our colonial possessions. We are aware that no power was ever yet known, voluntarily, to give up the dominion over a part of its territory. But if it could be made manifest to the trading and industrious portions of this nation, who have no honours, or interested ambition of any kind, at stake in the matter, that, whilst our dependencies are supported at an expense to them, in direct taxation, of more than five millions annually, they serve but a gorgeous and ponderous appendage to swell our ostensible grandeur, but, in reality, to complicate and magnify our government expenditure, without improving our balance of trade—surely, under such circumstances, it would become at least a question for anxious inquiry with a people so overwhelmed with debt, whether those colonies should not be preferred to support and defend themselves, as separate and independent existencies" (*Political Writings*, I, 30 f.). The leading spokesmen of the Manchester School, as will be seen, came closest to supporting the case for voluntary separation.

[11] It must be noted that the separationists, or the Little Englanders, too wise to believe that they could win over the nation to their radical programme, were very energetic propagandists of the second solution.

considerable reduction in the charge on the public purse would be the consequence. ... The official establishments in the Colonies should be revised, and reduced to what is merely necessary; excessive salaries should be diminished, and none but efficient officers should be appointed. All restrictions on colonial trade should be taken off, and then each colony should be made to contribute to the expense of its defence.[12]

There is no need here for presenting the various practical proposals that were advanced with the view of trimming the outlay on imperial expense.[13] The important point is that the colonies could not be made to shoulder a larger portion of their expense for government and defence without being granted an increasing amount of self-government. Considering the trends of the time, there was by necessity a direct relationship between these two processes: once the colonies carried the full cost of their government and defence, they would be virtually independent nations. Indeed, the gradual movement toward self-government within the Empire was sustained not by two but by three major causes: to the aspirations of the ruling groups in the colonies and the empire-wide programme of the metropolitan liberals[14] must be added the policy of the economy-minded faction in the mother country. As J. A. Roebuck remarked, that the colonies were a perpetual cause of waste did not make them by necessity "mischievous and costly."[15] When, in 1831, Joseph Hume brought in his motion for granting to the colonists direct representation in Parliament, he pointed out that the realization of this project would facilitate the partial transfer of the financial burden of imperial government and defence

[12]*On Financial Reform* (1830), p. 225.

[13]For interesting examples see Joseph Hume's perennial motions in the House of Commons and Molesworth's speech on Colonial Expenditures of July 25, 1848 (H. E. Egerton (ed.), *Selected Speeches of Sir William Molesworth on Questions relating to Colonial Policy* [London, 1903], pp. 154-213).

[14]"In 1831, in the course of the fight for the Reform Bill, Joseph Hume submitted a motion for the initiation of colonial representation in the House of Commons. He asked the House "why so important a portion of the King's dominions as the colonies ... should not come within the reach of so important a change as that now contemplated in the constitution of that House" (*Hansard*, third ser., VI, c. 111).

Another writer observed: "The desire for representative government was spreading among our own colonies ... it remains a disgrace to successive governments that the desire of our colonies for participation in the best privileges of the British constitution can scarcely obtain any attention. Next to Ireland, our colonies continue to be the opprobrium of our empire" (Harriet Martineau, *A History of the Thirty Years' Peace* [London, 1878], IV, 370 f.).

[15]*The Colonies of England* (London, 1849), p. 8.

to the colonies.[16] In the course of his speech on Colonial Expenditure in 1848, Sir William Molesworth declared:

I think I have sufficiently established my position that, in every portion of the globe, the British colonies are more economically and better governed in proportion as they are self-governed. . . . Hence I come to the conclusion that we should delegate to the colonies all powers of local legislation and administration which are now possessed by the Colonial Office, with the reservation only of those powers the exercise of which would be absolutely inconsistent with the sovereignty of this country, or might be directly injurious to the interests of the whole empire."[17]

In 1850, the Colonial Reform Society was founded. Its prospectus read in part: "The general object of the Society is to aid in obtaining for every dependency, which is a true colony of England, the real and sole management of all local affairs by the colony itself. . . . It will be a main object of the Society's endeavours, to relieve the Mother-country from the whole expense of the local government of Colonies, except only that of the defence of the colony from aggression by foreign powers at war with the Empire."[18] Writing in the early fifties, Earl Grey was able to say that the expense of civil government was met fully by the settlement colonies.[19] Regarding the item of defence cost the colonies were reluctant to assume greater responsibilities. Grey, however, voicing the majority opinion of the nation in this matter, intimated that the colonies must be called upon to provide for their own peace establishments.[20]

The arguments of the economy-minded faction did not remain unanswered. They were branded as narrow-minded economizers

[16]*Hansard*, third ser., VI, cs. 113, 123. In the same year Hume proposed to give Newfoundland a local legislative assembly which would relieve the metropolitan government of paying for a governor: ". . . 90,000 English subjects asked to be removed from under the arbitrary sway of one man, and to be allowed to conduct their own affairs. Was that unreasonable? They offered to do this without putting the country to the expense of 10,000l. or 20,000l. a-year, to which it was now liable" (*ibid*., c. 1383).

[17]*Selected Speeches*, pp. 199, 207.

[18]*The Spectator*, Jan. 5, 1850, p. 6.

[19]*The Colonial Policy of Lord J. Russell's Administration* (London, 1853), I, 43.

[20]*Ibid*., p. 44. After 1850, the Manchester party demanded categorically that the colonies bear the cost of their defence alone. Thus, Goldwin Smith wrote: "Why should not these free Communities pay the whole of their military expenses? They have received the full powers of self-government, why should they not undertake the full duty of self-defense?" (*The Empire* [Oxford, 1863], p. 73).

and "shopkeepers" who were bent on reducing everything to a matter of pounds, shillings, and pence. One writer declared:

> One of the main positions laid down by these theorists is, that no colony is worth retaining, unless the mother country derives from it a revenue equal to the expenditure upon it. This doctrine may unquestionably be considered as consistent with that bare, rigid, and penurious economy, which would reduce everything to a question of pounds, shillings, and pence. It is a creed suitable enough for the Domestic Economy of the merchant and the shopkeeper, who will do well to regulate all their transactions by it; but the views of a great nation, like England, should not be thus fettered by considerations of paltry gains, and calculations of how many shillings her important possessions may send into the treasury of the mother country.[21]

When, in 1832, Joseph Hume lodged one of his usual objections to the home government's generous grant of money for the government of the colonies, Sir Charles Wetherell exclaimed angrily: "I say that it is clear that this vote is not one penny more than it ought to be; and I trust, that the hon. member for Middlesex will in future abstain from insulting the House with his penny-farthing economy, and from daring to indulge in his contemptuous attempt to persuade us to adopt so paltry and miserable a policy."[22] Another writer criticized the Cobdenites in somewhat more restrained fashion:

> ... we must premise that we find a difference in limine between our views and those of the Financial Reformers as regards the paramount importance they assign to a mere curtailed amount of national expenditure. The cry for cheap government has been so pertinaciously raised during the last few years ... that it requires no ordinary courage to make head against it, or to hint that it may be carried to an injudicious and dangerous excess. Nevertheless, it is unquestionable that cheapness may be bought too dear; ... that ... there may be more important objects for our consideration than the saving of one or two millions to a people which so frequently spends fifty millions in some wild speculation, or some gigantic blunder.[23]

After the system of intra-imperial preferences had been abandoned and the settlement colonies were well on their way to become

[21]"The Political Importance of Our American Colonies," *Quarterly Review*, XXXIII (1825-6), 411 f.

[22]*Hansard*, third ser., XIV, c. 649.

[23]"Shall We Retain Our Colonies?" *Edinburgh Review*, XCIII (1851), 476 ff. A great many politicians and writers regarded the advantages of empire and the expenditure laid out on it as fundamentally incommensurable quantities. For example, Sir James Stephen, firmly convinced that Great Britain owed her superior strength and prestige to the colonies, declared in 1858 that in the Empire the mother country had laid up a treasure "which cannot be spanned by the theodolite or measured by the steelyard or weighed by the avoirdupois" (quoted in Paul Knaplund, "Sir James Stephen and British North American Problems," *Canadian Historical Review*, V [1924], 40).

Dominions, the expense of empire, indeed, was diminishing considerably. "The cost, fairly calculated, to Great Britain of her colonial empire is . . . something less than two millions yearly."[24] It also was argued that Great Britain, a wealthy country, could well afford the expense. "The British people . . . are wealthy beyond precedent in past or present times. They are generous and liberal in many things. They waste annually in bad debts and abortive speculations a sum larger than the whole annual expense of the State; yet they allow themselves to be persuaded that their weal or woe depends upon some trifling increase or diminution in a fraction of this expenditure."[25]

Finally, the nation was warned of the impracticability of keeping the colonies to a policy of free trade once they were burdened with the whole cost of their defence by conferring upon them the status of complete independence. In order to bear the full cost of independence the colonies would have to tap new sources of revenues. The sale of waste lands could never yield much. "Direct taxation is always burdensome, irritating, and unwelcome. . . . The source of indirect taxation alone remains. . . ."[26] Indirect taxation would mean higher customs duties.

> Now, in a densely populated and luxurious country like England, moderate duties suffice to procure a large revenue. . . . But this could not be the case in a thinly peopled colony; a low scale of duties could never raise an ample or adequate revenue. . . . The first effect, then, of our proclaiming the independence of our colonies must inevitably be, the enactment by them of a high tariff on all imported commodities; and as the commodities required by new countries are, by the nature of the case, articles of manufactured rather than of agricultural produce, and as England is the chief manufacturing country in the world, it would be chiefly on our productions that this high tariff would press, however unintentional such a result might be. . . .[27]

THE SPOILS OF EMPIRE

It has been shown previously that the imperial system of differential tariff duties was regarded by many as an arrangement by which the Few were able to exploit the Many.[28] Here we are

---

[24]"Shall We Retain Our Colonies?" *Edinburgh Review*, XCIII (1851), 486.

[25]G. W. Norman, *An Examination of Some Prevailing Opinions as to the Pressure of Taxation in This, and Other Countries* (3d ed.; London, 1850), pp. 75 f.

[26]"Shall We Retain Our Colonies?" p. 495.

[27]*Ibid.*, pp. 495 f.

[28]As Dr. Bowring said in 1843: ". . . the tax was levied by a class, which used the power of legislating to obtain privileges, and they made the labouring classes pay" (*Hansard*, third ser., LXX, c. 245).

concerned with the argument that the possession of colonies, by opening up new positions in the Home government, in the government and administration of the colonies, and in that part of the army and navy which was maintained for the protection of the colonies, put at the disposal of the government a prodigious source of patronage and created a great many "jobs" for the younger sons of the British ruling classes. Sir Alexander Malet declared: "The sole advantage which I have been able to discover that any portion of the inhabitants of this country reap from our connexion with the Canadas, is, in the quartering upon that country of certain official dependents of our aristocracy...."[29] Speaking of the value of Canada to the parent state, E. Baines said in 1838: "There was, however, one advantage derived from the possession of Canada ... and that was, a great extent of official patronage. If Canada was exalted to the rank of a free state, they should have much fewer governorships and secretaryships to bestow than at present, and much fewer appointments in the army, the navy, and the civil departments."[30]

It was argued, therefore, that the ruling class fostered distant colonies "as a source of patronage, and method of providing for clamorous and needy dependents,"[31] and that the dependencies were nothing "but the costly appendage of an aristocratic government."[32] Goldwin Smith asserted that the imperial system "rests on class interests and prejudices, ever triumphant, by their concentrated energy, over the public good.... It rests upon patronage, that foundation of adamant, upon which the puny assaults of reason and justice have so often spent, and will long spend, themselves in

[29] *The Canadas* (London, 1831), p. 13.
[30] *Hansard*, third ser., XL, c. 511.
[31] Malet, *The Canadas* (1831), p. 14.
[32] Cobden, *Political Writings*, I, 195. See also, Cobden, *Public Speeches*, I, 424 f. There follow two more quotations.

"These [the colonies] are a tremendous burthen on the resources of the mother country, chiefly to provide governorships, secretaryships, registrarships, agencies, and sinecures for the Aristocracy and their connexions" ([John Wade], *The Extraordinary Black Book* [London, 1831], p. 335).

"We are inclined, indeed, to believe, that the class which most profits by the outlet, afforded by the British dependencies, consists not of the poor, but of the rich.... How few are the families among the higher classes who do not look to Asia or America as affording a certain or a probable provision for some of their members" ("Lewis on the Government of Dependencies," *Edinburgh Review*, LXXXIII [1846], 551).

vain."[33] In 1849, Cobden wrote to his West Riding constituents: "I want you to raise the cry for colonial reform. . . . If you don't separate yourselves from the dominant class—in their attempt to keep the colonies as a field of patronage for their younger sons, and that the aristocracy may nominate the Government, you will have wars without end with your colonial fellow-subjects. . . ."[34] Excepting army, navy, and Colonial Office on the one hand, and India, the tropical colonies, and the naval stations on the other, the progressive constitutional reform of the Empire indeed gradually lessened the number of "places" available in the settlement colonies.[35] This change, however, left sufficient room for the criticism discussed in the present section.

THE POLITICAL BACKWASH OF IMPERIAL RULE

Bentham and James Mill had attributed a great deal of importance to the fact that autocratic rule in the dependencies was bound to have an adverse effect on constitutional government at home. This kind of argument continued to be used by those who doubted or denied the value of empire. First, there was the political corruption resulting from the patronage at the disposal of the government. "We may reckon amongst the disadvantages arising to the dominant country from the possession of dependencies, that it tends to generate or extend a system of official patronage in the dominant country, and thus to lower the standard of its political morality."[36] ". . . there is still another evil arising out of the Colonial administration, which merits observation. And this is, the malign influence of the Colonies upon our liberties and domestic government, through the patronage and power which they throw into the hands of the Executive. . . ."[37]

[33]*The Empire* (1863), p. 146. On another occasion Goldwin Smith remarked: "In the case of New Zealand, as of other dependencies, that which is officially styled the 'Empire' is patronage to a few, but to the nation expense, weakness, humiliation. . ." (*ibid.*, p. 147).

[34]Quoted in S. Maccoby, *English Radicalism, 1832-1852* (London, 1935), p. 349.

[35]This was pointed out by Earl Grey, *The Colonial Policy of Lord John Russell's Administration* (1853), I, 37 f.; Gladstone's speech of 1855 in Paul Knaplund, *Gladstone and Britain's Imperial Policy* (New York, 1927), p. 194.

[36]Lewis, *Government of Dependencies* (1841), p. 254.

[37]"The Colonial Expenditure," p. 29. The same writer pointed out that the enjoyment of monopolies rendered the monopolists hostile to the cause of political reform in England. "The possessors of the Colonial monopolies, are, as might be expected, the steady opponents of all Reform. The interests of this class in

Then, there was the contamination of a ruling class governing tropical territories in an autocratic fashion. This particular argument usually was advanced in connection with India, the most important case in point. Thus, Cobden wrote to George Combe in 1858: "I am afraid our national character is being deteriorated, and our love of freedom in danger of being impaired by what is passing in India. . . . It is more and more my conviction that the task of governing despotically 150 millions of people at a distance of twelve thousand miles cannot be executed by a constitutional Government."[38] And in 1860 he wrote to William Hargreaves: "Is it not just possible that we may become corrupted at home by the reaction of arbitrary political maxims in the East upon our domestic politics, just as Greece and Rome were demoralized by their contact with Asia?"[39] Similarly, Goldwin Smith remarked:

English politics have also suffered, and perhaps are destined to suffer still more, from our connexion with India. . . . It may . . . be said, generally, that the incorporation of a vast Empire such as India, which is not governed on free principles, with a free country, is apt to taint the political spirit of the free country, and to impair the vigour of its freedom. We may not be able as yet to point to specific evidences of this fact, but the influence is in its very nature impalpable, like a malaria in the air, and its pestilential effects may only become visible on looking back over a long range of history.[40]

Finally, it was maintained that the business of empire, of its government, preservation, and extension, served the ruling groups to divert the attention of the people from home politics. During the crisis generated by the Canadian rebellion, Sir George Cornewall Lewis wrote: "What possible advantage England derives from the

---

bad government, are represented by the extent of the Monopoly-tax. . . . It can hardly be necessary to remind the reader, that the parties here referred to, are the West-India quondam slave-holders, and the troublesome and noisy Shipping interest. These are to be seen, through their agents or their committees, browbeating and intimidating all ministries disposed to liberality, and through their representatives in both Houses of Parliament, aided by the representatives of the Corn monopolists, voting and declaiming against every popular measure" (*ibid.*, p. 30).

[38] John Morley, *The Life of Richard Cobden*, New ed. (London, 1883) p. 436.
[39] *Ibid.*, p. 532.
[40] *The Empire* (1863), pp. 286 ff. Interesting is the following note in Lord Elgin's diary: "It is a terrible business, the living among inferior races. I have seldom from man or woman since I came to the East heard a sentence which was reconcilable with the hypothesis that Christianity had ever come into the world. Detestation, contempt, ferocity, vengeance, whether Chinamen or Indians be the object" (quoted in W. H. Dawson, *Richard Cobden and Foreign Policy* [London, 1926], p. 198).

possession of Canada, I confess I am unable to see. If, however, the ministers irritate the Canadians into expressions and measures insulting to England, they will be able to appeal to the silly national pride of the people, and will probably be supported in a war. Perhaps, too, they may find it convenient to divert people's attention from internal to external politics."[41] Goldwin Smith observed:

The heaviest burden of all, however, is the general character of ostentation and wastefulness which the Empire gives to our Government, and the temptation which it holds out to ambitious Ministers when they cannot win the heart of the nation by good measures at home, to win it by swaggering abroad. The expedients of a government which thus maintains itself, in default of domestic measures of improvement, by pandering to the lust of imperial aggrandizement and to a passion for bluster usurping the name of glory, are certainly far less coarse, and may by some be thought far less degrading, than those of a government which maintains itself by the vulgar instruments of corruption; but they cost the people far more money, to say nothing of the blood.... The reckless invasion of Afghanistan, undertaken by a ministry bankrupt in reputation at home, in the hope of gaining glory abroad, cost twenty millions of money, besides the carnage and the dishonour.[42]

POWER AND PRESTIGE

Repetition of the various arguments according to which the colonies augmented the military power of the mother country is superfluous here. The counter-arguments also were largely the same as those advanced before. Joseph Hume told the Commons in 1823: "It was obvious, that the colonies, instead of being an addition to the strength of the country, increased its weakness; and he believed it would be better able to cope with any contingency which might arise, if those colonies were freed from their allegiance, and became their own masters."[43] Parnell stated: "Instead of furnishing a military force, the Colonies are always a great drain upon the military resources of the country, particularly in war, when they occupy a large portion of the army and fleet in their defence...."[44] Similarly, Goldwin Smith: "To protect dependent Colonies we not only burden our overtaxed people with gratuitous

[41]Sir G. F. Lewis (ed.), *Letters of Sir George Cornewall Lewis* (London, 1863), pp. 77 f.
[42]*The Empire* (1863), pp. 77 f.
[43]*Hansard*, sec. ser., VIII, c. 250.
[44]*On Financial Reform* (1830), p. 237. For a nearly verbatim presentation of this argument, see Wade, *Extraordinary Black Book* (1831), p. 335.

taxation, but scatter our forces, naval as well as military, over the globe, leaving the heart of England open to a sudden blow."[45]

The representations of those who held these views also professed complete indifference toward France's colonial expansion in North Africa. Thus, in 1859, Cobden wrote to Bright: "From what I hear, the Cabinet is concerned with the mighty question whether France is to take a bit of territory from Morocco.... For my part, if France took the whole of Africa, I do not see what harm she would do us or anybody else save herself."[46] Similarly, Goldwin Smith remarked: "We are told that the Emperor of the French ... envies our Colonial Empire, and desires a Colonial Empire of his own. Let us pray that he may obtain it. Nothing else can prevent him from being quite, as he is now almost, master of the destinies of Europe."[47]

J. A. Roebuck observed that Great Britain "may, by means of her colonies, acquire a power and influence which her own narrow territory might not permit her to attain."[48] "Influence," in this sense, meant prestige. Indeed, during the period under consideration, the argument that the possession of a large colonial empire bestowed upon the parent state a great deal of prestige, was of greater importance to politicians than the one that the possession of colonies meant an addition to the physical strength of Great Britain. Wakefield reported the argument of "a London banker" as follows:

[45] *The Empire* (1863), p. 2. See also *ibid.*, pp. 33 f., 110, 134.
[46] Morley, *Life of Cobden*, p. 454.
[47] *The Empire* (1863), pp. 129 f. One writer asserted that Great Britain was fortunate in having an empire where she could keep her army. "Like any power Britain needs to maintain a limited standing army. Standing armies, however, are always dangerous to public freedom. Hence, it is a great advantage that England is able to distribute her force, that is a large part of her standing army, among the distant transmarine settlements of the empire.... By means of the continual change which the British army undergoes from England to the colonies, the soldiers are kept as a body distinct from the people, with whom they are, therefore, not likely to form an intimacy dangerous to their discipline, or to become enlisted in behalf of either of the contending parties which strive for political mastery at home" (R. M. Martin, *Colonial Policy of the British Empire* [London, 1837], pp. 89 ff.). Indeed, when, after the close of the Napoleonic Wars, the English people reverted to their general dislike of everything military, the Duke of Wellington found colonies and naval stations very convenient as a way of hiding the army and concealing its size. See Douglas Woodruff, "Expansion and Emigration" in G. M. Young (ed.), *Early Victorian England, 1830-1865* (London, 1934), II, 352.
[48] *The Colonies of England* (1849), p. 11.

He began by admitting that possession of a colony may not make it better as a market; that it costs something in ordinary times; and that it exposes us to the risk of disputes with foreign nations, from which we should be free if the colony were independent. He admitted the whole argument of the merely scientific economist. But, on the other hand, said he, I am of opinion that the extent and glory of an empire are solid advantages for all its inhabitants and especially to those who inhabit its centre. I think that whatever the possession of our colonies may cost us in money, the possession is worth more in money than its money cost, and infinitely more in other respects. For by overawing foreign nations and impressing mankind with a prestige of our might, it enables us to keep the peace of the world, which we have no interest in disturbing, as it would enable us to disturb the world if we pleased. The advantage is, that the possession of this immense empire by England causes the mere name of England to be a real and mighty power; the greatest power that now exists in the world. . . . You tell us of the cost of dependencies: I admit it, but reply that the cost is the most beneficial of investments, since it converts the mere sound of a name into a force greater than that of the most costly fleets and armies. . . . Suppose that we gave them all up, without losing any of their utility as markets: I say that the name of England would cease to be a power; and that in order to preserve our own independence we should have to spend more than we do now in the business of defence.[49]

Earl Grey held the same opinion.

The possession of a number of steady and faithful allies, in various quarters of the globe, will surely be admitted to add greatly to the strength of the nation. . . . Nor ought it to be forgotten, that the power of a nation does not depend merely on the amount of physical force it can command, but rests, in no small degree, upon opinion and moral influence: in this respect British power would be diminished by the loss of our Colonies, to a degree which it would be difficult to estimate.[50]

It was for the sake of preserving British prestige that English statesmen refused to abandon any colony. Opposing the relinquishment of Canada, Huskisson declared in 1828:

Is this country, without necessity, without that right being challenged by anyone, to incur the indelible disgrace of withdrawing that protection? In contemplating such a question, I will not allow myself to say one word of the advantages, naval, commercial, and political, which we derive from our connexion with our colonies. But I may be allowed to speak of the political character of the country—of the moral impression throughout the world of such an abandonment as is here proposed. I may be allowed to say, that England cannot afford to be little. She must be what she is, or nothing. It is not Canada estimated in pounds, shillings, and pence—but the proudest

---

[49]Edward Gibbon Wakefield, *A View of the Art of Colonization* (London, 1849), pp. 98 f.
[50]*The Colonial Policy of Lord John Russell's Administration* (1853), I, 12.

trophies of British valour, but the character of British faith, but the honour of the British name, which we shall cast off. . . .[51]

When Lord Melbourne sent Lord Durham on his mission to Canada, he wrote to him: "The final separation of those colonies might possibly not be of material detriment to the interests of the Mother Country, but it is clear that it would be a serious blow to the honour of Great Britain. . . ."[52] Lord John Russell wrote to Earl Grey in 1849: "The loss of any great portion of our Colonies would diminish our importance in the world, and the vultures would soon gather together to despoil us of the other parts of our Empire."[53]

Gladstone was less partial to this consideration than the statesmen quoted above.

Then, again, people have a notion that for the reputation of this country it is desirable to possess colonies. I do not at all deny that the possession of colonies does contribute to the just reputation of this country, and does add to its moral influence, power and grandeur; but if it is meant by this doctrine that it is desirable to have colonies in order that we make a show in the world with which we have no substance to correspond, that I think you agree with me is not a good reason for desiring an extension of our colonial empire.[54]

The spokesmen of the Manchester School refused to see any virtue whatsoever in this argument. Typical of their attitude is the following quotation from Goldwin Smith.

"Prestige" goes with real strength, and with real strength alone. What would be thought of a general who should occupy more ground than he could cover, exhaust his resources, and wear out his men before the day of battle, in order to gain "prestige" in the eyes of his opponent? . . . Wooden artillery has been useful as a stratagem of war; but I never heard that it was useful, or that anything was risked by a wise Commander to preserve it, after the enemy had found out that it was wooden. . . . Not "apparent power," but most apparent weakness, is the true name for territories scattered over the globe, known to yield neither revenue nor military force to the possessors, and, from the moral feebleness which besets all dependencies, unprovided with any effective means of self-defence.[55]

Is "apparent power" really the object which the statesmen, in their imperial policy, pursue? Is this all that we gain by submitting to an immense

---

[51]Robert Walsh (ed.), *Select Speeches of William Windham and William Huskisson* (Philadelphia, 1845), p. 543.

[52]Quoted in A. J. Harrop, *The Amazing Career of Edward Gibbon Wakefield* (London, 1928), p. 103.

[53]Quoted in W. P. Morrell, *British Colonial Policy in the Age of Peel and Russell* (Oxford, 1930), p. 208.

[54]Speech of 1855 in Knaplund, *Gladstone and Britain's Imperial Policy*, p. 194.

[55]*The Empire* (1863), pp. 31 ff.

taxation? Do our people pay in the solid elements of strength and prosperity as well as in security, and receive in return "apparent power"?[56]

THE PRIDE AND GLORY OF EMPIRE

Pride of Empire and satisfaction of having built it constituted extremely powerful sentiments operating in favour of retention and even expansion of the oversea dominions of Great Britain. Quite understandably, they were seldom coined into an independent argument but found rich expression in many addresses. "Whatever may be the fate of the several British colonies at some future and distant period, it is something at least to have spread our laws and language, and moral character, over the most distant parts of the globe."[57] Speaking in the House of Commons about the Indian Empire, Macaulay said in 1833: "That a handful of adventurers from an island in the Atlantic should have subjugated a vast country divided from the place of their birth by half the globe . . . that we should govern a territory . . . larger and more populous than France, Spain, Italy, and Germany put together . . . a territory inhabited by men differing from us in race, colour, language, manners, morals, religion,—these are prodigies to which the world has seen nothing similar. Reason is confounded. We interrogate the past in vain. . . ."[58]

However, statements ridiculing and exposing the irrationality of such sentiments were also numerous. Buchanan remarked: "Colonies are frequently acquired by conquest, and hence are valued as the honourable trophies of successful war . . . and, at present, the cession of any of the numerous and expensive colonies of Britain, even for an equivalent, would probably draw on its adviser an equal share of popular odium, though no real injury might thence accrue to the country."[59] Sir George Cornewall Lewis stated dryly: "We will merely remark upon this imagined advantage, that a nation derives no true glory from any possession which produces no assignable advantage to itself or to other communities."[60] Again, the Manchester School was the most determined critic of the glory-motive. Cobden wrote in 1835:

[56] *Ibid.*, p. 34.
[57] "New Colony on Swan River," *Quarterly Review*, XXXIX (1829), 340.
[58] *Hansard*, third ser., XIX, c. 515.
[59] *Inquiry into the Taxation and Commercial Policy of Great Britain* (Edinburgh, 1844), p. 136.
[60] *Government of Dependencies* (1841), p. 233.

In truth, we have been planting, and supporting, and governing countries upon all degrees of habitable, and some that are not habitable, latitudes of the earth's surface; and so grateful to our national pride has been the spectacle, that we have never, for once, paused to inquire if our interests were advanced by such nominal greatness. Three hundred millions of permanent debt have been accumulated—millions of direct taxation are annually levied ... for the acquisition or maintenance of colonial possessions; and all for what? That we may repeat the fatal Spanish proverb—"The sun never sets on the King of England's dominions."[61]

John Bright said in 1858: "I believe there is no permanent greatness to a nation except it be based on morality. I do not care for military greatness or military renown. I care for the condition of the people among whom I live ... crowns, coronets, mitres, military display, the pomp of war, wide colonies, and a huge Empire, are, in my view, all trifles light as air, and not worth considering. ..."[62]

According to Goldwin Smith, the pride of empire "runs through" all the arguments offered for the retention of colonies.[63] The whole system of empire, he reasoned, "does not rest on argument. It rests on unreflecting pride, ignorant of the true sources of English greatness."[64] He pointed out that "the mere pride of empire, and the pleasure of indulging in it, belong only to the imperial class."[65] To the people, apparently, and to the Manchester party, England could "afford to be little." The glory-motive, indeed, seemed most dangerous to them because it was insusceptible to rational considerations. "Surely 'Empire' must be one of those strange intellectual spheres in which 'two and two make five.'"[66] And, in 1849, Cobden told his audience at Manchester: "It is through your national pride that cunning people manage to extract taxes from you."[67]

[61]*Political Writings*, I, 26.
[62]Trevelyan, *Life of John Bright*, pp. 274 f.
[63]*The Empire* (1863), Preface, pp. viii-ix.
[64]*Ibid.*, p. 146.
[65]*Ibid.*, pp. 74 f. Bright, arguing for the relinquishment of the Punjab and the province of Scinda in India, remarked: "It is not easy for great generals and statesmen who have been made earls and marquesses and had bronze statutes put up in their honour in our public squares—it is not easy for the statesmen who have done all this to turn round and reverse it all; they have not the moral courage to do it; ... it might appear a descent from the summit of empire and be wrongly construed throughout the world" (*Public Speeches*, I, 90).
[66]Goldwin Smith, *The Empire* (1863), p. 206.
[67]*Public Speeches*, I, 487.

THE SPREAD OF PEACE, ORDER, AND CIVILIZATION[68]

Addressing the Commons on the civil government of Canada, Huskisson declared in 1828:

> We cannot part with our dominions there, without doing an injustice to their fidelity and tried attachment, and tarnishing the national honour. We are not, Sir, at liberty to forego the high and important duties imposed upon us by our relative situation towards those colonies.... We have everywhere displayed marks of paternal government, and planted improvement, not only on our colonies there, but wherever our empire is acknowledged.... Sir, England is the parent of many flourishing colonies—one of them is become an empire among the most powerful in the world. In every quarter of the globe we have planted the seeds of freedom, civilization, and Christianity. To every quarter of the globe we have carried the language, the free institutions, the system of laws, which prevail in this country;—in every quarter they are fructifying and making progress; and if it be said by some selfish calculator, that we have done all this at the expense of sacrifices, we are still the first and happiest people in the world....[69]

Three ideas underlie this statement. First, Great Britain owes allegiance to her colonies. She is not at liberty to shirk or ignore the duty to protect, supervise, and assist them. Secondly, through the medium of world-wide colonization Great Britain is furthering the cause of freedom, peace, order, and Christian civilization "everywhere." Thirdly, it is Great Britain's lot to shoulder these tasks and duties even if they should involve material sacrifices. The urgency of this lofty mission is expressed in the following quotation:

> I am aware that the period in which we live is one of the most momentous epochs which mark the progress of our species in the ascending scale of knowledge, virtue, and happiness. I believe that England is intimately identified with that progressive perfection, and that on the permanent maintenance of her power is essentially dependent the welfare of mankind ... that Britain will be the nucleus around which all the nations of the earth will, eventually, form themselves in concentric circles, in proportion to their advancement in the scale of social bliss....[70]

It was Providence, of course, that destined Great Britain to perform this magnificent duty. To Alison it was "the obvious destiny of Great Britain."[71] "There never was a country so evidently destined by Providence, so nobly endowed by nature, with

---

[68]The theme of the white man's burden in relation to indigenous races wil be discussed in the next chapter.

[69]Walsh, *Select Speeches of W. Windham and W. Huskisson*, pp. 543 f.

[70]R. M. Martin, *Colonial Policy of the British Empire* (1837), pp. 80 f.

[71]Alison, *Essays*, I, 305.

all the gifts requisite to make it the heart and soul of all the European colonies over the globe, as Great Britain. . . . It is already the boast of her Transatlantic descendants, that to the Anglo-Saxon race is destined the sceptre of the globe."[72] Gladstone declared in 1855:

That is the great moral benefit that attends the foundations of British colonies. We think that our country is a country blessed with laws and a constitution that are eminently beneficial to mankind, and if so, what can be more desired than that we should have the means of reproducing in different portions of the globe something as like as may be to that country which we honour and revere? . . . It is the reproduction of the image and likeness of England—the reproduction of a country in which liberty is reconciled with order. . . . It is because we feel convinced that our constitution is a blessing to us, and will be a blessing to our posterity . . . that we are desirous of extending its influence, and that it should not be confined within the narrow borders of this little island; but that if it please Providence to create openings for us on the broad fields of distant continents, we shall avail ourselves in reason and moderation of those openings to reproduce the copy of those laws and institutions, those habits and national characteristics, which have made England so famous as she is.[73]

Following the discontinuation of the imperial system of tariff preferences, separationists were in a more favourable position than before; why, they asked, should the mother country be interested in preserving the connection with the Dominions? In addition to considerations of power and prestige, statesmen like Peel, Gladstone, Lord John Russell, Earl Grey, and like-minded politicians and writers referred to the duty-argument. Even if the maintenance of the imperial connection should involve material sacrifice, this duty should not be evaded. ". . . the maintenance of our connexion with the colonies was to be regarded rather as a matter of duty than one of advantage."[74] Earl Grey declared:

I conceive that, by the acquisition of its Colonial dominions, the Nation has incurred a responsibility of the highest kind, which it is not at liberty to throw off. The authority of the British Crown is at this moment the most powerful instrument, under Providence, of maintaining peace and order in many extensive regions of the earth, and thereby assists in diffusing amongst millions of the human race, the blessings of Christianity and civilization. Supposing it were clear (which I am far from admitting) that a reduction of our national expenditure (otherwise impracticable), to the extent of a few

---

[72]*Ibid.*, p. 304.

[73]In Knaplund, *Gladstone and Britain's Imperial Policy*, pp. 202 f.

[74]Gladstone speech of 1840 (*Hansard*, third ser., LIV, c. 730). R. M. Martin asked: "Does a wise parent begrudge the money expended on his children's rearing and education?" (*Colonial Policy of the British Empire* [1837], p. 100).

hundred thousand a year, could be effected by withdrawing our authority and protection from our numerous Colonies, should we be satisfied, for the sake of such a saving, in taking this step, and thus abandoning the duty which seems to have been cast upon us?[75]

"Very serious consequences" would result if Britain took such a step. In the West Indies "a fearful war of colour would probably soon break out . . . by which the germs of improvement now existing there would be destroyed, and civilization would be thrown back for centuries. In Ceylon a similar result would follow; its native races are utterly incapable of governing themselves . . . the most helpless anarchy would take place of that security which now exists. . . ."[76] In New Zealand, too, the result might be a war with the natives ending with their extinction. Retirement from the stations in West Africa would invite the reappearance of the slave trade in all its former magnitude and viciousness.[77] Even the settlement colonies, like New South Wales, might experience serious internal troubles.[78] Such a policy, Grey concluded, would be "unworthy of a great Nation."[79] Of course, it was assumed by these men that the settlement colonies would be able, at some future time, to do without the beneficial supervision and guidance of the parent state. "The rest," Sir James Stephen wrote, "are unfit for it—detached islands with heterogeneous populations—wretched burdens to this country, which in an evil hour we assumed, but which we have no right to lay down again."[80]

The assumption of this burden, it was hoped, would not remain entirely without material recompense. Having outlined the possible consequence of Great Britain's retirement from empire, Earl Grey remarked:

[75]*The Colonial Policy of Lord John Russell's Administration* (1853), I, 13 f.
[76]*Ibid.*, p. 14.   [77]*Ibid.*, pp. 14 f.   [78]*Ibid.*, p. 16.
[79]*Ibid.*, p. 17. Another writer argued similarly: ". . . not a single one of our colonies is inhabited by a homogeneous population. In none, is the British race the sole one; in scarcely any, is it the most numerous. . . . In Trinidad we have seven distinct races; in the Cape colony at least five; in Australia and New Zealand two . . . with what show of decency or justice could England abandon to their own guidance and protection countries peopled by such various, heterogeneous, and often hostile races. . . . What inevitable injustice such a step must entail upon one or other section of the colonists, what certain peril to the interests of them all, and of humanity at large . . . apart from this consideration, we have simply no right to abandon the Blacks to the possible oppression of the Whites, nor the Whites to the dubious mercies of the Blacks. We cannot do so without dereliction of duty, amounting to a crime" ("Shall We Retain Our Colonies," pp. 488 ff.). In this statement Britain's duty towards her colonies becomes clearly one with the white man's burden.
[80]C. E. Stephen (ed.), *Sir James Stephen. Letters* (Gloucester, 1906), p. 144.

To say nothing of higher motives, and of the duty which I conceive to be no less obligatory upon nations than upon individuals, of using the power and advantages entrusted to them by Providence to advance the welfare of mankind, I would ask whether, even in mere money, there would not be something to set off against the saving of expense from the abandonment of our Colonies? On the other side of the account we have to put the destruction of British property which would thus be occasioned, and the annihilation of lucrative branches of our commerce, by allowing anarchy and bloodshed to arrest the peaceful industry which now creates the means of paying for the British goods consumed daily in larger quantities, by the numerous and various populations now emerging from barbarism under our protection.[81]

Thus, quite often, the objects of Great Britain's effort at civilizing, particularly the coloured races, were also thought of as potential customers of English manufactures. The association of the two thoughts was not always as close as in the statement of a writer who, advocating the acquisition of the Barbary states, remarked: "We convert a nation of thieves and robbers into a nation of honest men and consumers of British manufactures at the same time."[82]

Sometimes the vigorous Anglo-Saxon expansionism found expression in bold projects like that of one writer who proposed the erection of a huge Oriental empire stretching from the Indian Archipelago to Northern Australia and inhabited by teeming populations of Chinese, Malays, and other Eastern races. The creation of new customers and the organization of the production of cotton, sugar, etc., was one objective. The other was that of Great Britain ruling over millions of unenlightened Orientals as the just arbiter and educator.[83]

Here, then, the magnificent problem of founding a free community of mixed races—an asylum for the victims of the various oppressions of the Eastern Archipelago—may possibly be worked out on a scale deserving of so vast an experiment. The principles which have proved so successful in the development of the little communities of Penang and Singapore—where tribes the most opposite in character live together in harmony—may here be applied to a Continent. There is room to receive the overflow of the swarming millions of China and the Islands; and to nurse the miscellaneous colony under the flat of Britain, until a new Union like that of America, though composed of men of . . . widespread different habits, may have spread itself over the tropical half of Australia.[84]

---

[81] *The Colonial Policy of Lord John Russell's Administration* (1853), I, 15 f.

[82] Lewis Goldsmith, "Observations on the Appointment of the Right Hon. Geo. Canning," *The Pamphleteer*, XXII (1823), 336.

[83] "Borneo and the Indian Archipelago," *Edinburgh Review*, LXXXIV (1846), 167-71.

[84] *Ibid.*, p. 173.

Many of these panegyrics on the expansion of Anglo-Saxon civilization and the unselfish duty owed to the colonies in particular and mankind in general, may have been sheer rationalizations. To many imperialists, no doubt, this cluster of arguments may have appeared more useful for propagation than the discredited reasons they actually had in mind. But to question the sincerity of the argument as such or of many who subscribed to it would be erroneous. While references to England's mission appeared at earlier and even at the earliest periods of British colonization, they increased steadily in number throughout the nineteenth century. Although it is impossible to adduce documentary evidence to that effect,[85] it is the opinion of the present writer that, over the same period, there occurred a corresponding increase in the sincere belief[86] that the Union Jack stood for a certain amount of justice, decency, chivalry, and generosity in regard to the relation between the White Man and the coloured races.

Nevertheless, not all English writers and politicians who advanced the claim did so with unquestionable sincerity and, no doubt, the manner in which the claim was put forth frequently was shockingly arrogant and self-complacent. The leaders of the Manchester School denied its validity altogether. Goldwin Smith, for example, declared:

Mission is a large word. All sorts of men and nations have missions, and some of their missions are of a very objectionable kind. Spain had a mission, undertaken in a most religious spirit ... to send buccaneering expeditions into the New World, and fill it with misery and blood. Prince Louis Bonaparte had a mission to strangle French liberty in its sleep. . . . "A mission," historically speaking, is little more than another name for a tendency to rapine. Providence no doubt puts conquered territories into the conqueror's hands; and Providence puts the stolen purse into the pocket of the thief. "Responsibility" is another word of the same kind. It is perhaps more frequently used than "mission" to defend the retention of what you have got in those special cases where the retention is very unprofitable to the nation at large, but profitable or agreeable to a class. In these cases, the class feels that, on whichever side the balance of political and economical advantage may be, it has "responsibilities" of a higher kind which it is not at liberty to resign.[87]

---

[85] It is equally impossible, of course, to prove the contrary thesis.

[86] Whether or not this belief was justified by the facts is a different question. However, even in this respect, it must have appeared to the critical Englishman that, on the whole, the British record compared favourably with that of other imperial nations.

[87] *The Empire* (1863), pp. 257 f.

As for the imposing dogma that "Providence" has put the Colonies into our hands, and that it is our duty to keep them, we must regard it not as an argument, but as a renunciation of argument. . . .[88]

In the case of India, however, John Bright and Goldwin Smith made an exception. There they conceived of a duty Great Britain had to discharge towards the native population. But it was a plain duty and not a mission imposed by Providence. The Indians had a claim upon their conquerors and the claim was based on English misrule and tyranny. The English nation had to make restitution. Cobden looked upon British rule in India "with an eye of despair."[89] John Bright, too, exposed British misgovernment in India with relentless intrepidity.[90] But he declared: "The people of India do not like us, but they scarcely know where to turn if we left them. They are sheep literally without a shepherd. They are people whom you have subdued, and who have the highest and strongest claims upon you—claims which you cannot forget—claims which, if you do not act upon, you may rely upon, if there be a judgment for nations . . . our children in no distant generation must pay the penalty which we have purchased by neglecting our duty to the populations of India."[91]

THE QUESTIONS OF SEPARATION AND ANTI-EXPANSIONISM

If Turgot had been right in saying that the ultimate emancipation of colonies was inevitable, and, until that stage was reached, colonies were extremely difficult to govern,[92] if sovereignty over

[88]*Ibid.*, p. 145.
[89]Morley, *Life of Cobden*, p. 532. He had "no faith in such an undertaking being anything but a calamity and a curse. . ." (*ibid.*).
[90]See his speeches of 1853 and 1858 (*Public Speeches*, I, 13-55).
[91]*Ibid.*, p. 61. Goldwin Smith wrote: "India, of course, stands upon a peculiar footing. There, all cant apart, we have not only taken up a position from which it is difficult to recede, but assumed responsibilities which we are bound, if we can, to discharge" (*The Empire* [1863], p. 8; see also, *ibid.*, pp. 257, 274-8, 292).
[92]". . . it must be confessed . . . that there is no problem in politics more difficult than the treatment of colonies. To watch and nurse their youth, and to mark the hour of their maturity;—to know on what occasions to enforce, and when to relax the strictness of parental superintendence—when to require unconditional obedience, and how to yield to supplication or remonstrance— . . . are amongst the most trying questions of legislative wisdom. . ." ("Spain and Her Colonies," *Quarterly Review*, XVII [1817], 532 f.).

colonies did not yield any advantage in itself,[93] and colonies were without value,[94] or "inventions for paying a quart to receive a pint,"[95] and if, actually, the colonists were exploiting and weakening the mother country,[96] then the casting off of the colonies should be considered a wise policy. Yet, in spite of the fact that these views were subscribed to by a large part of those people who formed articulate opinion in Great Britain—considering the period from 1815 to 1850 as a whole, and not particular crises like the Canadian rebellion—voices unequivocally demanding the separation of the colonies from the mother country were relatively few. It is necessary to note that the politicians, officials, and writers who were actively interested in the colonial question, constituted a very small minority of the people. The attitude of the majority of the ruling classes and, save an almost negligible portion, of the broad masses of the metropolitan population, was generally one of indifference. Not complete indifference, however, for though the symbols of empire were taken for granted, the loss of the empire or of any major part of it, undoubtedly would have been sensed as a shock, to say the least. As regards the articulate participants in the formation of English public opinion the problem presented itself as one of separation versus preservation, contraction versus expansion.

As documented by several statements quoted in the course of the present and the preceding chapter, there were cases in which the abandonment of the colonies was demanded explicitly. More frequently this recommendation was made implicitly, to be inferred from the statement that the colonies were without value or even a loss to the mother state. As a group, the Little Englanders, composed mainly of the leaders of the Manchester party, a few

---

[93]"We have not mentioned dominion among the advantages of the mother country. Fifty years ago, it would have been necessary to prove by argument that it is not necessary to govern a country in order to derive the greatest possible advantage from the only really profitable relations, those of commerce. The independence of the United States first revealed this secret" ("Emigration," *Edinburgh Review*, XLVII [1828], 205 f.).

[94]"It is now generally acknowledged, that colonies are of no real advantage to the mother country" (Buchanan, *Inquiry into the Taxation and Commercial Policy of Great Britain* [1844], p. 135).

[95]"Affairs of Canada," *Westminster Review*, XXIII (1835), p. 290.

[96]"In general, it may be said that one of the chief causes which weakens the power and diminishes the prosperity of a great and enterprising maritime nation, is its liability to be cramped, and weighed down and exhausted, by a parasitical growth of Dependencies" ("Lewis on the Government of Dependencies," p. 554).

economists like Buchanan and Radicals like Joseph Hume and Joseph Parkes[97] came out for separation. Yet, superficially viewed, even their advice lacked consistency. Goldwin Smith, though having pronounced that a policy of drifting was unworthy of a great nation,[98] remarked: "I do not say that we should hastily throw up anything; but I do say that since what we call our Empire was formed the world is changed, and that we ought to take practical note of the change."[99] Cobden declared in 1843 that "he did not wish to be misunderstood as to the course he was going to take. He was not opposed to the retention of colonies any more than hon. Gentlemen opposite. He was as anxious as anyone that the English race should spread itself over the earth; and he believed that colonization, under a proper system of management, might be made as conducive to the interests of the mother country as to the emigrants themselves. But he also believed that the system upon which our colonial affairs were now conducted was one of unmixed evil, injustice, and loss to the people of this country."[100] This statement was made before the inauguration of the British free-trade policy. Following that event, he said in 1848: "We have another argument to meet. We are told we must keep enormous armaments, because we have got so many colonies. People tell me I want to abandon our colonies; but I say, do you intend to hold your colonies by the sword, by armies, and ships of war? That is not a permanent hold upon them. I want to retain them by their affections."[101]

There is no fundamental incompatibility between Little Englandism and the kind of empire Cobden felt inclined to accept. If the imperial system were stripped of preferential tariff duties, the Empire thrown open to world trade, the dependencies granted full self-government and induced to assume the burden of their government and defence, if, in other words, the colonies, following a free-trade policy, were independent in everything but name, then the Empire could not in any way be objectionable to the Little Englander. To the proposition of a British Commonwealth of Nations minus Zollverein the Cobdenites would have gladly assented. This holds true of the majority of economists. McCulloch wrote in 1840: "We hope it will not be supposed, from any thing now stated,

[97]Philo-Bentham, *Canada. Emancipate Your Colonies. An Unpublished Argument by Jeremy Bentham* (London, 1838), Preface.
[98]*The Empire* (1863), p. 29.   [99]*Ibid.*, p. 8.
[100]*Hansard*, third ser., LXX, c. 205.
[101]Cobden, *Public Speeches*, I, 485 f.

that we consider the foundation of colonial establishments as, generally speaking, inexpedient. We entertain no such opinion. It is not to the establishment of colonies . . . but to the trammels that have been laid on their industry, and the interference exercised by the mother countries that we object."[102] Thirty years later John Stuart Mill wrote:

> I suspect that separation would still be a great shock to the general English public, though they justly dislike being taxed for the maintenance of the connection. For my own part I think a severance of it would be no advantage, but the contrary, to the world in general, and to England in particular; England would not oppose a deliberate wish on their part to separate, I would do nothing to encourage that wish, except telling them that they must be at the charge of any wars of their own provoking, and that though we should defend them against all enemies brought on them by us, in any other case we should only protect them in a case of extremity, such as is not at all likely to arise.[103]

There was in this respect little basic difference between the attitude of the Manchester School and that of Liberals like Gladstone, Lord John Russell, Earl Grey, on the one hand, and the bulk of the Colonial Reformers, such as Wakefield and Molesworth, on the other. They, too, accepted the free-trade principle and the proposition that the colonies must carry an increasing amount of the cost of government and defence. But, as with respect to increasing colonial self-government, they did not favour precipitate action on the part of the mother country and were inclined to place more emphasis on the preservation of the symbols of a united empire; united by bonds of sentiment if not by legal institutions.[104] The Colonial Reformers of the Wakefield school, moreover, favoured not only the preservation but also, by means of further colonization,

---

[102] *A Dictionary of Commerce and Commercial Navigation* (Philadelphia, 1840), I, 413.

[103] H. S. R. Elliot (ed.), *The Letters of John Stuart Mill* (London, 1910), II, 237 f.

[104] However, even in this respect the difference was only one of degree. Cobden, as has been shown, wanted the colonies "retained" by sentimental ties. Goldwin Smith said: "That connexion with the colonies, which is really a part of our greatness—the connexion of blood, sympathy, and ideas—will not be affected by political separation. And when our Colonies are nations, something in the nature of a great Anglo-Saxon federation may, in substance if not in form, spontaneously arise out of affinity, and mutual affection" (*The Empire* [1863], p. 6). This was basically in line with the Liberal standpoint. Gladstone declared in 1849: "If they [the colonies] were to be attached to us—if they were to follow our fortunes—they must be held by the cords of love, and in no other manner" (*The Spectator*, XXII [March 31, 1849], p. 290).

the extension of the Empire. Molesworth, for example, declared in 1838: "Those who cry 'Emancipate your colonies,' appear to have seen nothing but the abuses and evils; they have imagined that colonies and jobbing, colonial trade and colonial monopoly, were synonymous terms.... I should say distinguish between the evil and the good; do not 'Emancipate your colonies,' but multiply them and improve—reform your system of colonial government."[105]

Thus, the scrapping of the colonial system did not mean that "the giving-up system"[106] would force the disruption of the Empire. Indeed, during the period here under consideration, the public debate on the colonial problem was, fundamentally, not concerned with the question of separation versus preservation of the Empire, but with the specific character of the imperial system, of government, defence, and of commercial policies. The cry for the abolition of the system of tariff preferences and heavy financial outlays on the government and defence of the dependencies was a cry for separation only if the existing imperial system should prove incapable of change along these lines. The initiation of Great Britain's free-trade policy and constitutional reform did not amount to "discolonization" as the Die-hard Tories alleged.[107] Those who demanded a Little England under any circumstances were extremely few. To the vast majority of Little Englanders, Little Englandism and a liberal British Commonwealth of Nations were absolutely compatible objectives.[108]

[106] *Selected Speeches*, pp. 10 f.
[105] "Political Importance of Our American Colonies," p. 415.
[107] "Parliamentary Prospects," *Quarterly Review*, LXXXI (1847), 571. The same author asked: "If Canada is to be governed by a native Cabinet responsible to her own Legislative bodies—if her produce is to receive no favour in the English market, and English produce no favour in hers—and if British and Canadian shipping is to have no more advantage in the transport of either produce than French or American—will Lord Grey be pleased to tell us in what way Canada will differ, with regard to us, from one of the United States, except our being burdened with the EXPENSE of defending and the PERIL of losing it?" (*ibid.*). Grey, as has been shown above, gave this answer by pointing out why the Empire was worthy of preservation in spite of the loss of monopolies and "jobs."
[108] It should be kept in mind that, India apart, there were few British dependencies in 1850 which, within the near future, would not become capable of assuming the task of self-government and self-defence within the frame of a liberal empire. Aside from the future Dominions, there were only the West Indies and the naval stations.

CHAPTER XII

THE WHITE MAN'S BURDEN

THE idea of the white man's burden had gained popularity ever since the trial of Warren Hastings and the spectacular probing into the records of the East India Company. In the present chapter it will be attempted to draw a brief sketch of the humanitarian movement that commenced to affect broad sections of the British nation in the last quarter of the eighteenth century. This study will be focused upon the campaign against slave trade and slavery, the spread of missionary enterprise, and the new attitude towards the aborigines' problem.

The new humanitarian spirit sprang from two different sources. First, it originated in eighteenth-century enlightenment, in the intellectual temper that produced the French Revolution. Its spirit of egalitarianism and brotherhood and its belief in human perfectibility found expression in a novel code of humanitarian ethics. Secondly, it issued from the Evangelical movement which had been growing steadily since its inception by the early Methodists.[1] Thus, in respect of many objects of reform, there was an alliance, though not in spirit and motivation, between the Evangelicals and the Benthamites.[2]

THE CAMPAIGN AGAINST SLAVE TRADE AND SLAVERY

The twofold origin of the new humanitarianism is very obvious in the case of the anti-slavery campaign. On the one hand, the "prevailing rage"[3] for abolition sprang from "abstract metaphysical

---

[1] There is, of course, no necessary connection between Christianity and humanitarianism. In the course of its history the former has operated as a force both for and against humanitarianism. The charitable sentiment flowing from the new Evangelical ethos, moreover, was curiously selective in picking its objects. There was even a geographical fastidiousness in its partiality to helping the negro slave, the heathen, and the aborigine while charitableness was rather restrained with regard to the prostrate condition of large sections of the population at home. However, a discussion of these questions would be outside the scope of the present study and to state the facts, therefore, must suffice.

[2] See D. C. Somervell, *English Thought in the Nineteenth Century* (2d ed.; London, 1929), pp. 25 f.

[3] John Lord Sheffield, *Observations on the Slave Trade* (2d ed.; London, 1791), p. 2.

notions of liberty and equality."[4] Montesquieu, in the fifteenth Book of his *Esprit des Lois*, subjected the institution of slavery to a devastating attack, and Rousseau, creator of the "back-to-nature" movement, popularized the figment of the "noble savage," idealizing the virtuousness of backward peoples.[5] On the other hand, the Quakers were the earliest opponents of slave trade and slavery; later the Evangelicals took up the cause and in England the Clapham Sect became the backbone of the abolitionist movement.[6]

To a more callous age the negro slave had been but a commodity or a "raw material"[7] used in the manufacture of sugar. His conversion to Christianity did not alter his status.[8] To the abolitionist he was an innocent fellow-human who had been unscrupulously wronged and abused by his white and Christian brethren. The inhumanity of the slave-trader and the greedy cruelty of the slave-owner were greatly exaggerated.[9] Often, negro-phile enthusiasm contrasted sharply with the indifference exhibited by the same people toward the miserable lot of the Irish and English pauper. But, regardless of its merits, the abolitionist campaign was planned and executed with such propagandist skill and endeavour that it affected the sentiments of the overwhelming majority of the nation. For the purpose of the present study it is important to realize that this crusading spirit engendered by the abolitionist movement influenced imperial thinking in so far as it gave birth to a new sense of responsibility towards the backward races of the world,[10] and thus re-enforced the growing idea of the white man's burden. Suddenly it was acknowledged that the

[4] Joseph Marryat, *Thoughts on the Abolition of the Slave Trade* (3d ed.; London, 1816), p. 224.

[5] F. J. Klingberg, *The Anti-Slavery Movement in England* (New Haven, 1926), pp. 26, 34. Sièyes, Brissot, and Robespierre founded "La Société des Amis des Noirs" in 1783.

[6] See J. K. Ingram, *A History of Slavery and Serfdom* (London, 1895), pp. 155 ff.; C. M. MacInnes, *England and Slavery* (Bristol, 1934), pp. 125 ff., 140 ff.; E. C. P. Lascelles, *Granville Sharp* (Oxford, 1928), p. 127.

[7] Dr. Besset, *A Defence of the Slave-Trade on the Grounds of Humanity, Policy, and Justice* (London, 1804), p. 78.

[8] In 1741 the Bishop of London wrote: "The Freedom which Christianity gives, is a Freedom from the Bondage of Sin and Satan, but as to their outward Condition, whatever it was before, whether bond or free, their being baptiz'd, and becoming Christians, makes no manner of Change" (*Gentleman's Magazine*, XI [1741], p. 147).

[9] MacInnes, *England and Slavery*, pp. 49, 110 f.

[10] J. E. Botsford, *English Society in the Eighteenth Century* (New York, 1924), pp. 324 ff.

white Christian must assume a positive duty, an active trusteeship toward his vari-coloured brethren.[11]

Apart from this sentiment the abolitionist movement led to projects of opening up Africa to the commerce and civilization of Europe. Two considerations operated in this direction. On the one hand, it was believed that Europe in general and England in particular had to make restitution to the Africans for having so long upheld and sanctioned the iniquities of slave trade and slavery. Wilberforce declared in 1789: "Let us then make amends as we can for the mischiefs we have done to that unhappy continent. . . . Let us make reparation to Africa, so far as we can, by establishing a trade upon true commercial principles, and we shall soon find the rectitude of our conduct rewarded by the benefits of a regular and growing commerce."[12] Pitt voiced the same opinion[13] and told Thomas Clarkson that "it would be worthy of England to bestir herself for the civilization of Africa."[14] The other consideration was that in order to efface the slave trade it was necessary to stop it not only at the place of its final destination but also, or preferably, at the place of its origin.[15] Again, this object could be reached best by offering to the African slave-trader an adequate alternative in the pursuit of a lucrative trade in other African products.

The problem of suppressing the slave trade also led to such enterprises as the establishment of a colony at Sierra Leone and the famous Buxton-inspired Niger expedition.[16] Finally, at various

[11] R. Coupland, *The American Revolution and the British Empire* (London, 1930), p. 201.

[12] Quoted in R. Coupland, *Wilberforce* (Oxford, 1923), pp. 128 ff. This quotation shows clearly that the expectation of material reward was seldom quite absent from English indulgence in humanitarian enterprise. This fact, however, does by no means warrant the inference that the humanitarian feature was nothing but "window-dressing" and the desire for profit the real motive. Certainly, in the case of the anti-slave traders this would be a ludicrous misinterpretation. It could rather be argued that Wilberforce held out a bait to his less charitable countrymen in order to make humanitarian enterprise more palatable to them.

[13] *Ibid.*, pp. 168 ff.

[14] Quoted in R. D. Owen, *Threading My Way* (London, 1874), p. 111.

[15] See Klingberg, *Anti-Slavery Movement*, p. 321.

[16] Proposals for the elimination of the slave trade by the colonization and commercialization of Africa were heard with increasing frequency during the last two decades of the eighteenth century (Thomas Clarkson, *An Essay on the Impolicy of the African Slave Trade* [London, 1788], pp. 4-20; Rowland Hunt, *The Prosperity of Great Britain* [Shrewsbury, 1796], pp. 45 f.). As a result of the famous Somersett case, the Sierra Leone Company was founded in 1791 with the view to repatriating ex-slaves by settling them in West Africa. Both com-

stages demands were voiced for the annexation of African naval stations deemed particularly suitable for furthering the extermination of the traffic in slaves.[17] Thus, from a humanitarian point the slavery issue produced a state of mind that was conducive to British imperial expansion in Africa.

THE MISSIONARY MOVEMENT

Throughout the last half of the seventeenth and the first three-quarters of the eighteenth centuries, there were only a few isolated voices demanding large-scale missionary efforts on the part of the English clergy. The object of converting heathens to Christianity, moreover, was usually envisaged only as a means to some extraneous end. John Shebbeare, for example, wrote: "Were they [the English 'field-preachers'] sent to convert the Indians in America to the Christian faith, they would unite these nations more strongly to the English interest than every other power on earth; he who

---

mercial and humanitarian motives were behind this unprecedented project, but the latter were markedly more powerful than the former. In spite of the prodigious efforts of the Clapham Sect, and especially of Granville Sharp and Zachary Macaulay, the experiment failed. In 1807 Sierra Leone was made a Crown Colony and subsequently was retained by the Crown, despite vigorous parliamentary protests, in order to afford protection to the liberated slaves and to use the settlement as a *point d'appui* in Britain's campaign against the slave trade (*Hansard*, sec. ser., XX, c. 494; *ibid.*, third ser., XIV, c. 653).

Following the abolition of slavery within its Empire, Great Britain attempted vainly—in the eighteen-twenties and thirties—to effect, by naval and diplomatic means, a discontinuation of the slave trade outside the Empire. In 1838, Thomas F. Buxton conceived of the grandiose plan of uprooting this obnoxious trade at its source by offering to the Africans a substitute commerce equally lucrative and by teaching them the blessings of regular productive labour in the European manner. To accomplish this ambitious objective, Buxton proposed the establishment of agricultural companies in the interior of Africa. These settlements were not to be regular colonies but a group of rather autonomous protectorates (Thomas Fowell Buxton, *The African Slave Trade. Part II, The Remedy* [London, 1840]). Owing to the vicious adversity of tropical nature the Niger expedition ended in disaster and Buxton had to abandon his project. For two critical discussions of Buxton's scheme, the first favourable, the second unfavourable, see: "The Expedition to the Niger—Civilisation of Africa," *Edinburgh Review*, LXXII (1840-1), pp. 456-77; "Remedies for the Slave Trade," *Westminster Review*, XXXIV (1840), pp. 125-65.

[17]For example: "If it be considered as matter which really interests the government and the people of England, that an efficient check should be put to the slave trade in the very focus of that infamous traffic, the possession of Fernando Po, we do not hesitate to affirm, will do it more effectually than the whole squadron of men of war now employed on the station, and at a third part of the expense" ("Clapperton's Second Expedition into the Interior of Africa," *Quarterly Review*, XXXIX [1829], 182).

rules the soul, rules every thing. . . ."[18] The customary position, however, of those who discussed the possibility of carrying the Gospel to pagan nations, is expressed in the following quotation. "When some hear of 'Propagating of the Gospel in Foreign Parts,' they are apt to think of nothing else, but converting Heathen Nations to the Christian Faith. . . . But, whoever looks into our Charter, will find, that the first and principal End of this Corporation is, not to plant Christianity among Heathens, but, to restore, or to preserve it among Christians. . . . The converting Heathens, is a secondary, incidental Point."[19]

The beginning of the new missionary movement roughly coincided with that of the anti-slavery crusade.[20] Owing its inception to the earlier exploits of German pietism it fed on the same vigorous spirit of Evangelicalism. Following the Methodists, the Baptist Missionary Society was founded in 1792, the London Missionary Society in 1795, the Church Missionary Society in 1799, and the British and Foreign Bible Society in 1804. The movement was exceedingly popular and grew by leaps and bounds. The object was that of saving the souls of the benighted heathens. Referring to the East Indians, Wilberforce said in 1813:

Immense regions, with a population amounting . . . to sixty millions of souls, have providentially come under our dominion. They are deeply sunk, and by their religious superstitions fast bound, in the lowest depths of moral and social wretchedness and degradation. Must we not then . . . endeavour to raise these wretched beings out of their present miserable condition, and above all, to communicate to them those blessed truths, which would not only improve their understandings and elevate their minds, but would, in ten thousand ways, promote their temporal well-being, and point out to them a sure path to everlasting happiness.[21]

[18]John Shebbeare, *Letters on the English Nation* (2d ed.; London, 1756), I, p. 144. See also the Letter of Philo Indicus in *Gentleman's Magazine*, XXIV (1764), 125-8.

[19]Henry Stebbing, *A Sermon Preached before the Incorporate Society for the Propagation of the Gospel in Foreign Parts* (London, 1742), p. 18. Stebbing also was utterly sceptical of the possibility of Christianizing native Indians, "Of a general Conversion of the native Indians I see no great likelihood at present" (*ibid.*, p. 19). The civilizing of the heathens, he thought, was the prerequisite of successful conversion.

[20]See John Campbell, *Maritime Discovery and Christian Missions* (London, 1840), pp. 158-200; Robert Adler, *Wesleyan Missions* (London, 1842), pp. 1-7; J. H. Overton, *The English Church in the Nineteenth Century, 1800-1833* (London, 1894), chap. VIII; Louise Creighton, *Missions* (New York, 1912), pp. 56 ff.; E. C. Moore, *The Spread of Christianity in the Modern World* (Chicago, 1919).

[21]"Substance of the Speeches of William Wilberforce on the Clause in the East-India Bill for promoting the religious instruction . . . of the Natives of the British Dominions in India," *The Pamphleteer*, III (1814), 48.

During its first three decades the movement was powerful and expansive. Viewed in retrospect, its essence was an aggressive cultural imperialism, propaganda for the spread of European ideas and ideals over the face of the globe.[22] For Protestantism it was the missionary era *par excellence*.[23] The task, greatly romanticized, carried the gratifying flavour of adventure. Only in the forties began missionary enthusiasm to ebb. Actual achievements were disappointingly disproportionate to expectations and efforts. The romantic conception of the enterprise faded before the certainty of difficulties, hard labour, and slow success.[24] The various missionary societies experienced financial difficulties.[25]

Although the missionary movement was loosely connected with the European penetration of non-European continents, in England it was totally dissociated from the government. Unwittingly it may have assisted British colonial expansion, but it never intended to do so during the period under consideration. Former systems of government-assisted and -directed missionary enterprise were sharply rejected.

On the continents of Africa, India, and America, the Christianity imparted was that of European ecclesiastical establishments; she walked hand in hand with the civil power, in the paths of invasion, victory and conquest; the waving plume, the glittering sword, the roaring cannon, and the mingled swell of martial music, proclaimed her ap̱‚·ᵃ·ᶜ'. The erection of the fort of war and the house of prayer were contemporary operations. . . . In Polynesia, it was happily otherwise. The uncultivated isles, and untutored natives of the South, presented small temptation to the ambition and rapacity of European monarchs to send murderous armaments to extinguish their liberties. . . . The soldier and the missionary were not mess-mates. Gunpowder and the gospels were not carried in the same packet. The alternative of proselytism was not the gibbet. . . . Christianity, in her first approach to Polynesia, appeared arrayed in her native purity, with the olive-branch in her hand, with looks of love and accents of tenderness . . . Brethren and

---

[22]Moore, *Spread of Christianity*, p. 19.

[23]"The present age may be regarded as the Missionary era of the church and of the world. . . ." (Adler, *Wesleyan Missions* [1842], Preface, vi).

[24]"We have seen that in former years the missionaries over estimated their success, and, in relation to the prospects of the missionary cause, allowed themselves to indulge in hopes which facts have not justified. . . . But when God has destroyed the hopes of man, and the missionary cause is bereft of fascination and romance, and the shout of victory is exchanged for protracted and weary conflict, you are dispirited. . . . The mission is no longer an interesting mission, and you would like to be out of it. . . ." (Rev. David King, *The State and Progress of Jamaica* [London, 1850], pp. 120-3).

[25]Adler, *Wesleyan Missions* (1842), pp. 6 ff., 60.

Fathers ... secure the church of Christ against pollution from secular contact, and all the calamities consequent upon it.[26]

The indirect relationship between missionary movement and colonial expansion can best be studied in connection with the aborigines' problem.

THE ABORIGINES' PROBLEM

Until the last quarter of the eighteenth century, the colonizing nations of Protestant Europe were, on the whole, remarkably unconcerned over the fate meted out to the aboriginal peoples. The same age that felt disgust with the slave trade and was actuated by the urgent desire to confer the blessings of the Christian faith upon ignorant heathens, also broached the aborigines' question. Suddenly there were large numbers of people to whom no word was too harsh for describing the extent of the European crime committed against the helpless natives overseas. As early as 1776, Granville Sharp maintained that "the Europeans have taken upon themselves, for a long time past, to attack, destroy, drive out, dispossess, and enslave, the poor ignorant Heathen, in many distant parts of the world...."[27]

The following quotations show the spirit characteristic of this angry indignation.

For more than a thousand years the European nations have arrogated to themselves the title of Christians.... We have long laid to our souls the flattering unction that we are a civilized and a Christian people.... It is high time that we looked a little more rigidly into our pretences.... We talk of the heathen, the savage, the cruel, and the wily tribes ... how is it that these tribes know us?.... They know us chiefly by our crimes and our cruelty. It is we who are, and must appear to them the savages. What, indeed, are civilization and Christianity?[28]

It is shocking that the divine and beneficent religion of Christ should thus have been libelled by base pretenders, and made to stink in the nostrils of all people to whom it ought ... come as the opening of heaven.... They have visited every coast in the shape of rapacious and unprincipled monsters,

---

[26]Campbell, *Maritime Discovery and Christian Missions* (1840), pp. i-v. Indeed, the special interest shown by the missionary societies in the South Sea islands was partly inspired by the expectation that their lofty enterprise would not be contaminated there by the acquisitive expansionism of imperial nations (*ibid.*, pp. 201 ff.).

[27]Granville Sharp, *The Just Limitation of Slavery in the Laws of God* (London, 1776), p. 13.

[28]William Howitt, *Colonization and Christianity* (London, 1838), pp. 1-7.

and then cursed the inhabitants as besotted with superstition, because they did not look on them as angels.[29]

The cause of the aborigines is the cause of three-fourths of the population of the globe.[30]

Buxton asserted in 1835 that "British influence, wherever exerted, was uniformly injurious to those who, upon every ground of justice and right, were entitled to protection in the possession of their lands.... Of the 120,000 square miles now occupied or claimed by this country at the Cape of Good Hope, only a few acres were originally purchased."[31] The rest was stolen. Bannister spoke of "the sanguinary struggle between the white and coloured races"[32] and of "the long and melancholy story of Christian domination over the coloured races...."[33] Merivale wrote: "The history of the European settlements in America, Africa, and Australia, presents everywhere the same general features—a wide and sweeping destruction of native races by the uncontrolled violence of individuals and colonial authorities...."[34] The Report of the Parliamentary Select Committee on Aboriginal Tribes of 1837 constituted the high-mark of this self-accusatory line of argumentation. It is full of the most appalling and sometimes even shocking details.

The activities of Exeter Hall and allied groups were designed, first of all, to shake the British nation out of its indifference toward the aboriginal question by disseminating factual information. Secondly, they pressed the government to take up the cause of the helpless natives against encroachments on the part of British colonists and traders. In 1834, Buxton moved for the establishment of the above-mentioned committee. He declared: "... in every British Colony, without exception, the aboriginal inhabitants had greatly decreased, and still continued rapidly to dwindle away. This was the case in Australia and Africa and in North America, and ... British brandy and gunpowder had done their job in thinning the natives."[35] In 1836 the Aborigines Protection Society was founded and became, in short order, an exceedingly influential pressure group.

The core of the issue seemed to lie in the fact that wherever aborigines came into conflict with European colonists, trouble arose

[29]*Ibid.*, pp. 8 f.   [30]*Ibid.*, p. 507.
[31]*Hansard*, third ser., XXIX, c. 551.
[32]*British Colonization and Coloured Races* (London, 1838), p. 1.
[33]*Ibid.*, p. 6.   [34]H. Merivale, *Lectures* (London, 1841), II, p. 153.
[35]*Hansard*, third ser., XXIV, c. 1061.

and the natives were inevitably cheated or chased out of their lands. It was asserted, therefore, that parliamentary grants for purposes of colonization were in effect "so many premiums for human destruction."[36] The missionaries usually took up the cause of the natives. In 1809, for example, Methodist missionaries reported from Tahiti: ". . . we are afraid of colonizing, lest it should prove in time destructive to the liberty, or lives and property of the natives."[37] The history of New Zealand furnishes an interesting example of missionary opposition to colonization.

The missionaries who went out to convert native tribes in the Pacific area were not the allies of traders and colonists. Their sole motive was religious zeal.[38] Yet they found themselves unable to prevent traders from introducing European commodities and vices and thus, by compromising the prestige of the white man, obstructing the spread of the Gospel. The missionaries came to New Zealand in 1814. In the course of the next twenty years, they were followed by increasing numbers of whalers, traders, colonists, and escaped convicts from Australia. In their wake came vice, crime, and disturbances. In 1836, Wakefield described New Zealand as "the fittest country in the world for colonization. . . . It will be said that New Zealand does not belong to the British Crown and that is true, but Englishmen are beginning to colonize New Zealand. . . . Adventurers go from New South Wales and Van Diemen's land. . . . We are, I think, going to colonize New Zealand, but are doing so in a most slovenly and disgraceful manner."[39]

Wakefield, Francis Baring, Lord Durham, and Molesworth founded the New Zealand Association for the purpose of settling New Zealand in conformity with the principles of systematic colonization. According to this scheme, the Crown was to appoint an Inspector of the Natives and a tenth of all land purchased was to be set aside as an unalienable native reserve. Wakefield, furthermore, was willing to collaborate with the missionaries in New Zealand.[40] But from the beginning, Exeter Hall came out in bitter opposition to the project. Speaking for this group, Dandeson

---

[36]"Hottentots and Caffres," *London and Westminster Review*, XXVI (1836-7), 101 f.

[37]"Transactions of the Missionary Society in the South Sea Islands," *Quarterly Review*, II (1809), 55.

[38]K. L. P. Martin, *Missionaries and Annexation in the Pacific* (Oxford, 1924), p. 7.

[39]Quoted *ibid.*, pp. 36 f.   [40]*Ibid.*, p. 37.

Coates told a deputation of the New Zealand Association that he would "thwart the Association by every means in his power."[41] A pamphlet prepared by Coates maintained that, as past experience had abundantly proved, barbarous tribes inevitably suffered from intercourse with colonists of a superior race.[42] His pamphlet also revealed that the real missionary ideal of the time was the establishment of a theocracy. "Only let New Zealand be spared from colonization, and the Mission have its free and unrestricted course for half a century more, and the great political and moral problem will be solved—of a people passing from a barbarous to a civilized state, through the agency of Europeans, with the complete preservation of the Aboriginal race, and of their national independence and sovereignty."[43]

The Church Missionary Society commanded powerful influence with public opinion and governing circles. Lord Glenelg, the Colonial Secretary, and Mr. "Over-Secretary" Stephen, were both officials of the Society. For some time, indeed, the efforts of the New Zealand Association were successfully thwarted. In 1839, however, the Association resolved to colonize New Zealand without the sanction of the Colonial Office. The hand of the government was forced for, at the same time, the situation in the prospective colony was developing into a state of complete anarchy owing to the increased influx of adventurers and escaped convicts. Moreover, French designs of annexing New Zealand became known and in January, 1840, the British government reluctantly proclaimed the annexation of New Zealand to the Crown.[44]

Similar conflicts and intrigues developed in connection with the expansion of settlements in South Africa.[45] Two observations must be drawn from these incidents. First, under the influence of Exeter Hall, the government, and particularly the Colonial Office, became increasingly concerned over the fate of the aborigines. As friction between natives and settlers was inevitable, the government sometimes opposed, usually without success, further colonization and then was forced to follow an annexationist policy in order to be able to supervise effectively the relations between natives and settlers. Territorial expansion in South Africa was often dictated by purely humanitarian motives. Secondly, the

[41]*Ibid.*, p. 38.   [42]*Ibid.*, pp. 38 f.
[43]Quoted *ibid.*, p. 40.   [44]*Ibid.*, pp. 40 ff.
[45]See W. P. Morrell, *British Colonial Policy in the Age of Peel and Russell* (Oxford, 1930), pp. 23-7, chap. XII; H. E. Egerton, *A Short History of British Colonial Policy* (7th ed.; London, 1924), pp. 270 ff.

missionaries as a rule sided with the natives and took up their grievances against the settlers. Sometimes, as in the case of New Zealand, they were opposed to annexation, sometimes they asked for it, again for humanitarian reasons.

The demand for government intervention on behalf of the aborigines in all British colonies became increasingly urgent. Buxton wrote in 1834: "It appears to me that we ought to fix and enforce certain regulations and laws, with regard to the natives of all countries where we make settlements. Those laws must be based on the principles of justice. In order to do justice we must admit 1st. That the natives have a right to their own lands. 2dly. That as our settlements must be attended with some evils to them, it is our duty to give them compensation for those evils, by imparting the truths of Christianity and the arts of civilised life."[46] The Report of the Parliamentary Committee on Aboriginal Tribes suggested: "The protection of the Aborigines should be considered as a duty peculiarly belonging and appropriate to the executive government, as administered either in this country or by the governors of the respective colonies."[47] Another writer declared: "The government, then, must delay no longer to establish a wise system of justice and beneficence on behalf of the natives of all the Australias."[48] Merivale proposed "the appointment in every colony of a department of the civil service for that especial purpose, with one or more officers devoted to it."[49]

The Report of the Aborigines' Committee of 1837, under the chairmanship of Buxton, had expressed scepticism as to the beneficial influence of European commerce on the natives. It also had recommended the repression of further colonization in some instances and generally aimed at a policy of segregating indigenous tribes from white settlers. On the other hand, the West African Committee of 1842, under the chairmanship of Viscount Sandon and composed largely of the same members as the former committee, advocated, under strict supervision, the expansion of colonization and commerce as a means of civilizing the natives. The lapse of five years apparently had changed the minds of some of the English

[46] Charles Buxton (ed.), *Memoirs of Sir Thomas Fowell Buxton* (2d ed.; London, 1849), pp. 369 ff.

[47] Aborigines Protection Society (ed.), *Report of the Parliamentary Select Committee on Aboriginal Tribes* (London, 1837), p. 117.

[48] "Discoveries in Australia," *Eclectic Review*, XX, new ser. (1846), 624. See also S. Bannister, *Humane Policy* (2d ed.; London, n.d.), p. 3.

[49] *Lectures* (1841), II, 157.

philanthropists.[50] This different orientation was largely the outcome of the new theory that the African slave trade could only be effaced by opening up the interior of Africa to the commerce of the world.

One of the extreme exponents of this view was S. Bannister. He denied that European colonization and trade were necessarily destructive of the coloured races. Only "the corruption of some Christians . . . the short-sighted stupidity of some traders . . . the selfishness of some settlers" had brought about these "melancholy" results.[51] He extolled the civilizing effects of commerce[52] and declared "that colonization must afford even more powerful means of civilization to the natives. . . ."[53] Bannister offered a fanciful plan. He claimed "that white colonization and commercial enterprise, which no earthly power can, or ought to stop, should be accompanied by sufficient means for protecting and advancing coloured people in social and political union and intercourse with us, wherever we spread."[54] Thus, he looked forward to the "ultimate amalgamation" of the natives with the British.[55] In order to accelerate this process he also proposed a grandiose system for the large-scale education of aborigines in England.[56]

As mentioned before, all these proposals did not recommend themselves only on Christian and philanthropic grounds. Their authors seldom failed to point to the material advantages of a policy that would be patterned after their projects. William Howitt, for example, declared: "The idiocy of the man who killed his goose that he might get the golden eggs, was wisdom compared to the folly of the European nations, in outraging and destroying the Indian races, instead of civilizing them. Let any one look at the immediate effect amongst the South Sea Islanders, the Hottentots, or the Caffres, of civilization creating a demand for our manufactures, and of bringing the productions of their respective countries into the market. . . ."[57] Sir Fowell Buxton pointed out that kindness towards aborigines "would be far more preferable—that it would be far safer, far cheaper, and far more profitable than

[50]See Bannister, *Humane Policy*, Introd., pp. ix-x.
[51]*British Colonization and Coloured Tribes* (1838), p. 7.
[52]*Ibid.*, p. 188. The same view was expounded by the Rev. R. Raikes, the founder of the Sunday School. See *ibid.*, p. 184.
[53]*Humane Policy* (n.d.), p. 1.
[54]*Ibid.*, Introd., vi.
[55]*British Colonization and Coloured Tribes*, p. 274.
[56]*Ibid.*, p. 290 f.
[57]*Colonization and Christianity* (1838), p. 504.

coercion."[58] Bannister likewise maintained that his large-scale scheme of cultural imperialism would pay in the long run because the occurrence of costly wars with natives would diminish, markets would expand, and the value of the lands acquired in the colonies would rise correspondingly.[59]

This new humanitarian outlook in imperial thinking was not without opposition,[60] but it is no exaggeration to say that as a matter of principle and sentiment it was accepted by the British nation and permeated its councils. The idea of the Trusteeship over coloured peoples obviously was a powerful phenomenon in the thirties and forties of the nineteenth century. Of course, missionary imperialism of any kind, whether it embraces the spread of an entire culture or only parts of it, may constitute the conferring of benefits on peoples of a so-called inferior culture or religion from the point of view of the missionary nation. But as Bonn points out, it may turn out to be "a greater trial to subject races than a more primitive and not self-conscious form of exploitation."[61] For missionary imperialism does not even permit such peoples to live their own lives, to worship their Gods, and to preserve their institutions and customs.

[58] *Hansard*, third ser., XXIX, c. 549.

[59] *British Colonization and Coloured Tribes* (1838), p. 204.

[60] The colonists especially were outraged at the new trend. "Ye philanthropists—fallacious reasoners on subjects of which ye know nothing certain, who romanticise about savages and slavery till ye get entangled in a web of metaphysics of your own weaving. . . ." (Quoted from an appeal sent by South African frontier-settlers to the mother country: E. D. H. E. Napier, *Past and Future Emigration* [London, 1849], p. 3). This whole pamphlet is written against "the maudlin, vitiated, and mistaken popular feeling of the day, in favour of the 'oppressed and cruelly treated aborigines' " (*ibid.*, p. 13). To Napier the Kaffirs were nothing but "murderous," "treacherous," "brigands and cattle-robbers."

[61] M. J. Bonn, *The Crumbling of Empire* (London, 1938), p. 40.

CHAPTER XIII

THE PROBLEM OF CONVICT TRANSPORTATION

IN 1849, *The Times* declared: "If we are not to use our Colonies for Convict Settlements, what is the good of a Colony?"[1] This was a polemical statement, dictated by the exigencies of the moment, and it would be erroneous to conclude that the institution of transportation ever figured as a major argument for colonies and colonization. But among the minor arguments it had held its position over the centuries.

When the American War of Independence stopped the transportation of convicts to the New World, and the meagre facilities for their confinement in the metropolis had become woefully overcrowded, the government decided on the establishment of a penal colony in New South Wales. The cessation of transportation, indeed, would have necessitated a total revision of English criminal jurisprudence and a tremendous increase in the number of gaols in the metropolis. Thus, Australia became "the land of convicts and kangaroos," as Sydney Smith called it.[2]

The transportation system was firmly based on the legal and criminological theories of the time.[3] From the eighties of the eighteenth century on, however, the system was subjected to increasing criticism, especially by the utilitarian writers.[4] The views of Bentham and James Mill have been presented in Chapter VIII. In one form or other, and confirmed by recent experiences, they were restated by Archbishop Whately, Bishop Ullathorne, and William Molesworth. On the whole, the arguments brought forward in defence of the institution remained likewise unchanged. These arguments were:[5] (1) transportation was an effective and humane means of preventing crime and reforming the criminal;[6]

[1]Quoted in W. S. Childe-Pemberton, *Life of Lord Norton* (London, 1909), p. 73.
[2]"Botany Bay," *Edinburgh Review*, XXXII (1819), 28.
[3]See Eris O'Brien, *The Foundation of Australia* (London, 1936), book I, chaps. II-III.
[4]See *ibid.*, pp. 100-60.
[5]See J. D. Lang, *Transportation and Colonization* (London, 1837), pp. 18-32.
[6]Merivale recorded that "there was general confidence in the favourite theory, that the best mode of punishing offenders was that which removed them

(2) it was economical;[7] (3) it permanently ridded the mother country of "the irreclaimable portion of its culprit population;[8] and (4) in the colonies convict labour was turned to the best account for the public benefit and accelerated the economic development of the colonies.[9]

The principal counter-arguments, as marshalled by Archbishop Whately,[10] were: (1) transportation was inadequate as a punishment; (2) it was too expensive a system; and (3) it was prejudicial to the sound development of the colonies.

As to the first point, it was brought out that transportation lacked the very essence of punishment,—terror—, and, therefore, was not sufficiently dreaded to deter the prospective criminal from committing a crime.[11] Whately remarked in the House of Lords in 1840: "I found the relatives and former neighbours of transported convicts receiving such favourable accounts of the situation of those convicts—sometimes true, and sometimes false, but always alluring,—that the punishment of transportation had the effect of a bounty on crime...."[12] Another writer stated that transportation "cannot be amended. It has completely failed as a punishment; it has been still more ineffectual as a means of reformation; it has produced the most degraded community in the universe

---

from the scene of offence and temptation, cut them off by a great gulf of space from all their former connexions, and gave them the opportunity of redeeming past crimes by becoming useful members of society" (Herman Merivale, *Lectures* [London, 1841], II, pp. 17 f.). Thus, Lord John Russell said in the Commons in 1840: "Undoubtedly the most likely way to reform offenders and to prevent them from again committing the offence, was to remove them from temptation, and place them at once in a state of affluence" (*Hansard*, third ser., LIII, c. 1281). It was also asserted that the system of solitary confinement in prisons was inhumane. See Archibald Alison, "Crime and Transportation" (1849), in *Essays, Political, Historical, and Miscellaneous* (Edinburgh, 1850), I, pp. 560, 585.

[7]It was assumed that Britain would have to construct numerous penitentiaries and that building and operating costs would be enormous. See Alison, *Essays*, I, pp. 589 f.; and W. P. Morrell, *British Colonial Policy in the Age of Peel and Russell* (Oxford, 1930), p. 385.

[8]This was, of course, an unimpeachable argument as long as the advantage of the metropolis was considered exclusively. It will be discussed further in the following.

[9]This argument was based on the fact that in colonies labour invariably was scarce.

[10]*Thoughts on Secondary Punishment* (London, 1832), pp. 4-101; see also Richard Whately, *Remarks on Transportation* (London, 1834).

[11]H. G. Bennet, *Letter to Viscount Sidmouth ... on the Transportation Laws* (London, 1819), p. 44.

[12]*Hansard*, third ser., LIV, c. 252.

....".[13] The large expense of the system was attributed to the factors of distance and higher living costs in the colonies. Sydney Smith remarked: "Why we are to erect penitentiary houses and prisons at the distance of half the diameter of the globe, and to incur the enormous expense of feeding and transporting their inhabitants too, and at such a distance, is extremely difficult to discover. It certainly is not from a deficiency of barren islands near our own coast nor of uncultivated wastes in the interior...."[14] Herman Merivale maintained: "The labour of convicts is probably the dearest of all labour; that is, it costs more to some portion or other of society."[15]

As to the benefits that the system conferred upon the colonies, it was generally agreed, that it had been greatly profitable to them at the beginning, but, after a certain stage in their development had been reached, disadvantages were outweighing these benefits. Merivale wrote: "The causes of the early and rapid growth of wealth in these colonies are not difficult to trace. They were, in fact, almost wholly artificial—on the one hand an ample supply of labour, on the other a large government expenditure. Instead of being forced to support their own servants, the colonists received in truth a bounty for employing them, their produce being taken off their hands by the government at high prices, for the purpose of maintaining those very labourers."[16]

The advantage to the colonists, therefore, was in the form of an extremely wasteful subvention. Writing in 1841, Merivale maintained that the colonists "no longer depend in any essential degree on that government expenditure for their prosperity."[17] The Colonial Reformers, advocating large-scale emigration to the colonies, saw in the continuance of the transportation system only

[13]"Life in the Penal Colonies," *London and Westminster Review*, XXVII (1837), 92.

[14]"Collin's Account of New South Wales," *Edinburgh Review*, II (1803), 31 f. See also Bennet, *Letter to Viscount Sidmouth* (1819), p. 44.

[15]*Lectures* (1841), II, p. 7.

[16]*Ibid.*, II, p. 5.

[17]*Ibid.*, II, pp. 5 f. Similarly, Charles Buller declared in the House of Commons in 1840: "... whatever the merits of the transportation system might be, it was clear that there was a certain point in the condition of a colony, when it was no longer practicable to make it a penal colony, and it seemed to him that the colony of New South Wales had arrived at that point. The great object to be kept in view was to promote free emigration" (*Hansard*, third ser., LIII, c. 1301). This statement implies that it would be more profitable to have a larger influx of free labourers than of transportees.

an impediment to the out-flow of free workers because of the bad reputation of a convict-colony in the metropolis.[18] It also contaminated the very idea of empire.[19] As the British converted a portion of the Empire "into the moral dung-heap of Great Britain," it was logical to conclude that society in the colonies sustained grave damages in consequence of the transportation system. Sydney Smith said that New South Wales was "a sink of wickedness."[20] Observers pointed out that there was a great augmentation of crime in the convict colonies. "Crime has gone on gradually increasing in New South Wales, in a greater ratio than the increase of the convict population. The community has become, continually, more and more vicious."[21]

It was also believed that there was too great a disproportion between free settlers and convicts, that "there was not, in New South Wales, a sufficient infusion of that which was good and virtuous to give a tone to society."[22] Whately remarked: ". . . though it must be admitted that a community consisting of masters and slaves is bad, and that a nation of gaolers and prisoners—of criminals I may say, and executioners,—is bad, the union of the two in one system—the system of punishing criminals by assigning them as slaves to labour for the benefit of private individuals, is incomparably the worst of all."[23] And, in 1847, one author stated: "It is only of late that the system has fully revealed its gigantic capacities of evil. It was then but a nursling of hell; it is now a full grown demon."[24] Furthermore, it was observed that this continuous infusion of questionable characters retarded the process that would render Australia mature for self-government.[25] One writer

---

[18] ". . . the punishment of transportation excites amongst the common people a strong prejudice against emigration" (Edward Gibbon Wakefield, *A View of the Art of Colonization* [London, 1849], p. 138).

[19] Molesworth declared in 1849: "The noble Lord [Lord John Russell] had described the Colonial Empire as a glorious inheritance which we had received from our ancestors, and declared that he was determined at all risks to maintain it forever intact. Now, I ask him how do we treat that precious inheritance? By transportation we stock it with convicts; we convert it into the moral dung-heap of Great Britain. . . ." (quoted in Mrs. Fawcett, *Life of the Right Hon. Sir William Molesworth* [London, 1901], p. 282).

[20] "Botany Bay," p. 46.

[21] "Life in the Penal Colonies," p. 88.

[22] Speech of H. G. Ward in 1840 (*Hansard*, third ser., LIII, c. 1299).

[23] *Ibid.*, LIV, c. 256.

[24] "What is to be done with our Criminals?," *Edinburgh Review*, LXXXVI (1847), 224.

[25] See Buller's speech in 1840 (*Hansard*, third ser., LIII, c. 1302).

in the *Quarterly Review*, describing the evils of the system, declared:

In such a state of society, it required all the effrontery of modern Radicalism to set up a claim for a representative government. Yet such a claim is actually advanced and pressed by the 'felony' of Australia, and warmly supported by their political friends on this side of the water.... It will be obvious to all rational thinkers, that a great change, a great purification, the work of many years, must be carried into full effect, before the theory of popular representation can be safely adopted in a colony, so large a proportion of whose inhabitants are convicted thieves and their associates.[26]

The foes of the transportation system, of course, recommended the penitentiary system as a better alternative. To every rational mind their arguments were vastly more convincing than those of their opponents. What actually saved the system, in the face of attack and criticism, over so long a period of time, was partly the force of inertia against change, the pre-disposition among powerful circles, rather to "muddle through" somehow than boldly to embark upon an entirely new and untried policy. Too many influential people had not enough imagination to perceive that the penitentiary system was a satisfactory solution. The baffling question of "What to do with our criminals" really was the strongest argument in favour of the old system. Mundy wrote as late as 1852: " 'What is to be done with our criminals?' is still the cry. It is a fair puzzle. Are we to starve, flog, hang, draw and quarter them, with one school of disciplinarians, or to pet, educate, make modelprisoners of them ... with the opposite school?—or are we to provide some 'soft intermediate degree' of castigation—something between the truculent and the emolient—between Carlyle and Maconochie?"[27] Whately likewise remarked: "The opponents of transportation are indeed constantly met by the inquiry, 'What would you substitute?' as the sole and sufficient defence of the existing system...."[28]

To those who lacked confidence in the virtues of the penitentiary system, there seemed only a choice between convict colonies and Great Britain herself becoming a convict country. "Removing

[26]"New South Wales," *Quarterly Review*, LXII (1838), 491. The author approved of the conclusions of Molesworth's Transportation Committee (*ibid.*, p. 502).

[27]*Our Antipodes*, III, p. 108. The author favoured retention of a reformed system of transportation (*ibid.*, p. 109).

[28]*Hansard*, third ser., LIV, c. 260. Sir G. C. Lewis remarked that the system would "probably have been abandoned altogether before this time, if its abandonment would not lead to the necessity of building penitentiaries in England" (*An Essay on the Government of Dependencies* (1841), ed. C. P. Lucas [Oxford, 1891], p. 232).

the pestilence,"[29] then, was an absolute necessity. "What is to be the ultimate disposal of the prisoners, when their sentence has finally expired? . . . Are they all to be turned loose on the society which they have offended? . . . we cannot think without horror of the consequences of turning loose, even on our well-protected home society, 5,000 criminals a year. We should have some fear lest we should ourselves become a penal settlement."[30] Another writer asserted that the transportation system was indispensable owing to "the unavoidable necessity of ridding England of a monster evil of daily and formidable growth."[31] Even Lord Shaftesbury wrote to Adderley in 1851: "It would give me pleasure, I assure you, to aid in obtaining for the Colonies as much relief as is possible from the convict system, but I really do not see how we shall deal with the other question of Transportation. The thought of retaining all our convicts in England . . . is perfectly terrible. We shall very soon have twenty thousand forcats in this country, in addition to the floating mass of thieves and burglars which is already formidable enough."[32] With sad resignation Stephen remarked that "to colonize with convicts is to sow the seed of crime, misery, and waste, and although necessity may drive us to pursue that course, necessity will also compel us to reap as we have sown."[33] This state of mind explains the obstinate last-ditch defence of the system and the number of suggestions for its reform advanced in the forties and fifties.[34]

It has been said that with the appointment of Molesworth as chairman of the Transportation Committee of 1837-8, the battle

[29] G. R. Porter, *The Progress of the Nation* (London, 1851), p. 136.

[30] "What is to be done with our Criminals?" p. 262. This author assumed that convicts would be kept in penitentiary confinement only for a relatively short period of time.

[31] E. D. H. E. Napier, *Past and Future Emigration* (London, 1849), p. 349.

[32] Quoted in Childe-Pemberton, *Life of Lord Norton*, p. 94.

[33] Quoted in Morrell, *British Colonial Policy in the Age of Peel and Russell*, p. 43.

[34] For Lord Grey's defence of transportation see *ibid.*, chap. XVI. See also Earl Grey, *The Colonial Policy of Lord John Russell's Administration* (London, 1853), II, pp. 1-87.

It was left to Alison to suggest a truly fantastic remedy. In order to render the transportation of convicts palatable to the colonists he proposed that, with every shipment of convicts, the mother country transport "a certain number . . . of the untainted portions of the community" at public expense ("Crime and Transportation," [1849] in *Essays*, I, pp. 611 f.).

was really won.³⁵ More cautiously, Morrell stated that Molesworth's Report "scotched the snake" but did not kill it.³⁶ Indeed, in view of the prevailing state of mind on the subject, the system might have been preserved for a much longer period of time than it actually was—and the snake was not killed before 1867.

Mainly responsible for the discontinuation of the system was the increasingly hostile attitude of the colonists. In the case of Australia, the colonists, at first, had favoured the system. Between 1830 and 1850, however, there occurred a definite change in public opinion.³⁷ The squatters, the big land-owners,—a very influential part of the population—, for obvious reasons continued to approve of transportation.³⁸ But the increasing numbers of free labourers and immigrants were bitterly opposed to the system,— also for obvious reasons.³⁹ So were the freed convict-colonists.⁴⁰ When in 1849, because of stiff Australian protests, the government decided to send transportees to the Cape Colony, the violent remonstrations of the colonists there prevented the execution of the scheme.⁴¹

It may be remarked, finally, that as in the case of the anti-slavery and aboriginal questions the issue of transportation was largely a non-partisan issue.

[35] H. E. Egerton, *A Short History of British Colonial Policy*, (7th ed.; London, 1924), p. 322. For Molesworth's great speech of 1840 see *Hansard*, third ser., LIII, cs. 1236-79.

[36] Morrell, *British Colonial Policy in the Age of Peel and Russell*, p. 11.

[37] Woodruff, "Expansion and Emigration," in G. M. Young (ed.), *Early Victorian England* (London, 1934), II, p. 379.

[38] Egerton, *Short History of British Colonial Policy*, pp. 323 f. Mundy wrote "The squatters and other great employers of unskilled labour pray for renewal of convictism for the good of their trade, without reference to the benefit of the commonwealth—as the glazier prays for hail-storms, civic riots, and the revival of Tom-and-Jerryism, for his private ends.... There are a few 'parties' who would employ the Arch-fiend himself, if he would engage at low wages...." (*Our Antipodes* [1852], III, pp. 110 ff.).

[39] *Ibid.*, III, pp. 110 f.

[40] *Ibid.*, p. 111.

[41] When the *Neptune*, with a consignment of convicts, arrived at Capetown in September, 1849, tolling bells announced the unwelcome news to the inhabitants. Shops were closed and business was suspended. The boat was boycotted and could get no provisions from shore. Ultimately she sailed away with her cargo. The name of Adderly, who had taken up the cause of the Cape colonists, was given to the principal street in Capetown, while its only inhabitant who had refused to boycott the *Neptune* was knighted by the Home government for his patriotism (Childe-Pemberton, *Life of Lord Norton*, p. 75). For colonial protests against convictism in 1849 see *The Spectator*, XXII, pp. 583, 678, 750, 772, 867, 891, 913, 943, 1010, 1937.

CHAPTER XIV

A NOTE ON THE LAKE POETS AND THOMAS CARLYLE

NEITHER the Lake Poets nor Carlyle were interested in the colonies *per se*. Their treatment of the subject was incidental when they touched it at all and as far as they did pronounce any statements on the idea of empire and related questions, their influence on contemporaneous thought was well-nigh negligible.[1] They can be regarded only in a limited sense as forerunners of the later imperialism; for what did they have in common with Joseph Chamberlain's attitude? Their significance for the purpose of the present study is only an indirect one. The characteristic features of the early and mid-Victorian era in political, social, and intellectual respects, were the ascendancy of the higher middle classes—the *bourgeoisie*—over the landed nobility, of the manufacturer and trader over the landlord, of the city over the countryside, of Liberalism over Conservatism, of rationalism over traditionalism, and of materialism over idealism. Broadly speaking, the Lake Poets and Carlyle stood in opposition to the new values, and, as far as a later era rejected these values, these writers heralded the impending revolt.

One of the best statements on the basic antagonism between utilitarian and romantic thinking was given by a writer in the *Westminster Review*.

In considering this question, we must distrust the impressions of fancy and association. We must discard from our minds, if not all the susceptibilities of the poetic temperament, at least all its fictions and illusions. We must put far from us, not indeed all the pleasing dreams and images of poetry, but all such poetry as has its source and nutriment in the picturesque alone. For order, regularity, and a certain measure of uniformity, which are essential conditions of a nation's welfare, constitute the greatest enemies of the picturesque, and are utter abominations to a poet's fancy. The straightest road from one point to another is the best for all practical purposes of locomotion. Yet it is certainly the least attractive to the mind. The pursuits of commerce afford few materials to gratify a superficial fancy, however grand or beneficent their results may be. The history of an industrious, thriving, and contented people is proverbially dull.[2]

---

[1] Friedrich Brie, *Imperialistische Strömungen in der Englischen Literatur* (Halle, 1928), pp. 101, 139.

[2] "Resources of an Increasing Population: Emigration or Manufactures," *Westminster Review*, XL (1843), 106.

This expressed the position of the utilitarian thinker. The Lake Poets and Carlyle, on the other hand, assailed the fundamental premises and conclusions of liberal, utilitarian, and materialistic thinking, thus questioning the very attitude that, during the period here considered, largely determined British points of view with regard to empire and imperial problems.

THE LAKE POETS

Common to all Lake Poets[3] was the deep conviction that life dominated by "calculating, meddling reason" led to debasement of human kind.[4] They disliked the Age of Reason from which rationalism and utilitarianism had sprung and firmly believed in and defended the virtues of mysticism.[5] Their hostility toward Philosophical Radicals, political economists, and the Manchester School is very revealing in this respect. They were staunch conservatives, and, hence, opposed to the "de-bunking," questioning, reformist spirit of their intellectual adversaries. Wordsworth once remarked: "Can it, in a general view, be good that an infant should learn much which its parents do not know?"[6] The reaction to this question of a Benthamite or a "Manchester professor" can be well imagined. The attitude of the Lake Poets towards the meaning, function, and tasks of the State likewise differed vastly from the conception prevalent in their time. Laissez-faire doctrines, no doubt, must appear grossly incongruous if the State is conceived of as an "organic whole" and "moral unit," as was done by Coleridge.[7]

The views of the Lake Poets on the subject of material wealth were equally at variance with the utilitarians.[8] In their eyes,

[3]Wordsworth, Coleridge, and Southey, of course, partook of the Romantic movement. It would, however, be difficult to treat them as Romanticists with regard to the present problem, for the attitudes of such indisputable Romanticists as Byron, Shelley, and Keats, were fundamentally different in this respect. Sir Walter Scott, on the other hand, could be easily included, for he, "the eternal Conservative," shared most of the views of the "Lakers" that are relevant for the purpose of this study. See Crane Brinton, *The Political Ideas of the English Romanticists* (Oxford, 1926), pp. 111-19.

Thomas De Quincey will be included in this study.

[4]*Ibid.*, p. 48.

[5]*Ibid.*, pp. 56, 64 f., 90.

[6]Quoted: *ibid.*, p. 60.

[7]See Crane Brinton, *English Political Thought in the Nineteenth Century* (London, 1933), p. 82.

[8]See Brie, *Imperialistische Strömungen in der Englischen Literatur*, p. 91.

Englishmen, as a consequence of laissez-faire philosophy, were dominated by the vile shop-keeping spirit and devoured by an immoderate desire for material gain.[9] Although he was not opposed to a reasonable expansion of material wealth,[10] Coleridge, for example, in his Lay Sermon fulminated against the evils of "the spirit of barter." Vehemently, he condemned the new industrial society that was supplanting the old agricultural society of the country.[11] Like Wordsworth, he hated the temper of the large and throbbing industrial cities and nursed a strong dislike for the commercial classes.[12] It was with contempt that Coleridge spoke of "the great horde of manufacturers."[13] Southey likewise deprecated the "manufacturing greediness" of the nation.[14] He deplored that commercial speculation and competition were not "kept within the bounds of prudence and probity,"[15] and remarked: ". . . one might suppose, that the great fabric of British prosperity rested upon cotton; that the two purposes for which human beings are sent into this world, are to manufacture it and to wear it; that the proper definition of man is a manufacturing animal, and that the use for which children are created is to feed power-looms."[16]

The Lake Poets disliked not only the materialist spirit, they also were prejudiced against economy in the production of wealth. "What solemn humbug this modern political economy is," Coleridge said in his *Table Talk*.[17] Political economy, moreover, seemed vicious in its tendency to dissolve the irrational bonds that integrated national societies. "The entire tendency of modern or Malthusian political economy is to denationalize."[18] Coleridge felt no concern over the evils of a large national debt and heavy taxation, a consideration that was of great importance in the "tax-hating age."[19] He also upheld the virtues of economic self-sufficiency. "No state can be such properly, which is not self-

[9] Brinton, *English Political Thought in the Nineteenth Century*, p. 84.
[10] Brinton, *Political Ideas of the English Romanticists*, p. 83.
[11] See Brinton, *English Political Thought in the Nineteenth Century*, p. 83.
[12] See Brinton, *Political Ideas of the English Romanticists*, pp. 61, 83.
[13] Table Talk in W. G. T. Shedd (ed.), *The Complete Works of Samuel Taylor Coleridge* (New York, 1884), VI, p. 511.
[14] Robert Southey, *Essays, Moral and Political* (London, 1832), II, p. 267.
[15] *Ibid.*, II, p. 221. [16] *Ibid.*, II, pp. 267 f.
[17] *Works*, VI, p. 430. [18] *Ibid.*, VI, p. 516.
[19] "What evil results to this country . . . from the National Debt? I never could get a plain and practical answer to that question. As to taxation to pay the interest, how can the country suffer by a process under which the money is never one minute out of the pockets of the people? You may just as well say that a man is weakened by the circulation of his blood" (*ibid.*, VI, p. 431).

subsistent at least; for no state that is not so, is essentially independent. The nation that can not even exist without the commodity of another nation, is in effect the slave of that other nation."[20]

This brief review of the significant points of view of the Lake Poets shows that they were in fundamental disagreement with the ascending political and social forces that dominated English public opinion on the subject of colonies and imperial policies. Even from this short sketch of their attitudes it can be concluded that the Lake Poets were imperialists of the Tory brand. Indeed, the few remarks which they made on the subject corroborate this conclusion. In his *Table Talk*, Coleridge broached the subject of colonization: "Colonization is not only a manifest expedient, but an imperative duty of Great Britain. God seems to hold out his finger to us over the sea. But it must be a national colonization, such as was that of the Scotch to America; a colonization of Hope, and not such as we have alone encouraged and effected for the last fifty years—a colonization of Despair."[21] This statement is very typical of this school of thought: Colonization "of hope" versus colonization "of despair"; colonization motivated by some mysterious call of Providence or God rather than—from a utilitarian point of view—colonization because it is expedient and useful to society.

Southey's attitude is similar. Malthusianism is just "rubbish" to him.[22] "Till the whole earth be peopled to its utmost capacity, it is the fault of man if any checks to population exist...."[23] We have Canada with all its territory, we have Surinam, the Cape Colony, Australasia ... countries which are collectively more than fifty-fold the area of the British isles, and which a thousand years of uninterrupted prosperity would scarcely suffice to people. It is time that Britain should become the hive of nations, and cast her swarms; and here are lands to receive them. What is required of government is to encourage emigration by founding settlements, and facilitating the means of transportation."[24] The question of cost does not enter into the consideration. Everything is so simple. Besides, there is the vocation of cultural and religious imperialism, the sublime desire "for sowing the seeds of civilization in Africa, and for extending the blessings of Christianity to the degraded

[20]*Ibid.*, VI, p. 516.
[21]*Ibid.*, VI, pp. 446 f.
[22]*Essays*, I, p. 79.
[23]*Ibid.*, I, p. 91.
[24]*Ibid.*, I, p. 154.

nations of the East, the brutalized tribes of Polynesia, the Tartar hordes, the Negroes, and the poor Hottentots...."[25]

Pride of empire and the exultation of the British as the great colonizing nation in the world is particularly noticeable in Thomas De Quincey's writings. He boasted of "the colonizing genius of the British people."[26] The colonizing movement appeared to him a "machinery for sifting and winnowing the merits of races."[27] Speaking of Britain's achievement in India he declared: "We found many kingdoms established, and to these we have given unity; and in the process of doing so, by the necessities of the general welfare, or the mere instincts of self-preservation, we have transformed them to an empire, rising like an exhalation, of our own—a mighty monument of our own superior civilisation."[28] Thus, the pride-motive is joined to the idea of a cultural mission and of the English as the chosen people. De Quincey lamented that there had not been more expansion in the East: "Our Eastern rulers have erred always, and erred deeply, by doing too little rather than doing too much."[29] Expectation of future deeds inspired him to such arrogant language as this: "... the British race would be heard upon every wind, coming in with mighty hurrahs, full of power and tumult ... and crying aloud to the five hundred millions of Burmah, China, Japan, and the infinite islands, to make ready their paths before them."[30]

THOMAS CARLYLE

After Carlyle had sent his article on Burns to the *Edinburgh Review*, Jeffrey wrote back: "I wish there had been less mysticism about it, at least less mystical jargon, less talk and repetition about entireness, and simplicity, and exaggeration; and always the most dogmatism where you either are decidedly wrong or very doubt-

---

[25]*Ibid.*, I, p. 18. Being a poet, Southey duly versified this scheme:
"Queen of the Seas! enlarge thyself;
Redundant as thou art of life and power,
Be thou the hive of nations,
and send thy swarms abroad!
Send them like Greece of old,
With arts and science to enrich
The uncultivated earth...."
Quoted in Brie, *Imperialistische Strömungen in der Englischen Literatur*, pp. 86 f.
[26]Thomas De Quincey, "Ceylon," in *Works* (Edinburgh, 1862), XI, p. 3.
[27]*Ibid.*, p. 2.   [28]*Ibid.*, p. 4.
[29]*Ibid.*, p. 25.   [30]*Ibid.*, p. 2.

fully right."[31] Discussing Carlyle, Sir George Cornewall Lewis wrote, in 1838, to Sir Edmund Head: "He is interesting and even instructive to hear; though he belongs to a class whose business it is to deny all accurate knowledge, and all processes for arriving at accurate knowledge and to induce mankind to accept blindly certain mysterious dicta of their own."[32] These two contemporary critics sharply point out the outstanding shortcomings of Carlyle as a writer. Brinton is right in saying that any critical attempt at ascertaining what exactly Carlyle's political philosophy was, discloses the barrenness and scantiness of his political thoughts.[33] Nevertheless, a careful reading of his aphoristic dicta lays bare certain intellectual tendencies at least.

These attitudinal tendencies differed little, if at all, from those that characterized the thinking of the Lake Poets. There is the same worship of the mystical coupled with a studied under-valuation of rational thought and knowledge.[34] There also is the worship of the creative role to be played by the State. Carlyle castigated the hateful Liberalism of his epoch which to him meant nothing but "Anarchy plus the Constable."[35] While he extolled the virtues of strong leadership by aristocrats, laissez-faire was viewed as being, at bottom, "as good as an abdication on the part of the governors"[36] or "self-cancelling Donothingism."[37] Laissez-faire rule, Carlyle maintained, had a tendency to bring about the disintegration of society by dissolving traditional bonds[38] and by leaving its individual members without any ties to each other except that of "the sole nexus" of cash payments.[39] He was, of course, a passionate critic of utilitarianism whose influence on society he described as "paralytic."[40] His contemporaries' excessive quest for material wealth signified to him that they followed

[31] Quoted in D. A. Wilson, *Carlyle to "The French Revolution"* (London, 1924), p. 65.
[32] G. F. Lewis, *Letters of Sir G. C. Lewis*, p. 102.
[33] *English Political Thought in the Nineteenth Century*, p. 165.
[34] For an example see Thomas Carlyle, *Characteristics* (1831) in Harvard Classics (New York, 1909), XXV, p. 347.
[35] Thomas Carlyle, *Inaugural Address* (1866), in *Critical and Miscellaneous Essays* (Sterling ed.; Boston, n.d.), II, p. 414.
[36] Thomas Carlyle, *Chartism*, in *Essays*, II, p. 72.
[37] *Ibid.*, p. 82.
[38] Thus, in *Shooting Niagara*, he remarked that laissez-faire meant "a cutting asunder of straps and ties, wherever you may find them: pretty indiscriminate of choice in the matter: a general repeal of old regulations, fetters and restrictions . . . ." (*Essays*, II, p. 428).
[39] *Chartism*, p. 84.   [40] *Ibid.*, p. 105.

the "Gospel of Mammon," and that free trade—"the immense and universal question of Cheap and Nasty"—was a substitute for religion.[41] In 1830 he wrote about the economists: "Their whole Philosophy is an Arithmetical Computation—performed in words. Even if it were right! Which it scarcely ever is. The question of National Money-making is not a high but a low one: as they treat it, amongst the lowest . . . Political Philosophy should be a scientific revelation of the whole secret mechanism whereby men cohere in society; instead of which it tells us how 'flannel jackets' are exchanged for 'pork hams.' "[42]

Carlyle has been called a founder or "Bahnbrecher" of modern English expansionist imperialism.[43] That is an exaggeration as Bodelsen rightly observed.[44] He was not interested in the subject of colonies *per se* and his scattered references to it are nothing more than rather unrelated aphorisms. If he had an imperialist theory, he did not state it. Whatever influence he had—and he had more on the imperialism of his posterity than on that of his contemporaries—was through the propagation of a particular philosophy and the diffusion of an intellectual temper conducive to the development and acceptance of some components of later British expansionist imperialism. But even in this respect he has a claim to the noteworthiness of the propagator, not to that of the originator.

No doubt Carlyle held colonies to be useful to the metropolis, but as far as this belief was expressed in at all intelligible ideas, they were commonplace.[45] He was, however, much interested in emigration,—from the standpoint of the emigrant-to-be rather than from that of the mother country. Indeed along with Education (with a capital E, of course), he conceived Emigration as a panacea for the amelioration of the condition-of-England.[46] Full of contempt for the Malthusians and their creed, he remarked with Carlylean whimsicality, that their idea of the millenium was "twenty millions of working people . . . passing, in universal trades-union, a resolution not to beget any more till the labour-market

---

[41] *Shooting Niagara*, pp. 422, 449.

[42] Quoted in Wilson, *Carlyle to "The French Revolution,"* p. 171.

[43] Brinton, *English Political Thought in the Nineteenth Century*, p. 176; Brie, *Imperialistische Strömungen in der Englischen Literatur*, pp. 168 f.; G. von Schulze-Gaevernitz, *Britischer Imperialismus und englischer Freihandel* (Leipzig, 1906), p. 78.

[44] C. A. Bodelsen, *Studies in Midvictorian Imperialism* (Kjøbenhavn 1924), pp. 22 ff.

[45] See *ibid.*, p. 25.   [46] *Chartism*, p. 106.

become satisfactory."⁴⁷ "Over-population is the grand anomaly
.... Overpopulation? And yet, if this small western rim of
Europe is overpeopled, does not everywhere else a whole vacant
Earth, as it were, call to us, Come and till me, come and reap me!"⁴⁸
This is his solution.

... in the world where Canadian Forests stand unfelled, boundless Plains
and Prairies unbroken with the plough; on the west and on the east green
desert spaces never yet made white with corn.... And in an England with
wealth, and means for moving such as no Nation ever before had. With
ships; with war-ships rotting idle, which, but bidden to move and not rot,
might bridge all the oceans.⁴⁹

Must the indomitable millions, full of old Saxon energy and fire, lie cooped-up
in this Western Nook, choking one another, as in a Blackhole of Calcutta,
while a whole fertile untenanted Earth, desolate for want of the ploughshare,
cries: Come and till me...?⁵⁰

The younger-son problem was part of the condition-of-England
question. For him the "Earth" was likewise waiting to be "reaped."

In past years, I have sometimes thought what a thing it would be, could the
Queen 'in Council' pick out some gallant-minded, stout, well-gifted Cadet,—
younger Son of a Duke, of an Earl, of a Queen herself; younger Son doomed
now to go mainly to the Devil, for absolute want of a career; and say to him,
'Young fellow, if there do lie in you potentialities of governing, of gradually
guiding, leading and coercing to a noble goal, how sad is it they should be all
lost! They are the grandest gifts a mortal can have; and they are, of all, the
most necessary to other mortals in this world. See, I have scores on scores
of 'Colonies,' all ungoverned, and nine-tenths of them full of jungles, boa-
constrictors, rattlesnakes, Parliamentary Eloquence, and Emancipated
Niggers ripening towards nothing but destruction: one of these you shall
have, you as a Vice-King....⁵¹

Then, as an example, he described St. Dominica under the rule of
the "Vice-King": its upper portion, "salubrious and delightful for
the European, who might there spread and grow ... say only to a
population of 100,000 adult men; well fit to defend their island
against all comers, and beneficently keep steady to their work a
million of Niggers on the lower ranges...."⁵² Under the imperial
policies then obtaining in Great Britain—what was Dominica?
"Population of 100 white men (by no means of select type); unknown cipher of rattlesnakes, profligate Niggers and Mulattoes;
governed by a Pie-bald Parliament of Eleven (head Demosthenes
there a Nigger Tinman)...."⁵³

⁴⁷*Ibid.*, p. 114.
⁴⁸*Ibid.*, p. 113.
⁵⁰*Characteristics*, p. 368.
⁵²*Ibid.*, p. 436.
⁴⁹*Ibid.*, p. 116.
⁵¹*Shooting Niagara*, p. 435.
⁵³*Ibid.*

Carlyle had a strong belief in the superior racial qualities of the Anglo-Saxons.[54] As shown in the above statements he also thought that this chosen race, or, at least the younger sons of the aristocracy of this chosen race had a mission to fulfil in the world. A mission, different to be sure, from what the Buxtonites or Grey and Gladstone conceived it to be. Trusteeship over inferior races, not backward peoples, as Carlyle saw it, seemed to exhaust itself in governing them with iron rule and keeping them at work. His eulogizing defence of strong-man Governor Eyre[55] is rather unambiguous evidence.

The Jamaica Committee,[56] according to Carlyle, was composed of a "group or knot of rabid Nigger Philanthropists."[57] He cursed the false hypocrisy of Exeter Hall, of all those philanthropists who showed solicitude for the negro's welfare while "at home ... the British Whites are rather badly off; several millions of them hanging on the verge of continual famine...."[58] "Our beautiful Black darlings are at last happy; with little labour except to the teeth ... sitting yonder with their beautiful muzzles up to the ears in pumpkins, imbibing sweet pulps and juices ... while the sugar-crops rot round them uncut, because labour cannot be hired, so cheap are the pumpkins...."[59] It was unfortunate that pumpkins were so cheap or that the "Black Darlings" were so fond of pumpkin, for, according to Carlyle's philosophy, it is "the everlasting duty" of every man to work and he must be forced to work if circumstances do not compel him to do so.[60] The "nigger," in particular, "is born to be a servant, and, in fact, is useful in God's creation only as a servant."[61] The problem, therefore, as Carlyle viewed it, was "how to abolish the abuses of slavery, and save the precious thing in it."[62]

From this brief examination of the pertinent ideas of the Lake Poets and Carlyle, it becomes obvious that their direct contribution to the development of British colonial theories was rather insignificant. So was their influence on English public opinion in this particular respect. More important, however, was their indirect influence on the British attitude toward the Empire. They were

[54] See Bodelsen, *Studies in Midvictorian Imperialism*, pp. 28 f.
[55] See Lord Olivier, *The Myth of Governor Eyre* (London, 1933).
[56] The Committee included such men as Buxton, John Bright, Goldwin Smith, Professor F. W. Newman.
[57] *Shooting Niagara*, p. 431.
[58] *Occasional Discourse on the Nigger Question* (1849), in *Essays*, II, p. 294.
[59] *Ibid.*, p. 295. [60] *Ibid.*, p. 299.
[61] *Ibid.*, p. 311. [62] *Ibid.*, p. 312.

little concerned with the kind of arguments of which the broad stream of the British debate on the value of empire was composed. They questioned what these arguments had in common: the utilitarian outlook that fashioned them. The main ideals of the ascending middle class,[63] the ideals of Western European civilization under English leadership, was that of promoting the highest possible material standard of living and increased assurance of its undisturbed enjoyment by the largest possible number of individuals, the multiplication of material comforts.[64] Under such a guiding principle, the general frame of reference of the public debate on the imperial question had to be what has been described in this study. It would be ruled by the principle of economy and by balance-sheet rationality. To the philosopher, however, who questioned this guiding scale of values, most of the arguments advanced must have appeared irrelevant. The Lake Poets and Carlyle, in other words, were interested less in the means than in the ends of policies.

[63]This class, of course, had to share power, influence, and deference with the traditional elements of Great Britain's ruling groups and, correspondingly, their new scale of values did not gain universal acceptance, a fact which is manifest in the debate on the subject of empire. The Lake Poets and Carlyle partly identified themselves with traditional scales of values.

[64]Bound up with the ideal as to ends were corresponding ideas as to the political, social, and economic organization best adapted to the furtherance of these ends.

CHAPTER XV

THE MIDDLE CLASS AND THE EMPIRE

IN the second part of the present study, the important arguments, which reflected a change in English attitudes towards the value of colonies have been examined. The change of Great Britain's imperial commercial policy, the transition from the Empire of preferences—characterized by "reciprocity in disadvantage"[1]—to an Empire of free trade was the outcome of this change of ideas.[2] As regards the change of relevant ideas it is pertinent to inquire into their political genesis. Differences in party attitudes might be investigated with the view of discovering significant trends. However, as is typical of two-party states, the Tory-Conservative and the Whig-Liberal parties constituted motley coalitions of different groups. Throughout the eighteenth century, the struggle between Whigs and Tories was primarily one for power between rival factions. Both factions represented largely the aristocracy and gentry of the nation. The issue was one of struggle for office and the spoils of office rather than one of antagonistic principles of government. This state of affairs continued throughout the nineteenth century. But there existed, especially after the first Reform Bill, an increasing tendency for the parties to differ on points of political programmes.[3]

Except for the Peelites who later joined the Liberal party, it is a generally accepted observation that, during the forties, the majority of the Tories stood for protectionism while the bulk of the Whigs took up the cause of free trade. It cannot be said,

[1] John Davidson, *Commercial Federation and Colonial Trade Policy* (London, 1900), p. 14.

[2] It is unnecessary here to follow up this development as there exist a great many excellent accounts of the gradual alterations of policies. For example, see W. P. Morrell, *British Colonial Policy in the Age of Peel and Russell* (Oxford, 1930), pp. 166-269; R. L. Schuyler, "British Imperial Preference and Sir Robert Peel," *Political Science Quarterly*, XXXII (1917), pp. 429-49; R. L. Schuyler, "The Abolition of British Imperial Preference, 1846-1860," *ibid.*, XXXIII (1918), pp. 77-92.

[3] See on this point the interesting article of William Molesworth, "Terms of Alliance between Radicals and Whigs," *London and Westminster Review*, XXVI (1836-7), pp. 279 f.

however, that the Whigs were less interested in the preservation of the Empire than the Tories. They were merely less interested in the preservation of the basic imperial policies with which the Tories identified themselves. The difference lies in a different conception of empire. The Whigs, certainly in the forties, placed little if any value on the Empire of mutual preferences and monopolies, but they valued empire minus protectionism. More members of the Whig than the Tory party believed that the ultimate emancipation of the dependencies was inevitable and they were not willing to retain adult colonies within the Empire by compulsory means. It was particularly this consideration that led Whig leaders to replace the old bonds of mutual economic interests (preferences) by sentimental bonds and alliances. In consequence of these attitudes the Whigs were also more willing than the Tories to extend gradually the principle of colonial self-government.[4]

[4]Of other important political groups, the attitudes of the Radicals, the Manchester School, the Wakefield School, and the Evangelicals might be examined. Broadly speaking, and disregarding India, the Radicals were inclined to see the Empire as a heavy burden in economic and political respect up to about 1830. It must be kept in mind, however, that this negative attitude referred to the Old Colonial System rather than to the idea of empire as such. With the formation of the Wakefield School, the majority of the Radicals joined forces with the Colonial Reformers. There was, however, no perfect unity among them as becomes apparent from a study of the Radicals' reaction to the Canadian rebellion and Lord Durham's mission. See J. K. Buckley, *Joseph Parkes of Birmingham* (London, 1926), pp. 163-6; Mrs. Fawcett, *Life of the Right Hon. Sir William Molesworth* [London, 1901], pp. 188 f.; John Stuart Mill, "Radical Party and Canada," *London and Westminster Review*, XXVIII (1837-8), pp. 502-33.

The attitude of the Manchester School, as has been shown, was most consistent. They wanted to deliver the mother country from the burdens of empire (preferences, cost of imperial government and defence) even if the process made the dissolution of the Empire inevitable. They were not on principle opposed, however, to a British Commonwealth of Nations within which each member carried the burden of government and defence and which was free of protectionist arrangements.

The Wakefield School was a small but energetic and vociferous group. They had ardent faith in the future of the Empire which they wanted to preserve by granting complete self-government to the several settlement colonies. On the whole, they were Free Traders and opposed the retention of imperial preferences. Many of them supported the idea of having the colonies bear a proportionate share in the financial burden of the Empire. Pleading for further colonization theirs was an expansionist imperialism (Australia, New Zealand). On the other hand, as is clearly shown by the composition of the Colonial Reform Society in 1850, their ranks contained Tories (Godley, Adderley, Lyttleton), Radicals, Manchester reformers (Cobden, Milner Gibson) and their major principles enjoyed the approval of such men as Earl Grey, Gladstone, and Disraeli (see W. S.

An investigation into the composition of the House of Commons and the two major parties[5] reveals that, in the course of the period here under consideration, the House reflected fairly accurately the main trend of the economic development of Great Britain: representation of industry, commerce, finance, and the professions increased while representatives of the landholding interest diminished in number.[6] The comparative composition shows that the Whig-Liberal party was better fitted to express the points of view of Commerce, Industry, and Finance while the Tory-Conservative party was largely the mouthpiece of the landed interest.[7]

If this alteration in the composition of Parliament and parties reflected the change of Great Britain's development from a mainly agricultural into a mainly industrial society, then it also reflected the growing political weight of the ascending middle class—capitalists, entrepreneurs, managers—who pressed for more political influence, power, and prestige than that class had enjoyed before. Middle class in this connection meant upper middle class in the sense in which Brougham used the term in his much-quoted statement: "I speak now of the middle classes—of those hundred of thousands of respectable persons—the most numerous, and by far the most wealthy, order in the community;[8] for if all your Lordships' castles, manors, rights of warren and rights of chase, with all your broad acres, were brought to the hammer and sold at fifty years' purchase, the price would fly up and kick the beam when counterpoised by the vast and solid riches of those middle classes, who are also the genuine depositaries of sober, rational,

---

Childe-Pemberton, *Life of Lord Norton* [London, 1909], pp. 64-70; 78-89).

The Evangelicals, most important for having implanted in the English mind the idea of the Elect Nation, were inclined to be conservative in domestic politics but as regards the issues of imperial politics they may be regarded as a non-partisan body.

[5]See J. A. Thomas, *The House of Commons, 1832-1901* (Cardiff, 1939), pp. 4-7.

[6]In 1832, 489 representatives roughly identifiable with the landed interest were returned as against 248 representatives roughly identifiable with the industrial, commercial, and financial world. In 1865 the landed interest returned 436 members while Commerce, Industry, and Finance had 545 seats (*ibid.*, p. 5).

[7]*Ibid.*, pp. 10 f. This change in the composition of parties and Parliament, however, reflects the economic development of the country only in a rough manner. To gain a more accurate picture it would be necessary to examine the change of basic attitudes of members who are regarded as representatives of the landed interest, etc.

[8]Brougham here disregarded the "mobs," the broad masses of the people.

intelligent, and honest English feeling...."[9] He referred to the new propertied class and to these must be added the larger portion of the professional people and, above all, the intellectuals who are the typical product of middle-class emancipation.[10]

Through the Reform Bill of 1832 this ascending class gained formal recognition of its power by Britain's aristocracy. That law was the basis of the middle-class dominance which characterized the Victorian Era. The revolutionary modification of the legal framework of the country's commercial and imperial system was a consequence of that middle-class dominance.[11]

It was the middle class that opposed the philosophy of rationalistic common sense to political theorizing along traditionalist lines.[12] Most legislation that was enacted, whether by a Whig or by a Tory government, was of liberalist and utilitarian character and both Liberalism and Utilitarianism were, at that stage of English history, components of the middle-class creed.[13]

It was mainly the propagandist campaign of the Manchester party that secured the acceptance of the free-trade programme. The question, whether or not that effort was actuated exclusively by the selfish group-interest of the "shopocracy"[14] or "millocracy,"[15]

[9]Quoted in Crane Brinton, *English Political Thought in the Nineteenth Century* (London, 1933), pp. 34 f.

[10]See G. M. Young, *Victorian England* (Oxford, 1936), p. 6.

[11]Discussing the system of the political economists that was implemented by the ascending class, a staunch Tory like Alison remarked that a powerful agent in producing this result was "the class government which it is now apparent the Reform Bill has imposed upon the nation.... Whatever we were in the days when Napoleon said it, we are now, if not a nation of shopkeepers, at least a nation ruled by shopkeepers" (*Essays, Political, Historical and Miscellaneous* [Edinburgh, 1850], I, p. 479).

That the repeal of the Corn Laws, for example, constituted to some of the protectionists not only the change of a commercial policy but class legislation forced upon the nation by the "millocracy," is evidenced by the following excerpt of a letter written by John Robert Godley to Adderley: "I quite agree with you about the Jacobinical tone of the Anti-Corn Law League, but I think the way to meet it is not by maintaining that which is in the abstract indefensible, and thus giving them an opportunity of attacking, under cover of sound principles of Political Economy, the aristocratic influence of which they are the enemies" (quoted in Childe-Pemberton, *Life of Lord Norton*, p. 58).

[12]See Carl Brinckmann, *England seit 1815* (2d ed.; Berlin, 1938), p. 18.

[13]D. C. Somervell, *English Thought in the Nineteenth Century* (2d ed.; London, 1929), pp. 79 ff.; A. V. Dicey, *Lectures on the Relation between Law and Public Opinion in England during the Nineteenth Century* (London, 1905), p. 186.

[14]Expression coined by Cobden. See John Morley, *The Life of Richard Cobden* (New ed.; London, 1883), p. 80.

[15]G. C. Holland, *The Millocrat* (London, 1841).

cannot be examined here. It must suffice to point out that the demand for laissez-faire was an integral part of the whole Liberal programme.[16] Nevertheless, it is quite true that Cobden and Bright might have been unable to sway their "millocratic" backers and followers, had laissez-faire and free trade, economy at home and peace abroad not been in their particular interest in the forties and fifties. If the multiplication of material wealth and its undisturbed enjoyment are accepted as the principal ends of the middle-class movement, then the selfish interest of the "millocrats" of that time was not only their enlightened self-interest, but it also happened to coincide with the self-interest of the overwhelming portion of the people inside and outside the United Kingdom.

At any rate, the implementation of free trade in Britain and the object of realizing a world economy necessitated the break-up of the existing imperial system and the relinquishment of empire if it should be found without cohesion after the system had been changed.[17] This consideration plus the middle-class quest for economy, peace, and self-government constituted the main source of separationist sentiment.[18] Belief in the inevitability of ultimate colonial emancipation and the assumption that, from a utilitarian point of view, the possession of empire was unprofitable, added to separationist sentiment an attitude of indifference towards the colonies. Although exaggerated by many observers, this indifference was much more widespread a phenomenon than separation-

[16]Dunckley, for example, wrote: "Freedom of trade is properly included in the freedom of the individual. It forms part of that right of free action which is the inalienable possession of every man" (*The Charter of the Nations* [London, 1854], p. 20).

[17]It must be realized that the preferential imperial system was based not only on the assumption that these preferences were mutually profitable. They were also supposed to hold together the various parts of the Empire by making it a unit distinct from the outside world. If colonies were granted increasing powers of self-government, if, due to the quest for economy, the colonies were induced to carry an increasing part of the financial burden of statehood, if the preferential system was scrapped, what would keep the Empire from complete disintegration? Men like Lord Grey, as has been shown, perceived in all these steps measures which ultimately would put the Empire on a firmer foundation than before. The introduction of free trade and the development of Dominion status did not destroy the Empire. These processes only made for a different imperial conception.

[18]The abolition of the preferential system and, with increasing colonial self-government, a diminution in the financial burden of empire, rendered the principal arguments of the outright separationists obsolete. Indeed, even Cobden, as has been shown, approved of the idea of a British Commonwealth of Nations.

ism which was actively propagated only by a handful of writers and politicians. The two attitudes reached their climax in the sixties[19] when the free-trade policy of England seemed to be well on the way to becoming a policy adopted by other nations.

Against these forces stood a number of counteracting factors. Apart from certain metropolitan groups who still had a stake in the preservation of the Empire ("job"-holders, army, navy, etc.), there remained an interest in the British colonies as a field for emigration.[20] There also persisted such forces—whose strength is extremely difficult of measurement—as the pride of empire and the conviction that Anglo-Saxondom had a mission to fulfil, a mission to civilize backward races and to maintain peace and order wherever British influence was sufficiently strong. There also was what may be called the "habit" of empire; the habit of thinking in terms of Empire ("England cannot afford to be little") and of performing the functions of imperial government without inquiring into the utility of doing so. Then there was the fear of humiliation and of loss of prestige in the world if the colonies were relinquished. Last but not least, the colonists themselves, for sentimental or other reasons, did not want to be "given up."

The astonishing phenomenon in view of this current of separatism and indifference and the much stronger one of not wanting to augment the encumbrance of empire by extending its boundaries, is that even the period from 1815 to 1850 produced imperial increase and expansion. Much of it was inland expansion from coastal points and strips that had been in British possession before.[21] But that does not materially alter the point. Of course, in view of Britain's unchallenged command of the seas and the absence of foreign rivalry, it was easy for her to expand. Sometimes, as in India, territory was increased by the action of officials "on the spot" who were bent to "pacify" some frontier. Sometimes, as in South Africa, colonists poured forth across the frontier, often rendering its advancement necessary in order to protect the natives or the settlers.[22] Fear of French designs was operative in determining

[19]See R. L. Schuyler, "The Climax of Anti-Imperialism in England," *Political Science Quarterly*, XXXVI (1921), pp. 537-60.

[20]In 1850, for example, there occurred a new wave of interest in emigration to the United States and the colonies. See Morrell, *British Colonial Policy in the Age of Peel and Russell*, p. 473.

[21]See L. C. A. Knowles, *The Economic Development of the British Overseas Empire* (London, 1924), pp. 9 f.

[22]Cases of colonists outrunning the advance of the flag were quite frequent. Thus, one writer stated: "The despatch of the pioneer vessels of the South

the government to annex New Zealand. Sometimes, as in the case of the Gold Coast, territory was acquired for strictly humanitarian reasons (suppression of the slave trade). After Napoleon had been brought to St. Helena, Tristan D'Acunha and Ascension were occupied in order to prevent a repetition of his flight from Elba.[23] These few examples have been cited in order to demonstrate that during the period from 1815-50 imperial expansion was not the outcome of a consistent, determined, and planned policy of extending the frontiers of the Empire.

At any rate, the lack of determined and unyielding resistance to such expansion[24] can only be accounted for by the fact that prevailing attitudes of separatism and indifference to colonies, however vociferously expressed, were on the whole weaker than those forces which counteracted their influence. A policy of "scuttling" was never seriously taken up by any responsible English statesman.[25] Lecky denied that Little Englandism, though endorsed "by a large and powerful section of English politicians, ever penetrated very deeply into the English nation."[26] There can be no doubt that the successful propagation of Little Englandism depended on the successful spread of the free-trade movement and thus, directly and indirectly, on the complexion of international politics. Neither what Carlyle called "the Calico Millenium" nor the reign of peace for which Manchesterism hoped came, and with increasing disappointments in this respect, little Englandism was bound to wane.[27]

Australian Company without waiting for that official sanction which had so long been sought in vain . . . may be taken as a type of what happened at the founding of almost every settlement by British colonisers of that date. When the New Zealand Company . . . failed to pass its Bill in the House of Commons, and quietly fitted up the ship 'Tory' to convey a party under Colonel Wakefield, the British Government despatched the warship 'Druid' to chase the expedition and bring its leaders to their senses" (George Sutherland, *The South Australian Company* [London, 1898], p. 2). See also A. P. Newton, *A Hundred Years of the British Empire* (New York, 1940), p. 17.

[23]*Ibid.*, p. 34.

[24]As any history of the British Empire reveals, there were cases during the period here considered when such official opposition was determined, though, in the long run, usually without success.

[25]Newton, *A Hundred Years of the British Empire*, p. 28.

[26]W. E. H. Lecky, "The Empire: Its Value and Its Growth," *Historical and Political Essays* (London, 1908), p. 46.

[27]*Ibid.*, p. 47.

The odds, moreover, against which the Little Englanders had to fight, were quite prodigious. As early as 1848 Cobden wrote to Bright: "I believe there is as much clinging to colonies at the present moment amongst the middle class as among the aristocracy; and the working people are not wiser than the rest. . . . You may reason ever so logically, but never so convincingly as through the pocket. But it will take time even to play off John Bull's acquisitiveness against his combativeness."[28] Nor were the English people converted to the free-trade cause on a rational and, consequently, durable basis. The victory of the free-trade agitation, to a large extent, was a defeat of the Corn Laws, brought about by the unpopularity of a tax on bread.[29] In retrospect, Cobden in 1860 called the free-trade success "lucky": "To my eye . . . there seems a strange contempt of sober domestic politics among the English people. . . . I have often thought how lucky we were that when struggling for Free Trade in corn, the Continent was slumbering under Louis Philippe's soporific reign, and that we had to deal with statesmen like Peel and Lord Aberdeen, who were too honest and sedate to get up a war or foreign complications to divert attention from home grievances."[30] And in 1861, John Stuart Mill remarked:

I had learnt from experience that many false opinions may be changed for true ones, without in the least altering the habits of mind of which false opinions are the result. The English public, for example, are quite as raw and undiscerning on subjects of political economy since the nation has been converted to free-trade, as they were before; and are still further from having acquired better habits of thought or feeling, or being in any way better fortified against error, on subjects of a more elevated character. For, though they have thrown off certain errors, the general discipline of their minds, intellectually and morally, is not altered.[31]

It also seemed as if that part of the middle class which had taken the lead in fighting for the Reform Bill and the repeal of protectionist legislation, had exhausted itself. After 1850, the Radical party began to disintegrate. Efforts of Bright and Cobden to found a new "popular" party were abortive.[32] Among upper-middle class business men Non-conformism was giving way to churchmanship and liberalism to political conservatism while in

[28]Morley, *Life of Cobden*, pp. 322 f.
[29]See Dicey, *Lectures*, pp. 24 f.
[30]Morley, *Life of Cobden*, pp. 530 f.
[31]John Stuart Mill, *Autobiography*, Harvard Classics, XXV (New York, 1909), pp. 153 f.
[32]Morley, *Life of Cobden*, p. 321.

the sphere of social life they attempted to follow aristocratic patterns.[33] Cobden, Bright, and Goldwin Smith realized this change in the middle-class outlook. In 1859 Cobden wrote sadly of "the Court and aristocracy with whom the most powerful part of the middle class will be found sympathizing. . . ."[34] Three years later, disgusted with the snobbery of the "mercantile and manufacturing classes," he remarked: "I wish we could inspire the . . . manufacturing community with a little more self-respect."[35] And Goldwin Smith wrote in 1874 "that a community could not be reformed against the grain, and that the aristocracy kept the grain Tory."[36]

[33] See George M. Trevelyan, *The Life of John Bright* (6th ed.; London, 1913), p. 177.
[34] Morley, *Life of Cobden*, p. 225.
[35] *Ibid.*, p. 555.
[36] Arnold Haultain (ed.), *Goldwin Smith's Correspondence* (New York, 1913), p. 47.

INDEX

INDEX OF NAMES

Aberdeen, 4th Earl of, 407
Adderley, Sir C., 394, 395, 407, 409
Addison, J., 158
Adler, R., 380, 381
Albion, R. G., 113
Alexander, Sir W., 27, 55-6
Alison, A., 281, 315, 334, 343, 351, 366-7, 390, 394
Allen, J., 218
Almon, J., 133, 146, 148, 150
Althorp, Viscount, 322
Ancient Trades Decayed, Repaired Again, The, 99
Anderson, A., 85, 86, 99
Anderson, J., 205-6, 208, 209, 220-1, 222, 223, 229, 235, 241, 242, 244, 245
Andrews, C. M., 26
Annual Register, 84, 100, 115
Arguments Against a Spanish War, 107
Arkwright, R., 168
Ashley, J., 67, 68
Ashley, M. P., 134, 150
Ashworth, H., 170
Atkins, Alderman, 231
Atkins, Sir J., 138

Bacon, Sir Francis, 6-7, 11, 14, 16, 19, 26, 31, 36, 43, 46, 47, 49, 55, 62, 85
Baines, E., 346, 357
Baker, Alderman, 21
Bannister, S., 29, 30, 31, 32, 383, 386, 387, 388
Barbon, N., 21
Baring, A., 206, 321, 323
Baring, F., 384
Barnard, Sir J., 143
Bastiat, F., 168
Bedford, 4th Duke of, 109
Beer, G. L., 31, 38, 41-2, 50, 51, 59, 105, 134
Beer, M., 13
Bennet, H. G., 329, 390, 391

Bennet, J., 140
Bentham, Jeremy, 226, 251-6, 258-9, 261-8, 296, 341, 358, 389
Bentinck, Lord G., 344
Berkeley, G., 63, 113
Berkeley, Sir W., 83
Besset, A., 377
Bethel, S., 21, 69, 73, 110
Bindon, D., 70, 96, 97-8
Bitterman, H. J., 160
Bland, J., 137
Blewitt, G., 117
Bliss, H., 326, 327, 329-30, 331, 341
Bodelsen, C. A., 402, 404
Bolingbroke, Viscount, 99, 114
Bonar, J., 69, 221
Bonn, M. J., 5, 7, 19, 24, 130, 158, 388
Borough, J., 11
Bosanquet, C., 230, 238
Botsford, J. E., 377
Bowden, W., 150
Bowring, J., 329, 356
Brentano, L., 24
Brewster, Sir F., 25, 66, 67, 75, 78-9, 84, 86, 87, 89-90, 93, 95, 137
Brie, F., 27, 396, 397, 400, 402
Brief and Impartial Review of the State of Great Britain, A, 219
Bright, H., 278, 321
Bright, John, 166-72, 173, 200, 361, 365, 371, 404, 410, 413, 414
Brinckman, C., 409
Brinton, C., 397, 398, 401, 402, 409
Brissot, J.-P., 377
Britannia Languens, 15, 16, 70, 73, 74, 98, 110-12, 136, 137
Brougham, Henry, 224, 229-30, 235-6, 238, 243-4, 245, 248, 408-9
Brown, J., 15
Buchanan, D., 318, 319, 364, 372, 373
Buck, P., 24, 71, 83, 94, 98
Buckington, N., 235, 239
Buckley, J. K., 407

*Including authors of all books and articles cited, and titles of books or periodicals where work cited is anonymous.

417

418 BRITISH COLONIAL THEORIES

Buller, Charles, 269, 279, 284, 288, 293, 295, 296, 298, 302, 305-6, 314, 391, 392
Burchell, W. J., 292
Burghley, Lord, 20, 40
Burke, Edmund, 122, 131, 132-3, 134, 201, 214, 216-17, 234, 246
Burke, W., 23, 88, 91, 93, 107-8, 126
Burrough, S., 33
Burton, J. H., 338
Buxton, T. F., 378, 379, 383, 386, 387-8, 404
Byron, Lord, 397

Cabot, S., 29, 33
Campbell, Lord F., 202
Campbell, John (1708-75), 67, 75, 79, 88, 89, 94, 105, 126
Campbell, John (1794-1867), 380, 381-2
Carleill, C., 35, 51, 52
Carlile, C., *see* Carleill, C.
Carlyle, Thomas, 393, 396, 397, 400-5, 412
Carmathen, Lord, 130
Cartwright, J., 239
Cary, J., 67, 70, 78, 87, 89
Castell, W., 31
Castlereagh, Viscount, 244
[Cato], 107, 108, 113
Chalmers, G., 206, 207, 216, 217, 238
Chalmers, T., 272-3
Chamberlain, Joseph, 396
Chamberlayne, E., 63
Champion, R., 218-19
Chancellor, R., 33
Charles V, King of Spain, 36, 51
Child, Sir Josiah, 70, 74, 79, 80-1, 90, 137, 139
Childe-Pemberton, W. S., 408
Clapham, J. H., 225, 226, 235, 316, 344, 345, 347
Clark, G. N., 150
Clark, W. E., 117-20
Clarkson, T., 378
Coates, D., 384-5
Cobbett, William, 235, 236, 237, 238, 242
Cobden, Richard, 166-74, 200, 319, 321, 325, 336, 340, 350-1, 352, 357, 358, 359, 361, 364-5, 371, 373, 374, 407, 409, 410, 413, 414
Cockroft, G. A., 216
Coffin, Sir I., 325
Coke, Roger, 70, 73, 110, 111, 112-13, 135, 136
Coleridge, E. T., 212
Coleridge, S. T., 397, 398-9
Colquhoun, P., 224, 232, 238
Columbus, 35
Combe, G., 174, 359
Condorcet, M., 227
Considerable Advantages of a South Sea Trade, The, 77, 127
Considerations on the East India Trade, 99, 157
Considerations on the Expediency of a Spanish War, 66
Consolatory Epistle to the Members of an Old Faction, 109
Cooke, W. B., 314
Copland, P., 29
Cotton, J. H., 82
Coupland, R., 212, 247, 378
Coutts, T., 212
Crawford, S., 284, 293-4
Creighton, L., 380
Cropper, J., 323
Cunningham, W., 26, 40, 59, 149, 162, 188
Currie, J., 234, 235, 238
Curwen, S., 202

Dartmouth, Lord, 90-1, 104
Davenant, C., 12, 73, 74, 75-6, 79, 103-4, 106, 107-8, 110, 114
Davidson, J., 212, 213, 217, 318, 406
Decker, Sir M., 67, 72, 101, 135, 136, 144-5
Defoe, Daniel, 11, 15, 16, 89, 100-1, 129
Delbrück, H., 16
De Quincey, T., 397, 400
Deschamps, A., 57
Dicey, A. V., 409, 413
Discourse of the Common Weal of This Realm of England, A, 7, 14, 16
Discourse of the Nature, Use and Advantages of Trade, 70
Disraeli, B., 125, 349, 407
Don Pacifio, 165

Douglas, Sir H., 333
Douglas, J., 66
Drake, Sir F., 7
Dunckley, H., 318-19, 342, 410
Dundas, Henry, 250
Dupuis, C., 5
Durham, Lord, 277, 384, 407

Earle, G., 18-19
Eburne, R., 31, 44, 46-7, 58-9, 61, 149-50
Eclectic Review, 386
Eden, R., 33
Eden, W., 214-15, 216, 222
Edinburgh Review, 34, 243, 271, 273, 274, 275, 277, 278, 279, 280, 292, 296, 322, 345, 346, 347, 348, 350, 355, 356, 357, 368, 369, 372, 379, 389, 391, 392, 394, 400
Edwards, B., 127, 141, 148, 218
Egerton, H. E., 134, 138, 210, 385, 395
Elgin, Lord, 278-9, 336, 347, 359
Elking, H., 11-12, 19-20
Elliott, Sir G., 116
Ellis, C., 320, 321
Emancipation in Disguise, 230
Enquiry into the Causes of the Present High Price of . . . Sugars, An, 95, 140
Enquiry into the Melancholy Circumstances of Great Britain, An, 81, 83, 87
Ettinger, A. A., 76, 131
Ewart, W., 319
Ewing, J., 37

Fawcett, Mary C., 407
Fay, C. R., 187, 316
Filmer, Sir R., 134
Fortescue, J. W., 16
Fortrey, S., 73
Fox, Charles J., 212
Frobisher, Sir M., 33
Fuller, T., 29, 49
Furniss, E. S., 4, 8, 71

Galloway, J., 203
Gee, Joshua, 68, 76, 88, 102, 103, 148
Gentleman's Magazine, 21, 34, 64, 66, 74, 83, 84, 86, 90, 100, 377, 380
George III, 134
Gervaise, I., 99, 157

Gibson, M., 321, 407
Gilbert, Sir H., 33, 34, 35, 39, 40, 53, 58
Gillespie, J. E., 29, 48
Gladstone, Sir J., 295, 311, 334-5, 358, 363, 367, 374, 407
Glenelg, Lord, 385
Glover, R., 150
Godley, J. R., 407, 409
Goldsmith, L., 369
Goldsmith, Oliver, 107, 108
Gonnard, R., 5, 16, 25
Gorges, F., 41
Goulborn, H., 321
Goyau, G., 29
Grahame, J., 276-7
Grand Concern of England Explained, The, 71, 72
Grant, C., 323
Gratton, J., 275, 285
Gray, R., 30, 43, 61
Greg, W. R., 301
Grenville, G., 85, 92, 93, 104, 146
Grey, Earl, 267, 278, 322, 336, 341, 347, 354, 358, 362, 363, 367-8, 368-9, 374, 394, 407, 410
Grote, G., 267, 311
Guttridge, G. H., 150

H., C., 280, 281, 308
Haie, E., 28
Hakluyt, Richard, 15, 28, 30, 32, 34, 37, 38, 39, 42, 47, 52, 55, 58, 149
Hales, J., 41
Halévy, E., 266, 267
Hall, C., 242
Hall, F., 78, 86, 92-3
Hargreaves, W., 359
Haring, C. H., 35, 36
Harlow, V., 213
Harper, L. A., 24, 134, 139
Harrington, J., 62, 68-9
Harrop, A. J., 309
Hartley, D., 202
Hastings, Warren, 212, 246, 376
Hauser, H., 35, 50, 51, 57
Haversham, Lord, 12
Hawkesbury, Lord, 244
Hawtrey, R. G., 19
Head, Sir E., 401
Heathcote, G., 22, 82, 84

Heckscher, E., 8-9, 12, 17, 19, 71, 160
Henry VII, 29
Henry VIII, 51, 57
Hertz, G. B., 133, 134, 232, 233
Hewins, W. A. S., 188
Hillsborough, Earl of, 108
Himes, N. E., 227
Hinkhouse, F. J., 103, 104, 114, 115-16, 130
Hints On the Subject of the Timber Duties, 326, 330, 331
Hitchins, F. H., 269
Hobbes, Thomas, 6, 25
Hobson, J. A., 166, 172
Holland, B., 203, 210
Holland, G. C., 409
Home, H., 21, 103, 117
Home, M. J., 203
Horsley, W. A., 20, 113-14
Horton, Sir H. W., 270, 271-3, 276, 277, 278, 283, 284, 285, 286, 287, 294, 310
Hotblack, Kate, 150
Houghton, J., 78
Howitt, W., 382, 387
Hume, David, 116, 156, 159, 163, 187, 196, 220
Hume, James D., 319, 344, 345-6
Hume, Joseph, 282, 285, 289, 323, 350, 351-2, 353-4, 355, 360, 373
Hunt, R., 378
Huskisson, W., 316, 317, 322, 346, 362-3, 366
Hutchinson, T., 134

Iddesleigh, S. H. N., 148, 345, 347
Ingram, J. K., 377
Innis, H. A., 41

James I, 27
Jeffrey, F., 400-1
Jelly, T., 348
Jenks, L. H., 298
Johnson, E. A. J., 4, 8, 18, 24, 31, 37, 41-2, 58, 71
Johnson, E. R., 35, 134
Johnson R., 28, 30, 39, 43, 53, 55, 58
Johnson, S. C., 269, 281
Johnson, Samuel, 134
Judges, A. V., 3, 4

Kames, Lord, *see* Home, H.
Keats, J., 397
Keith, Sir W., 68, 86, 92, 95, 102-3, 114, 126, 145, 146-7
King, D., 381
King, J., 212
Klingberg, F. J., 377, 378
Knaplund, P., 295, 335, 355
Knight, G., 283
Knowles, L. C. A., 411
Knox, W., 92, 108, 203, 205, 212, 215-16
Knyvett, H., 42

Laing, S., 277, 282, 284, 309, 314-15
Lalor, J., 313, 333
Lang, J. D., 389
Lascelles, E. C. P., 377
Laudonnierre, R., 28
Laurie, D., 247
Lecky, W. E. H., 109, 412
Lee, W., 202
Leroy-Beaulieu, P., 298, 309
Leser, E., 162
Lewis, G. C., 292, 336, 340, 351, 358, 359-60, 393, 401
Lincoln, A., 200
Lindsay, P., 81, 83, 90, 92, 93, 142
Lipson, E., 8, 17, 19, 57, 68, 72
Littleton, E., 141-2
Locke, John, 63, 160
London and Westminster Review, see *Westminster Review*
Long, E., 217-18
Lord, E. L., 134
Lucas, Sir C., 31
Lynch, Sir T., 138
Lyttleton, G. W., 407

Macarthur, Major, 308-9
Macaulay, Lord, 324-5, 364
Macaulay, Z., 320, 323, 379
Maccoby, S., 311
McCulloch, J. R., 296-7, 299, 337, 338, 342, 373-4
M'Culloh, H., 66, 68
MacInnes, C. M., 34, 57, 68, 134, 139, 377
MacLean, C., 212
Macpherson, D., 36, 51, 134, 207, 208, 214, 218

NAMES, BOOKS AND PERIODICALS

Malet, Sir A., 326, 357
Malthus, T. R., 160, 220, 222, 223, 225-8, 264, 269, 270, 271-4, 283, 284, 286, 298, 300
Malynes, G., 14, 16, 18, 29, 44
Mandeville, B., 64
Manhart, G. B., 33
Manning, H. T., 210, 212, 213, 214
Marryat, James, 331, 333
Marryat, John, 321, 323, 332, 343
Marryat, Joseph, 377
Martin, K. L. P., 384, 385
Martin, R. M., 361, 366, 367
Martineau, Harriet, 353
Matthews, P., 274
Mauduit, I., 109, 145, 146, 202
Mazzei, J., 5
Melbourne, Lord, 363
Memoir on the Spirit and Reason of the Navigation Acts, 343
Merivale, H., 270, 282-3, 284-5, 298, 303, 309, 315, 318, 326, 337, 339, 341, 342, 346, 383, 386, 389-90, 391
Mildmay, Sir W., 23, 77, 88-9, 91, 108-9
Mill, James, 238, 251-63, 265-7, 296, 298, 352, 358, 389
Mill, John Stuart, 267, 268, 288, 300, 305, 349, 374, 407, 413
Mills, A., 276, 287
Minto, Earl of, 250
Molesworth, Sir W., 267, 310, 311, 334, 335, 337, 353, 354, 374, 375, 384, 389, 392, 393, 394, 395, 406
Monson, Sir W., 61
Montesquieu, C., 197, 199, 377
Moore, E. C., 380, 381
More, Sir Thomas, 45
Morini-Comby, J., 16, 17, 19, 24
Morley, J., 166-74, 413
Morrell, W. P., 336, 363, 385, 390, 394, 395, 404, 411
Mortimer, T., 223, 224, 238
Mountgomry, R., 63
Mowat, R. B., 5
Mulgrave, Lord, 244
Mun, T., 14, 16, 67
Mundy, G. C., 292, 393, 395

Namier, L. B., 133, 150, 202, 213

Napier, C. J., 273, 293, 314
Napier, E. D. H. E., 388, 394
Neill, E. D., 29, 33
Nelson, Admiral, 168
Newman, F. W., 404
Newton, A. P. A., 412
Nicholls, J., 208-9, 241
Nicholson, J. S., 187-90, 193
Norman, G. W., 356
North, Sir D., 110, 135
North, Lord, 134, 202, 205, 215
Northcote, S., 346

O'Brien, E., 389
O'Brien, W. S., 279, 283, 314
Oglethorp, J. E., 67, 71, 76-7, 90, 93, 100, 129, 131
Olivier, Lord, 404
Osgood, H. L., 150
Overton, J. H., 380
Owen, R. D., 378

Paley, W., 220, 222, 238
Palmerston, Viscount, 170
Parkes, J., 373
Parnell, H., 301, 322, 337, 352-3, 360
Paterson, W., 21, 65, 99
Peckham, Sir G., 30, 42
Peel, Sir R., 322, 367, 406, 413
Penn, William, 81
Perrin, W., 140, 142, 145-6
Perry, Alderman, 143
Petty, Sir W., 69, 71, 107
Petyt, W., see *Britannia Languens*
Philips, E., 17, 23, 86, 99
Pinsent, J., 310
Pitt, William, the Elder, 102, 109, 131, 132, 201
Pitt, William, the Younger, 212, 214, 215, 216, 217, 219, 237, 244, 246, 378
Place, F., 227, 267, 272, 273
Playfair, W., 229
Pollexfen, J., 95, 102
Popham, Sir H., 242
Popham, J., 27
Porter, G. R., 281, 319, 322, 339, 340, 342-3, 393-4
Postlethwayt, M., 22, 64, 67, 92, 96, 98, 103, 106, 107, 129, 130, 134, 147
Pownall, T., 109, 131, 132, 134, 144

Prentice, A., 289, 290, 292, 294
Preston, R. A., 41
Price, A. G., 309
Price, Richard, 60, 133, 134, 195-200, 201, 221, 222, 226
Priestley, Joseph, 133, 134, 195-8
Pulteney, W., 202, 209
Pütz, T., 163
Pym, J., 36

Quarterly Review, 275, 281, 286, 320, 337, 343, 348, 355, 364, 371, 375, 379, 384, 393

Rabelais, F., 33
Rae, J., 187-8, 195, 205
Raffles, S., 247
Ragatz, L. J., 317
Raikes, R., 387
Raleigh, Sir Walter, 15, 16, 28, 30, 35, 149
Ramsay, A., 131, 150, 161, 164
Rathbone, W., 173..
Read, C., 3, 24
Reasons for Raising a Fund for . . . a Colony at Virginia, 57, 129
Redfield, A., 148, 233
Rees, J. F., 140
Reflections and Considerations . . . for Taking off the Drawback on Foreign Linens, 115
Rein, A., 7, 33, 158
Remarks upon a Book . . . , 142
Reynell, C., 64, 72, 77, 93, 97, 106-7
Ricardo, David, 160, 251, 255-6, 261, 276, 296, 297, 298, 299, 300, 328, 329
Ricardo, J. L., 343, 345, 347, 349
Rice, T. S., 320
Richardson, R., 130
Roberts, L., 62
Robertson, H. M., 45, 149
Robespierre, M., 377
Robinson, F., 327
Robinson, H., 44, 54
Roebuck, J. A., 337, 353, 361
Rogers, J. E. T., 58, 167-8
Rooke, J., 306
Rose, G., 231, 244
Rouher, E., 170
Rousseau, J.-J., 377

Rowland, A. L., 33
Rudyard, B., 16, 36
Ruggiero, G., 160
Russell, Lord John, 167, 323, 363, 367, 374, 390, 392

Sandon, Viscount, 320, 386
Sandwich, Earl of, 87
Sandys, Sir E., 54
Savelle, M., 7
Say, H., 298, 299, 300
Schmoller, G., 8
Schulze-Gaevernitz, G. V., 27, 402
Schuyler, R. L., 118, 120, 406, 411
Scots Magazine, 34, 81, 82, 86, 90
Scott, Sir Walter, 397
Scott, W. R., 35, 149
Scrope, G. P., 27, 274, 278, 286-7, 308
Seeley, Sir J., 250
Selkirk, Earl of, 223-4
Selwyn, Sir J., 82
Senior, N. W., 279, 282, 306, 325, 338-9, 341, 342
Sepping, Sir R., 326
Shaftesbury, Lord, 394
Sharp, G., 379, 382
Shebbeare, J., 379-80
Sheffield, 1st Earl of, 214-16, 217, 218, 219, 244, 245-6, 248, 376
Shelburne, Earl of, 108, 134, 201, 208, 209, 214, 219
Shelley, P. B., 397
Sheridan, R. B., 246
Sheridan, T., 73
Shirley, W., 65
Short Answer to an Elaborate Pamphlet . . . , *A*, 140
Sidney, S., 290, 309
Sieyès, Abbé, 377
Silberner, E., 17, 20
Sinclair, Sir J., 195, 203-4, 212, 238, 240
Sismondi, J. C. L. S. de, 300
Sketches on Political Economy, 238
Smillie, E. A., 133
Smith, Adam, 8, 9, 10, 131, 134, 151, 155-64, 175-95, 196, 204-5, 214-15, 220, 228, 229, 234, 235, 237, 242, 245, 248, 251, 255, 296, 302, 310, 338, 341, 344
Smith, E. A., 48

Smith, Goldwin, 167-70, 172-4, 354, 357-8, 359, 360-1, 363-4, 365, 370-1, 373, 374, 404, 414
Smith, J., 28
Smith, Sidney, 275, 290
Smith, Sydney, 243, 247, 389, 391, 392
Smith, W., 232
Somervell, D. C., 376, 409
Southey, Robert, 397, 398, 399-400
Southey, T., 333
The Spectator, 354, 374, 395
Spence, W., 237, 238, 239, 240
Stair, Earl of, 205, 206, 234, 246
Stangeland, C. E., 69, 220
Stanley, Lord, 333
Stebbing, H., 380
Stephen, Sir J., 355, 368, 385, 394
Stepney, G., 67
Steuart, Sir J., 220
Stirling, Sir J., 345
Sutherland, G., 412
Suviranta, B., 13, 97
Sykes, D., 327
Symonds, W., 43

Temple, Sir W., 70
Thomas, J. A., 408
Thomas, P. J., 4, 8
Thomas, R., 198
Thompson, T. P., 170, 294, 341-2
Thorne, R., 33
Thoughts on a Question of Importance . . . , 107, 108, 113, 135
Tierney, G., 234
The Times (London), 188, 389
Tooke, T., 298
Torrens, Major Robert, 271, 276, 279, 281, 283, 286, 287, 288-9, 297, 298-9, 300, 303, 306, 307-8, 323, 324, 335
Trevelyan, G. M., 167-8, 170, 272
True and Sincere Declaration of the Purpose . . . of the Plantation Begun in Virginia, A, 43, 53, 60
True Declaration of the Estate of . . . Virginia, A, 30, 31, 39, 53, 55, 58
Tucker, Josiah, 117-25, 159, 195, 196, 201, 205, 207, 221, 310
Turgot, A.-R. J., 371
Twiss, T., 306-7

Ullathorne, Bishop, 389

V., S. F., 146, 148
Vanderlint, J., 73, 94, 110
Villiers, C. P., 302, 322, 328, 329, 330
Viner, J., 4, 8, 9, 10, 13, 14, 16, 18, 55, 94, 96, 98, 99, 156, 157, 159, 160
Violet, T., 14, 16

Wade, J., 273, 277, 286, 357, 360
Wagner, D. O., 185, 188, 310
Wakefield, Edward Gibbon, 107, 267, 270, 279, 288, 289, 292, 294-300, 302-6, 309-10, 311, 312, 322, 361-2, 374, 384, 392, 407, 412
Wallace, R., 220
Wallace, T., 316, 329
Ward, H. G., 392
Watt, J., 168
Wellesley, Marquess, 250
Wellington, Duke of, 168, 174
Wentworth, Sir J., 102
Westminster Review, 274, 275, 276, 290, 291, 295, 301, 309, 326, 328, 329, 330, 331, 346, 349, 350, 351, 352, 358, 359, 372, 379, 384, 390, 391, 392, 396, 406, 407
Wetherell, Sir C., 355
Whateley, Richard, 286, 287-8, 292, 308, 311-12, 313-14, 389, 390, 392, 393
Whiston, J., 15, 16, 20, 128
White, J., 40, 47-8, 49, 60
Whitworth, Sir C., 21-2
Wilberforce, William, 378, 380
Willes, R., 33
Williams, E., 38, 39, 44, 53, 56, 58
Willoughby, Sir H., 33
Willoughby, Lord, 138
Wingfield-Stratford, E., 246
Wood, H. T., 134
Wood, W., 67, 74, 84, 85, 89, 90, 93-4, 96, 102, 147
Woodruff, D., 361, 395
Wordsworth, William, 397, 398

Yarranton, A., 21
Young, Sir Arthur, 68, 86, 89, 90, 115, 128, 230-1, 238-9, 241-2, 245
Young, G. F., 332-3, 335-6, 343, 344
Young, G. M., 409

INDEX OF SUBJECTS

Aborigines' problem, 382-8
Aborigines' Protection Society, 383, 386
Africa, 50, 61, 67, 84, 102, 127, 175, 240, 249, 250, 361, 367, 369, 378-9, 381, 383, 385, 386, 387, 388, 399, 411, 412
American Intercourse Bill, 213-19, 244
Anti-imperialist attitudes, 59-62, 73-4, 105-17, 120-5, 210, 241-3, 248
Argentina, 304
Asia, 64, 127, 369, 400; *see also* India
Australia, 50, 211, 212, 243, 249, 250, 258-9, 290, 310, 315, 334, 367, 369, 383, 384, 389, 391, 392, 393, 395, 399, 407, 411-12

Baptist Missionary Society, 380
Bases
    naval, 64, 249-50, 361, 378-9; *see also* Naval stores
    strategic, 37-8, 63-6
Benthamites; *see* Philosophical Radicals
Bounties on colonial exports to the mother country, 150, 161, 163, 207; *see also* Tariff preferences on imports of colonial goods
British and Foreign Bible Society, 380
British exports; *see* Navigation Laws, criticism of
Bullion; *see* Gold

Canada, 65-6, 102, 115, 119, 126, 203, 205, 208-9, 211, 212, 215, 217, 218, 231, 239, 242, 269, 278-9, 285, 291, 325-31, 337, 347, 357, 359-60, 362-3, 366, 372, 375, 399, 403, 407
Cape of Good Hope, 240, 249-50, 383, 395, 399
Capital, belief in the existence of surplus capital in Great Britain, 233-4, 296-9; *see also* Colonies, advantages of, outlet for surplus capital; Colonies, disadvantages of, drain on capital

Central America, 64, 65
Ceylon, 368
Church Missionary Society, 380, 385
Clapham Sect, 377, 379
Classical economics, beginning of, 155-61
Coffee, 122, 230, 317, 319, 350
Colonial balance of power, 64, 243
Colonial exports; *see* Navigation Laws, criticism of; Bounties on colonial exports to the mother country
Colonial monopoly; *see* Monopoly of the colony trade
Colonial reform; *see* Empire reform
Colonial Reform Society, 354
Colonial shipbuilding; *see* Shipbuilding, colonial
Colonial system
    colonial manufacturing industries, opposition to, 92-3, 102-4, 124
    colonial rawstuff production, encouragement of, 92-3, 103, 128
    criticism of, 131-48, 177-83, 185-7, 206, 214-15, 217-19, 241, 249, 294, 316, 338, 341-2
    Huskisson's reform of, 316-17
    imperial self-sufficiency, 91-4, 129-30, 231, 232, 240, 332; *see also* Empire, as a Zollverein
    imperial trade monopoly as the chief objective, 126-8
    old system, 3, 106, 126-51, 203, 206, 210, 213-19, 407; *see also* Monopoly of the colony trade; Navigation Laws; Tariff preferences
    relative value of different colonies, 128
    subservience of colonies to the interests of the mother country, 128-30
Colonial theories, social genesis of, 149-51, 161-2, 164, 184-5, 406-14

INDEX OF SUBJECTS 425

Colonies, advantages to the mother country of
  battleground for European wars, 243-4
  carrying trade, 38-40, 88-9, 214-19; *see also* Navigation Laws
  complementarity of economic functions, 128-30
  emigration to non-British countries, discouragement of, 224, 290-1
  employment, increase of in the mother country, 78-80, 97-9, 222
  fisheries, 40-1
  free-trade extension through colonization, 236-7
  jobs for sons of ruling groups, 262-3
  markets, 56-9, 93, 95-105, 118, 126-7, 198, 215, 223, 229-31, 254, 256, 303-9, 330-7, 369
  missionary enterprise, encouragement of, 27-32, 60, 63, 379-82
  naval bases, 64, 249-50, 361, 378-9; *see also* Naval stores
  outlet for malcontent and poor, 74-7, 222, 224, 278-81
  outlet for surplus capital, 233-4, 248, 270, 302-5
  outlet for surplus population, 41-8, 74-81, 222, 223-4, 227-8, 248, 265-6, 267, 269-70, 275-81, 285-7, 302-9, 402-3
  outlet for undesirables and criminals; *see* Transportation
  population growth in the mother country, encouragement of, 78-80, 97-9, 222
  power, military, of the mother country increased, 360-4
  power, naval, of the mother country increased, 244-6, 248, 326-7, 343-5
  precious metals, 34-7, 63
  raw materials and foodstuffs, 18, 23, 50-6, 81-95, 118, 126-7, 198, 222, 230-1, 239, 255-6, 304-6, 330, 332-6
  re-export trade, 87-91, 128, 216
  revenue, 59
  seamen, nursery of, 38-40, 63-4, 66-8, 245
  shipping and shipbuilding, 39, 67-8, 215-16, 231
  strategic bases, 37-8, 63-6
  trading posts, 64, 127, 161
  see also Empire, as a Zollverein; Empire, duty of; Empire, mission of; Empire, prestige of; Empire, pride of; White Man's burden

Colonies, disadvantages to the mother country of
  burden of defence, 108-9, 123-4, 178, 183, 187-9, 192-5, 197, 199, 202, 207, 209, 215, 239, 245, 258, 354, 362-3
  causes of war, 197, 229, 241-2, 259, 263, 362
  colonial competition with metropolitan manufactures, 105-6, 115-16
  colonial competition with metropolitan shipping and shipbuilding, 112, 208, 216, 231
  corruption of metropolitan politics, 114, 123-4, 197, 242, 263-4, 356-60
  drain on capital, 60, 73-4, 238, 239
  drain on population, 60-1, 69, 72-81, 105, 107-8, 110, 119, 221-2, 283-4
  exploitation of mother country by the colonies, 213, 262, 318-25, 325-31, 339-40, 352, 372
  financial burden, 61-2, 107, 110, 116, 122-3, 130, 139, 178, 183, 187-9, 192-5, 197, 202, 207-10, 215, 234-6, 241, 249, 261-2, 284-6, 314, 318-25, 350-6, 365
  harmful effects on metropolitan production, 112-13, 122, 221

Colonies, indifference to, 213, 372, 410, 411, 412

Colonies, inutility to the mother country of (as regards special advantages claimed to accrue from ownership of colonies)

failure to provide revenue, 117-18, 260-1
inevitability of colonial emancipation, 60-2, 92-3, 114-16, 125, 208-9, 211, 223, 241-3, 249, 371
unprofitability, general, 61, 110, 183, 187, 207, 212, 372
unprofitability as a special investment field, 301
unprofitability as special markets, 110-11, 120, 147, 179-82, 205, 229, 231, 233, 237-9, 245, 251, 252-3, 254, 256, 314, 331, 339-40
unprofitability as special sources of raw stuffs, 111, 121-2, 208-9, 230-3, 237-9, 245-6, 251, 253, 256, 318-20, 325-31, 337-8, 339-40, 343
uselessness as outlet for surplus population, 227, 282-4, 306, 314
uselessness as special source of naval power, 113-14, 123-4, 212, 245, 256-8, 327-9, 345-7
Colonies, proposals for complete abandonment of, 116, 120, 187-92, 200, 204, 243, 248, 266, 352, 372-3, 410, 411, 412; see also Little Englanders
Colonies, proposals for the partial abandonment of, 93, 106, 209, 212, 218, 248, 365
Colonization
effect on European trade, 165-7
opposition to excessive, 62, 106-9, 207-8, 234-5, 241-3, 248, 249, 360
systematic, 294-315
versus free-trade, 301-9
Corn Laws, 165, 281, 294, 307, 308
repeal of, 165, 280, 302, 304, 347, 409, 413
Cotton, 88, 122, 148, 209, 232-3, 324, 333, 398

Dissenters, the English, 133-4, 195-200, 201
attitude towards colonies, 196-200

East India Company, 29, 51, 212, 246, 249, 267, 376
East India trade, 17, 95-6, 212, 247; see also India
Emigration to the colonies; see Colonies, advantages of, outlet for surplus population
Empire
as a commonwealth of nations, 49-50, 131-4, 187-8, 193-4, 198-9, 201-3, 310-11, 373, 407, 410
as a Zollverein, 308-9, 335-6, 373
duty of, 367-8, 374, 399, 404, 411
habit of, 211
mission of, 246-7, 248, 314-15, 364, 366-71, 399-400, 404, 411
prestige of, 362
pride of, 211, 262, 364-5, 400, 411
reform of, 191-5, 198-9, 201-3, 212-13, 353-4, 373-4, 407
Employment, mercantilist concept of, 13, 45, 47, 78-9
Employment, balance of, mercantilist concept of, 55, 96-9, 119, 180
Enumerated articles, 128, 140-1, 178
Enumeration Act, 128, 142
Evangelicalism, 155, 376-88, 407, 408
Exeter Hall, 383, 384-5, 404
Exports; see Colonies, advantages of; markets; International trade; Navigation Laws

Fisheries, North American, 40-1, 66, 208
Fisheries, source of naval power, 17, 40
Florida, 28, 38
Freeport Law (1766), 148
Freeports, 147-8
Free-trade movement in Great Britain, 165, 168, 172-3, 196, 214, 301-7, 316-17, 321-5, 329-49, 356, 373-4, 406, 407, 410, 411, 413; see also Laissez-faire

Georgia, 76, 82, 203
Gibraltar, 64, 195, 197, 212
Gold, 13, 17
Gold, functions of, 13-16, 18-23, 87, 89
Grain, 344

INDEX OF SUBJECTS 427

Imports; *see* Colonies, advantages of, raw materials and foodstuffs; International trade
India, 65, 211, 212, 231, 239, 240, 246-7, 249, 250, 260, 267, 333, 358, 359, 364, 365, 369, 371, 375, 380, 381, 400, 403, 407, 411; *see also* East India Company; East India trade
International division of labour
    classical economists' concept of, 157-9
    mercantilist concept of, 19
International politics
    concept of, in the era of economic liberalism, 164-74
    concept of, in the era of mercantilism, 8-17
International trade
    classical economists' concept of, 156-61
    mercantilist concept of, 18-23
    physiocratic concept of, 237-9
International trade, balance of, in mercantilist reasoning, 71, 85-7, 89

Jamaica Committee, 404
Jealousy, British
    of France, 20-2, 64-6, 68, 70, 88, 139-41, 143, 167, 385, 411-12
    of other nations, 196, 231
    of Spain, 15-16, 31, 35-8
    of the Netherlands, 21, 71, 112, 136-7, 139, 215

Laissez-faire, 227, 397, 401, 410
    classical doctrine of, 159-61
    early English support of, 135, 196, 200
Levant Company, 29
Little Englanders, 249, 372-5, 409-13; *see also*, Anti-imperialistic attitudes; Colonies, proposals for complete abandonment of
London Missionary Society, 380
Louisiana, 65
Lumber; *see* Timber

Manchester School, 10, 165-74, 195, 200, 350, 352, 354, 355, 363, 364, 370, 372, 374, 397, 407, 409, 412

views on international politics, 165-74, 365
Markets; *see* Colonies, advantages of, markets
Maryland, 83, 137, 138
Mercantilism
    classical refutation of, 155-61
    considerations of power, 8-17, 21-3, 71, 98
    considerations of wealth, 9-17, 22-3, 71-2, 98
    early opposition to, 119
    statecraft, 23-5
Minorca, 200
Missionary movement, 27-32, 379-82
Molasses Act (1633), 140-1, 146
Monopoly of the colony trade, 65, 127-8, 206, 213-19, 251-6; *see also* Colonial system, old; Navigation Laws
    criticism of, 111, 112-13, 120-1, 161-2, 177-83, 185-7, 202, 206, 214-15, 217-19, 229, 238-9, 241, 248, 251-4, 256
Muscovy Company, 33

National wealth; *see* Wealth, national
Naval bases; *see* Bases, naval
Naval power; *see* Power
Naval stores, 13, 16, 50-4, 83-7, 89-91, 93-4, 113, 118, 121, 239-40; *see also* Timber
Navigation Laws, 17, 24, 40, 64, 73, 92, 106, 132-3, 138-48, 150, 163, 178, 180, 186-7, 203, 214-19, 244-6, 248, 256, 328, 350
Navigation Laws, circumvention of, 148
Navigation Laws, criticism of, 132, 135-48, 177-83, 185-7, 214-15, 217-19, 248, 256-8, 327-9, 345-7
    benefit to special interest groups only, 135-6, 137-8, 219, 244, 263, 327, 329, 341-2
    diminish naval power, 218-19
    effect on sugar trade, 39-43, 214-19
    increase manufacturing costs, 136
    increase shipping costs, 136, 219, 329

restrain economic development of the colonies, 137-8
restrain trade, 135, 217-19, 345
restrict British exports, 136, 345
restrict colonial exports, 144-7
Navigation Laws, reform of, by Wallace and Huskisson, 316-17
Navigation Laws, repeal of, 347
New England colonies, 32, 40, 64, 87, 93-4, 96, 102, 103-4, 106-7, 112, 114, 116, 128, 129, 144-7, 213-15
Newfoundland, 60, 354
New York, 203
New Zealand, 211, 281, 290, 310, 334, 358, 368, 384-6, 407, 412
New Zealand Association, 384, 385
North Carolina, 83, 122, 203
Northwest Passage, 32-4, 63
Nova Scotia, 65, 203, 209, 212, 234; see also Canada

Penal settlements, opposition to, 258-9; see also Transportation
Pennsylvania, 81, 83
Philosophical Radicals, 155, 162, 166, 200, 210, 249, 267-8, 376, 397, 407
attitude towards colonies, 251-68
Physiocrats, 158, 205
attitude towards colonies, 236-40, 248
Population, 13, 18
British overpopulation, belief in, 42-5, 222, 223-6, 238, 249, 264, 269-75, 292-3, 294-6, 302, 403
British underpopulation, belief in, 69-73, 220, 222
early anti-mercantilist concepts of, 220
Malthusian doctrines of, 225-7, 249
mercantilist theories of, 47, 68-73, 107-8, 110, 118-19, 219-22
Potash, 50
Power
international balance of, 5-7, 20-2, 171, 243
national, 6-14, 20-3, 162-4, 186-7, 189-90, 256-8, 360-4

naval, 11-12, 17, 38-40, 66-8, 187, 208, 215-6, 244-6, 256-8, 326-7, 343-7
see also Colonial balance of power; International politics; Mercantilism, considerations of power
Protectionism
defence of, 99, 118
early opposition to, 99
see also, Colonial system, old; Colonies, advantages of, markets; Empire, as a Zollverein; Free-trade movement; Mercantilism, considerations of wealth; Monopoly of the colony trade; Navigation Laws; Tariff preferences on imports of colonial goods

Quakers, 377

Raw materials, 13, 17-18, 50-2; see also Coffee, Cotton, etc.; Colonies, advantages of, raw materials and foodstuffs; Colonies, inutility of, unprofitibility as special sources of rawstuffs; Tariff preferences on imports of colonial goods
Religious missionarism; see Missionary movement
Royal Society of Arts, 134
Sailors, training of, 16-17, 38-40; see also Colonies, advantages of; Power, naval; Seamen, nursery of
Seamen, nursery of; see Colonies, advantages of; Power, naval
Shipbuilding, colonial, 39, 67-8
Ships and shipbuilding, 13, 17, 38-40, 67-8, 215-16, 231; see also Colonies, advantages of, carrying trade, power, naval; Navigation Laws
Sierra Leone Company, 378-9
Silk, 50, 82-3, 90, 94
Slavery, suppression of, 318, 320, 323-5, 376-9, 380
Slave trade, 67, 382, 387
suppression of, 318, 323-5, 376-9, 387, 412
Somersett Case, 378
South America, 127

INDEX OF SUBJECTS

Stamp Act, 146
Sugar, 50, 51, 68, 86, 87-8, 93, 94-5, 111, 112, 113, 122, 139-44, 178, 213-19, 230-2, 240, 317-25, 344, 350
Sugar Act (1764), 145, 146

Tahiti, 384
Tariffs
    preferences on imports of colonial goods, 213, 231-2, 262, 281, 333, 339, 350, 410
    sugar duties, 317-25
    timber duties, 325-31
    see also Bounties on colonial exports to the mother country
Timber, 53, 86, 113, 145, 208, 213, 215, 217, 231, 239, 317, 325-31, 344, 350; *see also* Naval stores
Tobacco, 50, 54, 88, 93, 111, 113, 122, 137, 150, 178, 324
Trade, international; *see* International trade
Transportation of undesirables and convicts, 46, 48-50, 75-7, 250, 389-95; *see also* Penal settlements
Treasure; *see* Gold

United States, 214-19, 277, 278, 280, 288, 304, 313, 316, 317, 333, 369, 372, 379, 411; *see also* New England colonies; Florida, Georgia, etc.
    British emigration to, 277-8, 280, 291-2, 411
    satisfaction with the loss of, 201-2, 205-9, 216

Virginia, 29, 32, 35, 38, 60, 83, 122, 137, 138
Virginia Company, 29, 34, 36, 37

Wealth, national, 9-16, 18-23, 162-4
West Indies, 20, 36, 37, 60, 64, 67, 68, 88, 91, 93, 95, 96, 115, 122, 127, 128, 138, 139-48, 183, 197, 204, 209, 212, 213-17, 230-2, 239, 240, 244, 260, 317-25, 333, 368, 375, 403-4
White Man's burden, 266-7, 366, 376-88, 404; *see also* Empire, duty of, mission of
Wool, 51, 232, 333
Woollen exports, British, 90, 95-6, 99, 101-2, 104, 111

For Product Safety Concerns and Information please contact our EU representative GPSR@taylorandfrancis.com
Taylor & Francis Verlag GmbH, Kaufingerstraße 24, 80331 München, Germany

www.ingramcontent.com/pod-product-compliance
Lightning Source LLC
Chambersburg PA
CBHW071234300426
44116CB00008B/1031